Natural Computing Series

Series Editors: G. Rozenberg
Th. Bäck A.E. Eiben J.N. Kok H.P. Spaink

Leiden Center for Natural Computing

Juan Romero · Penousal Machado (Eds.)

The Art of Artificial Evolution

A Handbook on Evolutionary Art and Music

With 169 Figures, 30 Tables and DVD-ROM

Springer

Editors

Juan Romero
Department of Information
and Communication Technologies
University of A Coruña
Campus de Elvina
15071 La Coruña, Spain
jj@udc.es

Penousal Machado
CISUC
Dept. of Informatics Engineering
University of Coimbra
3030 Coimbra, Portugal
machado@dei.uc.pt

Series Editors

G. Rozenberg (Managing Editor)
rozenber@liacs.nl

Th. Bäck, J.N. Kok, H.P. Spaink
Leiden Center for Natural Computing
Leiden University
Niels Bohrweg 1
2333 CA Leiden, The Netherlands

A.E. Eiben
Vrije Universiteit Amsterdam
The Netherlands

Additional material to this book can be downloaded from http://extras.springer.com
ACM Computing Classification (2008): I.2, I.3, J.5, J.6

ISSN 1619-7127
ISBN 978-3-642-43666-6 Springer Berlin Heidelberg New York

Springer is a part of Springer Science+Business Media

springer.com

Softcover re-print of the Hardcover 1st edition 2008

Typesetting: by the Authors
Production: Integra Software Services Pvt. Ltd., Pondicherry, India
Cover Design: KünkelLopka GmbH, Heidelberg

Printed on acid-free paper 45/3100/Integra 5 4 3 2 1 0

To Alexandra and Raquel

Preface

Art is the Queen of all sciences communicating knowledge to all the generations of the world. Leonardo da Vinci

Artistic behavior is one of the most valued qualities of the human mind. Although artistic manifestations vary from culture to culture, dedication to artistic tasks is common to all. In other words, artistic behavior is a universal trait of the human species.

The current, Western definition of art is relatively new. However, a dedication to artistic endeavors — such as the embellishment of tools, body ornamentation, or gathering of unusual, arguably aesthetic, objects — can be traced back to the origins of humanity. That is, art is ever-present in human history and prehistory.

Art and science share a long and enduring relationship. The best-known example of the exploration of this relationship is probably the work of Leonardo da Vinci. Somewhere in the 19th century art and science grew apart, but the cross-transfer of concepts between the two domains continued to exist. Currently, albeit the need for specialization, there is a growing interest in the exploration of the connections between art and science.

Focusing on computer science, it is interesting to notice that early pioneers of this discipline such as Ada Byron and Alan Turing showed an interest in using computational devices for art-making purposes. Oddly, in spite of this early interest and the ubiquity of art, it has received relatively little attention from the computer science community in general, and, more surprisingly, from the artificial intelligence community.

In the initial years of artificial intelligence research the main source of inspiration was human intelligence. Recently, this traditional, somewhat anthropocentric, view of intelligence has given rise to the search for other potential sources of inspiration. There is a growing interest in biology-inspired computing techniques, a broad area of research that incorporates techniques such as evolutionary computation, swarm intelligence, ant colony optimization, and artificial life. These techniques offer a wide range of solutions and opportunities, for scientists, who have always made an effort to understand and model nature, and for artists, who have always used nature as a source of inspiration. The use of a metaphor that is relevant for scientists and artists helps to bridge the gap between the scientific and artistic communities, and fosters the collaboration and transfer of knowledge between the two domains.

In this line of thought, the seminal works of Richard Dawkins, Karl Sims and William Latham led to the emergence of a new research area, usually called *Evolutionary Art and Music*, which is characterized by the use of nature-inspired computation in artistic domains.

The early books edited by Peter Bentley and David Corne gave evolutionary art some important exposure. Over time, the growing interest in the area led to the appearance of dedicated scientific events and special issues, fostering the development of a strong research community and playing an important role in the establishment of evolutionary art and music as a meaningful research field. The current vitality of the area is reflected in the existence of dedicated annual workshops and special tracks at some of the main evolutionary computation conferences (e.g., *Evolved Art and Music* and *Evolutionary Design* at the IEEE Congress on Evolutionary Computation, and EvoMUSART, the Evo* Workshop on Evolutionary Music and Art). This thriving area of research is arguably at the verge of adulthood. Its current stage of development calls for a book that (1) provides a broad and coherent coverage of the field, (2) provides the necessary background information for newcomers, and (3) establishes directions for future research, thus providing a solid basis for its further development. These are the main objectives of the present book.

The book is aimed at a wide audience, including researchers and artists, beginners and experts in the field, and especially those who wish to explore the relationships between nature, science and art. We consider that it is important to shorten the gap between the scientific and artistic communities. Hopefully this book is a step in that direction, and this concern is reflected in the contents and structure of the book.

The book is divided into five parts: *Evolutionary Art*, *Evolutionary Music*, *Real-World Applications*, *Artistic Perspectives*, and *Future Perspectives.*

The first two parts of this book include some of the most interesting works on the application of evolutionary computation techniques in the fields of visual art, video, design (Part 1), sound, music and performance (Part 2). Although these chapters are mainly scientifically oriented, they all make relevant artistic contributions.

The first chapter, by Matthew Lewis, provides a thorough, and much needed, analysis of the state of the art in the fields of evolutionary art and design, introducing key concepts and terminology, reviewing nearly 200 publications, describing the most prominent approaches, and identifying some of the most relevant research topics in the area. In the second chapter John Collomosse describes the use of evolutionary computation techniques in the context of the non-photorealistic, painterly, rendering of images. Starting with an overview of artistic stylization algorithms, he then discusses the use of genetic algorithms to increase control over the level of detail in painting, and to enhance the usability of painterly rendering algorithms. The closing chapter of the first part of the book presents the "Electric Sheep" project, one of the largest and longest ongoing evolutionary art experiments, involving over 40,000 computers and people mediated using a genetic algorithm. Scott Draves offers a description of the representation, genotype–phenotype mapping and genetic operators that allow the evolution of fractal flames movies and still images, and he then focuses on the long-term behavior of the distributed system.

The fourth chapter takes us to the area of evolutionary sound synthesis. James McDermott, Niall J.L. Griffith and Michael O'Neill survey previous work in the area, and then focus on the problem of automatically matching a target sound using a given synthesizer, which involves building fitness functions that take into account timbral, perceptual, and statistical sound attributes. They report and thoroughly analyze the results attained in a comprehensive set of experiments aimed to determine the best combination of algorithm, parameters and fitness functions for this problem, drawing conclusions and indicating future work. Tim Blackwell describes the use of swarm intelligence and granular synthesis techniques for the generation of novel sounds, outlining the theoretical foundations of these techniques and the practical aspects involved in their usage. The explanation is illustrated by the detailed description of two swarm granulation systems, *Swarm Granulator* and *Swarm Techtiles*, and by the analysis of their behavior. In the sixth chapter, which concludes the Evolutionary Music part of the book, Rafael Ramirez, Amaury Hazan, Jordi Mariné and Xavier Serra tackle a challenging problem in computer music, producing an expressive performance of a musical piece. They use a genetic algorithm to build a computational model of expressive performance from a set of examples of jazz saxophone performances. Later, they use this model to automatically create performances of musical pieces.

The third part of the book comprises chapters that are characterized by the use of evolutionary art approaches for real-world applications, providing valuable case studies. Christian Jacob and Gerald Hushlak describe the use of evolutionary and swarm design techniques in art, music and design, showing how interactive breeding techniques can facilitate the creative processes, and presenting a wide variety of examples in areas that range from furniture design to swarm choreographies. In the eighth chapter, Martin Hemberg, Una-May O'Reilly, Achim Menges, Katrin Jonas, Michel da Costa Gonçalves and Steven R. Fuchs take us to the domain of architecture, describing *Genr8* — an evolutionary system that allows the evolution of surfaces generated through an organic growth algorithm — and reporting its use on six different architectural projects. Charlie D. Frowd and Peter J.B. Hancock describe *EvoFIT*, a system that allows the evolution of photorealistic human faces, and explore its use for the production of facial composites of criminals. Later, the artistic potential of *EvoFIT* is also analyzed, and other potential application areas discussed. In the tenth chapter, A.E. Eiben describes the modeling of the artistic styles of the famous Dutch painters Piet Mondriaan and M.C. Escher, giving particular emphasis to the mathematical modeling of Escher's tilings and to the construction of an evolutionary system that allows their generation.

One of the difficulties inherent to evolutionary art and music is the difference between the scientific and artistic perspectives. To lessen this problem the fourth part of this volume gives voice to artists who employ or analyze biology-inspired mechanisms in an artistic context. As such, it consists of chapters where the artistic perspective is the most fundamental. The interest of Nicolas Monmarché, Isabelle Mahnich and Mohamed Slimane in swarm intelligence, ant colony algorithms and self-organization leads them to an exploration of the artistic potential of these concepts for the creation of spatio-temporal structures, which is illustrated by the evolution of musical pieces and paintings. In the twelfth chapter, Günter Bachelier describes the three levels — basic, methodical and superordinate — of his art practice. His unique evolutionary art approach — which relies on a pixel-based representation, on the exchange of regions of interest, and on the application of transformations to these regions — is thoroughly described. Later he presents his novel evolutionary art approach, which also integrates aspects such as multi-sexual reproduction and image templates, and ontogenetic concepts such as spores or fruits. In the thirteenth chapter, Jeffrey J. Ventrella presents *Musical Gene Pool*, an application that allows the evolution of *liquid* music, i.e., nonlinear music whose structure is continually able to flow and rearrange, allowing serendipity. Alan Dorin presents a survey of the use of virtual ecosystem simulation in the context of generative electronic art. Based on a thorough analysis of these systems, he concludes that their major strengths lie in the ability to display multi-scaled complexity and to produce novelty, and that their major weakness lies in their unpredictable response to perturbation; he later describes methods to overcome this weakness. In the concluding chapter of this part, Philip Galanter, following the modernist tradition of the art manifesto, proposes a new art approach, entitled *Complexism*, which relies on the "application of a scientific understanding of complex systems to the subject matter of the arts and humanities". He compares it with modernist and postmodernist movements, arguing that *Complexism* subsumes both, and analyzes the relevance of evolutionary art practices in the context of the *Complexism* movement.

The final part of the book comprises chapters that focus on relatively unexplored areas of evolutionary art and on the identification of future trends and open problems. The sixteenth chapter, by Craig Neufeld, Brian J. Ross and William Ralph, describes the evolution of artistic filters. The use of multi-objective optimization techniques and of a bell curve model of aesthetics, based on the empirical evaluation of artworks, are some of the key contributions of this work, where a correlation between aesthetics and the application of the paint operator is shown. Gary R. Greenfield surveys co-evolutionary approaches to evolutionary art, making a detailed description and analyzing several instances of this type of approach. This analysis is followed by a discussion of the challenges, difficulties and opportunities posed by this type of approach. In the eighteenth chapter, Penousal Machado, Juan Romero and Bill Manaris describe a novel autonomous evolutionary art approach, where the competition between an artificial critic and an evolutionary creator leads to stylistic variation, presenting and analyzing the results attained across iterations and in validation experiments. In the closing chapter of the book, Jon McCormack looks into the future, examining the challenges and possibilities that lie ahead. He identifies and discusses several of the open problems of the field from a research and artistic perspective, presenting the background and motivation and discussing the theoretical issues involved.

Finally, the DVD of the book comprises demonstration programs, source code and valuable examples of images, music and videos that complement the materials presented throughout the chapters, allowing the reader to fully appreciate some of the evolved works.

As previously stated, evolutionary art and music research is reaching maturity, and part of this process is the growing awareness of the various social, artistic and scientific challenges the area faces.

The biggest social challenge for evolutionary art and music lies in the development of projects or tools that have a relevant social impact. Constructing tools that enhance or promote the creativity of the user is probably the most obvious way to address this goal. However, it is not sufficient — it is equally important to disseminate these tools and to improve the public's awareness of their potential.

From an artistic perspective, the acceptance of the evolutionary approach as a significant art practice is probably the greatest challenge. To meet it, it is particularly relevant to promote the participation of the artistic community in biology-inspired endeavors, disseminate evolutionary projects through the conventional art channels, and ensure their presence in the commercial art circuit. Although some evolutionary art practitioners and musicians have attained all of these objectives, the challenge the area faces is ensuring that these exceptions become the norm. The creation of art spaces devoted to evolutionary art may play an important role in attaining it.

From a scientific standpoint, the development of autonomous fitness assignment schemes that take into account aesthetic criteria, the creation of systems that are able to develop their own aesthetic concepts, the integration and interaction of these systems with the environment, embodiment, and the definition of new forms of human–machine interaction, are some of the most relevant challenges.

Acknowledgments

This book would never have become a reality without the enduring dedication of many. We would like to express our gratitude towards all the authors, who made this book possible, not only giving us such high quality materials, but also offering their enthusiasm, perseverance, patience and assistance. We would also like to thank Springer's editorial staff, and especially Ronan

Nugent, who provided encouragement and support throughout the entire process. We also acknowledge some of the early enthusiasts of this project, including Amílcar Cardoso, Ernesto Costa, Alejandro Pazos, Antonino Santos, and the EvoMUSART and Evo* communities. Finally, we are thankful to Jorge Tavares, Santiago González and Eva Celeiro, who provided valuable help in the revision and editing tasks; and to Erika González, who designed the DVD.

A Coruña
Coimbra
August 2007

Juan Romero
Penousal Machado

Contents

List of Contributors

Günter Bachelier
Drosselweg 11, D-66839
Schmelz, Germany
guba@vi-anec.de

Tim Blackwell
Dept. of Computing
Goldsmiths College
University of London
New Cross, London SE14 6NW, UK
t.blackwell@gold.ac.uk

John Philip Collomosse
Media Technology Research
Centre Dept. of Computer Science
University of Bath
Bath, BA2 7AY, UK
jpc@cs.bath.ac.uk

Alan Dorin
Centre for Electronic Media Art
Faculty of Information Technology
Monash University Clayton,
Australia 3800
aland@csse.monash.edu.au

Scott Draves
Spotworks
2261 Market St. #158
San Francisco, CA 94114, USA
spot@draves.org

A.E. Eiben
Dept. of Computer Science
Free University Amsterdam
De Boelelaan 1081a
1081 HV Amsterdam
The Netherlands
gusz@cs.vu.nl

Charlie D. Frowd
Dept. of Psychology
University of Stirling
Stirling FK9 4LA, UK
cdf1@stir.ac.uk

Steven R. Fuchs
Southern California Institute of
Architecture,
1022 W. 18th St., #3, San Pedro,
CA 90731, USA
steve_fuchs@sciarc.edu

Philip Galanter
Independent Artist
Atlanta, Georgia, USA
book@philipgalanter.com

Michel da Costa Gonçalves
Emergent Technologies and Design
Architectural Association School of
Architecture
2, rue Ferdinand Duval
F 75004, Paris, France
mdcg@aaschool.co.uk

Gary R. Greenfield
Mathematics and Computer Science
University of Richmond
Richmond, VA 23173
USA
ggreenfi@richmond.edu

Niall J.L. Griffith
Centre for Computational
Musicology and Computer Music
Dept. of Computer Science and
Information Systems
University of Limerick
Limerick, Ireland
niall.griffith@ul.ie

Peter J.B. Hancock
Dept. of Psychology
University of Stirling
Stirling FK9 4LA, UK
pjbh1@stir.ac.uk

Amaury Hazan
Universitat Pompeu Fabra
Ocata 1, Barcelona 08003, Spain
hazan@iua.upf.es

Martin Hemberg
Imperial College
Dept. of Bioengineering
Exhibition Road
London SW7 2AZ, UK
martin.hemberg@imperial.ac.uk

Gerald Hushlak
Dept. of Art
University of Calgary
2500 University Drive N.W.
Calgary, Alberta T2N 1N4, Canada
hushlak@ucalgary.ca

Christian Jacob
Dept. of Computer Science
University of Calgary
2500 University Drive NW
Calgary, Alberta T2N 1N4, Canada
cjacob@ucalgary.ca

Katrin Jonas
Bartlett School of Architecture
University College London
Wates House, 22 Gordon St.
London WC1H OQB, UK
and Buro Happold
17 Newman St.
London W1T 1PD, UK
katrin.jonas@ucl.ac.uk;
katrin.jonas@burohappold.com

Matthew Lewis
ACCAD
Ohio State University
1224 Kinnear Road
Columbus, OH 43212, USA
mlewis@accad.osu.edu

Penousal Machado
CISUC
Dept. of Informatics Engineering
University of Coimbra
3030 Coimbra, Portugal
machado@dei.uc.pt

Isabelle Mahnich
Ecole Polytechnique de l'Université
François Rabelais de Tours
Laboratoire d'Informatique
64 avenue Jean Portalis
37200 Tours, France
isabelle.mah@gmail.com

Bill Manaris
Computer Science Dept.
College of Charleston
Charleston, SC 29424, USA
manaris@cs.cofc.edu

Jordi Mariné
Universitat Pompeu Fabra
Ocata 1, Barcelona 08003, Spain
jmarine@iua.upf.es

Jon McCormack
Centre for Electronic Media Art
Faculty of Information Technology
Building 75
Monash University
Clayton, Victoria 3800
Australia
jonmc@csse.monash.edu.au

James McDermott
Centre for Computational
Musicology and Computer Music
Dept. of Computer Science and
Information Systems
Univ. of Limerick
Limerick, Ireland
jamesmichaelmcdermott@gmail.com

Achim Menges
Architectural Association
36 Bedford Square
London WC1B 3ES, UK
HfG Offenbach
University of Art and Design
Schlossstrasse 31
63065 Offenbach/M, Germany
achimmenges@aaschool.ac.uk;
menges@em.uni-frankfurt.de

Nicolas Monmarché
Ecole Polytechnique de l'Université
François Rabelais de Tours
Laboratoire d'Informatique
64 avenue Jean Portalis
37200 Tours, France
nicolas.monmarche@univ-tours.fr

Craig Neufeld
Dept. of Computer Science
Brock University
St. Catherines, Ontario L2S 3A1,
Canada
craig.neufeld@gmail.com

Michael O'Neill
Natural Computing Research &
Applications
School of Computer Science &
Informatics
University College Dublin
Belfield, Dublin 4, Ireland
m.oneill@ucd.ie

Una-May O'Reilly
Computer Science and Artificial
Intelligence Lab
Massachusetts Institute of
Technology
Cambridge, MA 02139, USA
unamay@csail.mit.edu

William James Ralph
Dept. of Mathematics
Brock University
500 Glenridge Ave.
St. Catharines, ON L2S 3A1
Canada
bralph@brocku.ca

Rafael Ramirez
Universitat Pompeu Fabra
Ocata 1, Barcelona 08003, Spain
rramirez@iua.upf.es

Juan Romero
Faculty of Computer Science
University of Coruña
CP 15071, Coruña, Spain
jj@udc.es

Brian J. Ross
Dept. of Computer Science
Brock University
500 Glenridge Ave.
St. Catharines, ON L2S 3A1
Canada
bross@brocku.ca

Xavier Serra
Universitat Pompeu Fabra
Ocata 1, Barcelona 08003,
Spain
xserra@iua.upf.es

Mohamed Slimane
Ecole Polytechnique de l'Université
François Rabelais de Tours
Laboratoire d'Informatique
64 avenue Jean Portalis
37200 Tours, France
mohamed.slimane@univ-tours.fr

Jeffrey Ventrella
335 Kentucky St.
Petaluma, CA 94952, USA
jeffrey@ventrella.com

Part I

Evolutionary Art

1

Evolutionary Visual Art and Design

Matthew Lewis

ACCAD, Ohio State University, Columbus, OH, USA mlewis@accad.osu.edu

Summary. This chapter presents an introduction to the different artistic design domains that make use of interactive evolutionary design approaches, the techniques they use, and many of the challenges arising. After a brief introduction to concepts and terminology common to most artificial genetic design, there is a survey of artistic evolutionary systems and related research for evolving images and forms. While the focus is primarily on purely aesthetic fitness landscapes, the survey also ventures into areas such as product design and architecture. The overview shifts from technique to application as organizational strategies, as appropriate. After briefly surveying additional information sources, the chapter concludes with a discussion of major topics of relevance to evolutionary system designers, providing context for the following chapters. It is hoped that this snapshot of the state of the field will increase exposure to projects and issues, discussion amongst participants, and ultimately the accessibility of these techniques and approaches.

1.1 Introduction

In the early 1990s, both Karl Sims and William Latham (with Stephen Todd) followed in the footsteps of scientist Richard Dawkins by combining evolutionary techniques and computer graphics to create artistic images of great complexity [1, 2, 3]. In the succeeding decades, a generation of artists/researchers have recombined, modified, and extended these techniques, beginning the exploration of possible applications of evolution to aesthetic design. This chapter will survey developments in this field, and introduce issues and concepts critical to the approaches described.

The beginning of this chapter briefly introduces basic concepts and terminology used in evolutionary art and design. The middle portion of this chapter presents an overview of many of the aesthetic domains, application areas, and techniques in which artificial evolution has been employed. Determining a categorization strategy from the many possible options was very challenging. At the top level of organization, examples are divided into two-dimensional, three-dimensional, and four-dimensional sections (image, form, and time). Within these categories, however, two different methods are used.

In the two-dimensional artifacts section, work is discussed primarily in terms of the technique used. Approximately 90% of the examples in the section are applications of nonrepresentational aesthetic image creation, with three to six examples of most techniques. The remaining 3D and 4D domains seem more readily divided by usage, given fewer examples of each individual approach, and greater diversity and balance of application areas. The overview of the field concludes with pointers to additional survey materials. While this chapter will not attempt to venture into the field of evolutionary music, it will frequently traverse the short distance between artistic/aesthetic and more design-oriented subjective fitness applications. While efforts have been made to provide references primarily to works published as papers, books, etc., due to the lack of reliability that accompanies Web-based references, there are quite a few relevant projects, companies, and other resources included that are available only online.[1]

In the space of evolutionary design research, the boundary around projects comprising "evolutionary art" is fuzzy. Are evolved creatures *art* when presented at an a-life conference versus a gallery installation? Are certain regions of software's potential design space *art*, while others are not? Which is the more critical task: the creation of evolutionary art interfaces or the crafting of the design spaces they represent? Very few of those capable of the technical demands of programming evolutionary design software have formal art training. While the products of evolutionary art systems are ostensibly tied to the aesthetic sensibilities of the user, the design of the solution space usually weighs much more heavily in the likely range of visual results.

The remainder of the chapter concludes by introducing a number of concepts and concerns prevalent in the field, including a summary of critical issues to provide context for the remaining chapters. Collectively, these point toward a future in which software, interface, and representation will work together to escape the local minima of current imagery and venture further into new regions in the possibility space of evolutionary art.

1.2 Concepts and Terminology

This section will briefly introduce the basic concepts upon which most evolutionary art and design approaches are based. In general, a design firm analogy can be of use. Given a particular design assignment, a staff of artists and designers creates a number of possible solutions. The director decides, using

[1] While this is intended to be a comprehensive survey providing brief coverage of representative works in a majority of the relevant areas, it is likely that many individuals, projects, and problem domains are not mentioned. Please continue to email missing references, which will be added to the growing online database [4].

whatever criteria he or she feels is most appropriate, which designs seem the most promising for further investigation. The team is then sent "back to the drawing board" to work on variations and combinations of the chosen *best* designs. It returns shortly to present its new solutions, which are again judged. The best are selected, and the process repeats until satisfactory designs are obtained.

To make use of a computer in this scenario, first the specific design problem must be represented numerically. A program produces a potentially large number of possible solutions. The quality or "fitness" of these solutions is then determined. In some cases, this can be done algorithmically, but in most of the examples discussed here, a human will judge subjectively. There are a number of means by which the best solutions can be combined and/or modified to produce new solutions similar to their antecedents. The method used is generally determined by the design representation. Approaches can be divided (very roughly) into two different methods, those using a fixed length string of numbers at the heart of their representation and those that make use of a hierarchical graph (usually representing an expression.)

1.2.1 Genetic Algorithms

Simple cartoon faces can be used to illustrate some of the basic principles of a *genetic algorithm (GA)*. A particular face can be described using a list of numbers (or parameters) that define traits like how wide the mouth is or how big the eyes are. Creating such a parametric model[2] implicitly creates a set of possible designs or a *solution space*. The list of parameters can be referred to as a *genotype*, with each number being thought of as a gene. The values of these genes determine the appearance of the face. The face can be referred to as the *phenotype*. A *population* of faces can be created by setting the values of the genes for each face to different values (e.g., see Fig. 1.9).

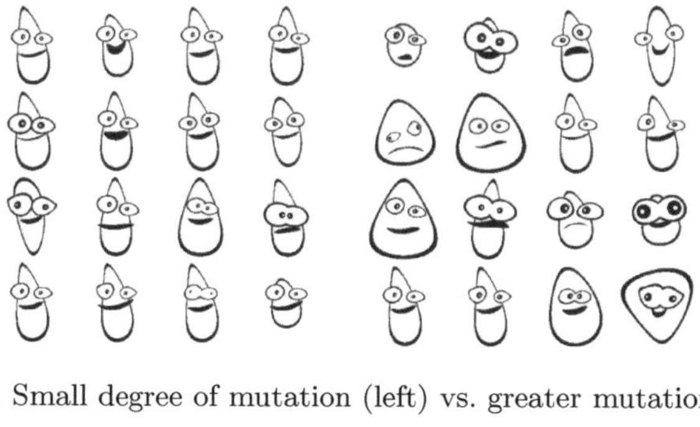

Fig. 1.1. Small degree of mutation (left) vs. greater mutation (right)

[2] The term "parametric" has several discipline-specific meanings. Here it will be used primarily when referring to entities defined by a set of parameters.

In a typical interactive evolutionary system, a population of individual faces is initially randomly generated and displayed to a software user. The user judges the population by selecting the most interesting faces, usually simply by clicking on them. The system then makes use of the user's choices to generate a new *generation* of faces. This process of evaluation, selection, and generation, is repeated until the user is satisfied.

The designs for two selected parent faces can be combined in different ways to produce a new set of offspring face designs. Each individual offspring may inherit some of the visual properties of one or both of the parents. Two faces are combined or *mated* by mixing genes, drawing some genes from one parent and the remaining genes from the other. One way this is commonly done is by using a technique called *crossover* wherein genes are copied in sequence from one of the parents, into the offspring. At some randomly determined point the copying process "crosses over" to the other parent, from whom it copies the remaining gene values. The child/offspring face could end up with the father's mouth but the mother's eyes as a result.

In addition to mating, new designs can also be produced by *mutation*. This involves producing variations of a current design solution by making random adjustments to some of the genes. Changing many genes usually results in significant differences, while minor gene modifications might produce correspondingly minor visual alterations to the phenotypes/faces (Fig. 1.1).

1.2.2 Genetic Programming

In evolutionary art, a different representation is also commonly used instead of the fixed-length list of numbers described above. In much of the work described in the next section, a mathematical expression is used as the genotype. An expression like $abs(sin(s * 3 * \pi) + cos(t * 4 * \pi))/2$ can be represented as a tree graph structure, made up of mathematical functions and operators at internal nodes, and constants or variables at the leaves. When the expression represented by the tree is evaluated at each pixel in an image by plugging in the pixel's coordinates, the resulting value can be used to determine the color of a pixel. The resulting image is the phenotype. While such systems are often still referred to as GAs by many, they are also often discussed as examples of *genetic programming (GP)*.

Images or forms thus created and selected can be mated using crossover techniques once again, but now instead of combining two lists of numbers, two node graphs must be combined. For example, one tree might be inserted randomly into the other, or subtrees might be exchanged. Mutation likewise still involves making small changes to the genotype. In this case, however, a change might be made to a subtree: changing a leaf node from a constant to a variable, inserting or deleting an internal operator node (e.g., addition becoming subtraction), or changing a node from one function to another. As will be seen in the following sections and chapters, there are many different techniques for representing genetic information as well as a very diverse set of

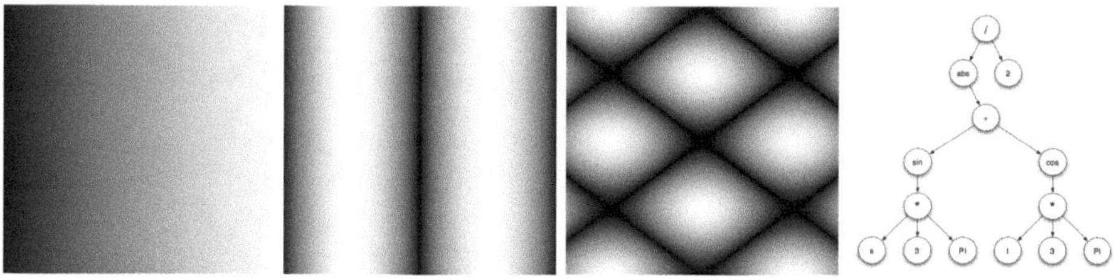

(a) (b) (c) (d)

Fig. 1.2. (a) Pixel intensity from horizontal s coordinate (b) pixel values from $abs(sin(s * 3 * \pi))$ (c) $abs(sin(s * 3 * \pi) + cos(t * 4 * \pi))/2$ (d) tree representation

application domains. Choices about what functions to use, how to map values, and so forth determine the breadth of phenotypes that can be created, and also influence the likelihood of finding interesting results.

1.3 Evolving 2D Artifacts

1.3.1 Expression-Based Imagery

In his 1991 paper Karl Sims introduced the expression-based approach to evolving images briefly described in the previous section [2]. His work resulted in complex and beautiful images like the ones in Fig. 1.3. In doing so, he created a template which has attracted the efforts of many artists and graphics programmers ever since. A number of artists have been inspired to create substantial bodies of work using expression-based image generation techniques. Through the 1990s, Steven Rooke in particular created one of the earliest major bodies of expression-based image work, about which a significant amount has been written [5, 6]. Rooke's Web site published extensive details about his process of evolving potentially hundreds of generations and then finally "tuning" the colors and region of image space presented by each image.[3]

Tatsuo Unemi is one of a few evolutionary artists who has continued breeding images from mathematical expressions for over a decade, using different versions of his SBART software [9, 10]. The work in his online gallery provides a rare opportunity to see a progression of color and form as his software's capabilities have been gradually extended (Fig. 1.4b).

More recently, David Hart [11] has put significant effort into developing a collection of images with a very different visual appearance from the majority of expression-based, evolved imagery (Fig. 1.4a). His interest, in particular in gaining control over the evolving colors and forms, is noteworthy. As such, his system's interface allows for extensive low-level tuning.

[3] An extremely informative resource, Rooke's Web site is unfortunately now only accessible through the Internet Archive's "Wayback Machine" site [7, 8].

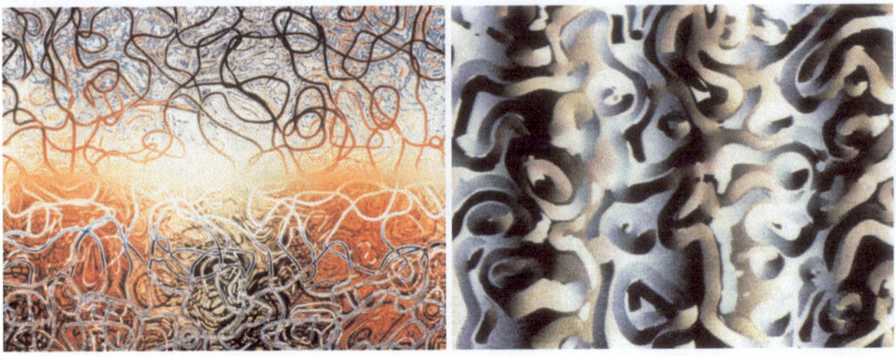

(a) (b)

Fig. 1.3. ©Karl Sims, 1991

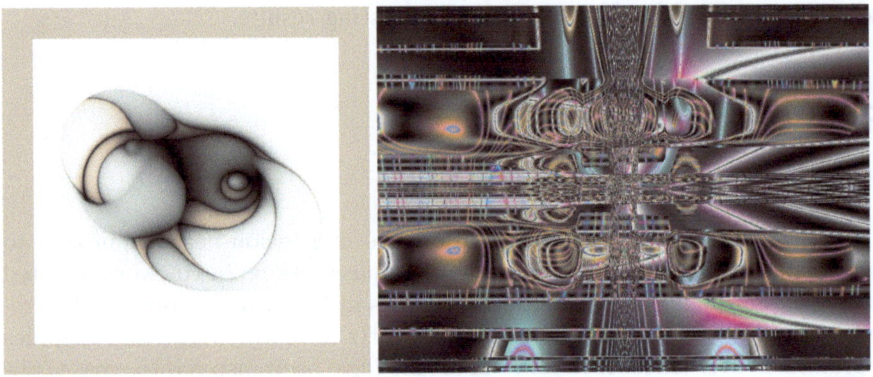

(a) (b)

Fig. 1.4. (a) ©2005 D. A. Hart (b) ©Tatsuo Unemi

The majority of expression-based image generation systems in the spirit of Sims use a reduced set of mathematical functions and often only local information for determining pixel color. In different systems it is often possible to recognize, in the images produced, emphasized reliance on specific techniques such as fractals, polar coordinate mappings, noise functions, etc.

It is common for there to be a dozen or more Web sites at any given time illustrating implementations of expression-based approaches. They are often either Java applets or downloadable PC programs, created as short-term student projects or by hobbyists, and many are unfortunately no longer accessible. It can be interesting to note the similarities and differences in image galleries produced using various systems. Information about the exact function sets used to construct genotypes is usually not available, but the characteristic results of different functions are sometimes evident. Some online examples include

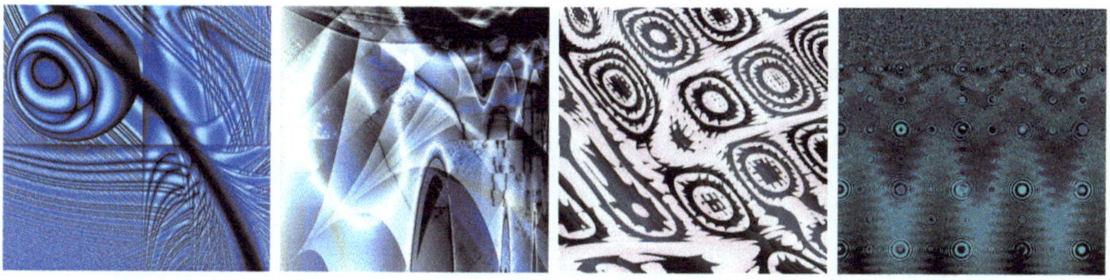

(a) (b) (c) (d)

Fig. 1.5. (a) ©Derek Gerstmann (b) ©David K. McAllister (c) ©Tim Day (d) ©Ashley Mills, 2005

work by Bacon [12], Davidson [13], Kleiweg [14], Maxwell [15], Mills [16], and Saunders [17].

Specific additions to the function set or other system extensions push system results in specific (often new) directions: Ellingsen's distortion and iteration operators [18], Gerstmann's HDR mapping (Fig. 1.5a) [19], or McAllister's evolved color palettes (Fig. 1.5b) [20] provide a few visual examples. Some hybrid systems using expression images such as Baluja's [21], Greenfield's evaluations of expression evolution [22, 23, 24], and Machado's NEvAr system [25] will be discussed later in this chapter (as well as in chapters 17 and 18.)

Image evolution software is occasionally released for others to use as an art-making tool with varying degrees of commercialization, interface development, and source code availability. A few examples include ArtMatic [26], Evolvotron (Fig. 1.5c) [27], Kandid [28], and Softology [29]. In particular, Kandid supports a large number of different representations in addition to expressions.

In a few cases evolution software has run in conjunction with a Web server, allowing those visiting the site to determine fitness by "voting" for images. The original example of this was a system by Mount, Neil-Reilly, and Witbrock [30, 31]. A more recent example is the python-based online voting system using tournament-style selection by Lee [32]. A few other voting/server systems will be mentioned below, including those of Draves [33], Gatarski [34], and Hemert and Jansen [35].

Besides 2D images, expressions have also been evolved to create textures for 3D geometry, most commonly using a surface point's coordinates as expression inputs. Sims demonstrated a few examples of his techniques applied to 3D geometry in his early work [2, 36]. Hobden focused on GP textures in the style of Sims [37]. RenderMan shaders making use of noise functions were evolved by Ibrahim [38]. Hewgill and Ross focused on obtaining textures based on sampled texture data [39].

A handful of other researchers have explored automatically evolving expressions using target images. Ibrahim [38] made some of the earliest attempts at replicating textures. DiPaola [40] recently focused on evolving expression images driven by portrait image targets (Fig. 1.6a). Ross's initial work in this

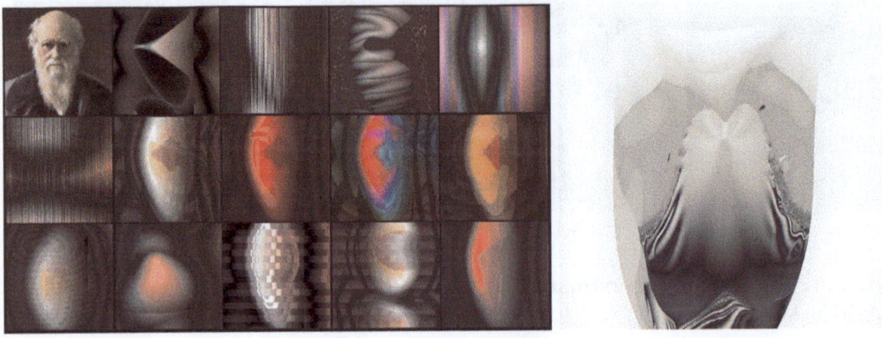

(a) (b)

Fig. 1.6. (a) Image target, upper left; ©Steve DiPaola, 2005 (b) ©JJ Ventrella, 2004

area with Wiens [41] sought to match simple test textures. Ross's more recent work attempts to generate expressions matching arbitrary artistic imagery [42] (see Chap. 16).

1.3.2 Fractals/IFS

Several researchers over the years have focused on fractals as their primary primitive, most typically using iterated function systems. An interesting example is the Electric Sheep project by Draves [43, 33] (discussed in Chap. 3). Implemented as a distributed screen saver with selection capabilities, Electric Sheep is likely the most widely used evolutionary design project to date. The genes consist of approximately 160 parameters (Fig. 1.7b).

Chapuis and Lutton's ArtiE-Fract project has produced a large gallery of images with a more traditional interactive selection interface using "nonlinear 2D functions (affine and non-affine), defined either in Cartesian or polar coordinates" [44, 45]. A Java applet with source code demonstrating a basic IFS interactive evolution system by Rowley is available online [46].

Yoshiaki provides software which explores a very different fractal image space based on the Mandelbrot set [47]. Ventrella generated imagery by evolving Mandelbrot parameter values using target portrait images (Fig. 1.6b) [48]. Rowley's "Toolkit for Visual Genetic Programming" [49] and Jourdan's Kandid [28] provide generic frameworks capable of evolving fractal imagery (Fig. 1.7a).

1.3.3 Neural Networks

Several projects have evolved neural networks to generate images. The Artificial Painter for example uses neural networks with inputs involving orientation and distance from landmark coordinates to either automatically or interactively evolve abstract imagery [50].

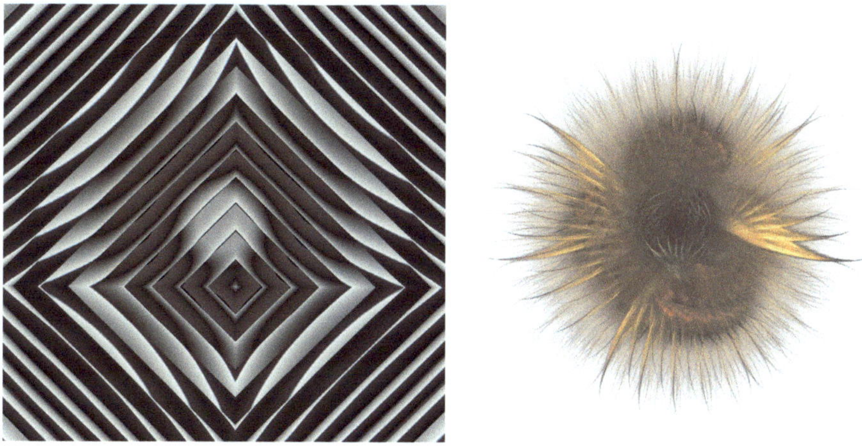

(a) (b)

Fig. 1.7. (a) ©Thomas Jourdan (kandid.org) (b) ©Scott Draves and the Electric Sheep (www.electricsheep.org)

Stanley's NEAT infrastructure was used by Fagerlund [51] to evolve complex networks for image generation (Fig. 1.8a). Stanley demonstrates the usage of the software for targeted evolution by interactively evolving networks which gradually refine a spaceship design [52]. This approach is replicated in a C# implementation by Ferstl (based on sharpNEAT) which adds several interface extensions, in particular giving the user greater control of color [53].

Others, such as Baluja, Machado, and Saunders, have investigated the use of artificial neural networks for fitness evaluation with the goal of automatically generating interesting images [21, 54, 55]. Automated image fitness evaluation will be discussed at the end of this chapter.

1.3.4 Image Processing

Quite a number of systems have used genetic techniques to process images provided as source material. A number of expression-evolving projects, including those by Sims, Unemi, and McGuire, have provided functions capable of drawing color from source images in addition to the usual math expressions greatly enhancing the palettes produced [2, 10, 56]. Other work that as focused specifically on image coloring includes Machado et al. and Greenfield [57, 58].

Graf and Banzhaf's work used image morphing and selective dissolving [59] while Poli and Cagnoni focused on image enhancement using a pseudo-coloring process [60]. There have been a few commercial products for image processing which allow users to interactively select from a set of images manipulated with different filters [61, 62].

Recently, a number of researchers have begun to use salience-based approaches to affect how different portions of an image are manipulated,

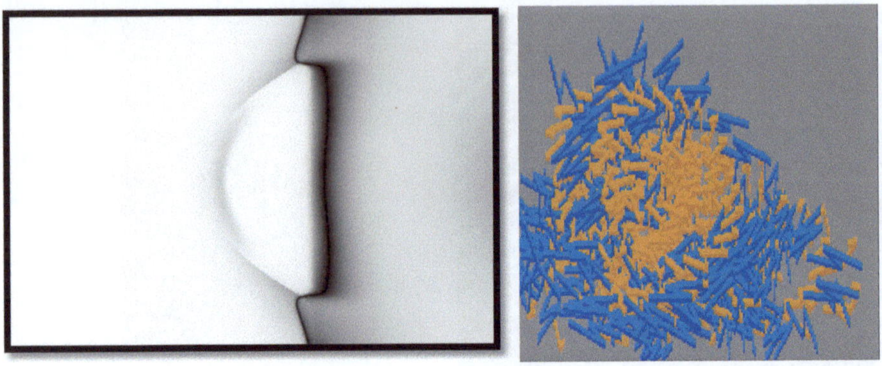

(a) (b)

Fig. 1.8. (a) ©Mattias Fagerlund, 2005 (b) ©Gary Greenfield

including work by Wolfer using neural networks [63] and by Collomosse [64, 65] (see Chap. 2). Neufeld and Ross evolve filters automatically based on a model of aesthetics and high-level paint stroke primitives (see Chap. 16).

Several researchers have worked to evolve images of faces, usually through image compositing and transformations. Among the earliest was the FacePrint work of Caldwell and Johnston. Initially put forth in a criminal sketch artist context, Johnston has since conducted a great deal of work on evolving numerical representations of facial aesthetics (and gender) [66, 67].

Hancock and Frowd [68] used principal components analysis in an approach based on eigenfaces to allow interactive creation of photographic face images (see Chap. 9). Takagi and Kishi [69] recombined face parts for one of their problem domains while studying user fatigue reduction. Lim [70] employed image warping, pushing and pulling appropriately placed anchor points to smoothly distort photos of faces to evolve facial expressions.

1.3.5 Lines and Shapes

Drawings, paintings, and shapes can be evolved using a wide array of techniques. Much evolutionary artwork in recent years has employed ant and swarm computing paradigms. Aupetit et al. use an interactive genetic algorithm (IGA) to evolve parameters for ant paintings [71] (see Chap. 11). Greenfield has evolved simulated ant and robot parameters, experimenting with different automated fitness functions to achieve varying aesthetic visual results [72, 73]. Urbano investigates consensual decision making among swarms of painter agents [74]. Moura and Ramos have also written extensively about swarm art [75, 76]. Jacob provides an in-depth discussion of swarm-based evolution [77] in Chap. 7.

Dudek developed an OS9 freeware program for interactively evolving drawings using a LOGO-like language, intended as a tool for teaching children

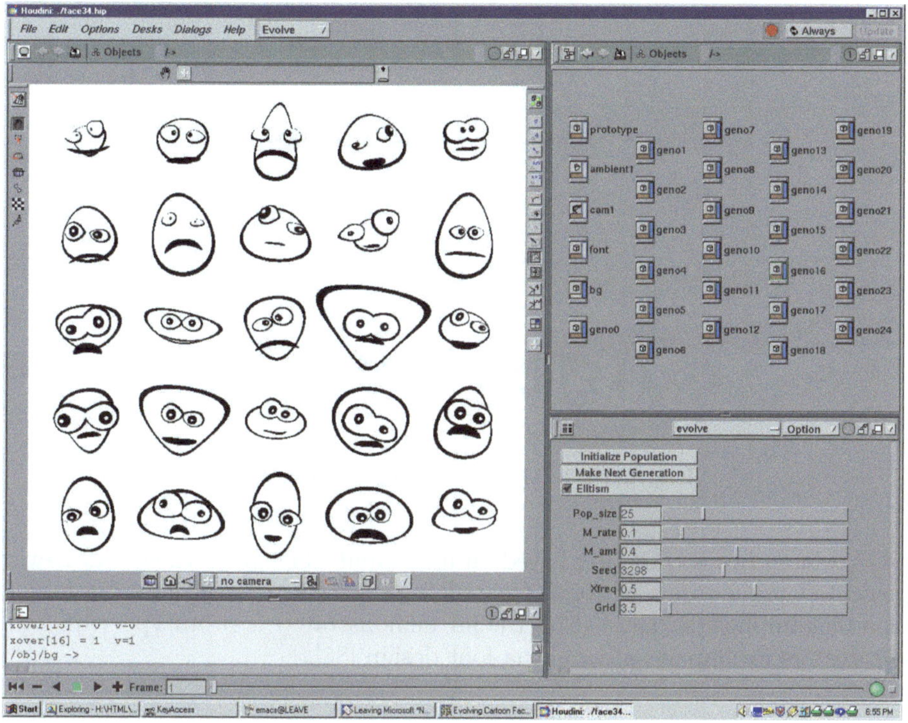

Fig. 1.9. ©Matthew Lewis, 2000

about evolution [78]. Dehlinger has written about his generative drawings in an evolutionary context [79]. In some of the earliest evolutionary work, Baker modified the positions of line segments, allowing a user to select the "best" images, from drawings of faces as one example [80].

Pagliarini and Parisi allowed users to evolve expressions on cartoon faces in a system intended to allow children to learn about facial expressions' conveyance of mood [81]. Nishio et al. created a cartoon face space with twelve parameters in order to study ways to reduce user fatigue by combining an IGA with different fitness assignment strategies [82]. The time to evolve a target face was compared for different approaches. Lewis used cartoon face evolution as one domain when developing the interactive evolutionary design platform "Metavolve" within a commercial 3D animation environment (Fig. 1.9) [83].

Lund used parametric fonts to compare interactive evolution and direct manipulation interfaces, observing that evolution yielded better results for creative exploration while direct manipulation was easier given a targeted design task [84]. Schmitz created a Flash-based program which allows the user to experiment with breeding different typefaces with an emphasis on drag-and-drop mating (Fig. 1.10) [85]. The Alphabet Synthesis Machine by Levin et al. creates abstract alphabets from a physically based writing simulation, using

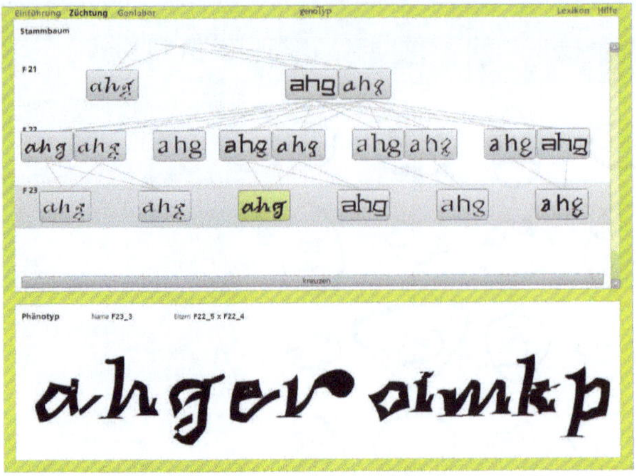

Fig. 1.10. ©Michael Schmitz, UdK Berlin

a GA with a fitness function based on user input [86]. Butterfield and Lewis presented populations of fonts created from letters deformed by groups of blending implicit surfaces [87]. Unemi demonstrated a prototype with ten parameters for Japanese Katakana font design [88].

1.3.6 Additional Techniques

Many other approaches to evolving 2D artifacts for a number of problem domains have been investigated. Ashmore employs "cartesian genetic programming" in which genotypes consisting of a string of numbers encode small function networks that map coordinates to colors [89]. Hemert and Jansen evolve Mondriaan, mandala, van Doesburg, and fractal style images using a CGI-based Web interface, which has the ability to collect data about people's aesthetic selections [35]. Lewis's image generation approach involves layering patterns created with varying degrees of irregularity, generated using procedural shader techniques with explicit embedding of basic principles of visual design [90].

Bachelier uses a process in which traditional art-making techniques are combined with computer-assisted methods such as selection masking, localized scaling, rotation, and translation, distortion, etc. to generate painterly images while working in an interactive evolution paradigm [91] (Fig. 1.11a and Chap. 12). McCabe's images combine interactive selection with automated fitness calculation based on diversity metrics measured at different scales (Fig. 1.11b) [92, 93].

Greenfield has continually explored a large number of varied image generation techniques with an eye primarily toward investigating potential noninteractive fitness functions. In addition to the drawing approaches mentioned

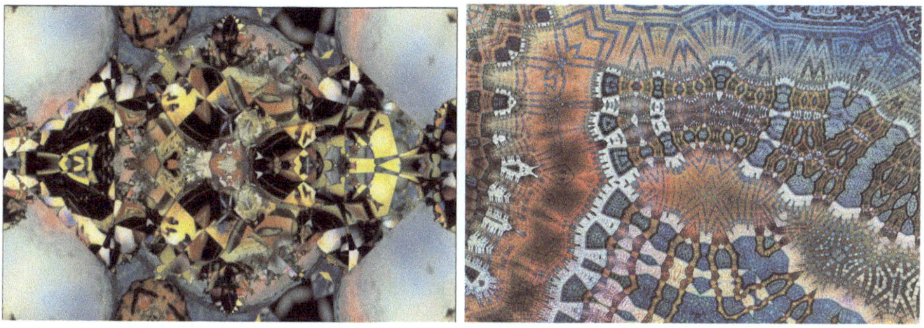

(a) (b)

Fig. 1.11. (a) ©Günter Bachelier, 2004 (www.aroshu.de) (b) ©Jonathan McCabe, 2006

earlier, other examples include his generated mosaics using image and convolution filter coevolution [94], as well as cellular processes [95] (Chap. 17).

Gatarski presented work in which banner advertisement designs for Web pages were automatically evolved using user click-through as a fitness metric [34]. Monmarché et al. investigated Web page visual design properties (colors, fonts, etc.) by interactively evolving style sheets [96]. Oliver et al. then extended this work to include page layout [97].

1.4 Evolving 3D Artifacts

Artists, scientists, and designers have used a wide range of techniques to evolve 3D geometry in a number of domains. The earliest efforts were the product of artist William Latham working with Stephen Todd of IBM UK around 1990 [3]. The complex branching (frequently animated) organic forms created using their software proved to be a strong inspiration for many of the earliest evolutionary artists.

There have been several implementations of their technique both as individual projects and as commercial software. Rowbottom's Form software provided an early PC-based implementation of Latham's approach [98]. Lintermann created a real-time installation (using a high-end SGI) called Morphogenesis [99]. Groboto is an interface which allows children to build and experiment with these sorts of forms [100] . A few commercial implementations existed, like Notting Hill's Cyberation/Dancer DNA [101], but are no longer available.

Todd and Latham's PC Mutator system expanded their infrastructure to allow their interactive genetic approach to interface with other arbitrary PC software packages ranging from drawing tools to spreadsheets [102, 103].

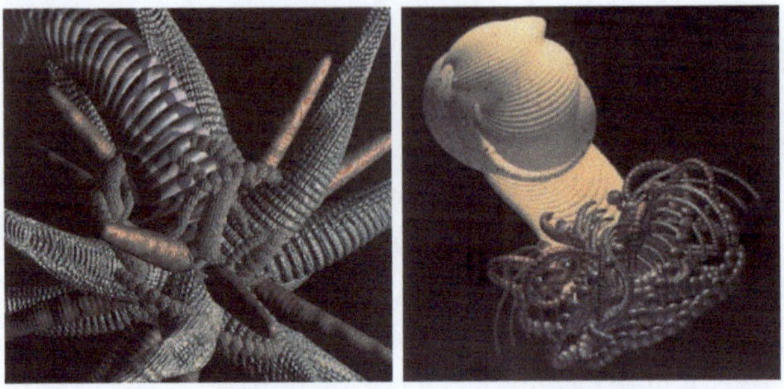

Fig. 1.12. Mutation Art. Artist: William Latham. Produced at the IBM UK Scientific Centre. Programmer Stephen Todd. Copyright William Latham, 1987 – 1993

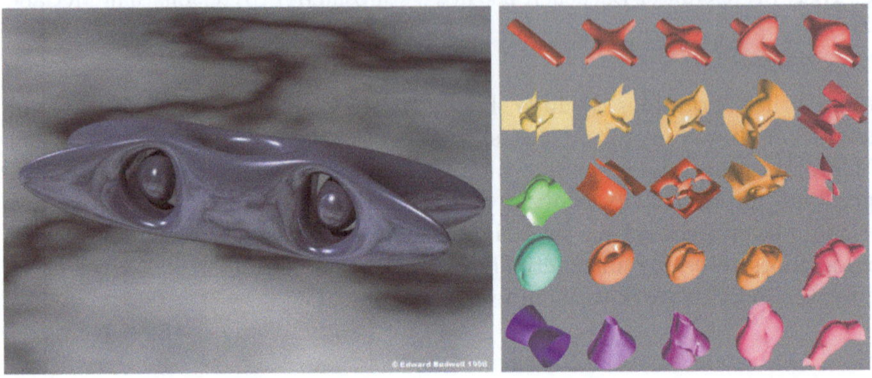

(a) (b)

Fig. 1.13. (a) ©Ted Bedwell, 1998 (b) ©Mark W. Jones

1.4.1 Abstract Form

Numerous geometric modeling techniques have been employed in an attempt to evolve arbitrary 3D forms using interactive evolution. Early examples were Watabe's lattice deformation approach [104] and Frank McGuire's sequences of polygonal operators [105].

A number of abstract form generation projects have employed implicit surfaces. Das, Bedwell, Jones, and Jacob all have presented implicitly defined volumetric primitives using GP-style crossover and mutation operations on equations to combine and then render them (Fig. 1.13b) [106, 107, 108, 109]. Nishino has used implicit primitives (superquadrics) combined with deformers in an interactive genetic algorithm (IGA) intended for free-form modeling [110].

Additional methods of evolving geometry have included surfaces of revolution [111], constructive solid geometry [112], surface curvature and form driven by simulated chemical reactions [113, 114], and VRML scene graphs [115, 116].

1.4.2 Consumer Design

A number of systems over the years have been developed to evolve consumer product designs. One of the earliest examples is the general evolution system described by Pontecorvo [117]. Rowland's research included an investigation into shampoo bottle evolution strategies [118, 115]. Bentley described his genetic spatial partitioning software which was shown to be useful in a number of evolutionary design domains [119].

A few researchers have applied genetic approaches to fashion design, using body parts with variable widths [120] or combining pre-modeled 3D garment geometry parts [121, 122]. Lee and Tang demonstrate the use of shape grammars in the generation of camera designs [123]. Hornby compares the strengths of a number of generative and non-generative representations, demonstrating the GENRE framework's performance evolving table designs [124].

A few companies offer evolutionary design systems for commercial design. Genometri's Genovate technology integrates with CAD software for form design [125]. Other emerging evolutionary consumer design systems include Icosystem's Hunch Engine [126] and Affinnova's IDDEA technology [127].

1.4.3 3D Computer Graphics

Modeling for 3D computer animation and virtual environments has provided a number of opportunities for evolutionary design. Several projects have used L-systems [128] to evolve plant geometry (as well as more abstract branching structures). In the early 1990s, Sims and artist Jon McCormack both evolved animated plant life in surreal landscapes [2, 129, 130]. Other efforts have included Traxler's evolution of realistic trees [131] and Jacob's Mathematica-based educational examples [132]. Grammidity is available as an open source package using Java for experimenting with grammar-based evolutionary programming [133].

Several genetic systems have been created to evolve human figure character geometry primarily for use in games and animation. Rowland's dissertation and Singular Inversion's FaceGen Modeller are two examples of systems for evolving high quality face geometry [118, 134]. DiPaola developed the FaceLift interface for evolving Sims2 game characters [135]. Lewis evolved both deformed polygonal and implicit surface-based body geometry within commercial computer graphics packages [136].

Aoki and Takagi used an IGA to build a lighting support system, comparing user performance in a manual lighting task with users employing an aesthetic selection interface [137, 138]. They have also conducted research into the evolution of particle system design, in the context of fireworks animations [139].

A common significant goal of creative evolutionary design approaches to artistic creation is to ease the difficulty inherent in using complicated visual design software. Lewis and his students have been working on approaches

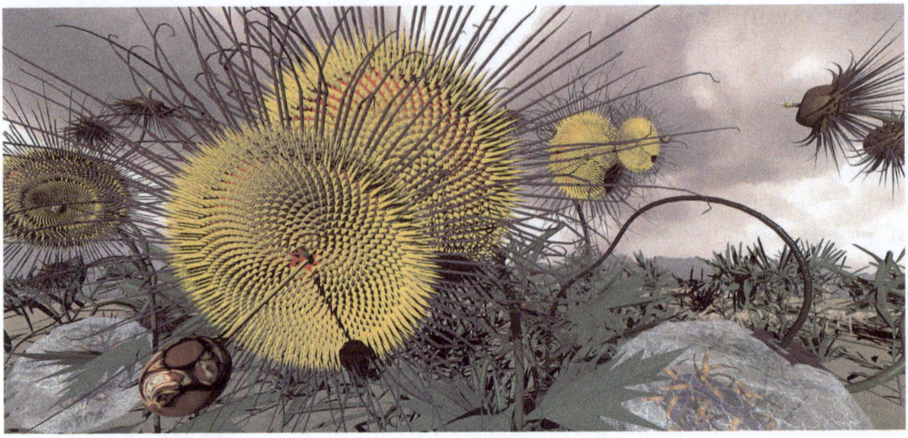

Fig. 1.14. Image from "Turbulence: an interactive museum of unnatural history," Copyright 1994 Jon McCormack

to allowing non-programmer visual artists and designers who are capable of creating parametric solution spaces in popular CG design software such as Maya, Houdini, and Jitter to explore interactive evolution design approaches without requiring custom programming. The domains of 3D modeling, lighting, surface materials, particle systems, and animation are all within this potential problem space [83, 140, 141, 142]. Marks et al. have provided an alternative approach in the same problem area in which populations of solutions are precomputed, with consideration given to encouraging maximum differences between the properties of individuals, to achieve sufficient coverage of a given CG domain [143].

1.4.4 Architecture

There is a very rich and complicated history of the use of evolutionary concepts and terminology in architectural design. It is very difficult to bound architectural usage of evolution because much of the work might more appropriately be broadly categorized as "generative design." Zarzar provides a critical analysis of the role of evolution in the work of several architects who make use of genetic design terminology, including Tsui, Soddu, Frazer, and Gero [144].

Frazer's long history of evolutionary architecture research has focused on procedures for controlling growth and development from seed forms into emerging structures rooted in biological analogies, drawing from a long list of generative and a-life techniques [145, 146].

Gero's research group's work has uniquely focused on very difficult problems such as representing stylistic knowledge, recognizing novelty, and extending state spaces in order to better model creative processes [147, 148, 149, 55].

Several interesting surface-generating systems using techniques such as L-systems and agents for surface generation have resulted from the Emergent Design Group at MIT, including Genr8 and Agency-GP [150, 151, 152] (see Chap. 18). Hemberg has also provided a simple GA implemented as a MEL script for generic evolution in Maya [153].

Paul Coates has made substantial use of L-systems and shape grammars to breed structures with fitness driven by performance, for example, in response to environmental conditions such as light and wind, and emphasizing structural properties like *enclosure* and *permeability* [154, 155].

1.5 Evolving 4D Artifacts

As is common in many of the above 3D domains, problem spaces in which evolved individuals vary over time can be challenging to evaluate. Animated characters, interactive systems, and dynamics simulations each require novel representations and interfaces.

Several researchers have used genetic approaches to generate character motion via interactive or automated fitness selection. Miller evolved human-like reaching movements through obstacle-filled 3D environments [156]. Shibuya also evolved natural arm motion but using an IGA in an effort to explore methods of automatically reducing the number of animations a user would need to evaluate [157]. Antonini further explored the use of IGAs for producing figure gestures for use by characters within avatar-based virtual environments [158].

Lim and Thalmann published a number of papers investigating IGAs for gait creation, including evolution from existing animation, methods for constraining the walk solution space, and, more generally, the use of tournament selection when evolving time-based solutions [159, 160, 161]. Lapointe demonstrates an approach to evolving dances using different choreographic mutations on sequences of movements. Both automated and interactive selection approaches are considered [162, 163].

Artificial life artwork and research has produced a vast amount of animated creatures employing varying degrees of evolutionary techniques. While the scope is too large to begin to provide adequate coverage here, a few jumping off points for further investigation include the physically simulated creatures of Sims, Ventrella, and Gritz [164, 165, 166] as well as several papers on the subject by Alan Dorin [167] (see Chap. 14). (The ant, swarm, and robot work referenced above also falls within this category.)

While this survey is not addressing genetic sound or music (which will be discussed in several later chapters), a number of systems have emerged for evolving results based on video material. Nemirovsky's work focuses on collaborative improvisational control of multiple media sources. The system allows users to specify fitness dynamically using *magnets*, which causes a GA to evolve the system's state in desired directions [168]. Henriques et al. have embedded video production knowledge (editing, montage, etc.) into fitness evaluation to generate video sequences. The system relies on both manually specified semantic information about the clips, as well as procedurally generated low-level information (e.g., histograms) [169]. Lewis demonstrated the evolution of arbitrary live-video processing filters in real time within a Max/MSP/Jitter-based framework [141]. Unemi extended SBART to allow movies to be both generated and used as input, using *boxels* to extract color volumes from the 3D movie space using expression-based GP with time varying cyclically as an additional variable [170].

A number of the previously mentioned image evolution artists/researchers have used their systems to produce animations within their respective genetic image spaces. These are often produced as either interpolative transitions between a sequence of one or more selected pairs of individuals, or sometimes with the insertion of *time* as a variable within an image or form-generating expression. Examples include animations by Latham, Sims, Unemi, and Hart [3, 2, 9, 171].

1.6 Overviews and Surveys

There are several excellent sources for further reading on different aspects of evolutionary art and design. In particular, Kelly's late 1990s book *Out of Control: The New Biology of Machines, Social Systems, and the Economic World* provides a very readable introduction to issues, techniques, and goals surrounding this discipline [54]. The survey texts edited by Peter Bentley, *Evolutionary Design by Computers* and *Creative Evolutionary Systems* (with co-editor Corne), provide a broad overview of most of the primary concerns in the wider field [172, 173].

Hideyuki Takagi has written a survey on interactive evolutionary computation which contains many references focusing on experiments in interface design and user fatigue [174]. Mitchell Whitelaw's book *Metacreation: Art and Artificial Life* contains in-depth analysis of several of the artists mentioned above, within an a-life context [6]. Finally, the Web site "Visual Aesthetic Evolutionary Design Links" provides a comprehensive list of online resources [4].

1.7 Concepts and Topics

Having reviewed the breadth of specific applications and techniques for applying evolution in the visual arts and design, this section will briefly introduce some challenges and research directions involved with developing such systems. Note that while the author has sometimes worn the hat of a computer scientist or an evolutionary artist, this section is written largely from the perspective of a *meta-designer*, his having been focused of late on the task of developing systems to enable others to make use of genetic approaches to art and design.

1.7.1 Solution Spaces

Meta-designers must carefully craft their solution spaces before they can be explored. Evolutionary algorithms are one way of traversing these abstract environments. Explicit parametric design can be very challenging since in a sense the range of desired possibilities must be considered in advance, which is difficult when the intent is the discovery of surprising solutions. In both interactive and automated fitness approaches, the design of the solution space is critical if there is to be any hope of satisfactory convergence.

Different fitness landscapes (as with landscape in the real world) vary considerably in form in large flat regions of similarity, continuous rolling hills, sharp peaks, abrupt cliffs, etc. More efforts like the examples by Hayashida et al. for visualizing multidimensional solution spaces would be worthwhile for studying the formal qualities of design spaces [138]. Although these spaces of possibilities are most commonly viewed only in terms of expressions, sets of functions, and ranges of values, by directly evaluating their shape these abstract environments could perhaps be sculpted and compared. Evaluating the fitness of solution spaces might allow them in turn to be evolved via mutation and recombination.

A number of writers have contrasted the control challenges of GP-based representations with the limitations inherent in GA representations [175, 22, 176, 177]. Control is a very significant challenge for expression-based genetic programming approaches. In many implementations, mating operations often result in offspring which resemble just one (or often neither) of the parents. Mutation operations can also be very difficult to control, in the sense of giving the user a slider which will accurately allow him to specify whether he wants primarily small visual changes. While automated fitness systems can tolerate large numbers of poor fitness offspring, the low population sizes of interactive system require design spaces with higher average fitness.

1.7.2 Shaping Fitness Landscapes

Iterative improvement of solution spaces (i.e., function sets, value ranges) is in many ways as equally challenging as developing techniques for searching for potential solutions. While much work focuses on innovative ways to assist in finding regions of high fitness, making the high-fitness regions large enough that they are easily discovered is also a frequent topic. This can be considered an "architectural" meta-design problem: how to modify solution spaces with the intent of them being traversed by artists and designers.

The *signature* or "style" of a given evolutionary design system very frequently seems stronger than the differences that might result from different users [98]. Most commonly this signature[4] is a result of biases toward certain

[4] McCormack refers to this as being "...of a certain class..." [178], while Musgrave refers to it as the "looks" and "characteristic patterns" of different genetic programs [176].

prevalent mathematical functions and techniques used to construct the images and solution spaces. Most systems make minimal attempts to allow this signature to be adjusted. Actually, in systems designed to be used to generate artwork by a single artist, such a signature is likely to be embraced and cultivated.

System balancing is a great challenge: highly constrained design spaces containing primarily similar designs naturally converge quickly. While they can have high initial average fitness "built in," they also have a very strong signature and few surprises. Design spaces in which the meta-designer has provided less constraints on what can exist also can have (in practice) a very strong signature because of their much lower average fitness (i.e., they can contain a great deal of junk). Their greater generality can yield more surprises, but only if those regions of creativity and novelty can be located.

In addition to navigating design spaces seeking high-fitness regions, there is also the option of reshaping the space itself. The majority of possible ranges for parameters are carefully tuned to be biased strongly toward acceptable results. The more these ranges are controlled, the less surprise becomes likely. The less these ranges are constrained, the more we are likely to be disappointed by purely random results. There is typically very little discussion in systems papers describing the manual tuning conducted, possibly because of the subjective aesthetic nature of the results which can detract from objective analysis of new techniques.

For example, in many of the expression-based image generation systems, color palette representation is frequently implicitly biased by mapping expression results into specific color (sub)spaces. One distinctive type of palette results from RGB mappings while another occurs from HSV or HSL mappings. System authors sometimes bias mappings within functions toward higher value or saturation, or index into tables of selected colors, but these choices are commonly hard-coded. While a given user can indeed attempt to breed individuals to reach specific color combinations, this may prove very difficult in spaces heavily biased toward specific classes of palettes [176].

1.7.3 Controlling Diversity

In the spirit of Simon's "every icon" artwork (which slowly displays every bitmap possible on a finite grid [179]), when generative design systems are under discussion there is frequent mention of the nearly infinite number of possibilities which can result from the algorithms in question. Galanter suggests a few ways to think about the significance of visible differences existing between possible design solutions [180] (see Chap. 15). Whether a given solution space actually contains a representation of every possible image is a commonly discussed topic (often using the Mona Lisa as a specific example [54, 181, 182, 178]). Many of the image spaces discussed indeed contain any given image if practical concerns are set aside, for example, with an expression which explicitly contains an appropriate value for each pixel. Whether or not one could practically find that image in a reasonable amount of time seems the more important question.

Eckert et al. suggest allowing the user to design and control biases in large solution spaces [183]. An example of this is Perlin's *bias* and *gain* functions, intended to give intuitive normalized tuning capabilities for parameter remapping. While *bias* pushes values controllably toward either extreme, *gain* can be used to pull values toward (or away from) the center of a range [184]. Allowing a user to sculpt solution spaces can be viewed as manipulating the abstract landscape such that there are always higher fitness peaks to climb [185].

Another such technique is the use of functions for mapping multiple arbitrary subranges of varying size yielding similar visual results into equally sized normalized regions. For example, a given parameter might yield one qualitatively similar set of visual results for values in $(0, 15)$, another set for $(15, 16)$, and a third set of visual results for values in $(16, 100)$. A simple mapping of a gene value into the $(0, 100)$ parameter range might never present individuals from the second qualitative class. But an interface which allows these classes to be identified and interactively remapped (for example, each occurring roughly one third of the time) can facilitate more rapid discovery of regions of higher aesthetic fitness [142].

Sources of signature often involve identifiable operations like recurrence of distinctive functions, deformations, unique values, etc. One strategy for reducing such signature is to actively control the frequency of the appearance of these visually dominant elements. Efforts can be made to make the chance of a trait being *activated* inversely proportional to its visual effect. Palettes of formal visual design traits can thus be selected and blended like the tables of colors mentioned above.

Symmetry is an example of a basic design trait one might wish to control. A common approach is to hope for properties like symmetry to gradually emerge by selecting for them. Another strategy is to build in symmetry functions which sometimes activate, appearing suddenly. However this leads to a lack of control, as offspring resulting from slight mutations (i.e., small steps in the solution space) bear little resemblance to their ancestors. One strategy is to explicitly attempt to make design traits parametric and visually continuous to make small steps correlate with small visual changes, for example, by using a variable symmetry operator, with parameters that determine the degree of symmetry, which (de)activate gradually [90].

1.7.4 Navigation

Interactive evolutionary design interfaces serve as navigation tools for parallel traversal of abstract spaces of design solutions. Interface controls adjust acceleration and velocity through exploration and refinement processes. Evolutionary approaches allow solution spaces to be navigated from many different regions simultaneously, with each step through the solution space representing a considered design.

Mating and mutation push and pull the diversity of a population, with users shifting between exploring and refining their areas of search. Precise manual refinement of genetic position through *genetic engineering* interfaces is sometimes an option, depending on the level of epistasis as well as the intuitiveness of correlations between individual genes and visual attributes.

Navigation is greatly aided if the rate of change visually in different dimensions can be coordinated in order to make small steps in the design space more visually continuous. Many interactive systems give the user one or more mutation controls which modulate the velocity through the solution space. Smoothing solution space continuity can help create a correspondence between distance traveled in the space and the amount of perceived visual change in the resulting phenotypes. This can be very difficult to do for multiple parameters simultaneously and little work has been done on providing solution space designers or artists with tools to facilitate this meta-design task. Continuity has the additional benefit of allowing the creation of animations when shifting between locations in the solution space [2, 3, 33, 11].

It remains an open question how necessary it is that a user of an interactive evolutionary design system be familiar with internal representations, evolutionary procedures, and design strategies in order to navigate solution spaces. Interface discussions are frequently centered around the ease-of-use of interactive evolutionary approaches: "simply select the ones you prefer and improved results will gradually evolve." The reality is often that certain attributes may *eventually* yield higher fitness results than others, and recognizing and selecting for these traits instead of other short-term gains can often improve the chances of satisfactory convergence. In short, one might prefer a given individual because of *experience* Knowing how the mutation or mating algorithms are implemented can also sometimes help the user improve fitness [22].

1.7.5 Fitness Evaluation

As mentioned above, some interactive evolutionary domains more easily lend themselves to rapid evaluation of individuals in a population, while others can prove more difficult. Grids of low-detail images can be quickly surveyed in large grids, while multidimensional individuals such as time-based pieces like music or animation, or 3-D objects, virtual environments, interactive entities, and simulations, all can require significant attention. Significant computation costs can cause long waits between generations or even individuals. Properties which vary at different scales can also be problematic: lower, more readily browsed resolution images might look great, but when selected, one discovers low-fitness details which require methodical higher-resolution viewing to discover. Or the opposite case occurs: individuals are dismissed for looking poorly at low resolutions, but examining higher resolution versions would have revealed desirable high-fitness traits.

Hierarchical evaluation interfaces are one approach. In one of the author's systems, a population of virtual environments could first be previewed and evaluated as a grid of maps. When chosen, an individual map could be examined as an interactively rotating 3D object, so that height relationships, for example, could be more easily observed. If further detail were desired, the map could be exported as a 3D environment and navigated through in a game engine, in order to further evaluate its fitness [140].

Takagi's research group has published a large number of papers investigating strategies for reducing user fatigue in interactive evolutionary computation applications [69, 174]. Examples of other recent papers discussing fatigue include those of Hsu and Huang, which try to quantify fatigue and satisfaction using a bottle design task [186], and the work of Saez et al., who use a low population size but with a large population of simulated human users [187].

There is much optimism that the computer could assist with image analysis. Automated fitness evaluation has emerged as one of the more active and challenging research areas in this field. Baluja's neural net approach to calculating fitness preceded most work in this area [21]. Since then, significant efforts have been made by Machado and Romero an others to develop autonomous art critics using a static fitness function based on complexity estimates for the purposes of filtering, fitness assignment, and seeding (non-random initialization) [188, 189, 190, 191]. Greenfield has published many experiments using different fitness functions for image generation. Some of his techniques have made use of digital and color filters with coevolution, and in the analysis of simulated robots and ant behaviors [24, 192, 58, 73, 72] (see Chap. 17). Greenfield additionally has proposed examining gaze data as an indicator of fitness [193]. Basa et al. also monitor users' physiological data, attempting to detect emotional responses [194]. McCabe uses multi-scale diversity metrics (Fig. 1.11b) [92, 93]. Saunder's work uses novelty-seeking agents with image complexity metrics [55].

There are numerous significant challenges to automating fitness in artistic domains. Researchers often write of a desire to collect information based on the user's selection, and to mine this data for objective evidence of aesthetic preferences. Aside from very substantial problems of shifting selection context and attributing user intent, and the challenges of computational aesthetics (see, e.g., Chap. 18 on this volume), practically speaking it has been very rare that sufficient usage data has been collected from these high-dimensional spaces to derive statistically significant aesthetic results. Online systems offer one potential solution but lack of experimental control seems problematic.

AI's "common sense" (or "general") knowledge problem seems to loom most heavily as an issue for fitness automation. We may prefer images or forms simply because they remind us of something else. It is difficult if not impossible for a system to be able to represent all of the knowledge we might have. This problem has at least two aspects. The first is theoretically possible to deal with: we may make selections based on recognized objective visual resemblances (such as when we see shapes of animals in clouds.) While this would be very challenging to implement in practice, it would not be impossible to make use of image similarity metrics, perhaps even aided by user-provided metadata about why the selection was made. The significantly more difficult problem would be automatically determining that an individual that was chosen had high fitness, because of completely subjective personal associations: a shape may be appreciated because it reminds someone of the toy he lost in the park as a child.

Ultimately, how should the results of automated fitness algorithms for evolutionary art be evaluated in a mixed culture of artists and computer scientists? Given two bodies of artistic images created using evolution, if knowledgeable computer scientists and computer artists disagree about which ones are a success and which ones are a failure, what are the mechanisms by which research proceeds? What are the criteria by which progress can be evaluated?

1.8 Conclusion

The overview of the field provided by this chapter has revealed the breadth of evolutionary visual art and design research. A primary attraction of many generative art and design approaches is the hope that algorithmic techniques can be used to produce many creative solutions on demand. While artists and researchers have focused their attention on ways to improve results, obviously numerous problems remain. Methods for identifying and measuring progress in aesthetic research, as always, remain uncertain.

The distinction between systems intended to produce art by their software's creator, as opposed to software intended to be used expressively by others, seems important to the interpretation of results and evaluation of success. The questions of stylistic signature and controllably increasing visual diversity strongly related to this goal remain present. How then to consider issues surrounding definitions of art, presentation contexts, intent, and authorship within this area seem additionally in need of investigation [195].

Indeed, this book concludes with an extended discussion of McCormack's list of open problems for this field [196] (Chap. 19). In his work (and also in Dorin's critique of aesthetic selection in artificial evolution [182]) the need is discussed for more art theory in evolutionary art. Doing so likely will require connecting knowledge from the disciplines of critical art theory, computer science, and philosophy. It is hoped that roadblocks to broader investigation of techniques and their implications will continue to be evaluated and discussed.

References

1. Dawkins, R. (1986). *The Blind Watchmaker.* Penguin Books
2. Sims, K. (1991). Artificial evolution for computer graphics. *ACM Computer Graphics*, **25**(4): 319–328
3. Todd, S., Latham, W. (1992). *Evolutionary Art and Computers.* Academic Press

4. Lewis, M. (2006). Visual aesthetic evolutionary design links. http://accad.osu.edu/~mlewis/aed.html
5. World, L. (1996). Aesthetic selection: The evolutionary art of Steven Rooke. *IEEE Computer Graphics And Applications*, **16**: 4
6. Whitelaw, M. (2004). *Metacreation: Art and Artificial Life.* MIT Press
7. Rooke, S. (2006). The Evolutionary Art of Steven Rooke. http://www.azstarnet.com/~srooke/
8. Internet Archive (2006). Wayback Machine. http://www.archive.org
9. Unemi, T. (1999). SBART2.4: Breeding 2D CG Images and Movies, and Creating a type of Collage. In: *The Third International Conference on Knowledge-based Intelligent Information Engineering Systems.* Adelaide, Australia, 288–291
10. Unemi, T. (2006). SBART home page. http://www.intlab.soka.ac.jp/~unemi/sbart/
11. Hart, D. (2006). D. a. hart abstract art. http://dahart.com
12. Bacon, D. (2003). geneticArt IV. http://www.accesscom.com/~darius/hacks/evoart/
13. Davidson, A. (1999). Biography – evolutionary image explorer. http://spaz.ca/aaron/SCS/biography/
14. Kleiwig, P. (2006). Genetic art. http://www.let.rug.nl/kleiweg/genart/genart.html
15. Maxwell, J.A. (2006). Image evolve applet. http://www.acm.vt.edu/~jmaxwell/evolve/
16. Mills, A. (2006). Evolutionary art gallery. http://www.ashleymills.com/?q=gallery
17. Saunders, R. (2006). Evol. http://wwwpeople.arch.usyd.edu.au/~rob/applets/genart/GenArt.html
18. Ellingsen, E. (2006). Steike genetic art. http://steike.com/GeneticArt
19. Gerstmann, D. (2004). Spawner. http://home.myuw.net/dgerstma/content/graphics/programs/spawner.shtml
20. McAllister, D. (2006). David McAllister's Genetic Art. http://home.comcast.net/~davemc0/GenArt/
21. Baluja, S., Pomerleau, D., Jochem, T. (1994). Towards automated artificial evolution for computer-generated images. *Connection Science*, **6**(2 and 3): 325–354
22. Greenfield, G.R. (1998). New directions for evolving expressions. In: *BRIDGES: Mathematical Connections in Art, Music and Science*
23. Greenfield, G.R. (1999). On understanding the search problem for image spaces. In: *BRIDGES: Mathematical Connections in Art, Music and Science*
24. Greenfield, G.R. (2000). Mathematical building blocks for evolving expressions. In: *BRIDGES: Mathematical Connections in Art, Music and Science*
25. Machado, P., Cardoso, A. (2003). NEvAr – system overview. In: *Proceedings of Generative Art 2003.* Milan, Italy
26. U&I Software, LLC (2003). Artmatic. http://www.artmatic.com/
27. Day, T. (2006). Evolvotron. http://www.bottlenose.demon.co.uk/share/evolvotron/
28. Jourdan, T. (2006). Kandid, a genetic art project. http://kandid.sourceforge.net/
29. Software, S. (2006). Genetic art gallery. http://softology.com.au/gallery/galleryga.htm

30. Witbrock, M., Neil-Reilly, S. (1999). Evolving genetic art. In Bentley, P.J., ed.: *Evolutionary Design by Computers.* Morgan Kaufmann, 251–259
31. Mount, J. (2006). geneticArt IV. `http://mzlabs.com/gart/g4.html`
32. Lee, J. (2006). Evolve. `http://artdent.homelinux.net/evolve/`
33. Draves, S. (2006). Electric sheep. `http://electricsheep.org/`
34. Gatarski, R. (1999). Evolutionary banners: An experiment with automated advertising design. In: *Proceedings of COTIM 99*
35. Hemert, J.I.V., Jansen, M. (2001). An engineering approach to evolutionary art. In: *Proceedings of the Genetic and Evolutionary Computation Conference.* Springer, 177
36. Sims, K. (1993). Interactive evolution of equations for procedural models. *The Visual Computer*, **9**: 466–476
37. Hobden, A. (1994). *Genetic Algorithms for Graphics Textures.* Technical Report EPCC-SS94-03. Edinburgh Parallel Computing Centre (EPCC)
38. Ibrahim, A.E.M. (1998). *Genshade: An Evolutionary Approach to Automatic and Interactive Procedural Texture Generation.* PhD thesis. Architecture, Texas A&M University
39. Hewgill, A., Ross, B.J. (2004). Procedural 3D texture synthesis using genetic programming. *Computers and Graphics Journal*, **28**(4): 569–584
40. DiPaola, S. (2005). a body of work. `http://dipaola.org/steve/`
41. Wiens, A.L., Ross, B.J. (2002). Gentropy: Evolutionary 2D texture generation. *Computers and Graphics*, **26**(1): 75–88
42. Ross, B.J., Ralph, W., Hai, Z. (2006). Evolutionary image synthesis using a model of aesthetics. In Yen, G.G., Lucas, S.M., Fogel, G., Kendall, G., Salomon, R., Zhang, B.T., Coello, C.A.C., Runarsson, T.P., eds.: *Proceedings of the 2006 IEEE Congress on Evolutionary Computation.* Vancouver, BC, Canada. IEEE Press, 1087–1094
43. Draves, S. (2005). The electric sheep screen-saver: A case study in aesthetic evolution. In Rothlauf, F., Branke, J., Cagnoni, S., Corne, D.W., Drechsler, R., Jin, Y., Machado, P., Marchiori, E., Romero, J., Smith, G.D., Squillero, G., eds.: *Applications of Evolutionary Computing, EvoWorkshops 2005: EvoBIO, EvoCOMNET, EvoHOT, EvoIASP, EvoMUSART, and EvoSTOC.* Vol. 3449 of Lecture Notes in Computer Science. Springer, 458–467
44. Chapuis, J., Lutton, E. (2001). ArtiE-Fract: Interactive evolution of fractals. In: *Proceedings of Generative Art 2001.* Milan, Italy
45. Lutton, E., Cayla, E., Chapuis, J. (2003). ArtiE-fract: The artist's viewpoint. In Raidl, G.R., Cagnoni, S., Cardalda, J.J.R., Corne, D.W., Gottlieb, J., Guillot, A., Hart, E., Johnson, C.G., Marchiori, E., Meyer, J.A., Middendorf, M., eds.: *Applications of Evolutionary Computing, EvoWorkshops2003: EvoBIO, EvoCOP, EvoIASP, EvoMUSART, EvoROB, EvoSTIM.* Vol. 2611 of LNCS. University of Essex, England, UK. Springer, 510–521
46. Rowley, H.A. (2006). Genetic art. `http://www.cs.cmu.edu/~har/GeneticArt.html`
47. Yoshiaki, I. (2006). Genetic programming fractal images. `http://www.bekkoame.ne.jp/~ishmnn/gallery/gp-image2.html`
48. Ventrella, J. (2004). Self portraits in fractal space. `http://www.ventrella.com/Tweaks/Portraits/`
49. Rowley, T. (1994). *A Toolkit for Visual Genetic Programming.* Technical Report GCG-74. The Geometry Center, University of Minnesota

50. Lund, H.H., Pagliarini, L., Miglino, O. (1995). Artistic design with genetic algorithms and neural networks. In Alander, J.T., ed.: *Proceedings of 1NWGA*. University of Vaasa, Vaasa
51. Fagerlund, M. (2006). GeneticArt. `http://www.cambrianlabs.com/mattias/GeneticArt/`
52. Stanley, K.O. (2006). Evolution of a spaceship. `http://www.cs.utexas.edu/users/kstanley/rocket.html`
53. Ferstl, H. (2006). Genetic art. `http://sephi.axinom.de/Blog/PermaLink.aspx?guid=a0affef8-eb07-4ad8-8942-be5d481dbc0f`
54. Kelly, M. (1999). Evol-artists – a new breed entirely. *EvoNews*, **11**
55. Saunders, R., Gero, J. (2001). The digital clockwork muse: A computational model of aesthetic evolution. In Wiggins, G., ed.: *Proceedings of the AISB Symposium on AI and Creativity in Arts and Science*. York, UK
56. McGuire, M. (2000). Artificial animator (evolver). `http://www.cs.brown.edu/people/morgan/aa/`
57. Machado, P., Dias, A., Duarte, N., Cardoso, A. (2002). Giving colour to images. In Cardoso, A., Wiggins, G., eds.: *AI and Creativity in Arts and Science*. Imperial College, United Kingdom A symposium as part of AISB'02.
58. Greenfield, G.R. (2004). Automated recoloring of evolved designs using evolved palettes. *Journal of Mathematics & Design*, **4**(1): 47–54
59. Graf, J., Banzhaf, W. (1995). Interactive evolution of images. In Fogel, D.B., ed.: *Proceedings of the Fourth Annual Conference on Evolutionary Programming*, 53–65
60. Poli, R., Cagnoni, S. (1997). Evolution of pseudo-colouring algorithms for image enhancement with interactive genetic programming. In: *Proceedings of the Second International Conference on Genetic Programming, GP'97*. Morgan Kaufmann, 269–277
61. Ransen Software (2006). Genetic art and natural color schemes. `http://www.ransen.com/Articles/GenArt.htm`
62. QBeo, Inc. (2001). PhotoGenetics 2.0. `http://www.imaging-resource.com/SOFT/PGEN2/PGEN2.HTM`
63. Wolfer, J. (2005). A neuro-genetic hybrid motif generator for genetic art. In: *Computer Graphics and Imaging*, 31–36
64. Collomosse, J.P., Hall, P.M. (2005). Salience-adaptive painterly rendering using genetic search. *Intl. Journal on Artificial Intelligence Tools (IJAIT)*, **14**(4)
65. Collomosse, J.P. (2006). Supervised genetic search for parameter selection in painterly rendering. In Rothlauf, F., Branke, J., Cagnoni, S., Costa, E., Cotta, C., Drechsler, R., Lutton, E., Machado, P., Moore, J.H., Romero, J., Smith, G.D., Squillero, G., Takagi, H., eds.: *Applications of Evolutionary Computing, EvoWorkshops2006: EvoBIO, EvoCOMNET, EvoHOT, EvoIASP, EvoInteraction, EvoMUSART, EvoSTOC*. Vol. 3907 of LNCS. Budapest. Springer, 599–610
66. Caldwell, C., Johnston, V. (1991). Tracking a criminal suspect through "face-space" with a genetic algorithm. In: *4th Int. Conf. on Genetic Algorithms*, 416–421
67. Johnston, V. (2006). FacePrints research site. `http://web.mac.com/vicjohn/iWeb/FacePrints/Welcome.html`
68. Hancock, P., Frowd, C. (1999). Evolutionary generation of faces. In: *Proceedings of the AISB Symposium on Creative Evolutionary Systems (CES)*.

The Society for the Study of Artificial Intelligence and Simulation of Behavior (AISB), 93–99

69. Takagi, H., Kishi, K. (1999). On-line knowledge embedding for an interactive EC-based montage system. In: *Interactive Evolutionary Computation: Fusion of the Capacities of EC Optimization and Human Evaluation.* Adelaide, SA, Australia, 280–283
70. Lim, I.S. (1995). Evolving facial expressions. In: *Proceedings of IEEE International Conference on Evolutionary Computation.* Perth, Australia, 515–520
71. Aupetit, S., Bordeau, V., Monmarche, N., Slimane, M., Venturini, G. (2003). Interactive evolution of ant paintings. In Sarker, R., Reynolds, R., Abbass, H., Tan, K.C., McKay, B., Essam, D., Gedeon, T., eds.: *Proceedings of the 2003 Congress on Evolutionary Computation CEC2003.* Canberra. IEEE Press, 1376–1383
72. Greenfield, G.R. (2005). Evolutionary methods for ant colony paintings. In Rothlauf, F., Branke, J., Cagnoni, S., Corne, D.W., Drechsler, R., Jin, Y., Machado, P., Marchiori, E., Romero, J., Smith, G.D., Squillero, G., eds.: *Applications of Evolutionary Computing, EvoWorkshops2005: EvoBIO, EvoCOMNET, EvoHOT, EvoIASP, EvoMUSART, EvoSTOC.* Vol. 3449 of LNCS. Lausanne, Switzerland. Springer, 478–487
73. Greenfield, G.R. (2006). Robot paintings evolved using simulated robots. In Rothlauf, F., Branke, J., Cagnoni, S., Costa, E., Cotta, C., Drechsler, R., Lutton, E., Machado, P., Moore, J.H., Romero, J., Smith, G.D., Squillero, G., Takagi, H., eds.: *Applications of Evolutionary Computing, EvoWorkshops 2006: EvoBIO, EvoCOMNET, EvoHOT, EvoIASP, EvoINTERACTION, EvoMUSART, and EvoSTOC.* Vol. 3907 of Lecture Notes in Computer Science. Springer, 611–621
74. Urbano, P. (2006). Consensual paintings. In Rothlauf, F., Branke, J., Cagnoni, S., Costa, E., Cotta, C., Drechsler, R., Lutton, E., Machado, P., Moore, J.H., Romero, J., Smith, G.D., Squillero, G., Takagi, H., eds.: *Applications of Evolutionary Computing, EvoWorkshops 2006: EvoBIO, EvoCOMNET, EvoHOT, EvoIASP, EvoINTERACTION, EvoMUSART, and EvoSTOC.* Vol. 3907 of Lecture Notes in Computer Science. Springer, 622–632
75. Moura, L., Ramos, V. (2006). Swarm paintings: Non-human art. `http://alfa.ist.utl.pt/~cvrm/staff/vramos/aswarm.html`
76. Ramos, V. (2002). On the implicit and on the artificial – morphogenesis and emergent aesthetics in autonomous collective systems. In Maubant, J.L., et al., eds.: *ARCHITOPIA Book, Art, Architecture and Science.* Institut d'art Contemporain, 25–57
77. Kwong, H., Jacob, C. (2003). Evolutionary exploration of dynamic swarm behaviour. In Sarker, R., Reynolds, R., Abbass, H., Tan, K.C., McKay, B., Essam, D., Gedeon, T., eds.: *Proceedings of the 2003 Congress on Evolutionary Computation CEC2003.* Canberra. IEEE Press, 367–374
78. Dudek, G. (2001). Genetic art. `http://www.cim.mcgill.ca/~dudek/ga.html`
79. Dehlinger, H.E. (1998). The artist's intentions and genetic coding in algorithmically generated drawings. In: *Proceedings of Generative Art 1998.* Milan, Italy
80. Baker, E. (1993). Evolving line drawings. In Forrest, S., ed.: *Proceedings of the Fifth International Conference on Genetic Algorithms.* San Mateo, CA. Morgan Kaufman

81. Pagliarini, L., Parisi, D. (1996). Face-It project. In: *Proceedings of XV Italian Congress on Experimental Psychology.* Italian Psychologist Association, 38–41
82. Nishio, K., et al. (1997). Fuzzy fitness assignment in an interactive genetic algorithm for a cartoon face search. In Sanchez, E., Shibata, T., Zadeh, L.A., eds.: *Genetic Algorithms and Fuzzy Logic Systems: Soft Computing Perspectives.* Vol. 7. World Scientific
83. Lewis, M. (2000). Aesthetic evolutionary design with data flow networks. In: *Proceedings of Generative Art 2000.* Milan, Italy
84. Lund, A. (2000). Evolving the shape of things to come: A comparison of direct manipulation and interactive evolutionary design. In: *Proceedings of Generative Art 2000.* Milan, Italy
85. Schmitz, M. (2004). genoTyp, an experiment about genetic typography. In: *Proceedings of Generative Art 2004.* Milan, Italy
86. Levin, G., Feinberg, J., Curtis, C. (2006). Alphabet synthesis machine. `http://alphabet.tmema.org`
87. Butterfield, I., Lewis, M. (2000). Evolving fonts. `http://accad.osu.edu/~mlewis/AED/Fonts/`
88. Unemi, T. (2003). An IEC-based support system for font design. In: *2003 IEEE International Conference on Systems, Man and Cybernetics*, 968–973
89. Ashmore, L. (2006). An investigation into evolutionary art using cartesian genetic programming. `http://www.emoware.org/evolutionary\_art.asp`
90. Lewis, M. (2001). *Creating Continuous Design Spaces for Interactive Genetic Algorithms with Layered, Correlated, Pattern Functions.* PhD thesis. Ohio State University
91. Bachelier, G. (2006). Evolutionary art. `http://www.vi-anec.de/Trance-Art/Evo-Kunst/Evo-Kunst-Beschreibungen/GBGesamt-Kunstprozess\_e.html`
92. McCabe, J. (2006). The front exhibition. `http://sf.anu.edu.au/~jrm900/The\_Front/`
93. McCabe, J. (2006). Personal communication
94. Greenfield, G.R. (2004). Tilings of sequences of co-evolved images. In Raidl, G.R., Cagnoni, S., Branke, J., Corne, D.W., Drechsler, R., Jin, Y., Johnson, C., Machado, P., Marchiori, E., Rothlauf, F., Smith, G.D., Squillero, G., eds.: *Applications of Evolutionary Computing, EvoWorkshops2004: EvoBIO, EvoCOMNET, EvoHOT, EvoIASP, EvoMUSART, EvoSTOC.* Vol. 3005 of LNCS. Coimbra, Portugal. Springer, 427–436
95. Greenfield, G.R. (2004). The void series – generative art using regulatory genes. In: *Proceedings of Generative Art 2004.* Milan, Italy
96. Monmarché, N., Nocent, G., Slimane, M., Venturini, G. (1999). Imagine: A tool for generating HTML style sheets with an interactive genetic algorithm on genes frequencies. In: *IEEE International Conference on Systems, Man, and Cybernetics (SMC'99).* Vol. 3. Tokyo, Japan, 640–645
97. Oliver, A., Monmarché, N., Venturini, G. (2002). Interactive design of web sites with a genetic algorithm. In: *Proceedings of the IADIS International Conference WWW/Internet.* Lisbon, Portugal, 355–362
98. Rowbottom, A. (1999). Evolutionary art and form. In Bentley, P.J., ed.: *Evolutionary Design by Computers.* Morgan Kaufmann, 261–277
99. Lintermann, B. (1997). Morphogenesis. `http://www.bernd-lintermann.de/morphogenesis.html`
100. Braid Media Arts (2006). GroBoto. `http://www.groboto.com/`

101. Notting Hill Publishing (2001). Cybertation. http://www.simonyi.ox.ac.uk/dawkins/WorldOfDawkins-archive/Dawkins/Work/CDROMs/cdrom.shtml
102. Todd, S., Latham, W. (1999). The mutation and growth of art by computers. In Bentley, P.J., ed.: *Evolutionary Design by Computers.* Morgan Kaufmann, 221–250
103. Latham, W. (2006). Design. http://www.doc.gold.ac.uk/~mas01whl/themes/design.htm
104. Watabe, H., Okino, N. (1993). A study on genetic shape design. In Forrest, S., ed.: *Proceedings of the Fifth International Conference on Genetic Algorithms.* Urbana-Champaign, IL, 445–450
105. McGuire, F. (1993). The origins of sculpture: Evolutionary 3D design. *IEEE Computer Graphics and Applications*, **13**(1): 9–11
106. Das, S., Franguidakis, T., Papka, M., DeFanti, T.A., Sandin, D.J. (1994). A genetic programming application in virtual reality. In: *Proceedings of the First IEEE Conference on Evolutionary Computation.* Vol. 1. Orlando, Florida, USA. IEEE Press, 480–484
107. Bedwell, E.J., Ebert, D.S. (1999). Artificial evolution of algebraic surfaces. *Proceedings Implicit Surfaces '99*
108. Jones, M.W. (1999). Direct surface rendering of general and genetically bred implicit surfaces. In: *Proceedings of the 17th Annual Conference of Eurographics (UK Chapter).* Cambridge, 37–46
109. Jacob, C., Kwong, H., Wyvill, B. (2001). Toward the creation of an evolutionary design system for implicit surfaces. In: *Western Computer Graphics Symposium.* Sun Peaks Resort, BC, Canada
110. Nishino, H., Takagi, H., Utsumiya, K. (2000). A Digital Prototyping System for Designing Novel 3D Geometries. In: *6th International Conference on Virtual Systems and Multimedia.* Ogaki, Gifu, Japan, 473–482
111. Tabuada, P., Alves, P., Gomes, J., Rosa, A. (1998). 3D Artificial Art by Genetic Algorithms. In: *Proceedings of the Workshop on Evolutionary Design at Artificial Intelligence in Design – AID' 98*, 18–21
112. Graham, I.J., Wood, R.L., Case, K. (1999). Evolutionary form design: The application of genetic algorithmic techniques to computer aided product design. In: *Proceedings of the 15th National Conference on Manufacturing Research (NCMR).* Vol. 13 of Advances in Manufacturing Technology
113. Kuriyama, S., Kaneko, T. (1999). Morphogenic synthesis of free-form shapes. In: *First Iteration Conference*, 106–115
114. Thomas, D. (2003). Aesthetic selection of morphogenetic art forms. *Kybernetes: The International Journal of Systems & Cybernetics*, **32**: 144–155
115. Rowland, D., Biocca, F. (2002). Evolutionary cooperative design methodology: The genetic sculpture park. *Leonardo*, **35**(2): 193–196
116. Ebner, M. (2003). Evolutionary design of objects using scene graphs. In Ryan, C., Soule, T., Keijzer, M., Tsang, E., Poli, R., Costa, E., eds.: *Proceedings of the 6th European Conference on Genetic Programming.* Essex, UK. Springer, 47–58
117. Pontecorvo, M.S. (1998). Designing the undesigned: Emergence as a tool for design. In: *Proceedings of Generative Art 1998.* Milan, Italy
118. Rowland, D.A. (1998). *Computer Graphic Control over Human Face and Head Appearance, Genetic Optimisation of Perceptual Characteristics.* PhD thesis. Michigan State University

119. Bentley, P.J. (1999). From coffee tables to hospitals: Generic evolutionary design. In Bentley, P.J., ed.: *Evolutionary Design by Computers.* Morgan Kaufmann, 405–423
120. Nakanishi, Y. (1996). Applying evolutionary systems to design aid system. In: *ALIFE V Poster presentations*, 147–154
121. Kim, H.S., Cho, S.B. (2000). Genetic algorithm with knowledge-based encoding for interactive fashion design. In: *Lecture Notes in Artificial Intelligence.* Springer, 404–414
122. Cho, S.B. (2002). Towards creative evolutionary systems with interactive genetic algorithm. *Applied Intelligence*, **16**(2): 129–138
123. Lee, H.C., Tang, M.X. (2004). Evolutionary shape grammars for product design. In: *Proceedings of Generative Art 2004.* Milan, Italy
124. Hornby, G. (2004). Functional scalability through generative representations: The evolution of table designs. *Environment and Planning B: Planning and Design*, **31**(4): 569–587
125. Genometri Ltd (2006). Genometri. `http://www.genometri.com`
126. Icosystem Corporation (2002). The hunch engine. `http://icosystem.com/hunch.htm`
127. Affinnova, Inc. (2006). Affinnova: From concept to launch. `http://www.affinnova.com`
128. Prusinkiewicz, P.W., Lindenmayer, A. (1990). *The Algorithmic Beauty of Plants.* Springer
129. McCormack, J. (1993). Interactive evolution of L-System grammars for computer graphics modelling. In Green, D., Bossomaier, T., eds.: *Complex Systems: From Biology to Computation.* ISO Press, Amsterdam
130. McCormack, J. (2004). *Impossible Nature: The Art of Jon McCormack.* Australian Centre for the Moving Image
131. Traxler, C., Gervautz, M. (1996). *Using Genetic Algorithms to Improve the Visual Quality of Fractal Plants Generated with CSG-PL-Systems.* Technical Report TR-186-2-96-04. Institute of Computer Graphics, Vienna University of Technology
132. Jacob, C. (2001). *Illustrating Evolutionary Computation with Mathematica.* Morgan Kaufmann Publishers
133. Putnam, J. (2003). Grammidity. `http://grammidity.sourceforge.net/`
134. Singular Inversions (2006). FaceGen Modeller. `http://www.facegen.com`
135. DiPaola, S. (2006). Sims FaceLift. `http://dipaola.org/steve/facelift.html`
136. Lewis, M. (2000). *An Implicit Surface Prototype for Evolving Human Figure Geometry.* Technical Report OSU-ACCAD-11/00-TR2. ACCAD, The Ohio State University
137. Aoki, K., Takagi, H. (1997). 3-D CG lighting with an interactive GA. In: *First International Conference on Knowledge-Based Intelligent Electronic Systems.* Adelaide, SA, Australia, 296–301
138. Hayashida, N., Takagi, H. (2000). Visualized IEC: Interactive evolutionary computation with multidimensional data visualization. In: *IEEE International Conference on Industrial Electronics, Control and Instrumentation (IECON2000).* Nagoya, Japan, 2738–2743
139. Takagi, H. (2004). Humanized computational intelligence with interactive evolutionary computation. `http://www.kyushu-id.ac.jp/~takagi/TAKAGI/IECpaper/IECtutorial100.pdf`

140. Lewis, M., Parent, R. (2002). Interactively evolving virtual environment maps with continuous layered pattern functions. In: *Computer Animation 2002 (CA 2002)*. Geneva, Switzerland. IEEE Computer Society, 49–54
141. Lewis, M. (2004). Aesthetic video filter evolution in an interactive real-time framework. In Raidl, G.R., Cagnoni, S., Branke, J., Corne, D.W., Drechsler, R., Jin, Y., Johnson, C., Machado, P., Marchiori, E., Rothlauf, F., Smith, G.D., Squillero, G., eds.: *Applications of Evolutionary Computing, EvoWorkshops2004: EvoBIO, EvoCOMNET, EvoHOT, EvoIASP, EvoMUSART, EvoSTOC*. Vol. 3005 of LNCS. Coimbra, Portugal. Springer, 409–418
142. Lewis, M., Ruston, K. (2005). Aesthetic geometry evolution in a generic interactive evolutionary design framework. *New Generation Computing*
143. Marks, J., et al. (1997). *Design Galleries: A General Approach to Setting Parameters for Computer Graphics and Animation.* Technical Report TR97-14. Mitsubishi Electric Research Laboratories, Inc.
144. Zarzar, K.M. (2003). *Use and Adaptation of Precedents in Architectural Design: Toward an Evolutionary Design Model.* Delft University Press
145. Frazer, J. (1995). *An Evolutionary Architecture.* Architectural Association. London
146. Frazer, J., Frazer, J., Xiyu, L., Mingxi, T., Janssen, P. (2002). Generative and evolutionary techniques for building envelope design. In: *Proceedings of Generative Art 2002*
147. Gero, J., Kazakov, V. (1996). An exploration-based evolutionary model of a generative design process. *Microcomputers in Civil Engineering*, **11**: 209–216
148. Gero, J.S. (1998). New models in evolutionary designing. In Bentley, P.J., ed.: *AID98 Workshop on Evolutionary Design, AID98, Lisbon*, 37–41
149. Schnier, T., Gero, J.S. (1998). From Frank Lloyd Wright to Mondrian: Transforming evolving representation. In Parmee, I.C., ed.: *Adaptive Computing in Design and Manufacture.* Springer. Berlin, 207–219
150. O'Reilly, U.M., Ramachandran, G. (1998). A preliminary investigation of evolution as a form design strategy. In Adami, C., Belew, R.K., Kitano, H., Taylor, C.E., eds.: *Proceedings of the Sixth International Conference on Artificial Life.* University of California, Los Angeles. MIT Press, 26–29
151. Testa, P., O'Reilly, U.M., Greenwold, S. (2000). Agent-based genetic programming for spatial exploration. Presented to the ACSA
152. Hemberg, M. (2006). Genr8. `http://projects.csail.mit.edu/emergentDesign/genr8/`
153. Hemberg, M. (2004). geneticEngine.mel. `http://projects.csail.mit.edu/emergentDesign/genr8/`
154. Coates, P., Broughton, T., Jackson, H. (1999). Exploring three-dimensional design worlds using lindenmayer systems and genetic programming. In Bentley, P.J., ed.: *Evolutionary Design by Computers.* Morgan Kaufmann, 323–341
155. Coates, P., Makris, D. (1999). Genetic programming and spatial morphogenesis. In: *Proceedings of the AISB Symposium on Creative Evolutionary Systems (CES).* The Society for the Study of Artificial Intelligence and Simulation of Behavior (AISB)
156. Miller, D.P. (1993). *The generation of human-like reaching motion for an arm in an obstacle-filled 3-D static environment.* PhD thesis. Ohio State University
157. Shibuya, M., Kita, H., Kobayashi, S. (1999). Integration of multi-objective and interactive genetic algorihtms and its application to animation design. In:

IEEE International Conference on System, Man, and Cybernetics (SMC'99). Vol. 3. Tokyo, Japan, 647–651

158. Antonini, R. (1999). Implementing an avatar gesture development tool as a creative evolutionary collaborative system. In Bentley, P.J., Corne, D., eds.: *Proceedings of the AISB Symposium on Creative Evolutionary Systems (CES)*. The Society for the Study of Artificial Intelligence and Simulation of Behavior (AISB)
159. Lim, I.S., Thalmann, D. (1999). Pro-actively interactive evolution for computer animation. In: *Proceedings of Eurographics Workshop on Animation and Simulation'99 (CAS '99)*. Milan, Italy. Springer, 45–52
160. Lim, I.S., Thalmann, D. (2000). Solve customers' problems: Interactive evolution for tinkering with computer animation. In: *Proceedings of ACM Symposium on Applied Computing (SAC 2000)*. Como, Italy, 404–407
161. Lim, I.S., Thalmann, D. (2000). Tournament selection for browsing temporal signals. In: *Proceedings of ACM Symposium on Applied Computing (SAC 2000)*. Como, Italy, 570–573
162. Lapointe, F.J. (2005). Choreogenetics: The generation of choreographic variants through genetic mutations and selection. In Rothlauf, F., ed.: *Genetic and Evolutionary Computation Conference, GECCO 2005, Workshop Proceedings*. Washington DC, USA. ACM, 366–369
163. Lapointe, F.J., Époque, M. (2005). The dancing genome project: generation of a human-computer choreography using a genetic algorithm. In: *ACM Multimedia*. ACM, 555–558
164. Sims, K. (1994). Evolving 3D Morphology and Behavior by Competition. In Brooks, R., Maes, P., eds.: *Artificial Life IV Proceedings*. MIT Press, 28–39
165. Ventrella, J. (1995). Disney meets Darwin: The evolution of funny animated figures. In: *Computer Animation '95 Proceedings*. Geneva, Switzerland
166. Gritz, L., Hahn, J.K. (1997). Genetic programming evolution of controllers for 3-D character animation. In Koza, J.R., et al., eds.: *Genetic Programming 1997: Proceedings of the 2nd Annual Conference*. Morgan Kaufmann, 139–146
167. Dorin, A. (2006). Animaland. `http://www.csse.monash.edu.au/~aland/`
168. Nemirovsky, P., Luger-Guillaume, R. (2004). Improvisational media space: Architecture and strategies for evolution. In Raidl, G.R., Cagnoni, S., Branke, J., Corne, D.W., Drechsler, R., Jin, Y., Johnson, C., Machado, P., Marchiori, E., Rothlauf, F., Smith, G.D., Squillero, G., eds.: *Applications of Evolutionary Computing, EvoWorkshops2004: EvoBIO, EvoCOMNET, EvoHOT, EvoIASP, EvoMUSART, EvoSTOC*. Vol. 3005 of LNCS. Coimbra, Portugal. Springer, 457–466
169. Henriques, N.A.C., Correia, N., Manzolli, J., Correia, L., Chambel, T. (2006). MovieGene: Evolutionary video production based on genetic algorithms and cinematic properties. In Rothlauf, F., Branke, J., Cagnoni, S., Costa, E., Cotta, C., Drechsler, R., Lutton, E., Machado, P., Moore, J.H., Romero, J., Smith, G.D., Squillero, G., Takagi, H., eds.: *Applications of Evolutionary Computing, EvoWorkshops2006: EvoBIO, EvoCOMNET, EvoHOT, EvoIASP, EvoInteraction, EvoMUSART, EvoSTOC*. Vol. 3907 of LNCS. Budapest. Springer, 707–711
170. Unemi, T. (2004). Embedding movie into SBART – breeding deformed movies. In: *2004 IEEE International Conference on Systems, Man and Cybernetics*, 5760–5764

171. Hart, D. (2006). Toward greater artistic control for interactive evolution of images and animation. SIGGRAPH Technical Sketch
172. Bentley, P.J. (1999). *Evolutionary Design by Computers.* Morgan Kaufmann
173. Bentley, P.J., Corne, D.W. (2001). *Creative Evolutionary Systems.* Morgan Kaufmann
174. Takagi, H. (2001). Interactive evolutionary computation: Fusion of the capabilities of EC optimization and human evaluation. *Proceedings of the IEEE,* **89**(9): 1275–1296
175. Boden, M.A. (1994). Agents and creativity. *Communications of the ACM,* **37**(7): 117–121
176. Musgrave, F.K. (1998). Genetic textures. In Ebert, D., ed.: *Texturing and Modeling: A Procedural Approach.* Academic Press, 373–384
177. Todd, S. (2000). Personal communication
178. McCormack, J. (2006). New challenges for evolutionary music and art. *SIGEVOlution: Newsletter of the ACM Special Interest Group on Genetic and Evolutionary Computation,* **1**(1)
179. Simon, Jr., J.F. (2001). Every icon. `http://www.numeral.com`
180. Galanter, P. (2003). What is generative art? complexity theory as a context for art theory. In: *Proceedings of Generative Art 2003.* Milan, Italy
181. Whitelaw, M. (2001). Breeding aesthetic objects: Art and artificial evolution. In Bentley, P.J., Corne, D., eds.: *Creative Evolutionary Systems.* Morgan Kaufmann
182. Dorin, A. (2001). Aesthetic fitness and artificial evolution for the selection of imagery from the mythical infinite library. In Kelemen, Sosik, eds.: *Proc. 6th European Conference on Artificial Life.* Prague. Springer, 659–668
183. Eckert, C., Kelly, I., Stacey, M. (1999). Interactive generative systems for conceptual design: An empirical perspective. *Artificial Intelligence for Engineering Design, Analysis and Manufacturing,* **13**: 303–320
184. Perlin, K. (1998). Noise, hypertexture, antialiasing, and gestures. In Ebert, D., ed.: *Texturing and Modeling: A Procedural Approach.* Academic Press, 209–274
185. Ray, T.S. (1999). Some thoughts on evolvability. `http://www.hip.atr.co.jp/~ray/pubs/evolvability/`
186. Hsu, F.C., Huang, P. (2005). Providing an appropriate search space to solve the fatigue problem in interactive evolutionary computation. *New Generation Computing*
187. Saez, Y., Isasi, P., Segovia, J., Hernandez, J.C. (2005). Reference chromosome to overcome user fatigue in iec. *New Generation Computing,* **23**(2): 129–142
188. Machado, P. (2006). Personal communication
189. Machado, P., Romero, J., Santos, M.L., Cardoso, A., Manaris, B. (2004). Adaptive critics for evolutionary artists. In Raidl, G.R., Cagnoni, S., Branke, J., Corne, D.W., Drechsler, R., Jin, Y., Johnson, C., Machado, P., Marchiori, E., Rothlauf, F., Smith, G.D., Squillero, G., eds.: *Applications of Evolutionary Computing, EvoWorkshops2004: EvoBIO, EvoCOMNET, EvoHOT, EvoIASP, EvoMUSART, EvoSTOC.* Vol. 3005 of LNCS. Coimbra, Portugal. Springer, 437–446
190. Machado, P., Romero, J., Cardoso, A., Santos, A. (2005). Partially interactive evolutionary artists. *New Generation Computing*
191. Romero, J., Machado, P., Santos, A., Cardoso, A. (2003). On the development of critics in evolutionary computation artists. In Raidl, G.R.,

Cagnoni, S., Cardalda, J.J.R., Corne, D.W., Gottlieb, J., Guillot, A., Hart, E., Johnson, C.G., Marchiori, E., Meyer, J.A., Middendorf, M., eds.: *Applications of Evolutionary Computing, EvoWorkshops2003: EvoBIO, EvoCOP, EvoIASP, EvoMUSART, EvoROB, EvoSTIM.* Vol. 2611 of LNCS. University of Essex, England, UK. Springer, 559–569

192. Greenfield, G.R. (2002). Simulated aesthetics and evolving artworks: A coevolutionary approach. *Leonardo*, **35**(3)
193. Greenfield, G.R. (2003). Computational aesthetics based on gaze patterns. Presentation at ISAMA 2003 and the 6th Annual Bridges Conference
194. Basa, T., Go, C.A., Yoo, K.S., Lee, W.H. (2006). Using physiological signals to evolve art. In Rothlauf, F., Branke, J., Cagnoni, S., Costa, E., Cotta, C., Drechsler, R., Lutton, E., Machado, P., Moore, J.H., Romero, J., Smith, G.D., Squillero, G., Takagi, H., eds.: *Applications of Evolutionary Computing, EvoWorkshops 2006: EvoBIO, EvoCOMNET, EvoHOT, EvoIASP, EvoINTERACTION, EvoMUSART, and EvoSTOC, Budapest, Hungary, April 10–12, 2006, Proceedings.* Vol. 3907 of Lecture Notes in Computer Science. Springer, 633–641
195. Danto, A. (1981). *The Transfiguration of the Commonplace.* Harvard University Press
196. McCormack, J. (2005). Open problems in evolutionary music and art. In Rothlauf, F., Branke, J., Cagnoni, S., Corne, D.W., Drechsler, R., Jin, Y., Machado, P., Marchiori, E., Romero, J., Smith, G.D., Squillero, G., eds.: *Applications of Evolutionary Computing, EvoWorkshops 2005: EvoBIO, EvoCOMNET, EvoHOT, EvoIASP, EvoMUSART, and EvoSTOC.* Vol. 3449 of Lecture Notes in Computer Science. Springer, 428–436

2

Evolutionary Search for the Artistic Rendering of Photographs

John P. Collomosse

Department of Computer Science, University of Bath, Bath, U.K.
jpc@cs.bath.ac.uk

Summary. This chapter explores algorithms for the artistic stylization (transformation) of photographs into digital artwork, complementing techniques discussed so far in this book that focus on image generation. Most artistic stylization algorithms operate by placing atomic rendering primitives "strokes" on a virtual canvas, guided by automated artistic heuristics. In many cases the stroke placement process can be phrased as an optimization problem, demanding guided exploration of a high dimensional and turbulent search space to produce aesthetically pleasing renderings. Evolutionary search algorithms can offer attractive solutions to such problems.

This chapter begins with a brief review of artistic stylization algorithms, in particular algorithms for producing painterly renderings from two-dimensional sources. It then discusses how genetic algorithms may be harnessed both to increase control over level of detail when painting (so improving aesthetics) and to enhance usability of parameterized painterly rendering algorithms.

2.1 Introduction to Artistic Rendering

Research in computer graphics has traditionally focused on attaining *photorealism*; simulating physical interactions between light and modelled objects to produce scenes lit in an ostensibly natural manner. Over the past decade the development of rendering styles outside the bounds of photorealism has gathered significant momentum — so-called *non-photorealistic rendering* or *NPR*. In particular, algorithms for generating artistic renderings for the purpose of aesthetics (for example pen-and-ink hatchings [1, 2], or paintings [3, 4]) have received considerable attention from NPR researchers. Artists typically draw not only to convey scene content, but also to convey a sense of how that content is to be perceived. Artistic renderings therefore offer numerous advantages over photorealistic imagery, including the ability to stylize presentation, abstract away unimportant detail and focus the viewer's attention.

The development of automated artistic rendering algorithms arguably began in the early 1990s with Paul Haeberli's machine assisted painting environments [5]. Despite the advances in artistic media modelling made during the late 1980s, Haeberli observed that convincing impressionist style paintings remained unobtainable in digital paint systems. Blaming the time overhead required to select new colors from the palette, Haeberli devised a novel stroke based rendering system based on source image point sampling.

In Haeberli's system the user starts with a source photograph that they wish to paint, and is supplied with a virtual canvas on which to produce the painting. The user then moves a cursor over the virtual canvas creating brush strokes as is common in typical digital paint systems. The color of the brush stroke is determined by point sampling the source image at the location of the cursor. Stroke orientation may also be determined automatically by point sampling intensity edge gradient (computed using a Sobel operator) while other brush attributes, such as brush size and style, can be varied interactively by the user. A painting is thus represented as an ordered list of strokes, each stroke exhibiting a mixture of user and system defined attributes. This semi-automatic painting approach was judged highly effective by users who were able to construct renderings quickly and easily. Thereafter, Haeberli's combination of source image point sampling and stroke based rendering became something of an NPR paradigm and has been incorporated in to most painterly rendering algorithms subsequently developed.

2.1.1 Fully Automatic Painting Algorithms

The novelty and high aesthetic quality of Haeberli's renderings prompted research efforts into both alternative artistic styles for NPR, and further automation of the painting process (for example, to facilitate painterly animations). In this chapter we focus on the topic of painterly rendering, and so review only the latter body of work.

The earliest attempts to derive fully automate the stroke placement process simply substituted the user interactive components of Haeberli's system (e.g., brush stroke size, or stroke painting order) with pseudo-random processes [6]. This led to a disappointing loss of detail in paintings, as brush strokes from visually important (often termed "salient") image regions tended to become overlapped and obscured by strokes from unimportant (non-salient) regions. To mitigate against this problem, various image data driven algorithms were developed that place strokes and modulate their attributes according to image content. These fully automatic algorithms encode procedural heuristics designed to emulate the human artistic process.

The first heuristics appearing in the literature were driven by low-level image processing operators. Litwinowicz presented an algorithm for painterly rendering using rectangular brush strokes [3] which were clipped against thresholded Sobel edges detected in the image. As with Haeberli's system, strokes were oriented tangential to edge gradient. Litwinowicz's system was thus prevented from painting "outside the lines" of edge features in images, so avoiding the problematic loss of detail caused by earlier pseudo-random systems. Statistical image measures were employed by Treavett and Chen [7],

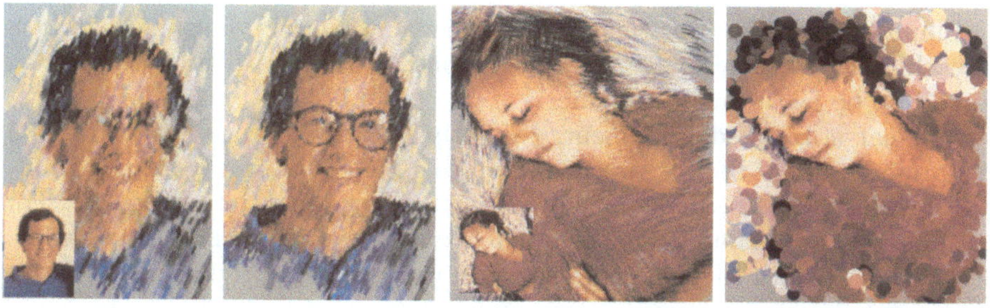

Fig. 2.1. Paintings produced interactively using Haeberli's impressionist system. The user clicks on the canvas to create strokes, the color and orientation of which are point sampled from a reference photograph (inset). Reproduced from [5]. Courtesy Paul Haeberli. (c) 1990 ACM, Inc. Reprinted by permission

and later by Shirashi and Yamaguchi [8]. These systems compute statistical moments of pixel intensity within a small pixel window local to a stroke's intended position. Strokes are then painted tangential to the axis of least variance within that window.

In these early automated painterly algorithms, the generated "brush strokes" were little more than textured stamps centered, rotated and composited on canvas as directed by the painterly rendering algorithm. The late 1990s saw the development of a new generation of algorithms that paid greater attention to the complexities of stroke placement. Hertzmann developed a painting algorithm that made use of curved spline brush strokes fitted to strong Sobel edge detected in the source image. Stroke control points were formed by modelling a particle that "hopped" between pixels along stroke image edges in a similar fashion to the algorithm described later in Sect. 2.2.4. Hertzmann also adopted a multi-resolution approach to producing his paintings, initially producing a coarse scale painting using large strokes painted on a heavily sub-sampled image. The painting was then refined iteratively by painting increasingly finer strokes on canvas using decreasingly sub-sampled versions of the source image. Curved strokes were also used in Curtis et al.'s watercolor painting system [9], accompanied by a sophisticated model of watercolor pigment and substrate.

2.1.2 More Sophisticated Approaches to Painterly Rendering

Most of the painterly rendering algorithms developed in the 1990s can be characterized as spatially local, non-linear filtering operations. Strokes are positioned on canvas solely on the basis of information extracted from a small pixel neighborhood centered upon the stroke's location. This observation was made explicit by the "Image Analogies" system of Hertzmann et al. [10] which, when presented with a photograph and a painterly rendering of that photograph, was able to learn painterly rendering transformations by example. This was accomplished by modelling the mapping between corresponding pixel windows in each image. Simple linear transformations such as sharpening or blurring could also be learnt in this manner.

At that stage of development, painterly rendering heuristics focused on the preservation of high frequency detail (e.g., edges or fine texture) to mitigate against loss of salient image content during the painting process. For example in Hertzmann's "Paint by Relaxation" systems [11] (discussed in Sect. 2.2.1), paintings were created via an optimization process in which the objective function minimized discrepancies between detail in the original and painted images. This tends to produce a machine-generated signature in the resulting painterly renderings; human painters do not seek to preserve all content when rendering a scene, but rather paint to emphasize the perceptually *salient* detail in that a scene whilst abstracting away non-salient details. The emphasis placed on a particular region within a painting is therefore a function of the relative importance of that region to the artist. Such observations have most recently motivated a trend away from use of local low-level image processing operators towards the incorporation of mid-level computer vision techniques in stroke placement heuristics (in particular, image salience measures [12] and color segmentation algorithms [13, 14]). Notably, DeCarlo and Santella produced a segmentation based painting system [14] in which an eye tracker was used to monitor a user's interest in regions of a source photograph, so producing an salience map of the image interactively. Presenting a user with a photograph would cause his or her gaze to automatically fixate upon perceptually salient regions of the image. The location and duration of these fixations governed level of detail in DeCarlo and Santella's painting process. In Sect. 2.2.2 we discuss a fully automatic approach to producing salience adaptive painterly renderings [12].

We conclude this review by observing that various attempts have been made to produce painterly animations from video. This is a challenging problem; the presence of video noise or process non-determinism in painterly rendering algorithms frequently induces a distracting flickering or in the painted animation that prohibits the independent rendering of video frames. A naive solution to this problem is to fix the positions of brush strokes, allowing only their colors to change. This gives the impression of video moving "behind a shower door" [15] and is aesthetically poor in most cases. Litwinowicz was the first to produce a solution, making use of *optical flow* algorithms to estimate the motion of pixels from one video frame to the next [3]. The idea is straightforward, paint strokes are generated on the first frame of video and translated to subsequent frames based on the inter-frame motion estimate. This technique was applied in parts of the movie "What Dreams may Come", which won an Academy Award for "Best Visual Effects" in 1998. Unfortunately optical flow estimates are often inaccurate in general video, and the errors that accumulate and propagate throughout the animation require extensive manual correction to prevent flicker in videos of a practical size. Other temporally local algorithms, making use of inter-frame differencing rather than optical

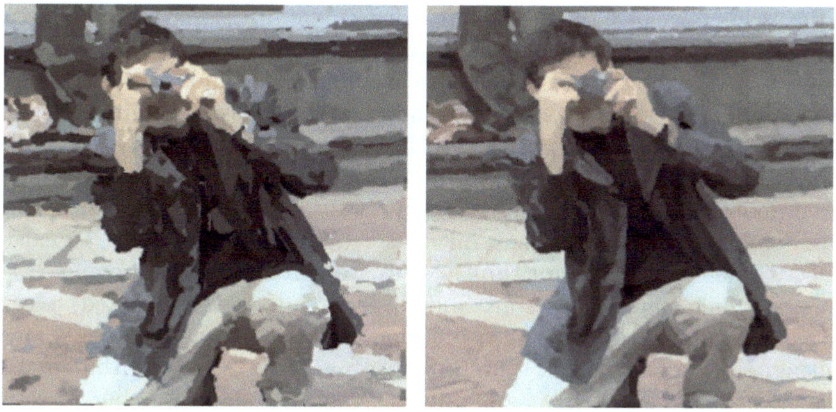

Fig. 2.2. Curved B-spline stroke paintings produced by Hertzmann's original, single-pass algorithm [4] (left) and by Hertzmann's active contour (snake) optimization process [11] (right). Note the improvements in stroke placement precision using the latter. Reproduced from [10]. Courtesy Aaron Hertzmann. Copyright 2001 IEEE

flow, were presented in [16]. Most recently, researchers have begun to explore the avenue of spatio-temporal optimization in video for painterly rendering, with some promising results addressing the problem of stroke flicker [17, 18].

2.2 Painting as an Optimization Problem

Most painting rendering algorithms treat painting as a "single-pass" process; pixels in the image are examined in turn, and strokes placed according to various artistic heuristics. Although the image might be processed repeatedly at different scales (producing successive coarse to fine layers of strokes [4, 8]), once a particular stroke is placed there is no subsequent adjustment of its position or attributes to improve the painting in a more global sense. Recently researchers have begun to address this shortcoming by phrasing the painterly rendering process as a global goal-directed search (optimization) problem.

2.2.1 Paint by Relaxation

Although optimization approaches to painting were first suggested by Haeberli [5] it was not until a decade later that the first algorithmic solution was presented by Hertzmann [10]. Hertzmann extended his single-pass curved stroke painterly algorithm [4] by treating each stroke as an active contour or "snake". Snakes are a computer vision innovation developed in the late 1980s by Kass et al. for the purpose fitting of curves to edges detected in images [19]. A snake is typically a piecewise curve whose control points are iteratively updated to minimize an energy function; a process termed *relaxation*. Ideally, this has the effect of moving the curve incrementally closer to the edge over time. The energy function for a snake is a weighted sum of "internal" energy parameters, guarding against sharp discontinuities or "kinks" appearing along the curve, and "external" energy parameters which serve to minimize distance between the curve and edges detected in the image.

In Hertzmann's optimization system, a single painting is created from the source photograph and iteratively updated to converge toward an aesthetic ideal. Strokes are placed in their initial positions on canvas using an existing curved stroke painting algorithm [4]. An iterative optimization phase then begins in which snake strokes are added, deleted or moved (relaxed) over the canvas to minimize an objective function that evaluates the quality of the painting. Hertzmann deems a high quality painting to be one that matches the source image as closely as possible, using a minimal number of strokes but covering the maximum area of canvas in paint. His objective function is a summation of four weighted scalar functions which assess the current painting "P" with respect to these attributes.

$$E_{\text{app}}(P) = \omega_1 \sum_{x=1}^{\text{width}} \sum_{y=1}^{\text{height}} |\underline{P}(x,y) - \underline{G}(x,y)| \tag{2.1}$$

$$E_{\text{area}}(P) = \omega_2 \sum_{S \in P} \text{Area}(S) \tag{2.2}$$

$$E_{\text{nstr}}(P) = \omega_3 \cdot (\text{number of strokes in } P) \tag{2.3}$$

$$E_{\text{cov}}(P) = \omega_4 \cdot (\text{number of unpainted pixels in } P). \tag{2.4}$$

Weights $\omega_{1,\ldots,4}$ control the influence of each quality attribute and are determined empirically. Vector functions $P(x,y)$ and $G(x,y)$ refer to RGB pixel color at point $[x,y]^T$ in the painting and source photograph respectively. Expression $S \in P$ refers to all strokes comprising painting P. Summing the areas of strokes in (2.3) yields a value analogous to the quantity of paint used in producing the painting.

Figure 2.2 demonstrates the significant improvements in accuracy that can be obtained using an optimization approach to painting. However the consistently high level of detail returned within the painting can cause the rendering to tend back toward photorealism, and is arguably inconsistent with the selective process of abstraction with which artists paint. Furthermore the snake relaxation process is prone to falling into local minima. Artifacts may appear in paintings where snake relaxation falls into local minima causing strokes to be painted erroneously across salient features in the image. In most cases this can be resolved by tweaking weights $\omega_{1,\ldots,4}$ and re-running the optimization. Snake relaxation is also computationally expensive, and this places significant limitations on the usability of the system for experimentation and exploration of potential artistic styles. A typical painting containing tens of thousands of snake strokes can take many hours to optimize.

2.2.2 A Search for Salient Paintings

Art historian E.H. Gombrich writes that "works of art are not mirrors" [20] — rather, artists commonly paint to capture the structure and elements of a scene that they consider to be visually important (salient). In an addendum to Hertzmann's "Paint by Relaxation" paper (Sect. 2.2.1) users could draw masks over regions of the image to reduce the influence of (2.2), so interactively attenuating non-salient detail in these areas (a precursor to DeCarlo and Santella's gaze driven painting system, Sect. 2.1.2). In this section we describe an algorithm for rendering images in an impasto oil painted style, *automatically* identifying salient regions in the source image and concentrating painting detail there. The algorithm was developed by Collomosse and Hall [12] and extends an earlier pilot study [21] which demonstrated that ordering the placement of virtual brush stroke with respect to image salience can enhance both accuracy and sense of composition within a painterly rendering.

Collomosse and Hall's algorithm makes use of a genetic algorithm (GA) to search the space of possible paintings, so locating the optimal painting for a given photograph. Their *optimality criterion* is a measure of the strength of correlation between the level of detail in a painting and the salience map of its source image (later defined more formally in (2.14)). Their GA approach was motivated through consideration of Haeberli's abstraction of a painting; an ordered list of strokes [5] (comprising control points, thickness, etc. with color as a data dependent function of these). Under this representation the space of possible paintings for a given source image is very high dimensional, and the aforementioned optimality criterion makes this space extremely turbulent. Stochastic searches that model evolutionary processes, such as GAs [22], are often cited among the best search strategies in such situations; large regions of problem space can be covered quickly, and local minima more likely to be avoided [23, 24]. Furthermore the GA approach adopted allows different regions within a painting to be optimized independently, and later combined to produce improved solutions in later generations.

We now outline the trainable salience measure that forms the basis of the fitness function for the GA. The GA is then described in Sect. 2.2.4.

2.2.3 A Trainable Image Salience Measure

Image salience measures map a color image to a scalar field, in which the value of any point is directly proportional to the perceived salience of the corresponding image point. This scalar field describes the importance (salience magnitude) of image regions and is referred to as a "salience map". Producing a salience map is a subjective task; for example, different faces photographed in a crowd will hold different levels of salience to friends or strangers. A priori user training is one way of incorporating this notion of subjectivity into an automated salience measure. The salience measure used by Collomosse and

Hall [25] is trainable, and combines three operators which compute the *rarity*, *visibility* and the *classification* of local image artifacts.

The first operator (P_{rare}) performs unsupervised global statistical analysis to evaluate the relative rarity (P_{rare}) of image artifacts, a technique inspired by Walker et al. [26] who observe that salient features are uncommon in an image. However, not all rare artifacts should be considered "salient". In particular, salient artifacts should also be visible, and the salience measure incorporates a second, perceptually trained, operator which estimates the visibility (P_{visible}) of image artifacts. Finally, the user may perceive certain classes of artifact, for example edges or corners, to be more salient than others. The salience measure incorporates a third operator which users train by highlighting salient artifacts in photographs. Signals corresponding to these artifacts are clustered to produce a classifier which may be applied to artifacts in novel images in order to estimate their potential salience (P_{class}). The three operators are computed independently, yielding three probabilities which are combined to estimate the final probability of an image artifact being salient:

$$P_{\text{salient}} = P_{\text{rare}} \cdot P_{\text{visible}} \cdot P_{\text{class}}. \tag{2.5}$$

The three operators are computed for each pixel location $\underline{p} = (i,j)^T$ in the source image by analyzing a signal (hereafter written $\underline{x}(\underline{.})$) obtained via a circular sampling technique. Image data is sampled under a series of rings of radius ρ, each centered at $\underline{p}$. The image is uniformly sampled around each ring's circumference at angular positions θ, hence obtaining a discrete "circular" signal $\underline{x}(\rho,\theta;\underline{p}) \in \Re^3$; colors are in RGB space. Suitable sampling rates for ρ and θ are cited as 0.5 in range $[1,3]$, and $\pi/16$ in range $[0,2\pi]$ respectively.

Operator 1: Feature Rarity

Image rarity is computed by modelling the statistical distribution of a set of measures locally associated with each pixel, and isolating the outliers of this distribution. For each pixel location $\underline{p} = (i,j)^T$ the discrete image signal $\underline{x}(\rho,\theta;\underline{p})$ is rewritten as a column vector. An eigenmodel is created from the collection of vectors $\underline{x}(.)$ sampled over from each pixel within the image. The Mahalanobis distance $d(.)$ is then computed for all pixels $\mathcal{P}$ in the image.

$$d^2(\underline{x}(.)) = (\underline{x}(.) - \underline{\mu})^T \underline{\underline{U}}\ \underline{\underline{\Lambda}}\ \underline{\underline{U}}^T (\underline{x}(.) - \underline{\mu}). \tag{2.6}$$

The probability of an individual pixel $\underline{q} \in \mathcal{P}$ being rare is given by a quotient measuring the fraction of the sample density which is less rare than the pixel $\underline{q}$:

$$\mathcal{Q} = \{\underline{r} : d(\underline{x}(\underline{r})) \leq d(\underline{x}(\underline{q})) \wedge \underline{r}, \underline{q} \in \mathcal{P}\} \tag{2.7}$$

$$P_{\text{rare}}(\underline{q}) = \frac{\sum_{\underline{p}\in\mathcal{Q}} d(\underline{x}(\underline{p}))}{\sum_{\forall \underline{p}\in\mathcal{P}} d(\underline{x}(\underline{p}))}. \tag{2.8}$$

Operator 2: Feature Visibility

The second operator is perceptually visibility measure, calibrated as a one-off process prior to processing. It is simplistically assumed that for each RGB color $\underline{r}$ there is distance $\tau(\underline{r})$, also in RGB space beyond which it is possible to perceptually distinguish colors from $\underline{r}$. This unit of distance is termed the "just noticeable difference" (JND). Together the color and the distance specify a sphere of RGB colors $(\underline{r}, \tau(\underline{r}))$. No color interior to the surface of the sphere can be perceptually discriminated from the centre color, whilst all exterior colors can be so discriminated. The distance $\tau(\underline{r})$ is one JND at the color $\underline{r}$, and is measured experimentally using a process described in [25]. The sphere radius can vary depending on experimental conditions, and after several experimental trials τ emerges as the mean radius accompanied by an associated standard deviation σ.

To evaluate the visibility of artifacts local to a point $\underline{p}$, we compute the differential magnitude of circular signal $\underline{x}(\rho, \theta; \underline{p})$ as:

$$d(\rho, \theta; \underline{p}) = \left\| \left| \frac{\delta \underline{x}(\rho, \theta; \underline{p})}{\delta \rho} \right|^2 + \left| \frac{\delta \underline{x}(\rho, \theta; \underline{p})}{\delta \theta} \right|^2 \right\|^{1/2} . \qquad (2.9)$$

The probability $\phi(.)$ that this change is visible is computed as:

$$\phi(\rho, \theta; \underline{p}) = \mathrm{erf}((d(\rho, \theta; \underline{p}) - \tau)/\sigma) \qquad (2.10)$$

where τ and σ are the JND and its deviation for the color sample at $\underline{x}(\rho, \theta; \underline{p})$ in the local window. Ideally, if a signal grazes the edge of the disk it should register as visible, but not strongly because it will not pass through all rings. The probability of the region local to location $\underline{p}$ being visible is thus:

$$P_{\text{visible}} = \sum_{\rho=1}^{\rho_{\max}} \max(\phi(\rho, \theta; \underline{p})). \qquad (2.11)$$

Operator 3: Feature Classification

The final operator enables users to train the system to identify certain classes of low-level artifact as potentially salient. This not only introduces a subjective property to the salience measure but also enables the salience measure to classify the type of salient feature it encounters. This additional functionality is useful later (Sect. 2.2.4) where it enables different types of stroke to be painted for different features such as edges or ridges.

Each ring in circular signal $\underline{x}(\rho, \theta; \underline{p})$ is processed separately, and later combined to produce a value P_{class} for location $\underline{p}$. Here we outline the classification process for a single ring (i.e., ρ is constant), and refer the reader to [25] for details, including the method for combining signals from multiple rings.

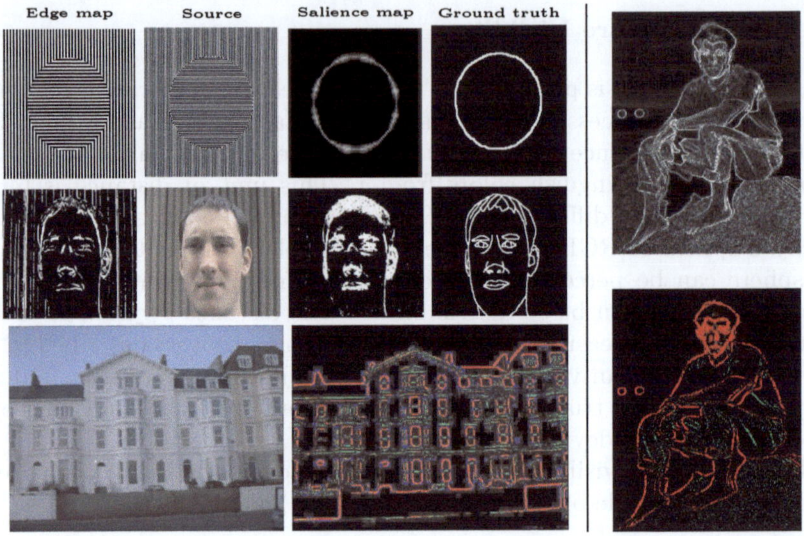

Fig. 2.3. Left: Comparison of images edge detected and salience mapped [25], with a hand-sketched ground truth. The salience maps are qualitatively closer to sketches, and can "pick out" the circle and face where local methods such as edge detection fail. Such examples motivate the use of global salience maps rather than local edge detection in the production of artistic renderings. The salience measure described in Sect. 2.2.3 both estimates salience magnitude and classifies salient artifacts into trained categories (bottom row). In this example edges are drawn in red, ridges green, and corners blue. Right: Sobel edges (top) and salience map (bottom), corresponding to the MODEL painting included on the DVD. Salient edges are discriminated from non-salient high frequency texture, which allows the GA fitness function in Sect. 2.2.4 direct level of painterly detail correctly

The operator begins by transforming the circular signal $\underline{x}(\rho, \theta; \underline{p})$ into a useful invariant form amenable to feature classification. We simplify notation here by writing the periodic signal (at location $\underline{p}$ with constant ρ) as $\underline{y}(\theta)$. To obtain the invariant form, $\underline{y}(\theta)$ is transformed into the spectral domain using a Fourier transform. The magnitude (absolute value) of the Fourier components $|F[\underline{y}(\theta)]|$ are computed, normalized to unit power, and the d.c. component dropped to yield a feature vector $\underline{f}(\omega)$:

$$\underline{f}(\omega) = \frac{|F[\underline{y}(\theta)]|}{\left(\sum_{\theta} |\underline{y}(\theta)|^2\right)^{\frac{1}{2}}} \tag{2.12}$$

$$\underline{f}(\omega) \leftarrow \underline{f}(\omega) \setminus \underline{f}(0). \tag{2.13}$$

By disregarding phase the feature vector $\underline{f}(\omega)$ becomes rotationally invariant. In addition, dropping the d.c. component and normalizing offers some invariance to changes of brightness and contrast over the image.

The classification operator requires the user to specify training examples of salient and non-salient features $\underline{f}(\omega)$, in order to build an a priori model of the features the user finds subjectively important. Precise details of the modelling process are beyond the scope of this chapter, but details may be found in [25]. In summary, this "training" occurs over several images, and requires the user to interactively highlight artifacts they regard as salient. The user may choose a number of classes of artifacts (such as edge, ridge, or corner), and identify a class label with each artifact they highlight.

During painting, classification of location $\underline{p}$ begins by sampling to obtain $\underline{f}(\omega)$. A probability vector is computed (one element per class of feature trained) to determine if the region local to $\underline{p}$ contains a potential salient feature. P_{class} is computed as the maximum value in this probability vector.

2.2.4 Initializing the Painting Population

Collomosse and Hall's system accepts as input a source image I; paintings derived from I are points in the search space. The algorithm begins by applying the salience measure to I; obtaining both a salience map and a classification probability for each pixel. An intensity gradient image is also computed using Gaussian derivatives, from which a gradient direction field is obtained. Once this pre-processing is complete, a fixed size population of 50 individuals is initialized. Each individual is a point in the search space, represented by an ordered list of strokes that, when rendered, produces a painting from I. Each individual (painting) is derived from the source image via a stochastic process.

Stochastic Stroke Placement and Growth

Seed points are scattered over the canvas, from which brush strokes will be subsequently "grown". Seeds are scattered stochastically, with a bias toward placement of seeds in more salient regions of source image I. A painting is formed by compositing curved Catmull–Rom spline brush strokes on a canvas of identical size to the source image. Brush strokes are grown to extend bi-directionally from each seed point; each end grows independently until halted by one or more preset criteria. Growth proceeds in a manner similar to Hertzmann's algorithm [4]. Starting from the pixel at given seed point, the algorithm "hops" between pixels in the direction tangential to their intensity gradient (Fig. 2.4). The list of visited pixels forms the control points for the stroke.

Recognizing that noise forms a component of any real image, Collomosse and Hall treat hop directions as samples from a stochastic distribution. Given a locally optimal direction estimate θ a hop direction is selected by adding Gaussian noise $G(0, \sigma)$. The value σ is an estimate for the level of noise in the image, and is calibrated using a procedure outlined elsewhere [12] (typical σ values vary between 2 and 5 degrees, depending on the imaging device that acquired the photograph). The magnitude of the hop is also Gaussian distributed, but inversely proportional to the local value of the salience map

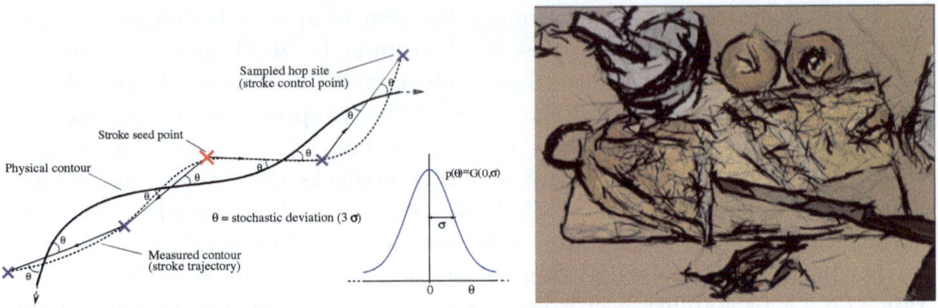

Fig. 2.4. Left: Stochastic growth of strokes from a seed pixel. The departure angle of a "hop" is drawn from distribution $p(\theta) = G(0, \sigma)$. Right: A "loose and sketchy" painting in the style of Matisse, rendered prior to the GA optimization step of Sect. 2.2.5. Note the variation in stroke style when rendering edges and ridges

measured at the seed point of the stroke. The growth of a stroke end is halted when either the curvature between adjacent pixels, or the difference between the color of the pixel to be appended and the mean color of visited pixels exceeds a threshold. This method initially yields a sub-optimal trajectory for the stroke with respect to our optimality criterion. However, for a "loose and sketchy" paintings this is often desirable (see Fig. 2.4, right).

Rendering an Individual Painting

At this stage it is possible to either render one of the paintings in the initial population (to produce a single-pass "loose and sketchy" painting), or proceed to Sect. 2.2.5 to optimize the painting — each iteration of the latter process also requires paintings to be rendered to evaluate fitness.

Rendering a painting is a straightforward process of scan-converting and compositing its list of curved spline brush strokes. Stroke thickness is set inversely proportional to *stroke salience*; taken as the mean salience over each control point. Stroke color is uniform and set according to the mean of all pixels encompassed in the footprint of the thick paint stroke. During rendering, strokes of least salience are laid down first, with more salient strokes being painted later. This prevents strokes from non-salient regions encroaching upon salient areas of the painting. The ability of our salience measure to differentiate between classes of salient feature (e.g., edge, ridge) also enables us to vary brush style styles. Fig. 2.4 shows a painting where the classification probability of a feature has been used as a parameter to interpolate between three stroke rendering styles *flat*, *edge* and *ridge*.

2.2.5 Iterative Search Step of the GA

Genetic algorithms (GAs) simulate the process of natural selection by breeding successive generations of individuals through crossover, mutation and fitness-proportionate selection [24]. In Collomosse and Hall's system such individuals are paintings; their genomes are ordered lists of strokes. A description of a single iteration (generation) of their GA search now follows. Iteration continues until the improvements gained over previous generations are marginal (the change in both average and maximum population fitness over a sliding time window falls below a threshold).

Evaluation and Fitness Function

The entire population is first rendered, and edge maps of each painting are produced by convolution with Gaussian derivatives, which serve as a quantitative measure of local fine detail. The generated maps are then compared to a precomputed salience map of the source image. The mean squared error (MSE) between maps is used as the basis for evaluating the fitness quality $F(.)$ of a particular painting; the lower the MSE, the better the painting:

$$F(I, \psi) = 1 - \frac{1}{N} \sum |S(I) - E(\Psi(I, \psi))|^2 . \tag{2.14}$$

The summation is computed over all N pixels in source image I. $\Psi(.)$ is our painterly process, which produces a rendering from I and a particular ordered list of strokes ψ corresponding to an individual in the population. The function $S(.)$ signifies the salience mapping process described in Sect. 2.2.3, and $E(.)$ the process of convolution with Gaussian derivatives.

The population is evaluated according to (2.14) and individuals are ranked according to fitness. The bottom 10% are culled, and the best 10% of the population pass to the next generation. The middle 80% are used to produce the remainder of the next generation — two individuals are selected stochastically using roulette wheel selection. These individuals are bred via crossover to produce a novel offspring for the successive generation.

Crossover and Mutation

Two difference images, A and B, are produced by subtracting the edge maps of the parents from the salience map of the original image, then taking the absolute value of the result. Large values in these difference images (A and B) indicate large discrepancies between level of detail in the painting, and salient detail detected in the source image. These discrepancies are undesirable, given the fitness criterion defined in (2.14).

We define the $>$ (greater than) operator to act on images, outputting a binary image mask that indicates where pixels in one image hold larger values than those in corresponding locations in a second image. By computing the binary image $A > B$, and likewise $B > A$, it is easy to determine which pixels in one parent contribute toward the fitness criterion to a greater degree than those in the other. Since the primitives of paintings are thick brush

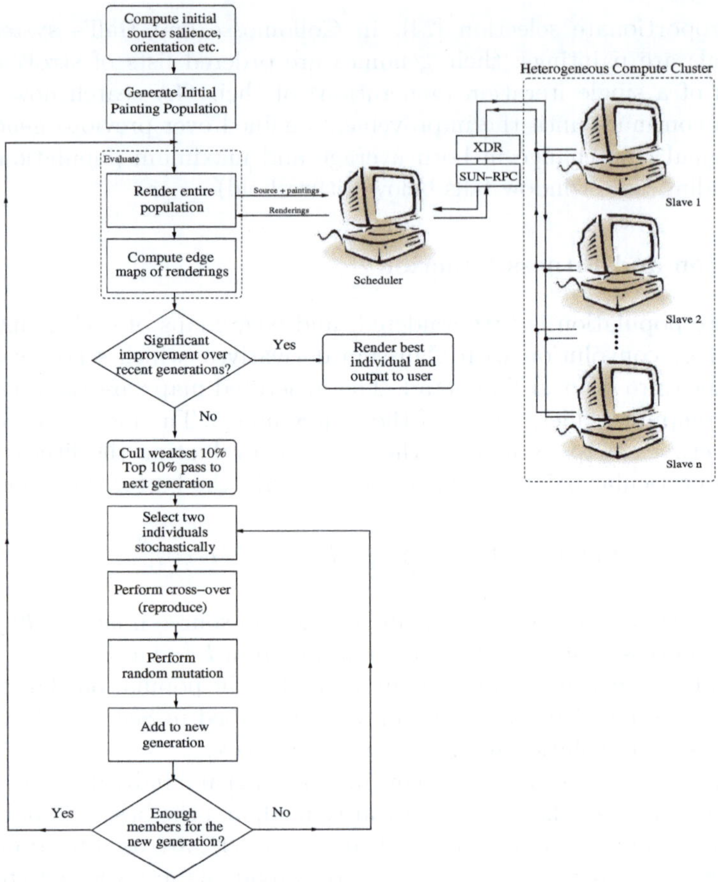

Fig. 2.5. Control flow in the genetic painting algorithm. Population evaluation is performed in parallel over a distributed computing cluster

strokes rather than single pixels, we perform several binary dilations to both images to mark small regions local to these "fitter" pixels as desirable. A binary AND operation between the dilated images yields mutually preferred regions (i.e., where $A = B$). These conflicting regions are masked with a coarse chequerboard texture (of random scale and phase offset) to decide between parents in an arbitrary fashion. Strokes seeded within the set regions in each parent's mask are cloned to create the offspring individual (Fig. 2.6).

When a bred individual passes to a successive generation it is subjected to a random mutation. A new "temporary" painting is synthesized (though never rendered), and a binary mask produced containing several small disks scattered within it. The number, location and radius of the disks are governed by random variates. Strokes seeded within set regions of the binary mask are

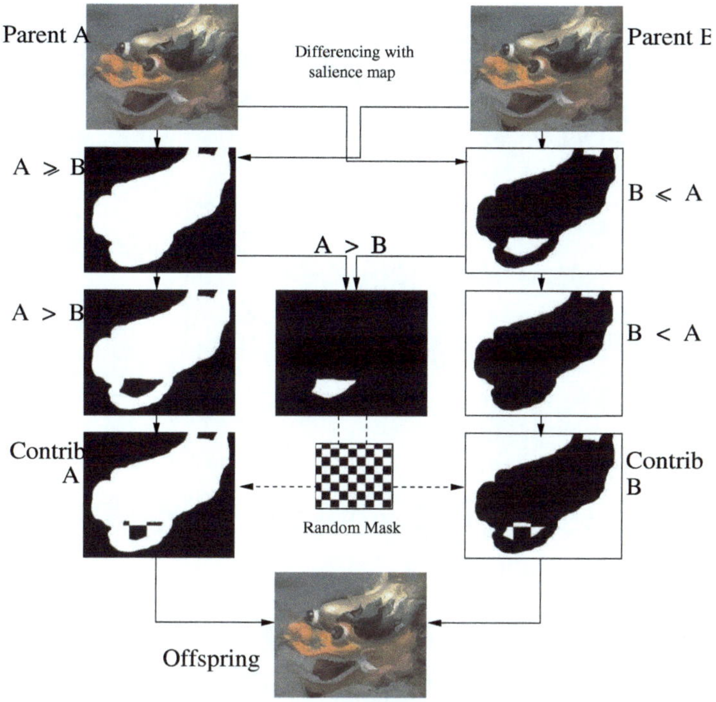

Fig. 2.6. Visualization of crossover (using the DRAGON from Fig. 2.8, manually marked up for illustration). Two parent paintings, A and B, are rendered and compared to the pre-computed salience map. If a region from one parent preserves salient detail to a greater degree than the corresponding region from the other parent, the former region's strokes are adopted by the new offspring — see Sect. 2.2.5

substituted for those in the temporary painting; the temporary painting is then discarded. Mutation occurs over approximately 4% of the canvas.

2.2.6 Parallel Implementation

In practice, evaluation is the most lengthly part of the process and the rendering step is farmed out to several machines concurrently. In Collomosse and Hall's implementation, paintings are evaluated in parallel using the Sun RPC/XDR interface to communicate over a small heterogeneous (Pentium III/UltraSPARC) compute cluster. The typical time to render a 50 painting generation is cited as approximately 15 minutes over six workstations. Optimization of the painting can therefore take in the order of hours, but significant

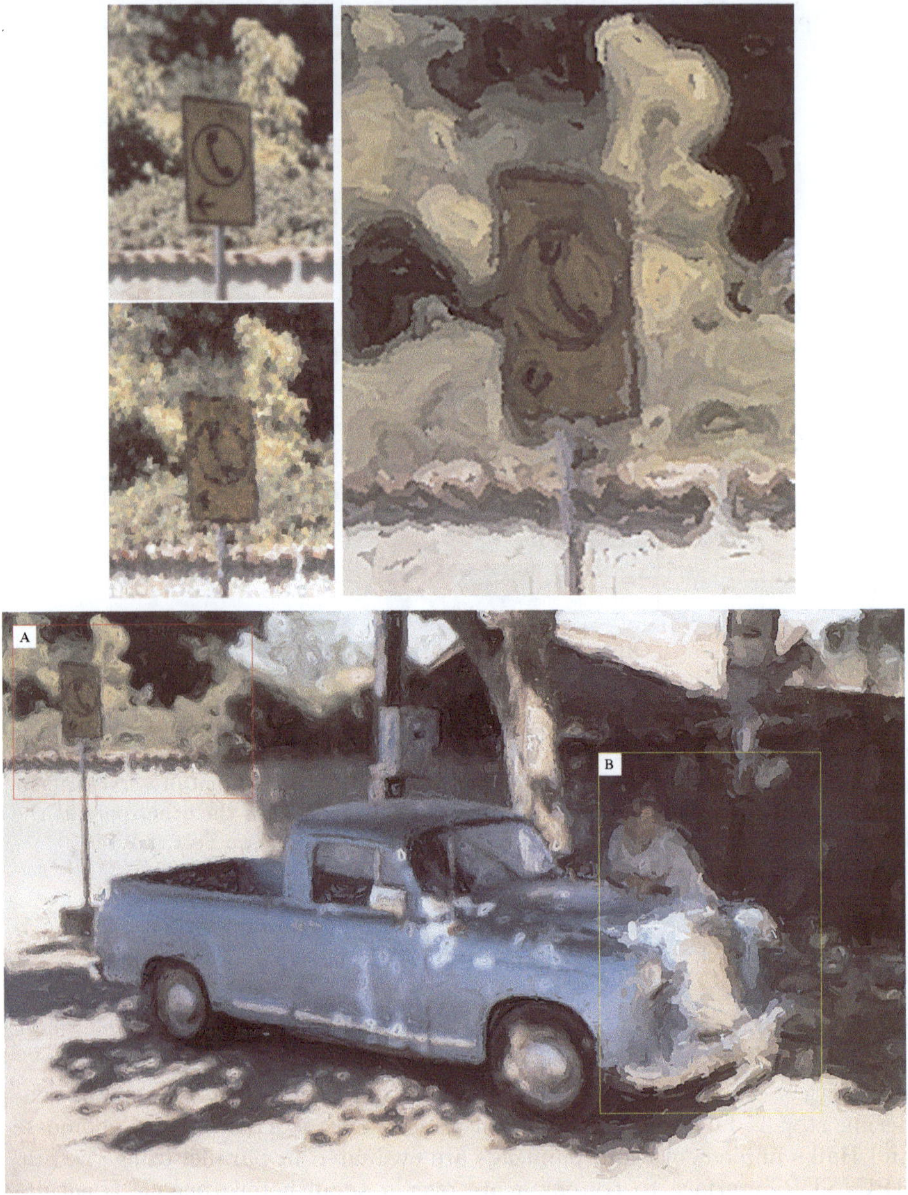

Fig. 2.7. Salience adaptive painting of the TRUCK image. Bottom row: Salience map values within region **B** have been artificially reduced to demonstrate visual abstraction of detail. Top-left: Region **A** source image exhibiting salient detail (sign) against non-salient detail (shrubbery). Top-middle: Litwinowicz's painterly rendering algorithm [3] affords equal emphasis to all features. Top-right: Collomosse and Hall's algorithm abstracts away non-salient detail with coarse brush strokes whilst preserving salient detail on the sign

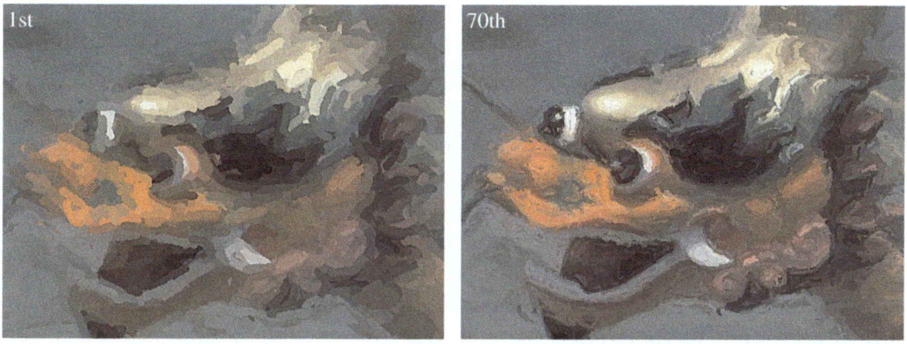

Fig. 2.8. Detail in the salient region of the DRAGON painting sampled from the fittest individual in the first, and 70th generation of the GA search

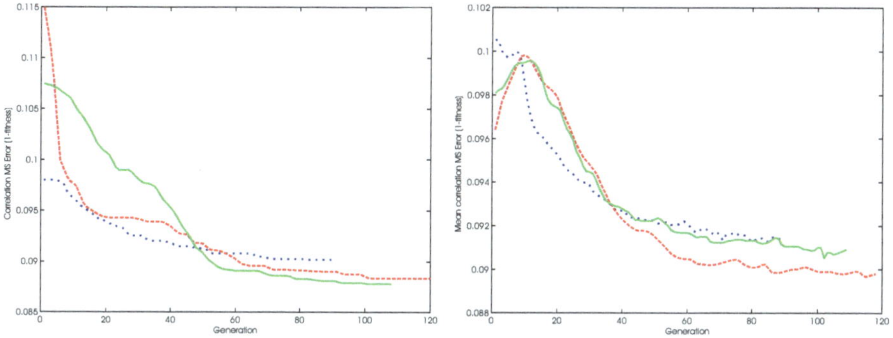

Fig. 2.9. Population fitness graphed during optimization. Left: MSE of the fittest individual plotted against time. Right: MSE averaged over each generation. Red-dashed line indicates the DRAGON (Fig. 2.8, video of optimization on DVD), green-solid line the TRUCK (Fig. 2.7), and blue-dotted line the MODEL (included on the DVD)

improvements in stroke placement can be achieved — see Figs. 2.7 and 2.8. In particular note the variation in level of detail present in Fig. 2.7 as a function of the salience map defined in Sect. 2.2.3. Additional paintings and a video of the optimization process for Fig. 2.8 are included on the DVD.

2.3 Interactive Genetic Search for Parameter Selection

Artistic rendering algorithms are commonly motivated as creative tools, for example helping to improve accessibility to art (perhaps allowing young children to produce digital paintings or create cartoon animations from videos of their toys [27, 18]), or permitting experimentation with new forms of dynamic art (such as artistic stylization of digital video [17, 18]). In fully automated painterly rendering algorithms, creative control is expressed through setting various user parameters governing internal operation of the algorithm. For example, Hertzmann's curved stroke painterly algorithm [4] contains many stylistic parameters controlling properties such as maximum stroke length or random color jitter, as well as data dependent parameters controlling the scale at which images are filtered to detect edges. By manipulating these parameters it is possible to emulate a wide gamut of styles including "pointillist", "impressionist", "expressionist" and "abstract" paintings.

Unfortunately the large number of parameters that accompany many painterly rendering algorithms can be time consuming to set — both due to their number, but also due to their low-level nature, which can make them non-intuitive for inexperienced users to manipulate when aiming for a conceptually high level effect (for example, a dark, gloomy painting or an energetic, cheerful composition). Moreover, parameters can interact in complex ways leading to emergent behavior within the painting that the user may not expect or understand. The end result is often a slow, iterative trial and error process before the user is able to instantiate their desired results.

This parameter selection problem can be overcome, as before, by framing the painterly rendering problem as a goal-centered evolutionary search [28], and resorting to a form of IEC system (see, e.g., Chap. 1). A population of paintings is iteratively evolved towards a user's aesthetic ideal using a GA. The user is presented with a sample of the population for fitness evaluation in each evolutionary cycle. Through this interface the user affects selection in the GA, and so the composition of paintings in subsequent generations.

2.3.1 A Fast Segmentation-Based Painterly Algorithm

Here we illustrate an interactive GA system for parameter selection using a simple, but fast, single-pass painterly rendering algorithm (from [28]). The algorithm operates by segmentation alone. A source image is first segmented into regions of homogeneous color using the EDISON [29] algorithm. Each segmented region is rendered using a combination of "interior" and "boundary" strokes; each stroke is curved and takes the form of a spline, textured and bump mapped to give a 3D relief effect reminiscent of oil paintings [30].

Interior strokes are used to fill the interiors of regions, and are painted tangential to the principal axis running through the region (except for very large regions, which are rendered using horizontal straight strokes). Boundary strokes are painted around the exterior perimeter of a region vectorized using a standard contour walking technique (chain codes). The color of brush strokes is sampled from the source image as with other painterly rendering algorithms. Care is taken when placing each stroke to prevent (a) the stroke spanning pixel regions of greatly differing color (b) the stroke bending at too acute an angle. Both problems cause distortion and smearing of detail, and are avoided by fragmenting the stroke into multiple, smaller strokes.

Algorithm Parameterization

There are eight parameters $p_{1,\ldots,8} = [0, 1]$ governing this algorithm which, as with [4], are capable of creating significant stylistic variation in the output of the algorithm. A full description of the mathematical function of each parameter is beyond the scope of this text (but may be found in [28]). Instead we now summarize the function of these parameters. Figure 2.11 gives an indication of the various painterly effects attainable.

p_1 **Color jitter:** The maximum distance in RGB space by which the color of strokes may be randomly offset from their "true" color sampled from the source image.

p_2 **Maximum stroke angle:** The maximum angle a spline stroke may bend during placement, before it becomes fragmented into smaller strokes. This tends to govern stroke size and expressiveness.

p_3 **Region turbulence:** Boundary stroke placement may be repeatedly performed, each time shrinking the area (and so the perimeter) of the region being painted. Under few repetitions, the interior of a region is comprised mainly of strokes oriented in a common direction. Under many repetitions, the interior becomes more chaotic, formed of series of concentric boundary strokes with reduced visual structure.

$p_{4,5}$ **Color mood:** The color of strokes is subjected to a transformation process, according to vector (p_4, p_5) which represents a point in Russell's 2D pleasure-arousal space [31]. Russell's space is used to represent emotional state; an emotion such as anger would be positioned low on the "pleasure" axis and high on the "arousal" axis, for example. A complex series of color transformations, derived from the color psychology literature, are performed on the original stroke color according to the value of point (p_4, p_5). Interested readers can find further details in [28].

p_6 **Stroke jaggedness:** Brush strokes are splines, created by interpolating control points generated during the stroke placement process. In one possible extreme ($p_6 = 0$), interpolation is performed smoothly using Catmull–Rom splines; in the other ($p_6 = 1$) using only linear interpolation (so creating jagged strokes).

p_7 **Stroke undulation:** Sinusoidal variation can be introduced along each brush stroke, causing inaccuracy in stroke placement and conveying a different visual aesthetic to the painting. p_7 controls the magnitude of this variation.

p_8 **Region dampening:** The effects of stroke undulation parameter p_7 can affect either the interior or boundary strokes, depending on this parameter.

2.3.2 Interactive Evolutionary Search

Within this parameterized rendering framework, the painting process is reduced to a search for the point in parameter space $[p_1, p_2, ..., p_8] \in \Re^8$. The genome of an individual in the GA search is thus represented as eight normalized scalar values. The system creates a population of 1000 such individuals, initially with random genome. As is explained in the next subsection, the user will explicitly evaluate only a fraction of this population on each generation (the remainder will be evaluated by extrapolation). The algorithm then enters an iterative stage in which individuals are bred to produce improved paintings. When successive improvements fall below a threshold, the algorithm terminates; in practice this usually takes only 20–25 iterations.

Interactive Evaluation

The first step in each iterative cycle is population evaluation, in which the proximity of each individual's phenotype to the user's "ideal" aesthetic in measured. Specifically we require a mapping $M([p_1 p_2 ... p_8]) \mapsto f \in \Re$ where f is a normalized fitness score; higher values correspond to aesthetically superior paintings. As our aim is to assist the user creatively in style specification it is not possible to write an automatic function for $M(.)$. Our objective is therefore twofold. First, to estimate the mapping function $M(.)$ through user interaction. Second, to search for the point $\underline{p} \in \Re^8$ that maximizes $M(\underline{p})$.

The first of these problems can be addressed by sparsely evaluating $M(.)$ over a subset of the population, and use this data to extrapolate the behavior of $M(.)$ over the entire population. A simple user interface, allowing the user to be prompted for the fitness of a given individual drawn from the population (so obtaining a sparse domain sample of $M(.)$). The user is supplied with a graduated color bar, and asked to rate the aesthetics of the painting rendered from a given individual on a continuous scale spanning red (bad), amber (neutral) and green (excellent). The user is presented with the nine fittest individuals from the previous iteration, and asked to rate the individual that they feel most strongly about.

The sparse set of user interactions are transformed into a continuous estimate for $M(.)$. Each time a user evaluates an individual we obtain a point $\underline{q}$ and a user fitness rating $U(\underline{q}) = [-1, 1]$. These data are encoded by adding a Gaussian to a cumulative model, built up over successive user evaluations. Each Gaussian distribution is centered at point $\underline{q}$, and multiplied by the factor $U(\underline{q})$. The integral under the Gaussian is assumed to be well approximated by unity in space $\Re^8 \in [0, 1]$, and so the continuous function $M(.)$ is written:

$$M(\underline{p}) = 0.5 + \begin{cases} 0 & \text{if } N = 0, \\ \frac{1}{2N} \sum_{i=1}^{N} U(\underline{q}_i) G(\underline{p}, \underline{q}_i, \sigma) & \text{otherwise} \end{cases} \tag{2.15}$$

where $\underline{p}$ is an individual to be evaluated in the current generation, $\underline{q}_i$ are individuals evaluated by the user in the previous N iterative cycles, and $U(\underline{x})$ is the user's score of a given genotype $\underline{x}$. The function $G(\underline{x}, \underline{\mu}, \sigma)$ denotes a Gaussian distribution with mean $\underline{\mu}$ and standard deviation σ, evaluated at $\underline{x}$. The standard deviation σ governs the locality in problem space over which a single user evaluation holds influence; $\sigma = 0.1$ for typical results

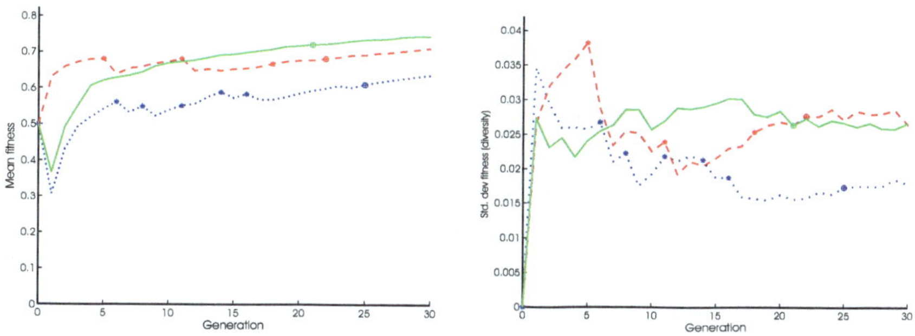

Fig. 2.10. Population statistics from three runs of the GA system, corresponding to Fig. 2.11 top left (blue, dotted), top right (red, dashed), and bottom left (green, solid). Left: Mean fitness over time. Right: Fitness diversity over time. The + symbol indicates algorithm termination. * indicates a negative fitness rating from the user

Selection and Propagation

Once the current population has been evaluated, pairs of individuals are selected and bred to produce the next generation of painting solutions. Parent individuals are selected with replacement, using a stochastic process biased toward fitter individuals. A single offspring is produced from two parents via stochastic crossover and mutation operations. Each of the eight parameters that comprise the genome of the offspring has an equal chance of being drawn from either parent. Mutation is implemented by adding a random normal variate to each parameter. These variates have standard deviations of 0.1; 97% of mutations will produce less than ± 0.3 variation in a rendering parameter.

Improvements in Usability

The population statistics gathered during several runs of the GA search (Fig. 2.10) show a steady improvement in fitness over time, punctuated by short-term dips. These correspond to the occasions when the model $M(.)$ does not tally with the user's aesthetic ideal, requiring correction, in the form of a negative ratings issued by the user. These dips become less pronounced over time as $M(.)$ more closely matches the users expectations.

In small scale usability studies conducted with this system, non-expert users were given a target aesthetic objective, for example "produce a happy, cheerful composition". Using the GA system users were able to manifest their desired aesthetic using approximately 20–25 mouse clicks (one click per generation), in an average of one minute. The same users were asked to re-create the results using a bank of eight sliders (each controlling an independent painting parameter). The results were reproducible but usually took around 4–5 minutes due to the number of parameters and unexpected emergent visual properties caused by interactions between the parameters. The number

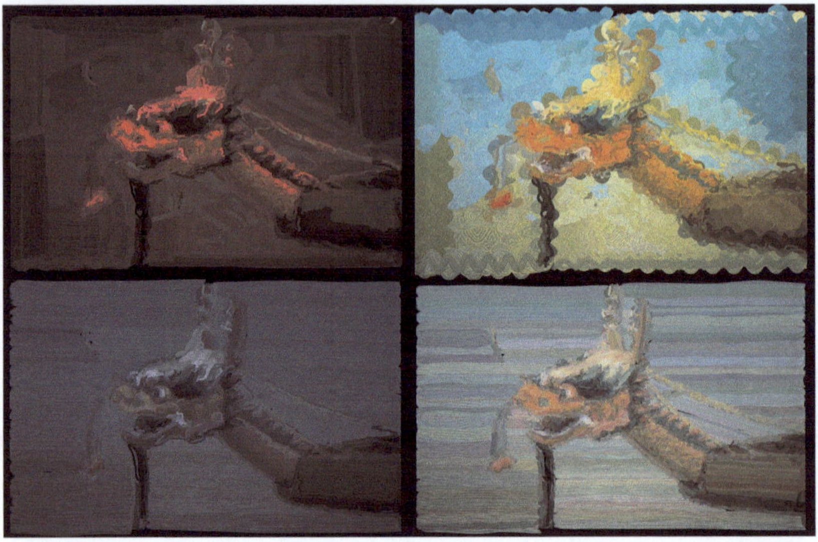

Fig. 2.11. A variety of paintings rendered from the DRAGON image using the algorithm outlined in Sect. 2.3.1, parameterized using the interactive GA

of mouse clicks required to use the sliders was significantly larger than the GA system; between 100 to 200 interactions in all cases.

2.4 Summary and Conclusions

In this chapter we have explored the topic of artistic stylization, presenting two algorithms that harness evolutionary search algorithms to produce synthetic oil paintings from photographs. We began by reviewing a brief history of artistic rendering algorithms, which evolved from artistic media emulation work in the mid-1980s, to semi-automated paint packages, to fully automatic stylization algorithms in the late 1990s (Sect. 2.1). We described how these automatic painting processes can be phrased as optimization problems; as a search to identify the "best" configuration and arrangement of paint strokes for a given source image (Sect. 2.2). We then provided a detailed exposition of Collomosse and Hall's evolutionary search algorithm that develops paintings where emphasis (expressed through level of brush detail) is focused upon the areas of visual importance or "image salience" (Sect. 2.2.2).

Collomosse and Hall's algorithm [12] presented two key technical contributions: (i) a perceptually based measure of image salience; (ii) a genetic algorithm driven relaxation process that automatically produces "optimal" synthetic oil paintings under a definition derived from (i). Adopting a salience adaptive approach to painting was shown to improve the aesthetics of renderings; abstracting away non-salient detail with coarse brush strokes and emphasizing salient detail with fine strokes (Figs. 2.7 and 2.8). The ability of the salience measure to classify image artifacts (for example edges, ridges, or corners) was also harnessed to parameterize stroke style, yielding attractive artistic effects.

In addition to directly manipulating strokes during painting, we also discussed how genetic algorithms can be applied to aid user parameter selection for painting algorithms (Sect. 2.3.2). Often artistic rendering algorithms are capable of a wide gamut of styles, but the parameterizations of that gamut is counter-intuitive for non-expert users. By framing the painting problem as a goal-centered evolutionary search with interactive aesthetic evaluation (i.e., an IEC system) we described how users can efficiently control a painting algorithm without detailed knowledge of its underlying parameterization.

Artistic rendering is a comparatively young field within computer graphics, and much of the groundwork has been laid down only within the last 10–15 years. However over this period we have already observed an marked increase in the complexity of stroke placement algorithms; from simple random stroke placement [6], to image filtering and edge detection based techniques [3, 4, 8], to approaches drawing on sophisticated mid-level computer vision [13] and models of perceptual salience [14, 12]. Strong convergence trends are now emerging between artistic rendering and fields such as computer vision and cognitive science. As this cross-pollination of ideas yields increasingly complex stroke placement heuristics, contributing to new algorithms with diverse artistic capabilities, it is likely that evolutionary algorithms will continue to find application in the design and control of artistic rendering software.

References

1. Salisbury, M.P., Anderson, S.E., Barzel, R., Salesin, D.H. (1994). Interactive pen-and-ink illustration. In: *Proc. ACM SIGGRAPH.* Florida, USA, 101–108
2. Salisbury, M.P., Wong, M.T., Hughes, J.F., Salesin, D.H. (1997). Orientable textures for image-based pen-and-ink illustration. In: *Proc. ACM SIGGRAPH.* Los Angeles, USA, 401–406
3. Litwinowicz, P. (1997). Processing images and video for an impressionist effect. In: *Proc. ACM SIGGRAPH.* Los Angeles, USA, 407–414
4. Hertzmann, A. (1998). Painterly rendering with curved brush strokes of multiple sizes. In: *Proc. ACM SIGGRAPH*, 453–460
5. Haeberli, P. (1990). Paint by numbers: Abstract image representations. In: *Proc. ACM SIGGRAPH.* Vol. 4, 207–214, Figs. 1 and 4. `http://doi.acm.org/10.1145/97879.97902`
6. Haggerty, M. (1991). Almost automatic computer painting. *IEEE Computer Graphics and Applications*, **11**(6): 11–12
7. Treavett, S., Chen, M. (1997). Statistical techniques for the automated synthesis of non-photorealistic images. In: *Proc. Eurographics UK*, 201–210
8. Shiraishi, M., Yamaguchi, Y. (2000). An algorithm for automatic painterly rendering based on local source image approximation. In: *Proc. ACM NPAR*

9. Curtis, C., Anderson, S., Seims, J., Fleischer, K., Salesin, D.H. (1997). Computer-generated watercolor. In: *Proc. ACM SIGGRAPH*, 421–430
10. Hertzmann, A., Jacobs, C., Oliver, N., Curless, B., Salesin, D.H. (2001). Image analogies. In: *Proc. ACM SIGRGAPH*, 327–340
11. Hertzmann, A. (2001). Paint by relaxation. In: *Proc. Computer Graphics Intl. (CGI)*, 47–54
12. Collomosse, J.P., Hall, P.M. (2005). Genetic paint: A search for salient paintings. In: *Applications of Evolutionary Computing, EvoWorkshops 2004*. Vol. 3449 of LNCS, 437–447
13. Gooch, B., Coombe, G., Shirley, P. (2002). Artistic vision: Painterly rendering using computer vision techniques. In: *Proc. ACM NPAR*, 83–90
14. DeCarlo, D., Santella, A. (2002). Abstracted painterly renderings using eye-tracking data. In: *Proc. ACM SIGGRAPH*, 769–776
15. Meier, B. (1996). Painterly rendering for animation. In: *Proc. ACM SIGGRAPH*, 447–484
16. Hertzmann, A., Perlin, K. (2000). Painterly rendering for video and interaction. In: *Proc. ACM NPAR*, 7–12
17. Wang, J., Xu, Y., Shum, H.Y., Cohen, M. (2004). Video tooning. In: *Proc. ACM SIGGRAPH*, 574–583
18. Collomosse, J.P., Rowntree, D., Hall, P.M. (2005). Stroke surfaces: Temporally coherent non-photorealistic animations from video. *IEEE Trans. Visualization and Comp. Graphics*, **11**(5): 540–549
19. Kass, M., Witkin, A., Terzopoulos, D. (1987). Active contour models. *Intl. Journal of Computer Vision (IJCV)*, **1**(4): 321–331
20. Gombrich, E.H. (1960). *Art and Illusion.* Phaidon Press Ltd.. Oxford
21. Collomosse, J.P., Hall, P.M. (2002). Painterly rendering using image salience. In: *Proc. Eurographics UK*, 122–128
22. Holland, J. (1975). *Adaptation in Natural and Artificial Systems. An Introductory Analysis with Applications to Biology, Control, and Artificial Intelligence.* University Michigan Press
23. de Jong, K. (1988). Learning with genetic algorithms. *Machine Learning*, **3**: 121–138
24. Goldberg, D. (1989). *Genetic Algorithms in Search, Optimization, and Machine Learning.* Addison-Wesley. Reading, MA ISBN: 0-201-15767-5.
25. Hall, P.M., Owen, M., Collomosse, J.P. (2004). A trainable low-level feature detector. In: *Proc. Intl. Conf. on Pattern Recognition (ICPR)*. Vol. 1, 708–711
26. Walker, K.N., Cootes, T.F., Taylor, C.J. (1998). Locating salient object features. In: *Proc. British Machine Vision Conf. (BMVC)*. Vol. 2, 557–567
27. Agarwala, A. (2002). Snaketoonz: A semi-automatic approach to creating cel animation from video. In: *Proc. ACM NPAR*, 139–147
28. Collomosse, J.P. (2006). Supervised genetic search for parameter selection in painterly rendering. In: *Applications of Evolutionary Computing, EvoWorkshops 2006*. Vol. 3907, 599–610
29. Christoudias, C., Georgescu, B., Meer, P. (2002). Synergism in low level vision. In: *Intl. Conf. on Pattern Recog. (ICPR)*. Vol. 4, 150–155
30. Hertzmann, A. (2002). Fast paint texture. In: *Proc. ACM NPAR*, 91–96
31. Russell, J.A. (1997). Reading emotion from and into faces: Resurrecting a dimensional-contextual perspective. In Russel, J.A., Fernández-Dols, J.M., eds.: *The Psychology of Facial Expression.* Cambridge University Press, 295–320

3

Evolution and Collective Intelligence of the Electric Sheep

Scott Draves

Spotworks, San Francisco, CA, USA `spot@draves.org`

Summary. *Electric Sheep* is a collective intelligence composed of 40,000 computers and people mediated by a genetic algorithm. It is made with an open source screen-saver that harnesses idle computers into a render farm with the purpose of animating and evolving artificial life-forms known as *sheep*. The votes of the users form the basis for a fitness function for exploring a space of abstract animations. Users also may design sheep by hand for inclusion in the gene pool.

The name *Electric Sheep* is an homage to Philip K. Dick's novel *Do Androids Dream of Electric Sheep*; the basis for the film *Blade Runner*. The metaphor compares the screen-saver to the computer's dream.

After the introduction, we dig into the system starting with Sect. 3.2 on its architecture and implementation. Sect. 3.3 covers the genetic code, including its basis in the equations of classic Iterated Function Systems. The equation is then generalized into the Fractal Flame algorithm, which translates the genetic code into an image. The next two sections treat color and motion.

Section 3.4 shows how the genetic algorithm decides which sheep die, which ones reproduce, and how. Section 3.5 defines the primary dataset and its limitations, and reports some of its statistics. Section 3.5.1 uses the dataset to determine that the genetic algorithm functions more as an amplifier of its human collaborators' creativity rather than as a traditional genetic algorithm that optimizes a fitness function.

The goal of Electric Sheep is to create a self-supporting, network-resident life-form. Section 3.6 speculates on how to make the flock support more of a self-sustaining reaction rather than functioning as an amplifier. Finally, Sect. 3.6.1, explains how *Dreams in High Fidelity* addresses the support issue.

3.1 Introduction

The Electric Sheep project began in 1999, and is ongoing [1]. To the public, it appears as a screen-saver client that can be downloaded and installed on almost any computer. When one of these computers is idle and goes to sleep,

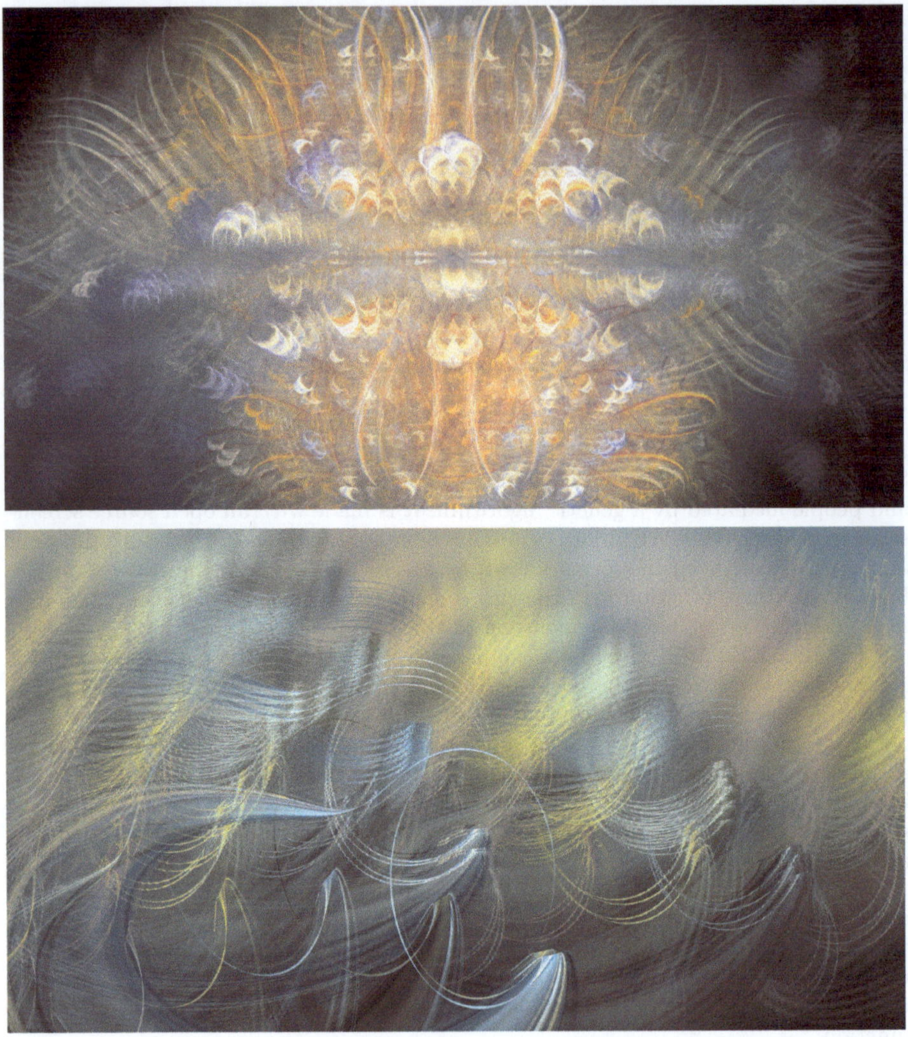

Fig. 3.1. Above is sheep 191.21054 (sheep generation 191, number 21054) and below is sheep 198.19616, born in August and December 2005, respectively

the sheep animations appear, and in parallel the computer goes to work rendering new sheep and sharing its results with all other users. It was inspired by the SETI@Home distributed screen-saver [2].

Figure 3.1 shows still images of two example sheep. After installation, no interaction is required for a user to enjoy the imagery and for her/his computer to contribute to its creation.

Each sheep's shape, motion, and color are specified by a genetic code, a string of hundreds of floating-point numbers. When the users see a sheep they

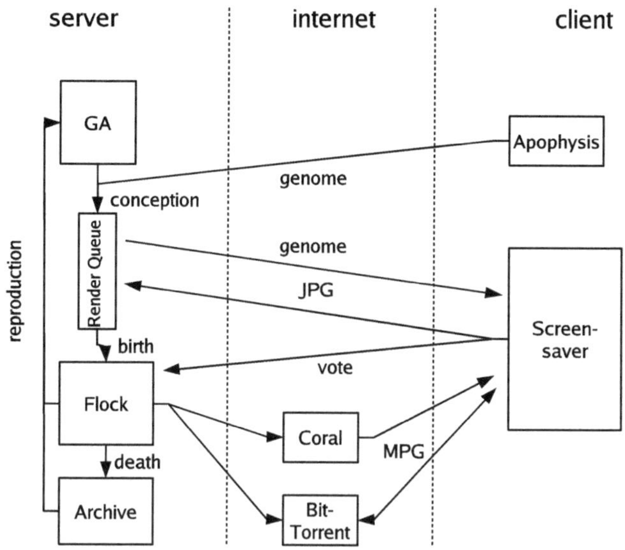

Fig. 3.2. System block diagram. The dotted lines divide the diagram into three parts: on the left are the components that run on the server, on the right those that run on the client, and in the middle is the Internet. A sheep is conceived by the genetic algorithm (GA, described in Sect. 3.4), sits in the render queue until all its frames have been received, and then is born into the flock. It can then be downloaded to the client and voted upon until its death. Apophysis is the sheep design GUI (see Sect. 3.4.1). Coral and BitTorrent are download accelerators (see Sect. 3.2.1)

like, they can press the up arrow key to vote for it, and increase its rating. Sheep with higher ratings live longer and are more likely to reproduce. This fitness function captures the desire of the audience; hence the sheep are a product of aesthetic evolution, a concept first realized by Karl Sims [3].

Users can also download GUI software called *Apophysis* [4] to design sheep genomes and post them to the server. If they prove popular they may interbreed with the artificially evolved population. Hence a human design team collaborates and competes with the artificial intelligence.

3.2 Architecture and Implementation

Electric Sheep has a client/server architecture as illustrated in Fig. 3.2. The client initiates all communication between them, and if no client were running, the server would not run at all.

The screen-saver client has three main threads. One thread downloads sheep animations from the server to a local disk cache. It downloads those with the most votes first. The default size of the cache is 1 GB (enough for 216 animations) but the user may change it. Another thread reads the sheep from the cache and displays them in a continuous sequence on the screen. The third thread contacts the server, receives a genome specifying a frame to render, renders the frame, and then uploads the resulting JPEG file.

The server maintains several collections of sheep. Sheep are numbered as they are created and are identified by this sequence number. Freshly conceived genomes start out in the render queue. Each frame is sent out to a different computer. When all the frames of a sheep have been received, they are compressed into MPEG and deleted, and the sheep is made available for download and voting. Sheep average 4.6 MB each. Eventually the sheep dies (Sect. 3.4.2 explains when) and the MPEG file is deleted.

All these sheep are referred to collectively as a generation. Each time the server is reset the database is wiped, all sheep are deleted from the server and from all client caches, the generation number is incremented, and evolution starts afresh. The generation in November 2006 was 202, and the sheep that are analyzed below are members of generation 165, from 2004. The major generations last for many months, contain thousands of sheep, and are preserved on the server. Most generations last only a few moments during debugging and are discarded.

3.2.1 Bandwidth

The primary server is a commodity Linux x86 server running Apache. It runs the evolutionary algorithm, collects frames and votes, compresses frames, and sends genomes to clients for rendering. This server receives 220 Kb/s from the clients and transmits 260 Kb/s to them (measured average of July to October 2004). On average since its inception in 1999, the server traffic has doubled every nine months. This machine does not have nearly enough bandwidth available to distribute the MPEG files to all the clients. With the current audience size, this would require 20 TB/day (1.8 Gb/s)!

Over the years the mechanism and source for the bandwidth have changed. Right now, the primary server copies them to a high-volume server with 15 Mb/s allocated to sheep. This machine feeds the Coral WebCache, an NSF-funded network of hundreds of servers located worldwide. Coral limits Electric Sheep to 250 GB/day of traffic.

Because each user only gets a fraction of the flock, his/her experience is less than ideal. A freshly installed client may take a *long* time to download its first sheep. When it does run, the playback will probably be repetitive and discontinuous because the client has only a subset of the flock. Right now this is the factor limiting user growth. Bandwidth is the bottleneck.

To address this, the sheep are adopting BitTorrent, a peer-to-peer file sharing protocol [5]. The idea is to share the bandwidth load among the clients in the same way the computational load already is shared. A client with BitTorrent built-in has been released and is delivering about 2 TB/day of sheep. Unfortunately BitTorrent depends on each user configuring the personal firewall to allow the computer to act as a server. Only about 15% of them do so successfully, and this subset cannot support the whole network. Because the sheep are batched into torrents of 100 MB each (about 22 sheep), with this protocol the download is not prioritized by rating.

The system is open source and the code is licensed under the GPL (General Public License version 2) [6]. The fractal flame utilities are written in C and, alas, the server is written in Perl. The clients are written in C, C++, and Objective-C. The genome format is XML.

3.3 The Genetic Code

Fractal flames [7] were developed in 1992 as a generalization and refinement of the Iterated Function System (IFS) category of fractals [8]. The genetic code used by Electric Sheep is the parameter set for these fractals. It consists of up to several hundred floating-point numbers. The parameters control the scattering of billions of particles from which an image emerges.

The genetic code is a visual language and the core of the system. The language is intended to be abstract, expressive, and robust. *Abstract* means that the codes are small relative to the images. *Expressive* means that a variety of images can be drawn. And *robust* means that useful codes are easy to find. These are conflicting goals.

3.3.1 Iterated Function Systems

A classic IFS consists of a recursive set equation on the plane:

$$S = \bigcup_{i=0}^{n-1} T_i(S).$$

The solution S is a subset of the plane (and hence a two-tone image). The T_i are a small collection of n affine transforms of the plane, and S is their fixed point. Affine transformations consist of combinations of scale, rotate, translate, and skew. Hence S is composed of several distorted copies of itself. Normally each copy is smaller than the whole. This is illustrated in Fig. 3.3. Overlap is allowed.

The process is closely related to both video feedback (with each camera corresponding to one transformation), and iterated photocopying with zoom and cut-and-paste. Its implementation however is more like a particle system: the transformations are iterated to generate a stream of colored particles, each of which contributes luminance to a pixel. Unlike a regular particle system, the particles' positions are not saved, and with each frame they are all generated

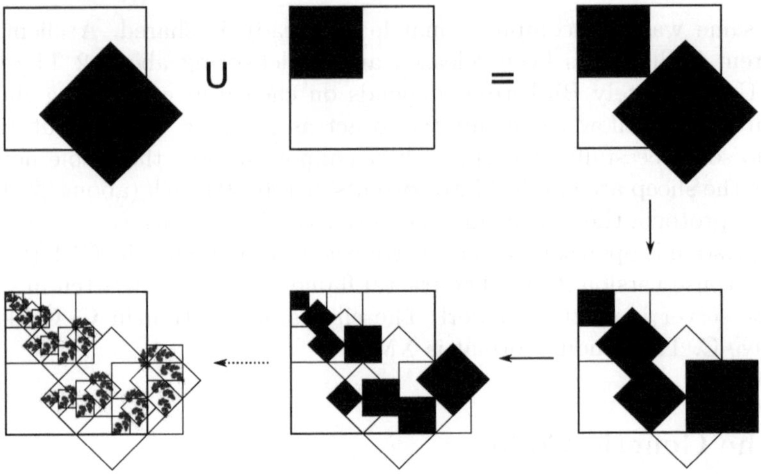

Fig. 3.3. Construction of S from two transformations T_0 and T_1. The first two diagrams in the top row represent T_0 and T_1 by showing how they map the biunit square (outlined) into a smaller square (shaded). Their union is the top-right diagram. The bottom row represents further applications of the transformations, right to left. The solution S appears in the lower left along with the first four levels of construction squares

from scratch using just the genome. This allows the renderer to run in parallel across many computers.

3.3.2 Fractal Flames

A fractal flame is based on the same recursive equation, but the transforms may be nonlinear and the solution algorithm produces a full-color image. The transforms are linear blends of a set of 31 basis functions known as *variations*. The variations are composed with an affine matrix, like a classic IFS. So each transform T_i is

$$T_i(x, y) = \sum_j v_{ij} V_j(a_i x + b_i y + c_i, d_i x + e_i y + f_i)$$

where v_{ij} are the blending coefficients for T_i, and a_i through f_i are six affine matrix coefficients. The V_j are the variations, for example,

$$\begin{array}{ll} V_0(x, y) = (x, y) & V_3(x, y) = (r\cos(\theta + r), r\sin(\theta + r)) \\ V_1(x, y) = (\sin x, \sin y) & V_4(x, y) = (r\cos(2\theta), r\sin(2\theta)) \\ V_2(x, y) = (x/r^2, y/r^2) & V_5(x, y) = (\theta/\pi, r - 1) \end{array}$$

where r and θ are the polar coordinates for the point (x, y) in rectangular coordinates. V_0 is the identity function, so this space of nonlinear functions is a superset of the space of linear functions. See [7] for the complete list.

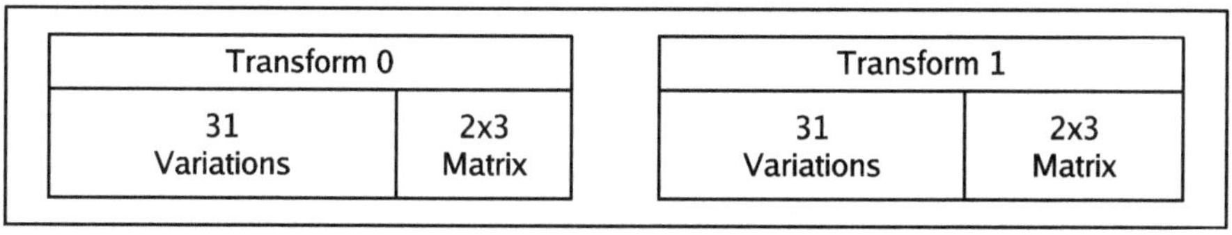

$$S=(\sum_j v_{0j} V_j(a_0x+b_0y+c_0, d_0x+e_0y+f_0))(S) \cup (\sum_j v_{1j} V_j(a_1x+b_1y+c_1, d_1x+e_1y+f_1))(S)$$

$$S=T_0(S) \cup T_1(S)$$

Fig. 3.4. A genome with two transforms, its formula, and its formula again written more abstractly

There are three additional parameters for density, color, and symmetry. Density affects the relative brightness; color affects which part of the palette is used, and symmetry affects the motion. They are also explained in [7]. Together these 40 (31 for v_{ij}, plus six for a_i to f_i, plus three) parameters make up one transform, and are roughly equivalent to a gene in biological genetics. The order of the transforms in the genome does not effect the solution image. Many transforms have visually identifiable effects on the solution, for example, particular shapes, structures, textures, angles, or locations. The genome and its relation to the recursive set equation is depicted in Fig. 3.4.

On average there are five transforms in the function system, making for 200 (5×40) floating-point numbers in the genome. Note however that most sheep have most variational coefficients set to zero, which reduces the effective dimensionality of the space. However, some sheep have many more than five transforms. When the XML representation of a large collection of genomes were compressed with gzip, they averaged 1.7 KB each.

At the time of generation 165, there were only up to six transforms in the function system, and there were only 18 variations, resulting in 162 dimensions. The next version has 40 variations plus 24 additional parameters per transform.

3.3.3 Color and Palettes

The colors of the image are determined by a palette, which is a map from [0, 1] to color. During generation 165, the palette was determined by a single number, which selected one of several hundred built-in palettes. This integer color parameter has since been replaced with an arbitrary palette (768 bytes) in the genome. This is like a classic color map of an 8-bit frame buffer, but it is used just to determine the color of each particle, which is then drawn into a full-color image.

The original palettes were algorithmically derived from photographs of landscapes and famous paintings. The algorithm extracts colors from an input image (the trivial part) and then orders them to reduce the difference between adjacent colors in the palette (the hard part—finding an optimal solution is equivalent to the Traveling Salesman Problem). Today users who submit genomes can use their own source images to create palettes with this algorithm, or import arbitrary palettes.

This contrasts with the more common genetic approaches to colors, which are to evolve either an algebraic expression for the palette or separate expressions for each color component (red, green, and blue, or hue, saturation, and value). The problem with these methods is that the color-space used (RGB or HSV) predominates, resulting in either mostly grays and unsaturated colors (from RGB) or garish rainbows (from HSV).

3.3.4 Animation and Transitions

The previous sections described how a single image is defined by the genome. To create animations, Electric Sheep rotates over time the 2×2 matrix part (a_i, b_i, d_i, and e_i) of each of the transforms. After a full circle, the solution image returns to the first frame, so sheep animations loop smoothly. Sheep are 128 frames long, and by default are played back at 23 frames per second making them 5.5 seconds long.

The client does not just cut from one looping animation to another. It displays a continuously morphing sequence. To do this the system renders transitions between sheep in addition to the sheep themselves. The transitions are genetic crossfades based on pair-wise linear interpolation, but using a spline to maintain C^1 continuity with the endpoints. This means that the derivative of the motion is also continuous; hence the motion is free of jerks.

Transitions are also 128 frames long. For each sheep created, three transitions are also created: one from another random flock member to the new sheep, one from the new sheep to a random flock member, and one between two other random members. Most of the rendering effort is spent on transitions.

3.4 The Genetic Algorithm

There are three parts of the genetic algorithm: the rating system that collects the votes and computes the fitness of individual sheep, the genetic operators used to create new genomes, and the main loop that controls which ones live and which ones die.

As already mentioned, users can vote for a sheep they like by pressing the up arrow key. If the sheep is alive its rating is incremented. Pressing the down arrow key decreases the rating. Votes for dead sheep are discarded. Votes during transitions are discarded. Users may also vote for or against a sheep by pressing buttons on its Web page.

The ratings decay over time. Each day the ratings are divided by four with integer arithmetic rounding down.

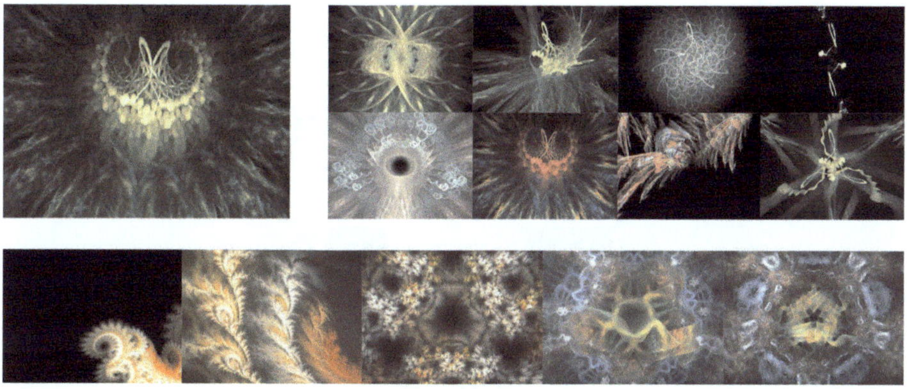

Fig. 3.5. Sheep 165.15875 (generation 165, number 15875), on the top left, was born on August 16 and died 24 hours later after receiving one vote. It was one of 42 siblings. It was reincarnated on October 28 as sheep 165.29140, received a peak rating of 29, lived seven days, and had 26 children, eight of which appear to its right. Below are five descendants of a sheep in order of parent to child, starting on the left. Their numbers are 165.01751, 165.01903, 165.02313, 165.02772, and 165.02975. The last is a result of mutation, the previous three of crossover; the first was posted by Liz Tomchek

3.4.1 Genetic Operators

There are four sources of genomes for new sheep: randomness, mutation, crossover, and posts from Apophysis. The parents for mutation and crossover operators are randomly picked from the current population weighted by rating. The probability of being selected is proportional to $\log_2(1+r)$, where r is the rating . Sheep that have received no votes have rating zero and so cannot be selected. When the study below was conducted, the probability was linear in the rating. The results appeared to follow a winner-take-all pattern though, with a few popular sheep dominating reproduction. Sample families appear in Figs. 3.5 and 3.6.

Randomness The affine matrix coefficients are chosen with uniform distribution from [-1, 1]. The variational coefficients are set to zero except for one variation chosen at random that is set to one.

Crossover The crossover operation has three methods. The main method creates a genome by taking each transform (gene) from one parent or the other at random. Another method does pair-wise linear interpolation between the two parent genomes, where the blend factor is chosen uniformly from [0, 1]. The last method takes the union of the two genomes. 1/10 crossovers use union, 2/10 use interpolation.

Mutation The mutation operator has several different methods: randomizing just the variational coefficients, randomizing just the matrix coefficients

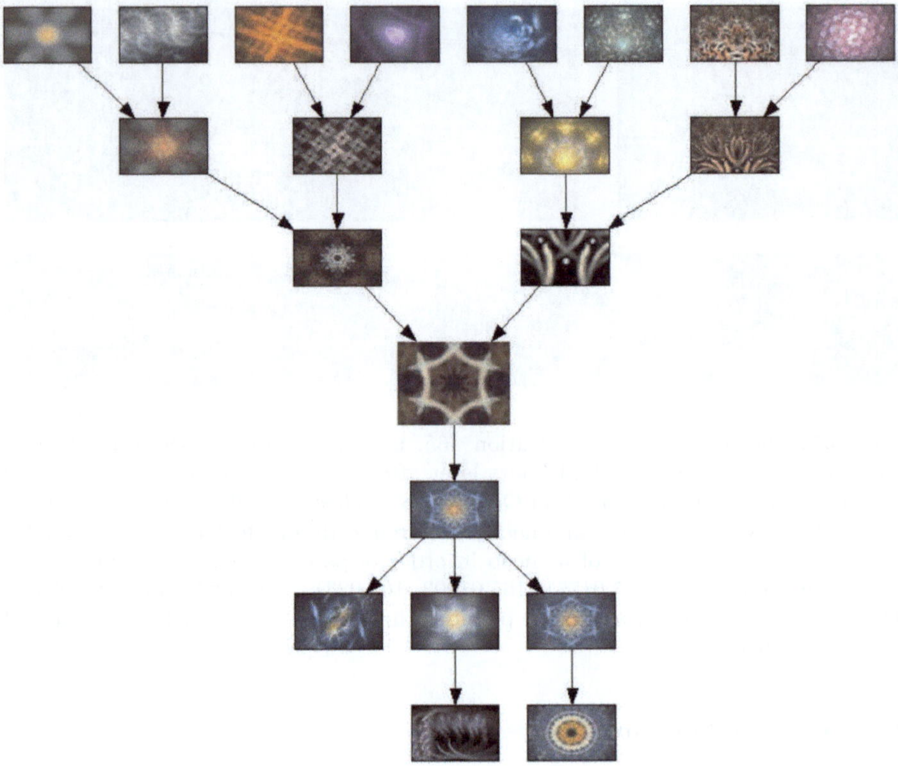

Fig. 3.6. The closest ancestors and descendants of Sheep 202.43868, the brown snowflake-symmetric sheep drawn slightly larger in the center. This sheep and these ancestors were generated by crossover, so each has two parents. The in-laws of the descendants generated by crossover are not shown, so whether they are mutants or children is not depicted

of one transform, adding noise (-10 decibels, or numbers from [-0.1, 0.1]) to all the matrix coefficients, changing just the colors, and adding symmetry.

When applying these three automatic operators, the server renders a low-resolution frame and tests if the image is too dark or too bright. The operator is iterated until the resulting genome passes. For random genomes, 43% are rejected (in a test run 177 tries were required to get 100 passing genomes). This is a simple viability test.

Post Human designers may post genomes to the server with Apophysis. Apophysis represents the matrix coefficients as triangles that the designer can drag, scale, and rotate. The variations are represented with type-in boxes, and the rest of the parameters are editable in one of several dialog windows. Apophysis is scriptable, and scripts are also often shared. Scripts are essentially user-defined, high-level genetic operators. Discovery plays a large role in working with Apophysis.

In generation 202, all genomes are required to be under the Creative Commons Attribution license [9] to allow derived works, such as by the genetic algorithm. As a result, anyone can download any sheep, learn from its genome, improve it, and repost it.

The server has a queue of sheep and transitions that are currently being rendered. When the queue is left with fewer than about 60 sheep, it is filled with genomes derived with one of the three automatic operators, or posted genomes if any are available.

In addition to picking parents for mutation and crossover from the current population, there are two additional sources of genomes. One is an archive of dead sheep from the current generation with peak rating of 2 or more, the other is a gene-bank of the sheep from previous generations with peak ratings of 4 or more. A sheep's peak rating is the highest rating obtained during its lifetime. The gene-bank is not represented in Fig. 3.2.

In contrast with the older genetic algorithm used during generation 165, the GA now substitutes previous good sheep for most random sheep. It also favors crossover over mutation. See Sect. 3.6 below for an explanation of *broods*, a further improvement of the genetic algorithm.

3.4.2 The Main Loop

The server maintains a single flock of sheep and continuously updates their ratings, creates new sheep, and kills off old ones. During generation 165, the server had 510 MB of disk space for storing sheep animations, enough for 28 sheep and 83 transitions. Now it has 2.5 GB. Each time a sheep is born, when it finishes rendering, the sheep with the lowest rating is killed to make room. If several sheep are tied for the worst rating, then the oldest is taken (usually several sheep have received no votes and are tied with a rating of zero). Sheep also have a maximum lifespan of seven days.

Killing a sheep removes the animation file from the server, but not from clients who may have allocated more disk space to their caches. The other records, including the peak rating, parentage, genome, a filmstrip of 16 thumbnails, and the first frame are kept. This archive may be browsed on the server, sorted either by peak rating, as extended family trees, or by designer.

This online or steady-state approach contrasts with the more traditional genetic algorithm's off-line main loop that divides the population into generations and alternates between rating all the individuals in a generation, and then derives the next generation from the ratings. Note that Electric Sheep does have "generations", but it means something else, as explained in Sect. 3.2.

3.5 Empirical Results

The primary dataset of 4,100 genomes was collected from the server's database, starting 13 July 2004, until 13 October 2004. Previous versions of the server did not keep a record of the sheep: when they died they were completely deleted from the server. The data we have collected are a starting point to understanding the system and its behavior. However, they are somewhat misleading:

- The client uses the ratings to prioritize downloading. Since the server is busy enough that most clients cannot download all the sheep, this causes a snowball effect where a high rating itself causes more votes.
- The audience is fickle: sheep with identical genomes regularly receive completely different ratings (see Fig. 3.5). Possibly the audience becomes fatigued by repeated exposure to variations of a successful genome, and stops voting for them. Even once-popular sheep reintroduced much later do not necessarily fare well.
- Designers enlist others to vote for their sheep, post many similar sheep, or repost the results of automatic evolution. There are three administrators who occasionally kill sheep; explicitly direct mating, mutation, and reincarnation; and vote without limit.

In April 2006 there were 30,000 users of the screen-saver almost everyday. About 900 of them voted by pushing the arrow keys on the keyboard, and 20 voted while browsing the database on the Web. On average each day, 14 genomes were submitted by eight different designers. Over the six months of generation 198, 44 people submitted five or more genomes. By September 2006 the number of daily users had increased to 40,000.

Previously, user counts had to be estimated from unique IP addresses [1], but starting May 2005 with v2.6 the client generates a unique identifier (like a Web cookie). By comparison over a one-day period, the IP address estimate was 10% higher, but if counted over weeks, it was about double.

The collective intelligence has other more traditional channels as well: In the past month the general client user forum has averaged 13 messages per day. The genetic design discussion list has received 1.5 messages per day, and the Apophysis email list has received 10 messages per day. Wikis are used to supplement traditional documentation.

3.5.1 Amplification of Creativity

In a system with human-computer collaboration, we propose defining the *creative amplification* as the ratio of total content divided by the human-created content. If we compare the posted genomes with their evolved descendants we can measure how much creative amplification Electric Sheep provides.

In the primary dataset there were 21% hand-designed, posted sheep and 79% evolved sheep. If the sum is weighted by rating, then we get 48% to

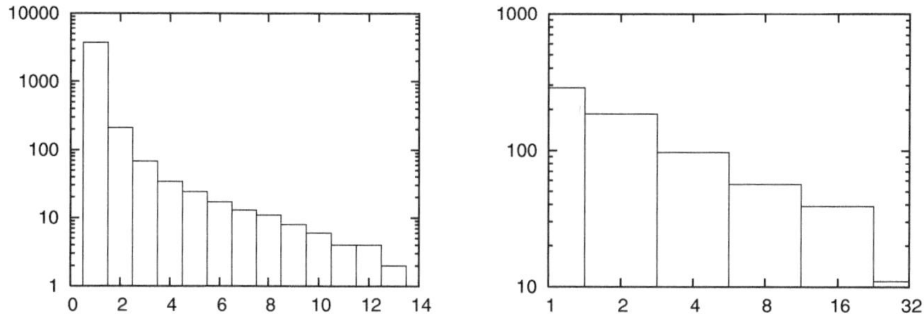

Fig. 3.7. On the left is a histogram of lengths of lineages. The length is on the horizontal axis, and the number of sheep is on the vertical. On the right is a histogram of the ratings of the sheep. Again, the rating is on the horizontal and the number of sheep is on the vertical

52%, for an amplification factor of 2.08 (1+52/48). One could say the genetic algorithm is doubling the output of the human posters.

Of the 79% evolved sheep, 42% of them result from the totally random genetic operator. Their fraction of total ratings is only 3.8%.

There are some caveats to this metric. For example, if the genetic algorithm just copied the posted genomes, it might receive some votes for its "creativity". Or if it ignored the posted genomes and evolved on its own, it would receive some votes but they would not represent "amplification".

Figure 3.7 shows the distribution of lengths of lineages of the sheep. The lineage length of a sheep is the maximum number of parent-to-child relationships that issue from it. Sheep with no children are assigned 1, and sheep with children are assigned 1 plus the maximum of the lineage lengths of those children. Instead of fitness increasing along lineages, we find it dying out: the rating of the average parent is 6.7 but the average maximum rating of direct siblings is only 3.8.

The decay in ratings may result from the audience losing interest in a lineage because it fails to change fast enough, rather than from a decay of absolute quality of those sheep. The viewpoint of watching the screen-saver and seeing sheep sequentially is different from the viewpoint of browsing the archive and comparing all the sheep. Neither can be called definitive.

Genetic algorithms normally run for many tens to hundreds or thousands of generations. In contrast, the lineages of the sheep are very short: the longest is 13.

3.6 Motivation and Direction

Electric Sheep illustrates the process in which the longer and closer one studies something, the more the detail and structure appear. It investigates the role of experiencers in creating the experience. If nobody ran the client, there would be nothing to see.

Because the collective guides the evolution, no one has the burden of voting. Instead people act on inspiration. The network is used to assemble these bits of judgment efficiently. This avoids the common pitfall of aesthetic evolution, which is a dearth of human input.

The sheep are parasites of human attention. The goal of Electric Sheep is to create a self-supporting, network-resident life-form. Right now the sheep depend on a central server, requiring disk, bandwidth, and administration. Hopefully these inputs can be eliminated and the network can be made symmetric by using Distributed Hash Tables [10] and BitTorrent (see Sect. 3.2).

Furthermore, the genetic algorithm depends on input from human designers. Our goal here is not to remove the input, but to improve what the genetic algorithm does with it: to increase the creative amplification factor. The ultimate goal then is divergence of the factor. In *Can a machine do anything new?* [11], Alan Turing wrote:

> One could say that a man can "inject" an idea into the machine, and that it will respond to a certain extent and then drop into quiescence, like a piano string struck by a hammer. Another simile would be an atomic pile of less than critical size: an injected idea is to correspond to a neutron entering the pile from without. Each such neutron will cause a certain disturbance which eventually dies away. If, however, the size of the pile is sufficiently increased, their disturbance caused by such an incoming neutron will very likely go on and on increasing until the whole pile is destroyed. Is there a corresponding phenomenon for minds, and is there one for machines? ... Adhering to this analogy we ask, "Can a machine be made to be supercritical?"

A big problem with the Electric Sheep's genetic algorithm is that the population size is too small. Good mutations are rare. So just eliminating the constraints of the central server and increasing the population might help. If sheep have more children their chance of having one whose rating exceeds their own increases. The question is, will the audience become bored first?

A more direct way to improve the genetic algorithm would be to develop a model of the historic sheep ratings, and then use this model to screen the output of the genetic algorithm. This would be a more sophisticated viability test than the one described in Sect. 3.4.1. One useful input to this model could be the fractal dimension of the sheep, as it correlates well with aesthetics [12]. A histogram of total rating by dimension has a characteristic sharp peak between 1.5 and 1.7 [13]. This risks homogenizing the sheep, however.

In the meantime we are experimenting with putting a human filter on the genetic algorithm, a technique we call the *brood*. The server now daily generates 256 potential children, but only renders one frame of each (this is about as expensive as rendering two ordinary sheep). The shepherd picks the best 40 or so of the brood. Future invocations of the genetic algorithm then use these picks, if available. Early indications are that the lengths of lineages have increased: so far the maximum in generation 202 is 30, compared to 13 for generation 165 (see Sect. 3.5.1).

A more fundamental problem with achieving open-ended evolution is the finiteness of the genetic code. One way to address that may be to replace the current fixed set of variations and coefficients with algebraic expressions, as in Genetic Programming [14]. Another would be to embed the current genetic code into a per-pixel, image-arithmetic language, like Sims' [3].

3.6.1 Dreams in High Fidelity

One way that the Electric Sheep are *not* self-supporting is financially: the developers are volunteers. There are many ways of supporting open source software; for the Electric Sheep, donations, DVD sales, and advertisements on the Web site have proved to be inadequate. The new plan is to turn the bandwidth bottleneck (see Sect. 3.2.1) to our advantage.

Dreams in High Fidelity consists of a small computer driving a large 1280×720 liquid crystal display: a painting that evolves. It plays animations rendered by the Electric Sheep, but at triple the resolution and six times more frames per sheep. The image quality is striking on a large display. It requires 20 times the computation to make a high-fidelity sheep.

The artist selects his favorite sheep (not the most popular ones) from the archives and public flock, and sends them back to be re-rendered at higher resolution: heaven for an electric sheep. So far two such flocks have been completed. The first is 55 GB, totaling eight hours if played end-to-end, and requiring over one million CPU hours to render. The second is 100 GB.

The *Dreams* have a symbiotic relationship to the screen-saver. The free version provides the design laboratory and gene pool from which the best sheep are extracted. It also provides the distributed supercomputer needed to realize the high-fidelity content. Ideally the hi-fi version will fetch the income required to keep the whole project in operation, and develop it further.

3.7 Conclusion

The Electric Sheep demonstrate the feasibility of large-scale distributed interactive evolution. The network serves both as artwork and as a platform for further research. In particular, this framework can be applied to other genetic codes besides fractal flames.

I believe the free flow of code is an increasingly important social and artistic force. The proliferation of powerful computers with high-bandwidth network connections forms the substrate of an expanding universe. The Electric Sheep and we, their shepherds, are colonizing this new frontier.

I look forward to many more generations of sheep at ever higher resolutions, with more expressive genetic codes, in three dimensions, responding to music, performing feats not yet imagined.

Acknowledgments

Many thanks to Dean Gaudet, Paul Graham, Scott Hassan, Tristan Horn, Nick Long, David McGrath, Erik Reckase, Matt Reda, Jeremy Richardson, Mark Townsend, and Chris Ursitti.

References

1. Draves, S. (2005). The electric sheep screen-saver: A case study in aesthetic evolution. In: *Applications of Evolutionary Computing, LNCS 3449.* Springer
2. Anderson, D., et al. (2002). SETI@home: An experiment in public-resource computing. *Communications of the ACM*, **45**: 56–61
3. Sims, K. (1991). Artificial evolution for computer graphics. In: *Proceedings of SIGGRAPH.* ACM
4. Townsend, M. (2004). Apophysis. `http://apophysis.org`
5. Cohen, B. (2003). Incentives build robustness in bittorrent. In: *Workshop on Economics of Peer-to-Peer Systems*
6. Parens, B. (1999). The open source definition. In: *Open Sources: Voices from the Open Source Revolution.* O'Reilly
7. Draves, S. (2004). The fractal flame algorithm. `http://flam3.com/flame.pdf`
8. Barnsley, M. (1988). *Fractals Everywhere.* Academic Press
9. Lessig, L. (2002). *The Future of Ideas.* Vintage
10. Balakrishnan, H., Kaashoek, M.F., Karger, D., Morris, R., Stoica, I. (2003). Looking up data in p2p systems. *Communications of the ACM*, **46**(2): 43–48
11. Turing, A. (1950). Can a machine do anything new? *Computing Machinery and Intelligence*, **59**: 433–460
12. Sprott, J.C. (1994). Automatic generation of iterated function systems. *Computers and Graphics*, **18**: 417–425
13. Draves, S., Abraham, F., Abraham, R., Sprott, J.C., Viotti, P. (2005). Aesthetics and the fractal dimension of electric sheep. Presented at the annual meeting of the Society for Chaos Theory in Psychology and the Life Sciences
14. Koza, J. (1992). *Genetic Programming: On the Programming of Computers by Means of Natural Selection.* Complex Adaptive Systems. The MIT Press

Part II

Evolutionary Music

4

Evolutionary Computation Applied to Sound Synthesis

James McDermott,[1] Niall J. L. Griffith,[2] and Michael O'Neill[3]

[1] University of Limerick jamesmichaelmcdermott@gmail.com
[2] University of Limerick niall.griffith@ul.ie
[3] University College Dublin m.oneill@ucd.ie

Summary. Sound synthesis is a natural domain in which to apply evolutionary computation (EC). The EC concepts of the genome, the phenotype, and the fitness function map naturally to the synthesis concepts of control parameters, output sound, and comparison with a desired sound. More importantly, sound synthesis can be a very unintuitive technique, since changes in input parameters can give rise, via non-linearities and interactions among parameters, to unexpected changes in output sounds. The novice synthesizer user and the simple hill-climbing search algorithm will both fail to produce a desired sound in this context, whereas an EC technique is well-suited to the task.

In this chapter we introduce and provide motivation for the application of EC to sound synthesis, surveying previous work in this area. We focus on the problem of automatically matching a target sound using a given synthesizer. The ability to mimic a given sound can be used in several ways to augment interactive sound synthesis applications. We report on several sets of experiments run to determine the best EC algorithms, parameters, and fitness functions for this problem.

4.1 Introduction

A typical synthesizer is controlled in two ways. Aspects of performance, such as choice of note or frequency, note length, and note volume, are specified through a device such as a MIDI keyboard or in a saved performance file. Aspects of timbre are controlled by a set of user-variable input parameters. These are generally continuously-variable, though a synthesizer may interpret some parameters discretely.

In applying EC to sound synthesis, we are generally concerned with the problem of setting the input parameters: that is, choosing a point – in the continuous, multi-dimensional space defined by the set of parameters – which corresponds to a desired sound or timbre.

4.1.1 Motivation

There are several reasons why this is a difficult task for users to perform manually. Firstly, parameters are mathematical entities which do not in general relate directly to perceptible attributes of the sound. They are named in a way that is off-putting to non-technical users, and there may be a large number of them – up to 200 or more in some cases, though a range of 20–40 is typical. In many cases, the user does not have a definite target sound in mind, but is rather engaging in simultaneous exploration of possibilities and search for an under-defined goal. The synthesizer can often appear to respond non-linearly to some parameters (a small change in the parameter space can cause a large change in the sound), and often the response to one parameter is dependent on the value of others. In particular, a parameter can in some circumstances have no effect on the sound.

All of this makes synthesis control a difficult and unintuitive process for a beginner; even experienced and technically-oriented users, while composing with a complex synthesizer, sometimes prefer to pursue a desired sound through an intuitive process with immediate feedback rather than switching into analytical, parameter-setting mode. In other situations the ability to automatically match a target sound is required. Evolutionary techniques offer the potential to take away some of the workload involved and make synthesis control more accessible.

4.1.2 EC in the Context of Sound Synthesis

In many EC applications, the fitness function is determined by the problem to be solved, and the choice of representation (the genetic encoding, the genotype–phenotype mapping, and the evolutionary operators) is open for research.

The situation with sound synthesis is somewhat different. Typical synthesizers already possess a natural encoding of parameters as floating-point arrays (some tree-structured exceptions will be seen in Sect. 4.1.3), and the synthesizer itself performs the map from the input parameters (genotype) to a piece of digital audio (phenotype); the choices of evolutionary operators and fitness function to be used are therefore the main areas studied in EC sound synthesis research. Most such research has used the genetic algorithm (GA) [1].

The fitness function in particular is crucial. The basis for defining any fitness function for synthesizer control is the idea of a *distance function* on the sound space: a non-negative real-valued function of two sounds which measures the distance between them. The idea that humans perceive a distance function on the sound space is supported by, for example, Grey [2] and McAdams and Cunibile [3]; however perception of timbre is not fully understood and therefore difficult to model in computational and signal-processing terms. There are therefore two possibilities: we can define automatically-computable distance functions, in the knowledge that at best they approximate human perception, and use them to compare candidate sounds to pre-specified targets (where evolution is towards individuals which closely match the targets); or we can allow a user to rate sounds according to their aesthetic value (where evolution is towards individuals with higher aesthetic value). In this paper we concentrate on the former: see Sect. 4.3.1 for more on the latter.

4.1.3 Literature Review

Several authors have used more or less standard GAs with spectral-comparison (i.e., discrete Fourier transform-, or DFT-based) fitness functions for matching target sounds. In most cases, the individuals in the GA population consist of floating-point arrays, with each element corresponding to a single synthesizer parameter. Each individual can be regarded as a synthesizer preset, and is mapped by the synthesizer to an output sound.

GAs were used by Horner et al. [4] in emulating the spectra of real instruments using FM synthesis. The GA was used to determine the best carrier-to-modulator frequency ratios and (time-invariant) modulation indices. They achieved good results, especially when using several carriers. The fitness function used was a direct comparison of the target and candidate sounds' spectra.

A GA was used by Riionheimo and Välimäki [5] to match target sounds using a plucked-string synthesizer. Here the fitness function used was a comparison of the perceptually-transformed spectra of the candidate and target sounds: the perceptual transformation was motivated by the fact that a comparison of untransformed spectra gives equal weight to all areas of the spectrum, whereas the human ear does not.

Others have used a genetic programming (GP) [6] approach in matching target sounds, evolving the synthesizer itself rather than the parameter settings for a fixed synthesizer. Both Wehn [7] and Garcia [8] defined a small set of synthesis primitives which could be linked together into tree-structures, thus forming complete synthesizers. Again, the fitness functions used in this research were a DFT comparison (in the former case) and a weighted DFT comparison (in the latter).

Spectral-comparison fitness functions tend to lead to rugged fitness landscapes, which can impact on search performance. Mitchell and Pipe [9] used a windowed DFT fitness function, eliminating a proportion of local optima in the fitness landscape. See Sect. 4.2.4 for more on this issue.

In general, authors have not compared their methods experimentally with alternative parameters, algorithms, or implementations. The experiments described in Sect. 4.2 begin to address this.

4.2 Experiments with Automatically-Computable Fitness Functions

In this section we discuss experiments run to determine the best EC algorithms, parameters, and fitness functions for the problem of automatically matching a target sound using a particular synthesizer.

4.2.1 Experimental Setup

All software used in this research is included on the accompanying DVD.[4]. It is described next.

Synthesizer

The synthesizer used is a slightly restricted version of the XSynth synthesizer [10], an analog-modular style subtractive synth written in C, featuring two oscillators, two assignable envelopes, one assignable low-frequency oscillator, and a six-mode filter. The assignable features make the parameters very interdependent, increasing the difficulty of the problem. The full version of the synthesizer has 32 input parameters: however to avoid an instability in the filter, and to prevent very large pitch vibrato, a few of the parameter ranges have been restricted, and in three cases closed off altogether. The resulting synthesizer effectively has 29 floating-point parameters, of which four are really integer-valued but encoded as floating-point.

The experimental setup could incorporate other synthesizers as plug-in replacements for XSynth. Search success in this case is likely to depend on the number of synthesizer parameters, and their degree of interdependence. This is an open question for possible future work.

Target Sounds

All sounds (both candidate and target) used in this study were 1.5 seconds long, generated using XSynth by sending a note-on signal with MIDI note number 69 (concert A), followed 1 seconds later by a note-off, after which a "release tail" of 0.5 seconds was recorded.

For each evolution, a new target sound was generated by setting the synthesizer according to a randomly-generated set of parameters. An alternative possibility is to use recorded samples of real sounds as the targets. This is the more likely real-world application of the system. It is likely that searching for a recorded sound will be less successful than searching for a sound originally generated by the synthesizer, since in general a synthesizer cannot exactly reproduce every possible sound. We avoid this complication in our experiments by using sounds known to be achievable using the given synthesizer: again, this is a possible area for future work.

[4] Updated versions may be available for download at `http://www.skynet.ie/~jmmcd/research.html` and via email from `jamesmichaelmcdermott@gmail.com`.

GA Parameters

The EA used here was a steady-state GA over 100 generations with 100 individuals in the population. Each individual genome consisted of 32 floating-point values, one per synthesizer parameter. The synthesizer, in mapping from the parameters to digital audio, performed the genotype–phenotype mapping. The replacement probability was 0.5, one-point crossover had a probability of 0.5, and Gaussian mutation had a per-gene probability of 0.1 (except in Experiment 2, which investigates different values for crossover and mutation). Selection was by the roulette wheel algorithm. This amounts to a fairly typical floating-point GA.

4.2.2 Fitness Functions

A fitness function, in this context, is a measure of similarity between a candidate sound and a target. Several fitness functions were implemented, each returning a fitness value of the form $1/(1 + d(t, c))$ ($\in [1/2, 1]$), for a target sound t and candidate sound c, where d ($\in [0, 1]$) is the *distance* between the two sounds, calculated in a different way for each fitness function.

Timbral, Perceptual, and Statistical Sound Attributes

Distance functions can be defined based on timbral, perceptual, and statistical attributes extracted from the target and candidate sounds. Some attributes, such as attack time, are intended to mimic as closely as possible aspects of human audio perception of audio. Some, such as pitch vibrato rate, are known to be significant determiners of timbre, e.g., in differentiating between the orchestral instruments. Some, such as zero-crossing rate, are statistical in nature. Almost all of these attributes have been used in recent machine learning research. Many are described by, among others, Jensen [11], Eronen and Klapuri [12], and Lu et al. [13]; and our previous work [14] describes our choice of attributes. Table 4.1 lists them together with their ranges and a key name for each.

The attributes we have chosen do not break down neatly into hierarchical subsets: for example, pitch vibrato depth fits in both the partial-domain and the periodic subsets, and neither is a subset of the other. We have chosen to classify attributes into nine overlapping groups, as shown in Table 4.2.

Attribute Differences

We can calculate a measure of the difference between two sounds by comparing their respective attribute values. A few of the attributes used here are known to be perceived logarithmically: for example, the difference between sounds of 220 Hz and 440 Hz is perceived to be the same as the difference between sounds of 440 Hz and 880 Hz (each is an octave jump), even though the

Table 4.1. Attributes and their ranges: log-domain attributes are marked *

Attribute		Key	Min	Max
Attack	*	att	0.0	1.0
Mean RMS	*	rms	0.0	1.0
Zero-crossing Rate		zcr	0.0	22050.0
Crest Factor		crest	0.0	1.0
Mean Centroid		cen	0.0	512.0
Spectral Spread		sprd	0.0	1.0
Spectral Flatness		flat	0.0	1.0
Mean Flux		flx	0.0	1.0
Presence	*	pres	0.0	1.0
Spectral Rolloff		roff	0.0	1.0
Fast Modulation		fastm	0.0	1.0
RMS Vibrato Depth		vdpth.rms	0.0	1.0
RMS Vibrato Rate		vrate.rms	0.0	20.0
Centroid Vibrato Depth		vdpth.cen	0.0	1.0
Centroid Vibrato Rate		vrate.cen	0.0	20.0
RMS Temporal Centroid		tcn.rms	0.0	1.0
Centroid Temporal Centroid		tcn.cen	0.0	1.0
RMS Temporal Peakedness		tpk.rms	0.0	1.0
Centroid Temporal Peakedness		tpk.cen	0.0	1.0
RMS HFVR		hfvr.rms	0.0	1.0
RMS LFVR		lfvr.rms	0.0	1.0
Centroid HFVR		hfvr.cen	0.0	1.0
Centroid LFVR		lfvr.cen	0.0	1.0
Zero-crossing Rate HFVR		hfvr.zcr	0.0	1.0
Zero-crossing Rate LFVR		lfvr.zcr	0.0	1.0
RMS Heuristic Strength	*	hs.rms	1.0	10.0
RMS Delta Ratio	*	dr.rms	0.1	10.0
Centroid Heuristic Strength	*	hs.cen	1.0	10.0
Centroid Delta Ratio	*	dr.cen	0.1	10.0
Pitch	*	pit	20.0	10000.0
TWM Pitch Error		twm.err	0.0	40.0
Pitch Vibrato Depth		vdpth.pit	0.0	1.0
Pitch Vibrato Rate		vrate.pit	0.0	20.0
Inharmonicity		inh	0.0	1.0
Irregularity (Jensen's)		irr	0.0	10.0
Tristimulus 1		tri1	0.0	1.0
Tristimulus 2		tri2	0.0	1.0
Tristimulus 3		tri3	0.0	1.0
Odd Harmonic Ratio		odd	0.0	1.0
Even Harmonic Ratio		evn	0.0	1.0

Table 4.2. Attributes listed by group

Group name	Keys
Basic	rms, cen, pit, att
RMS	rms, tcn.rms, tpk.rms, hs.rms, dr.rms, hfvr.rms, lfvr.rms, vdpth.rms, vrate.rms
Centroid	cen, dr.cen, hs.cen, hfvr.cen, lfvr.cen, tcn.cen, tpk.cen, vdpth.cen, vrate.cen
Partial domain	evn, inh, irr, odd, tri1, tri2, tri3, pit, twm.err, vdpth.pit, vrate.pit
Trajectory	dr.rms, dr.cen, hs.rms, hs.cen, tcn.rms, tcn.cen, tpk.rms, tpk.cen
Periodic	vdpth.rms, vrate.rms, vdpth.cen, vrate.cen, vdpth.pit, vrate.pit
Statistical	hfvr.rms, hfvr.cen, lfvr.rms, lfvr.cen, hfvr.zcr, lfvr.zcr
FFT domain	cen, sprd, flat, flx, pres, roff
Time domain	rms, crest, att, zcr, fastm

linear differences between the pairs are not the same. Attack time and RMS energy are also known to be perceived in this way. Attributes seen as log-domain require a different comparison function from those seen as linear-domain. Table 4.1 indicates those attributes measured in the log domain.

For each attribute, a difference function is defined which depends on the attribute's theoretical upper and lower bounds, and on whether the attribute is supposed to have a logarithmic or a linear quality:

$$d_i(x, y) = |f_i(v_i(x)) - f_i(v_i(y))|. \tag{4.1}$$

Here x and y are the two sound signals, and $f_i(v) \in [0, 1]$ is a scaling function:

$$f_i(v) = \frac{v - lb_i}{ub_i - lb_i} \tag{4.2}$$

for linear-domain attributes, and

$$f_i(v) = \log(1 + \frac{v - lb_i}{ub_i - lb_i}(e^k - 1))/k \tag{4.3}$$

for log-domain attributes. $v_i(x)$ is the ith attribute value extracted from a sound x, and ub_i and lb_i are the theoretical upper and lower bounds, respectively, for the ith attribute. k is a constant controlling the shape of the logarithmic mapping: here it is assigned the value 5, as used by, e.g., the Sineshaper synthesizer [15]. Note that $d_i \in [0, 1]$ $\forall$ i.

We make an overall attribute comparison between two sounds by combining the individual attribute differences:

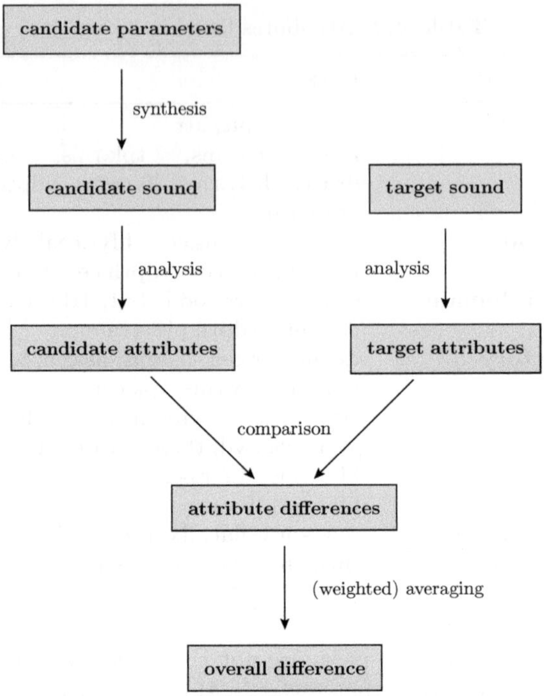

Fig. 4.1. Synthesis, analysis, and comparison using an attribute-difference fitness function

$$d_A(x,y) = \frac{\sum_{i=1}^{n} w_i d_i(x,y)}{\sum_{i=1}^{n} w_i} \tag{4.4}$$

where the weights w_i are taken to be equal to 1 if we require simple averaging, rather than weighting.

This system can be summarized as in Fig. 4.1.

Other Distance Functions

Other types of distance functions can also be defined, such as the *pointwise metric*:

$$d_P(x,y) = \frac{\sum_{t=0}^{T} |x_t - y_t|}{2T} \tag{4.5}$$

where x and y are the sound signals. This is the *DFT metric*:

$$d_F(x,y) = \frac{\sum_{L \in \{256,1024,4096\}} d_{F_L}(x,y)}{3} \tag{4.6}$$

where

$$d_{F_L}(x,y) = \frac{\sum_{j=0}^{N} \left(\sum_{i=0}^{L/2} |X_j(i) - Y_j(i)| \right)}{N} \tag{4.7}$$

where L is the transform length, X_j and Y_j are the normalized outputs from the jth transforms of the sound signals x and y, and N, the number of transforms for each sound, is determined on the basis of 2×-overlapping Hann windows.

We can also form a *composite metric*:

$$d_C(x,y) = \frac{\sum_{d \in \{d_A, d_P, d_F\}} d(x,y)}{3}. \tag{4.8}$$

4.2.3 Experiment 1: Different Types of Fitness Function

This experiment is intended to compare the performance of four types of fitness function, based on the distance measures (Pointwise, DFT, Attribute, and Composite) described in Sect. 4.2.2.

Each fitness function was used to drive 30 evolutions, each with a different target sound. The best individual found in each of the 30 runs was then evaluated under all four of the fitness functions, to allow their performance to be compared. Figures 4.2 and 4.3 show the results.

The Pointwise function awards a high score to the results of all the other functions. It has a bias towards quiet sounds, in that (by definition) two dissimilar quiet sounds will be judged to be closer together than two dissimilar

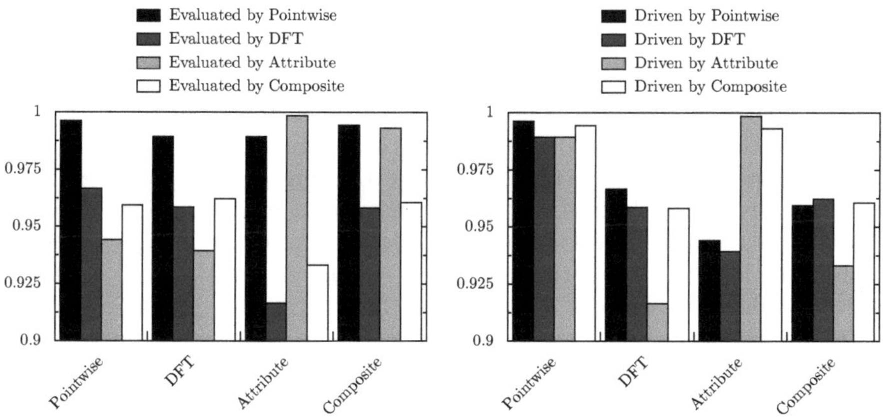

Fig. 4.2. Best fitness averaged over 30 runs driven and then evaluated by each of the four fitness functions, grouped by driving fitness function (left), and the same results, grouped by evaluating fitness function (right). For example, the highest bar indicates the high score of GAs driven by the Attribute fitness function *when evaluated by* the same function; the lowest bar indicates the low score of GAs driven by the Attribute fitness function but evaluated by the DFT function

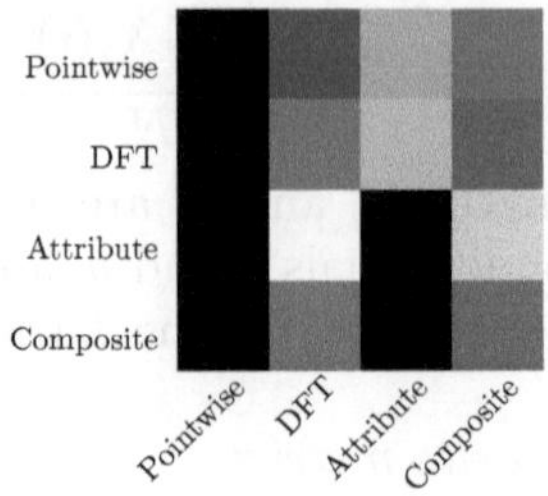

Fig. 4.3. The same results as shown in Fig. 4.2, with scores indicated by intensity, where darker means higher. Driving fitness function is on the y-axis and evaluating fitness function is on the x-axis

loud sounds. In an experiment where the randomly-generated targets were often relatively quiet, this made the Pointwise function very forgiving. The DFT function has a similar bias towards quiet sounds.

Each of the DFT and Attribute functions awards a high score to itself and a low score to its counterpart. The Composite function probably performs best overall. Overall, the lack of an objective method of evaluating performance makes it impossible to draw a definite conclusion.

This experiment is similar to an experiment we have previously reported [16], although that work used a single-modulator FM synthesizer, and a set of simple additively-synthesized target sounds. The Pointwise and DFT fitness functions performed much worse in that experiment, partly because the target sounds were much louder, on average, than those used here.

Relative Improvements in Fitness

Another way to analyze the same results is to consider the relative change in fitness over the course of evolution. For each distance measure, and for each of 30 runs, we calculate the fitness before evolution (i.e., the average fitness of an unevolved population), the best fitness after evolution driven by the corresponding fitness function, and the relative improvement, calculated by dividing the latter by the former. We then average across the 30 runs. These results are shown in Table 4.3.

Table 4.3. Results for four fitness functions, averaged across 30 runs

	Pointwise	DFT	Attribute	Composite
Average best fitness (random search)	0.994	0.953	0.955	0.961
Average fitness before evolution	0.985	0.881	0.884	0.913
Average best fitness after evolution	0.995	0.965	0.974	0.974
Average relative improvement	1.010	1.097	1.102	1.066

The relative improvement for the Attribute fitness function is better than that for the other fitness functions: according to t-tests, it out-performs both the Pointwise and Composite fitness functions with more than 99% confidence, but its advantage over the DFT fitness function is not statistically significant. These results show that the Pointwise fitness function does not perform well. The poor performance of the Composite fitness function is probably due to the influence of the Pointwise function. The DFT and Attribute fitness functions are seen to perform the best: since DFT is the function most commonly used in EC sound synthesis, this justifies further study of the Attribute function.

Also in Table 4.3, we show the best fitness found using a random search algorithm, averaged over the same 30 targets. The random search was over 5000 individuals, the same number processed by our GA, and therefore results for the GA and the random search can be compared. Of the four fitness functions, only the Attribute fitness function drives a GA to perform better than the random search, at a 99% confidence level. Again, this justifies further study of the Attribute fitness function.

4.2.4 Induced Fitness Landscapes

The results of Sect. 4.2.3 can be partly explained with reference to the *fitness landscape*, i.e., the surface corresponding to the (indirect) map from the genome to the fitness value. In our case, for a given target sound, the fitness landscape is the map from the set of synthesizer input parameters to the measured distance between the corresponding candidate sound and the target. In general, the more a fitness landscape exhibits ruggedness and multiple peaks, the more difficult it is to apply any type of machine learning to the problem. Different methods of measuring distance induce different fitness landscapes, and so it is useful to compare the landscapes induced by each of the distance functions discussed in Sect. 4.2.2.

Because there are a large number of input parameters we cannot picture the entire space: however we can look at general trends in the landscape, and form cross-sections of the landscape using parameter-space interpolation.

For Fig. 4.4, we randomly generate 30 target and candidate points, and for each pair interpolate from target to candidate, so that distance to the target (as measured in the parameter space) increases linearly as we move along the x-axis from left to right: at each point in the interpolation we calculate the distance from the current point to the target using each of the four distance functions used in Experiment 1. Averaging across the 30 runs yields a picture of general trends in the four fitness landscapes.

Figure 4.4 demonstrates some of the strengths and weaknesses of the distance measures. The Pointwise distance measure is shown to have an almost totally flat landscape, with only a tiny area in which evolutionary selection is meaningful. The other landscapes show smooth gradients leading towards the target, and so appear to be relatively "easy": however, the averaging process has smoothed out individual features of these gradients, so in Fig. 4.5 we also

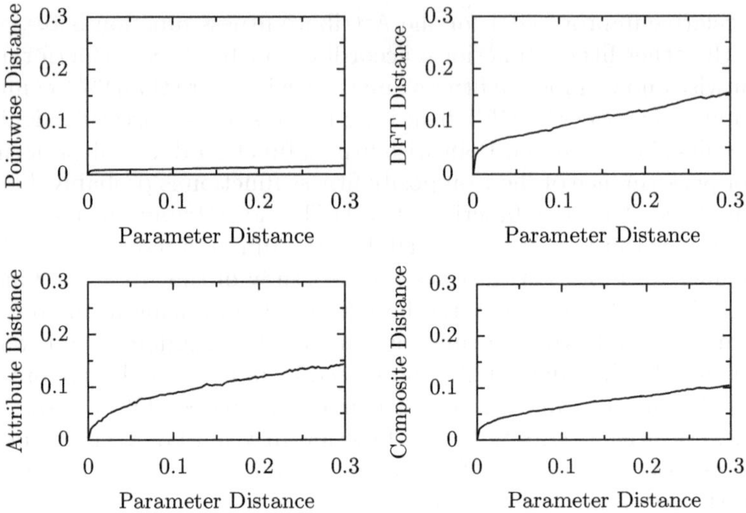

Fig. 4.4. General trends in the fitness landscapes induced by different distance functions. The curves show how each distance measure (indicated on the y-axis) varies with Parameter distance (indicated on the x-axis), averaged over 30 interpolations from target to candidate sounds

examine a single typical cross-section of the landscape. Here, the interpolation was generated in the same way as in Fig. 4.4, but only one interpolation is shown – the same one for each distance function – rather than an average over all 30.

Coupled with the results presented in Fig. 4.4, the cross-sections in Fig. 4.5 provide some additional evidence to suggest the strengths and weaknesses of the various distance measures. The Pointwise measure leads to a very flat landscape with a very small area of decreasing distance: thus evolution becomes a random search for this area. The DFT measure induces quite a smooth landscape, but for much of the interpolation shown the DFT measure is decreasing while Parameter distance is increasing: this presents a difficulty for evolution. The Attribute measure is largely aligned with Parameter distance, except for the addition of many small changes of direction. These, as indicators of local optima, can be detrimental to search performance. Finally, the Composite distance measure combines the strengths and weaknesses of the other measures.

We can also attempt to *quantify* the "difficulty" of a fitness landscape. One method of doing this is to measure the amount of *Monotonicity* in landscape cross-sections such as Fig. 4.5. The larger the number of directional changes the greater the probability of local optima, which can impact performance in many types of search technique. Another method is to use *Fitness Distance Correlation* or FDC [17], which is a measure of to what extent distance – as

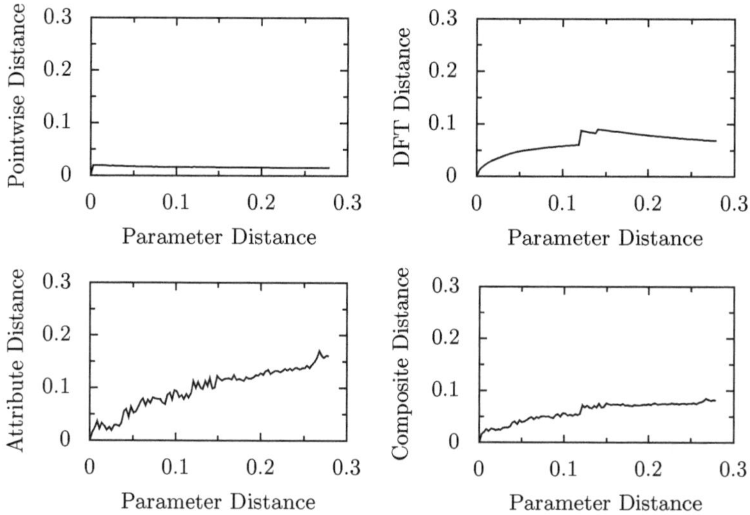

Fig. 4.5. A typical cross-section from the fitness landscapes induced by different distance functions. The curves show how each distance measure (indicated on the y-axis) varies with Parameter distance (indicated on the x-axis)

measured by the fitness function – is correlated with distance – as measured on underlying parameters.

We can estimate the FDC for the fitness landscapes induced by the four distance functions as follows. We take a sample of 30 target points, and for each target, 10 candidate points, both target and candidate points being randomly generated in the parameter space. For each of the 300 pairs, we calculate the underlying parameter distance between the points, and the distance between the pair as calculated by the various distance functions. We then perform a Pearson correlation between the underlying parameter distances and each of the other datasets, to find the FDC in each case. Similarly, we can estimate the Monotonicity by calculating, for each distance measure, 1 minus the average number of changes of direction per point, across all 30 interpolations described for Fig. 4.4.

Table 4.4. Measures of fitness landscape difficulty

Difficulty measure	Pointwise	DFT	Attribute	Composite
FDC	0.103	0.080	0.273	0.153
Monotonicity	0.839	0.907	0.404	0.432

The larger the FDC or Monotonicity value, the easier the fitness landscape. Examining the results we see that these two methods of estimating landscape difficulty give somewhat contradictory evidence in this case: the highest FDC values correspond to the lowest Monotonicity values, and vice versa. The FDC is the difficulty measure endorsed in the literature [17], and so we conclude at this time that the Attribute distance function leads to the "easiest" fitness landscapes – with the caveat that the EA must be designed to avoid premature convergence to local optima, since according to the Monotonicity measure the Attribute distance function leads to more of these.

Considering the relative merits of the fitness functions we have assessed, for subsequent experiments we concentrate on fitness functions based on the Attribute distance measure, and measures derived from it.

4.2.5 Experiment 2: Varying GA Parameters

This experiment compares the performance of GAs, driven by the attribute-based fitness function, in which the mutation and crossover probabilities were varied. Typical values from the GA literature for the two probabilities are compared with more extreme values. We wish to confirm that typical values are appropriate to the particular case of sound synthesis EC.

Figure 4.6 shows the results. According to t-tests, the typical probabilities of (0.5, 0.1) for crossover and (per-gene) mutation perform better than the (0.1, 0.01), (0.1, 0.3), and (0.7, 0.3) combinations, at the 99% confidence level. Their advantage over other combinations is not statistically significant.

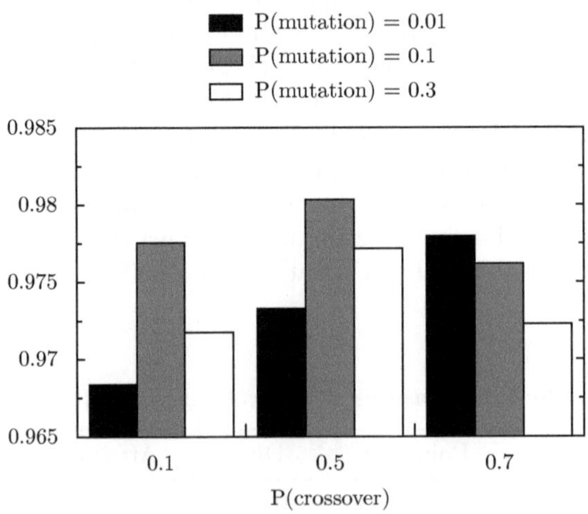

Fig. 4.6. Best fitness averaged over 30 runs for GA with Attribute fitness function and varying values for crossover and mutation probabilities

4.2.6 Experiment 3: Increasingly Discriminating Fitness Functions

We define a set of Increasingly Discriminating Fitness Functions (IDFFs), motivated by the idea that in some search problems, the fitness landscape is characterized by large flat areas of low fitness, and small peaks, with steep sides, of high fitness. When the population is stuck on a flat area, selection becomes meaningless, and evolutionary progress is dependent on chance. An IDFF can reshape the fitness landscape by rewarding minor progress at each stage which is not rewarded by an ordinary fitness function. This idea, "layered learning", has been applied in other areas of EC, such as in robotics control applications [18]. Here, we compare the performance of IDFFs with that of an ordinary GA with an attribute-based fitness function, a GA run with a weighted-attribute fitness function, and a random search algorithm. Eight experiments were defined:

One-stage Here, the fitness function consisted of *all* attributes: in other words, this is an unmodified GA. It was run 30 times with a different randomly-generated target sound for each run.

Two-stage Here, the IDFF consisted of a single attribute for the first 50 generations, and of all attributes for the final 50 generations. Thus there were 40 variations on this experiment, one per attribute: each was run 30 times with a different target sound for each run.

Eight-stage The 100 generations were divided into eight stages of 12 and 13 generations each. The IDFF consisted of five attributes for the first stage, and increased by five attributes for each subsequent stage. The ordering in which attributes were added was randomly generated. Thirty different orderings were used: each was run 30 times with a different target sound for each run.

Nine-stage groups Here, the attributes were divided into the nine groups discussed in Sect. 4.2.2. The 100 generations were divided into nine stages of 11 and 12 generations each. The IDFF consisted of one group of attributes for the first stage, and increased by one group for each subsequent stage. The ordering in which groups were added was randomly generated. Again, 30 different orderings were generated, and each was run 30 times with a different target sound each time.

Twenty-stage This case was similar to that of the eight-stage IDFF evolutions, except that here the 100 generations were divided into 20 stages of five generations each. Evolution began with just two attributes, and two were added for each subsequent stage.

Random search This used a fitness function based on all attributes. In order to compare the performance of different search algorithms, it is only necessary to arrange that they make the same number of calls to the fitness function: hence the random search was conducted over 5000 individuals, the same number as are evaluated by a steady-state GA with the parameters described in Sect. 4.2.1. 5000-individual random search was run 30 times, in each case with a different target sound.

Ordered by difficulty This case was similar to the eight-stage IDFF evolutions, though the ordering, instead of being randomly generated, was chosen to add the most difficult attributes (as reported in Table 4.5) earliest in the evolution. This ordering was run 30 times with a different target sound each time.

Weighted by difficulty This case was a one-stage evolution where the overall fitness function was defined by weighting the attribute differences according to their difficulty, rather than simply averaging them. This evolution was run 30 times with a different target sound each time.

The best individual from each of the 30 runs of the random search was used to calculate an average error for each attribute: these are given in Table 4.5, and were used for the weighting and ordering in the final two experiments.

Table 4.5. Average error by attribute for random search

Attribute	Error	Attribute	Error
att	0.1134	rms	0.0590
zcr	0.0233	crest	0.0280
cen	0.0120	sprd	0.0128
flat	0.0053	flx	0.0104
pres	0.0319	roff	0.0590
fastm	0.0481	vdpth.rms	0.0260
vrate.rms	0.0890	vdpth.cen	0.0339
vrate.cen	0.1167	tcn.rms	0.0223
tcn.cen	0.0314	tpk.rms	0.0192
tpk.cen	0.0182	hfvr.rms	0.0439
lfvr.rms	0.0307	hfvr.cen	0.0005
lfvr.cen	0.0000	hfvr.zcr	0.0724
lfvr.zcr	0.1121	hs.rms	0.0563
dr.rms	0.0485	hs.cen	0.1304
dr.cen	0.0239	pit	0.0303
twm.err	0.0919	vdpth.pit	0.0910
vrate.pit	0.1096	inh	0.0548
irr	0.0163	tri1	0.0589
tri2	0.0437	tri3	0.0508
odd	0.0483	evn	0.0402

Results

The final fitness values reported by each evolution are calculated in terms of *all* attributes, and the **weighted by difficulty** results are evaluated, after evolution has finished, *without* weightings. Therefore it is possible to directly

Table 4.6. Results for eight search techniques, averaged over 30 or more runs (see text for details)

Experiment	Mean	Max	StdDev
Random search	0.955	0.985	0.013
One-stage GA	0.980	0.995	0.010
Two-stage GA	0.968	1.000	0.012
Eight-stage GA	0.973	0.999	0.013
Nine-stage GA	0.973	1.000	0.012
Twenty-stage GA	0.970	1.000	0.013
Ordered by difficulty	0.969	0.992	0.013
Weighted by difficulty	0.972	0.992	0.012

compare results from the weighted evolutions, the IDFF evolutions, the random search, and the unmodified GA.

Table 4.6 shows the results for the random search, the unmodified (i.e., one-stage) GA, the IDFF variations, and the weighted one-stage GA. For each technique, the dataset consists of the highest fitness achieved in each of 30 evolutionary runs (1200 in the case of two-stage, and 900 in the cases of eight-, nine- and 20-stage: see below). For each dataset we give the mean, maximum, and standard deviation.

T-tests show that all of the GA techniques perform better than the random search, at a 99% confidence level. Also, t-tests show that the unmodified GA (one-stage GA) outperforms the modified versions at a 99% confidence level, or higher. However the unmodified version's advantage is not large.

However, this is not the full story: the dataset for each of the two, eight, nine, and 20-stage modified versions is composed of results for 30 (40 for two-stage) *orderings*, each repeated 30 times. Several of the modified versions show high best scores, though means are low. Since we want to test whether some orderings perform better than others, we also look at means and t-tests for individual orderings.

However Table 4.7 shows that these high "best" scores do not come from correspondingly high datasets. In fact, every one of the 30 repetitions for each of the 30 orderings of the eight, nine and 20-stage experiments, and for each of the 40 possible two-stage experiments, performs worse than the one-stage experiment, at the 99% confidence level or higher. This leads us to conclude that the unmodified GA performs better than any of the tested orderings.

The (eight-stage) evolution in which the addition of attributes was *ordered* according to their difficulty does not show improvement over the comparable results (the other eight-stage orderings). Similarly, the technique of *weighting* the attributes according to their difficulty shows a disimprovement in performance, against the comparable results (the unmodified one-stage evolution).

Table 4.7. Results for selected orderings, averaged over 30 runs: the label associated with each two-stage GA indicates the single attribute used to drive evolution for the first of the two stages

Experiment	Mean	Max	StdDev
Two-stage GA, irr	0.981	0.997	0.010
Two-stage GA, sprd	0.982	0.997	0.011
Two-stage GA, lfvr.cen	0.980	0.994	0.010
Nine-stage GA, ordering 0	0.973	1.000	0.014
Nine-stage GA, ordering 8	0.978	1.000	0.010
Nine-stage GA, ordering 16	0.972	1.000	0.015
Twenty-stage GA, ordering 1	0.970	0.997	0.011
Twenty-stage GA, ordering 2	0.975	1.000	0.010
Twenty-stage GA, ordering 6	0.970	0.996	0.012

4.3 Conclusions and Future Work

We have compared the performance of several different types of fitness functions, different values for GA parameters, weightings for timbral attributes, and various increasingly discriminating fitness functions.

The results from the first experiment (Sect. 4.2.3) are hardest to interpret, since the performance of each fitness function can only be described in terms of the others. No clear-cut best function emerges. An alternative analysis, in terms of relative improvement over the course of evolution, may indicate that the Attribute distance fitness function performs slightly better than the others: certainly its performance is competitive, and therefore further work on this method is justified. One thing that is clear is that a fitness function based on timbral, perceptual, and statistical attributes has the potential to be used for constructing sounds in the abstract, perhaps by allowing a user to "sculpt out" desired areas of the attribute space. This is one reason why we have focused on this type of fitness function for later work.

The results on fitness landscapes (Sect. 4.2.4) give contradictory evidence on the question of which fitness functions give the easiest fitness landscapes. The two methods of comparing fitness landscape difficulty (Fitness Distance Correlation and Monotonicity) do not agree. However, comparing these results with those of Sect. 4.2.3 may indicate that Fitness Distance Correlation is the better method of measuring landscape difficulty.

The results on varying GA parameters (Sect. 4.2.5) are not surprising: they confirm that the typical parameters used in the GA literature are applicable to the problem of EC sound synthesis.

The final experiment (Sect. 4.2.6) fails to uncover any technique which can be used to improve on the performance of the unmodified GA. The failure of the IDFFs can perhaps be explained by noting that the fitness landscape for an attribute-based fitness function does not conform to the picture, described in Sect. 4.2.6, of large flat areas of low fitness with small islands of high fitness. In such a situation selection is often effectively random, so evolutionary search is unsuccessful, and a layered technique such as IDFFs can be useful. Instead, the fitness landscape is as shown in Sect. 4.2.4: an individual randomly generated in the parameter space will often have several attributes at least somewhat close to their desired values, and small decrements in parameter distance to the target tend to lead to small increments in fitness. Therefore, selection becomes meaningful and the evolutionary operators make progress. Since the IDFF technique decreases the number of generations available to evolve under the true fitness function, it turns out to be a hindrance rather than a help.

The same applies to another modification, that of weighting the values of the attributes in an attribute-based fitness function. The general conclusion is that, at least in these cases, the longer evolution is allowed to proceed with the "true" fitness function (i.e., the eventual evaluator), the more successful it will be. However the search remains open for a combination of timbral, perceptual and statistical attributes which both reflect true similarity between sounds and lead to good EC performance.

4.3.1 Future Work

Our experiments on automatically-computable fitness functions leave some work remaining to be done, including comparing the performance of other automatic EC search techniques, such as the particle swarm, differential evolution, and evolutionary Strategies; comparing other synthesizers; and using non-synthesized target sounds. The evaluation of EC performance using subjective listening tests is another very important area for future work.

The area of interactive EC (IEC) for sound synthesis has also been explored by several authors [19, 20, 21]. Much work remains to be done both in exploring new IEC ideas and in quantitatively comparing innovations with standard IEC and non-EC methods of interacting with synthesizers.

We have implemented two new techniques:

- *Background evolution* works by allowing the user to specify a target sound for automatic ("background") evolution, and to continue to work on interactive ("foreground") evolution. The best individuals from the background are periodically added to the foreground population. This technique can thus be seen as a way of combining the strengths of human and machine.
- *Sweeping* is a new population interface, which takes the place of explicit fitness evaluation and also functions as a genetic operator. The user controls an interpolation (at the genetic level) between individuals of the population, thus hearing a great variety of sounds, quickly eliminating unsuitable sounds, and focusing in more closely on interesting areas.

Usability studies comparing these techniques with standard EC and non-EC synthesizer interfaces are ongoing.

4.4 Acknowledgements

Co-author James McDermott gratefully acknowledges the guidance of his co-authors and supervisors, and is supported by IRCSET grant no. RS/2003/68.

References

1. Goldberg, D. (1989). *Genetic Algorithms in Search, Optimization and Machine Learning.* Addison-Wesley. Reading, MA
2. Grey, J.M. (1976). Multidimensional perceptual scaling of musical timbres. *J. Acoust. Soc. Am.*, **61**(5): 1270–1277
3. McAdams, S., Cunibile, J.C. (1992). Perception of timbral analogies. *Philosophical Transactions of the Royal Society*, **336**(Series B): 383–389
4. Horner, A., Beauchamp, J., Haken, L. (1993). Machine tongues XVI: Genetic algorithms and their application to FM matching synthesis. *Computer Music Journal*, **17**(4): 17–29
5. Riionheimo, J., Välimäki, V. (2003). Parameter estimation of a plucked string synthesis model using a genetic algorithm with perceptual fitness calculation. *EURASIP Journal on Applied Signal Processing*, **8**: 791–805
6. Koza, J.R. (1992). *Genetic Programming: On the Programming of Computers by Means of Natural Selection.* MIT Press
7. Wehn, K. (1998). Using ideas from natural selection to evolve synthesized sounds. In: *Digital Audio Effects (DAFX)*
8. Garcia, R.A. (2001). Growing sound synthesizers using evolutionary methods. In Bilotta, E., Miranda, E.R., Pantano, P., Todd, P., eds.: *Proceedings ALMMA 2001: Artificial Life Models for Musical Applications Workshop (ECAL 2001)*
9. Mitchell, T.J., Pipe, A.G. (2005). Convergence synthesis of dynamic frequency modulation tones using an evolution strategy. In Rothlauf, F., et al., eds.: *EvoWorkshops 2005.* Berlin Heidelberg. Springer, 533–538
10. Bolton, S. (2005). XSynth-DSSI. `http://dssi.sourceforge.net/` Last viewed 2 March 2006.
11. Jensen, K. (1999). *Timbre Models of Musical Sounds.* PhD thesis. Dept. of Computer Science, University of Copenhagen
12. Eronen, A., Klapuri, A. (2000). Musical instrument recognition using cepstral coefficients and temporal features. In: *Proceedings of the 2000 IEEE International Conference on Acoustics, Speech, and Signal Processing.* IEEE, 753–756
13. Lu, L., Zhang, H.J., Jiang, H. (2002). Content analysis for audio classification and segmentation. *IEEE Transactions on Speech and Audio Processing*, **10**(7): 504–516
14. McDermott, J., Griffith, N.J., O'Neill, M. (2006). Timbral, perceptual, and statistical attributes for synthesized sound. In: *Proceedings of the International Computer Music Conference 2006.* International Computer Music Association
15. Luthman, L. (2005). Sineshaper. `http://ll-plugins.sourceforge.net` Last viewed 1 September 2006.
16. McDermott, J., Griffith, N.J., O'Neill, M. (2005). Toward user-directed evolution of sound synthesis parameters. In Rothlauf, F., et al., eds.: *EvoWorkshops 2005.* Berlin. Springer

17. Jones, T., Forrest, S. (1995). Fitness distance correlation as a measure of problem difficulty for genetic algorithms. In: *Proceedings of the 6th International Conference on Genetic Algorithms*. San Francisco, CA, USA. Morgan Kaufmann Publishers Inc., 184–192
18. Gustafson, S.M., Hsu, W.H. (2001). Layered learning in genetic programming for a cooperative robot soccer problem. In Miller, J.F., Tomassini, M., Lanzi, P.L., Ryan, C., Tettamanzi, A., Langdon, W.B., eds.: *Proceedings of EuroGP 2001*. Springer, 291–301
19. Johnson, C.G. (2003). Exploring sound-space with interactive genetic algorithms. *Leonardo*, **36**(1): 51–54
20. Mandelis, J. (2001). Genophone: An evolutionary approach to sound synthesis and performance. In Bilotta, E., Miranda, E.R., Pantano, P., Todd, P., eds.: *Proceedings ALMMA 2001: Artificial Life Models for Musical Applications Workshop*
21. Dahlstedt, P. (2001). Creating and exploring huge parameter spaces: Interactive evolution as a tool for sound generation. In: *Proceedings of the International Computer Music Conference 2001*

5

Swarm Granulation

Tim Blackwell

Centre for Cognition, Computation and Culture, Goldsmiths College
New Cross, London, UK
t.blackwell@gold.ac.uk

Summary. Swarm granulation, as a union of swarming behaviour and sonic granulation, holds much potential for the generation of novel sounds. Theoretical and practical aspects of this technique are outlined here, and an explanation of how musical interactions with swarms can be enabled using an analogue of the biological process of stigmergy. Two manifestations of swarm granulation are explained in some detail. Social criticality, an inter-particle communication that is driven by a critical system such as a sandpile, and its use in determining the rendering of sound grains, is introduced.

5.1 Introduction

Swarm granulation, as a sound synthesis technique, is capable of producing highly textured and organised streams of sound. 'Granulation' refers to the process of packing very short samples of sound into tiny grains, which are subsequently rendered in dense clouds. In this technique, the flow and dynamic patterning of a virtual swarm is matched to the sonic properties of the grain cloud by a relationship between particles and grains; the organisation of the swarm in a space of grain parameterisations is manifest as a sonic organisation in a space of textural possibilities.

This chapter presents two manifestations of this technique, Swarm Granulator and Swarm Techtiles. A distinctive feature of these systems is that they are interactive. In Swarm Granulator [1], the swarm flies through a space of possible grain parameterisations. External sounds are parameterised and positioned in this space as 'attractors', in analogy with the biological process of stigmergy [2]. If the swarm discovers these attractors, it will explore near-by regions of space, producing a sonic stream that has a resemblance to, but is not a copy of, the captured sound.

The mechanism of interaction differs in Swarm Techtiles [3]. In this system, the swarm flies above an image of the incoming sound and searches for regions of high micro-texture, as quantified by the evaluation of a mathematical measure. The images are constructed from live sound using a mapping known as woven sound. Attractors are deposited by the swarm at maximally textured regions, encouraging further exploration in a process similar to particle swarm optimisation [4].

The possibility of musical interpretations of the spontaneous, organisational behaviour of swarms has not remained unnoticed by computer musicians. *Visualisations* of music in terms of swarms and flocks has been explored by various workers. An early example is [5]; the behaviour of a boid animation is controlled by acoustical information supplied by musicians. The flocks do not themselves produce sounds however.

Sonifications of swarms have also been attempted. Spector and Klein [6] were inspired by Swarm Music [7] to add musical events to their swarm and flock simulations, implemented in the BREVE simulation system. Notes are associated with certain events within the system, for example, feeding. Different instrument timbres are associated with each of the three species, and gradual musical transitions occur as each species enjoys a period of feeding. In this system, sounds derive from agent behaviour and not directly on flock spatial patterning. The authors report that in an extension, spectral and amplitude information from recorded music was used to alter constants in the swarm update formula, although few details are given.

Non-sonic interactions with swarms may proceed through physical gestures, rather than by music. Unemi and Bisig [8] have developed an interactive boid simulation that acts as a virtual instrument. The boids move in a 3D space, with boid coordinates interpreted as pan, pitch and loudness. Users interact with the flocks by making physical movements which are captured by a camera. The user can change the instrumentation, and the melodic and rhythmic patterns of the flock.

Sonic interactions with swarms were introduced in the Swarm Music family of virtual improvisers [7, 1, 3]. The musical contributions of an external (human) musician are mapped to objects, known as attractors, and placed either directly (Swarm Granulator) or indirectly (Swarm Techtiles) in the space of the virtual swarm. The group of attractors form an image of the external music or sonic environment and can be considered as a second type of swarm whose movements are determined by the external participants. Positions of particles as they organise themselves around the attractors are re-interpreted and rendered as sonic grains or MIDI sound events by a synthesizer.

Section 5.2 presents an overview of swarming, proceeding from a discussion of principles, to a formal statement as a dynamical system, and ending with an account of implementation as a real-time simulation.

Section 5.3 outlines Swarm Granulator, an experimental artificial improviser. The connection between free improvisation, interactivity and stigmergy is introduced as a motivation for system design, and a general modular architecture for such improvisers (known as 'live algorithms') is presented. This section ends with a discussion on swarm-attractor behaviour, and how this corresponds to perceived system behaviour.

Section 5.4 describes the development of Swarm Techtiles and covers unusual features of the algorithm (woven sound, attractor consumption and micro-texture washing) that do not appear in the swarming algorithms presented in Sect. 5.2 . Self-organised criticality and the sandpile model are introduced, and their use in determining which particles are rendered as sound grains (social criticality) is motivated and explained.

A number of resources (images of woven sound, screenshots of Swarm Techtiles, a concert performance of Swarm Granulator and a swarm simulation) has been placed online at [9]. Further information and reference materials on the topics covered in this chapter is also available at the author's website (follow the link at [9]).

5.2 Swarm Algorithms

Reynold's discovery [10] that convincing swarm, flock, herd, shoal and school animations can result from local, de-centralised rules has done much to support the hypothesis that social animal groups are self-organizing. In this model, the collective behaviour of the group is emergent in the sense that the local rules concerning individual movement does not contain any notion of the whole. In a centralised approach, animations would be scripted with every individual movement described in full. Swarming (henceforth we shall take the example of a swarm as the prototypical animal group) behaviour would not then be emergent because it is built into the script from the outset.

It seems very unlikely that actual swarm behaviour would derive from any type of script or centralised control because such rigid control structures are not robust and cannot cope with the many small variations that occur in natural environments. De-centralisation is demonstrably robust, and furthermore explains the scalability of natural swarms. The variation of swarm sizes over six orders of magnitude suggests that (models of) the interactions between swarming individuals must have linear complexity. If individuals were aware of the entire swarm, the number of interactions would increase quadratically with swarm size, with, presumably, an increase in brain size amongst individuals from large swarms. However even very small animals might swarm in vast numbers. In fact it is believed that an individual is only aware of other individuals and attractors in a finite region of space centred on that individual.

A broad classification of swarm algorithms would distinguish *non-social* from *social* swarms. In this context, 'social' refers to an additional mechanism of information transfer between individuals, taking place through a topological information network. This network might bear no relationship to the spatial configuration of the swarm; individuals within a social sub-group can communicate irrespectively of their spatial separation, rather like sub-groups of humans can with mobile phones. The dynamics of individual movement in any swarm, however, still derives from the spatial configuration of the individuals.

Although some swarming systems are used as scientific models of natural systems (for example, the biological swarm and flock models of Couzin et al. [11]), other swarms are developed primarily as real-time simulations. Prominent examples of simulation swarms include bird flocks [10], bat swarms and penguin flocks in the motion picture *Batman Returns* and the wildebeest stampede in the cartoon *The Lion King*.

Optimisation swarms include the transfer of information over a social network. These swarms are used to solve mathematical problems, as in ant colony optimisation [12] and particle swarm optimisation [13]. Real-space swarms may be adapted for discrete and combinatorial problems, in which case individuals 'move' in a discrete rather than a continuous space [13, 14]. Optimisation swarms may be visualised as real-time simulations, but this is not necessary.

5.2.1 Principles

At a high level of abstraction, a set of swarming rules govern the movement of any individual in a virtual swarm. Each individual may:

1. move away from any neighbour who is too close (Separation);
2. attempt to match velocities with neighbours (Alignment);
3. move towards other individuals in its neighbourhood (Cohesion);
4. move closer to any nearby object of interest (Curiosity);
5. communicate with other individuals in a social group (Society).

Separation and cohesion are sufficient to produce the spatio-temporal patterns of organisation so typical of real-life swarms and are implemented in all virtual swarms. Alignment applies to collectives where individuals have a tendency to move in unison, such as flocks, herds and schools (a school is a polarised shoal). Curiosity gives the swarm a preferred direction of motion, and the rule of society allows non-spatial communication. These last two rules are used in optimisation swarms.

Arguably alignment, and hence flocking, is less suitable for sonically interacting swarm systems because they are *too* organised; the flock movement is interpreted as a regular transition through grain and sound event parameter space, an effect that is too restricting. The two systems described in this chapter do not, therefore, use this rule.

5.2.2 Swarms as Dynamical Systems

This, and the following, subsection present a rather formal statement of the swarming principles and their implementation as a real-time simulation. Readers who do not care about these details may skip these parts.

At a low level of abstraction, a swarm algorithm is implemented as a dynamical system. Formally an individual i is represented as a point particle at position x_i and velocity v_i in a d-dimensional Euclidean space. A map M_i updates the dynamical state $\sigma_i = (x_i,\ v_i)$ at successive steps t

$$\sigma(t+1) = M_i(\sigma_i(t)). \tag{5.1}$$

The map is a discretisation of Newton's laws, but with $dt = 1$. The update of particle i at iteration t of swarm S is

$$a_i = \frac{1}{m} f(\{x_j, p\} \in D_i, \alpha) \tag{5.2}$$

$$v_i(t+1) = v_i(t) + a_i \tag{5.3}$$

$$x_i(t+1) = x_i(t) + v_i(t+1). \tag{5.4}$$

A *swarm update* or iteration corresponds to a single update of each particle in the swarm. The force f is a function of the positions of any particles j and attractors p within a spatial neighbourhood D_i of i, and parameters α which specify the strengths of the interactions. The inertial mass m governs the overall responsiveness of i to forces and is usually set to unity because re-scaling can take place via the α's. The terms "force" and "acceleration" can therefore be used interchangeably.

Particle positions are vector quantities, usually restricted to a bounded region of d-dimensional Euclidean space E, for example $[0,\ X]^d$ where X is the linear size of the box. (In a general formulation of swarming, x is a vector in any bounded subspace of a vector space H.) Particle velocities, which are the difference of two vectors in E are vectors in a larger space, $v_i \in [-X,\ X]^d$ in our example. Updates that might take a particle outside E are dealt with in a number of ways. For example, a particle might be reflected from the edge of the space, or might be re-positioned on the edge with zero velocity. Toroidal boundary conditions can also be implemented, so that a particle leaving at one face reappears through the opposite face. However, for musical swarms, toroidal conditions may produce a discontinuity in parameter values q, unless the parameterisations are themselves circular in some way (for example, q is a phase angle, $q \in [0,\ 2\pi]$). For this reason, reflective boundary conditions are used in the systems described in this chapter.

Equation (5.3) is often replaced with a speed clamp which can be used to limit particle speed in the case of high accelerations,

$$v = v_i(t) + a_i \tag{5.5}$$

$$v_i(t+1) = \min(v,\ v_{\max}). \tag{5.6}$$

Particle motion can also proceed at fixed speed c by replacing (5.6) with

$$v_i(t+1) = c\hat{v} \tag{5.7}$$

where $\hat{v} = v/|v|$ is a unit vector pointing in the direction of v.

The calculation of the acceleration, a_i, in (5.2) consists of attractive (cohesion and curiosity) and repulsive (separation) terms. Particles perceive each other within a spatial neighbourhood D_i, which may be divided into two distinct separation and cohesion zones. The separation zone is a hypersphere of radius r_{sep} and the coherence zone is an encircling shell of radius $r_{\mathrm{coh}} > r_{\mathrm{sep}}$. Figure 5.1 illustrates the general idea. Bio-swarms use three concentric neighbourhoods; separation applies in an inner zone, alignment in a middle zone, and cohesion in an outer zone [11]. Individuals may even have a blind volume in which neighbours are undetectable.

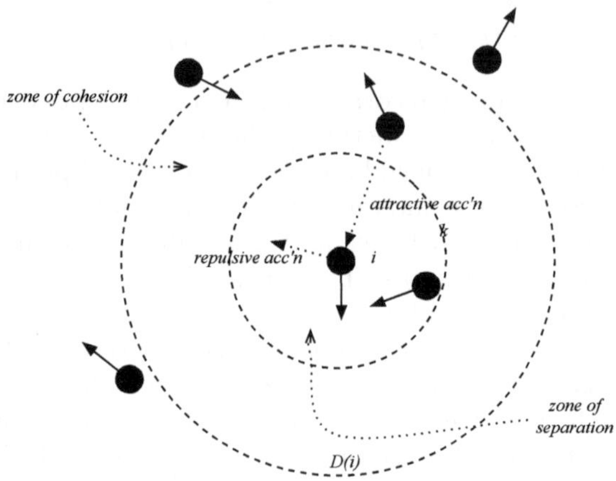

Fig. 5.1. The spatial neighbourhood D_i of a particle contains separate zones of coherence and separation

Bio and some simulation swarms use a swarming function, (5.2), that produces accelerations of fixed magnitude. For example, the attraction of a particle at x_i towards a neighbouring particle at x_j might be an acceleration of unit magnitude,

$$a_{ij}^{\mathrm{coh}} = \hat{x}_{ij},\ j \neq i \tag{5.8}$$

where the displacement vector is $x_{ij} = x_j - x_i$. Another method (used in the two systems described in this chapter) is to calculate vectors to the centroids of particles in the separation and coherence zones and to attractors (see below) in a curiosity zone D_{cur}. The total acceleration for a particle at x_i is

$$a_i = -\frac{1}{n_{\mathrm{sep}}} \sum_{j \in D_{\mathrm{sep}}} x_{ij} + \frac{1}{n_{\mathrm{coh}}} \sum_{j \in D_{\mathrm{sep}}} x_{ij} + \frac{1}{n_{\mathrm{cur}}} \sum_{j \in D_{\mathrm{cur}}} x_{ij} \tag{5.9}$$

where $n_{sep,coh,cur}$ are the numbers of particles or attractors in each zone. The negative sign in front of the first term of (5.9) corresponds to a repulsive force. Separation of particles, which is desirable in any swarm except for optimisation swarms (which require convergence), can also be implemented by assigning a 'charge' Q to particles [15], and calculating an electrostatic repulsion

$$a_{ij}^{\mathrm{sep}} = -\frac{Q^2(r_{ij})}{|r_{ij}|^3}. \tag{5.10}$$

A single expression which includes both repulsion and attraction can also be implemented; for example the Lennard-Jones function [16]

$$a_{ij}^{\mathrm{coh}} + a_{ij}^{\mathrm{sep}} = \left(\frac{B}{|r_{ij}|^{\beta}} - \frac{A}{|r_{ij}|^{\alpha}}\right) r_{ij} \tag{5.11}$$

where A, B, a, $b > 0$.

As previously mentioned, *attractors* may also exist in H. Attractors in dynamical systems theory are points x^* with the property $M(x^*) = x^*$ and are asymptotically attained by dissipative systems. The interactive swarming systems which are the subject of this chapter are not dissipative and the attractor itself is never attained by any particle. Accelerations towards attractors can be steering, towards the centroid of the attracting group, or spring-like as in particle swarm optimisation (PSO)

$$a_{ip}^{\mathrm{cur}} = C(p - x_i) \tag{5.12}$$

where C is a spring constant and p is a good (as defined by an objective function) location previously visited by particle i, and/or by any other particle in i's social network. Convergence, which is desirable in PSO, is obtained by including a frictional drag force in the calculation of a_i. Particle displacements about p_i become progressively smaller as energy is dissipated from the system, leading to finer exploration of the area around p_i. The attraction of a particle to a previous best position can be viewed as a stigmergetic (see Sect. 5.3.1) interaction. Particles leave attractors p_i at promising locations. These attractors are available to any other particle in the same social network, irrespective of distance. Particles in social swarms such as PSO possess a *social state* as well as a dynamic state; in this case they retain a memory of best location visited.

The scalar constants Q, α, β, A, B, C, r_{sep}, r_{coh}, r_{cur} occurring in the above equations are acceleration constants, collectively denoted α.

5.2.3 Swarms as Real-Time Simulations

The previous subsection described swarms as dynamical systems, using a map to advance particle state step by step; the parameter t is merely a counter, counting logical steps. In order to run the dynamical system as a real-time simulation, t must be linked to an actual interval of time τ. There are arguments for ensuring that interactive, musical swarms are real-time simulations of possible swarms. The introduction of an interval τ links the algorithm to the real-time process of musical interaction. It is hard to see how one may interact with an abstract dynamical system. Moreover, a visualisation of the underlying generative process greatly facilitates performer and spectator engagement with the machine. Without τ, a computer would run a loop consisting of (5.2)–(5.4) just as fast as it could. The resulting animation would be erratic, and machine dependent, even if the parameters α were adjusted to give slow particle speeds.

In order to control the real-time running of the animation, two parameters, contained in (5.2)–(5.6) must be related to physical requirements. The physical scales of the simulation are display size L, measured in pixels, and desired frame rate F, measured in frames per second. The internal scales are box size X (the single physical length scale in the algorithm) and particle speed in units of the box length, c/X (or $v_{\max}/X$).

Suppose a particle screen speed V (several hundreds of pixels per second) is required and that the update loop, (5.2)–(5.4) is designed to run at one swarm update per frame. This can be achieved by halting the program for a small time interval τ at the end of each swarm update. If the actual time needed to perform the update calculations is τ_{CPU} then $\tau_{\mathrm{CPU}} + \tau = 1/F$. In practice, τ_{CPU} will vary at each cycle and discrepancies are either made up at the next loop. The particle screen speed in pixels per frame is $L\,(c/X)$ giving an actual screen speed of $V = FL\,(c/X)$ pixels per second. The relation between the algorithmic constants X, c and the physical parameters frame rate, screen size and particle screen speed is

$$\frac{V}{FL} = \frac{c}{X}. \tag{5.13}$$

Swarm and Attractors, a swarm simulation written in Processing (a variant of Java) can be accessed at [9]. The application displays a 3D simulation and a control panel, allowing for adjustment of system and swarm parameters. Particles are depicted as white blobs and attractors as red squares. Any particle that has entered the zone of influence of an attractor will be coloured green. Attractors can be placed within the space by a mouse click (the depth of the attractor is random). The box length L and internal dimension X are fixed at 500 pixels. V and F can be adjusted in accordance with (5.13). (The desired frame rate might not be achievable; no correction for discrepancies between desired and actual frame rates has been implemented.)

Centroid accelerations are used in the simulation, with the addition of a random acceleration ξ. This is added to the acceleration as calculated in (5.9). The resulting acceleration is added to the velocity and clamped in accordance with (5.7). The amplitude of ξ and the radii of the zones in pixels are displayed on the control panel. Additionally, attractors will vanish after a user-defined number of visits. The dynamics of this demonstration swarm is essentially the same as the dynamics of Swarm Granulator and Swarm Techtiles.

5.3 Swarm Granulator

Swarm Granulator is a real-time performing system, developed in collaboration with the composer Michael Young. Swarm Granulator can be viewed as a prototype artificial improviser, able to take part in a freely improvised performance with other musicians. Analysis of incoming audio and sound synthesis is programmed in Max/MSP and the swarm simulation, programmed in Java, runs on a separate machine. The computers communicate by exchanging datagrams, with information packed according to the Open Sound Control protocol (`http://www.opensoundcontrol.org/cnmat`). A recording of Swarm Granulator, with Mette Bille (voice), Tim Blackwell (sax) and Michael Young, at the Live Algorithms concert, London, 18th December 2005 is available for download at [9].

5.3.1 Free Improvisation and Stigmergy

Free improvisation, originating in the free jazz movement of the 1960s, but blended with a European sensibility for colour and timbre, is an expressive performative practice that eschews "conventional" musical elements of rhythm, melody and harmony, in favour of improvised timbre and texture [17, 18]. Typically, an improvised performance will proceed with no prior agreement on form and content; it has been conjectured that any long time-scale structure is emergent [19]. There are reasons to believe that an artificial improviser might participate in such a genre. The main advantage for any autonomous system engaged in free improvisation is the relative unimportance of conventional musical syntax and form. According to the conjecture of Blackwell and Young, the structure of a freely improvised performance is a function of how the performers respond to each other, irrespective of the precise nature of the sonic material itself. In this sense, the performance is built from local interactions.

At this stage of analysis, a biological parallel becomes appealing. Consider for example the nests of social insects. Despite the complexity of these nests, there is no evidence to suggest that individual workers possess a global representation of the structure. Indeed, it is proposed that nest building is a de-centralised activity built by cooperative, autonomous individuals which have, in part, random behaviour, but also have access to, and can respond to, local information (see [12] and references therein). This information is communicated in a process known as stigmergy [2], an indirect interaction between insects caused by a modification of the environment. In a computational model of self-assembly, Theraulaz and Bonabeau [20] demonstrate the emergence of architectures reminiscent of wasp nests from a simple agent system. In this system, agents move in a 3D discrete space, depositing new "bricks" according to rules based solely on the local configuration of bricks in the immediate neighbourhood of the agent.

Blackwell and Young have proposed an interactive model, analogous to nest construction [21]. Form emerges in a free improvisation through a stigmergetic interaction between musicians. Instead of bricks, musicians have the option of depositing sound "objects". A sound object can be thought of as a musical event of finite duration, or as a perceived element of an ongoing event. The advantage of this model, from the perspective of the deign of interactive music systems, is representational. Sound objects, defined by the analysis of an incoming stream of sound into parameters, become dynamical entities within the formal system.

In Swarm Granulator, the image of external sound objects deriving from other musicians are attractors in the internal space of the swarm. Swarm movement is contingent, but not determined by the attractors, so that there is an illusion of autonomy; if the swarm is drawn towards the attractors, the re-interpretation of particle position will correspond to sonic output that is associated with the heard external objects. Alternatively, the exploration of internal space away from attractors would correspond to contrasting contributions. All this will depend on a rich interpretation of possible states as synthesis parameters, and a swarm dynamics that enables convergent, as well as exploratory, movement.

5.3.2 Granulation

Swarm Granulator uses a *granulator* for the sonic interpretation of particles. Granulation (a form of granular synthesis) is well suited to textural improvisation since the output is potentially diverse and not obviously related to a conventional instrument. The basic idea of granular synthesis is to superpose many grains of sound into a larger cloud or stream of sound [22, 23, 24]. A grain of sound is a short duration (tens of milliseconds) burst of sound and represents the smallest duration of sound that has a perceivable timbre. Shorter burst are heard as clicks, whatever their spectral content. The grains themselves can be built synthetically, or can derive from sampled sound (as in granulation). In the latter case, sampled sound is stored in a buffer and grains are constructed by entering the buffer at a particular position and reading consecutive samples. Grains must be carefully enveloped in order to prevent phase discontinuities which are heard as clicks. Granulation utilises the rich timbres already present in natural sounds and presents many possibilities for the generation of sonic texture, often producing sound streams with considerable "flow", not unlike natural sound textures such as running water.

5.3.3 System Overview

A general design for an artificial improviser or "live algorithm" might be based on the modular design of Swarm Music [15], and its descendant, Swarm Granulator. The architecture is depicted in Fig. 5.2 This design informally acknowledges three functionalities of an improviser: listening (P), generation of response and/or new ideas (f) and articulation by means of instrumental gestures (Q).

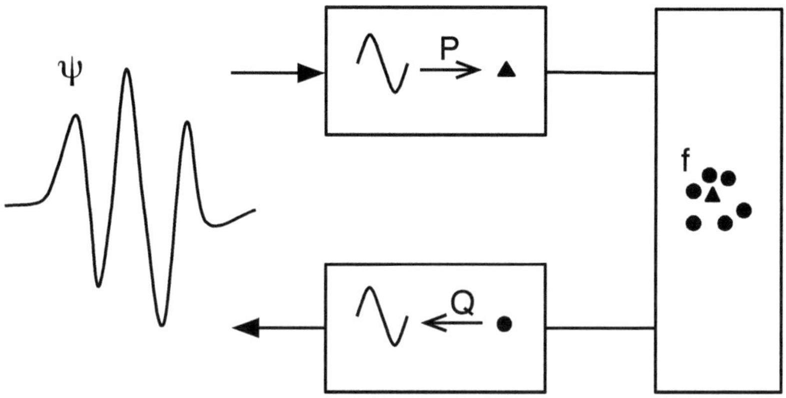

Fig. 5.2. Modular PQf architecture for Swarm Granulator. An incoming event ψ is parameterised by the analysis module P and placed in the swarming space as an attractor (triangle). Particles (blobs) swarm around the attractor (f) and positions are interpreted as re-synthesis parameters by Q

The first Swarm Granulator analysed incoming into four parameters: event pitch, amplitude, duration and interval between successive events. The analysis module had control of four granulation parameters: buffer scanning speed (pitch), amplitude, grain duration and interval between successive grains. In addition, the operator could manually specify envelope characteristics (attack and decay characteristic times). The granulator consisted of three grain guns or output streams; grains were emitted in turn by each gun.

The current version of Swarm Granulator is a slimmer system, operating in three dimensions. The biggest change has been an attempt to interpret sonic timbre. The dimensions of the internal space are: pitch, amplitude and timbre, where timbre is defined as the centroid (weighted average) of the Fourier spectrum over small windows of incoming sound. In effect, this analysis component builds up a map between a list of incoming timbres and buffer position (measured in numbers of received samples). One component of particle position represents timbre and is interpreted as a convenient buffer entry point for the granulator. The other two components determine the amplitude and scanning speed of the buffer. Swarm Granulator now has twenty simultaneous, unsynchronised grain streams; each grain gun is fired in turn upon arrival of a particle position. The increased number of guns allows for denser texture since up to 20 grains can be rendered at any one time.

5.3.4 Behaviour

The essence of the interactivity between musicians and Swarm Granulator is governed by the dynamic response of the swarm to attractors, and by attractor characteristics. Attractors in Swarm Granulator (and Swarm Techtiles) have a local spatio-temporal neighbourhood; they have a finite life span and can only influence particle motion over a local spatial neighbourhood.

In analogy with the depletion of a food source, attractors are gradually consumed upon each visit by a particle. Attractors with a finite life span enhance exploration of the internal space of grain parameterisations, and diversify output so that it may at times appear uncorrelated to the input. If no new external sounds are available, attractor consumption will prevent stagnation. The system appears to have more autonomy, and hence becomes closer to the ideal of the live algorithm.

Spatial neighbourhoods are important because they prevent the system from becoming dominated by a single attractor and therefore also aid autonomy; a lone particle i is only aware of attractors p within a neighbourhood D_{cur} and its trajectory will be affected by p according to the swarming function f described in Sect. 5.2. For example, the particle may be drawn into an orbit within p. However, if i is part of a subswarm S_i, the force of mutual attraction between i and other members of S_i mean that one of a number of scenarios might be played out.

Other particles might follow the deviation if i away from S_i and towards p, thereby pulling yet more members of S_i towards p, until the subswarm as a whole orbits p. This is a direct working of fluctuation amplification, a mechanism that is believed to be an important pre-requisite of self-organisation [12]. A second scenario is that S_i will fracture; i and some other members of S_i will be drawn towards p, but the fluctuation will not propagate throughout S_i due to the finite size of the neighbourhoods that surround each particle. A separate sub-swarm will then move away from p. The degree of amplification, which is dependent on the initial configuration (the relative positions and velocities of the particles) of S_i when the fluctuation occurred, is not sufficient to affect the entire sub-swarm. This second scenario is a mechanism for swarm division. The third scenario is that i is merely disturbed by p, but the attraction to S_i is overwhelming and i rejoins S_i which as a whole remains unperturbed by p.

The delivery of a new sound object to the system therefore has one of three outcomes. Perhaps the entire swarm becomes trapped momentarily by p. Interpretation of particle positions will correspond to synthesis parameters that are close to the perceived parameters of the external object. The resulting output will be heard by an interacting musician as a supporting texture, at least until the attractor is consumed and the swarm moves away. The new attractor might cause swarm splitting, with a smaller sub-swarm in local orbit. Sonically this will cause a bifurcation in the output grain stream, with two perceivable textures, only one of which is related directly to the found object. Finally, the ensuing attractor might be far from any sub-swarm, or the new attractor might be placed close to a sub-swarm and the third scenario described above is played out. In either case, the attractor will be ignored, at least for a while. The musical significance is that output will be in contrast to the current sound environment; this state of affairs is not uncommon in freely improvised music.

The possibility of any of these three outcomes, and the consumption of attractors, enhances the perceived behaviour of the system, since a musician cannot know for sure what affect her contribution will have.

5.4 Swarm Techtiles

Swarm Techtiles combines elements of optimisation and social swarms within the swarm granulation framework described in the previous section. In this application, particles fly above a landscape, searching for optimal regions as quantified by evaluation of an objective function which measures local image texture. The landscape itself is a two-dimensional textured pattern that is built from incoming audio in a process known as "woven sound".

The fitness at a location (x, y) is calculated as the value of a function evaluated at a small tile centred on (x, y). This defines micro-texture. Numerous measures are available from the domain of machine vision [25] and the author has experimented with maximum entropy and maximum variance measures. The latter is computationally more efficient, an important criterion since the system has the major real time computational tasks of weaving sound, swarm animation and visualisation, local texture evaluation and sound granulation.

Attractors are left by particles at locations of high micro-texture, serving as an invitation to other particles. As the particles explore, local image elements, corresponding to tiles or threads and centred on the particle position's are unwoven and granulated. In Swarm Techtiles, only selected particles are chosen for rendering at each swarm iteration. Swarm Granulator produces a continuous stream of textured sound because every particle is rendered at each iteration; however Swarm Techtiles produces clouds of varying grain density that are emitted in bursts. The mechanism for choosing which particle to render at each iteration is based on social communication.

The background to Swarm Techtiles is the arts project "A Sound You Can Touch", developed in conjunction with the textile artist Janis Jefferies. This project is an investigation of aural, visual and haptic texture and their connections. Within the auspices of this project, Swarm Techtiles provides a link between aural and visual texture and a study of how our attention wonders over a textured surface.

5.4.1 Woven Sound

There are many possible mappings from 1D linear time onto a 2D image. A rather literal approach is taken in "A Sound You Can Touch"; the incoming stream of audio samples is likened to a thread with sample values shifted and scaled to pixel values. Left and right channels provide two threads, which are woven as warp and weft and displayed. An image of several hundreds of pixels represents a few seconds of sound at a sample rate of 44.1kHz. Surprisingly, the images bear a resemblance to their sonic origin. A pure tone of several hundred Hz produces regular variations in pixel values, easily perceived since the wavelength is commensurate with the image size (several hundred pixels). Noise and other non-periodic sounds, on the other hand, produce random patterns of lines and dots. The woven sound images at [9] include a saxophone multiphonic and a weave of non-pitched sounds. The multiphonic contains a superposition of frequencies, a feature that is clearly visible on the image. The non-pitched sounds are more random.

5.4.2 Design Specification

It was decided at the outset to use a large swarm (80–100 particles) and a high frame rate (the quantity F in Sect. 5.2.3 set to 80 frames per second). These choices can produce a good quality animation. In this case, the animation is reminiscent of gnats dancing above water. Furthermore, it was decided to use a single computer for the entire application. However, the capability of the computer to complete all the computational tasks means that some alterations to the Swarm Granulator implementation must be made.

Swarm Techtiles, like Swarm Granulator, uses 20 asynchronous grain guns. This means that up to 20 grains/particles may be rendered at once. The animation runs an 81 particle swarm (the choice of a perfect square will be explained below) at 80 frames (complete swarm updates) per second. This means that each particle is updated every 12.5 ms and that there are 6480 potential grains in each second. Sound grains typically last for tens of milliseconds, so with 20 guns, the synthesizer can accommodate only up to 2000 grains (for very small grains of 10 ms duration). Clearly, with these settings, some particle positions must be overlooked. Furthermore, the process of granulation is computationally taxing, and can slow the visualisation. An experiment showed that if each particle is rendered at each iteration, on a 1.5 GHz Mac G4, the swarm moves very slowly and exploration of the textured surface is much reduced. (Swarm Granulator uses smaller swarms (typically 10 particles) and the computational tasks are split between two machines, so it is possible to render each particle at each update.)

Trials showed that, if only a sub-swarm is rendered at each update, the swarm can attain its desired speed and all computations can be achieved. Further investigations of granulations of sub-swarms of varying size revealed that the ensuing variation in grain density, enhanced sonic interest, even producing bursts of activity, punctuated by pauses, perceivable as events. However, the problem remains as to which particles to render at each update. Various schemes have been tried, such as rendering only those particles that have found attractors, or rendering a randomly chosen sub-swarm. Eventually a scheme for rendering based on "social criticality" was found to produce a satisfactory diversity in grain densities and events. Although this decision relies on a subjective evaluation, there is some theoretical support for this methodology.

5.4.3 Self-organised Criticality

A study has suggested that the distributions of various music-theoretic elements such as pitch, duration and note distance in various genres of music are describable by power laws [26]. It is possible that the textural sound world of improvised music displays similar properties; the relevant measurable attributes are quantities such as energy, event density, spectral density and micro-texture. In an investigation of this proposal, the sonic texture delivered by Swarm Techtiles consists of grain clouds with a power law distribution of cloud size. Self-organised criticality (SOC) is a well known generator of events with power law distributions of event size.

SOC is manifest in open, dissipative systems and is characterised by a critical state at the edge of instability [27]. The critical state displays an inverse power law distribution of "avalanches". An avalanche will start at a critical location, i.e., the state of an object at that location has become unstable. A state transition to sub-criticality occurs. Associated with this transition is a re-distribution of "criticality" to neighbouring objects. If, as a result, these neighbours also become critical, there will be further transitions and the avalanche progresses until no neighbour is critical. The size of the avalanches, measured, for example in numbers of participating objects, follows a power law so that large avalanches occur less often than small ones, but are not exponentially unlikely. Theoretically, SOC is a model of the natural distribution of strengths of catastrophic events such as earthquakes and actual avalanches.

The sandpile model [28] is the prototypical implementation of SOC. In a single update of this model, a unit of sand is added at a random point (i, j) on a bounded square grid. If the height of sand h at (i, j) exceeds three units, $h(i, j)$ is reduced by four units (this is known as a toppling) and the sand is equally dispersed to the four neighbours of the site, except if (i, j) lies on the boundary of the grid, in which case sand is lost from the pile. The sandpile is initialised with random heights $h \in [0 : 3]$ and after a few updates the pile enters a critical state. As mentioned, the critical state has a power law distribution in the avalanche size s measured in topplings. Figure 5.3 show a plot of avalanche size for a 9^2 grid.

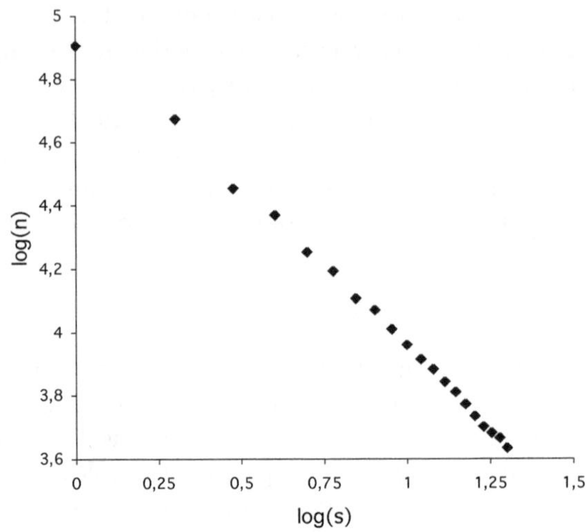

Fig. 5.3. Plot of $\log_{10}(n)$, n number of avalanches, versus $\log_{10}(s)$, size s of avalanche for the sandpile model on a 9^2 grid. The figure shows data for 10^6 sandpile updates. The graph shows a power distribution, $n \sim s^{-\alpha}$, $\alpha > 0$

SOC has been employed with optimisation swarms [29]. In this work, the distribution of criticality occurs through a spatial neighbourhood and it serves to increase swarm diversity and mitigates against premature convergence. In contrast, Swarm Techtiles uses *social* SOC for the distribution of criticality.

5.4.4 Social Criticality

In this scheme, known here as social criticality, each particle is part of a social network and inter-particle communication is driven by a sandpile model. A particle is randomly chosen after δt_{SOC} swarm updates and its criticality is increased by one. The particle is granulated if (metaphorically) it can no longer resist the urge to communicate (i.e., becomes critical) and "topples". Micro-textures from social neighbours that also topple are also rendered at this moment. The result is that the numbers of grains s in the ensuing cloud are power-law distributed. One virtue of using social criticality, rather than the spatial SOC of Lovbjerg and Krink, is that contributions from particles that are not encircling attractors are more likely to be included, which increases the diversity of the grain cloud. After the avalanche, which precipitates a grain cloud with s grains, the SOC update interval δt_{SOC} is set to s. This leads to an approximate power-law distribution of intervals δt_{bursts} between bursts of sound grains. The distribution is noisy, since, although the δt_{SOC}'s will be power-law distributed, avalanches do not certainly occur whenever sand is added. (On a 9^2 grid, empirical investigations show there is a 39% chance that an avalanche will occur whenever sand is added.)

5.4.5 Algorithm Overview

The main loop of Swarm Techtiles is given in Algorithm 1. The loop starts with analysing (module P) a full audio buffer for any events. The audio buffer holds enough samples to weave a complete image (typically 800 × 800 pixels) and takes several seconds to fill. If any events are found (as defined by a threshold), the buffer is woven and displayed, all attractors are removed and the overall best micro-texture set to zero. The next step in Algorithm 1 removes, if necessary, attractors, according to a tally of the number of individual particle visits. The loop continues with a complete swarm update, and then with the application of stigmergy. Due to the computational expense of the evaluation of the texture function, only one particle is chosen for evaluation. With an 81 particle swarm, and a frame rate of 80 s^{-1}, each particle is tested, on average, about once a second.

Algorithm 1 Swarm Techtiles in pseudocode

```
loop
  if an audio event is found then
    weave sound, remove attractors and set best micro-texture to zero
  for all attractors do
    if attractor is consumed then
      remove attractor
      update best micro-texture
  // swarm update
  for all particles in swarm do
    move particle
  // stigmergy
  choose a particle at random from the swarm
  evaluate local micro-texture at location of chosen particle
  if new micro-texture is better than any known to swarm then
    place an attractor at this location
    update best micro-texture
  // sandpile
  if t = δt_SOC then
    increase criticality of chosen particle
    while any particle is critical do
      granulate critical particle, reduce criticality of critical particle
      wash local micro-texture
    set δt_SOC to size of avalanche
```

Particle dynamics are implemented with centroid vectors (5.9). Noise, in the form of a unit vector pointing in a random direction can be added to (5.9). Stochasticity has little affect on particle motion within a sub-swarm, since the dynamics of a few interacting particles are already chaotic, but it does enhance the appearance of free particle motion, which in the absence of any interactions, would otherwise be linear.

Swarm techtiles employs attractor consumption and micro-texture *washing* in order to promote exploration and sonic diversity. Washing is simply the weakening of micro-texture at each rendering, according to an exponential rule that reduces the image RGB pixel values at the local region to uniformity): $\{R, G, B\} = 128 + 0.5(\{R, G, B\} - 128)$. The effect of micro-texture washing is to divert the swarm to other, more textured regions of the image (even if these regions were initially weaker), with a corresponding enhancement in the diversity of sonic output.

5.5 Concluding Remarks

This chapter has explained how swarms might organise the streams of sonic grains delivered from a granular synthesizer, and how musicians might interact with these grains, not by adjusting control parameters, but by playing an instrument. Without a mechanism for interaction, a swarm would wonder rather aimlessly in the space of grain parameterisations. Although the grain clouds might reflect the patterning of the swarm, there would not otherwise be any structure to the output, unless this should happen by chance. Interaction, however, feeds information into the system by virtue of the structuring abilities of collaborating musicians. This structure is represented in Swarm Granulator and Swarm Techtiles as a dynamic configuration of attractors.

An interactive model based on biological stigmergy lies at the heart of these systems. The requirement of musical diversity is met by ensuring that attractors and particles have local neighbourhoods of influence, and that attractors have a finite life-time. The aim of the swarm is to find attractors and the musical behaviour of the system is a sonification of this search. This picture arises from the observation that improvisation might be regarded as an exploration of the possibilities contained within the system, whether human or artificial.

An artificial improviser or live algorithm, must be able to generate rich timbres and textures if it is to participate in the activity of free improvisation. Granular synthesis, which is capable of producing very complex and detailed textures, is a natural choice. A clear advantage of granulation, which packs sampled rather than synthetic sound into grains, is that the raw material is already intricate and varied. Overall, the purpose of the swarm is to mutate, fragment and otherwise transform sampled sound. The organisation of swarming particles about one another and about attractors is directly related to the perceived behaviour of the autonomous system as a whole, inviting creative involvement.

Swarm Techtiles deploys self-organised criticality as a means of determining which particles render local micro-textures into sound, and when this happens. The result is that the distribution of grain cloud sizes is power-law. Such distributions have been shown to describe musical attributes in non-improvised music, suggesting that attributes of improvised music (e.g., texture, as measured in grain density) might have similar properties. Swarm Techtiles actually uses social criticality; the communication network connecting neighbours does not depend on spatial positions, ensuring that micro-textures throughout the landscape can be rendered.

Future research might take one of many directions, since the ultimate potential of these systems is far from understood. For example, the omission of memory, and hence of learning, prominent in human endeavour, is missing. Various mechanisms for the inclusion of memory are immediately apparent. One idea would be to introduce pheromone trails, familiar from insect swarms; particles might be inclined to follow paths that they have previously followed. This would introduce repetition, familiar in human music. The evaporation of such trails could be employed to prohibit excessive similarity. A notion of history could profitably be introduced into Swarm Techtiles. Previous sheets of woven sound could be retained and stored in a block. Motion of the swarm through this block would uncover textures previously encountered, linking temporally separated events.

Despite the complexity of the systems described in this chapter, a very simple intuition remains intact: a connection between the spontaneous, flickering behaviour of swarms and the extemporary, free-form musical patterning of free improvisation.

References

1. Blackwell, T.M., Young, M. (2004). Swarm granulator. In Raidl, G.R., ed.: *Applications of Evolutionary Computing.* Vol. 3005 of LNCS. Springer, 399–408
2. Grassé, P. (1959). La reconstruction du nid et les coordinations inter-individuelles chez bellicosi-termes natalensis et cubitermes sp. la theorie de la stigmergie: essai d'interpretation des termites constructeurs. *Insect Societies*, **6**: 41–83
3. Blackwell, T.M., Jefferies, J. (2005). Swarm tech-tiles. In Rothlauf, R., ed.: *Applications of Evolutionary Computing.* Vol. 3449 of LNCS. Springer, 468–251
4. Kennedy, J., Eberhart, R. (1995). Particle swarm optimization. In: *Proceedings of the 1995 IEEE International Conference on Neural Networks*, 1942–1948
5. Rowe, R., Singer, E. (1997). Two highly-related real-time music and graphics performance systems. In: *Proc. Int'l Computer Music Conf.*, 133–140
6. Spector, L., Klein, J. (1997). Complex adaptive music systems in the breve simulation environment. In Bilotta, et al., eds.: *8th Int'l Conf. on the Simulation and Synthesis of Living Systems.* University of New South Wales, 167–170

7. Blackwell, T.M., Bentley, P. (2002). Improvised music with swarms. In: *Congress on Evolutionary Computation*, 1462–1467
8. Unemi, T., Bisig, D. (2005). Playing by interaction among two flocking species and a human. In: *Proc. of the Third Int'l Conf. on Generative Systems in Electronic Arts*, 171–179
9. Blackwell, T.M. (2006). `http://art-of-artficial-evolution.doc.gold.ac.uk/`
10. C.Reynolds (1987). Flocks, herds and schools: a distributed behavioral model. *Computer Graphics*, **21**: 25–34
11. I. Couzin, K. Krause, G.R.G., Franks, N. (2002). Collective memory and spatial sorting in animal groups. *J. Theor. Biol.*, **218**: 1–11
12. E.Bonabeau, M., G.Theraulaz (1999). *Swarm Intelligence.* Oxford University Press
13. J. Kennedy, R., Y.Shi (2001). *Swarm Intelligence.* Morgan Kaufmann
14. Clerc, M. (2006). *Particle Swarm Optimization.* ISTE publishing company
15. Blackwell, T.M., Bentley, P.J. (2002). Dynamic search with charged swarms. In Langdon, W.B., et al., eds.: *Genetic and Evolutionary Computation Conference.* Morgan Kaufmann, 19–26
16. Bourg, D., Seeman, G. (2004). *AI for Game Developers.* O'Reilly
17. Jost, E. (1974). *Free Jazz.* Da Capo
18. Bailey, D. (1992). *Improvisation: its Nature and Practice in Music.* The British Library Sound Archive, London
19. Blackwell, T.M., Young, M. (2004). Self-organised music. *Organised Sound 9*, **9**: 123–136
20. Theraulaz, G., Bonabeau, E. (1995). Coordination on distributed building. *Science*, **269**: 686–688
21. Blackwell, T.M., Young, M. (2005). Live algorithms. *Society for the Study of Artificial Intelligence and Simulation of Behaviour Quarterly*, **122**: 7
22. Gabor, D. (1947). Acoustical quanta and the theory hearing. *Nature*, **159**: 591–594
23. Miranda, E. (1998). *Computer Sound Synthesis for the Electronic Musician.* Focal Press
24. Roads, C. (2001). *Microsound.* CUP
25. R. Jain, R. Kasturi, J.S. (1995). *Machine Vision.* McGraw-Hill
26. Manaris, B., Vaughan, D., Wagner, C., Romero, J., Davis, R. (2003). Evolutionary music and the zipf-mandelbrot law: developing fitness functions for pleasant music. In Rothlauf, R., et al., eds.: *EvoWorkshops.* Vol. 2611 of LNCS. Springer, 522–534
27. Bak, P. (1996). *How Nature Works: The Science of Self-Organized Criticality.* Copernicus Press
28. Bak, P., Tang, C., Wiesenfeld, K. (1987). Self-organized criticality: an explanation of the 1/f noise. *Phys. Rev. Lett.*, **59**: 381–384
29. Lovbjerg, M., Krink, T. (2002). Extending particle swarm optimizers with self-organized criticality. In: *Proc. Congress on Evolutionary Computation.* IEEE, 1588–1593

6

Evolutionary Computing for Expressive Music Performance

Rafael Ramirez, Amaury Hazan, Jordi Marine, and Xavier Serra

Pompeu Fabra University
Music Technology Group
Ocata 1, 08003 Barcelona, Spain
{rafael,ahazan,jmarine,xserra}@iua.upf.edu

Summary. We describe an evolutionary approach to one of the most challenging problems in computer music: modeling the knowledge applied by a musician when performing a score of a piece in order to produce an expressive performance of the piece. We extract a set of acoustic features from jazz recordings, thereby providing a symbolic representation of the musician's expressive performance. By applying an evolutionary algorithm to the symbolic representation, we obtain an interpretable expressive performance computational model. We use the model to generate automatically performances with the timing and energy expressiveness of a human saxophonist.

6.1 Introduction

Evolutionary computation is being considered with growing interest in musical applications. One of the music domains in which evolutionary computation has made the most impact is music composition. A large number of evolutionary systems for composing musical material have been proposed (e.g., [1, 2, 3, 4]). In addition to music composition, evolutionary computing has been considered in music improvisation applications where an evolutionary algorithm typically models a musician improvising (e.g., [5]). Nevertheless, very little research focusing on the use of evolutionary computation for expressive performance analysis has been reported (e.g., [6]).

In the past, expressive performance has been studied using different approaches (e.g., [7]). The main approaches to empirically study expressive performance have been based on statistical analysis, mathematical modelling, and analysis-by-synthesis. In all these approaches, a person is responsible for devising a theory or a mathematical model which captures different aspects of musical expressive performance. The theory or model is later tested on real performance data in order to determine its accuracy. In this chapter we describe an approach to investigate musical expressive performance based on evolutionary computation. Instead of manually modelling expressive performance and testing the model on real musical data, we let a computer execute a *sequential-covering genetic algorithm* to automatically discover regularities and performance principles from real performance data: audio recordings of jazz standards. The algorithm combines sequential-covering [8] and genetic algorithms [9]. The sequential component of the algorithm incrementally constructs a set of rules by learning new rules one at a time, removing the positive examples covered by the latest rule before attempting to learn the next rule. The genetic component of the algorithm learns each of the new rules by applying a genetic algorithm. The algorithm provides an interpretable specification of the expressive principles applied to an interpretation of a piece of music and, at the same time, provides a generative model of expressive performance, i.e., a model capable of generating a computer music performance with the timing and energy expressiveness that characterizes human-generated music.

The use of evolutionary techniques for modeling expressive music performance provides a number of potential advantages over other supervised learning algorithms. By applying our evolutionary algorithm, it is possible to (1) explore and analyze the induced expressive model as it "evolves", (2) guide and interact with the evolution of the model, and (3) obtain different models resulting from different executions of the algorithm. This last point is very relevant to the task of modeling expressive music performance since it is desirable to obtain a nondeterministic model capturing the different possible interpretations a performer may produce for a given piece.

The rest of the chapter is organized as follows: Section 6.2 reports on related work. Section 6.3 describes how we extract a set of acoustic features from the audio recordings in order to obtain a symbolic description of the different expressive parameters embedded in the recordings. In Sect. 6.4 we describe our evolutionary approach for inducing an expressive music performance computational model; and finally Sect. 6.5 presents some conclusions and indicates some areas of future research.

6.2 Related Work

Evolutionary computation has been considered with growing interest in musical applications [10]. A large number of experimental systems using evolutionary techniques to generate musical compositions have been proposed, including Cellular Automata Music [11], a Cellular Automata Music Workstation [12], CAMUS [13], MOE [14], GenDash [15], CAMUS 3D [16], Vox Populi [17], Synthetic Harmonies [18], Living Melodies [2] and Genophone [19]. Composition systems based on genetic algorithms generally follow the standard genetic algorithm approach for evolving musical elements such as melodies, rhythms and chords. Thus, such composition systems share the core approach with the one presented in this chapter. For example, Vox Populi [17] evolves populations of chords of four notes, each of which is represented as a 7-bit string. The genotype of a chord therefore consists of a string of 28 bits (e.g., 1001011 0010011 0010110 0010101) and the genetic operations of crossover and mutation are applied to these strings in order to produce new generations of the population. The fitness function is based on three criteria: melodic fitness, harmonic fitness and voice range fitness. The melodic fitness is evaluated by comparing the notes of the chord to a reference value provided by the user, the harmonic fitness takes into account the consonance of the chord, and the voice range fitness measures whether or not the notes of the chord are within a range also specified by the user. Evolutionary computation has also been considered for improvisation applications such as [5], where a genetic algorithm-based model of a novice jazz musician learning to improvise was developed. The system evolves a set of melodic ideas that are mapped to notes considering the chord progression being played. The fitness function can be altered by the feedback of the human playing with the system.

Nevertheless, very few works focusing on the use of evolutionary computation for expressive performance analysis have been published. In the context of the ProMusic project, Grachten et al. [6] optimize the weights of edit distance operations by a genetic algorithm in order to annotate a human jazz performance. They present an enhancement of edit-distance-based music performance annotation. In order to reduce the number of errors in automatic performance annotation, they use an evolutionary approach to optimize the parameter values of cost functions of the edit distance. In another study, Hazan et al. [20] propose an evolutionary generative regression tree model for expressive rendering of MIDI performances. Madsen at al. [21] present an approach to exploring similarities in classical music piano performances based on simple measurements of timing and intensity in 12 recordings of a Schubert piano piece. The work presented in this chapter is an extension to our previous work [22] where we induce expressive performance classification rules using a genetic algorithm. Here, in addition to considering classification rules, we consider regression rules, and while in [22] rules are independently induced by the genetic algorithm, here we apply a sequential-covering algorithm in order to cover the whole example space.

There have been several approaches for addressing expressive music performance using machine learning techniques other than evolutionary techniques. The work most related to the research presented in this chapter are those by Ramirez et al. [23, 24] and Lopez de Mantaras et al. [25].

Lopez de Mantaras et al. report on SaxEx, a performance system capable of generating expressive solo performances in jazz. Their system is based on case-based reasoning, a type of analogical reasoning where problems are solved by reusing the solutions of similar, previously solved problems. In order to generate expressive solo performances, the case-based reasoning system retrieves, from a memory containing expressive interpretations, those notes that are *similar* to the input inexpressive notes. The case memory contains information about metrical strength, note duration, and so on, and uses this information to retrieve the appropriate notes. However, their system does not allow one to examine or understand the way it makes predictions.

Ramirez et al. explore and compare different machine learning techniques for inducing both, an *interpretable* expressive performance model (characterized by a set of rules) and a *generative* expressive performance model. Based on this, they describe a performance system capable of generating expressive monophonic jazz performances and providing "explanations" of the expressive transformations it performs. The work described in this chapter has similar objectives but by using a genetic algorithm it incorporates some desirable properties: (1) the induced model may be explored and analyzed while it is "evolving", (2) it is possible to guide the evolution of the model in a natural way, and (3) by repeatedly executing the algorithm different models are obtained. In the context of expressive music performance modeling, these properties are very relevant.

With the exception of the work by Lopez de Mantaras et al. and Ramirez et al., most of the research in expressive performance using machine learning techniques has focused on classical piano music where the tempo of the performed pieces is not constant and melody alterations are not permitted (in classical music melody alterations are considered performance errors). Thus, in these works the focus is on global tempo and energy transformations while we are interested in note-level tempo and energy transformations as well as in melody ornamentations which are a very important expressive resource in jazz.

Widmer [26, 27] reports on the task of discovering general rules of expressive classical piano performance from real performance data via inductive machine learning. The performance data used for the study are MIDI recordings of 13 piano sonatas by Mozart performed by a skilled pianist. In addition to these data, the music score is also coded. The resulting substantial data consists of information about the nominal note onsets, duration, metrical information and annotations. When trained on the data an inductive rule-learning algorithm discovers a small set of quite simple classification rules [26] that predict a large number of the note-level choices of the pianist.

Tobudic et al. [28] describe a relational instance-based approach to the problem of learning to apply expressive tempo and dynamics variations to a piece of classical music at different levels of the phrase hierarchy. The different phrases of a piece and the relations among them are represented in first-order logic. The description of the musical scores through predicates (e.g., *contains(ph1, ph2)*) provides the background knowledge. The training examples are encoded by another predicate whose arguments encode information about the way the phrase was played by the musician. Their learning algorithm recognizes similar phrases from the training set and applies their expressive patterns to a new piece.

Other inductive machine learning approaches to rule learning in music and musical analysis include [29, 30, 31, 32]. In [29], Dovey analyzes piano performances of Rachmaninoff pieces using inductive logic programming and extracts rules underlying them. In [30], Van Baelen extends Dovey's work and attempts to discover regularities that could be used to generate MIDI information derived from the musical analysis of the piece. In [31], Morales reports research on learning counterpoint rules. The goal of the reported system is to obtain standard counterpoint rules from examples of counterpoint music pieces and basic music knowledge from traditional music. In [32], Igarashi et al. describe the analysis of respiration during music performance by inductive logic programming. Using a respiration sensor, respiration during a cello performance was measured and rules were extracted from the data together with knowledge such as harmonic progression and bowing direction.

There are a number of approaches which address expressive performance without using data mining techniques. One of the first attempts to provide a computer system with music expressiveness is that of Johnson [33]. Johnson developed a rule-based expert system to determine expressive tempo and articulation for Bach's fugues from *The Well-Tempered Clavier*. The rules were obtained from two expert performers.

A long-term effort in expressive performance modeling is the work of the KTH group [34, 35, 36]. Their *Director Musices* system incorporates rules for tempo, dynamics and articulation transformations. The rules are obtained from both theoretical musical knowledge and experimentally from training using an analysis-by-synthesis approach. The rules are divided into *differentiation rules* which enhance the differences between scale tones, *grouping rules* which specify what tones belong together, and *ensemble rules* which synchronize the voices in an ensemble.

Canazza et al. [37] developed a system to analyze the relationship between the musician's expressive intentions and her performance. The analysis reveals two expressive dimensions, one related to energy (dynamics), and another related to kinetics (rubato).

6.3 Melodic Description

In this section, we summarize how we extract a symbolic description from the monophonic recordings of performances of jazz standards. We need this symbolic representation in order to apply a sequential-covering genetic algorithm to the data. Our interest is to model note-level transformations such as onset deviations, duration transformations and energy variations. Thus, descriptors providing note-level information are of particular interest in this context.

6.3.1 Algorithms for Feature Extraction

Figure 6.1 represents the steps performed to obtain a melodic description from audio. First of all, we perform a spectral analysis of a portion of sound, the analysis frame, whose size is a parameter of the algorithm. This spectral analysis consists of multiplying the audio frame with an appropriate analysis window and performing a Discrete Fourier Transform (DFT) to obtain its spectrum. In this case, we use a frame width of 46 ms, an overlap factor of 50%, and a Keiser-Bessel 25 dB window. Then, we perform a note segmentation using low-level descriptor values. Once the note boundaries are known, the note descriptors are computed from the low-level and the fundamental frequency values.

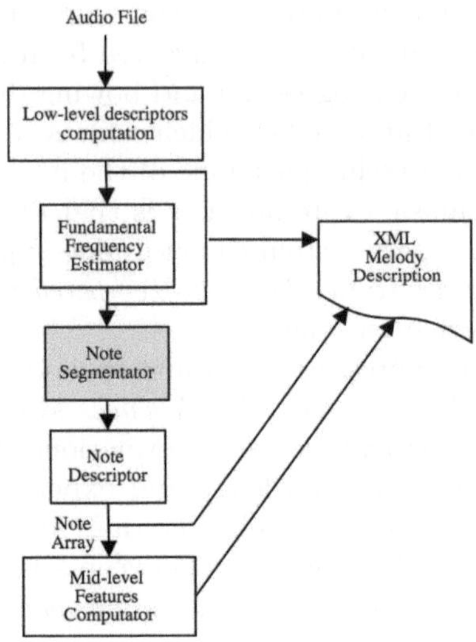

Fig. 6.1. Block diagram of the melody descriptor

6.3.2 Low-level Descriptors Computation

The main low-level descriptors used to characterize expressive performance are instantaneous energy and fundamental frequency.

Energy Computation

The energy descriptor is computed on the spectral domain, using the values of the amplitude spectrum at each analysis frame. In addition, energy is computed in different frequency bands as defined in [38], and these values are used by the algorithm for note segmentation.

Fundamental Frequency Estimation

For the estimation of the instantaneous fundamental frequency we use a harmonic-matching model derived from the two-way mismatch (TWM) procedure [39]. For each fundamental frequency candidate, mismatches between the harmonics generated and the measured partials frequencies are averaged over a fixed subset of the available partials. A weighting scheme is used to make the procedure robust to the presence of noise or absence of certain partials in the spectral data. The solution presented in [39] employs two mismatch error calculations. The first one is based on the frequency difference between each partial in the measured sequence and its nearest neighbor in the predicted sequence. The second is based on the mismatch between each harmonic in the predicted sequence and its nearest partial neighbor in the measured sequence. This two-way mismatch helps us avoid octave errors by applying a penalty for partials that are present in the measured data but are not predicted, and for partials whose presence is predicted but which do not actually appear in the measured sequence. The TWM procedure has also the benefit that the effect of any spurious components can be counteracted by the presence of uncorrupted partials in the same frame.

Figure 6.2 shows the block diagram for the fundamental frequency estimator following a harmonic-matching approach. First, we perform a spectral analysis of all the windowed frames, as explained above. Second, we detect the prominent spectral peaks. These spectral peaks are defined as the local maxima in the spectra with magnitude greater than a threshold. The spectral peaks are compared to a harmonic series, and a TWM error is computed for each fundamental frequency candidate. The candidate with the minimum error is chosen to be the fundamental frequency estimate.

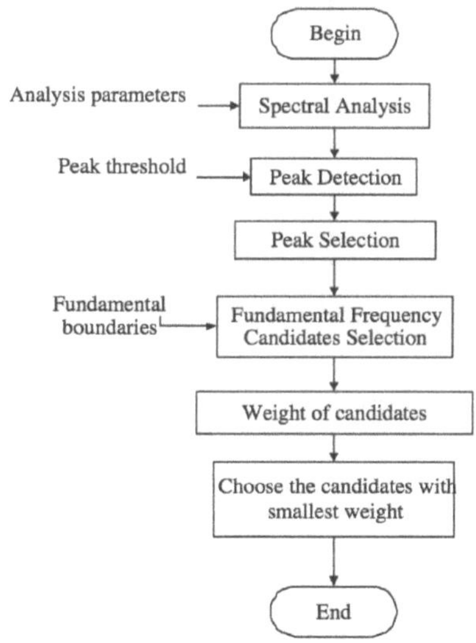

Fig. 6.2. Flow diagram of the TWM algorithm

After a first test of this implementation, some improvements to the original algorithm were added to deal with some of the algorithm's shortcoming.

- Peak selection: a peak selection routine has been added in order to eliminate spectral peaks corresponding to noise. The peak selection is done according to a masking threshold around each of the maximum magnitude peaks. The form of the masking threshold depends on the peak amplitude, and uses three different slopes depending on the frequency distance to the peak frequency.
- Context awareness: we take into account previous values of the fundamental frequency estimation and instrument dependencies to obtain a more adapted result.
- Noise gate: a noise gate based on some low-level signal descriptors is applied to detect silences, so that the estimation is only performed in non-silent segments of the sound.

6.3.3 Note Segmentation

Note segmentation is performed using a set of frame descriptors, which are fundamental frequency and energy (in different frequency bands). Energy onsets are first detected following a band-wise algorithm that uses psycho-acoustic knowledge [38]. In the second step, fundamental frequency transitions are also detected. Finally, both results are merged to find the note boundaries (onset and offset information).

6.3.4 Note Descriptor Computation

We compute note descriptors using the note boundaries and the low-level descriptor values. The low-level descriptors associated with a note segment are computed by averaging the frame values within it. Pitch histograms have been used to compute the pitch note and the fundamental frequency that represents each note segment, as found in [40]. This is done to avoid taking into account mistaken frames in the fundamental frequency mean computation.

First, frequency values are converted into cents, by the following formula:

$$c = 1200 \cdot \frac{\log\left(\frac{f}{f_{ref}}\right)}{log2} \tag{6.1}$$

where $f_{ref} = 8.176$. Then, we define histograms with bins of 100 cents and hop size of 5 cents and we compute the maximum of the histogram to identify the note pitch. Finally, we compute the frequency mean for all the points that belong to the histogram. The MIDI pitch is computed by quantization of this fundamental frequency mean over the frames within the note limits.

6.4 Learning the Expressive Performance Model

In this section, we describe our inductive approach for learning an expressive music performance model from performances of jazz standards. Our aim is to obtain a model capable of automatically generating a music performance with the expressiveness that characterizes human-generated music. In other words, we intend to generate automatically human-like expressive performances of a piece given an inexpressive description of the piece (e.g., a textual description of its score).

We understand that not all the expressive transformations performed by a musician can be predicted at a local note level. Musicians perform music considering a number of abstract structures (e.g., musical phrases) which makes expressive performance a multilevel phenomenon. In this context, our aim is to obtain a computational model of expressive performance which combines note-level and structure-level information. As a first step in this direction, we have based our music analysis on the *implication/realization model*, proposed by Narmour [41, 42].

6.4.1 Musical Analysis

The implication/realization model is a theory of perception and cognition of melodies. The theory states that a melodic music line continuously causes listeners to generate expectations of how the melody should continue. An individual's expectations are motivated by two types of sources: innate and learned. According to Narmour, on one hand we are all born with innate information which suggests to us how a particular melody should continue. On the other hand, learned factors also influence our expectations, and these factors are a result of exposure to music throughout our lives and our familiarity with music styles and particular melodies.

Any two consecutively perceived notes constitute a melodic interval, and if this interval is not conceived as complete, it is an *implicative interval*, i.e., an interval that implies a subsequent interval with certain characteristics. That is to say, some notes are more likely than others to follow the implicative interval. Two main principles recognized by Narmour concern *registral direction* and *intervallic difference*. The principle of registral direction states that small intervals imply the same registral direction (a small upward interval implies another upward interval, and analogously for downward intervals), and large intervals imply a change in registral direction (a large upward interval implies a downward interval, and analogously for downward intervals). The principle of intervallic difference states that a small (five semitones or less) interval implies a similarly sized interval (plus or minus two semitones), and a large interval (seven semitones or more) implies a smaller interval. Based on these two principles, melodic patterns or groups can be identified that either satisfy or violate the implication as predicted by the principles. Figure 6.3 shows prototypical Narmour structures.

A note in a melody often belongs to more than one structure. Thus, a description of a melody as a sequence of Narmour structures consists of a list of overlapping structures. We parse each melody in the training data in order to automatically generate an implication/realization analysis of the pieces. Figure 6.4 shows the analysis for a fragment of *All of me*.

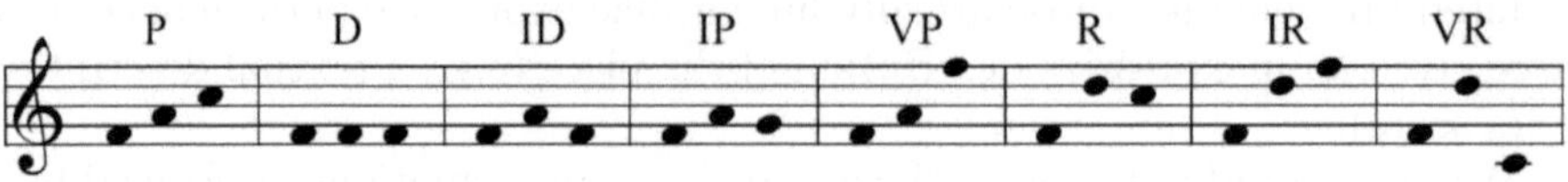

Fig. 6.3. Prototypical Narmour structures

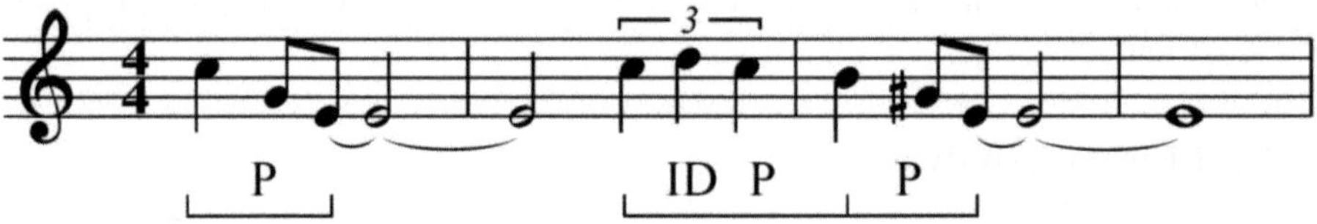

Fig. 6.4. Narmour analysis of *All of Me*

6.4.2 Training Data

The training data used in our experimental investigations are monophonic recordings of four jazz standards (*Body and Soul*, *Once I Loved*, *Like Someone in Love* and *Up Jumped Spring*) performed by a professional musician at 11 different tempos around the nominal tempo. For each piece, the nominal tempo was determined by the musician as the most natural and comfortable tempo to interpret the piece. Also, for each piece, the musician identified the fastest and slowest tempos at which a piece could be reasonably interpreted. Interpretations were recorded at regular intervals around the nominal tempo (five faster and five slower) within the fastest-slowest tempo limits. The data set is composed of 4,360 performed notes. Each note in the training data is annotated with its corresponding performed characteristics and a number of attributes representing both properties of the note itself and aspects of the context in which the note appears. Information about the note includes note duration and the note metrical position within a bar, while information about its melodic context includes performed tempo, information on neighboring notes, and the Narmour structure in which the note appears (we focused on the Narmour group in which the note appears in the third position since this is where it provides the best indicator of the degree to which the note is expected).

6.4.3 Learning Task

In this chapter, we are concerned with note-level expressive transformations, in particular transformations of note duration, onset and energy. Initially, for each expressive transformation, we approach the problem as a classification problem, for example, for note duration transformation we classify each note to belong to one of the classes *lengthen, shorten* and *same*. Once we obtain a classification mechanism capable of classifying all notes in our training data, we apply a regression algorithm in order to produce a numerical value representing the amount of transformation to be applied to a particular note. The complete algorithm is detailed in Sect. 6.4.4.

The performance classes that interest us are *lengthen*, *shorten*, and *same* for duration transformation; *advance*, *delay* and *same* for onset deviation; *soft*, *loud* and *same* for energy; and *ornamentation* and *none* for note alteration. A note is considered to belong to class *lengthen* if its performed duration is 20% (or more) longer than its nominal duration, for example, its duration according to the score. Class *shorten* is defined analogously. A note is considered to be in class *advance* if its performed onset is 5% (or more) of a bar earlier than its nominal onset. Class *delay* is defined analogously. A note is considered to be in class *loud* if it is played louder than its predecessor and louder than the average level of the piece. Class *soft* is defined analogously. We decided to set these boundaries after experimenting with different ratios. The main idea was to guarantee that a note classified, for instance, as lengthen was purposely lengthened by the performer and was not the result of a performance inexactitude. A note is considered to belong to class *ornamentation* if a note or group of notes not specified in the score has been introduced in the performance to embellish the note in the melody, and to class *none* otherwise.

6.4.4 Algorithm

We applied a genetic sequential-covering algorithm to the training data. Roughly, the algorithm incrementally constructs a set of rules by learning new rules one at a time, removing the positive examples covered by the latest rule before attempting to learn the next rule. Rules are learned using a genetic algorithm evolving a population of rules with the usual mutation and crossover operations.

For each class of interest (lengthen, shorten, same), we collect the rules with best fitness during the evolution of the population. For obtaining rules for a particular class of interest (e.g., lengthen), we consider as negatives the examples of the other two complementary classes (shorten and same). It is worth mentioning that although the test was running over 40 generations, the fittest rules were obtained around the twentieth generation.

In the case of note duration, onset and energy, once we obtain the set of rules covering all the training examples, for each rule we apply linear regression to the examples covered by it in order to obtain a linear equation predicting a numerical value. This leads to a set of rules producing a numerical prediction, not just a nominal class prediction. In the case of note alteration we do not compute a numerical value. Instead we simply keep the set of examples covered by the rule. Later, for generation, we apply a standard k-nearest neighbor algorithm to select one of the examples covered by the rule and adapt the selected example to the new melodic context, i.e., we transpose the ornamental note(s) to fit the melody key and ornamented note pitch. The algorithm is as follows:

```
GeneticSeqCovAlg(Class,Fitness,Threshold,p,r,m,Examples)
Pos = examples which belong to Class
Neg = examples which do not belong to Class
Learned_rules = {}
While Pos do
      P = generate p hypothesis at random
      for each h in P,
         compute fitness(h)
      while max(fitness(h)) < Threshold do
         create a new generation Pnew
         P = Pnew
         for each h in P,
            compute fitness(h)
      Return the hypothesis Newrule from P that
                                        has the highest fitness
      Rpos = members of Pos covered by NewRule
      compute PredictedValue(Rpos)
      NumericNewRule = NewRule with Class replaced by
                                               Regression(Rpos)
      Learned_rules = Learned_rules + NumericNewrule
      Pos = Pos - Rpos
Return Learned_rules
```

The outer loop learns new rules one at a time, removing the positive examples covered by the latest rule before attempting to learn the next rule. The inner loop performs a genetic search through the space of possible rules in search of a rule with high accuracy. At each iteration, the outer loop adds a new rule to its disjunctive hypothesis, `Learned_rules`. The effect of each new rule is to generalize the current disjunctive hypothesis (i.e., to increase the number of instances it classifies as positive) by adding a new disjunct. At this level, the search is a specific-to-general search starting with the most specific hypothesis (i.e., the empty disjunction) and terminating when the hypothesis is sufficiently general to cover all training examples. `NumericNewRule` is a rule where the consequent `Regression(Rpos)` is a linear equation

$$X = w_0 + w_1a_1 + w_2a_2 + \cdots + w_ka_k$$

where X is the predicted value expressed as a linear combination of the attributes $a_1, \ldots a_k$ of the training examples with predetermined weights

$w_0, \ldots w_k$. The weights are calculated using the set of positive examples covered by the rule `Rpos` by linear regression. In the case of note alteration, i.e., when dealing with ornamentations, `Regression(Rpos)` is simply the set examples covered by the rule.

The inner loop performs a finer-grained search to determine the exact form of each new rule. This is done by applying a genetic algorithm with the usual parameters r, m and p, specifying the fraction of the parent population replaced by crossover, the mutation rate, and the population size, respectively. The exact values for these parameters are presented in Table 6.1. In the inner loop, a new generation is created as follows:

1. **Select:** probabilistically select $(1-r)p$ members of P to add to P_s. The probability of $Pr(h_i)$ of selecting hypothesis h_i from P is

$$Pr(hi) = \frac{Fitness(hi)}{\Sigma(h_j)} \qquad (1 \leq j \leq p).$$

2. **Crossover:** probabilistically select $r \times p/2$ pairs of hypothesis from P (according to $Pr(h_i)$ above). For each pair, produce an offspring by applying the crossover operator (see below) and add it to P_s.
3. **Mutate:** Choose $m\%$ of the members of P_s with uniform probability and apply the mutation operator (see below).

Table 6.1. Parameter values of the genetic algorithm

Parameter	Identifier	Value
Crossover rate	r	0.8
Mutation rate	m	0.05
Population size	p	200

Hypothesis representation. The hypothesis space of rule preconditions consists of a conjunction of a fixed set of attributes. Each rule is represented as a bit-string as follows: the previous and next note duration are represented each by five bits (much shorter, shorter, same, longer and much longer), previous and next note pitch each by five bits (much lower, lower, same, higher and much higher), metrical strength by five bits (very weak, weak, medium, strong and very strong), tempo by three bits (slow, nominal and fast) and Narmour groups by three bits (coding the eight groups in Fig. 6.3). For example, in our representation the rule

"if the previous note duration is much longer and its pitch is the same and it is in a very strong metrical position and the current note appears in Narmour group R then lengthen the duration of the current note"

is coded as the binary string

00001 11111 00100 11111 00001 111 110 001

The exact meanings of the adjectives which the particular bits represent are as follows: previous and next note durations are considered much shorter if the duration is less than half of the current note, shorter if it is shorter than the current note but longer than its half, and same if it is the same as the current note. Much longer and longer are defined analogously. Previous and next note pitches are considered much lower if the pitch is lower by a minor third or more, lower if the pitch is within a minor third, and same if it is the same. Higher and much higher are defined analogously. The note's metrical position is very strong, strong, medium, weak, and very weak if it is on the first beat of the bar, on the third beat of the bar, on the second or fourth beat, offbeat, and in none of the previous, respectively. The piece is played at slow, nominal, and fast tempos if it is performed at a speed slower than 15% or more of the nominal tempo (i.e., the tempo identified as the most natural by the performer), within 15% of the nominal tempo, and faster than 15% of the nominal tempo, respectively. In the case of the note's Narmour groups we decided to code only one Narmour group for each note. That is, instead of specifying all the possible Narmour groups for a note, we select the one in which the note appears in the third position (if there is no such group, we consider one in which the note appears either in the first or the second position, in that order).

Genetic operators. We use the standard single-point crossover and mutation operators with two restrictions. In order to perform a crossover operation of two parents the crossover points are chosen at random as long as they are on the attribute substring boundaries. Similarly, the mutation points are chosen randomly as long as they do not generate inconsistent rule strings; for example, only one class can be predicted so exactly one 1 can appear in the last three-bit substring.

Fitness function. The fitness of each hypothesized rule is based on its classification accuracy over the training data. In particular, the function used to measure fitness is

$$\frac{tp^{\alpha}}{(tp+fp)}$$

where *tp* is the number of true positives, *fp* is the number of false positives, and α is a constant which controls the true positives to false positives ratio. Often α is set to one, which results in the standard fitness function $tp/(tp+fp)$. This fitness function favors individuals covering a small number of true positive and zero false positives (resulting in a fitness value of one) over individuals covering a large number of true positives and one false positive (resulting in a fitness value of less than one). In our application this is an undesirable property of the fitness function since we are interested in inducing general expressive performance rules covering a large number of examples (possibly including a small number of false positives). Thus, in our algorithm we have set $\alpha = 1.15$ which, for our application, is a good compromise between coverage and accuracy.

6.4.5 Results

It is always difficult to evaluate formally a model which captures subjective knowledge, as it is the case with an expressive music performance model. The ultimate evaluation may consist of listening to the transformations the model performs. In the DVD which accompanies this book, we have included samples of transformations performed by the model (inexpressive transcriptions of a musical score and their corresponding expressive versions as generated by our model).

Alternatively, the model may be evaluated by comparing the model's transformation predictions and the actual transformations performed by the musician. Figures 6.5 and 6.6 show the note-by-note duration ratio predicted by two different models induced by different executions of the algorithm and compare them with the actual duration ratio in the recording. Similar results were obtained for the predicted onset deviation and energy variation. As illustrated by Figs. 6.5 and 6.6, the induced model seems to accurately capture the musician's expressive performance transformations (despite the relatively small amount of training data).

The correlation coefficients for the onset, duration and energy submodels are 0.80, 0.84 and 0.86, respectively. These numbers were obtained by performing a ten-fold cross-validation on the data. At each fold, we removed the performances similar to the ones selected in the test set, i.e., the performances of the same piece at tempos within 10% of performances in the test set.

We ran the sequential-covering genetic algorithm 20 times in order to observe the differences between the correlation coefficients of different runs. We observed no substantial differences. As a result of executing the genetic algorithm several times we obtained different models. These models clearly share similar performance trends but at the same time generate slightly different expressive performances.

We allowed the user to influence the construction of the expressive model by imposing "readability constraints" on the shape of the rules. That is, the user was able to restrict the rule format (for example, allow only some bit sequences) during the evolution in order to enhance the interpretability of the induced rules. We examined some of the classification rules the algorithm induced (before replacing the class with the numerical predicted value). We observed rules of different types. Some focus on features of the note itself and depend on the performance tempo while others focus on the Narmour analysis and are independent of the performance tempo. Rules referring to the local

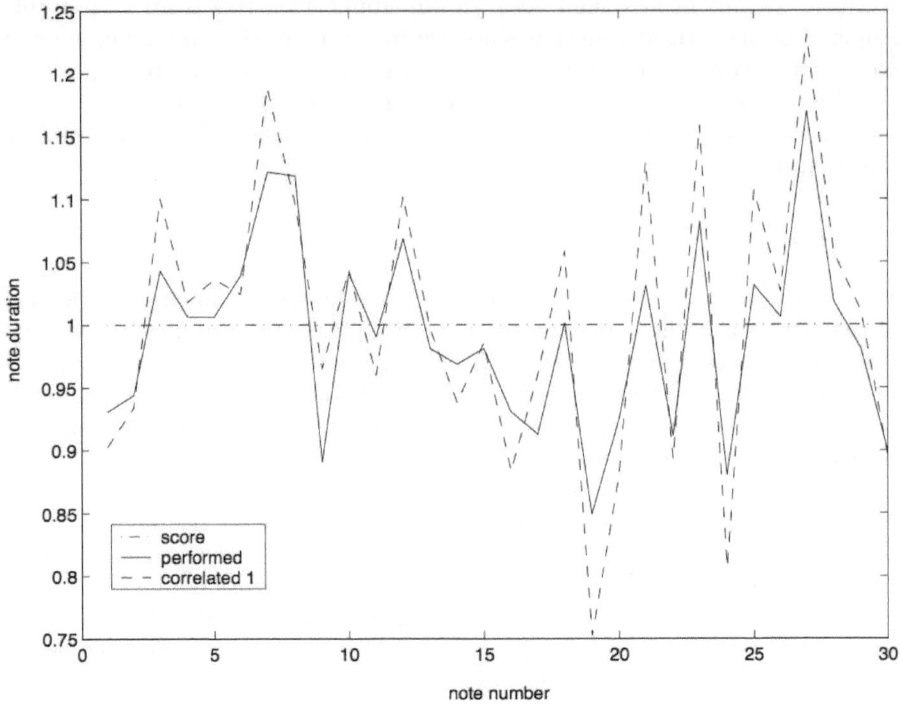

Fig. 6.5. Correlation between model predicted duration values and the actual performed values in *Body and Soul* at a tempo of 65

context of a note, i.e., rules classifying a note solely in terms of the timing, pitch and metrical strength of the note and its neighbors, as well as compound rules that refer to both the local context and the Narmour structure, were discovered. In order to illustrate the types of rules found we present some examples of duration rules:

RULE1: 11111 01110 11110 00110 00011 010 010 001

"In nominal tempo, if the duration of the next note is similar and the note is in a strong metrical position and the note appears in a D Narmour group then lengthen the current note."

RULE2: 00111 00111 00011 01101 10101 111 111 100

"If the previous and next notes durations are longer than (or equal to) the duration of the current note and the pitch of the previous note is higher then shorten the current note."

RULE3: 01000 11100 01111 01110 00111 111 111 010

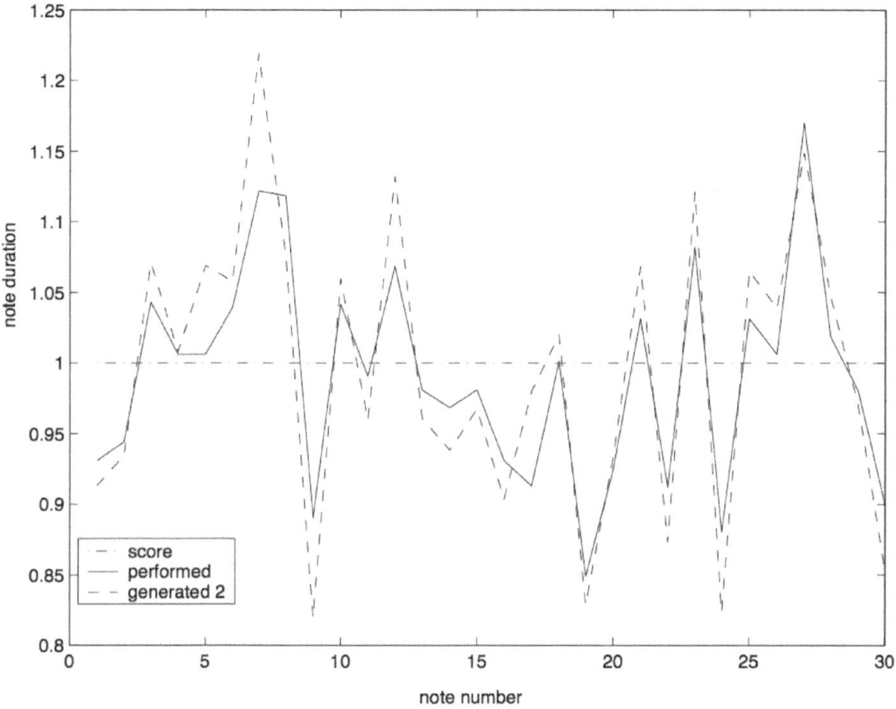

Fig. 6.6. Correlation between model predicted duration values and the actual performed values in *Body and Soul* at a tempo of 65

"If the previous note is slightly shorter and not much lower in pitch, and the next note is not longer and has a similar pitch (within a minor third), and the current note is not on a weak metrical position, then the duration of the current note remains the same (i.e., there is no lengthening or shortening)."

These simple rules turn out to be very accurate: the first rule predicts 92%, the second rule predicts 100% and the third rule predicts 90% of the relevant cases. Some of the rules turn out to be of musical interest; for instance, RULE1 above states that a note is to be lengthened if the two previous notes have the same pitch (i.e., appear in a D Narmour group) and it has duration similar to the following note. This rule may represent the performer's intention to differentiate the last note of a sequence of notes with the same pitch.

6.5 Conclusion

This chapter describes an evolutionary computation approach for learning an expressive performance model from recordings of jazz standards by a skilled saxophone player. Our objective has been to find a computational model which predicts how a particular note in a particular context should be played (for example, longer or shorter than its nominal duration). In order to induce the expressive performance model, we have extracted a set of acoustic features from the recordings, resulting in a symbolic representation of the performed pieces, and then applied a sequential-covering genetic algorithm to the symbolic data and information about the context in which the data appear. Despite the relatively small amount of training data, the induced model seems to accurately capture the musician's expressive performance transformations. In addition, some of the classification rules induced by the algorithm have proved to be of musical interest. Currently we are in the process of increasing the amount of training data as well as experimenting with different information encoded in it. Increasing the training data, extending the information in it and combining it with background musical knowledge will certainly generate more models. As future research we are planning to extend our model to be able to predict not only note-level timing and energy transformations but also intra-note expressive features such as vibrato and instantaneous energy. We plan to extend the model by characterizing the notes in the data set by their pitch, energy, and timbre features and to learn to predict these features of a note according to its musical context.

Acknowledgments

This work was supported by the Spanish TIC project ProMusic (TIC2003-07776-C02-01) and the TIN Project ProSeMus (TIN2006-14932-C02-01). We would like to thank Emilia Gomez, Esteban Maestre and Maarten Grachten for their invaluable help in processing the data.

References

1. Horner, A., Goldberg, D. (1991). Genetic algorithms and computer-assisted music composition. In: *Proceedings of the International Computer Music Conference*
2. Dahlstedt, P., Nordhal, M.G. (2001). Living melodies: Coevolution of sonic communication. *Leonardo Music Journal*, **34**(3): 243–248
3. Tokui, N., Iba, H. (2000). Music composition with interactive evolutionary computation. In: *Proceedings of the International Conference on Genetic Algorithms*
4. Phon-Amnuaisuk, S., Wiggins, G.A. (1999). The four-part harmonisation problem: A comparison between genetic algorithms and a rule-based system. In: *Proceedings of AISB'99*. Edinburgh, Scotland
5. Biles, J.A. (1994). GenJam: A genetic algorithm for generating jazz solos. In: *Proceedings of International Computer Music Conference*
6. Grachten, M., Arcos, J.L., López de Mántaras, R. (2004). Evolutionary optimization of music performance optimization. In: *Proceedings of Computer Music Modeling and Retrieval*

7. Gabrielsson, A. (1999). *The Performance of Music.* Academic Press.
8. Michalski, R.S. (1969). On the quasi-minimal solution of the general covering problem. In: *Proceedings of the First International Symposium on Information Processing*
9. Holland, J.M. (1975). *Adaptation in Natural and Artificial Systems.* University of Michigan Press
10. Miranda, E.R. (2004). At the crossroads of evolutionary computation and music: Self-programming synthesizers, swarm orchestras and the origins of melody. *Evolutionary Computation*, **12**(2)
11. Millen, D. (1990). Cellular automata music. In: *Proceedings of the International Computer Music Conference*
12. Hunt, A., Kirk, R., Orton, R. (1991). Musical applications of a cellular automata workstation. In: *Proceedings of the International Computer Music Conference*
13. Miranda, E.R. (1993). Cellular automata music: An interdisciplinary music project interface. *Journal of New Music Research*, **22**(1)
14. Degazio, B. (1999). La evolucion de los organismos musicales. In Miranda, E.R., ed.: *Musica y Nuevas Tecnologias: Perspectivas para el siglo XXI.* ACC L'Angelot, 137–148
15. Waschka II, R. (1999). Avoiding the fitness bottleneck: Using genetic algorithms to compose orchestral music. In: *Proceedings of the International Computer Music Conference.* San Francisco, California. ICMA, 201–203
16. McAlpine, K., Miranda, E.R., Hogar, S. (1999). Composing music with algorithms: A case study system. *Computer Music Journal*, **23**(2)
17. Manzolli, J., Moroni, A., von Zuben, F., Gudwin, R. (1999). An evolutionary approach applied to algorithmic composition. In: *Proceedings of the Brazilian Symposium on Computer Music*
18. Bilota, E., Pantano, P., Talarico, V. (2000). Synthetic harmonies: an approach to musical semiosis by means of cellular automata. In: *Proceedings of Artificial Life*
19. Mandelis, J. (2001). Genophone: An evolutionary approach to sound synthesis and performance. In: *Proceedings of the International Workshop on Artificial Models for Musical Applications*
20. Hazan, A., Ramirez, R., Maestre, E., Perez, A., Pertusa, A. (2006). Modelling expressive performance: A regression tree approach based on strongly typed genetic programming. In: *Proceedings of the European Workshop on Evolutionary Music and Art.* Budapest, Hungary
21. Madsen, S.T., Widmer, G. (2005). Exploring similarities in music performances with an evolutionary algorithm. In: *Proceedings of the International FLAIRS Conference.* AAAI Press
22. Ramirez, R., Hazan, A. (2005). Understanding expressive music performance using genetic algorithms. In: *Proceedings of the European Workshop on Evolutionary Music and Art.* Lauzane, Switzerland
23. Ramirez, R., Hazan, A., Gomez, E., Maestre, E. (2005). Understanding expressive transformations in saxophone jazz performances. *Journal of New Music Research*, **34-4**: 319–330
24. Ramirez, R., Hazan, A., Maestre, E., Serra, X. (2006). A Data Mining Approach to Expressive Music Performance Modeling. In: *A Data Mining Approach to Expressive Music Performance Modeling.* Springer
25. Lopez de Mantaras, R., Arcos, J.L. (2002). AI and music from composition to expressive performance. *AI Magazine*, **23**(3)

26. Widmer, G. (2002). Machine discoveries: A few simple, robust local expression principles. *Computer Music Journal*
27. Widmer, G. (2002). In search of the horowitz factor: Interim report on a musical discovery project. In: *Proceedings of the International Conference on Discovery Science*
28. Tobudic, A., Widmer, G. (2003). Relational ibl in music with a new structural similarity measure. In: *Proceedings of the International Conference on Inductive Logic Programming*
29. Dovey, M.J. (1995). Analysis of rachmaninoff's piano performances using inductive logic programming. In: *Proceeding of the European Conference on Machine Learning.* Springer
30. Van Baelen, E., De Raedt, L. (1996). Analysis and prediction of piano performances using inductive logic programming. In: *Proceedings of International Conference in Inductive Logic Programming*
31. Morales, E. (1997). PAL: A pattern-based first-order inductive system. *Machine Learning,* **26**
32. Igarashi, S., Ozaki, T., Furukawa, K. (2002). Respiration reflecting musical expression: Analysis of respiration during musical performance by inductive logic programming. In: *Proceedings of Second International Conference on Music and Artificial Intelligence*
33. Johnson, M.L. (1992). An expert system for the articulation of Bach fugue melodies. In Baggi, D.L., ed.: *Readings in Computer-Generated Music.* IEEE Computer Society, 41–51
34. Bresin, R. (2000). *Virtual Virtuosity: Studies in Automatic Music Performance.* PhD thesis. Kungliga Tekniska Högskolan
35. Friberg, A. (1997). *A Quantitative Rule System for Musical Performance.* PhD thesis. Kungliga Tekniska Högskolan
36. Friberg, A., Bresin, R., Fryden, L. (2000). Music from motion: Sound level envelopes of tones expressing human locomotion. *Journal of New Music Research,* **29**(3): 199–210
37. Canazza, S., De Poli, G., Roda, A., Vidolin, A. (1997). Analysis and synthesis of expressive intention in a clarinet performance. In: *Proceedings of the International Computer Music Conference*
38. Klapuri, A. (1999). Sound onset detection by applying psychoacoustic knowledge. In: *Proceedings of the IEEE International Conference on Acoustics, Speech and Signal Processing*
39. Maher, R.C., Beauchamp, J.W. (1994). Fundamental frequency estimation of musical signals using a two-way mismatch procedure. *Journal of the Acoustic Society of America,* **95**
40. Ramirez, R., Hazan, A. (2007). Inducing a generative expressive performance model using a sequential-covering genetic algorithm. In: *GECCO 07: Proceedings of the 9th Annual Conference on Genetic and Evolutionary Computation.* New York, NY, USA. ACM Press, 2159–2166
41. Narmour, E. (1990). *The Analysis and Cognition of Basic Melodic Structures: The Implication Realization Model.* University of Chicago Press
42. Narmour, E. (1991). *The Analysis and Cognition of Melodic Complexity: The Implication Realization Model.* University of Chicago Press

Part III

Real-World Applications

7

Evolutionary and Swarm Design in Science, Art, and Music

Christian Jacob[1,2], and Gerald Hushlak[3]

[1] Department of Computer Science, University of Calgary cjacob@ucalgary.ca
[2] Department of Biochemistry & Molecular Biology, University of Calgary
[3] Department of Art, University of Calgary hushlak@ucalgary.ca

Summary. Evolutionary design can take many forms. In this chapter, we describe how different evolutionary techniques — such as genetic programming and evolution strategies — can be applied to a wide variety of nature-inspired designs. We will show how techniques of *interactive evolutionary breeding* can facilitate the creative processes of design. As practical examples we demonstrate how to use implicit surface modeling to create virtual sculptures, and furniture designs through evolutionary breeding.

Rather than creating variations of blueprints through an evolutionary process, we then focus on the evolution of 'design programs'. That is, instead of a static description (blueprint) of an object, we evolve recipes or algorithms to build objects. This leads to a much wider repertoire of variability on the designer's side and can be implemented in a straightforward manner using genetic programming. Starting with a simple breeding approach of fractals, we give examples of how to — either automatically or interactively — evolve growth programs for plants with particular characteristics, which we illustrate using a garden of artificial flowers. We use evolvable Lindenmayer systems (L-systems) to capture growth processes.

The evolution of choreographic swarm interactions leads to new ways of 'swarm programming', where changes in control parameters result in emergent agent behaviours. Swarm grammars, as we will show, combine swarming agents with developmental programs as an extension of L-systems. We demonstrate how to use this technique to generate virtual paintings on 2D and 3D canvases. These *SwarmArt* implementations have also been exhibited in various museums as interactive computer installations, which we will use to describe how to integrate music and sound generation into evolutionary swarm systems.

7.1 Interactive Evolutionary Breeding

Design processes can be seen as iterative and evolutionary. As a designer one has to work within a given particular context. Let us say we want to design an everyday household item, such as a new set of containers that can be used to drink juice. Usually, we will first go through an exploratory 'brain storming' phase, during which we give ourselves the liberty to explore a larger variety of different designs. At this stage, we are not concerned about whether any of these solutions are actually feasible in the sense of whether the designs are easy to fabricate, how expensive they would be, or how practical to use. From this initial set of solutions we might get inspirations regarding specific aspects of our designs: in the case of our intended containers, for example, we might come across an unusual but attractive shape; an elegant colour scheme; a different way of adding a handle; or an artistic, but hardly practical configuration (see Fig. 7.5 for a glimpse ahead).

After this inspirational phase, we might then take a more goal-oriented approach. We filter out and keep the practically feasible solutions. We want to take specifically interesting aspects of different solutions and combine them into one design. We then work on the finer details of our designs: change colours, play with different materials, try variations in the proportions of smaller modules, etc.

Ideally, we have found a solution we are satisfied with. But normally design processes are much more time consuming, as the design cycle will have to start again: creating more variations from the current solutions, re-evaluating the new designs, filtering and identifying promising new design paths and ideas, and then, again, fine-tuning. Some constraints regarding the overall design might have changed on the way as well. Only certain materials are available, which could constrain the variety of shapes (e.g., containers made out of clay have more constraints than using modern, highly flexible and formable plastics), or weight and size could be a factor.

Hence, one might consider design processes to be evolutionary. Solutions have to pass the designer's fitness criteria, surviving solutions get modified. Mostly slight modifications are performed, but dramatic diversions from an original solution are welcome as well, as these will act as an 'inspirational pool'. Design modifications are accomplished by variations (mutations) of current solutions or by recombinations of aspects of a number of different solutions into a new design.

With this in mind, one interesting question regarding design practice arises: How many different designs are usually considered or produced in practice? Would the inspirational brain-storming phase benefit from an expanded pool of suggested designs than current designers have the time to consider? Would a computer-based evolutionary design system expand a designer's options to explore a wide array of solutions? Would this help to come up with unique design ideas, and then utilize the evolutionary system again to work out the details during a fine-tuning phase?

In collaboration with artists and designers, we have developed *Inspirica* [1], a programming environment and run-time evolutionary design system. We think that *Inspirica* provides enough flexibility from a programmer's perspective as well as ease-of-use for a designer. On the one hand, a wide range of design tasks can be tackled with the system through simple plug-in interfaces. On the other hand, the artist/designer does not need to learn how to program or manipulate computer code in order to use the system.

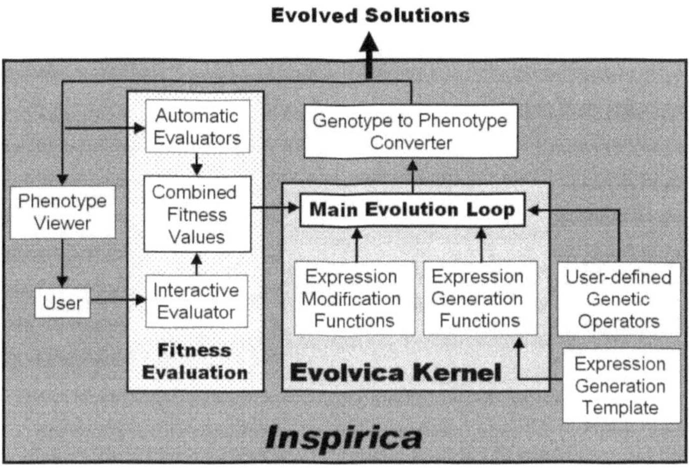

Fig. 7.1. Overview of the *Inspirica* system [1]

Figure 7.1 gives an overview of the *Inspirica* architecture. An evolutionary kernel (*Evolvica* [2]) sits at the center and provides the basic functionality of a genetic programming system (solution generation, modification, and selection based on fitness). Depending on the problem domain, the user selects from a set of standard genetic operators (a number of mutation operators as well as crossover, deletion, duplication, and en-/decapsulation) or adds new, tailored operators. As usual in genetic programming, a problem-specific set of building blocks (in the form of symbolic expressions) has to be defined as well. Fitness evaluation can then either be performed automatically (if a fitness function is specified) or interactively through user input. A combination of both is also possible, where the automatic fitness function acts as a pre-filter before the actual evaluation by the user. A genotype-to-phenotype converter will transform the internal design representations (based on symbolic expressions) into visualizations in the form of graphical objects or animations in 2D or 3D space.

In the following sections we will present a variety of design tasks such as the evolution of containers that can hold liquid, furniture in the form of chairs, and virtual sculptures, for all of which we have used the *Inspirica* system.

7.1.1 Virtual Sculptures: Evolutionary Exploration

Systems for evolving engineering designs — such as tables, stairs, heat sinks, optical prisms, boat bows and hulls, and car bodies — have been created in the past [3, 4]. However, none of these evolutionary design systems have used implicit surfaces, which allow us to easily model curved shapes [5, 6, 7]. Another advantage of using implicit surfaces is the ease with which one can

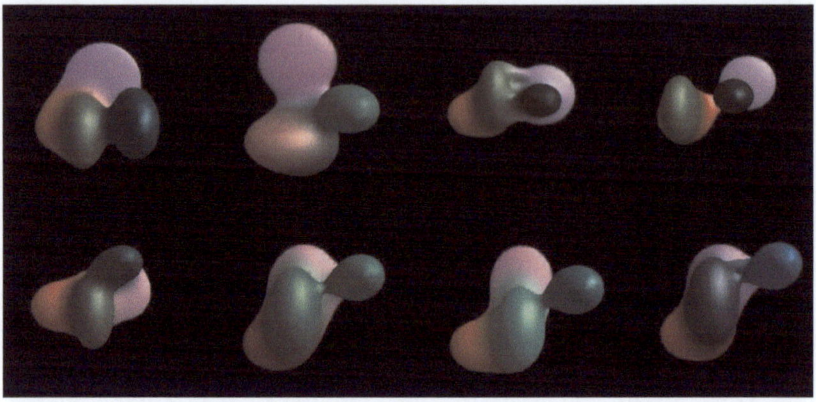

(a) Seven steps of mutation on blob sculptures

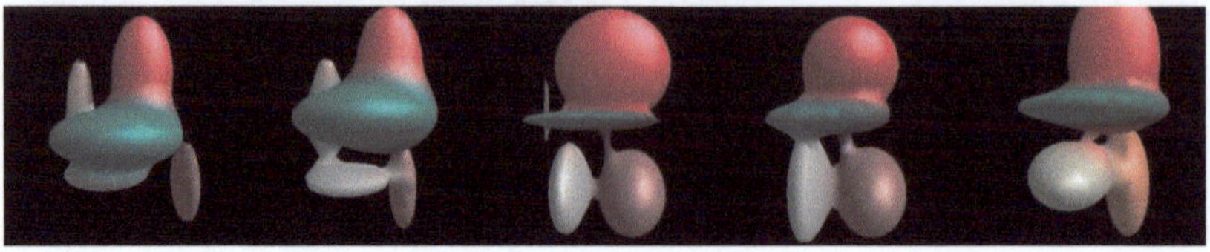

(b) Four mutation steps

Fig. 7.2. Example mutations on blob sculptures

create blended objects. Such objects are created by combining a set of skeletal primitives (points and lines) using operations such as blend, union, intersection, difference, and spatial warps [8]. A *BlobTree* is a hierarchy of nodes for primitives, operators, affine transformations, warps, and attributes [9]. The primitives provide sources of field values, similar to a magnetic or electrical field emanating from a point source. Implicit surfaces are then defined as the points in 3D space that share the same field value.

Figures 7.2 and 7.3 illustrate what kind of designs are typically achieved from BlobTrees[4]. Looking at the top left form in Fig. 7.2a, the 'sculpture' consists of four sub-components, all of which have a spherical shape. Each of these 'blobby' components is characterized by its coordinate in 3D space, its colour, and its scaling factor along the x-, y-, and z-axis. Through simple mutations of these defining values one can get from one sculptural form to another, as is illustrated in Fig. 7.2a for seven and in Fig. 7.2b for four mutation steps. For a glimpse of the underlying genotypic representations of these blob structures see Fig. 7.8a.

In addition to mutation operators, we also use recombinations, which merge aspects (colours, coordinates, shapes, and blob points) among two designs. Figure 7.3 gives a few examples of sculptural forms that were created

[4] See Figure 7.8 for an example of how these blob structures are encoded.

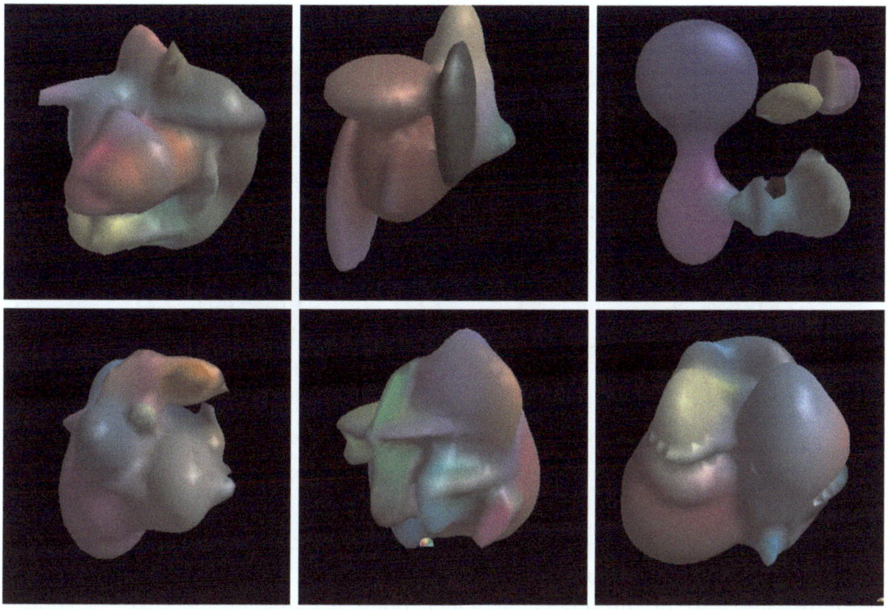

Fig. 7.3. Examples of evolved blob sculptures

through a small number (typically 10 to 20 iterations) of interactive evaluations, with a population size of six solutions to be considered at a time. At the time these experiments were conducted, we were not able to also bring these virtual sculptures to real life. Today, however, rapid prototyping printers can turn these into real sculptural forms of various materials that accurately represent the colours as well. The step from virtual designs to physical realizations has become much more feasible.

7.1.2 Evolving Functional Designs: Containers

Sculptures usually do not have a particular function. They are artistic objects to be exhibited, but normally are static designs. When it comes to functional design, not only aesthetics play a role, but one also has to incorporate aspects of functionality. Let us consider the design of containers that can hold fluids. If one describes the container forms through implicit surfaces, then the evolved forms have to be evaluated with respect to their ability to hold a certain amount of fluid.

Figure 7.5 gives examples of such evolved containers, modeled through implicit surfaces. The actual designs were evaluated both manually by a designer inspecting the overall aesthetics of the generated form and an automatic fitness filter, which simulates the dripping of water onto these solutions and

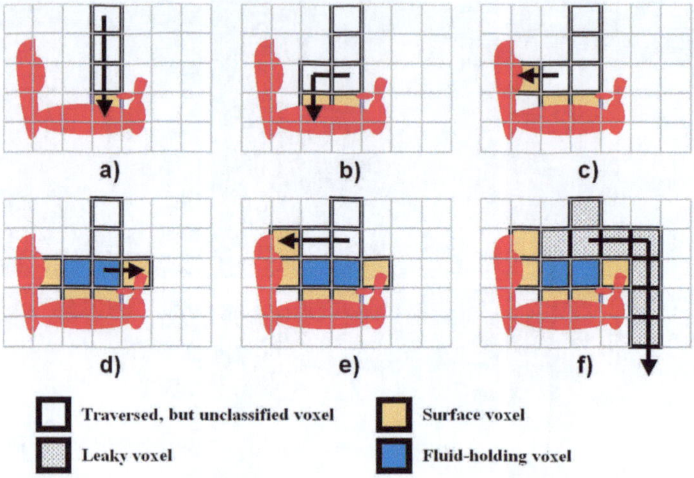

Fig. 7.4. How much fluid can a design hold? (a) A fluid particle drops from the top until it reaches part of the object, at which point it classifies the voxel (a volume pixel) as a surface element and returns to the previously visited voxel. (b) The particle recursively attempts to go around the object. (c) The particle is hindered on the left. (d) The particle is constrained on the right and is trapped as a result. All unclassified voxels on its lateral plane are designated as fluid-holding voxels. The particle returns to the voxel on the previous level. (e) The particle bounces off on the left. (f) The particle discovers a path to the bottom of the object's bounding box, at which point all unclassified voxels are considered as leaky [1]

measures how much fluid is maintained within the structure. Figure 7.4 explains for the 2D case how the evaluation is performed.

The selection of evolved containers in Fig. 7.5 gives a sample of the design variety. All these containers can hold fluids, some are quite shallow, but have a unique design, others are combinations of two containers, or come with interesting handles. The 'goblet'-shaped solution (top right) is one example of an obviously practical design. The cup is a little shallow, but this can be rectified by simply changing one parameter by hand.

7.1.3 Evolving Furniture: The Next Generation of Product Design?

Product design, however, may take a different path, where one already has a specific, well-established and well-tested design solution as a starting point. In the case of furniture design, let us consider a chair. Chairs have certain characteristics that have — in most cases — proven to be useful: a chair has four legs for stability, there is a surface to sit on, and a back part. In this case it seems reasonable to start with a prototypical chair design, and then see which

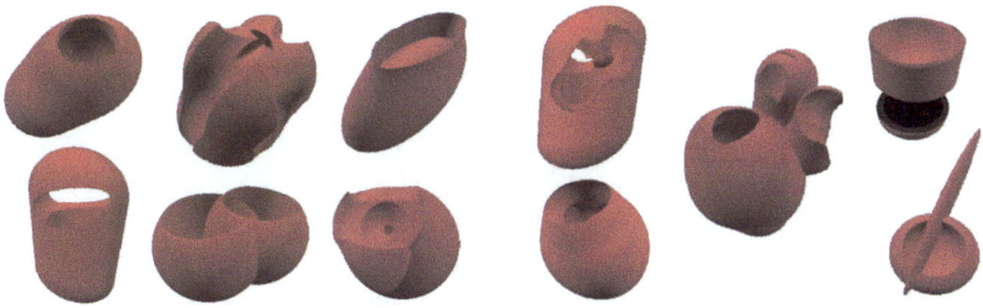

Fig. 7.5. A selection of evolved containers for fluids using implicit surface models

variations of that scheme can be achieved. This is the approach illustrated in Fig. 7.6, where we created an implicit surface model of a chair, for which we show different evolutionary paths over three iterations. Genetic operators of colour, scale, and position mutation are applied. Most of the interesting design outcomes for these chair evolutions are the result of mutations as exemplified in Fig. 7.8a. We show the symbolic expression data structure and a set of typical mutations together with their effects on the phenotypical chair representations.

Figure 7.7 shows a few more examples of innovative ideas for chair designs. Here we did not add a fitness function that would filter out non-functional designs. In fact, it turns out to be rather difficult to write such an evaluation function. It is easy to check for connectivity of all components (otherwise the chair would fall apart), but it is more challenging to decide whether only four-leg designs are acceptable (some of the interesting designs do not have four legs), enforce a back part, or require other aspects of structural stability (components wide enough to support weight or make the chair stand level). Indeed, the system is more useful if fewer constraints are applied to the solutions, as this enables the creation of a wider variety of designs. The designer, who inspects the proposed solutions, can then easily pick out the interesting aspects of each design or dismiss some completely.

In Fig. 7.8b we illustrate such a case. Three chair designs are the result of taking two non-functional chairs and combining some of their features into a functional chair. This recombination can either be done by changing the underlying genotypical expressions (Fig. 7.8a) or by directly working on the phenotypical chair representations. Of course, these 'designs' themselves can only serve as inspirations for the then following actual design process, in which the selection of material, cost, producibility etc. play essential roles. However, from our experience working with designers and artists using our system, having an exploratory tool such as *Inspirica* at their disposal can definitely help expand their world of creativity. In many cases new tools and new technology prompt innovation; this is no different for artistic design.

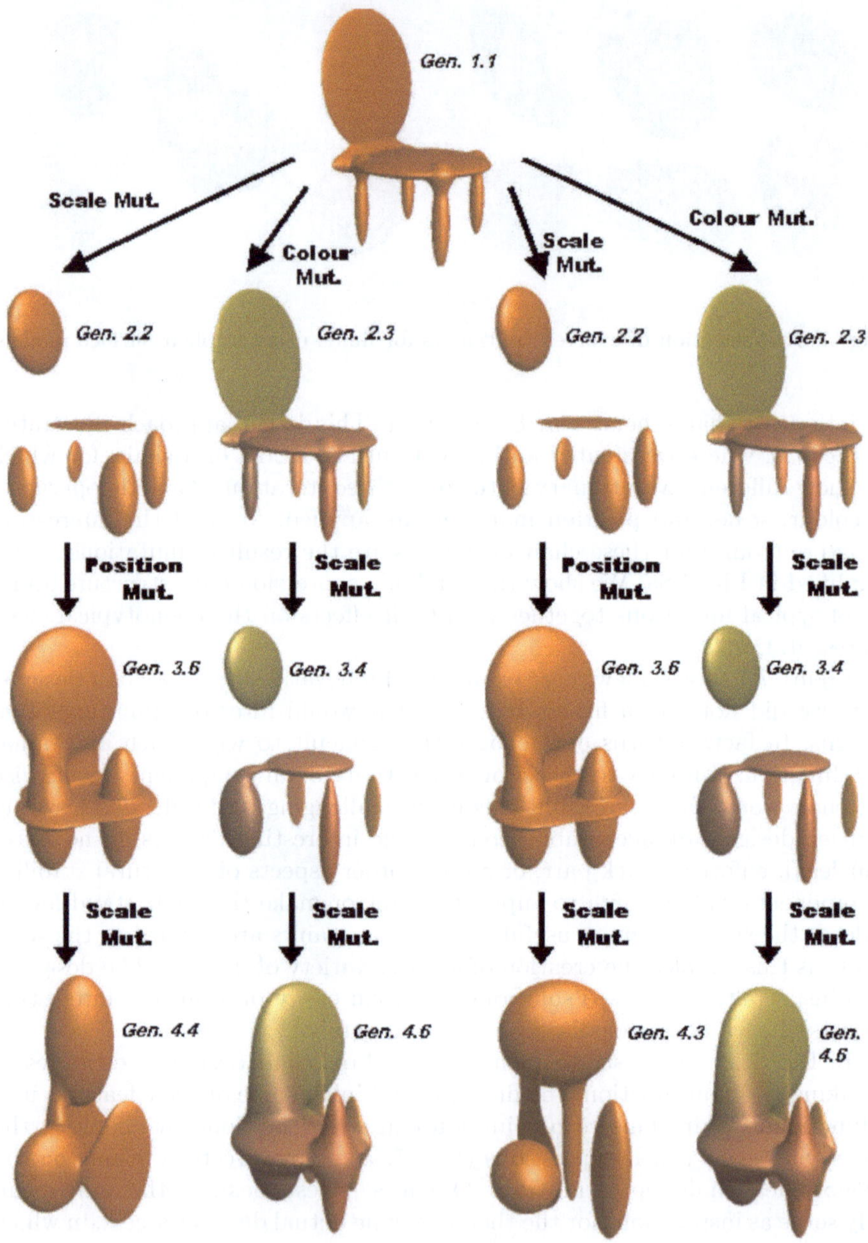

Fig. 7.6. Examples of evolutionary variations starting from a manually designed chair

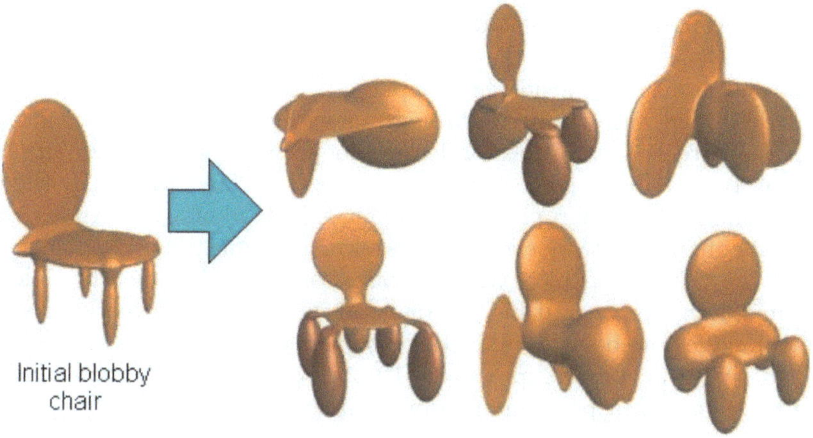

Fig. 7.7. Further examples of evolved Blob Furniture

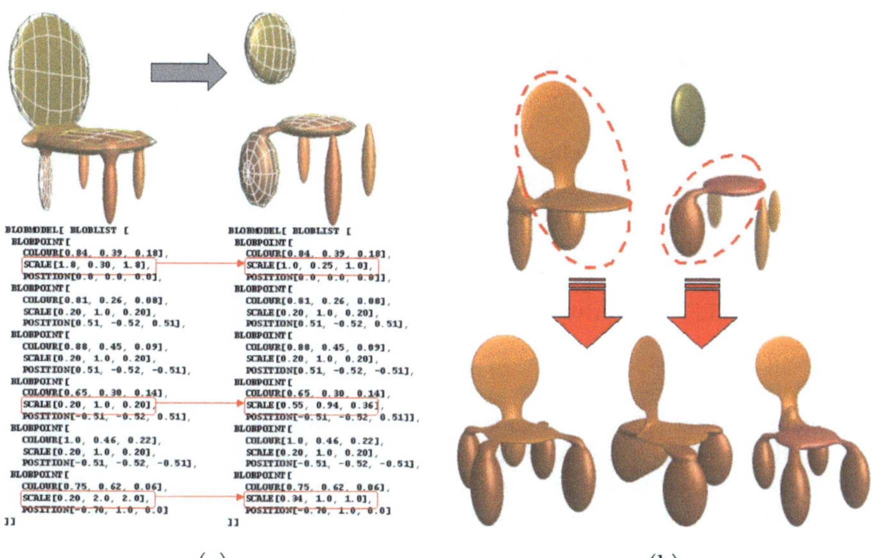

Fig. 7.8. (a) Encoding of the blob chairs and mutation effects. (b) The chair forms at the bottom are a composition of different parts (indicated by the dotted circles) from the purely evolved, non-functional chair forms above

7.2 Evolution of Developmental Programs

Artistic design may be considered as a process. To a certain extent, processes can be described and captured through algorithms, procedures, or recipes. Rather than creating variations of design blueprints through an evolutionary technique (as we did in the examples discussed so far), we will now focus on the evolution of 'design programs'. That is, instead of a static description (blueprint) of an object, we evolve recipes or algorithms to build objects. The designer can therefore explore a much wider repertoire of variability and has a dynamic design process at his/her disposal. Furthermore, genetic programming techniques can be utilized for the evolution of design programs, encoded as tree-based or symbolic expressions [10, 2]. For the following examples we have used *Evolvica*, a programming environment for evolutionary optimization, design and exploration of developmental processes. *Evolvica* is described in detail in [2]; it is based on *Mathematica* [11] and can be downloaded from the *Swarm-Design.org* Web site listed at the end of this chapter.

7.2.1 Evolution of Fractals: Advantages of Rewriting Systems

In order to illustrate the power of design programs to specify models of developmental processes, we choose a simple version of so-called Lindenmayer systems (L-systems) as examples of rewriting systems that have been successfully used for specifying a wide range of growth processes, mainly in the area of botanical branching structures [12, 13, 14, 2].

The bottom of Fig. 7.9 shows a simple rewrite system. Starting from an *axiom* of FLFLFLF, we iteratively apply the replacement rule

$$\texttt{F} \longrightarrow \texttt{FLFRFRFFLFLFRF}.$$

This means that each symbol F in the axiom is replaced by the symbols on the right-hand side of the rule. We can then repeat this rewriting on the resulting strings several times, which creates a larger and larger, recursively constructed string. Each symbol F, L, and R represents a command for a drawing device, a so-called *turtle*: move forward, turn left, and turn right (90 degrees), respectively. This is a straightforward translation from a one-dimensional string into a 2-dimensional graphical representation. Now imagine we create an evolutionary system (in fact, we used a precursor of *Inspirica*) that can mutate both the axiom and the replacement rule [15]. What kind of 2-dimensional structures are we going to get? Figure 7.9 gives a few examples. These fractal structures are the result of a few evolution runs, with interactive selection where we evaluated the aesthetics of the fractals. Starting from an axiom, each associated replacement rule was applied five times, which creates truly recursive structures. The designs range from symmetric to curly line-like structures, from geometric (squared and circular) to more natural-looking shapes, and from intricately detailed to rather straightforward fractal patterns.

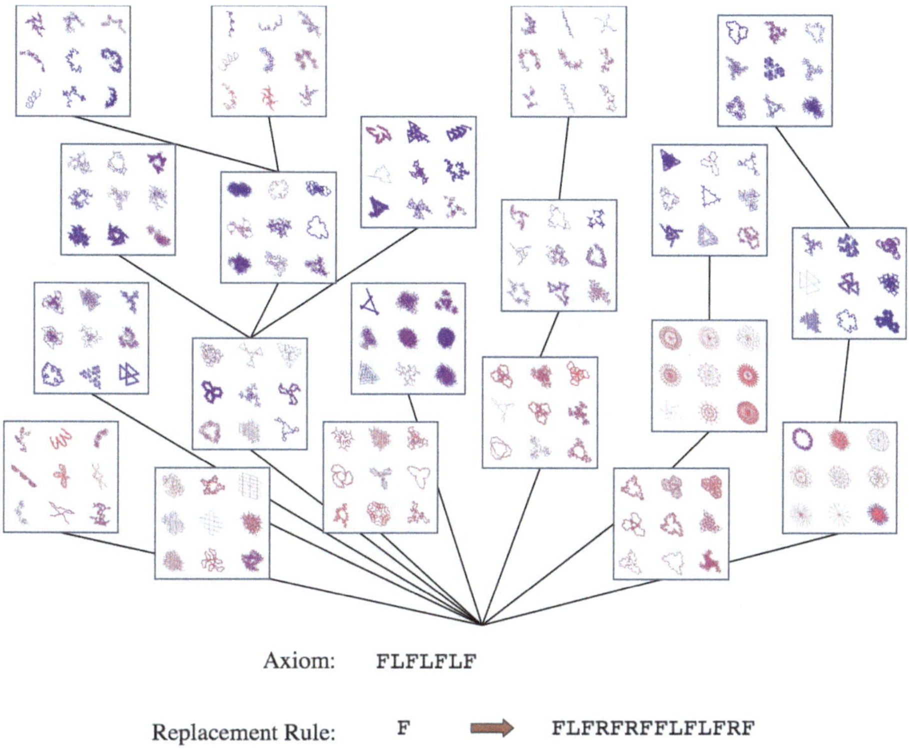

Fig. 7.9. Fractal structures evolved from an axiom and a single replacement rule

7.2.2 Evolving ArtFlowers: A Variety of Botanical Structures

The same principles apply when we look at L-systems to which we apply a turtle interpretation in three dimensions. Now commands like pitch, yaw, and roll — similar to maneuvering an airplane in 3D space — come into play. In order to create plant-like structures, we can also add macro commands to add flowers, leaves, and other attributes that relate to plant modules (e.g., thickness, colour, and texture of stem sections).

Figure 7.10 shows a collection of evolved blooming plants. The plant structure on the top-left is a model of the rose champion *Lychnis coronaria*. All other plants were evolved from this *Lychnis* L-system, similar to the chair evolution as discussed previously. Fitness evaluation is performed both automatically and by visual inspection [2]. The automatic fitness function measures the size of the plant (in x-, y- and z-direction) and counts its leaves and blooms. The more leaves and blooms and the more expansive a plant is, the higher its fitness. The second row in Fig. 7.10 shows some strange growing patterns, which are nevertheless also found in nature. The third row plants carry considerably more flowers. The next two rows are plants that

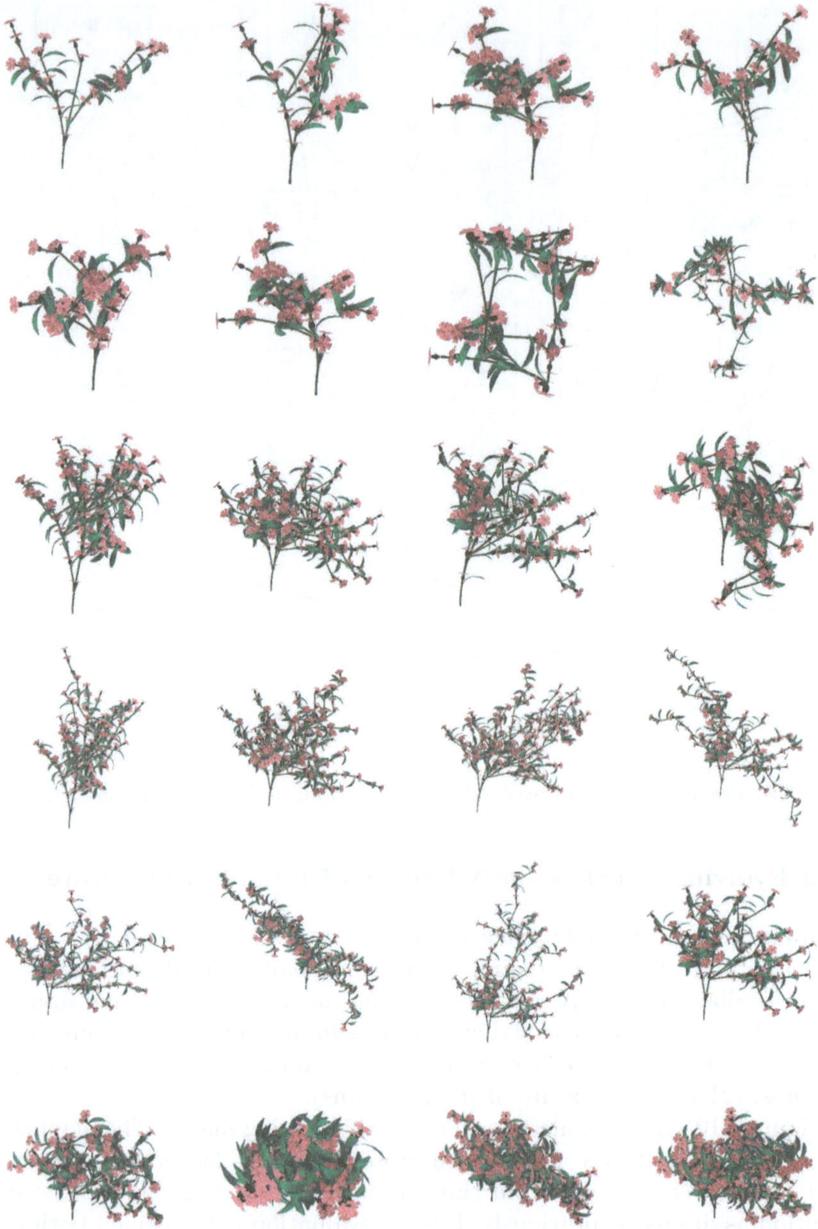

Fig. 7.10. A selection of evolved ArtFlowers. All L-systems are interpreted and visualized using CPFG [14]

were tuned to grow high and wide, instead of deep. Hence, they are similar to wall-climbing plants. The last row of plants is particularly interesting as these have a 'bushy' appearance. This is a typical example where it is not obvious at all how to incorporate certain characteristics of plants, such as 'bushiness', into an automatic fitness evaluation. Only after having examples of bush-like structures evolved is one able to analyze what makes a plant appear bushy. It turns out that this appearance depends not only on a single variable or replacement rule. It is a combination of various rules and parameter settings, as, for example, rather large leaves combined with a higher degree of branching. But all these factors are relative to the overall proportion of the plant. Hence, there are some great lessons to learn, regarding features that are obvious to any human, but are extremely hard to incorporate into an automatic design system. Consequently, we now see the human designer as an essential part of any evolutionary design process. Attributes like 'bushiness' are easy to detect by human observers, and the combination of interactive evaluation and automatic fitness calculations makes an evolutionary system even more powerful and useful. The next section will give yet another example of this human-enhanced approach towards evolutionary design.

7.3 Evolved Swarm Choreography

Let us, once again, expand our view of the systems we want to design. In the last section we introduced growth programs to capture the actual process of developing an object. Many patterns and morphogenetic (structure forming) processes in nature are the emergent result of interactions among a relatively large number of 'agents'. Take a flock of birds, for example. From a single bird's perspective, we can define rules of interaction with other birds in its immediate neighbourhood. Following Craig Reynold's 'Boids' model [18], a bird agent should have rules for *cohesion* (the tendency to keep close to other flock mates), *separation* (avoiding collisions with other birds), and *alignment* (moving in the average direction and with a similar speed to neighbouring birds). These rules are already enough to realistically simulate bird flocking patterns. The same principle applies to other 'swarm intelligence' systems, such as ant colonies [19], pedestrian and vehicular traffic [20, 21], and interactions among biomolecules [22, 23], cells [24], and bacterial colonies [25, 26].

An interesting question arises with the simulation of swarm intelligence systems: To what extent can global properties — such as birds flying in a particular arrangement (e.g., V-shape) — be controlled either through the agent interaction rules or through fine-tuning of simulation control parameters? Can one use an evolutionary approach to breed or design choreographed swarm behaviours?

This is what we were trying to explore with the following experiments. Figure 7.11 shows a selection of examples of evolved swarm choreographies of bird-like agents flying through a 3-dimensional world. Using an interactive

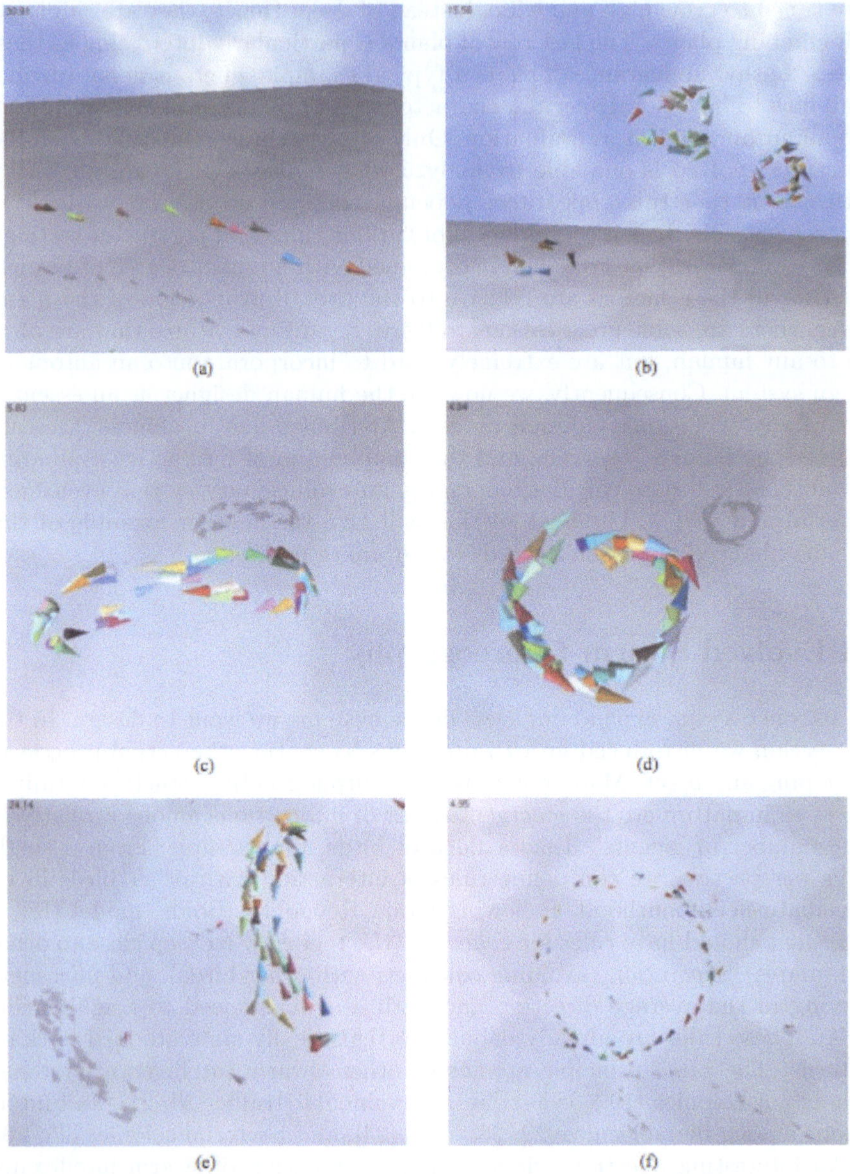

Fig. 7.11. (a) A simple evolved line formation. (b) Evolved loose swirling ring formations. (c) A figure-eight formation that evolved as a recombination of (a) and (b). (d) A ring formation that evolved from (a) and (b). In this formation, the agents fly in both clockwise and counterclockwise directions, like a figure-eight formation where the two end-loops have folded in on one another. Note that the shape of these ring formations are more defined than those in (b). (e) A messy figure-eight that evolved from (c). The figure-eight shape is not as well defined as the one in (c). (f) A larger ring that evolved from (d) with agents more spread out

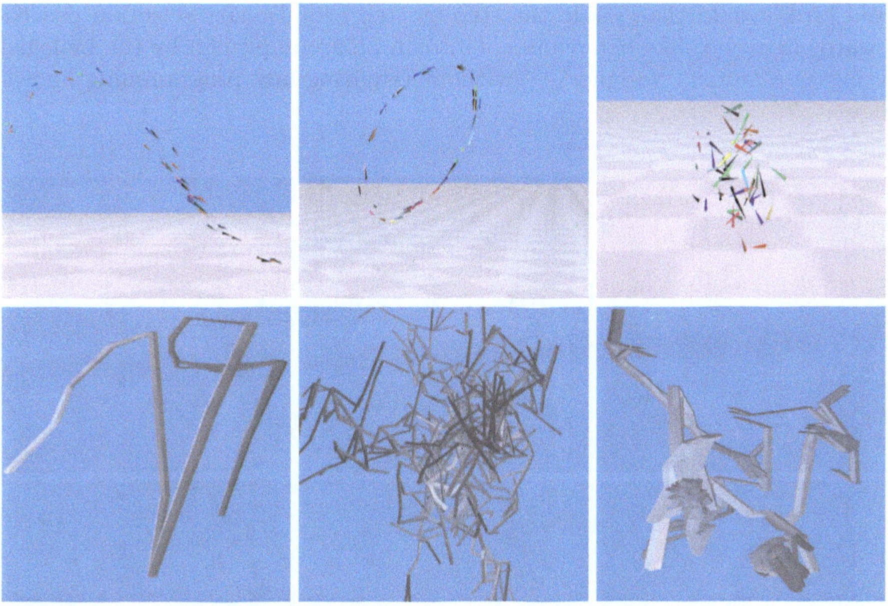

Fig. 7.12. Choreographed swarm behaviours and their corresponding swarm grammar representations [16, 17]

evolutionary approach, we were able to breed specific flight patterns, such as line, figure-eight or ring formations. In this case, only swarm control parameters were manipulated by the evolutionary system (for details see [27, 28]).

Figure 7.12 shows an artistic approach to these choreographed swarms, where we applied concurrent turtle interpretations through swarm grammars [16], which utilize agent interactions based on the rewrite systems and their turtle interpretations discussed in Section 7.2. This results in artistic arrangements representing the areas covered by the swarm agents. The swarm builder agents leave trails of cylindrical elements within the 3D canvas. The resulting sculptures represent static snapshots of the dynamic construction and interaction processes among the swarm particles. This system relies on a multiagent variation of the single-turtle interpretation used in L-systems and is described in detail in [17].

There is another interesting aspect to this 'genetic swarm programming' approach. Imagine that we have constructed a simulation of bird flocking, as described above. A biologist, interested in social insects, might want to study the behaviours of bees. Can the bird model help to develop a bees model? Intuitively, it can. Let us assume that an expert in social insects would use the evolutionary breeder system starting from the bird simulations, and interactively evaluate the population of simulations on the computer screen. Looking for specific aspects in the flight and interaction patterns that distinguish bees from birds would then guide the step-by-step evolutionary selection process towards more bee-like behaviours. This can be accomplished by the biologist acting as a 'swarm designer' — without requiring any programming knowledge.

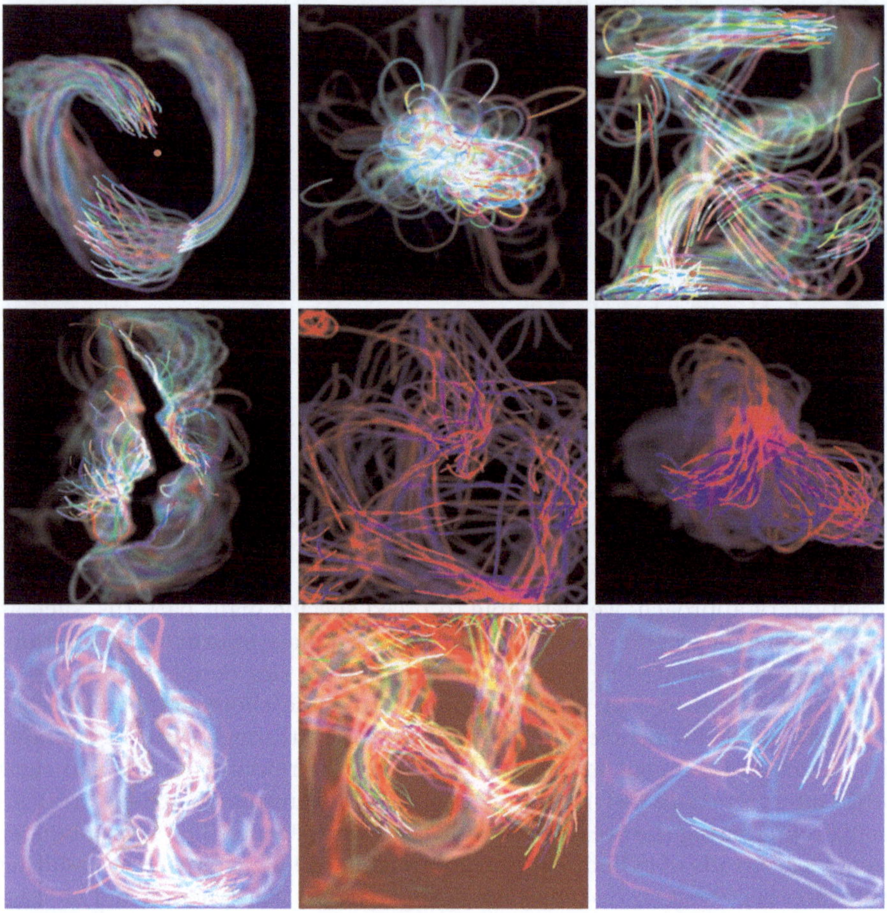

Fig. 7.13. BoidLand swarm drawings by *SwarmArt.com*

7.4 Evolutionary SwarmArt Installations

Our team is enjoying a long-term collaboration between the Faculty of Fine Arts (Department of Art), the Faculty of Science (Department of Computer

Science) and the Faculty of Medicine (Department of Biochemistry & Molecular Biology). From our interdisciplinary exchanges we have learnt how to form close connections between art and science. In our case, this is mainly facilitated by the use of state-of-the-art techniques and methodologies in computer science and engineering, such as multimedia processing, video and image manipulation, computer graphics, computer-aided design, and collective intelligence algorithms. Our investigations of biological and medical systems through simulations and computer modeling [25, 24, 22, 29, 23, 30] provide an ideal vehicle for the incorporation of scientific concepts and results into artistic computer exhibitions. This, in turn, leads to a welcome side effect: many visitors to an art gallery become indirectly engaged in scientific explorations, simply by playfully interacting with our *SwarmArt* installations (`www.swarmart.com`). We will briefly describe some of our installations in this section (for more details see [28, 31, 32]).

7.4.1 Creative Interaction with Swarm Art

The swarm drawing examples in Fig. 7.13 illustrate how simulated swarming can be used to generate abstract paintings on a virtual canvas. Here the swarm agents follow a user-directed cursor (red dot), which can influence the movement of the swarm. Each agent has a particular colour assigned and leaves a trail behind while it is moving across the 2D or 3D canvas. Over time, the trails are fading, which introduces depth and a sense of temporal dynamics into the pictures. Any obstacle, such as the outline of a specific shape, can be put inside the simulation space, with the agents floating around it. Several versions of this swarm drawing interface were installed in the Nickle Arts Museum in Calgary. The evolution of this and other *SwarmArt* installations is described in more detail in [28] and [31].

7.4.2 The Sounds of Swarms

Creating a seamless interface for controlling swarm behaviours, especially in a museum or gallery setting, is crucial as complicated technical setups are hard to maintain by museum personnel. Visitors should be able to interact with the installation without having to use specific devices, such as a mouse or sensor gloves. We therefore opted for a video-based interface, as illustrated in Fig. 7.14. This video interface was implemented for a museum installation in 2005 that incorporated a set of swarms which would blend over live video streams taken within the exhibition space. An iSight camera is connected to an Apple Mac mini^{TM} computer. Subsequent image frames from the camera are analyzed to identify any moving objects (similar to [34, 33]). Visitors entering the space would activate the movement detector. Depending on where movements are identified within the video image, different musical instruments would start to play (keyboard, piano, choir, drum set, etc.). As the swarms that move over the image also trigger instruments, the viewer establishes an

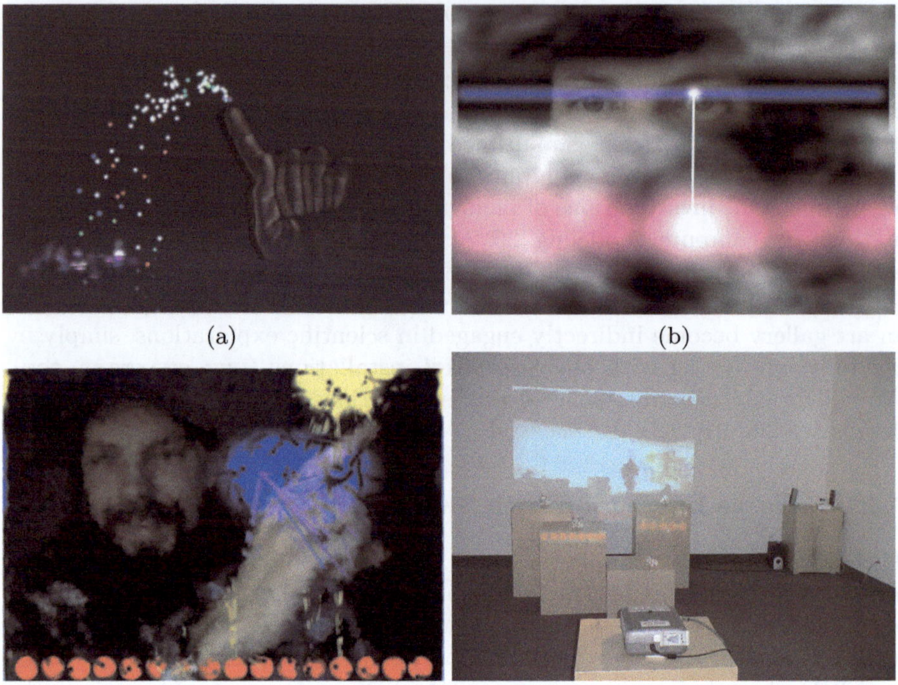

(a) (b) (c) (d)

Fig. 7.14. Controlling swarms through a video interface [33]. (a) A swarm of particles follows the movements of the finger tip. (b) Blinking with one eye triggers an action; the bright spot represents a musical instrument that plays a particular key. (c) Larger movements, such as moving a hand, identifies movement regions. The video image is subdivided into areas within which instruments are triggered. The bottom row of red bulbs represents a percussion set. The middle area plays strings (blue), whereas the top area triggers piano sounds (yellow). (d) The actual setup of the installation in the Nickle Arts Museum, Calgary

immediate musical communication with the swarm system. The user acts as a composer, who, however, is not in complete control of the actual composition, but rather influences the emergent musical paths that the swarms decide to follow.

Figure 7.15 shows the installation in action. Several visitors are interacting with the system and triggering different tunes by entering the camera space. Any movement detected by the camera is projected into the swarm simulation space, where the agents gravitate towards the coordinates of the detected motion points.

As an additional element, we also included i-dogs^{TM}, three of which are sitting on the boxes in front of the projection screen. These little robot dogs have built-in microphones. Depending on the musical patterns they receive,

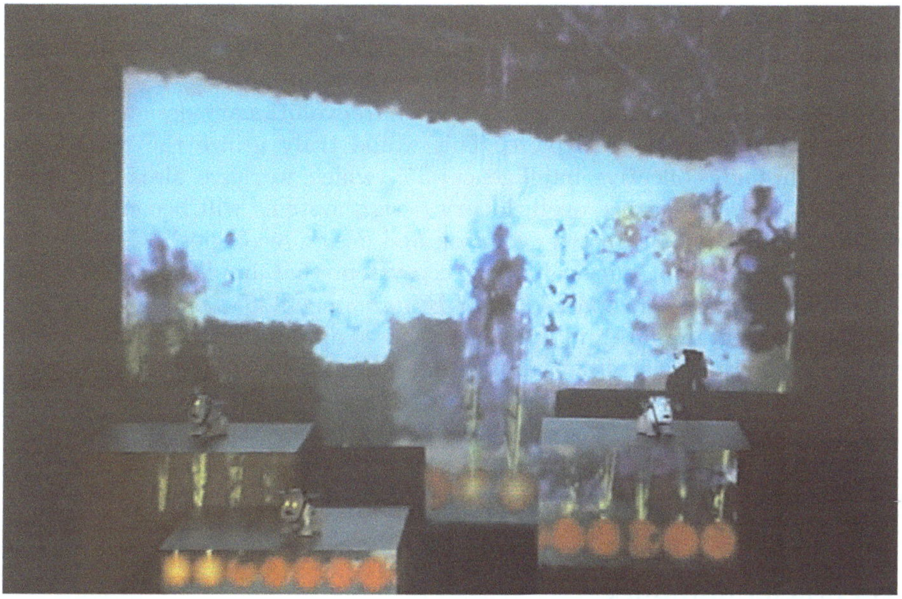

Fig. 7.15. Close-up of the 2005 SwarmMusic installation at the Nickle Arts Museum in Calgary

the dogs start moving their heads and ears. Having the i-dogs sit in front of the camera creates an interesting feedback loop: the swarms play musical tunes, the i-dogs listen to the music and start to move after a short while. These movements, in turn, trigger more music. Hence, the i-dogs have started and will maintain an interaction cycle — without any human intervention.

7.5 Conclusion

By example of our *Inspirica* system we have demonstrated how automatic evolutionary design in combination with interactive selection by a human designer can provide a wider variety of design solutions (blob sculptures, chairs, and containers). As an expansion to static design blueprints, using developmental approaches can help to capture dynamic processes that lead to designed outcomes. We have shown two examples of these emergent designs (fractals and plants) generated through genetic L-system programming. Adding swarms of agents to a virtual design space expands the range of possible structures even further. However, remaining in tight control of these swarm interaction processes is more challenging, as we have illustrated through the evolution of choreographed swarm behaviours and their swarm grammar expansion. Applying these nature-inspired design principles within artistic settings and bringing them to life in art gallery exhibitions is highly gratifying and establishes a fruitful interaction between science, art, and an engaged audience.

As video-based user interfaces will become more and more easy to use, the incorporation of audience interactions into evolutionary design processes will be a further path to explore. This would truly utilize the 'wisdom of crowds' through collective intelligence [35], which we have already started to investigate [31]. Future evolutionary design systems will become hybrids of interactive, human-directed evolution and design 'ecologies', where design solutions compete for survival in an ecosystem that implicitly defines the constraints of the design spaces. In our *Evolutionary & Swarm Design Lab* we will use swarm grammars and other agent-based approaches to further explore this avenue of emergent design ecologies.

The examples discussed in this chapter as well as further material, such as videos and sample source code, are available online at:

`http://www.swarm-design.org` and `http://www.swarmart.com`.

Acknowledgements

The described projects were funded by NSERC, the Natural Sciences and Engineering Research Council of Canada, and the Canada Council for the Arts. We thank the following students and colleagues at the University of Calgary for their contributions to these projects: Euan Forrester (BoidLand), Henry Kwong (Inspirica), Sebastian von Mammen (Swarm Grammars), Scott Novakowski (musical video swarms), Dr. Przemyslaw Prusinkiewicz (CPFG), Ryan Schmidt (Blob Sculptures), Dr. Brian Wyvill (BlobTree), and Jing Yu (evolved fractals).

References

1. Kwong, H. (2003). *Evolutionary Design of Implicit Surfaces and Swarm Dynamics.* Master's thesis. Department of Computer Science, University of Calgary. Calgary, AB, Canada
2. Jacob, C. (2001). *Illustrating Evolutionary Computation with Mathematica.* Morgan Kaufmann Publishers
3. Bentley, P. (1999). From coffee tables to hospitals: Generic evolutionary design. In Bentley, P., ed.: *Evolutionary Design by Computers.* Morgan Kaufmann, San Francisco, CA
4. Bentley, P. (2001). *Generic Evolutionary Design of Solid Objects Using a Genetic Algorithm.* PhD thesis. University of Huddersfield
5. Bloomenthal, J., Bajaj, C., Blinn, J., Cani-Gasuel, M., Rockwook, A., Wyvill, B. (1998). *Introduction to Implicit Surfaces.* Morgan Kaufmann, San Francisco, CA

6. Bedwell, E., Ebert, D. (1998). Artificial evolution of implicit surfaces. In: *ACM SIGGRAPH Technical Sketch*
7. Tigges, M., Wyvill, B. (2000). Python for scene and model description for computer graphics. In: *Proc. IPC 2000*
8. Wyvill, B., Galin, E., Guy, A. (1999). Extending the CSG tree. Warping, blending and boolean operations in an implicit surface modeling system. *Computer Graphics Forum*, **18**(2): 149–158
9. Fox, M. (2001). *Animated Blobtrees for the Impatient.* Master's thesis. University of Calgary. Calgary, AB, Canada
10. Koza, J.R., Keane, M.A., Streeter, M.J., Mydlowec, W., Yu, J., Lanza, G. (2003). *Genetic Programming IV — Routine Human–Competitive Machine Intelligence.* Kluwer Academic Publishers. Norwell, MA
11. Wolfram, S. (1996). *The Mathematica Book.* 3rd edn. Cambridge University Press. Cambridge
12. Lindenmayer, A. (1968). Mathematical models for cellular interaction in development, parts I and II. *Journal of Theoretical Biology*, **18**: 280–315
13. Prusinkiewicz, P., Hanan, J. (1989). *Lindenmayer Systems, Fractals, and Plants.* Vol. 79 of Lecture Notes in Biomathematics. Springer. New York
14. Prusinkiewicz, P., Lindenmayer, A. (1990). *The Algorithmic Beauty of Plants.* Springer. New York
15. Yu, J. (2004). *Evolutionary Design of 2D Fractals and 3D Plant Structures for Computer Graphics.* Master's thesis. Department of Computer Science, University of Calgary
16. von Mammen, S. (2006). *Swarm Grammars. A New Approach to Dynamic Growth.* Technical Report 2006-835-28. Department of Computer Science, University of Calgary. Calgary, AB, Canada
17. Jacob, C., von Mammen, S. (2007). Swarm grammars: Growing dynamic structures in 3D agent spaces. *Digital Creativity*, **18**(1)
18. Reynolds, C.W. (1987). Flocks, herds and schools: A distributed behavioral model. In: *Int. Conference on Computer Graphics and Interactive Techniques, SIGGRAPH.* ACM, 25–34
19. Suen, G. (2004). *Modelling and Simulating Army Ant Raids.* Master's thesis. University of Calgary, Dept. of Computer Science. Calgary, Canada
20. Hoar, R., Penner, J., Jacob, C. (2002). Evolutionary swarm traffic: If ant roads had traffic lights. In: *IEEE World Congress on Computational Intelligence.* Honolulu, Hawaii. IEEE Press
21. Penner, J., Hoar, R., Jacob, C. (2002). Swarm-based traffic simulation with evolutionary traffic light adaptation. In Ubertini, L., ed.: *Applied Simulation and Modelling.* International Association of Science and Technology for Development, IASTED. Crete, Greece. ACTA Press, Zurich, 289–294
22. Jacob, C., Burleigh, I. (2004). Biomolecular swarms: An agent-based model of the lactose operon. *Natural Computing*, **3**(4): 361–376
23. Jacob, C., Barbasiewicz, A., Tsui, G. (2006). Swarms and genes: Exploring λ-switch gene regulation through swarm intelligence. In: *IEEE Congress on Evolutionary Computation*
24. Jacob, C., Litorco, J., Lee, L. (2004). Immunity through swarms: Agent-based simulations of the human immune system. In: *Artificial Immune Systems, ICARIS 2004, Third International Conference.* Catania, Italy. LNCS 3239, Springer

25. Penner, J., Hoar, R., Jacob, C. (2003). Bacterial chemotaxis in silico. In: *ACAL 2003, First Australian Conference on Artificial Life.* Canberra, Australia
26. Hoar, R., Penner, J., Jacob, C. (2003). Transcription and evolution of a virtual bacteria culture. In: *IEEE Congress on Evolutionary Computation.* Canberra, Australia. IEEE Press
27. Kwong, H., Jacob, C. (2003). Evolutionary exploration of dynamic swarm behaviour. In: *IEEE Congress on Evolutionary Computation.* Canberra, Australia. IEEE Press
28. Boyd, J., Hushlak, G., Jacob, C. (2004). SwarmArt: Interactive art from swarm intelligence. In: *ACM Multimedia.* ACM Multimedia. ACM
29. Jacob, C., Burleigh, I. (2005). Genetic programming inside a cell. In Yu, T., Riolo, R.L., Worzel, B., eds.: *Genetic Programming Theory and Practice III.* Springer
30. Jacob, C., Steil, S., Bergmann, K. (2006). The swarming body: Simulating the decentralized defenses of immunity. In: *Artificial Immune Systems, ICARIS 2006, 5th International Conference.* Oeiras, Portugal. Springer
31. Nguyen, Q., Novakowski, S., Boyd, J., Jacob, C., Hushlak, G. (2006). Motion swarms: Video interaction for art in complex environments. In: *ACM Multimedia.* ACM
32. Jacob, C., Hushlak, G., Boyd, J., Nuytten, P., Sayles, M., Pilat, M. (2007). SwarmArt: Interactive art from swarm intelligence. *Leonardo*, **40**(3): 248–254
33. Novakowski, S. (2005). Interactive swarm music. CPSC 503 Project Report, Department of Computer Science, University of Calgary
34. Unemi, T., Bisig, D. (2004). Playing music by conducting boid agents. In Pollack, J., et al., eds.: *Proceedings of the Ninth International Conference on the Simulation and Synthesis of Living Systems.* Boston, MA. MIT Press, 546–550
35. Surowiecki, J. (2005). *The Wisdom of Crowds.* Anchor Books

8

Genr8: Architects' Experience with an Emergent Design Tool

Martin Hemberg,[1,2] Una-May O'Reilly,[3] Achim Menges,[2] Katrin Jonas,[4,5] Michel da Costa Gonçalves,[2] and Steven R. Fuchs[6]

[1] Department of Bioengineering, Imperial College London martin.hemberg@imperial.ac.uk
[2] Emergent Design and Technologies, Architectural Association achimmenges@aaschool.ac.uk, mdcg@aaschool.ac.uk
[3] Computer Science and Artificial Intelligence Lab, Massachusetts Institute of Technology unamay@csail.mit.edu
[4] Adaptive Architecture and Computation, Bartlett School of Architecture, University College London katrin.jonas@ucl.ac.uk
[5] Buro Happold Engineering, London
[6] Southern California Institute of Architecture steve@virtual-architect.com

Summary. We present the computational design tool Genr8 and six different architectural projects making extensive use of Genr8. Genr8 is based on ideas from Evolutionary Computation (EC) and Artificial Life and it produces surfaces using an organic growth algorithm inspired by how plants grow. These algorithms have been implemented as an architect's design tool and the chapter provides an illustration of the possibilities that the tool provides.

8.1 Introduction

The human eye is intuitively drawn to the organic shapes of sand dunes, curling vines, rolling hills and other natural phenomena. Because of its strong aesthetic appeal, our particular interest is in generating biologically inspired form for architects. In the past, architectural form was constrained by material and structure and was able to reflect only a small degree of natural form in examples such as rounded pillars and domed roofs. In an exciting paradigm shift in architecture, contemporary computer-aided design and manufacturing in interaction with integrated, human-designed materials have largely unleashed today's architects from these shackles. They can now move beyond simply appreciating the graceful form of an emerging flower that bends in response to the sun's position or admiring the evolved shape of a natural shelter that responds to seasonal elements.

Beyond the aesthetic appeal delivered by natural form, such form is often very efficient in terms of structural capacity and economy of materials. See

Tsui [1] for an excellent discussion of this from an architectural perspective. In addition, D'Arcy W. Thompson, [2], observed, "The form of any particle of matter, whether it be living or dead, and the changes in form which are apparent in its movements and in its growth, may in all cases be described as due to the action of force." Unlike most man-made designs, structures found in nature are often robust to a wide range of failures and can fulfill multiple functions.

Thompson famously counseled that form follows function. Likewise, for achieving form akin to nature, our approach has been to have form follow process – the growth and evolutionary process that occurs in the living world. Essentially, this approach of mimicry allows designers to capitalize on nature's strategies which, arguably, are the most compelling means of achieving nature's outcome. The manifestation of this conceptual statement of our goals is a computational design tool named Genr8. It allows an architect or designer to both *grow* and *evolve* three-dimensional *digital* forms or surfaces. At the core of Genr8 is a "growth engine" that executes and visualizes a set of growth instructions (more formally a "HEMLS" or Hemberg Extended Map L-system grammar). When Genr8 executes a set of growth instructions, it mimics growth by expanding a planar surface (specified by the instructions) much like a primitive cell of a leaf expands into a complete leaf. Just as a growing leaf twists and shapes itself in response to environmental factors such as gravity and sunlight, Genr8's expanding (digital) planar surface grows in reaction to an environment of digital physical boundaries, attractors and repellors. In concert with Genr8's growth engine, an evolutionary algorithm selects, genetically varies and adapts the growth instructions and their resulting surfaces. This exploitation of evolution relieves the architect of the cognitively cumbersome task of providing Genr8 with a specific set of growth instructions.

In an effort to capture the combined technical and application aspects of Genr8, this chapter is co-authored by Genr8's developers (Hemberg and O'Reilly) and architects who have used Genr8 (Fuchs, Gonçalves, Jonas, and Menges). In Sect. 8.2 we set the context for Genr8 in terms of related work. Section 8.3 describes the organic growth algorithm at the core of Genr8 and its evolutionary algorithm. We aspire to making these comprehensible to a reader who may be either a developer or a technically adept designer. A graphical user interface and scripting language, described in Sect. 8.4, are the interface to design control. We then devote the remaining sections to relating designers' experiences with Genr8. Each experience has multiple facets and is unique due to a designer's personal goals, experience, and approach to interacting with Genr8. In Sect. 8.5 the authors who are architects are given voice. From goal, through methodology, to outcome, each describes, with illustrations, how he or she conducted a project with Genr8. This informative material then sets the stage for a discussion in Sect. 8.6 where the developers and architects collectively explore their impressions of Genr8's effectiveness, the sources of that effectiveness, and its general implications for architectural form design.

8.2 Related Work

A number of architectural design groups have explored generative or growth processes. One of the early pioneers was John Frazer who began his work at the Architectural Association (AA) in the 1960s [3]. Throughout the years Frazer has been involved in a large number of projects exploring generative concepts. Particularly noteworthy is his Universal Constructor which is based on Cellular Automata [4]. Interestingly, many of his experiments are direct physical implementations of growth or evolutionary algorithms using custom-built hardware, sensors and actuators. Another example is a predecessor to Genr8, the MOSS project by the Emergent Design Group at MIT. MOSS explored the use of hand-designed Lindenmayer Systems (L-systems) that were digitally visualized. The L-system grammars were quite restricted in their syntax to allow a planar region to be delineated by segments because L-systems rather than Map L-systems were employed. A project resembling Genr8 was undertaken by Coates et al. [5]. They combine L-systems and Genetic Programming and grow 3D forms on an iso-spatial grid influenced by an environment. Hornby and Pollack contribute a demonstration of the advantages of using generative encodings for evolutionary design systems [6]. An edited volume by Kumar and Bentley [7] provides an introduction to computational development and provides examples in the realm of robotics and neural network design.

When one considers approaches that are not restricted to combining growth and evolutionary computation for design purposes the field widens. For example, the use of evolutionary algorithms has been explored by various authors (e.g., [8, 9, 10, 11, 12]). Numerous applications of evolutionary computation to design are documented in the collections edited by Bentley [13] and Bentley and Corne [14].

8.3 Genr8's Algorithms

Genr8 is a plug-in for Alias|Wavefront's 3D design tool Maya and it was developed by the Emergent Design Group at MIT in 2001. More information can be found on `http://projects.csail.mit.edu/emergentDesign/genr8/`. The Emergent Design Group was an interdisciplinary group that developed new ideas in architecture by bringing together researchers in Artificial Intelligence and architects. A more technical description of Genr8's core growth and evolutionary algorithms can be found in [15].

8.3.1 Organic Growth Algorithm

At the heart of Genr8 is the growth algorithm for generating surfaces. The algorithm is based on L-systems which have been widely and successfully used to model plant growth [16]. An L-system is a *grammar*, consisting of a *seed* and a set of *production rules*, plus a *rewrite* process in which production rules are repeatedly applied to the seed and its successive states. In its most stripped down form, an L-system can be considered as a system for rewriting strings of symbols. In combination with a graphical interpretation of the generated strings, they are a powerful means of generating graphics. By far the most popular method of representing L-systems graphically is *turtle graphics*, where the symbols are interpreted as instructions for an imaginary turtle moving about in 3D space drawing lines. An L-system should be understood as a set of instructions for how to create a specific form rather than as an exact blueprint detailing every coordinate. A specific characteristic of L-systems, which is responsible for the organic appearance, is that at each growth step the entire surface will be modified concurrently rather than by the sequential addition of elements.

A limitation of the basic L-system model is that it can only create arboreal topologies. To generate surfaces one has to employ the *Map L-systems* algorithm [16]. In Genr8, the Map L-systems algorithm has been further extended and we use Hemberg Extended Map L-systems (HEMLS) to create surfaces in 3D which are grown in a reactive simulated physical environment. An example of a simple HEMLS grown in an empty environment is shown in Fig. 8.1. An HEMLS requires the specification of a seed (or initial planar

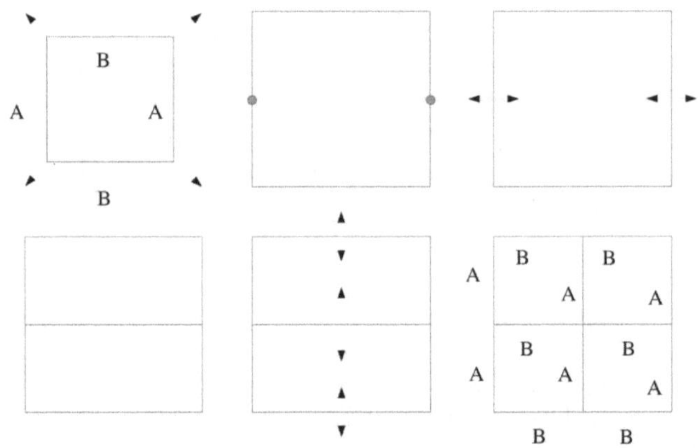

Fig. 8.1. One derivation step of a HEMLS rewrite system for creating symmetric squares described in the main text. Each growth step has three phases. Starting from the seed at the top left and moving along the row, each phase is illustrated. First the size of the surface is increased by a simple scaling factor. Each vertex is moved away from the geometrical centre of the surface as indicated by the arrows. In the second phase the rewrite rules are applied to each edge in the surface. Here the A edges are split and the new vertices are indicated by circles. In the final phase, the branches are drawn and connected. The same procedure is applied to the B edges in the middle panel at the bottom. The label for each edge is only shown at the top left and the bottom right, which shows the surface with new labels after one iteration of the rewrite rules

surface), a set of production rules and two additional parameters; we label this collection a rewrite system. The square rewrite system shown in Fig. 8.1 is built in to Genr8 and it can be defined as:

```
A + B + A + B
A -> A [ [ + B ] - B ] A
B -> B [ [ + A ] - A ] B
Angle  90
```

The instructions for the seed, a square, are provided on the first line. The next two lines are the production rules and the final line is the turn angle parameter required for the turtle graphics. The second parameter is a boolean determining what type of strategy should be used to join the branches. The square rewrite system uses the asynchronous mode, which is the default; to use the synchronous mode the keyword `sync` should be included in the rewrite system. The alphabetic symbols represent edges and the non-alphabetic symbols are turtle graphics commands. The ``+'' and ``-'' are turn commands and the left and right brackets are push and pop instructions, respectively, for branching.

Genr8's environment is specified by the designer and it has a significant impact on the outcome of the growth process. There are two types of elements in the environment: forces and boundaries. Forces can either be point-like attractors or repellors which act like magnets to make the surface grow toward or away from their location. There is also a gravitational force which uniformly directs the growth along one of the principal coordinate axes. The boundaries can either be placed as obstacles or used as bounding boxes to enclose the surface. Examples of the environment are shown in Fig. 8.2.

8.3.2 Evolutionary Computation

Creating a rewrite system that grows interesting surfaces by hand is a complicated task. This stems mainly from the difficulties of imagining what a given rewrite system will look like after repeated iterations. The influence of the environment only serves to exacerbate this problem. Additional complications arise from the difficulty of making sure that the rewrite system is syntactically correct. It is with these concerns in mind that an Evolutionary Algorithm (EA) was incorporated into Genr8. The EA automatically generates selectively adaptive and syntactically valid rewrite rules. The designer exerts high-level control over the process by specifying the fitness function and the environment.

The particular type of EA used in Genr8 is called Grammatical Evolution (GE) [17]. The main advantage of GE is that it combines the strengths of Genetic Algorithms (GAs) [18] and Genetic Programming (GP) [19]. GP is a powerful algorithm because it evolves executable structures represented as trees. For example, in Genr8 the executable structures are rewrite systems that are later grown in the simulated environment. Unfortunately, the genetic

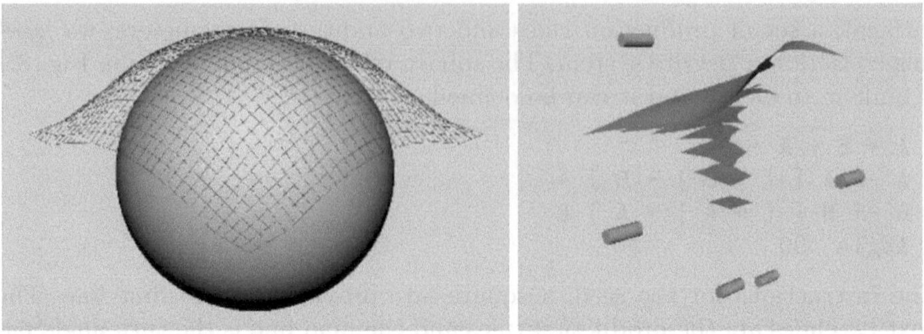

Fig. 8.2. Two examples of the square rewrite system in Fig. 8.1 grown in two different environments. Left: the seed was placed above the sphere and pulled down by gravity as it grew. The surface was prevented from growing through the sphere and instead it drapes the sphere. Right: there are five repellors, each located at a single point, but drawn as a cylinder. The initial surface is pushed upwards by the two repellors beneath it. During subsequent development it was further deformed by the more distant repellors. The figure shows all derivation steps overlaid. The overall shape of the seventh surface is far from the original flat square and it is composed of four-sided non-uniform cells

operations often become very complicated when one deals with subtrees that have to be type compatible when swapped. GAs on the other hand are very convenient when one applies the genetic operators since the genome is represented as an array of integers as a representation of the genotype. The key invention in GE is to map a GA-style linear genome into a GP-like tree structure. This is achieved by mapping the set of integers to the desired language via a Backus-Naur Form (BNF) representation of the grammar. This powerful technique can be applied to any language which can be represented by a context-free grammar. All constraints of the language are handled by the BNF, and GE thus provides a strict separation between the representation of the genome and the target language.

Unlike many other EC applications, Genr8 has an additional mapping step. Once the genome has been mapped to a rewrite system, it is grown in the simulated physical environment. As illustrated in Fig. 8.2, the environment can have a significant impact on the outcome of the growth process. Once the surface has been grown, it is assigned a fitness value based on a number of distinct attributes. Consequently, changing the environment can lead to the surface attaining a different fitness value.

A crucial part of an EA is the fitness evaluation which guides the search towards better solutions. In design, there is no general way of algorithmically defining a "good" surface. Coming up with a useful fitness evaluation scheme for design applications is still an open research question [20]. In Genr8 we use a fitness evaluation scheme that gives the designer high-level control of the evolutionary search. This has been implemented as a multi-parametric fitness function. Each parameter represents a specific feature of the surface.

The designer may set target values for each parameter as well as weights to determine the importance of each criterion. The total fitness is $F_{tot} = \sum w_i F_i$, where i runs over the six different criteria and the weight w_i is a non-negative real number indicating the relative importance of each criterion. The six criteria are size (the extent in the x and y directions), symmetry, soft boundaries (growing through walls is allowed but can be penalized within the fitness function), subdivisions (measure of how refined the surface is), smoothness and undulation (local and global measures of the variation in the z direction).

It is important to point out that in most situations there are many different ways to attain a given fitness value. That is, the fitness function is degenerate in mapping the surfaces to a single fitness value. Consequently, there are many different surfaces which are equally good solutions for a given set of fitness criteria. This can be advantageous since it makes it easier to maintain a diverse population. Moreover, some of the criteria are more or less in conflict with each other. This means that the EA must negotiate a trade-off between the different criteria. These situations usually lead to the most interesting outcomes and help increase the variability of the population.

8.4 Using Genr8

Genr8's use of growth and evolution yields an unconventional, stimulating and indirect design process for an architect. Conceptually, the interaction and control between the architect and tool are changed. The designer has three means of controlling the design that emerges from interaction between the computer and herself: 1) by setting up the digital physical environment, 2) by supplying the growth instructions, and 3) by interactively guiding the evolutionary algorithm. In practical terms, the designer can interface with Genr8 via either a graphical user interface or Maya's built-in scripting language.

The environment is set up before the growth is started, but can also be modified at a later stage between evolutionary generations. The designer has considerable freedom in specifying the environment. There are separate commands for creating attractors and repellors in the Maya scene. The attractors and repellors are represented as standard Maya cylinders and can be manipulated as standard Maya objects. In principle, any Maya object can be used as an obstacle or boundary. However, in practice, for boundaries the best results are achieved if they are smooth (such as regular polyhedra and spheres) and not placed too close to the seed.

Our experience has shown that designers are usually reluctant to give up any form of creative control to a computational tool. Thus, with respect to interactive control, our intent is that the overall design experience be analogous to the designer driving a car (in the driver's seat) where the evolutionary algorithm acts as engine. In terms of high-level control, the car drives forward based on the designer-chosen parameter values of the fitness function. These values guide selection of fitter parents for creating the next generation of off-spring. The designer uses Genr8's "interruption, intervention and resumption" (IIR) control mode like the steering wheel, brakes and gas pedal. When the designer hits the brakes ("interrupt"), the current results can be inspected and the evolutionary process can be redirected ("intervene and resume"). In terms of inspection, the designer has flexible access to detailed information about the population. The rewrite system for each surface is available for replaying the growth steps and for closer inspection. The surfaces' fitness is factored into the six different fitness criteria, making it possible to determine to what degree the different criteria contribute to the fitness score. There are also many options for redirection. For example, the designer can use standard Maya commands to investigate and modify surfaces. The computed fitness value of a surface can also be overwritten to emphatically select it more often because the designer subjectively prefers it very strongly. Moreover, any parameter such as mutation rate or the fitness function weights can be changed. Typically, to evolve a family of designs from one "run" of the evolutionary algorithm, the designer periodically adjusts it and resumes for a few more generations.

In fact, Genr8 has a large array of parameters that can be adjusted by its designer. The drawback of these multiple degrees of freedom is that it can be difficult for the designer to fully comprehend the consequence of each parameters and intuit how they relate to each other. We have observed that the most frequently used strategy is to hold most parameters constant and focus only on exploring the possibilities provided by modifying a small set. The interactions of even a small set of parametric variations are sufficiently rich for a large variety of outcomes.

8.5 Genr8 Projects

The previous section discussed strategies for someone trying to run Genr8. However, it is important to emphasize that Genr8 is intended as a computational tool to assist the designer. It was developed to be as open-ended as possible to make it easy for architects to incorporate it into their design process. Genr8 has the capability to produce a vast amount of output in a short time. This can be overwhelming for the user and it may be difficult to make sense of the variety of surfaces. To get the most out of Genr8 it is paramount that the user have a clear idea of what he or she is trying to achieve with the tool. A useful way of approaching this task is to formulate the goal in terms of some criterion which can not be directly represented by the parameters or the fitness function. The key is then for the designer to understand how the available settings (including the environment) are related to this specific goal.

Genr8 has been used in student projects for the Emergent Design and Technologies (EmTech) program at the AA, London, UK, since 2003. Since it is available free on the Internet, it has also been used by architects worldwide. In this section we describe six different projects which used Genr8. Each project is presented by its designer and is situated by his or her perspective. This implies a varying level of detail in each description. The variation serves to emphasize that Genr8 is a collaborative creative tool: once it is adopted by a designer its role becomes highly personalized and the design process follows a unique trajectory.

Designer: Steven Fuchs
Project: Butterfly Machines (2005)
Goal: To explore the implications of creating a family of designs under simple conditions that allow environmental influences to be directly interpretable. The aim of the project was to explore double-curved self-intersecting surfaces with the intent of allowing them to promote, provoke or suggest a design object or model.

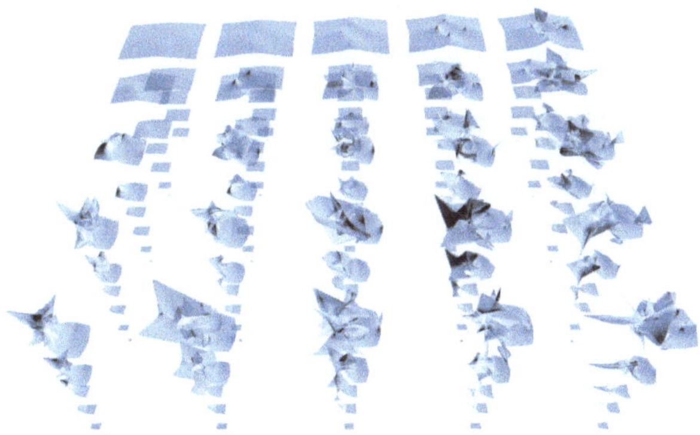

Fig. 8.3. Butterfly Machines Project: Fuchs used Genr8 to assemble multiple families of Genr8 surfaces that were self-intersecting. Each family is a simple parametric variation of the square rewrite system. Across families, the location of attractors and repellors varies. Placement was chosen to promote the chance of self-intersection during growth. Within a family, different surfaces are generated by experimenting with the strengths of attractors and repellors at fixed locations. This image captures one family both in time and in repellor and attractor spaces. Each surface "grows" along the vertical (time) axis. A vertical slice of the three-dimensional projection shows the family's surfaces responding to different attractor and repellor strengths at a (time) step in the development

Methodology: In the Butterfly Machines project the square rewrite system in Fig. 8.1 is used. By incrementally changing the parameters and the environment, a whole set of self-intersecting shapes was obtained. See Fig. 8.3 for one family of surfaces. Instead of relying on the EA for selection, Fuchs controlled it according to his interest among a population. He started to see elements of a chair, such as a seat and seat back, emerge and he tried to encourage evolution toward more chair-like elements. The surface curvature additionally suggested ergonomics as a design driver. This pairing of computation-based discovery with a designer's interpretation encouraged a subsequent step in the design project wherein a physical model could (and would?) eventually be constructed. One of the surfaces that was chosen for subsequent investigations is shown in Fig. 8.4.

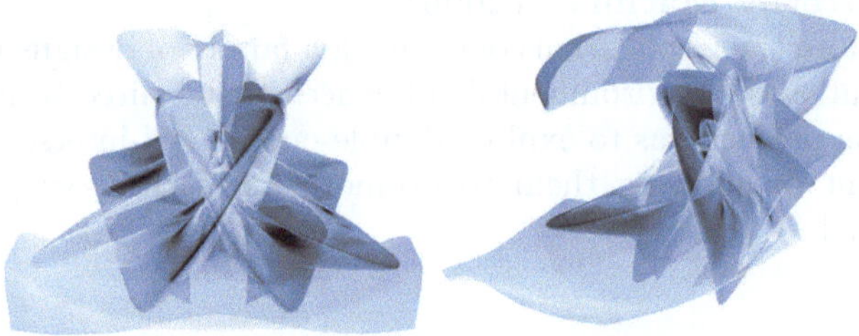

Fig. 8.4. Left: an example of a symmetric self-intersecting surface from the Butterfly Machines project. The aim of this project was to develop a chair, a rendering of which is shown on the right. This surface is an intermediate growth step and it was selected based on aesthetic considerations with respect to the amount of self-intersection of the surface and ergonomic considerations. The ergonomic viability of the surface was evaluated using a script in Digital Projects/Catia

Designer: Achim Menges
General Intent: To utilize Genr8 to embed the possibilities and constraints of fabrication and assembly processes directly into the computational form generation process.
Project: Sectional Surfaces (2003)
Goal: To synthesize digitally evolved geometry and computer-aided fabrication processes through the definition of fitness criteria that embed manufacturing properties and material constraints as generative drivers in the morphogenetic process.
Methodology: The experiment commences from the possibility of describing the geometry of a surface with varying curvature as a system of tangential and perpendicular construction planes. These planar elements are later used as input into the fabrication process which involves the computer-aided laser-cutting of sheet material. Genr8 was employed to initiate the co-evolution of two interlocking surfaces with increasingly complex geometric articulation. Thus, a number of geometric constraints were used when choosing the parameters for the fitness function and thereby ensuring that the elements ended up in the correct planar fashion.

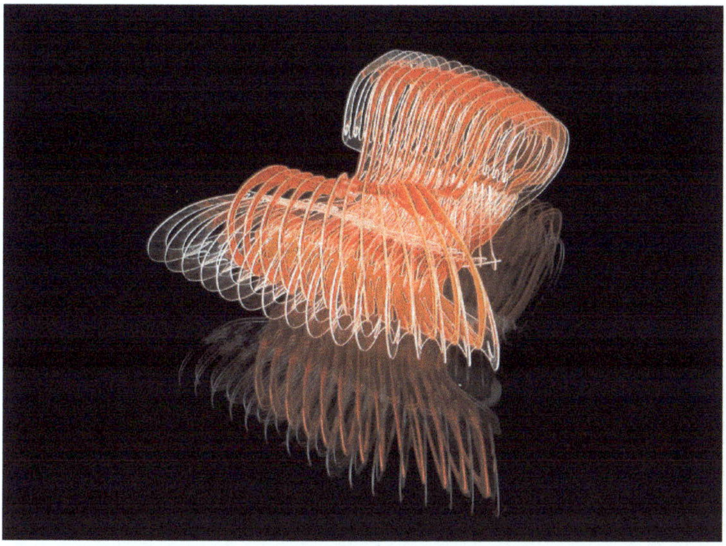

Fig. 8.5. A photograph of the sectional surface model

Project: Pneumatic Strawberry Bar (2003)
Goal: A design for a pneumatic strawberry bar for the Architectural Association's annual end-of-year party, intended to utilize the evolutionary dynamics of reproduction, mutation, competition and selection as design strategies.
Methodology: The possibilities and limits from initial form generation to the actual fabrication process were explored by shifting the investigation towards performative patterns that evolve as species across populations and successive generations whilst maintaining structural capacity and geometric characteristics. The starting point of the Genr8-driven development process was a relatively simple pneumatic component geometrically defined by the cut pattern of two trapeziform surfaces that were aligned at the plane of the connecting seams. Once inflated the component attains a three-dimensional form defined by the different length of the surfaces in relation to the defining points. These simple geometric relations, defined as generic 3D cut patterns, provide the basis for the subsequent evolutionary process. Rather than breeding just one surface, three sub-populations were used in the scheme based on co-evolution. A feedback loop was initiated where the most recently evolved surface was used as a bounding box for the current surface. This method preserved the properties of the pneumatic component in a larger system but dissolved the distinction between environmental constraints and individual response. Another feedback loop utilized digital form-finding in a dedicated membrane engineering software, and additional physical test modelling further informed the evolutionary process and its evaluation.

After running Genr8 for over 600 generations, 144 species were identified and catalogued according to specific patterns of relevant geometric features.

Since the structural behavior of the pneumatic system relied primarily on specific geometric relations such as alignment and proportional distances of definition points, the individuals that shared these geometric features were selected. Then the individual of the chosen species that grew in the last and most developed generation was picked. The genotype of this individual incorporated the genomes of three geometry-defining surfaces, establishing a degree of phenotypic plasticity that allowed the resulting pneumatic system to adjust to the constraints of a digital cutting pattern and computer-aided manufacturing process.

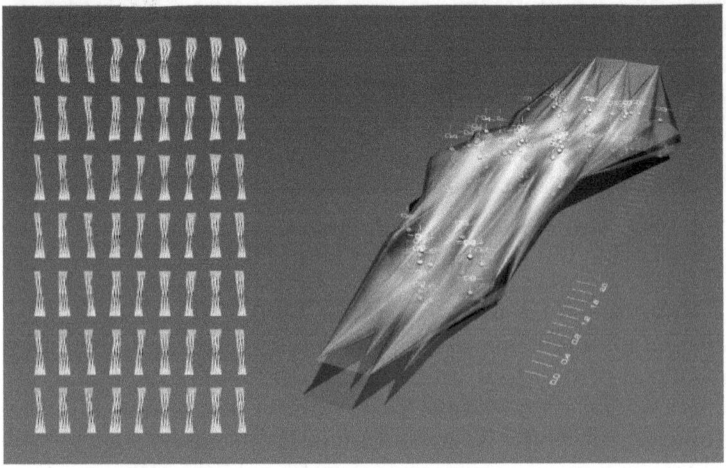

Fig. 8.6. Left: a selection of surfaces evolved for the strawberry bar. Right: a rendered model of the pneumatic strawberry bar

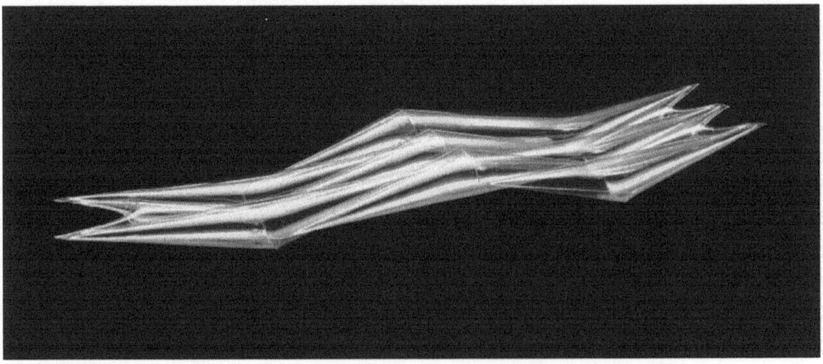

Fig. 8.7. A photograph of the pneumatic strawberry bar

Project: Fibrous Surfaces (2005)
Goal: To investigate possibilities of combining digital growth and associative parametric modelling to evolve a differentiated surface.

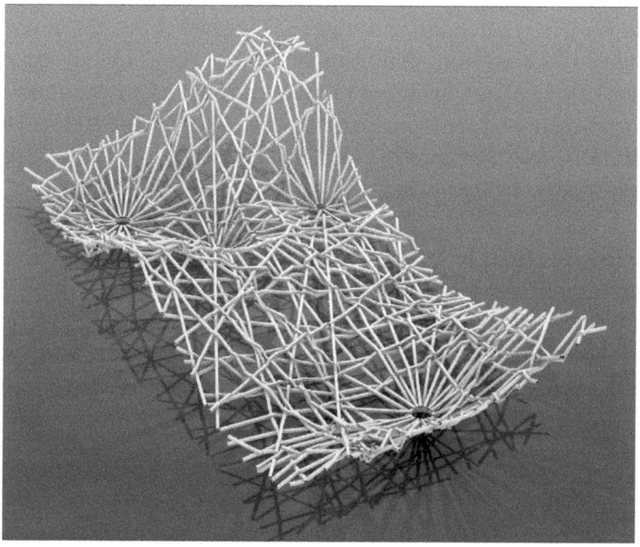

Fig. 8.8. A view of the fibrous surface model. This prototype has almost 90 members and 1,000 joints

Methodology: The structure consists of a dense network of interlocking members from a basic array of simple, straight elements. The basic system constituent is defined as a jagged, planar strip cut from sheet material on a three-axis CNC router. First a generic digital component is established in a parametric software application through the geometric relationships that remain invariant in all their possible instances as well as the variable production constraints of the intended machining technology and process. The use of this parametric component is then based on three interrelated inputs: The primary input influencing the particular geometry of a specific system type is given by a gestalt envelope. Based on the derived surface another input for the implementation of the material elements is generated. In response to particular geometric surface features derived through Genr8, a variable distribution algorithm establishes a network of lines on the surface indicating the position of each element and the related node type. Instances of the generic parametric component then populate the system accordingly. In the resultant organization crossing members only intersect if they are perpendicular due to the embedded manufacturing constraints. If not, they pass under or over crossing elements, similarly to a bird's nest, and thereby form a geometrically defined, self-interlocking, stable structure. This complex correlation of geometric definition, structural behavior and production considerations does not remain coherent only in a single system, but is also integral to the generation process itself. This is of particular importance if one considers that the surface defining the critical morphogenetic input is constructed through a bottom-up process in which all parts respond to local interactions and the environment. As these internal and external interactions are complex and the interpretation of the L-system is nonlinear, the outcome of the growth process remains open-ended. This continual change combined with the long chain dependencies of the subsequent parametric component population enables the growth of different system types of member organization, system topology and consequent performative capacity.

Designer: Katrin Jonas
Project: Surface Envelopes (2003)
Goal: As part of a general investigation into using surfaces to define inhabitable spaces, the objective of this project was to explore how external conditions would influence the growth of surfaces which create a covered space underneath.

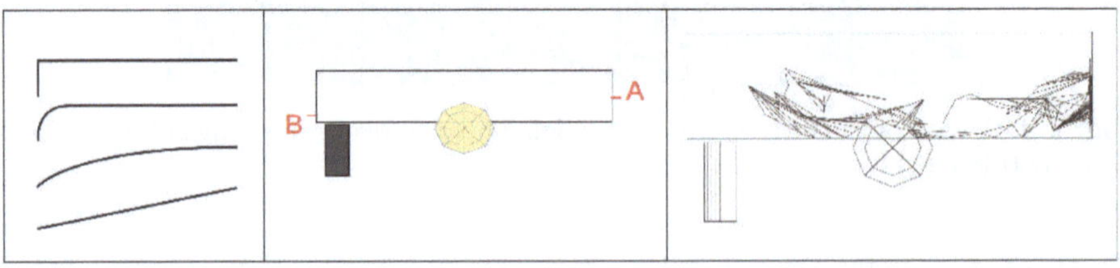

Fig. 8.9. Left: the conceptual sketch for the environment prior to using Genr8 for the surface envelopes. Centre: elevation view of the environment used in Maya; the cylinder at the bottom left represent two attractors (one cannot be seen as it is placed directly behind the other), a sphere and a bounding box. Right: an example of an evolved surface from the experiment

Methodology: The environment as shown in Fig. 8.9 included a spherical obstacle, two attractors at a lower level than the starting point and a bounding box. The size of the bounding box was made smaller than the surfaces so that they would collide with it and expand along the walls, creating a rim of overlapping geometries.

The setup allowed us for a clear definition of a design problem and it also allowed to form expectations of what the outcome might look like. The expected abstracts of surfaces which describe a path from a higher to a lower level in space were challenged by the multitude of outcomes that actually emerged. The surfaces which evolved in this environmental setup responded in an unexpected, yet intelligible way. Where the sphere was hampering the growth, the surfaces would yield and expand upwards. The attractors produced a number of different outcomes: some surfaces grew downwards as was expected; others split into two branches before descending with each branch reaching into the direction of one of the attractors, while others did not decline after splitting into two branches.

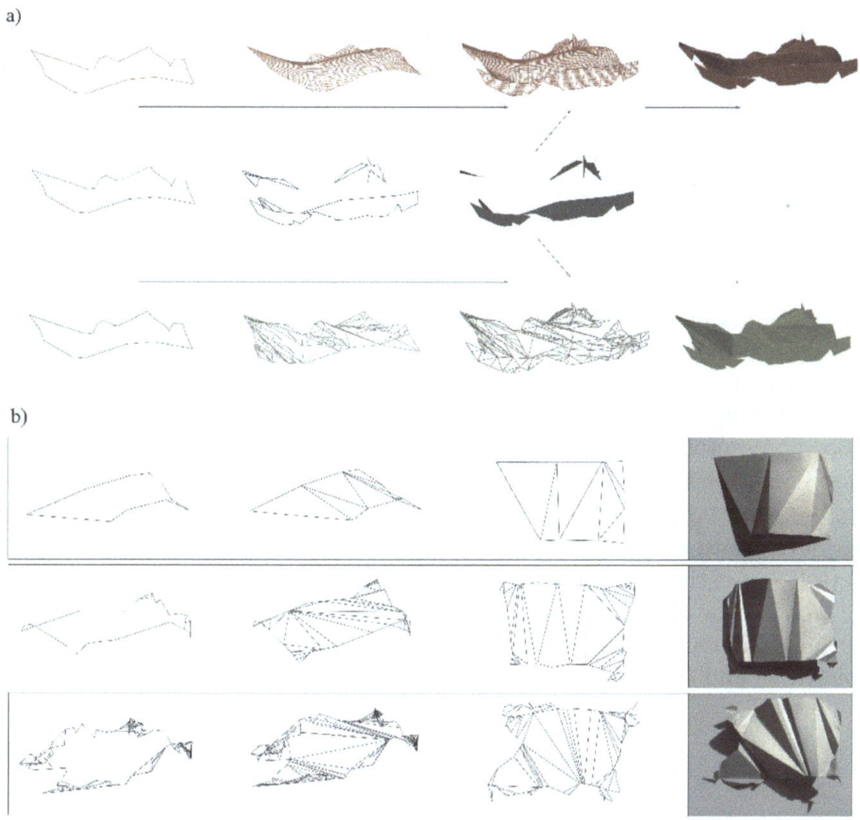

Fig. 8.10. (a) How fundamentally different objects can be produced through different methods of interpreting a particular surface outline. The middle row shows the processing of the initial Genr8 rim, in that geometries which overlay each other were filtered to share a single outline. The upper and lower rows each show the development of a central body definition. Starting from the rim outline in the upper sequence a smooth definition is applied; and, in the lower row, a folded definition is applied. Subsequently the filtered outrigger of the rim are reattached. (b) Three different Genr8 surfaces with the same fitness values but different degrees of complexity in their articulation. The surfaces are triangulated and unfolded to create a pattern which can be used for laser cutting and scoring. The first column shows the outlines obtained from the Genr8 surfaces and the second the triangulation which was obtained using Maya. The third column shows the unfolded version; and, finally, there are photographs of the produced surfaces

The next step was to select a number of surfaces for further analysis and production of physical models. Here the fitness function proved useful as the system produced several distinct solutions with similar fitness values. Despite their dissimilarity in the arrangement of geometric elements, all surfaces shared the common feature of sharp edges. One of the challenges with the forms however was that there was no definition of the centre part of the surfaces when shading them. The individuals all just described polygonal outlines. In preparation for the computer-aided manufacturing of the design, focus was placed on defining the corpus of the forms. This was achieved by post-processing the output in a number of different software applications. A single Genr8 surface outline would allow for a number of valid interpretations as shown in Fig. 8.10a. Three Genr8 surface outlines with similar fitness values, but with different degrees of complexity were chosen to produce physical models. The geometries were triangulated, filtered and finally unfolded to obtain a scoring and cutting pattern that could be supplied to a laser cutter.

For the manufacturing, aluminum was chosen since it allows for an uncomplicated manual folding process. The metal sheets can be folded along score lines without deforming the faces. After processing the pattern, the sheets were folded up into the final physical objects. Each model as shown in Fig. 8.10b represented one possible interpretation of a Genr8 surface.

Designer: Michel da Costa Gonçalves
Project: Nested Cubes (2004)
Goal: To investigate the use of Genr8 as a semi-automated spatial sketching tool and to consider how Genr8 can propose contrasting hands-off "design solutions" that inhabit a particular environment. This will test the opposing explorative and exploitive capabilities inherent to the EA.

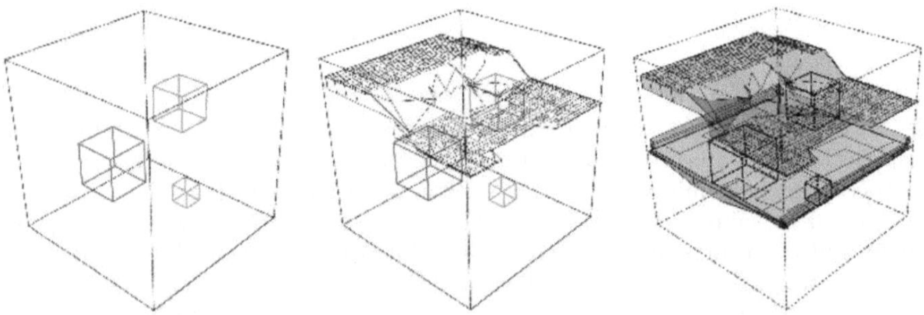

Fig. 8.11. The leftmost image shows an example of the boundaries used in the Nested Cubes project. The middle image shows an upper evolved surface and the last image shows the upper and the lower evolved surfaces

Methodology: The project used a literal illustration of inhabitable constraints such as overall limitation and internal desirable layout of spaces. The graphic interpretation is taken as a direct representation of a material envelope. The skin-like surfaces are interpreted as spatial enclosures filling a physical setting. The environment comprises a bounding box enclosing the growing surface as well as smaller obstacles impeding the growth. The external boundary is represented by a cube containing up to three smaller cubes as shown in Fig. 8.11. A script was developed to automatically set up the environment and assign random positions to the inner cubes. The environment also included repellors that would push the surfaces up or down, forcing them to interact with the obstacles.

Since there is no direct representation of structural constraints, this project forgoes such issues and instead focuses on investigating the spatial divisions attained by the tool. The obstacles' positions were representative of a given architectural layout while fitness parameters simulated inhabitable characteristics. Spatial configurations were generated by filling the environment in accordance with its embedded criteria. Fitness was prioritized towards local continuity, giving weight to smoothness criteria. The selection criteria also included a balance between local variations of the "envelope" and degrees of conformity to a given configuration. Furthermore, the parameters controlling the growth had to be tuned in such a way that the grown surfaces would fit inside the bounding box. For the parameters related to the EA, the goal was to find a relationship between Genr8's fitness criteria and the recurrent features of the environment. As shown in Fig. 8.11, an upper and a lower surface were created for each configuration.

A script was developed that would automatically loop through the relevant parameter ranges. In this way it was possible to create 1,008 configurations and 168 "optimized" enclosures which were later grouped in comparative charts to identify the relevant dependencies between the parameters. In addition to fitness criteria, the tuning phase studied the growth algorithm by establishing the scale ratio between the surface cell and the overall environment. The results were reviewed according to modes and degrees of interactions such as the proportional relation between cell and frame, surface coverage and spatial conformity. The process included discarded conditions where the surfaces displayed limited occupancy or overcame obstacles and boundaries.

The results were exported, rebuilt and transformed in different manners in order to recreate the continuity between the surfaces following the boundary limits. For example, one operation sought spatial coherence by locally increasing the curvature continuity of separate contours. After being reconstructed and lofted, these profiles generated a seamless envelope. Successively, the same conditions were rebuilt with a regular meshing related to a proportional structural meshing.

This project explores how basic architectural requirements can be explored with Genr8 to provide envelope solutions generated according to spatial criteria. The process could be largely extended by giving more control over the

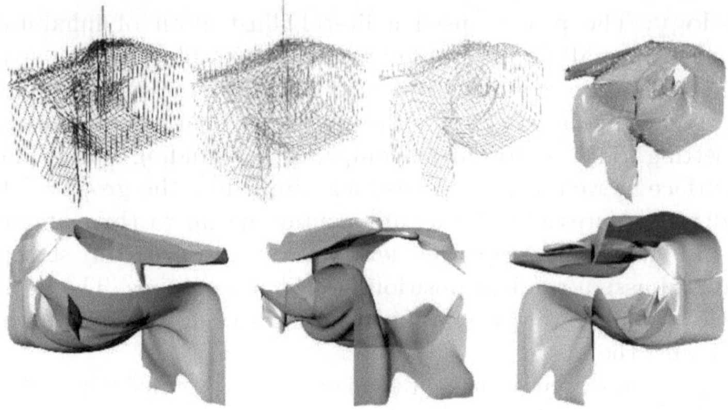

Fig. 8.12. An illustration of the sequences of transformations of the evolved surfaces from Fig. 8.11. Through a number of different operations, a smooth spatial envelop is created

range of fitness values in relation to design criteria. The project illustrates an abstract transcription of design variables different in nature and scale. It includes different levels of "external" constraints influencing the surfaces' generation combining the intangible criteria guiding the generation/creation with fixed geometrical/spatial layout. By domesticating seemingly unpredictable tools, it offers consideration for added design characteristics: dissociated generations of fitted results.

EAs are based on seemingly contradictory principles of exploration and exploitation. This allows them to operate in a nonlinear way to find the optimal solution of hard problems. However, it requires that the designer understand how to manage the equilibrium between converging fitness and the variability of the population. The redundant fitness function facilitates this process by allowing for potentially distinct solutions of a given problem. This hints at the difference between Genr8 and other digital design tools: the dissociation between the user of form generation and the seemingly unpredictable character of the procedure. Design expertise, and to a certain extent creativity, could be reconsidered for the integration of nonlinear formal generation within a design process.

8.6 Discussion

The designers agree that Genr8 is different from any other design tool they have used and that it presents them with new possibilities as well as new challenges. Genr8 uniquely offers the designer a chance to engage in a nonlinear generative bottom-up design process. However, in order to exploit this opportunity, the designer must relinquish some conventional aspects regarding her role. With Genr8 the control of the design process is shifted slightly out of the hands of the designer. The designer must accept the fact that she no longer has complete and direct control, and consequentially adjust to a new mode of control. The new mode of control is indirect: the designer controls the elements that affect the outcome but not the outcome directly. These control elements are the definition of the environment, the specification of parameters and interactive guidance of the evolutionary selection process.

The developers' aim was to develop a design tool that would empower designers who had only rudimentary knowledge of evolutionary computation and L-systems. However, the designers found it challenging to understand the distinction between the behavior of the growth algorithm and the behavior of the evolutionary algorithm while they observed that this is necessary to exploit the tool to its greatest potential. A designer using Genr8 does not have to understand the algorithmic details within it but must have a coherent and sufficiently accurate mental model of the tool's behavior. An inaccurate mental model creates a frustrating gap between desired and actual outcomes. Over time, especially through teaching at the AA by Hemberg and Menges, improved explanations of Genr8 that enable better mental models have been formulated.

Since both the evolutionary and growth algorithms influence the complex output that arises as a result of reacting to the environment, it is initially difficult to disentangle their individual roles in the output. There is a learning process during initial experimentation when the designer comes to discern the separate aspects of the two algorithms. The tool must be experimented with quite a bit before it can be used to fulfill project goals.

The two interacting algorithms also set up a considerable tool adoption challenge: how to best exploit Genr8 to accomplish a set of goals. To do this, the designer's task becomes one of figuring out how to express her design criteria in ways that are amenable to Genr8's framework. Since so many new and unorthodox concepts are incorporated into Genr8, this task is reported as often being non-intuitive. Genr8 is sometimes experienced as being unwieldly. The challenge for the designer lies in combining and understanding the abstract parameters and the behavior and outcome of the evolutionary and the growth algorithms with the geometrical and spatial layout at hand. The environment fortunately is much more intuitive to work with. It provides a powerful means of representing a wide range of influences, both physical and more conceptual notions. The designer gradually acquires an appreciation of the solutions proposed by Genr8. The designer also gradually learns to recognize how the tool has negotiated among different constraints and performance criteria.

Genr8 was originally conceived as a sketching tool to be used at an early stage in the design process. It was predicted to be useful for deriving broad conceptualizations of form that would subsequently undergo more detailed definition and analysis with respect to structure or material. It was expected that the lack of structural and material analysis in Genr8 would limit its specific value. Although the environment can be set up to reflect the physical reality to a certain extent, the fitness criteria and the parameters are inherently geometric. This forces the designer to interpret the structural or material constraints in geometric terms (for example, by restraining certain angles or the distances between support points).

By interacting with the designers using Genr8 the developers have learned that it is more powerful than they initially predicted. Architects have and will continue to exploit the tool with unanticipated techniques and solutions that surmount its limitations regarding structure and material considerations. One such example is the work of Achim Menges presented in Sect. 8.5 which is a result of his insight that the constraints of the manufacturing process can be mapped to the environment and parameters of Genr8. One instance of a "bug" becoming a feature emerged in the course of the Butterfly Machines project which is based on the concept of self-intersecting surfaces. Originally, self-intersecting surfaces were a "bug". They arise when multiple attractors and repellors are placed close to the seed. The developers thought no one would want them but they also could find no simple means of preventing them. In hindsight, it is quite fortunate that the "bug" was left untouched.

The overall scenario of early-stage use was indeed adopted by the designers. Nevertheless, the designers did not perceive geometric interpretations to be as big of an obstacle as originally feared. Instead they considered Genr8's approach to creating surfaces through a generative growth algorithm to be an opportunity. Paraphrasing an early feedback comment: "In contrast to most contemporary design, Genr8's approach is not based on the artificial distinction between processes of form definition and making. Instead it derives morphology from the inherent constraints and possibilities of production and construction. Thus Genr8 becomes not only an enabling software tool but also a strategic vehicle for understanding and instrumenting the design process as truly morphogenetic, in which process formation and materialization are always inherently and inseparably related." Another interesting aspect of design tools based on EC is that they provide a family of designs, and we have shown how they can be successfully embraced to provide highly interesting and exciting options. For example, a designer can obtain surfaces which are equally well adapted to the given fitness criteria, but nevertheless quite distinct as illustrated in Fig. 8.10*b*.

At the outset of Genr8's development in 2001, the developers had many goals: provide a proof of concept that ideas from evolutionary computation and Artificial Life could be useful in architectural design, address the complicated issue of developing natural shapes with biologically inspired computational processes, and develop a unique software that aims to be creative by being able to come up with new ideas in tandem with the designer. Both Genr8's developers and the designers who are co-authors of this chapter agree that Genr8 has achieved its goals.

8.7 Synthesis

We have developed an open-ended, creative, surface design tool which uses an organic growth model and an evolutionary algorithm. The surfaces are grown in a parallel fashion with all parts changing and expanding at the same time during each growth step. Growth occurs in response to a 3D environment with force and boundary elements. One technical underpinning of Genr8 is a graphics-based algorithm that implements extended map L-systems that generate surfaces in 3D space. Another is Genr8's use of Grammatical Evolution to evolve rewrite systems which are interpreted to form surfaces. The fitness function is a weighted combination of specific surface features. Genr8 is interactive and attempts to maximize the possibilities for the user to maintain creative control. Genr8's generative process handles what is hard for a human designer to specify and predict. It is arguably impossible for a designer to directly specify an outcome similar to Genr8's. Nor can a designer usually fully anticipate what Genr8's outcome will be. Thus, open-ended is a good characterization of Genr8.

The paradox of making Genr8 open-ended is that, while it does not constrain the designers who use it, predicting how it will be used is impossible. Through observing Genr8 in use it has at least been possible now to elucidate some strategies that successfully exploit it. Yet, we remain certain that not all of its possibilities and potential have been enumerated to date. If Genr8 continues to be disseminated in a way wherein its adopters must figure out how to use it by themselves, it will continue to be integral to many creative and inventive design interactions.

Acknowledgements

We would like to thank Peter Testa, Devyn Weiser, Simon Greenwold and all the other members of the Emergent Design Group at MIT for their contributions to developing Genr8. We are also grateful to Michael Hensel and Mike Weinstock at the AA for stimulating discussions. Finally, we would like to thank all the students and other designers who have provided valuable feedback over the years.

References

1. Tsui, E. (1999). *Evolutionary Architecture: Nature as a Basis for Design.* John Wiley
2. Thompson, D. (1961). *On Growth and Form.* Cambridge University Press
3. Frazer, J. (1995). *An Evolutionary Architecture.* Architectural Association. London
4. von Neumann, J. (1966). *The Theory of Self-Reproducing Automata.* University of Illinois Press

5. Broughton, T., Coates, P., Jackson, H. (1999). Exploring 3d design worlds using Lindenmayer systems and genetic programming. In Bentley, P.J., ed.: *Evolutionary Design by Computers.* Morgan Kaufmann
6. Hornby, G.S., Pollack, J.B. (2001). The advantages of generative grammatical encodings for physical design. In: *Congress on Evolutionary Computation*
7. Kumar, S., Bentley, P.J., eds. (2003). *On Growth, Form and Computers.* Elsevier
8. Murawski, K., Arciszewski, T., Jong, K.A.D. (2000). Evolutionary computation in structural design. *Eng. Comput. (Lond.)*, **16**(3-4): 275–286
9. Shi, X.G., Gero, J.S. (2000). Design families and design individuals. *Eng. Comput. (Lond.)*, **16**(3-4): 253–263
10. Maher, M.L. (2000). A model of co-evolutionary design. *Eng. Comput. (Lond.)*, **16**(3-4): 195–208
11. Gero, J.S., Kazakov, V. (2000). Adaptive enlargement of state spaces in evolutionary designing. *AI EDAM*, **14**(1): 31–38
12. Gero, J.S., Kazakov, V. (2001). A genetic engineering approach to genetic algorithms. *Evolutionary Computation*, **9**(1): 71–92
13. Bentley, P.J., ed. (1999). *Evolutionary Design by Computers.* Morgan Kaufmann
14. Bentley, P., Corne, D., eds. (2001). *Creative Evolutionary Systems.* Morgan Kaufmann
15. O'Reilly, U.M., Hemberg, M. (2007). Integrating generative growth and evolutionary computation for form exploration. *Genetic Programming and Evolvable Machines*, **8**(2): 163–186
16. Prusinkiewicz, P., Lindenmayer, A. (1991). *The Algorithmic Beauty of Plants.* Springer
17. O'Neill, M., Ryan, C. (2003). *Grammatical Evolution – Evolving Programs in an Arbitrary Language.* Kluwer Academic Publishers
18. Mitchell, M. (1996). *An Introduction to Genetic Algorithms.* MIT Press
19. Koza, J.R. (1992). *Genetic Programming: On the Programming of Computers by Means of Natural Selection.* MIT Press
20. Romero, J., Machado, P., Santos, A., Cardoso, A. (2003). On the development of critics in evolutionary computation artists. In Raidl, G.R., Cagnoni, S., Cardalda, J.J.R., Corne, D.W., Gottlieb, J., Guillot, A., Hart, E., Johnson, C.G., Marchiori, E., Meyer, J.A., Middendorf, M., eds.: *Applications of Evolutionary Computing, EvoWorkshops2003: EvoBIO, EvoCOP, EvoIASP, EvoMUSART, EvoROB, EvoSTIM.* Vol. 2611 of LNCS. University of Essex, England, UK. Springer-Verlag, 562–573

9

Evolving Human Faces

Charlie D. Frowd[1], and Peter J. B. Hancock[2]

[1] Department of Psychology, University of Stirling, Stirling FK9 4LA, UK
cdf1@stir.ac.uk
[2] Department of Psychology, University of Stirling, Stirling FK9 4LA, UK
pjbh1@stir.ac.uk

Summary. Witnesses and victims of serious crime are normally requested to construct a picture of the criminal's face. These pictures are known as facial composites and are typically produced by a witness recalling details of the face and then selecting individual facial features: hair, eyes, nose, mouth, etc. While composites remain an important tool for the apprehension of criminals, research has suggested that, even under favorable conditions, they are rarely recognized. In the current chapter, we present a new method called EvoFIT whereby users select complete faces and a composite is "evolved" using a Genetic Algorithm. While considerable development was required to tune the new approach, research indicates that EvoFIT now produces more identifiable composites than those produced from the traditional "feature" systems. Novel applications of the technology are also discussed.

9.1 Introduction

Creating a drawing of someone's face requires considerable skill and practice and is usually a job for an artist. Most people cannot produce a recognizable face. However, a victim of or witness to a crime may be asked by the police to create such an image of the person he saw. Unable to do so alone, he works with either a skilled sketch artist or a specially trained police officer operating a photo-composite system. While sketch artists can produce quite good renditions of a target face, results from computer composite systems are typically relatively poor (e.g., [1, 2, 3, 4]). This chapter describes how the artistic potential of an evolutionary-based face generation system may be exploited to produce a system that allows users to produce a passable likeness with relatively little help.

The current procedure requires a witness first to describe the appearance of a face and then to select individual facial features: hair, face shape, eyes, brows, nose, mouth, and ears. A sketch artist draws the face by hand using pencils and crayons, while the composite systems use features cut from photographs of a large number of faces. The term facial "composite" is used to describe an image produced from any technique, including a sketch artist.

Facial composites are circulated within a police force, and sometimes more widely in the newspapers and on TV, in an attempt to identify a suspect and promote an arrest.

Methods for producing facial composites have changed considerably. About 40 years ago, a system called Photofit was popular in the UK (and was similar to another called Identikit in the US). Photofit contained facial features printed on jigsaw-like pieces that fitted into a template to build up the face. The approach was simple to use, but research suggested that the faces produced were rather poor renditions of the persons concerned (e.g., Ellis et al. [5]). While part of the reason for this turned out to be limitations in the available facial features (Davies [6]), a more serious problem was that witnesses were required to select facial features in isolation from a complete face [7]. There is good evidence that we recognize faces as "wholes" (e.g., Tanaka and Farah [8]) and the absence of a complete face for selecting the facial features interferes with this process. Modern systems not only contain a better range of facial features, but witnesses select the features in the context of an intact face.

There are many of these "feature"-type composite systems available throughout the world, and most are computerized. In the UK, there are two systems, E-FIT and PRO-fit; in the US, there are more: FACES, Identikit 2000 and ComPhotofit are examples. It is apparent that a good rendition of a face is now possible with these techniques when a person works directly from a photograph of a face, essentially an exercise in copying [1, 9]. However, laboratory research clearly demonstrates that a different story emerges when a person constructs a face from memory. It turns out that composites are correctly identified only about 20% of the time when a target has been seen quite recently [1, 2, 9, 3, 4], but after a delay of several days, the norm for real witnesses, correct identification levels fall to just a few percent, in spite of some careful experimental designs which have attempted to mirror police procedures as far as possible [10, 11, 12].

This result is particularly alarming in the light of the considerable developments made in the production systems and the forensic importance of composites. The consequence is that few criminals are likely to be apprehended using current procedures and technology. But, why should this be? We believe that the basic procedure of selecting individual facial features is an unnatural process, even if carried out in the context of a complete face. As mentioned above, faces are perceived as wholes, not parts, and, as such, approaches based on the selection of individual features are essentially flawed. The traditional process clearly involves an element of recalling information, and describing and selecting facial features, an exercise similar to remembering items in a shopping list, and is subject to quite rapid decay (Ellis et al. [13]); this would appear to be the reason why composite quality diminishes with increasing delay. However, while face recall decays rapidly, face recognition does not, and instead remains more stable for longer periods (e.g., Shepherd [14]). Indeed, this contrast reflects a more general division within human cognition between the recognition and the recall of information (e.g., [15]). It would appear therefore that an approach based more on recognition rather than recall is likely to be more successful for the production of composites.

9.2 A Recognition-Based Face Evolving System

Given the deficiencies of the traditional "feature" approach, a better composite system is likely to be one that capitalizes on our ability to recognize a face as a whole, rather than recalling specific details of a face and selecting individual facial features. For the past ten years we have been designing such a system: EvoFIT [16, 17, 18]. Users of EvoFIT are presented with sets of complete faces, initially with random though plausible facial characteristics, and select a few that best match their memory of a target. These faces are then bred together to combine their characteristics, and users select again. Repeated a couple of times, the faces become more like each other and more like that of a target. Ultimately, the face with the best likeness is saved as the composite. A composite is therefore evolved by the supervised process of selecting whole faces. A Genetic Algorithm (GA) is used to breed the selected faces together, to provide a user with alternatives, and, in doing so, to carry out a search in the space of possible faces.

We are aware of two other systems that evolve faces in a similar way, one developed by Chris Solomon [19], the other by Colin Tredoux [20]; while we are not aware of a formal evaluation involving these alternatives, one comparing EvoFIT and the ID system [20] has recently been proposed [21]. The general approach was inspired by Richard Dawkins [22], but has also been popularized in Michael Crichton's novel, *Prey* [23].

In the following sections, the mechanism used to generate faces within EvoFIT is described, along with details of the GA used and the enhancements made to the basic system; a more detailed account may be found in [16] and [18].

9.2.1 Generating Faces

There are a number of possible ways to synthesize good-quality human face images that could be presented to witnesses when constructing a composite. Perhaps one of the most obvious is to generate faces with facial features – eyes, nose, mouth and so forth – which have been sampled from a conventional "feature"-based composite system. This approach would present a number of candidate faces to a witness for rating of best likeness. Features in the faces with higher likeness scores would be combined to produce further candidate faces for rating. This general approach was followed by Caldwell and Johnston [24] who generated faces containing features sampled from the Photofit kit. While informal evidence was given for its success, there are inherent problems. One of the most pressing is perhaps the coding mechanism used to represent the facial features along the genetic strings: it is unclear how to classify features satisfactorily in this way. A better approach would be to move away from a feature-based coding system to one where faces are represented in their entirety. In this respect, the model used to generate faces would be broadly similar to the whole face mechanism we use to recognize faces [8].

Arguably the best known method for generating a holistic representation of a face, and the approach followed here, is to use Principal Components Analysis, or PCA (for a review of PCA refer to [25]). PCA is a statistical technique that extracts the main axes of variation within a set of data – in this case, faces. It provides a compact coding scheme, namely a set of PCA coefficients for each item of data, along with a set of reference vectors called *eigenvectors* (or sometimes *eigenfaces*, *eigenshapes* and *eigentextures* when modeling faces). The eigenvectors provide a code which influences the overall appearance of a face, and thus are holistic in nature. As can be seen in the animations on the DVD accompanying this book, some of the eigenvectors provide a coding scheme which appears to be psychologically based [26] – by changing a face's width, length or age – but most have quite complex behaviours, such as a combination of head rotation plus nodding. The eigenvectors also provide a mechanism which allows the original data to be reconstructed by a weighted combination (a set of PCA coefficient values) of eigenvectors. In the current application, combining the eigenvectors in different random proportions allows a novel face to be generated.

To provide a natural variation in facial appearance, two such PCA models are required: one is referred to as facial *shape*, the other facial *texture*. We note that other approaches, such as Cootes et al. [27], combine these models into a unified one, but are kept separate here to accelerate the process, as discussed later. The initial procedure to construct these two models with PCA requires the careful positioning of about 250 coordinate points around key facial features in a set of reference faces, as shown in Fig. 9.1.

These coordinate locations are then subjected to a PCA which provides a statistical *shape* model. This model describes not only the shape and position of the features of the inner face, but also the outline of the face and the shape of the hair, ears and neck. The model contains a set of reference shapes, known as *eigenshapes* in this context, which are combined in random proportions (the PCA shape coefficients) to produce a novel face shape. For the second model, *texture*, the reference images are first distorted or *morphed* to a common average shape, also illustrated in Fig. 9.1, so that the features of each face are aligned. A second PCA is applied to the pixel intensities of these aligned images, which describes the colour of the eyes, brows and mouth as well as the overall appearance of the facial skin. This model contains a set of reference textures, or *eigentextures*, which are similarly combined in random proportions (PCA texture coefficients) to produce a random texture.

The generation of a novel face is the result of a random facial texture from the texture model morphed to a novel face shape from the shape model. In

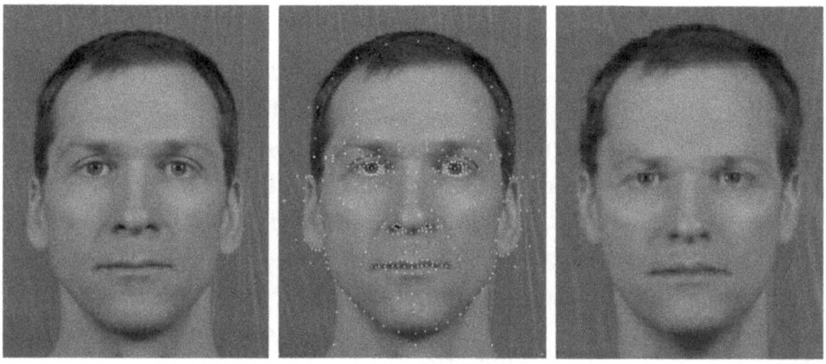

Fig. 9.1. Image preprocessing. The first stage to building a face generator is the careful positioning of facial landmarks (centre). The landmarks are used to build a facial shape model and also to morph each face to an average shape (right) in readiness for constructing a facial texture model. The image on the left is the original

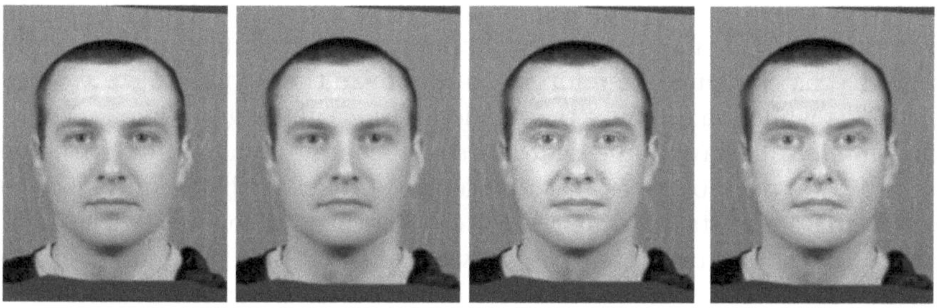

a) Hair, ears, neck b) Shape c) Texture d) Combined image

Fig. 9.2. Representations used in the production of a novel face: a) hair, ears and neck – the external facial features – with average face shape and texture; b) random shape with landmarks overlaid (average texture); c) random texture (average shape); and d) final image comprising the random texture morphed to the random shape

practice, users select an appropriate set of "external" facial features – hair, ears and neck – at the start of the process and the texture is blended into this reference image, with shape changes applied thereafter. Repeating this procedure with different random PCA shape and texture coefficients produces plausible, but different-looking new faces. Refer to Fig. 9.2 for an example of the representations used in the production of a novel face.

In the following section, the evolutionary mechanism employed to locate a specific face within a face model is discussed, along with results from computer simulations, which were used to fine-tune the process, and several formal evaluations of system performance.

9.2.2 Evolving a Composite Face

The face model at the heart of EvoFIT is capable of producing a very large number of different-looking faces. The construction of a composite using this model is essentially a search problem: to locate a face with a good likeness within the space of possibilities, a problem ideally suited to an evolutionary approach. It is apparent that given an appropriately constructed face model, a large population size and many breeding cycles, that it should be possible to produce a face with a good likeness to a target.

Clearly, the size and constitution of the faces used to build the face models will influence the range of faces able to be generated. Early work involved models built from 36 adult faces generally in their thirties [16], but the formal evaluations described below used 72, a number comparable to that used in other PCA face research (e.g., [25, 28]). More recent work, as mentioned in Sect. 9.3.1, explores the role of more carefully selected face sets. Note that merely increasing the size of the face model, in an attempt to increase the range of faces produced, does not necessarily improve performance [29] since the complexity of the face space is also likely to increase.

Witnesses to crime are unlikely to have seen the suspect for very long and their memory of this face may suffer interference if too many other faces are presented. The challenge therefore is to minimize the number of faces shown to witnesses while maximizing the chances of locating a good likeness within the face model. We have found that users are generally comfortable with being shown up to about 500 faces in total, a size similar to that found elsewhere [30], and this suggests an upper limit on face production per witness. The approach taken was to present users with sets of 18 faces, a number close to the maximum that can be sensibly displayed on a computer monitor. An example screenshot is presented in Fig. 9.3 overleaf.

In an initial implementation by Peter Hancock [31], user feedback on the subjective likeness of a screen of 18 such faces was via a rating scale (a Windows slider). The underlying GA based the selection of parents on higher rating scores (proportional fitness selection) and a new generation of 18 faces was bred comprising of a random mix of PCA coefficients from both parents (uniform crossover), with a small amount mutation applied to the coefficient values. The same basic approach was used in the current implementation, though rating scales were removed since rating about 500 faces might be a rather arduous task for a witness. It turns out that about one in ten faces are produced from the models with a likeness somewhat similar to a target face, or two faces in a set of 18. We therefore simply ask users to select two faces per screen, and give each selected face an equal breeding opportunity in the GA (unity selection pressure).

A series of computer simulations were run to estimate settings for the evolutionary parameters [16, 18], the results of which are summarized in Table 9.1. These simulations used randomly generated faces as targets and a face selection procedure that was based on the overall error between a population and a target face. Specifically, faces were selected with the lowest mean-square error (MSE) for image pixel values for a target. The general approach is rather problematic, as evolutionary parameters tend to interact with each other (e.g., Mitchell [32]), although indications were that better performance

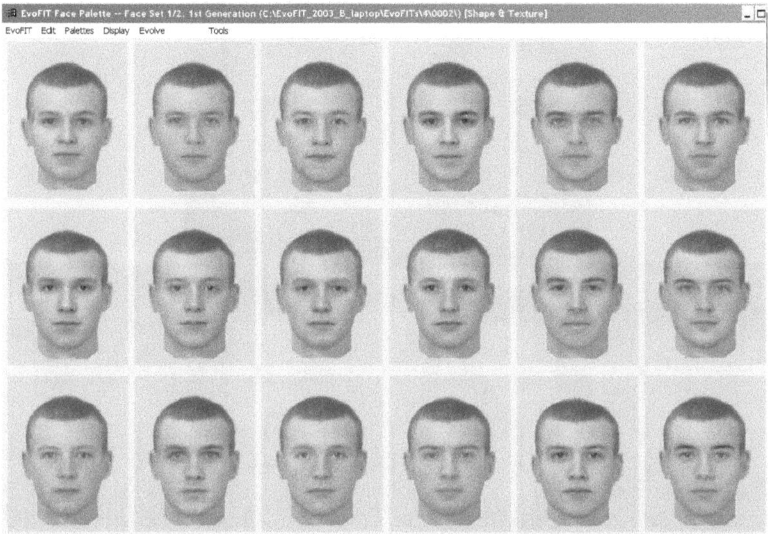

Fig. 9.3. An example screen of EvoFIT faces. The faces shown contain random shape and texture characteristics (within the range of a young adult white male) and are presented with a hairstyle selected by the user

was produced with a small probability of mutation (a rate of about 1 in 20) and following at least three cycles of breeding. The effect of crossover and mutation operators is illustrated in Fig. 9.4.

The work clearly demonstrated that even a single cycle of breeding produced a much better likeness of a target than just a random generation of faces. The work also found value in carrying forward the best likeness to the next generation, a so-called elitist approach, since this avoids a preferable likeness being lost through breeding; specifically, via crossover and mutation operators. In addition, more rapid evolution emerged by giving this best (elitist) face twice the number of breeding opportunities relative to the other selected faces. Further, it was found valuable to separate the selection of facial shape and texture. This is because sometimes a face with an appropriate texture may have a poor shape, and vice versa. To accommodate this improvement, the system was expanded with extra screens to first present facial shape, and then facial texture. As can be seen by Fig. 9.5, a quite good likeness could now be evolved using targets which had been randomly generated from within the system.

Two further improvements were made prior to carrying out a more formal test. Firstly, although users were asked to base their selections on an overall (holistic) impression of a face, they sometimes requested more feature-like operations to be carried out on the evolved faces, such as making them thinner or lowering the faces' eyebrows. A small utility called the Feature Shift tool was designed to allow such modifications, and was offered for use not just

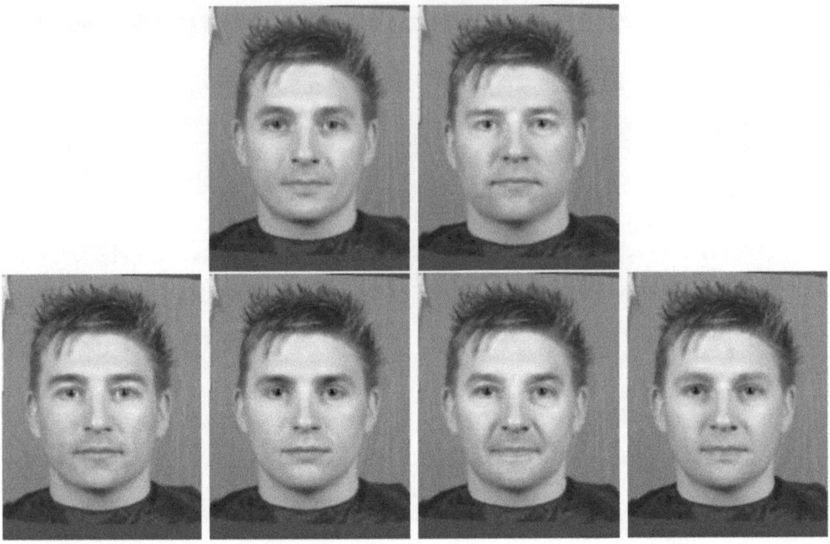

(a) (b) (c) (d)

Fig. 9.4. The effect of crossover and mutation operators. The shape and texture PCA coefficients of the "parent" faces (top row) were mixed together via a uniform crossover operator to produce four different "offspring" faces (bottom row). Faces (a) and (b) were bred without mutation; (c) and (d) illustrate the effect when a small amount of mutation (one in 20 parameters) was applied: (c) illustrates a positive age mutation and (d) illustrates a mutation which has lightened the eyebrows

Table 9.1. Summary of parameter settings emerging from computer simulations

Parameter	**Setting**
Population size	10-32
Generations	5-12 (depending on population size)
Mutation rate	0.1 (probability per parameter)
Breeding opportunities	2:1 (Best face : other selected faces)
Elitism	Enabled
No. of selected faces	Fewer is better (lower limit 3 or 4)
Selection of shapes and textures	Separate

when evolution was complete, but to enhance the best (elitist) face selected at the end of each generation, thus further accelerating convergence. The second improvement attempted to make face selection easier for users. Recall that shapes are selected first, and then textures. In the first generation, no texture would have been selected, and so the shapes are presented with an average texture (see Fig. 9.2). In the second generation, a preferable texture would have already been identified that contained in the best face, and thus the shapes were given the texture from this elitist face. A similar idea was applied when displaying textures, with these faces morphed into the shape of

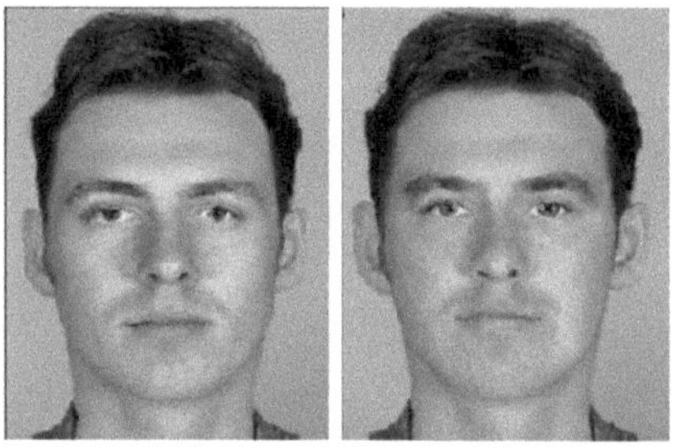

Fig. 9.5. An example composite (left) evolved by a user of a randomly generated target (right). An early version of face model was used and system settings were suggested by simulation

the best likeness presented on the previous shape screen. Subjective feedback was positive from users regarding these additional enhancements.

9.2.3 Evaluation and Development

EvoFIT has been subjected to a number of more formal evaluations [9, 4, 10, 16, 18, 33, 17]. Such investigations are normally quite complicated in design but typically involve recruiting participants to act as "witnesses", exposing each person to a target face for a short time, and asking him to evolve a composite. Note that we have generally avoided constructing EvoFIT composites directly from a target photograph, unlike that carried out with the feature systems [1, 9]. While such "in view" construction focuses more on the capability of the system by minimizing memory load, users may be tempted to inspect the individual features of the faces, as is likely with such comparative procedures [4], and thus detract from a whole face selection mechanism. Instead, we have generally opted to evolve highly familiar faces when more optimal conditions are required.

For a baseline, we compare the quality of EvoFIT composites with composites constructed by another group of witnesses who use one of the "feature" systems, such as the UK E-FIT or PRO-fit. In addition, witnesses are normally required to describe the appearance of their target face prior to composite construction, to reflect police procedures, although this is not necessary with EvoFIT. Further, the work normally involves a "facial imaging specialist", a person who assists witnesses recall their target face and operates the computer software. The resulting composites are then given to a further group of participants who evaluate them by attempting to give each a name, or to match them to photographs of the targets. These latter, more auxiliary measures of composite quality are often quite important as composite naming is generally very poor when construction occurs a couple of days after a target has been seen (e.g., [9, 10]).

The first such EvoFIT evaluation by Frowd et al. [18] used 30 photographs of well-known famous male faces as targets; examples included Tom Cruise,

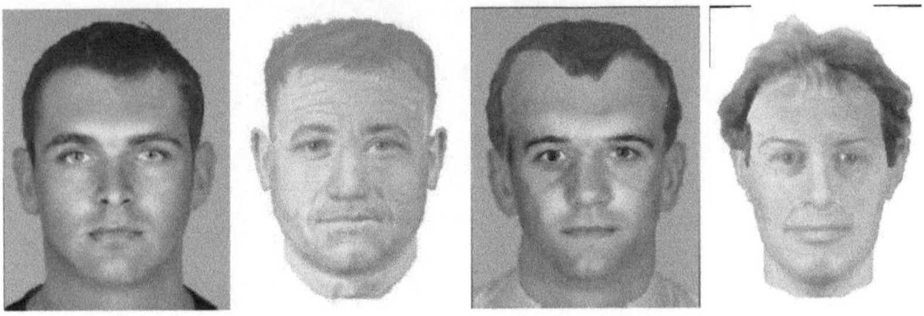

Fig. 9.6. Example EvoFIT and E-FIT composites produced in the study. They are of the American actor Bruce Willis (left pair) and British Prime Minister Tony Blair (right pair). The EvoFIT is the left image for each pair

Tony Blair, Michael Owen and Robert De Niro. Thirty people looked at the photograph of a celebrity for 60 seconds, described his face and then evolved a composite. To do this, they first chose a hairstyle, and were then nominally shown four screens of 18 facial shapes, and selected two per screen up to a maximum of six, and four screens of 18 facial textures, and similarly selected six – that is, an approximate population size of 60 shapes and 60 textures. After selecting the best overall likeness, the elitist face, the faces were bred together. Witnesses made use of the Feature Shift tool on the best face as necessary and three generations were normally run (i.e., the initial generation of faces plus two complete breeding cycles). Any additional artistic enhancements, such as darkening the eyebrows or adding shading to the facial texture, which is sometimes necessary with all systems,[3] was carried out using Adobe Photoshop. Example composites are shown in Fig. 9.6.

Another group of 30 people followed the same procedure as above but prepared a composite with the UK E-FIT system instead of EvoFIT. To do this, they selected individual features contained in the system, and positioned and resized each as necessary in order to create the best possible likeness.

Analysis revealed that the E-FIT composites were correctly named 17% of the time, the norm for feature systems with immediate construction [1, 2, 9] or when the delay is only a few hours in duration [4], but the EvoFITs were correctly named only 10% of the time. While this result was somewhat disappointing for EvoFIT, it turns out that most of the targets used were much older than the average age in the EvoFIT model, which had an average of 30 years, and demonstrated that the PCA model did not generalize well by

[3] We have examined the effect of artistic enhancement on a set of 20 PRO-fit and Photofit composites constructed by realistic procedures in the laboratory (from Frowd et al. [4]). Results suggested that the presence of artwork changes (carried out on the composites as part of the construction procedure) approximately doubled the naming rate, thus underscoring the importance of this procedure (unpublished data). An example of artwork improvements can be seen in the EvoFIT of Tony Blair in Fig. 1.6 which includes under-eyes bags and shading along the jowls.

age. A good example of this is the EvoFIT produced of Tony Blair, who does indeed look young.

A more realistic evaluation was carried out later by Frowd et al. [10], and this compared EvoFIT with a range of composite systems in police use. Participant witnesses again looked at a photograph of a famous face, only this time the target was checked to be unfamiliar to them (as in real life) and was kept in memory for a realistic two days. A new similarly sized face model was also built, one that was capable of constructing faces up to an age of about 40 years and was also suitable for police use (the previous one was for research only). Targets were age-appropriate for the EvoFIT face model. Five groups of 10 people took part in the study, and each group constructed a single composite with one of five systems: E-FIT, PRO-fit, EvoFIT, FACES (a US system) and a sketch artist; refer to Fig. 9.7 for examples.

The overall level of composite naming was very poor for this experiment, a few percent correct, and the best performance was found for those people who worked with the police sketch artist, a mean of 8.1% correct – see Table 9.2 for details. The result was again disappointing for EvoFIT, though these composites were nonetheless named significantly more often than those constructed with E-FIT and PRO-fit.

While there was anecdotal evidence that EvoFIT could sometimes produce a good-quality composite, and therefore a good representation of the target face existed within the face model, evaluations such as those mentioned above suggested that the evolution was not reliably converging on a good likeness of a target. We have since found a much better method for the user to identify the face with the best likeness at the end of each generation. The new method is to simply present all combinations of selected facial shape and facial texture, a total of 36 faces (six shapes × six textures), and to ask witnesses to select the best likeness. This is somewhat like a tournament selection method, where

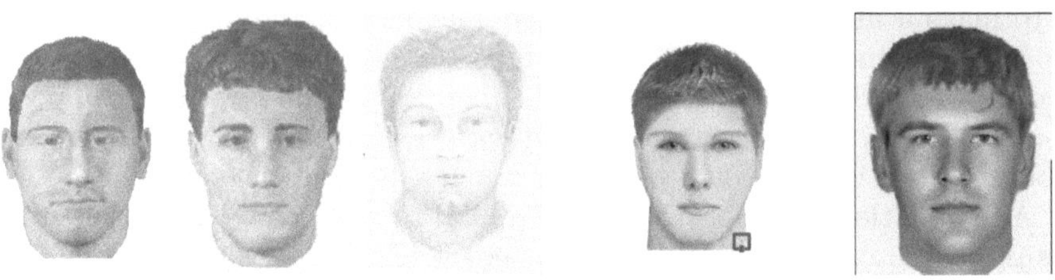

Fig. 9.7. Example composites each constructed of the US actor Ben Affleck. They were produced by different witnesses after a two-day delay from (left to right) E-FIT, PRO-fit, a sketch artist, FACES and EvoFIT

Sketch	**EvoFIT**	**FACES**	**PRO-fit**	**E-FIT**
8.1	3.6	3.2	1.3	0.0

Table 9.2. Mean naming level of the composites produced in the two-day study. Values are percent correct

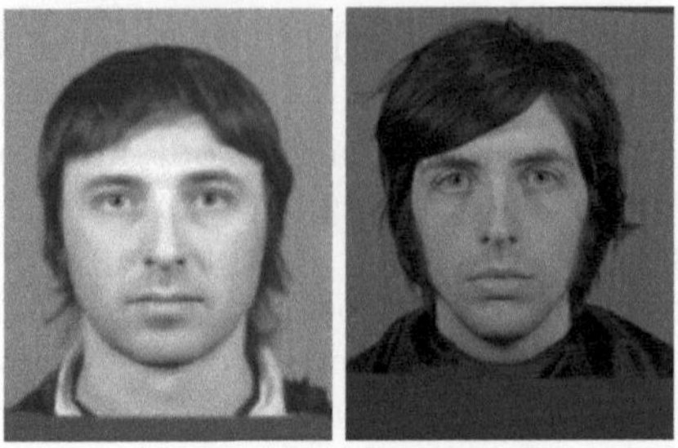

Fig. 9.8. An example composite (left) evolved from the memory of a face (right) using the enhanced method for selecting the best face

candidates compete with each other for pole position, but the result has had a quite dramatic effect on system convergence, as found in the next evaluation. An example composite produced from memory using this method is presented in Fig. 9.8.

A version of the system containing the shape-texture combinations was evaluated by Frowd et al. [9] in the same way as [10], using unfamiliar target faces and a two-day delay. Since celebrities such as film stars tend to be relatively attractive, we used UK footballers, not generally known for their good looks, as targets. This had the added advantage that they would be genuinely unfamiliar to people with no interest in the game, who would construct the composites, but potentially identifiable by fans, who would evaluate them. In this study, the method participant witnesses used to remember or encode their target face was also manipulated. It is known that people may consciously attempt to remember the appearance of a face, and thereby scrutinize the face feature-by-feature, or they may perceive the face more passively and form a more overall (holistic) impression [34]. In the study, participant witnesses were asked either to study the features of their target face, a feature encoding, or to make a number of personality judgments, which are known to encourage a holistic encoding (e.g., [35]). Each person made a composite using either EvoFIT or PRO-fit. It was expected that the traditional "feature" composites from PRO-fit would be better under a feature encoding but that composites evolved from EvoFIT would be better under a holistic encoding.

An evaluation of the composites (Fig. 9.9) revealed that the overall level of composite naming was consistently better for the EvoFITs than the PRO-fits (8.0% vs. 4.3%), demonstrating success in the new method for identifying the best face. This procedure appears to improve the search of face space with only a modest increase in the number of faces presented to users (about 100 faces more per person).

There were two slightly curious results found in this study. The first was that both approaches benefited from scrutinizing a target face by its features. This type of coding may assist EvoFIT users by allowing them to verbalize the face better, which would then be helpful when improving the size and

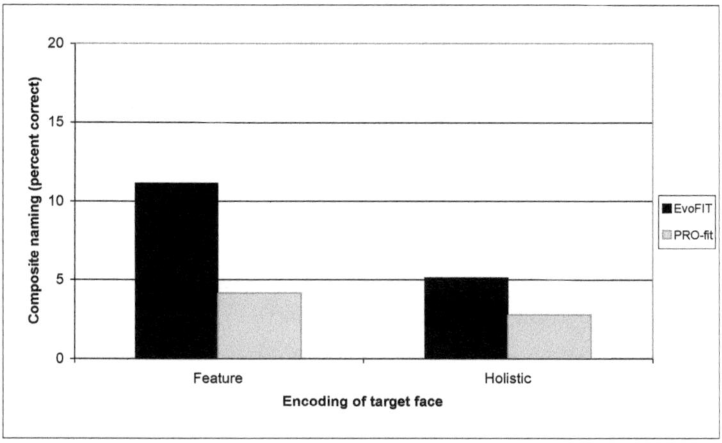

Fig. 9.9. Naming of the EvoFIT and PRO-fit composites in the two day footballers' study. The target faces were unfamiliar to the participant witnesses

placement of features using the Feature Shift tool. The significant gain in naming under feature encoding, relative to the currently used PRO-fit system, has suggested, along with other research [33, 17], that while performance is by no means perfect, the system would be of value to the police at this stage. As such, the UK police have now been given a full system for use in criminal investigations; this software may also be used for research and is provided on the accompanying DVD. Secondly, a supplementary analysis revealed that the quality of the hairstyles on the EvoFITs was a little better than those on the PRO-fits, in spite of the hair being taken throughout from the PRO-fit system in this evaluation (to maintain a tight comparison). It is most likely that a better hairstyle was produced since the shape of the hairstyle is part of the evolving process (recall that it is morphed along with the rest of the face shape) and an overall better likeness could be gained through breeding.

9.2.4 Operation Mallard

EvoFIT was first used forensically a few years ago in a UK criminal investigation, Operation Mallard. This case involved a series of sexual assaults which took place in Southern England between 1999 and 2001. Several composites were constructed in this investigation and several public appeals were made for information on the BBC Crimewatch program, though the perpetrator was not located. One of the most recent victims had difficulty in recalling the appearance of the assailant's hair and this was likely to have limited the effectiveness of the overall sketch. About a year later, however, the victim was reminded of a more appropriate hairstyle, first on TV and then in the street, and an updated sketch was prepared for the hair, ears and neck. It was

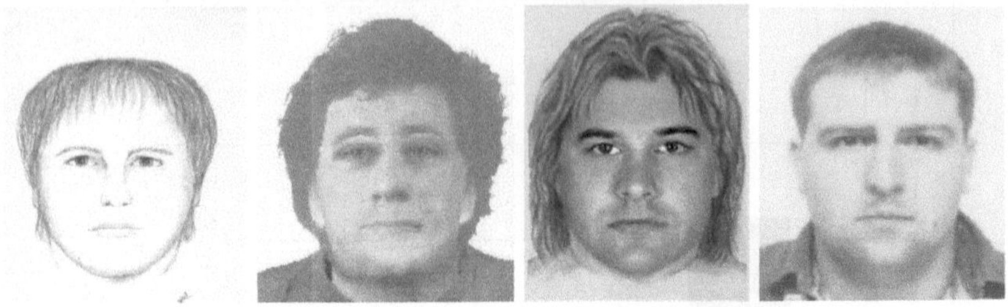

Fig. 9.10. The Sketch, E-FIT and EvoFIT constructed in the Operation Mallard investigation. A photograph of the assailant is on the right

decided that this image be used as a starting point for the construction of an EvoFIT with this victim.

This new sketch was resized and the outline of the face and hair morphed so that it could be used as a set of external features. The construction of an EvoFIT was carried out as normal, by the selection of shapes and textures, but without the improved method of obtaining a best face, and three generations of faces were required to evolve a good likeness of the assailant (see Fig. 9.10). The EvoFIT evoked a powerful reminder of the incident and the victim found it quite uncomfortable to look at.

The perpetrator of these crimes was recently identified by familial DNA (a family member was on the UK National DNA database) and has been convicted. We have now carried out a small evaluation [33] of the composites produced from the latest victim. While the main aim of this study was to explore the effectiveness of averaging together the composites produced, since this can enhance target identification [2], the sketch was found to be generally best, the EvoFIT second-best, and the E-FIT third-best; the EvoFIT appeared to have the best individual features. Overall, the results suggested that EvoFIT could produce good results when used in a criminal investigation.

9.3 Exploring the Artistic Potential of EvoFIT

EvoFIT was designed for a specific purpose, to transfer the memory of a face into a form (a picture) that can be communicated to and recognized by another person. Evolving a face is clearly a creative process: it is in essence a person's expression of an image held in memory. Of course, witnesses or victims may not be able to recall the appearance of the face, they are much more likely to recognize the similarity in a given face; hence the value of EvoFIT; but such images may still be considered "works of art". There are of course limits to the appropriateness of a witness's artistic expression, largely constrained by the seriousness of the application, and it may be inappropriate for witnesses to over-exaggerate a composite to make it look too aggressive, too threatening or too "criminal" in appearance, even if these traits better reflect a particular crime. In the laboratory, it has been shown that the subjective opinion held by a participant witness of a target can indeed influence the appearance of a composite (e.g., Shepherd et al. [36]). However, it is also likely that composites are better recognized by other people (who are typically close friends or family members of the suspect) when the composite itself is portrayed with a more neutral, or even positive, expression. This suggests that composites exhibiting less extreme expressions may be more identifiable. EvoFIT can, however, clearly be used creatively in other ways; for example to explore a range of human percepts such as attractiveness, intelligence and arrogance. These arguably more subjective notions of appearance are explored below in conjunction with other applications of the technology.

9.3.1 Evolving Generic Face Types

Social psychology informs us that we make judgments of people based on facial appearance. For example, it has been shown that the simple act of wearing glasses can give the impression of greater intelligence. We also have a clear notion of what an attractive face looks like [37] even if we are unable to express it verbally. One possible way to explore the presence of stereotypes is to simply ask people to "evolve" a generic face type. Another evolutionary face system, FacePrints, been used in this way to demonstrate that it is indeed possible to evolve attractive faces [38], or faces that are highly masculine or feminine [39].

EvoFIT has similarly been used to evolve attractive faces of women [40]. Howdle tested two groups of 15 men: those native to Britain and those who had grown up in Africa but were students at Stirling. Each person was presented with three screens of 18 randomly generated faces (each face changed by both shape and texture) and were asked to select two from each screen that seemed most attractive. They then chose the best of these six and a new generation of faces was produced; this was repeated for three generations. The face model used was of young Caucasian women, so it was understood that the faces generated might not be ideal for the African group, but nevertheless they were able to choose faces that seemed relatively attractive to them. The hair for all faces was the same, a relatively short, dark style.

The generated images were evaluated by pairing one from a British participant and one from an African. Eight such pairs were then shown to 12 African and 12 British students, who were asked to select which of each pair they preferred. The results showed a significant interaction, with each race choosing more of the images generated by members of his own race. Visual inspection suggested that the African participants generated faces which were rounder and had more prominent eyes than those produced by the British participants

We have also started exploring whether it is possible to evolve other generic face types: do we have a stereotype of what an intelligent person might look like? Might the same be true for an artist, a footballer, a celebrity, or even a

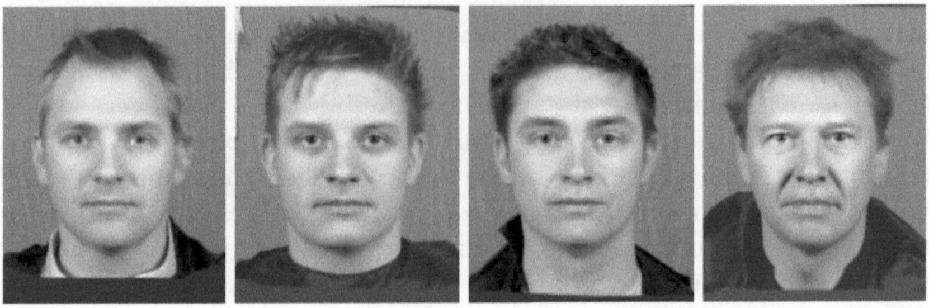

Fig. 9.11. Evolving generic face types. Faces were selected to be most intelligent (left pair) and most like an artist (right pair). Each attempt was constructed by a different person

scientist? To do this, a different face model was employed, one much larger than that currently used for policework, or for evolving attractive faces. This model contains 200 white male faces with an age range of 16 to 75 years and is being used more generally to improve system performance by biasing the initial faces more appropriately – by making them appear thin, middle aged, masculine, or attractive, if that is what is required – rather than presenting faces containing random characteristics. In the current pilot work, faces were selected on the basis of appearing intelligent, or being most those of artists. Examples are presented in Fig. 9.11; the best likenesses evolved after three generations. While we have used the system in this way only for a few people, it is interesting to note how similar the evolved faces appeared to each other for intelligence, but not for "artist", perhaps indicating a more consistent representation for the former dimension.

9.3.2 Evolving an Artist's Impression

EvoFIT now appears to produce composites that are more identifiable than other UK computerized systems when tested using procedures which mirror real witnesses as far as possible [9, 10, 33]. Part of the current work, as mentioned above, is to improve the evolution by providing a better set of initial faces. Another approach might be to change the appearance of the faces altogether. Research by Frowd et al. [10] has demonstrated that composites produced after a two-day delay when people work with a sketch artist are generally better than when produced using modern computerized systems. As illustrated in Fig. 9.12, a sketch constructed in this way can be quite sparse, presumably because facial texture is difficult to describe. However, it is possible that sketches are more accurate overall than other approaches which produce more photographic-like quality images, if not for any other reason than because there is less information to be inaccurate! The presence of "blank" regions in a sketch may also prompt our visual system to actively reconstruct these areas and to provide a more accurate probe for recognition.

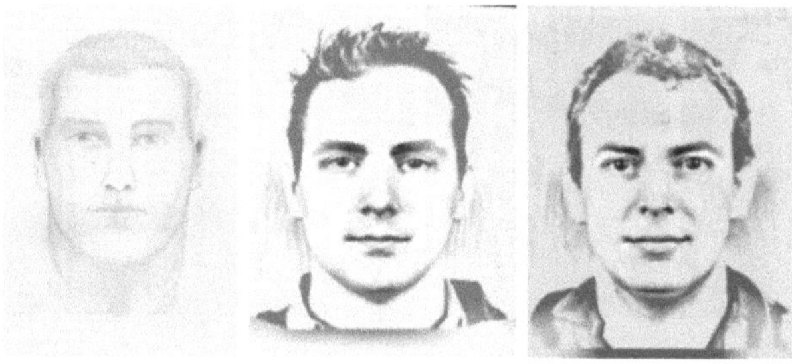

Fig. 9.12. An artist's sketch of the footballer Michael Owen (left) and evolved sketches of the Irish pop singer Ronan Keating (centre) and the UK Prime Minister Tony Blair (right)

We have built an EvoFIT face model to broadly mirror the images produced by a sketch artist. To do this, we preprocessed the faces to remove the main facial texture while leaving the features largely intact. A small study, involving a dozen people evolving celebrity faces using this model, has demonstrated (Fig. 9.12) that sometimes it is possible to construct a very good likeness using this image mode. The images produced are rather interesting aesthetically with the features appearing quite pronounced in the face.

9.3.3 Predicting the Appearance of Children

To our knowledge, no reliable mechanism exists to predict the facial appearance of human children, although such a system would appear to be of interest, even if for entertainment purposes. We have developed a version of EvoFIT that allows photographs of pairs of faces to be imported into a mixed gender face model, to obtain PCA coefficients for each face, and then to produce an offspring face via a random mix of these coefficients. Note that we make no strong claims as to the accuracy of this procedure compared with faces produced by natural breeding.

Such a fun application was developed by Frowd et al. [41] by constructing a new 200 item face model, in colour, and using an equal number of male and female adult faces. Then, the parent photographs first had their major facial landmarks identified, for the construction of the face model itself, to allow the PCA shape coefficients of the face to be obtained (a best fit in the shape model). The parent faces were then morphed into the average face shape and the pixel intensities were similarly projected onto the texture model. This resulted in a pair of parameters, one for shape and one for texture, for each parent face. Simply mixing together the shape coefficients from both parents, and likewise for the texture coefficients, enabled an offspring face to be "bred".

An example of a pair of parent faces that were imported into the model and bred together is shown in Fig. 9.13. Since the mix of coefficients from the two parents is random, a different offspring face is produced each time a child

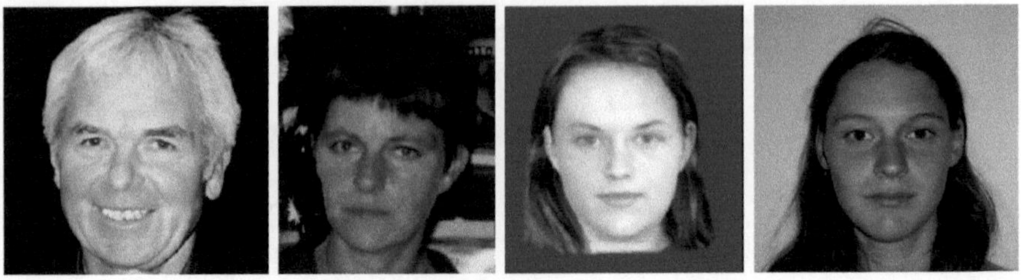

Fig. 9.13. A breeding example. Photographs of two parent faces are on the left, followed by a "daughter" face that was "bred" from the parents. As the average age of the face model is about 30 years, the breeding procedure produces offspring also as adults. Far right: a photograph of one of the couple's four real daughters, illustrating that a close likeness is possible with the technique (albeit by a chance mixing of face coefficients)

is generated. This version of EvoFIT has generated a large amount of public interest, in spite of it being marketed as a fun application of the technology. We have, nonetheless, carried out a small evaluation to demonstrate that the offspring of parent faces produced using this method may be identified among others faces above the level of chance [41], as is the case for "real" offspring [42].

9.4 Future Directions

We believe that significant research is still required before highly identifiable composites are consistently produced by the evolutionary approach. There are several promising avenues. One approach might be to simplify the appearance of the faces, as discussed above. Another might be to provide a face model which better matches a suspect's memory of a criminal. The current version of EvoFIT given to the police initially presents witnesses with faces containing random characteristics, within the general classes of race and sex. However, witnesses often recall details about a suspect's face, and this information may be used as part of constructing an EvoFIT; this information is important for the E-FIT and PRO-fit systems to help locate specific features. For example, they may provide an estimate of a suspect's age (e.g., early forties), the shape of the face (e.g., wide) and the overall facial appearance (e.g., unhealthy skin). Thus, it should be possible to build a face model with characteristics that broadly match this description (early forties, wide, unhealthy). Evolving a face using such a user-defined model, which may not need to contain as many as 72 faces, should enable a better likeness to be produced relative to a more generic model.

It is clear that even with constraining the face model in this way, there is still an element of chance involved: if the initial random faces are by chance not distributed well, perhaps important regions of the face space may not be

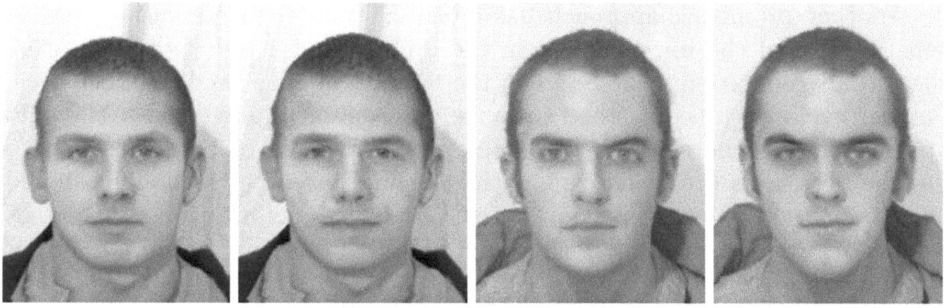

Fig. 9.14. Evolving more than one composite of the same celebrity. The pair of images on the left are of the British footballer David Beckham; the images on the right are of the British pop singer Robbie Williams

searched appropriately by the GA. One promising approach is simply to ask users to construct more than one composite. As the initial sets of faces are randomized for each run, we have found that the chance of producing a good likeness increases with a second attempt. In one evaluation, by Frowd et al. [17], a user looked at a celebrity face for one minute, then ran the evolver twice. Examples are presented in Fig. 9.14. Results supported the notion that the set of initial faces were important to the evolved likeness, given that sometimes a better likeness was constructed first, and sometimes second. Importantly, the user was able to reliably identify which of the two composites constructed was the best, thus providing a mechanism to improve the problem of a chance poor set of initial faces. We have recently shown [29] that this benefit similarly extends to a more realistic design involving unfamiliar faces and a two-day delay, suggesting that the method may also be of forensic use.

In these Frowd et al. [29, 17] studies, users constructed two composites from the memory of a target face. In both studies the average composite naming rate for each target ranged from a few percent to nearly 70% correct, while the quality of users' first and second attempts (as measured by naming) were highly correlated ($r = 0.8$). These data suggest that the main problem concerns the ability to generate faces, rather than to select faces from memory. Indeed, in [17], targets were highly familiar to the user, and therefore forgetting was unlikely to be a problem; yet naming attained only 27% correct overall. This is perhaps not too surprising since a relatively small number of faces – 72 in this case – were used to build the face models that were required to evolve a good likeness of *any* target (for a specific race and age range); thus, some targets were constructed very well, and some not so well. In a more recent evaluation, Frowd et al. [43] compared two similarly sized face models using the design and procedure of [17]. It was found that composite identification was markedly different for half of the targets between the models, supporting the notion that a particular face model does not generalize sufficiently well and, crucially, that a user-defined face model, as suggested above, is a promising next step.

Another promising approach has emerged from the observation that in general most of the improvement in the evolution of a target occurs during the second generation; that is, when the faces have been bred together once. Further cycles of breeding tend to make only minor improvements. It would appear sensible therefore to employ several shorter evolution runs and to use the best faces produced from each in a final breeding cycle. This should overcome the problem of a poor set of initial faces, as mentioned above, as well as of carrying out a more thorough search of face space from a good set of starting positions.

9.5 Conclusion

Obtaining a good likeness of a suspect's face can be crucial to solving a crime, although the traditional "feature" computer systems used by the police are far from ideal. The approach presented in this chapter simply requires witnesses to select from an array of alternative faces and a likeness is "evolved" over time. The main problem has been to limit the number of faces presented, while carrying out a thorough search of the face space. Through a process of selecting facial shapes and facial textures, and then combinations thereof, we have found that the new EvoFIT method works better than the traditional one. We are currently exploring mechanisms for improving performance, including limiting the complexity of the face space, or running the system more than once per witness. There are other interesting applications of the technology that we have also been exploring, such as of predicting the offspring of faces or of producing generic face types.

Acknowledgements

We would like to thank the EPSRC, whose contribution has enabled EvoFIT to be developed, as well as David and Cindy Frowd for kindly proofreading an early version of this chapter.

References

1. Davies, G.M., van der Willik, P., Morrison, L.J. (2000). Facial composite production: A comparison of mechanical and computer-driven systems. *Journal of Applied Psychology*, **85**(1): 19–124
2. Bruce, V., Ness, H., Hancock, P.J.B., Newman, C., Rarity, J. (2002). Four heads are better than one. combining face composites yields improvements in face likeness. *Journal of Applied Psychology*, **87**: 894–902
3. Brace, N., Pike, G., Kemp, R. (2000). Investigating e-fit using famous faces. In: *Forensic Psychology and Law Krakow.* Institute of Forensic Research Publishers, 272–276

4. Frowd, C.D., Carson, D., Ness, H., Richardson, J., Morrison, L., McLanaghan, S., Hancock, P.J.B. (2005). A forensically valid comparison of facial composite systems. *Psychology, Crime and Law*, **11**: 33–52
5. Ellis, H.D., Shepherd, J., Davies, G.M. (1975). Use of photo-fit for recalling faces. *British Journal of Psychology*, **66**: 29–37
6. Davies, G.M. (1983). Forensic face recall: the role of visual and verbal information. In Lloyd-Bostock, S.M.A., Clifford, B.R., eds.: *Evaluating witness evidence.* John Wiley and Sons Ltd., 103–123
7. Davies, G.M., Ellis, H.D., Shepherd, J. (1978). Face identification: The influence of delay upon accuracy of photofit construction. *Journal of Police Science and Administration*, **6**(1): 35–42
8. Tanaka, J.W., Farah, M.J. (1993). Parts and wholes in face recognition. *Quarterly Journal of Experimental Psychology: Human Experimental Psychology*, **46**(A): 225–245
9. Frowd, C.D., Bruce, V., Ness, H., Bowie, L., Paterson, J., Thomson-Bogner, C., McIntyre, A., Hancock, P.J.B. (2007). Parallel approaches to composite production. *Ergonomics*, **50**(4): 562–585
10. Frowd, D., Carson, D., Ness, H., Mcquiston-Surrett, D., Richardson, J., Baldwin, H., Hancock, P. (2005). Contemporary composite techniques: The impact of a forensically-relevant target delay. *Legal and Criminological Psychology*, **10**(1): 63–81
11. Frowd, C.D., McQuiston-Surrett, D., Anandaciva, S., Ireland, C., Hancock, P.J.B. (2007). An evaluation of US systems for facial composite production. *Ergonomics*
12. Koehn, C.E., Fisher, R.P. (1997). Constructing facial composites with the mac-a-mug pro system. *Psychology, Crime and Law*, **3**: 215–224
13. Ellis, H.D., Shepherd, J.W., Davies, G.M. (1980). The deterioration of verbal descriptions of faces over different delay intervals. *Journal of Police Science and Administration*, **8**: 101–106
14. Shepherd, J.W. (1983). Identification after long delays. In: *Evaluating Witness Evidence.* Wiley, 173–187
15. Eysenck, M.W., Keane, M.T. (2005). *Cognitive Psychology: A Student's Handbook.* 5th edn. Psychology Press, UK
16. Frowd, C.D. (2002). EvoFIT: A holistic, evolutionary facial imaging system. `http://www.psychology.stir.ac.uk/staff/cfrowd/Thesis.txt`
17. Frowd, C.D., Hancock, P.J.B. (2006). Facial composites: image modality and multiple attempts. In: *IEEE Crime and Security.* London
18. Frowd, C.D., Hancock, P.J.B., Carson, D. (2004). EvoFIT: A holistic, evolutionary facial imaging technique for creating composites. *ACM Transactions on Applied Psychology (TAP)*, **1**: 1–21
19. Gibson, S.J., Solomon, C.J., Pallares-Bejarano, A. (2003). Synthesis of photographic quality facial composites using evolutionary algorithms. In Harvey, R., Bangham, J.A., eds.: *British Machine Vision Conference*, 221–230
20. Tredoux, C., Rosenthal, Y. (1999). Face reconstruction using a configural, eigenface-based composite system. In: *SARMAC III.* Boulder, Colorado
21. Schmidt, H. (2006). Personal communication
22. Dawkins, R. (1996). *The Blind Watchmaker: Why the Evidence of Evolution Reveals a Universe Without Design.* W. W. Norton
23. Crichton, M. (2002). *Prey.* Harper-Collins. London

24. Caldwell, C., Johnston, V.S. (1991). Tracking a criminal suspect through "face-space" with a genetic algorithm. In: *Fourth International Conference on Genetic Algorithms.* Morgan Kaufmann, 416–421
25. Sirovich, L., Kirby, M. (1987). Low-dimensional procedure for the characterization of human faces. *Journal of the Optical Society of America*, **4**: 519–524
26. Hancock, P.J.B., Bruce, V., Burton, A.M. (1997). Testing principal component representations for faces. In Bullinaria, J.A., Glasspool, D.W., Houghton, G., eds.: *4th Neural Computation and Psychology Workshop.* Springer. London, 84–97
27. Cootes, T.F., Walker, K.N., Taylor, C.J. (2000). View-based active appearance models. In: *FG '00: Proceedings of the Fourth IEEE International Conference on Automatic Face and Gesture Recognition.* Washington, DC, USA. IEEE Computer Society, 227–232
28. Brunelli, R., Mich, O. (1996). SpotIt! an interactive identikit system. *Graphical models and image processing: GMIP*, **58**(5): 399–404
29. Frowd, C.D., Bruce, V., McIntyre, A., Hancock, P.J.B. (2006). Lost in space. Unpublished
30. Pike, G., Brace, N., Turner, J., Kynan, S. (2005). Making faces with computers: Witness cognition and technology. *Pragmatics and Cognition*, **13**: 459–479
31. Hancock, P.J.B. (2000). Evolving faces from principal components. *Behavior Research Methods, Instruments and Computers*, **32**: 327–333
32. Mitchell, M. (1996). *An introduction to genetic algorithms.* MIT Press. Cambridge, MA, USA
33. Frowd, C.D., Bruce, V., Storås, K., Spick, P., Hancock, P.J.B. (2006). An evaluation of morphed composites constructed in a criminal investigation. In: *16th Conference of the European Association of Psychology and Law*
34. Olsson, N., Juslin, P. (1999). Can self-reported encoding strategy and recognition skill be diagnostic of performance in eyewitness identification? *Journal of Applied Psychology*, **84**: 42–49
35. Shapiro, P.N., Penrod, S.D. (1986). Meta-analysis of facial identification rates. *Psychological Bulletin*, **100**: 139–156
36. Shepherd, J.W., Ellis, H.D., McMurran, M., Davies, G.M. (1978). Effect of character attribution on photofit construction of a face. *European Journal of Social Psychology*, **8**: 263–268
37. Ellis, H.D. (1975). Recognizing faces. *British Journal of Psychology*, **66**: 404–426
38. Johnston, V.S., Franklin, M. (1993). Is beauty in the eye of the beholder? *Ethology and Sociobiology*, **14**: 183–199
39. Johnston, V.S., Hagel, R., Franklin, M., Fink, B., Grammer, K. (2001). Male facial attractiveness: evidence for hormone-mediated adaptive design. *Evolution and Human Behavior*, **22**(4): 251–267
40. Howdle, J. (2005). A cross cultural comparison of the attractiveness preferences of African and British males
41. Frowd, C.D., Bruce, V., Hancock, P.J.B. (2006). Predict your child: a system to suggest the facial appearance of children. Unpublished
42. Bressan, P., Grassi, M. (2006). Parental resemblance in one-year-olds and the gaussian curve. *Evolution and Human Behavior*, **25**: 133–141
43. Frowd, C.D., Bruce, V., Hancock, P.J.B. (2006). A comparison of police and future EvoFIT face models. unpublished

10

Evolutionary Reproduction of Dutch Masters: The Mondriaan and Escher Evolvers

A.E. Eiben

Free University Amsterdam gusz@cs.vu.nl

Summary. Creative evolutionary systems are often concerned with producing images of high artistic quality. A key challenge to such a system is to be human-competitive by producing the same quality. Then, mimicking existing human artists could be seen as a canonical benchmark, not unlike the Turing test for intelligence. This chapter discusses two applications aimed at evolving images in the styles of two well-known Dutch painters: Mondriaan and Escher. For both cases we have an evaluation criterion based on "style-fidelity" as perceived and judged by the users. In other words, here we have a target style, which makes the (subjective) selection less free than in applications solely aiming at nice images. Technically, the Mondriaan evolver is less difficult, given that his most popular style "simply" uses horizontal and vertical lines, and primary colours to fill the resulting rectangles. The Escher evolver project is more challenging. First, because Escher's style is less simple to capture. Second, the system is tested in vivo, in a real museum, posing requirements on the interface. We describe how to meet the style challenge based on the mathematical system behind Escher's tiling. Designing a suitable representation and the corresponding variation operators based on this system specifies an appropriate search space guaranteeing the Escher style to some extent and leaving enough freedom for the selection. As for the second objective, we describe two versions that differ in the way the images are presented to, respectively evaluated by the visitors. The experiences gained during a six-month exhibition period in the City Museum in The Hague, The Netherlands, are discussed from the visitors' perspective as well as from the algorithmic point of view and are illustrated with some "evolved Escher's".

10.1 Introduction

Creative evolutionary systems are often concerned with producing images of high artistic quality [1, 2]. A fundamental question raised by evolutionary art projects is: Who is creative here? Is it the user who executes (subjective) selection, or is it the evolution that produces the items to be selected by means of reproduction? Clearly, the answer depends on the definition of creativity. Discussing such a definition in depth exceeds the scope of this paper, but we note that many (implicit) definitions emphasize either the creation of something new and innovative or the creation of something with aesthetic qualities. For evolutionary processes it holds in general that reproduction is the power pushing novelty – by creating new stuff through crossover and mutation – and selection is the force behind quality – by propagating good stuff [3]. From this perspective, the question whether selection or reproduction is the creative force translates to whether novelty or quality accounts (more) for the creative experience of the users. This dichotomy neatly coincides with the two interpretations of creativity, innovativeness vs. aesthetic qualities, hence making the answer a judgement call. The work described here does not take a stance, but, rather, it emphasizes the role of the applied representation. As we will see, representation plays an essential role in systems aiming at the evolutionary reproduction of images of existing artists.

10.2 The Mondriaan Evolver

P.C. Mondriaan is considered one of the most prominent 20th century geometric painters. In 1917 he and three others founded the journal "De Stijl" wherein Mondriaan published 12 chapters on his vision on new art. Around that time he started painting only in abstract and some years later he took this style one step further by using only primary colours and straight horizontal and vertical black lines that intersect at right angles.

The Mondriaan project is rooted in the author's university course on evolutionary computation including a programming assignment: implementation of an evolutionary system that creates images in the style of Mondriaan. The first version of such a Mondriaan Evolver was implemented together with J. van Hemert [4], later adjusted by B. Craenen.[1] As for representing Mondriaan-like images (the phenotypes) by simple code (the genotypes), there are numerous simple options. In the first version of our system, chromosomes consist of two parts, one standing for the colour and one for the composition. The decoding (genotype – phenotype mapping) is done by a recursive function. This function takes the canvas and starts dividing it up into smaller planes using the data in the chromosomes to decide where to split and what colours to use for the resulting planes. Such a straightforward linear chromosome structure allows the use of simple genetic operators: single-point crossover and n-point mutation. Alternatively, a tree-representation can be used as well. Within such a tree an internal node specifies a split of the rectangle by the nodes label (horizontal/vertical) and its three child nodes that determine the position of the line to split and the colours of the resulting two subplanes. Instead of a colour, a child can be another internal node, leading to a simple recursive system. Figure 10.1 illustrates this system.

As for selection, it takes place through a GUI presenting 9 images to the user who can grade them on a given scale. This can be 1 to 10, or in later

[1] `http://www.xs4all.nl/~bcraenen/EArt.html`

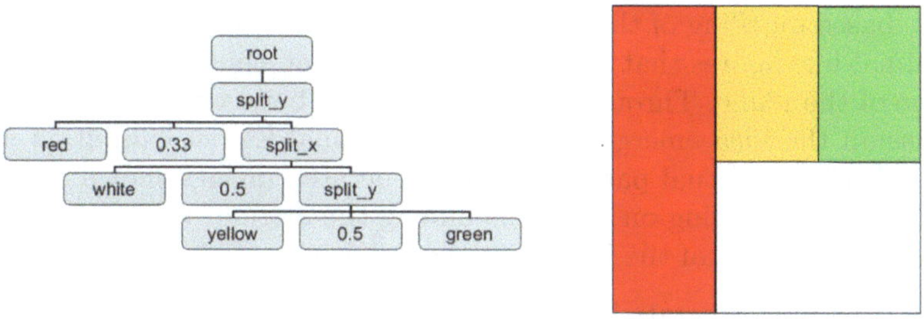

Fig. 10.1. Tree-based representation of Mondriaan style images using arbitrary (i.e., not necessarily Mondriaan-like) colours

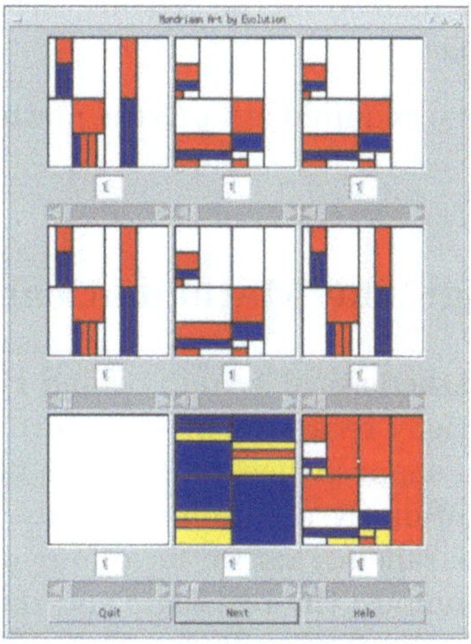

Fig. 10.2. Graphical user interface of the Mondriaan evolver

versions 1 to 3: good, neutral, bad. This GUI is illustrated in Fig. 10.2, showing a screenshot from the online Mondriaan Evolver.[2]

10.3 The Escher Evolver

The project described here emerged from a cooperation with the City Museum in The Hague, The Netherlands, that intended to organize a large exhibition devoted to the works of M.C. Escher [5]. Although Escher had no background in mathematics, his insights and self-study led him to an art form that is based on the geometry of two- and three-dimensional spaces. Very popular are his

[2] `http://www.cs.vu.nl/ci/EvolutionaryArt.html`

pictures based on tiling of the two-dimensional plane [6, 7]. These images feature animal-like figures that complement each other, thus forming a complete coverage of the plane. Through informal contacts between the university and the museum the idea emerged that the traditional Escher exhibition should be extended by a virtual part: computer-generated images shown to visitors on LCD screens hanging on the walls among the original works of the artist. The essential aspects of the idea were the following.

1. The computer-generated images should be in the style of Escher's tilings.
2. Images should be generated by an evolutionary process, that is, random variation and fitness-based selection on a population of images.
3. The visitors should be able to control the evolution by subjective selection. That is, looking at the pictures they could vote on the images and thereby set the fitness values, defined as the balance between votes in favour of and against a given picture.

The key to meet the first requirement was the mathematical system behind Escher's tilings.

10.4 Escher's Tiling: The Mathematical System

A nice overview of the mathematical system behind Escher's tiling is given in [7], pp. 31–69. Here we briefly recap the most important aspects of it. Escher used two different ground shapes when creating his tessellations: triangles or parallelograms. Our evolutionary program uses only parallelograms. Including special cases of the parallelogram we have four different ground shapes: the parallelogram, the rhombus, the rectangle and the square. To fill a plane with one of these ground shapes one can use three different transformations: translation, rotation and glide reflection (a combination of a reflection and a translation). Using these transformations one can create 10 different transformation systems for filling the plane. These are numbered traditionally with Roman numbers as I, II, ..., X. During this project we did not consider transformation system X since it operates on triangles. A few translation systems work on all ground shapes, the others assume equal side length (rhombus or square) or square corners (rectangle or square). Table 10.1 shows all possible combinations of ground shapes and systems after [7], p. 58. All of these systems are repeating, that is, we can always create a block of these shapes that can fill the plane using only translation.

The left-hand side of Fig. 10.3 shows the details for system II using a simple rotation. The right-hand side illustrates system IV which uses 2 glide-reflections. System VI (not illustrated here) is the most complicated, 2 rotations and 2 glide-reflections are used in such a way that only a block of 16 shapes is large enough to fill the plane by translation only.

Table 10.1. Possible combinations of shapes and transformations

	I	II	III	IV	V	VI	VII	VIII	IX
A. Parallelogram									
B. Rhombus									
C. Rectangle									
D. Square									

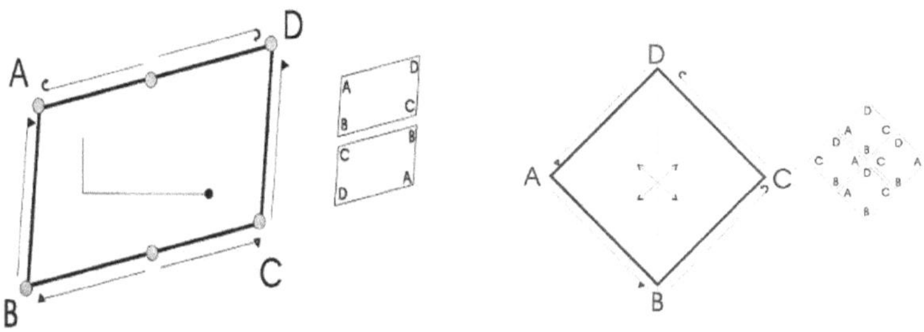

Fig. 10.3. Transformation systems II (left) and IV (right)

10.5 Evolvable Representation of Escher's Tilings

The computational engine behind the Escher Evolver is an evolutionary algorithm. In the whole algorithm design it is the representation that forms the greatest challenge, because it determines the syntax (set of genotypes) and its corresponding semantics (set of images encoded by these genotypes). Thus ultimately it determines what kind of pictures can evolve at all. The other components of the evolutionary system, genetic operators, parent selection, and population update rule (survivor selection), are more straightforward.

The algorithm operates on a genotype consisting of an array of integers. Several steps are needed to transform these into an Escher-like image. The first step in generating an image is calculating image properties such as size, shape and colours using the genetic information. These are used to create several affine transformations used to transform and paint the building blocks, i.e., the tiles forming the basic units of the final image, onto our drawing canvas. Second, the curves forming the contour of a single building block are calculated, then the filling of the block is done. We then have a vector image of a single building block. Using the affine transformations this is extended to a tiling and transformed into a bitmap before being drawn onto the canvas. Next we take a detailed look at these steps beginning with transforming the genotype into image properties. Table 10.2 shows the genes we use and the properties they determine.

Table 10.2. Escher representation. For more details, see the corresponding subsections

Gene no.	Trait	Converted into range	Note
		GROUND SHAPE	
0	Ground Shape	A,B,C,D	
1	Ground Shape angle	amin ... 180-amin	A and B only
2	Edge-Ratio	emin ... emax	A and C only
3	Transformation System	1 ... 10	
4...5	Vertex Displacement		Unused
		PLANE TRANSFORMATION	
6	Plane Scaling factor	smin ... smax	
7	Plane Rotation Angle	0 ... 359	
8...9	Old colour		Unused
		FILLING OF THE SHAPE	
10	Type of view	Top / side view	
11	Head Corner	1 ... 4	
12	Eye distance	0.1 ... 0.3	
13	Mouth type	none, loose, beak	Side view only
14	Wing type	none or one of 4 types	
15	Number of wing lines	2 ... 5	
16	Wing width	0.2 ... 0.5	
17	Wing length	0.3 ... 0.8	
18	Tail type	none, full	
19	Number of tail lines	3 ... 6	
20	Tail edge length	0.2 ... 0.5	
21	Tail center length	0.2 ... 0.5	
22	Spine	true, false	Top view only
		colourS	
23...25	Foreground colour	HSB-colour	
26...28	Background colour	HSB-colour	
		CURVES	
29...38	curve 1	3rd-order Bézier curve	
39...48	curve 2	3rd-order Bézier curve	
49...58	curve 3	3rd-order Bézier curve	
59...68	curve 4	3rd-order Bézier curve	

10.5.1 Ground Shape and Transformation System

In our genotype we store the ground shape and translation system. Both can be changed independently during crossover and mutation. Therefore we apply a repair algorithm after the reproduction phase. This algorithm reverts an invalid combination to a neighbouring valid combination. The vertex displacement genes were to be used for distorting the image by moving the cornerpoints of the shapes, but we never implemented these displacements. Escher used them in numerous images though.

10.5.2 Curves

The contour of a shape is build up out of 2, 3, or 4 different curves. How many curves are needed, where each curve is placed and which direction they are facing is determined by the transformation system in use. For each of the 9 systems we separately encoded this into the drawing algorithm. To represent the curves we use high-order Bézier curves (see Fig. 10.4) because we can use as many control points as necessary, and Bézier curves have a convex nature which ensures that our curves do not cross each other. In the final implementation 5 control points are used.

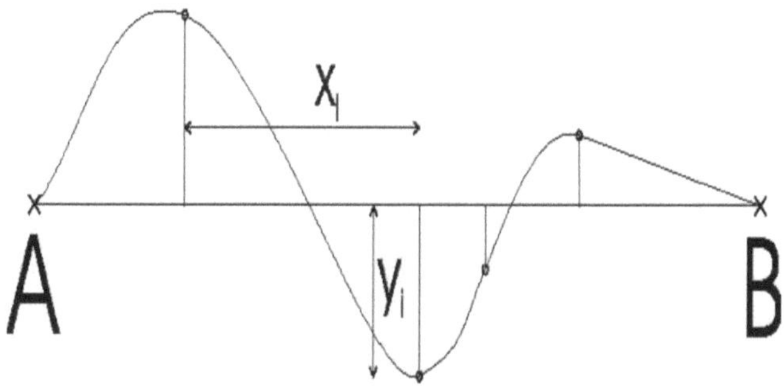

Fig. 10.4. Representation of a curve

10.5.3 Filling the Shape

Use only a contour, the drawing will never look like an animal such as a bird, fish or reptile. We have to use eyes, wings and tails for this. First we tried to use curves for the fillings too, assuming that curves that make the figure look alive would emerge over time through the evolutionary process driven by the user selection. This, however, did not work very well. So we chose a set of predefined curves to fill the shapes. First we have a bit that decides whether the picture is a side-view (birds, fish) or top-view (fish, reptiles). The top-view has 2 eyes and possibly a spine. The side view has one eye

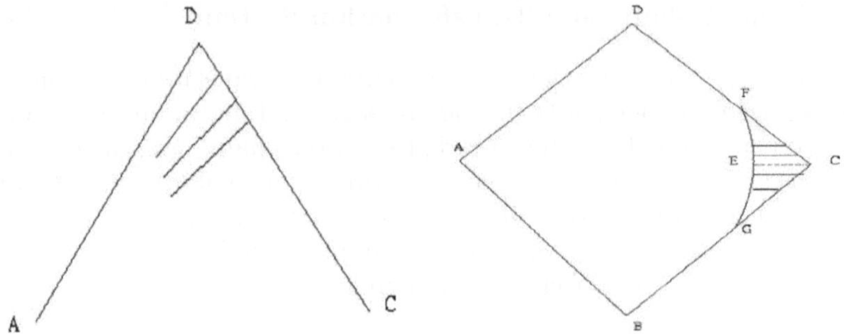

Fig. 10.5. Illustrations of filling a shape: diagonal wing (left) and tail (right)

only and can have a mouth. Both types can have several types of wings. The left-hand side of Fig. 10.5 shows a diagonal wing. The direction, number and length of winglines are genetically determined. The same applies for the tail section. Here the curve closing the tail and the number of tail lines are drawn using several genes. The right-hand side of Fig. 10.5 displays a typical tail configuration. Before drawing, the entire filling is clipped to the shape area, so the wings and tail lines always end at the contour.

10.5.4 Colours

The image has 2 colours, a foreground and a background colour. Both are represented in a HSB (Hue-Saturation-Brightness) colour model. Not all values for H, S and B are possible, for example the foreground colour is a little bit brighter than the background colour. The old colour genes (one integer per colour) are not used anymore. They did not produce enough different colours.

10.5.5 Plane Transformation

After the entire image has been made in vector format it needs to be transformed into a bitmap. The plane scaling factor multiplied by a target dependent factor form the size (in pixels) of one shape. Fig. 10.6 shows an image obtained through this representation. The one shown here was named "The Flatfish".

10.6 Reproduction and selection operators

The initial evolutionary algorithm was based on simple operators: one-point crossover, random change mutation, tournament selection, and generational replacement. After having gained experience with the resulting system we had to conclude that none of these choices was the right one, and we chose alternatives for all of them. We briefly discuss the four main operators below.

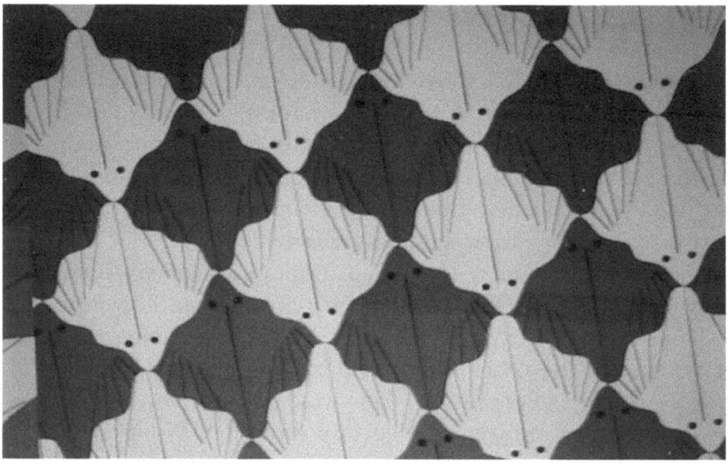

Fig. 10.6. Illustration of a possible image phenotype: The Flatfish

N-point crossover. One-point crossover did not satisfy our needs; for instance the two old colour genes were located next to each other. Because of this the offspring often had both colours of one single parent. Using uniform crossover, the curves did not cross very well. After a number of comparative experiments we found that N-point crossover (with a random number of crossover points) provides a better mixture of genes, keeping parts of the curve structure intact.

Gaussian mutation. When we used replacement of genes with random values, strange mutations occurred. For example, curves became totally different, or radical colour shifts and huge size variations occurred. For users (experimenters) such changes were too big, the process looked rather more like a random walk than gradual evolution. A more subtle approach was required, where a gene was not replaced by a random value but was mutated by an increment. The value for this increment was chosen from a Gaussian distribution with mean = 0 and $0.2 \cdot gene_{max}$ as standard deviation. This value (positive or negative) is then added to the existing gene value.

Roulette wheel selection. To perform parent selection we first applied tournament selection as used in the Mondriaan Evolver. However, experiments during development indicated that it did not work as expected. Simple roulette wheel selection worked well, and was therefore chosen for the final implementation.

Steady-state replacement. As for the survivor selection mechanism, we started the exhibition period using a generational model, where all present individuals die and are replaced by the offspring. Later on we changed to a steady-state model (only replacing part of the actual population), see next section.

10.7 Working of the System

Two implementations of the above algorithm were exhibited at the City Museum, The Hague. Both are networked systems that use flat LCD screens to gain votes, based on the same standalone version. The main differences between the first and second version are the evolutionary model used (generational vs. steady state) and the way the visitors vote (either for/against a single picture or a choice between two given pictures).

In the standalone version the whole population of six images is shown to one user in one screen. The evolutionary mechanism is completely hidden (that is, the user cannot experiment with different mutation rates, or various crossover types), all the user needs to do is to evaluate the images and press the button for the next generation. This way, the user can quickly see how to direct the evolutionary process to a certain direction. We used this version to test the genetic decoder and to compare different algorithmic setups.

10.7.1 First Networked Version

The first networked version was actually a copy of the standalone version. Here, six flat screens were hung on the walls of the museum, among the regular works, and one image was shown on each screen. Note that, hereby, the population size was limited to the number of screens (six), which resulted in a rather small population. Based on this setup a collective of visitors, rather than one user, was evaluating the images, thereby delivering the necessary votes to compute the fitness values of the pictures. Physically, each screen was connected to a client PC, and these clients were all connected to a server.

The work was divided between the server and the clients. The server actually runs the genetic algorithm and it sends the genetic information to the clients, one individual to each client. The client decodes the genotype it receives and shows it on the screen. The visitors can use 2 buttons under the screen to vote "yes, I like this picture" or "no, I do not like this picture". At a regular interval each client sends its vote count to the server. After an interval between 5 and 30 minutes (depending on the number of votes received) the server counts all the votes and calculates the fitness of each individual. This is simply the percentage of "yes" votes using some bias to handle the situation of no votes at all. Finally the server performs an evolutionary cycle (parent selection, reproduction, survivor selection) to calculate the next generation, which replaces the current one and is sent to the clients again.

Although the software worked fine, the evolution did not work well. There were not enough votes and there was much convergence, i.e., very similar pictures in the population. The causes were found in the user interface and algorithm setup:

1. The population size of 6 was too small to hold enough diversity.

2. Sometimes – even when running on 30-minute intervals – the total number of votes was only 20 per interval. This resulted in individuals that became very dominant in one or two generations.
3. Visitors thought the voting instructions were unclear. Some interpreted them as "Do you like the picture?", others as "Is the picture Escher-like?". Furthermore, it turned out that people would prefer voting in the context of other pictures, using picture(s) A (B,C, ...) as a reference to judge picture X. This was impossible because of the distribution of the screens in different rooms in the museum.
4. When a visitor voted, he or she only got a "thanks for your vote" message as feedback on the screen. This was neither amusing nor interesting enough to motivate them to vote at other screens too. Apparently, people expect an immediate effect after pushing a button.
5. The variance in colour was not sufficient, we had only light foreground and dark background colours.

All these factors together made the screens and the whole virtual exhibition not attractive enough. Therefore, a second version was implemented to overcome these problems, while still using the same hardware and genetic representation.

10.7.2 Second Networked Version

Apart from introducing the new colour system, which uses 3 genes per colour instead of one, the genetic structure was unchanged. The main novelties were in the reproduction mechanism and the user interface.

We had to increase both the population size and the number of votes received, but we could only use six flatscreens. To accomplish the larger population we allocated 5 individuals to each flatscreen, which made a total of 30 individuals in the population. We could not generate 30 new individuals each generation, we did not have enough votes. A steady-state algorithm – where not the whole population is replaced in one cycle – could solve the problem, because an individual that stays in the population for many (approx. 5–10) cycles can get many more votes. In this model the raw fitness of an individual is calculated just as in the old model. The fitness values used for reproduction and survival are calculated using age-dependent transformations of the raw fitness values. This protects young individuals from dying quickly and makes old ones reproduce less and die faster. The age correction for reproduction is as follows. The fitness of an individual that has been around in the population is transformed to lie between zero and L_r, where L_r is an age-dependent limit. L_r is 100 for individuals two generations old, and reduces by 10 for each age up to age seven and by a decrement of 20 afterwards. After age nine $L_r = 0$. Using roulette wheel selection based on this age-corrected fitness values means that only individuals between two and nine generations old will ever be selected as parents for reproduction. The correspondence between fitness and survival in the population is treated differently, as follows. Individuals of zero (newborn) or one generation old are given maximum fitness $L_s = 100$. The fitness of an individual two generations old is scaled between $L_s = 60$ and $L_s = 100$, that is, ensuring a survival fitness of at least 60. Individuals from five to nine generations get constrained by a maximum of $L_s = 90, 80, 70, 50,$ and 30, respectively, and individuals after nine generations have $L_s = 0$.

The user interface now has the task of accumulating votes for different individuals. It manages this task by showing two pictures at the same time on a split screen, see Fig. 10.7. The user can vote in favour of one of them. Note that the meaning of the two buttons under the screen changed from yes/no for one picture to yes for left/right picture. Each time a vote was made, the client thanked the visitor by replacing the "loser" with an instruction text. A few seconds later two new pictures, drawn randomly from the pool of 5 individuals available to the client, are shown. The user may then vote again.

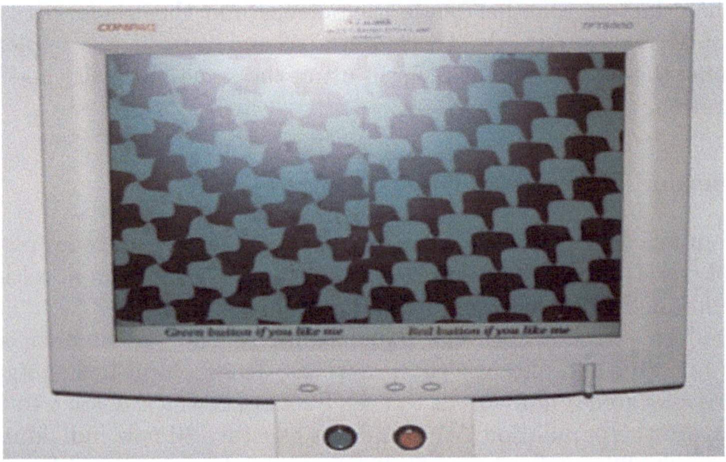

Fig. 10.7. Split screen in the second version of the system in the City Museum, The Hague. Viewers press the buttons below the display to indicate their preferred image

The pictures that emerged in the museum during the approximately thousand generations do show resemblance to Escher's tilings, but they could never be mistaken for a real Escher. We conjecture that there were two factors that prevented the evolution of convincing Escher-like images. One lies in the subjective selection of the ever-changing set of visitors. The collective intelligence, or, rather, the collective taste, was arguably not consistent enough to direct the process towards a specific type of image. This effect would obviously not occur in a standalone system controlled by a single user. The other one is rooted in the limitations of the representation. This could only be helped by designing more complex genotypes and corresponding decoders.

The exhibition was visited by thousands of people who actively participated in an evolutionary process of breeding art. Even though the "style-fidelity" of the images was limited, the visitors' reactions were mainly positive. An interesting aspect was the cognitive experience of the visitors. As discussed above we noticed a preference for comparing images, as opposed to simply voting for/against one picture. Nevertheless, the overall evaluation of the museum management was very positive; the combination of traditional art and new media, together with the active involvement of the visitors in creating the art shown, was greatly appreciated.

10.8 Concluding Remarks

Systems using interactive evolution, i.e., evolutionary algorithms with subjective user selection, have proven capable of creating objects with artistic value, see [1, 2]. Depending on how one defines creativity, it can be argued that such systems are creative through the influence of the user (selection) or through the evolutionary operators (reproduction). In this chapter we approach the issue from a different perspective. Paraphrasing Koza et al. [8] it could be said that the ultimate challenge to a creative evolutionary system is to be human-competitive by producing the same quality. Then, mimicking existing human artists forms a canonical benchmark, not unlike the Turing test for intelligence.

In this chapter we described two projects, concerning the Mondriaan and the Escher Evolvers. Of these two, the Mondriaan showcase was easier. The reason is that the underlying structure is easier to represent in a computer. The Escher Evolver needs more sophisticated representations to be really convincing. These experiences suggest that the representation is the most essential system component when aiming at the evolutionary reproduction of images of existing artists. Furthermore, for the time being, imitating existing art using evolutionary processes remains a great challenge.

Acknowledgements

The author is grateful to all former colleagues who contributed to these projects, the software code, and previous publications on the subject. Special thanks goes to I. Booij, B. Craenen, H. Labout, R. Nabuurs, and J. van Hemert.

References

1. Bentley, P., ed. (1999). *Evolutionary Design by Computers.* Morgan Kaufmann

2. Bentley, P., Corne, D., eds. (2002). *Creative Evolutionary Systems.* Academic Press
3. Eiben, A., Smith, J. (2003). *Introduction to Evolutionary Computing.* Springer
4. van Hemert, J., Eiben, A. (1999). Mondriaan art by evolution. In Postma, E., Gyssens, M., eds.: *Proceedings on the Eleventh Belgium-Netherlands Confererence on Artificial Intelligence (BNAIC'99).* AI, 291–293
5. Eiben, A., Nabuurs, R., Booi, I. (2002). The Escher evolver: Evolution to the people. In Bentley, P., Corne, D., eds.: *Creative Evolutionary Systems.* Academic Press, 425–439
6. Escher, M., Bool., F. (1986). *Regular Divisions of the Plane at the Haags Gemeentemuseum.* Haags Gemeentemuseum
7. Schattschneider, D. (1990). *Visions of Symmetry: Notebooks, Periodic Drawings, and Related Work of M.C. Escher.* W.H. Freeman and Company
8. Koza, J., Keane, M., Yu, J., Bennett, F., Mydlowec, W. (2000). Automatic creation of human-competitive programs and controllers by means of genetic programming. *Genetic Programming and Evolvable Machines*, **1**(1): 121–164

Part IV

Artistic Perspectives

11

Artificial Art Made by Artificial Ants

Nicolas Monmarché, Isabelle Mahnich, and Mohamed Slimane

Université François Rabelais, Tours
Laboratoire d'Informatique
nicolas.monmarche@univ-tours.fr

Summary. We present how we have considered the artificial ant paradigm as a tool for the generation of music and painting. From an aesthetic perspective, we are interested in demonstrating that swarm intelligence and self-organization can lead to spatio-temporal structures that can reach an artistic dimension. In our case, the use of artificial pheromones can lead to the creation of melodies thanks to a cooperative behavior of the ant-agents but also to the emergence of abstract paintings thanks to competitive behaviors within the artificial colonies. The user's point of view is also taken into account through interactive genetic algorithms.

11.1 Introduction

Algorithms inspired by Nature such as genetic algorithms or artificial neural networks are now well known and widely used. More recently, researchers have created heuristics based on ants' collective and self-organizing capabilities (see [1] for an overview of the fertile topic of swarm intelligence). In this paper we focus our study on the automatic production of digital art works inspired by ants' behavior. As Nature has always been a predominant source of inspiration for arts, its implication in computational arts is shown here as the translation of an artificial life and artificial intelligence paradigm producing dynamic systems able to create both music and paintings.

Science and arts have a long common history made of mutual interactions like for instance in musical composition [2]. Scientific results can often be emphasized with a well-chosen representation using sounds or graphics. Symmetrically, science and technology can help artists produce more realistic live performances (for instance, in case of artificial music instruments). Nevertheless, a detailed analysis of these interactions is beyond the scope of this chapter.

This paper investigates more detailed relations between artistic works and science with computer-generated music [3] and paintings [4] from the swarm intelligence point of view. We will describe how the collective behavior of ants can lead to a compositional and a painting system.

After a short introduction to ant algorithms, we will first present the AntMusic project and give some details about the algorithm and its parameters. Then the AntPainting project will be described. We will concentrate our study on two aspects: first, we will describe how ants can produce paintings without any human direction and second, we will introduce an evolutionary mechanism allowing users to interact with artwork production. Last, we will suggest future artistic or scientific directions.

11.2 About Artificial Ants and Computer Arts

11.2.1 From Real Ants' Behavior to Artificial Stigmergy

Ants are social insects widely adapted to their various natural environments [5]. Their communication abilities are often very complex and have inspired computer science researchers, mainly to solve combinatorial optimization problems such as the classical traveling salesman problem [6]. The natural mechanisms that have been adapted are those which take place during mass recruitment of workers to find and exploit food resources. Different species are able to deposit olfactive substances, called pheromones, on the ground to guide workers toward food. This kind of communication, called stigmergy, is indirect because it relies on the ground and allows auto-catalytic reinforcement mechanisms to appear: the more ants are numerous to find a food site, the more they will deposit pheromones and the more other ants will be attracted by this olfactive path. Moreover, pheromones' intensity decreases with time (evaporates) and in this way, ants can loose a path that leads to an empty site.

This collective behavior has been modeled by a population of agents that take their decisions in a probabilistic way according to the pheromone intensities they encounter during their moves. In many successful works that deal with combinatorial optimization (see a review in [1, 7]), artificial pheromones are real values that are used with a positive feedback mechanism which reinforce promising solutions. These agents follow simple behavioral rules and are often simple in comparison to the complexity of the tasks they perform collectively.

11.2.2 Generating Music with AI

Artificial intelligence (AI) has been used to conceive computer music systems since the beginning of computer science (see a review in [8]). Several models have been proposed to capture musical knowledge such as finite and infinite automata [9], neural networks [10, 11], analogical reasoning [8], constraint programming [12], multi-agent systems [13] or evolutionary computation (EC) (see for instance [14] and [15, 16] for longer reviews).

These systems can be classified in three fields: composition, improvisation and performance. In the following section, we will focus on the two first types since the last one, which consists in producing artificial realistic performances, is far from our work. In the former category, we can quote the pioneering work of Hiller and Isaacson's (in 1958) in which notes are pseudo-randomly generated by Markov chains and selected according to classical harmony and counterpoint rules. In the EMI project [17], the style of various composers was emulated by searching patterns in a few of their pieces. In the latter category, for instance, neural networks are used to learn how to improvise jazz solos [18]. We can also listen to music improvised by an interactive genetic algorithm, improved since 1994 by J. Biles [19]. This system, called GenJam, maintains hierarchically related populations of melodic ideas and plays its solos over the accompaniment of a standard rhythm section, while a human mentor gives real-time feedback. Then, users' appreciation of proposed melodies can be taken into account through an interactive genetic algorithm [14] but also through his/her body gestures [20]. Users can also participate during the generation process: for instance they can play a MIDI instrument and then play the role of particular agents within the multi-agent system [13].

In this chapter, we will use the collective behavior of ants to produce music. Todd and Miranda [21] have established that there are three ways to generate music with an artificial life system:

1. Music can be an expression of the movement of agents which are not aware of what they produce. In this case, music can be considered as a representation of the artificial world.
2. Each individual produces music and its survival depends on it. This approach belongs to evolutionary algorithms techniques.
3. Agents produce music that has an influence on other agents' behavior.

Our system would belong to the first category because ant-agents are not aware of what they produce and would also belong to the third because music is the result of multiple social interactions of these agents.

In the context of collective intelligence, we can consider the work of T. Blackwell [22, 23] (see also Chap. 5), with his Swarm Music and Swarm Granulator, who has experimented with collective behaviors to create improvised and interactive music. Even if other swarm systems could be presented, as far as we know, artificial ants have never been used to generate music before.

11.2.3 Painting with Ant-Like Robots or Ant-Like Agents

Automatic painting systems that use ants are still rare. For instance, in [24], the author describes ants that are able to pick up and deposit paint which represents food in order to produce images and then to analyze the emerging complexity and the regulation that appears in this kind of systems. With a greater artistic will, L. Moura and V. Ramos[1] have produced swarm

[1] `http://www.lxxl.pt/aswarm/aswarm.html`.

paintings in a computational art approach. And more recently, L. Moura, with H. Garcia-Pereira, has followed his ideas of "Making the Artists that Make the Art" with a colony of autonomous robots [25]. P. Urbano has also been interested with pheromones' role in artistic multiagent swarms [26] and G. Greenfield has recently studied how the fitness measures can influence the results obtained by a genetic algorithm used to find parameters for ant paintings as described in Sect. 11.4. Other works consider an image as a playground for artificial ants and even for spiders but without any artistic goal, for instance to perform edge detection [27, 28].

11.3 The AntMusic Project

In the AntMusic project, we use artificial ants to build a melody according to transition probabilities and taking advantage of the collective behavior of marking paths with pheromones. Graphs, or more precisely networks, have already been considered for musical analysis and composition [29], but in our case, melody building does not only rely on graph connectivity but also on pheromones' depositing and evaporation dynamics.

11.3.1 Artificial Ants on the Graph of Notes

Artificial ants are agents that are located on vertices in a graph and can move and deposit pheromones on edges. The more ants choose a particular edge, the more pheromones will be present there and the more other ants will choose this edge. As mentioned in Sect. 11.2, this general principle has been exploited for combinatorial optimization problems like the well-known Traveling Salesman Problem (TSP). One of the first algorithms designed to deal with this problem was called Ant System (AS) [30]; we have adopted in this project the same principles. In our case, the vertices are MIDI events and a melody corresponds to a path between several vertices. A MIDI event fully describes the parameters for one note (pitch, duration, volume, ...). Each edge (i, j), between vertices i and j, is weighted by a positive pheromone value τ_{ij} (see Fig. 11.1).

A transition rule is used to decide which of the vertices an ant will choose when located in vertex i: the probability of choosing vertex j is given by:

$$p_{ij} = \frac{\tau_{ij} \times \eta_{ij}^{\beta}}{\sum_{k \in N_i} \tau_{ik} \times \eta_{ik}^{\beta}} \tag{11.1}$$

where η_{ij} represents the desirability and which is set to $1/(d(i, j) + 1)$ with $d(i, j)$ representing a distance (in our case it corresponds to the number of half tones between the two notes i and j but we could use another formula based on musical scales). This desirability encourages ants to choose closest notes from their current position to form a melody. The parameter β controls the

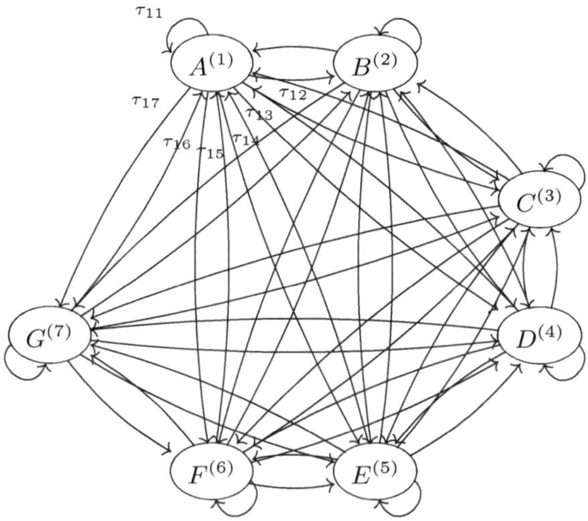

Fig. 11.1. Example of graph with seven vertices: each vertex is a MIDI event (but here, only the note $A, \ldots, G$ have been represented and numbers are vertex indices) on which ants can move (pheromones have only been represented when moving from note A)

influence of the desirability: high values increase the probability to produce small intervals between consecutive notes and low values give more importance to the pheromone values for the transition choices between notes. Finally, N_i stands for the set of possible vertices that can be reached from i.

Each time an ant moves from a vertex i to a vertex j, it deposits a pheromone quantity τ_0:

$$\tau_{ij} \leftarrow \tau_{ij} + \tau_0. \tag{11.2}$$

Finally, as it occurs in natural systems, pheromones slowly evaporates:

$$\tau_{ij} \leftarrow (1 - \rho) \times \tau_{ij} \tag{11.3}$$

where ρ is a parameter called evaporation ($0 \leq \rho \leq 1$).

For one ant, the algorithm that simulates its movements on the graph and generates a melody of $T_{\max}$ notes is given in Fig. 11.2.

The same algorithm can be used simultaneously for several ants in order to compose several voices for the selected instrument. Finally, the evaporation step is performed regularly and independently from the ants movements.

Usually, pheromones' evaporation allows the search process not to be stuck in local minima. This phenomenon is very useful in optimization methods. Applied to our compositional system, the generated melody evolves during long runs: even if predominant paths exist in the graph they can slowly evolve. All ants can lay down pheromones as we can see in step 2(b) in Fig. 11.2, but we can also introduce silent ants that do not play the MIDI event they encounter (step 2(c)). These ants are used to increase quickly the amount of

1. Initialization:
   (a) randomly choose a vertex for the initial position of each ant
   (b) initialize pheromone values: $\tau_{ij} \leftarrow \tau_0 \quad \forall i, j$
   (c) $t \leftarrow 0$
2. while $t < T_{\max}$ do
   (a) choose the next MIDI event j according to the transition rule (formula 11.1)
   (b) deposit pheromones on chosen edge (formula 11.2)
   (c) move to vertex j and play the corresponding MIDI event
   (d) $t \leftarrow t + 1$

Fig. 11.2. Algorithm for AntMusic

pheromones within the graph: then a few ants (i.e., voices) play the instrument while a large number collectively build the melody and remain silent.

The main underlying principle that we emphasize in this system is that a musical melody is often identified by the human mind as a repetition of notes and rhythms in the same way than presented in [31]. So, the reinforcement performed when an ant lays down pheromones can be considered as an encouragement to repeat cycles in the graph.

11.3.2 Implementation Details

Pauses Between Notes

Since pauses are important in a piece of music, we have introduced special pause vertices with only a duration value. When one ant goes through this kind of vertex, of course, it produces no new sound thus stopping the previous note played by this same ant.

Several Instruments

Since many levels of complexity can be added to the system, we have introduced several instruments that can be played at the same time. In this case, we only have to build one graph for each desired instrument and different ants can move independently on these graphs in the same way that has been described before.

Limiting the Graph Size

A graph containing all possible MIDI events would be very large. In order to decrease its size, we can use any MIDI file to initialize the graph: the file is scanned to build a graph that only contains the MIDI events that are present in the file. Moreover, pheromones can be initialized according to the MIDI event transitions that can be found in the file. In this case, ants will not only use the same events, they will also have a tendency to build a melody that sounds like the melody contained in the MIDI file.

Summary of Parameters

In order to let the user define his/her will, for each instrument, the following parameters can be independently set (default values are indicated within brackets):

- tempo (1–360)
- instrument: one of the 128 MIDI instruments (0: piano)
- minimum and maximum values of notes (0–127)
- volume (0–127)
- length of the melody: $T_{\max}$ (25)
- number of ants: silent (0) and playing ones (1)
- style: parameter β (1.0)
- possible duration ratios: 2, 1, 1/2, 1/4 (1)
- quantity of pheromones laid down by ants: τ_0 (0.1)
- evaporation: parameter ρ (0.01)

11.3.3 Musical Results

The score of Fig. 11.3 has been generated with the following parameters: one instrument (piano), three playing and 10 silent ants, 50 and 70 as minimum and maximum notes, $\beta = 1.5$, $T_{\max} = 15$, possible duration ratios are $1, 1/2, 1/4$, $\tau_0 = 0.1$ and $\rho = 0.01$. We can observe that three voices can be found (three notes can be played at the same time) because we have used three playing ants.

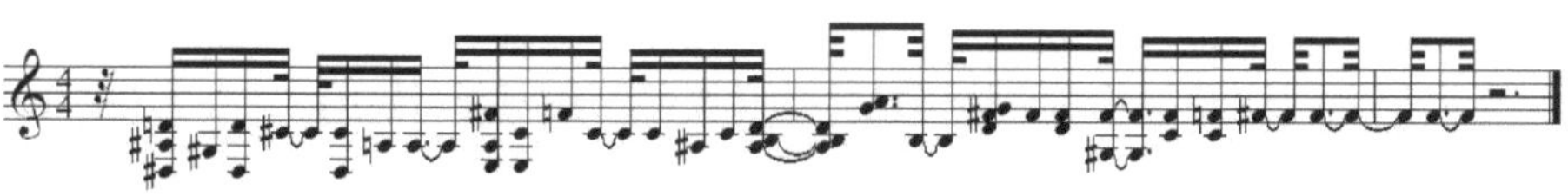

Fig. 11.3. Example of score obtained with three playing ants (see the text for other parameters)

The score of Fig. 11.4 has been generated with the following parameters: two instruments (two pianos), for the first one: only one playing ant, 60 and 80 as minimum and maximum notes, $\beta = 2.0$, $T_{\max} = 15$, possible durations are $1, 1/2, 1/4$, $\tau_0 = 0.1$ and $\rho = 0.01$. For the second piano: two playing and five silent ants, 40 and 65 as minimum and maximum notes, $\beta = 1.5$, $T_{\max} = 15$, possible duration ratios are $2, 1, 1/2$, $\tau_0 = 0.3$ and $\rho = 0.01$.

This example shows how it is possible to use two instruments to obtain two independent voices for the same instrument: the first piano plays in a high range of notes (60–80) whereas the second one plays in a low range (40–65).

The last example in Fig. 11.5 shows a score obtained with three instruments: two pianos and one string.

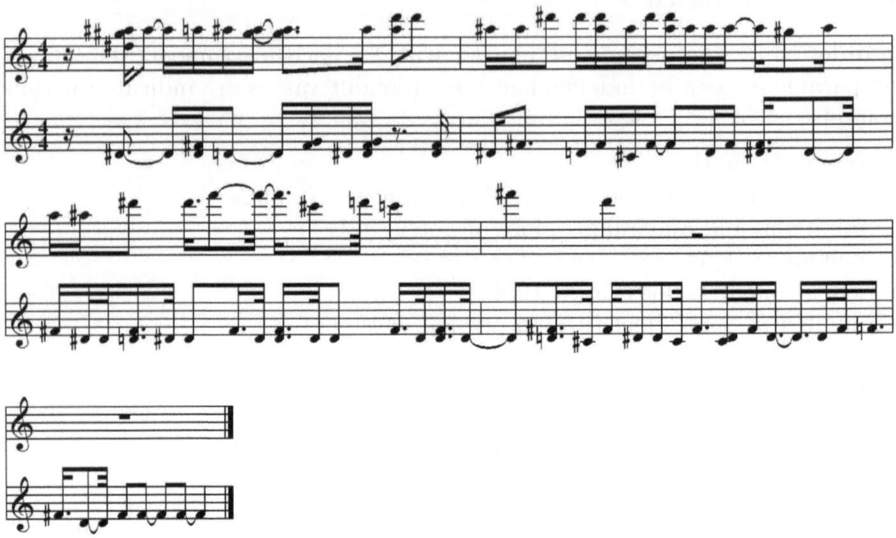

Fig. 11.4. Example of score obtained with two pianos (see the text for other parameters)

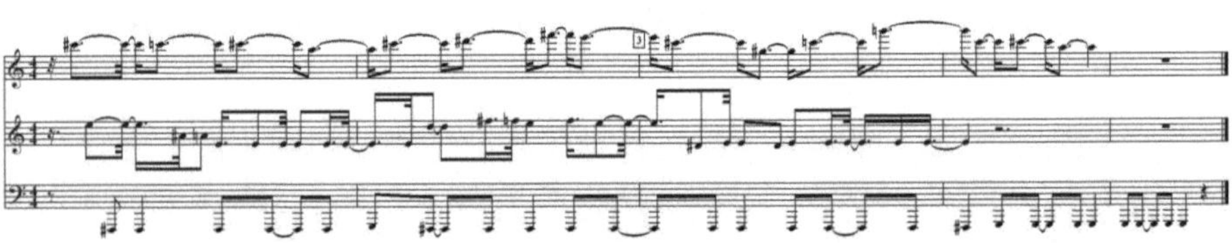

Fig. 11.5. Example of score obtained with three instruments (piano and strings)

We have noticed that the parameters β (weight for desirability) and ρ (evaporation) have an obvious impact on the generated music: the former allows us to build melodies without any wide gap between notes (the style of the music is smoother) and the latter allows us to control how often the sequences of notes are repeated. The influence of this last parameter also depends on the number of ants on the graph, either playing or silent ones.

Recently, we have introduced an XML notation for the parameters in order to simplify the user's work. For instance, the XML text given in Fig. 11.6 has produced the score of Fig. 11.7. This allows us to quickly build new sets of parameters and then to generate much more music. All these example can listen from the accompanying DVD.

```
<melody tempo="80">
  <voice instrument="0">
    <colony nb_ants="1" max_time="10000" initial_graph_weight="0.1"
       rho="0.1" alpha="5" beta="0.5" tau="0.8" />
    <style>
      <pitch value="G5" /> <pitch value="A5" /> <pitch value="Bb5" />
      <pitch value="B5" /> <pitch value="C6" /> <pitch value="C#6" />
      <pitch value="D6" /> <pitch value="E6" /> <pitch value="F6" />
      <pitch value="G6" />
      <duration value="48" /> <duration value="24" />
    </style>
  </voice>
  <voice instrument="0">
    <colony nb_ants="1" max_time="10000" initial_graph_weight="0.1"
      rho="0.1" alpha="5" beta="0.5" tau="0.8" />
    <style>
      <pitch value="G2" /> <pitch value="G3" /> <pitch value="D4" />
      <pitch value="G4" />
      <duration value="48" /> <duration value="72" />
    </style>
  </voice>
</melody>
```

Fig. 11.6. Example of XML code for parameter settings for the score of Fig. 11.7

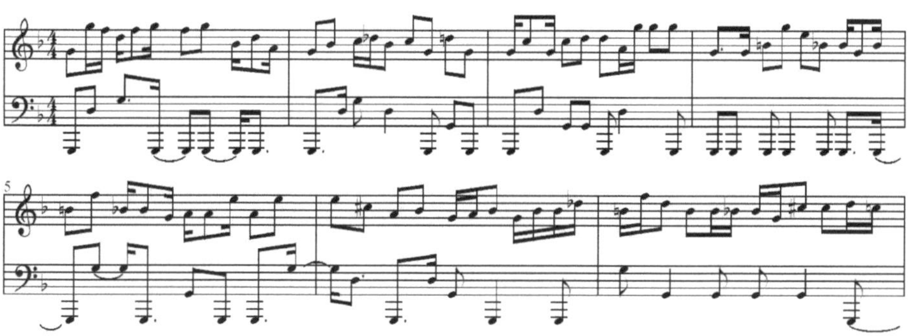

Fig. 11.7. Example of the first seven bars of a bluesy score

11.4 Painting Ants

In this ant paradigm application, ant like agents can move on a virtual painting, which is a bitmap picture, laying down paint of different colors. At each step, an ant chooses the next pixel to reach in a stochastic manner: it tends to prefer movements which preserve its direction. Thus, two kinds of movements are possible: oblique or right angle movement (Fig. 11.8).

For each ant, three parameters represent the probabilities to turn left (P_l), right (P_r) and to go straight ahead (P_a), and so we have $P_l + P_r + P_a = 1$.

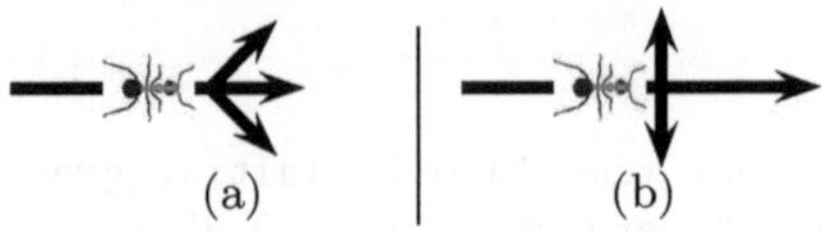

Fig. 11.8. Example of ant with an oblique movement, referred by D_o (a) and with a right angle movement, referred by D_d (b)

The paint which is deposited corresponds to pheromones paths from which the color is specific to each ant. This color is defined by its RGB components (C_R, C_G, C_B).

Moreover, at each step, the ant inspects its neighborhood looking for a pheromone path of another ant. The color it is looking for is also defined by its RGB components (F_R, F_G, F_B). A luminance comparison is then performed between the color of the pixel and the color that is searched by the ant:

$$\text{Lum}(R, G, B) = 0.2426 \cdot R + 0.7152 \cdot G + 0.0722 \cdot B \tag{11.4}$$

where R, G and B are the components of the pixel inspected by the ant

$$\varDelta(F_R, F_G, F_B, R, G, B) = |\text{Lum}(F_R, F_G, F_B) - \text{Lum}(R, G, B)|. \tag{11.5}$$

If the value $\varDelta$ is below a given threshold (fixed to 40), the ant recognizes the color and can decide to follow it with a probability P_s and so will deposit its own color on the searched color. This mechanism can produce a competition between ants by the mean of their colors.

In order to give a diffusion aspect, the color laid down by an ant is deposited on the painting by a discrete convolution product on the nine neighboring cells. This product is performed thanks to the following matrix:

$$M_c = \begin{pmatrix} 1 & 2 & 1 \\ 2 & 4 & 2 \\ 1 & 2 & 1 \end{pmatrix}.$$

Finally, the painting has no border (it is a toroid picture) to permit the visualization of the painting as a mosaic.

Then, for each painting, we have to fix the number of ants, and for each ant we need to define the following parameters:

- the color laid down: (C_R, C_G, C_B),
- the color it is looking for: (F_R, F_G, F_B),
- its movement probabilities: (P_l, P_r, P_a),
- its kind of movement: D_o or D_d,
- its probability to follow the color it is looking for: P_s.

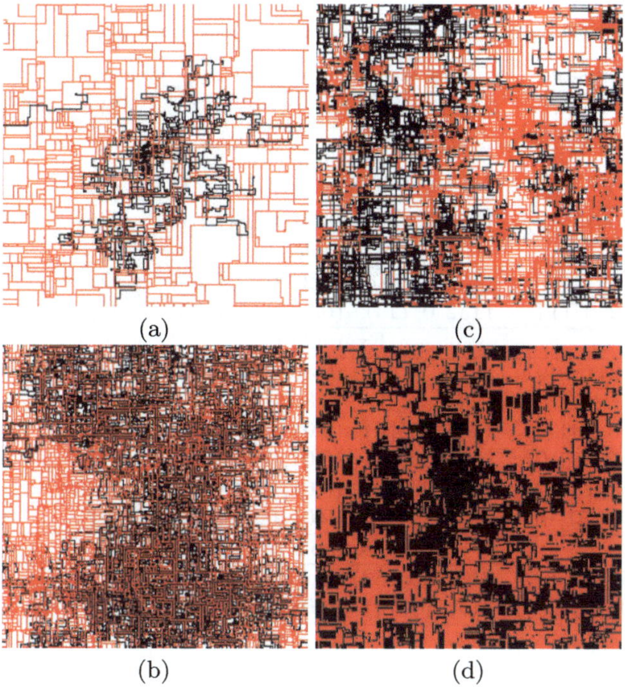

Fig. 11.9. Paintings obtained with different parameter settings. Each ant follows its own color: (a) after 10^5 iterations, and (c) after 10^6 iterations. Each ant follows the color deposited by the other ant: (b) after 10^5 iteration, and (d) after 10^6 iterations

11.4.1 Results

When parameters are fixed, the simulation starts and the user can watch the building of the painting without any interaction, he can only suspend and resume the process by clicking on the picture.

Let us consider various simple examples (i.e., with few ants). Consider two ants: a black one and a red one. Both ants are given the same probabilities but in one case the red ant follows the red color and the black ant follows the black color (Fig. 11.9(a) and (b)) and in the other case, the red ant follows the black color and the black ant follows the red color (Fig. 11.9(c) and (d)). We can see that results can be very different according to this behavioral change.

Other examples are shown in Fig. 11.10 and parameters used to produce these paintings are listed in Table 11.1.

Putting aside the aesthetic feeling which is subjective, we can notice that the dynamic and collective building of the painting highlights the competition that occurs between colors laid down by ants: each ant tries to replace the color deposited by one of its rivals by its own color and we can see how movement parameters can be an advantage or not. Consider for instance the

Table 11.1. Parameters of painting ants used to obtain examples of Fig. 11.10

Ant	Deposited color (C_R, C_G, C_B)	Followed color (F_R, F_G, F_B)	Movement probabilities (P_l, P_r, P_a)	Movement type $D_{d\|o}$	Following probability P_s
			Example (a)		
1	(192, 0, 255)	(255, 155, 3)	(0.04, 0.95, 0.01)	D_d	0.7852
2	(255, 155, 3)	(76, 68, 181)	(0.01, 0.98, 0.01)	D_d	0.8409
			Example (b)		
1	(145, 0, 94)	(145, 0, 94)	(0.24, 0.73, 0.03)	D_d	0.99
2	(132, 0, 114)	(132, 0, 114)	(0.27, 0.68, 0.05)	D_d	0.99
			Example (c)		
1	(5, 211, 149)	(255, 12, 0)	(0.80, 0.10, 0.10)	D_d	0.80
2	(145, 11, 149)	(255, 12, 0)	(0.80, 0.10, 0.10)	D_o	0.80
3	(255, 204, 0)	(255, 255, 0)	(0.01, 0.98, 0.01)	D_d	0.75
4	(255, 255, 0)	(255, 204, 0)	(0.01, 0.98, 0.01)	D_d	0.75
5	(255, 153, 0)	(255, 204, 0)	(0.01, 0.98, 0.01)	D_o	0.75
6	(255, 51, 0)	(255, 255, 0)	(0.01, 0.98, 0.01)	D_d	1.00
			Example (d)		
1	(14, 108, 15)	(210, 193, 253)	(0.18, 0.40, 0.42)	D_d	0.67
2	(210, 193, 253)	(14, 108, 15)	(0.08, 0.01, 0.91)	D_d	0.81

case of two ants, each having a different color and trying to find the color of the other (see ants 1 and 2 of the example (d) in Table 11.1): we can notice in Fig. 11.10(d) that the first ant (green one) has covered a smaller surface than the other ant which has very different parameters of movement and which is more "aggressive" because of its probability of 0.81 to follow the green color.

Finally, another characteristic of the system can not be shown in this paper: we are only presenting static paintings but ants can paint during many hours, continuously offering a new painting. Demo files can been found on the accompanying DVD.

11.5 Interactive Evolution of Ants' Paintings

In order for the ant-paintings to evolve according to the user's preferences we use a standard interactive evolution approach.

11.5.1 IGA + Painting Ants = Evolutionary Art

First, as we have seen in Sect. 11.4, a painting generated by ants strongly depends on initial parameters that have been chosen. A consequence is that the search space is very large:

- the number of ants can vary from one to a limit imposed by the CPU capabilities,

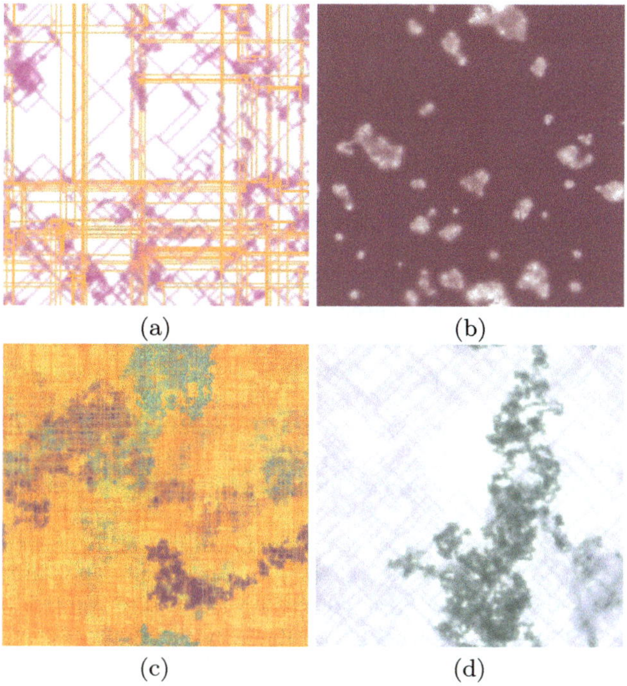

Fig. 11.10. Paintings obtained with different parameter settings

- the color dropped by one ant is determined by three RGB components, that is 256 × 256 × 256 different colors,
- the color followed by one ant can also be defined on the same color space,
- the direction can be set to D_o or D_d,
- the probabilities P_l, P_r, P_a, and P_s are real values in $[0, 1]$.

Second, the quality of a painting depends on the user who is watching it. IGAs are a well suited method to tackle this kind of problem: GAs can deal with large search spaces and interactivity is the best way to take into account the user preferences when it is difficult to obtain a fitness function.

Thus, an individual is a parameter setting that can be used to generate a painting. The length of its genome is not fixed because it depends on the number of ants. In order to reduce the parameter space, we have decided to adjust the followed color of an ant to the color dropped by another ant (in fact an ant can also follow its own color and that can lead to interesting results: see Fig. 11.10(b)). Moreover, the number of ants can vary from two to six and the probabilities must verify the following property $P_l + P_r + P_a = 1$.

The details are given hereafter.

11.5.2 Algorithm

The main steps of the method are given in Fig. 11.11.

1. Generate an initial population of N individuals with randomly generated parameters
2. Display the individuals: the N parameter settings are used to initialize N ant paintings
3. Possibly Stop: the user may be satisfied of one painting
4. Select individual(s): the user checks the individuals that he prefers
5. Generate a new population: keep the N_{select} checked individuals for the next generation, discard the others and replace them with newly generated individuals according to:
   a) $N_{\text{select}} = 0$: the whole population is regenerated (random creation as in step 1),
   b) $N_{\text{select}} = 1$: $N - 1$ new individuals are generated with the mutation of the selected individual,
   c) $N_{\text{select}} = N$: the next generation is identical to the current one,
   d) $N_{\text{select}} \in \{2, \ldots, N-1\}$: each of the $(N - N_{\text{select}})$ new individuals are generated with the crossover operator which is applied to two randomly selected parents among the checked individuals in order to create one offspring. In the end, the mutation operator is applied to these offsprings.
6. Go to step 2 in order to display the new generation

Fig. 11.11. Main IGA algorithm

The population size N has been limited to nine because it is important from the user point of view to display all the individuals on the same screen and because a larger population would be more time consuming.

Initialization: N individuals are generated with random parameters.

Crossover: If the selected parents are more than two, every non-selected individual is replaced by an offspring o which is computed from two parents p_1 and p_2 randomly chosen within selected ones. The number of ants for the offspring o is randomly chosen between the number of ants of p_1 and p_2 and for each ant, its parameters are randomly chosen within parameters of a randomly selected ant of p_1 and a randomly selected ant of p_2. If only one parent has been selected, offsprings are obtained by the mutation of this parent.

Mutation: The mutation operator can modify the parameters of each ant: colors' components are slightly increased or decreased. Moreover, while there are selected parents, the mutation intensity of colors decreases at each generation in order to narrow around the users' favorite individuals:

$$x \leftarrow \text{int}\left(\min\left\{\max\left\{x + \mathcal{U}(\{-80, 80\}) \times \frac{1}{g+1}, 0\right\}, 255\right\}\right) \quad (11.6)$$

where $x \in \{C_R, C_G, C_B\}$, int() returns the integer value of its argument, $\mathcal{U}(\{-80, 80\})$ gives a random integer uniformly generated in $\{-80, \ldots, +80\}$ and g stands for the number of generations where at least one parent have been checked. If no parent is selected the mutation intensity is set to its initial value ($g \leftarrow 0$). Probabilities (P_l, P_r, P_a, P_s) are also decreased or increased (one chance out of two) but without any relation with the number of generations:

$$P_i \leftarrow P_i \pm 10\% \quad \forall i \in \{l, r, a, s\}. \tag{11.7}$$

After that, probabilities are normalized ($P_l + P_r + P_a = 1$ and $P_s \leftarrow \min\{P_s, 0.999\}$). At the end, a new movement type is generated with a probability of 0.5.

These settings give the user the feeling that his choices are taken into account and nevertheless let the IGA explore a lot of possibilities.

11.5.3 Results

The IGA has been implemented using PHP language and a Java applet to draw the paintings.

In Fig. 11.12 we present the web interface that allows the user to:

- select individuals that will be considered as parents for the next generation (with the check box: here two individuals are selected),
- stop or restart one painting (by clicking on it),
- see a larger view with detailed parameters (with ),
- modify parameters (with ).

From the artist's point of view, this last item is very important: even if the genetic process should converge to what he wants, we need to offer him a way to change all the parameters.

Moreover, as it can be seen in the Fig. 11.12, all usual parameters of evolutionary methods are hidden to the user: he can only select individuals and ask for the next generation to be computed. Parameters such as mutation probability have been fixed by us in order to create an "easy to play" impression.

In Fig. 11.13 the next generation obtained after the one in Fig. 11.12 is presented. We can notice that the selected parents of Fig. 11.12 remain in the same position and are still checked. If the user changes his mind, he can uncheck them and choose new parents. At the end, in Fig. 11.14, the possibility of modifying parameters is presented.

This system can be experimented from this webpage: `http://www.hant.li.univ-tours.fr/webhant/index.php?pageid=18`.

11.6 Conclusion

This chapter has presented our work in the artistic field of music and painting production. We have been specially interested by artificial ants and their

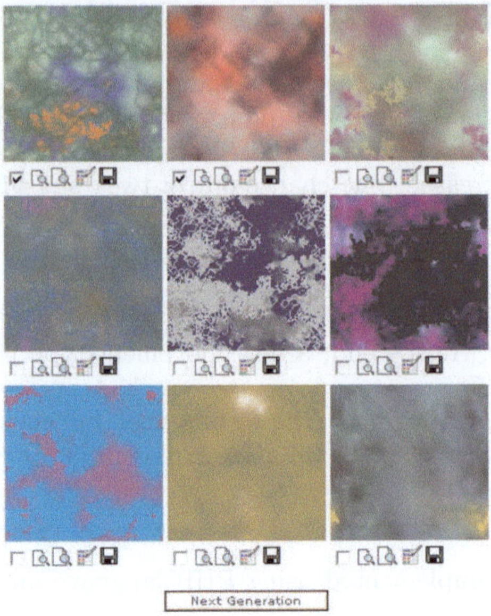

Fig. 11.12. Example of AGI interface when two individuals are selected

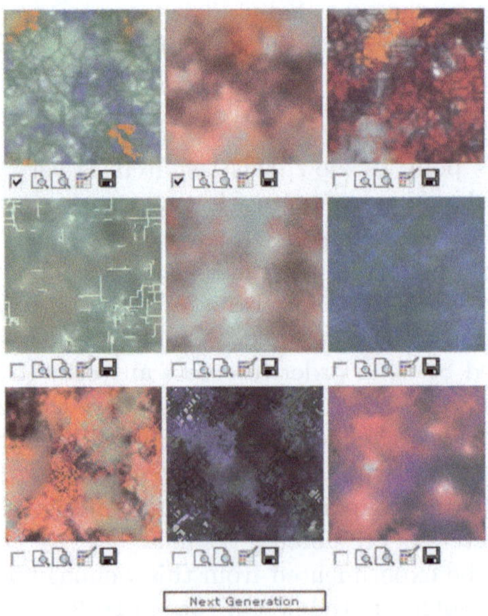

Fig. 11.13. Example showing generated individuals with the selected parents of Fig. 11.12

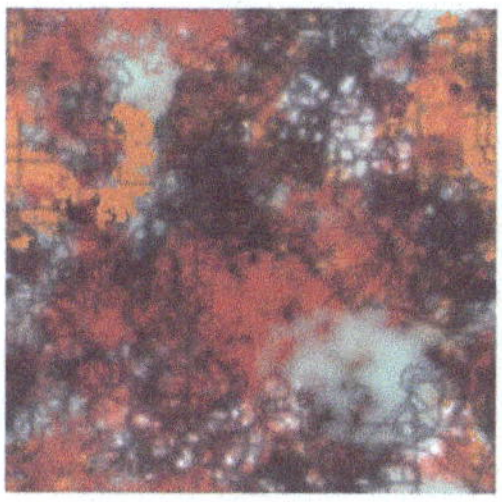

Ant Number			Deposited Color				Followed Color					Initial position		Dir.	Size.	Type of Mvt.	Probabilities			
			R	G	B	Color	R	G	B	#ant	Color	x	y				Left	Front	Right	Follow
0	☑	Rand	176	255	205		48	0	68	-		0.56	0.70	6	2	d	0.5586012	0.4281846	0.0132140	0.4794062
1	☑	Rand	213	12	112		48	0	68	-		0.42	0.05	4	1	d	0.2612126	0.6237320	0.1150552	0.6202926
2	☑	Rand	48	0	68		213	12	112	-		0.55	0.85	2	1	o	0.0213145	0.7955315	0.1831538	0.999
3	☑	Rand	234	85	57		176	255	205	-		0.74	0.04	6	0	d	0.7186032	0.2010222	0.0803745	0.4527926
4	☐	Rand	0	0	0		0	0	0	-		0.5	0.5	0	0	d	0.3	0.4	0.3	0.5

Reset See OK

Fig. 11.14. Modification interface

stigmergetic collective behaviors. These works have already been presented in various public manifestations (such as described in [32]) and international conferences in computer science [33, 3, 4].

Many directions of improvement can be drawn. Concerning painting ants, they produce a dynamic artwork but their parameters are fixed at the beginning of the run: nevertheless we can imagine many ways to enrich paintings. For instance, with the notion of food, ants could be reinforced by their capacity to survive and weak ants could die. Moreover, the default initial state of the painting is white, we can start with a picture on which ants move. This improvement leads to more personalized artworks if we let the user decide about the initial picture (see Fig. 11.15).

Since it is difficult to judge the quality of the obtained paintings, we have recorded how the interactive and evolutionary process could be useful for the user: for instance, since the beginning of the experiment, out of 618 user events, 442 new generations have been asked within 133 sessions, and when individuals were selected, an average of 2.88 individuals were selected by generation. The high number of individual checkings or modification (28 %) confirms that the user is very fond of details about the process he is playing around with. But only 193 generations out of the 442 have at least one individual selected. This can be due the fact that many visitors first try the "next generation" button before reading instructions ...

It is interesting to look at one of the recent works of G. Greenfield [34] who has considered our AntPainting process with a non-subjective and consequently non-human fitness function. Then, convergence of parameters is easily observed and this method can be useful to choose the kind of fitness function instead of only choosing pleasant paintings.

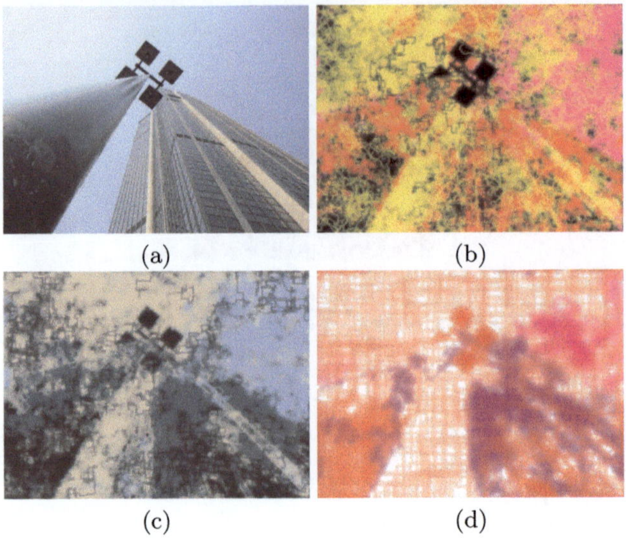

Fig. 11.15. Paintings obtained when an initial image (a) is used as pheromone field

For the compositional system presented in this chapter, many directions remain to be explored. For instance, in its current version, the system can produce melodies for different instruments simultaneously but without any harmonization between them. This could be addressed by introducing harmonization rules that would reduce the N_i sets at the transition step. Moreover, the style variation can only be influenced by the β parameter and its influence only concerns the distance between notes. Several ways can be considered: we can add a MIDI entry which could be used by a MIDI instrument musician or by a given MIDI file to influence the pheromone values either as an initialization step or as an interactive and real time system.

From the user point of view, one drawback of this compositional system is its large number of parameters and consequently the huge number of possible melodies (but for the system itself it is of course a good property). To improve this point, and then to reduce the chance that the user could be lost and discouraged, we need to help him find easily the parameters that will produce a music he/she appreciates. As it has been done with ant paintings, one possible way is to use an interactive genetic algorithm to perform an intuitive and very subjective exploration of this huge search space.

Finally, we plan to merge the two systems to build a compositional systems with a graphical aesthetic view of the musical process; this type of experiment can be found in [35].

References

1. Bonabeau, E., Dorigo, M., Theraulaz, G. (1999). *Swarm Intelligence: From Natural to Artificial Systems.* Oxford University Press. New York
2. Root-Bernstein, R. (2001). Music, creativity and scientific thinking. *Leonardo,* **34**(1): 63–68
3. Guéret, C., Monmarché, N., Slimane, M. (2004). Ants can play music. In: *Fourth International Workshop on Ant Colony Optimization and Swarm Intelligence (ANTS 2004).* Lecture Notes in Computer Science. Université Libre de Bruxelles, Belgique. Springer, 310–317
4. Aupetit, S., Bordeau, V., Monmarché, N., Slimane, M., Venturini, G. (2003). Interactive Evolution of Ant Paintings. In: *IEEE Congress on Evolutionary Computation.* Vol. 2. Canberra. IEEE Press, 1376–1383
5. Hölldobler, B., Wilson, E. (1990). *The Ants.* Springer
6. Stützle, T., Dorigo, M. (1999). ACO algorithms for the Traveling Salesman Problem. In Miettinen, K., Mäkelä, M., Neittaanmäki, P., Periaux, J., eds.: *Evolutionary Algorithms in Engineering and Computer Science: Recent Advances in Genetic Algorithms, Evolution Strategies, Evolutionary Programming, Genetic Programming and Industrial Applications.* John Wiley & Sons
7. Dorigo, M., Stützle, T. (2004). *Ant Colony Optimization.* MIT Press
8. Lopez de Mantaras, R., Arcos, J. (2002). AI and music, from composition to expressive performance. *AI magazine,* **23**(3): 43–57
9. T., J. (1996). *Self-Similar Melodies.* Edition 75
10. Chen, C., Miikkulainen, R. (2001). Creating melodies with evolving recurrent neural networks. In: *Proceedings of the 2001 International Joint Conference on Neural Networks (IJCNN–2001)*, 2241–2246
11. Eck, D., Schmidhuber, J. (2002). Finding temporal structure in music: Blues improvisation with LSTM recurrent networks. In Bourlard, H., ed.: *Proceedings of IEEE Workshop on Neural Networks for Signal Processing XII*, 747–756
12. Henz, M., Lauer, S., Zimmermann, D. (1996). COMPOzE — intention-based music composition through constraint programming. In: *Proceedings of the 8th IEEE International Conference on Tools with Artificial Intelligence.* Toulouse, France. IEEE Computer Society Press, 118–121
13. Wulfhorst, R.D., Flores, L.V., Nakayama, L., Flores, C.D., Alvares, L.O.C., Viccari, R.M. (2001). An open architecture for a musical multi-agent system. In: *Proceedings of Brazilian Symposium on Computer Music*
14. Moroni, A., Manzolli, J., Von Zuben, F., Gudwin, R. (2000). Vox populi: An interactive evolutionary system for algorithmic music composition. *Leonardo Music Journal,* **10**: 49–54
15. Todd, P., Werner, G. (1998). Frankensteinian Methods for Evolutionary Music Composition. In Griffith, N., Todd, P., eds.: *Musical Networks: Parallel Distributed Perception and Performance.* MIT Press/Bradford Books
16. Bentley, P., Corne, D., eds. (2001). *Creative Evolutionary Systems.* Morgan Kaufmann
17. Cope, D. (1990). Pattern matching as an engine for the computer simulation of musical style. In Association, I.C.M., ed.: *Proceedings of the International Computer Music Conference.* San Francisco, 288–291
18. Franklin, J. (2001). Multi-phase learning for jazz improvisation and interaction. In: *Proceedings of the Eighth Biennal Symposium on Art and Technology.* New London, Connecticut

19. Biles, J. (1994). GEMJAM: a genetic algorithm for generating jazz solos. In: *Proceedings of the International Computer Music Conference*. San Francisco. International Computer Music Association, 131–137
20. Morales-Manzanares, R., Morales, E., Danenberg, R., Berger, J. (2001). SICIB: An interactive music composition system using body movements. *New Music Research*, **25**(2): 25–36
21. Todd, P., Miranda, E. (2003). Putting some (artificial) life into models of musical creativity. In Deliege, I., Wiggins, G., eds.: *Musical Creativity: Current Research in Theory and Practise*. Psychology Press
22. Blackwell, T., P., B. (2002). Improvised music with swarms. In: *Proceedings of the World Congress on Evolutionary Computation (CEC'2002)*, 1462–1467
23. Blackwell, T., M., Y. (2004). Swarm granulator. In Raidl, G.R., et al., eds.: *Applications of Evolutionary Computing, EvoWorkshops2004: EvoBIO, EvoCOMNET, EvoHOT, EvoIASP, EvoMUSART, EvoSTOC*. Lecture Notes in Computer Science. Coimbra, Portugal. Springer, 399–408
24. Tzafestas, E. (2000). Integrating drawing tools with behavioral modeling in digital painting. In: *Proceedings of the 1st International Workshop "Bridging the Gap: Bringing Together New Media Artists and Multimedia Technologists"*. Los Angeles, CA
25. Moura, L., Garcia Pereira, H. (2004). *Man + Robots: Symbiotic Art*. Institut d'art contemporain. Villeurbanne, France
26. Urbano, P. (2005). Playing in the pheromone playground: Experiences in swarm painting. In Rothlauf, F., et al., eds.: *Applications on Evolutionary Computing: EvoWorkkshops 2005: EvoBIO, EvoCOMNET, EvoHOT, EvoIASP, EvoMUSART, and EvoSTOC*. Lecture Notes in Computer Science. Lausanne, Switzerland. Springer Berlin/Heidelberg, 527
27. Ramos, V., Almeida, F. (2000). Artificial ant colonies in digital image habitats – a mass behaviour effect study on pattern recognition. In Dorigo, M., Middendoff, M., Stützle, T., eds.: *From Ant Colonies to Artificial Ants: Proceedings of the Second International Workshop on Ant Algorithms (ANTS'2000)*. Brussels, Belgium, 113–116
28. Bourjot, C., Chevrier, V., Thomas, V. (2003). A new swarm mechanism based on social spiders colonies: from web weaving to region detection. *Web Intelligence and Agent Systems: An International Journal – WIAS*
29. Campolongo, G., Vena, S. (2006). Science of networks and music: A new approach on musical analysis and creation. In Rothlauf, F., et al., eds.: *Applications of Evolutionary Computing, EvoWorkshops2006: EvoBIO, EvoCOMNET, EvoHOT, EvoIASP, EvoInteraction, EvoMUSART, EvoSTOC*. Lecture Notes in Computer Science. Springer, 642–651
30. Dorigo, M., Maniezzo, V., Colorni, A. (1996). The Ant System: Optimization by a colony of cooperating agents. *IEEE Transactions on Systems, Man, and Cybernetics–Part B*, **26**(1): 29–41
31. Minsky, M. (1993). Music, Mind and Meaning. In Schwanauer, S., Levitt, D., eds.: *Machine Models of Music*. MIT Press, 327–354
32. Lebocey, P., Fortune, J., Puret, A., Monmarché, N., Gaucher, P., Slimane, M., Lastu, D. (2006). On the popularization of artificial insects: an interactive exhibition for a wide audience to explain and demonstrate computer science and robotic problem solving taking inspiration of insects. In Dorigo, M., Gambardella, L., Birattari, M., Martinoli, A., Poli, R., Stützle, T., eds.: *Ant Colony*

Optimization and Swarm Intelligence, 5th International Workshop, ANTS 2006. Lecture Notes in Computer Science. Bruxelles, Belgium. Springer, 476–483
33. Monmarché, N., Slimane, M., Venturini, G. (2003). Fourmis artistiques ou l'art artificiel pictural et musical. In: *Hypertextes et Hypermédias, Réalisations, Outils & Méthodes (H2PTM'03).* Paris, France. Hermes, 109–118
34. Greenfield, G. (2005). Evolutionary methods for ant colony paintings. In Rothlauf, F., et al., eds.: *Applications on Evolutionary Computing: EvoWorkkshops 2005: EvoBIO, EvoCOMNET, EvoHOT, EvoIASP, EvoMUSART, and EvoSTOC.* Lecture Notes in Computer Science. Lausanne, Switzerland, 478
35. Lesbros, V. (1996). From images to sounds, a dual representation. *Computer Music Journal*, **20**(3): 59–69

12

Embedding of Pixel-Based Evolutionary Algorithms in My Global Art Process

Günter Bachelier

Drosselweg 11, 66839 Schmelz, Germany guba@vi-anec.de

Summary. My art comprises three levels: basic, methodical, and superordinate. The basic level refers to the production of individual works of art. At the methodical level, I am concerned with the development of artistic processes, in this case, inspired by evolutionary concepts. Finally, at the superordinate level, social sculpture, "Health Art", is considered.

Between 1995 and 2003 I developed and used several pixel-based evolutionary art processes. These artistic approaches resort to biologically inspired concepts, such as population, variation, and selection. The individuals were pixel images. In the reproduction phase two (or more) individuals were selected as parents and the images were recombined by the exchange of image parts (Regions-of-Interest). Variation (mutation) was performed by means of image processing operations such as the rotation of image parts with random but constrained parameters. Parents and offspring were evaluated by the aesthetic preferences of the artist and the best individuals built the next generation.

A unique and more complex evolution art process was developed in 2004, with no direct correspondence to known evolutionary algorithms like GA, ES, or GP. It uses some additional evolutionary concepts, such as a global pool of images and multi-sexual recombination, together with ontogenetic concepts, such as spores or fruits, and other concepts such as image templates. In a narrow sense, there is no change of generations of image individuals. Selected individuals are directly inserted into the global image pool, being also involved in a second reproduction process where they are transformed by mathematical symmetry operations. The resulting images are also inserted into the global image pool, while all the images in this pool build the basis for recombination in the next generation.

Future plans, about file formats, other image reproduction operators, image databases, and aesthetic preference modelling, are also discussed.

12.1 The Three Levels of My Current Art

In the next sections I explore the scientific and artistic issues that arise at the three levels – basic, methodical, and superordinate – of my work as an artist.

12.1.1 Basic Level: Individual Work of Art

The first level raises purely artistic questions about shape, composition, and color. I was strongly influenced by art styles such as Informel [1, 2, 3, 4], Abstract Expressionism [5], and Action Painting, as well as by artists such as Hans Hartung [6] and Jackson Pollock [7]. Pollock's dripping technique led me to the development of different methods of self-organizing painting [8], long before I came across the term "self-organizing painting" – I was about 13 years old. I was, and still am, fascinated by the ability of materials to build complex structures only by means of their physical and chemical properties. These structures are dynamic and the most interesting of them are far from balance. Therefore, capturing these interesting structures by photographing them was natural to me, which led me to abstract photography. A large archive of abstract photographs was accumulated over the years and they were digitized in the early 1990s. This marks a turning point because my work shifted from conventional visual art, such as painting, to computer-aided art, using, however, conventional image processing methods.

These abstract (macro) photos have associations to satellite images of the earth and other planets. This is no coincidence because the dynamic effects that shape landscapes and atmospheric structures belong to the same class as the effects that shape the structures in self-organizing painting (dynamic structures in fluids; see Fig. 12.1).

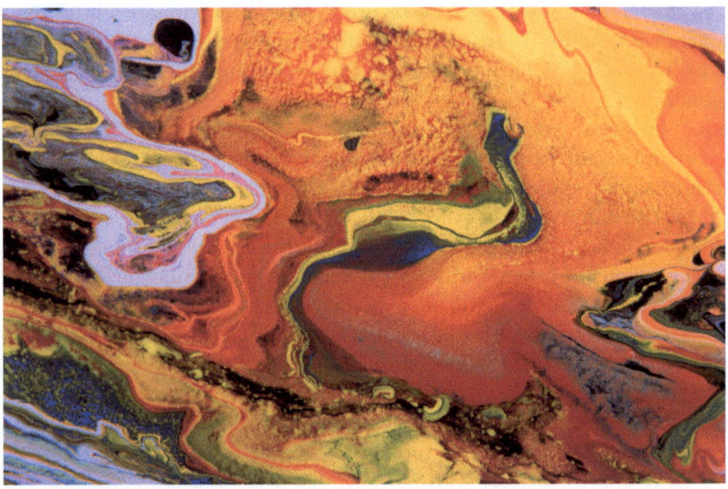

Fig. 12.1. Example of a digitized macro photo as part of a self-organized painting

The idea of a "contrast aesthetics" developed over the years and I tried to recombine contrasting and partially contradicting concepts to create both aesthetic and interesting works. The biological concept of symbiosis constituted an increasingly important metaphor for this integration. To date, the following concepts have been integrated into my works:

- symbiosis of self-organizing painting (Informel, Abstract Expressionism) and geometric/constructive art (concrete art [9])
- symbiosis of biomorphic and hard-edge painting shapes
- symbiosis of symmetry and symmetry breaking
- symbiosis of local and global symmetry.

Questions about symmetry and symmetry breaking have come specially under focus in the last two years. Bilateral symmetry is used in most cases because there are neural and evolutionary biological correlations to aesthetic feelings. This is shown by the scientific research on aesthetics which can be exemplified by studies about the attractiveness of faces.

Given that as social beings humans depend on recognizing and interpreting faces and facial expressions, a large part of the visual system is focused on face recognition.

Faces have an overall bilateral symmetry, although they present plenty of small local symmetry breaking (the same can be said about the bodies of most animals). Therefore, the visual system specializes in recognizing bilateral symmetry and its deviations.

There is a long standing hypothesis according to which symmetric faces are more often selected, given the task to select faces with higher attractiveness [10]. Some empirical studies validate this hypothesis [10] specially if female subjects are selecting male faces, although other studies came to inconclusive results ([11] or [12]). The attractiveness of symmetric faces could be explained by evolutionary biology. The deviation from a symmetric ideal could point towards development alterations which might be caused by genetic defects or by parasitic influences. Both cases would possibly affect reproduction success; therefore, reproduction partners with symmetric properties are preferred. Such an explanation would indicate that aesthetics has an established foundation in evolutionary biology [13].

The starting point for me to develop a meta-strategy to find a balance between symmetry and symmetry breaking was based on the positive correlation between symmetry and aesthetic feeling (on the one hand) and between symmetry and boredom after some time of perception (on the other), so as to find aesthetic and interesting works of art.

12.1.2 Methodical Level: Evolutionary Art

The second level is the methodical level, where I transfer evolutionary concepts and methods to develop evolutionary art processes that enable me to create nonrepresentative works of art that fit my aesthetic preferences. I view an art process as a sequence of actions by an artist or group of artists whose outcome is a work of art (e.g., image, sculpture) or the process itself is a work of art (e.g., performance, dance).

In this context, an evolutionary art process can be defined as an artistic process where the three evolutionary concepts population, variation, and selection are used. This does not necessarily mean that the whole process is computerized, or even that a specific evolutionary algorithm is incorporated, because evolutionary art can be done with paper, pencil, and a dice. For instance, William Latham was doing evolutionary art on paper long before his ideas were converted into a computational approach [14]. Such a definition includes cases where an implemented evolutionary algorithm is only a part of the whole process, specially if the outcome of the algorithm can be optimized by the artist. If the desired output of an art process is a complex image, it is natural to use the aid of computers to generate image individuals; otherwise the change of generation would take too long. The resulting evolutionary art process might be style and material independent.

The background for this development dates back to around 1995, when my scientific interests shifted from Neural Networks [15] and specially self-organizing maps [16, 17] to Evolutionary Algorithms and particularly Evolution Strategies [18, 19, 20]. I first became aware of Evolutionary Art when reading the exhibition catalog of Ars Electronica 1993, about Artificial Life and Genetic Algorithms [21]. I realized immediately that this could be a crossroads, a junction bringing together my research and artistic interests.

In the first stage I developed an integration of my conventional art process, (self-organizing painting), and an evolutionary art process that uses the basic concepts: population, variation, and selection. I used the digital images in my archives for the initialization of the whole of my early evolutionary art runs and I evolved these images over some years (see Fig. 12.2 for example).

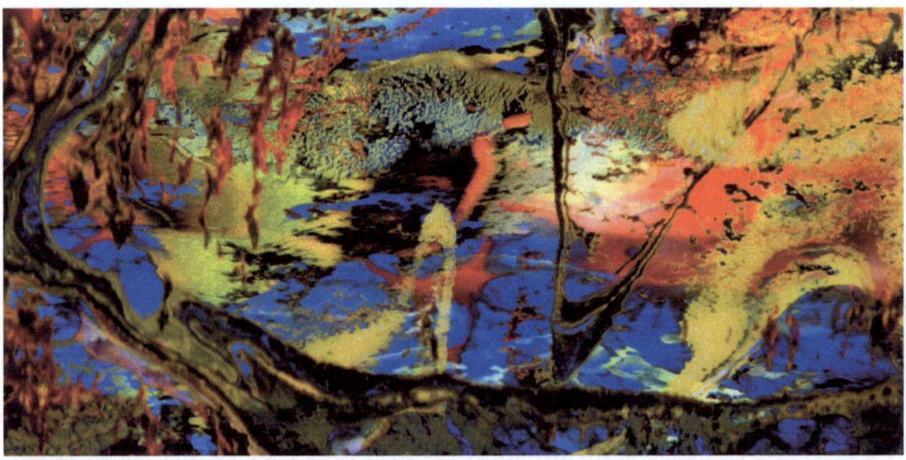

Fig. 12.2. Image individual from the end of my first evolutionary art phase

I also used the results for post-processing operations – such as the creation of abstract panoramas (see Fig. 12.3) which were developed until 2003. They can be viewed on the Web with a specific panorama viewer (see `http://www.vi-anec.de/Trance-Art/Gesamt-Panoramen.html`). A physical transformation of this kind of art is difficult because panoramas often have a height: width proportion of 1:10.

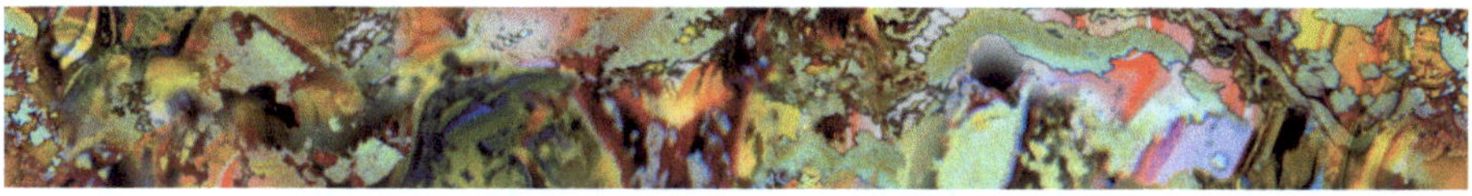

Fig. 12.3. Example of an abstract panorama

Around 2002, I realized that this kind of evolutionary art process was ending. So, in the context of my contrast aesthetics, I began to play with the idea of how to combine contradicting approaches (such as geometric, constructive, and concrete art) with the images derived from the nonrepresentational art of self-organizing painting. The combination of geometric shape and nonrepresentational content opened a new dimension to my work and the combinatorial properties of evolutionary art were suitable for exploring this new dimension.

Geometric forms naturally lead to questions about symmetry, so I combined this development with the wish to work with biomorphic shapes by applying the supershape formula [22] in many of my new works. Figure 12.4 shows some examples from the repository of masks generated from supershapes.

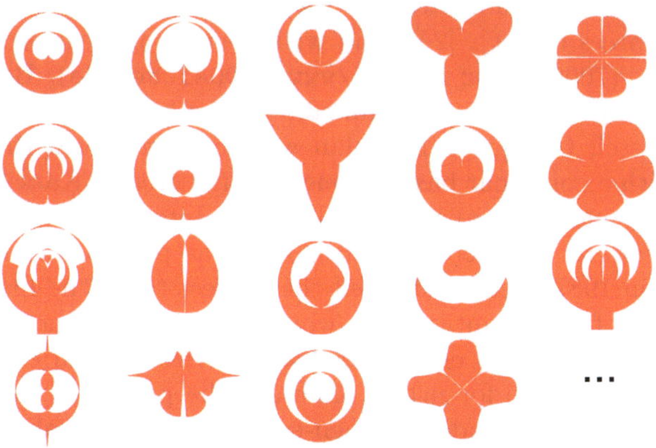

Fig. 12.4. Examples of supershape masks

The new questions about symmetry, symmetry breaking, and biomorphic shapes required a new adapted kind of evolutionary art process. Such a unique and more complex evolutionary art process is being developed since 2004, dealing with these new requests and using additional concepts, namely, multi-sexual recombination, and global image pools, as well as ontogenetic concepts, i.e., spores.

12.1.3 Social Sculpture: Health Art

Since 2004, I have embedded the first two levels into a larger artistic process, a social sculpture ([23], `http://www.social-sculpture.org`) called "Health Art" invented by me. Health Art is a completely new way to combine art and health within the environment, and a new answer to the old questions about the effects and benefits of art. Health Art works, in general, possess an intended and objectively quantifiable influence on environmental factors which positively affects health. This general concept is specialized in AROSHU® Health Art by integrating in my art works absorber materials which neutralize and/or bind a large number of gaseous air pollutants. The effectiveness of the absorber materials was scientifically confirmed by several research institutions such as the DW-Institute (`http://www.dwi.rwth-aachen.de`) at the technical University of Aachen and the Eco Umweltinstitut (`http://eco-umweltinstitut.de`) in Cologne. A unique AROSHU® picture frame was developed in which the absorber material is suspended in such a way that it allows a multiple area of absorber material surface (up to four times indicated AROSHU®-4). An AROSHU® picture of one square meter has approx. Four square meters of integrated absorber surface, capable of cleaning a room with approximately 80 cubic meters of air.

The social sculpture of Health Art has connections to the work of Joseph Beuys specially to his examination of the connections between medicine and art ("healing forces of art", [24]) and with socio-ecological projects like the "7000 Eichen", (7000 Oaks; `http://www.7000eichen.de`). Beuys's project 7000 Oaks started in 1982 at Documenta 7, the large international art exhibition in Kassel, Germany. The plan was to plant seven thousand trees, each paired with a columnar basalt stone through greater Kassel. The project was carried out under the auspices of the Free International University and it took five years to complete. The last tree was planted at the opening of Documenta 8 in 1987. Beuys intended the project to be the first stage in an ongoing scheme of tree planting that would extend throughout the world as part of a global mission to effect social and environmental change. Locally, the action was a gesture for urban renewal. The projects "7000 Oaks" and "Health Art" are both intended as open-ended growing social sculptures that integrate artistic, ecological, and social aspects.

Health Art integrates the additional aspect of human health because indoor air pollution is a large, but underestimated problem and many millions of people in industrialized countries are affected by environmental diseases like allergies, sick building syndrome (SBS), or multiple chemical sensitiveness (MCS).

12.2 The First Evolutionary Art Processes (1995–2003)

As previously stated, in this context evolutionary art is seen as art created by a method that resorts to evolutionary concepts.

Since I use the help of computers in my evolutionary art method, it can be explained by the description of a generic evolutionary algorithm with four main components: population, evaluation, selection, and reproduction. The goal was to transfer these components to an artistic context (here, visual art) and determine what could be the meaning of these central concepts in its scope. There is no obvious or single answer to this question, since a huge variety of possible evolutionary art processes are possible.

12.2.1 Population and Individuals

Although most conventional evolutionary art approaches resort to expression-based image representation, all the individuals in my evolutionary art processes are bitmap images. The population is simply a set of such individuals, i.e., it has no other internal structure such as a graph. In contrast to expression-based representations, I have named this approach "data-based" evolutionary art.

It is possible to use the whole range of concepts that have been implemented in graphic file format, such as alpha channels and layers. File formats using meta-information (commentary, IPTC-Header, XML tags, etc.) can be used directly as image individuals, since the fitness value can be saved as a kind of meta-information in the file.

The seeding operation, i.e., the creation of the first population, is an important part of my approach. Typically, in expression-based approaches, the individuals of the first population are created through the random generation of the corresponding expression trees. A random initialization in the case of data-based evolutionary art is not reasonable because such an image would not have any structures. It is more efficient and effective to start with images from outside an evolutionary process which have already satisfied to some extent the aesthetic preferences of the artist.

12.2.2 Evaluation and Selection

After the initialization and after the generation of offspring, the individuals are evaluated. In most evolutionary algorithms this is done with a fitness function. However, in the case of interactive evolutionary art, the quality of an individual reflects the aesthetic preference of the artist who is evaluating the image individuals. In my evolutionary art processes there is no explicit fitness function; therefore this is an interactive evolution approach, requiring input from an external source, the artist.

A binary evaluation is applied as strategy to select the individuals and parents for the next generation. My evolutionary art process depends solely on my aesthetic judgments, images that do not satisfy my aesthetic needs are not selected and are deleted at a later stage.

12.2.3 Reproduction

Reproduction is the operation by which new individuals (offspring) are produced from the genetic code of one or more mature individuals (parents). It is necessary to define recombination and mutation operators suitable for data-based evolutionary art.

If we use bitmap images as individuals, the interpretation of reproduction with the two components (recombination and mutation) is not that obvious, but it is clear that the interpretation is different from expression-based evolutionary art. My solution, in 1995, was to apply some image processing functions as reproduction operators and to use random but constrained parameters of such functions so as to introduce variations in the next generation.

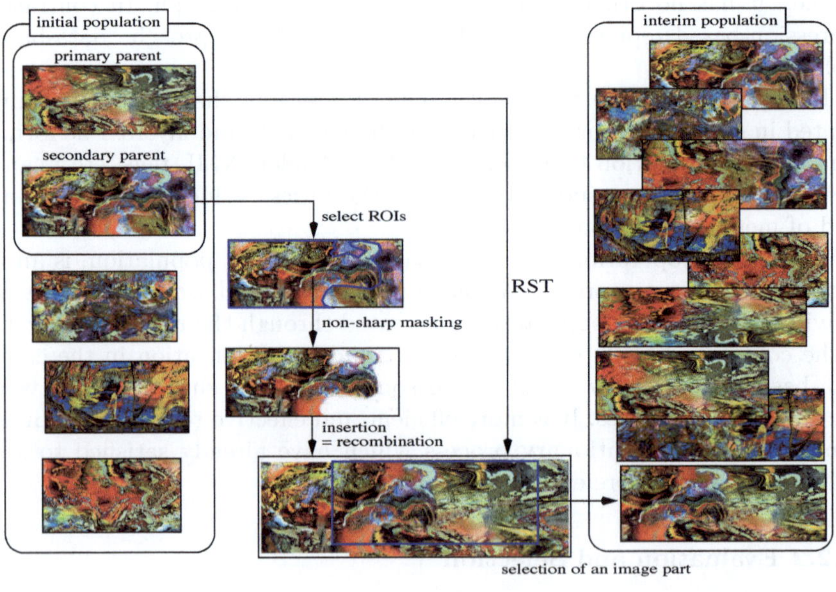

Fig. 12.5. Recombination and mutation in the first evolutionary art processes

Recombination

One possible definition of recombination, used in my art process, is an analogy to the crossover operations in genetic algorithms, or to the discrete recombination operator in evolutionary strategies.

Segments of one parent image are selected which, in turn, build an offspring image with the complementary parts of the second image. The concept through which this is achieved is called regions-of-interest (ROIs), i.e., possible overlapping segments of an image defined by the artist.

A simple reproduction strategy that was used first selects at random two parents from the image population (see Fig. 12.5). One of them is selected randomly as the primary parent who is copied to one layer of the offspring individual. Then ROIs of the secondary parent are selected randomly and they are masked with non-sharp edges and later copied to a higher layer of the offspring.

This reproduction strategy can be generalized to multi-sexual reproduction if the offspring obtain their genetic material (image components) from more than two parents; i.e., the second, third, and so on parent inserts its selected ROIs in the copied primary image.

Mutation

Copying images and image parts in an offspring individual is the recombination part of the reproduction process. Additional variation (mutation) is introduced by transforming the transmitted regions by means of image processing operations with randomized parameters with certain constraints. The primary image is not just copied but also undergoes transformations. In most cases, a RST transformation (Rotation, Scaling, Translation) was used, i.e., the image of the primary parent and the ROIs are rotated by an angle between 0 and 360 degrees, scaled by a scaling factor, for example, between 0.8 and 2.4, and moved in the x and y direction.

After recombination with mutation, the parents and offspring build an interim population and the elements from this population are evaluated, i.e., the artist decides if the images are compatible with his aesthetic preferences. The images that survive this evaluation are selected for the next generation.

12.3 Current Evolutionary Art Process (2004-Ongoing)

My current evolutionary art process was developed in 2004 using some additional concepts, such as a global image pool, image templates (as an analogy to the genome), multi-sexual recombination and specific types of meme reproduction, as a translation of the ontogenetic concept of spores or fruits.

12.3.1 Overview

The process begins with the definition of a template image that consists of several masks, each on one layer (see point 2 in Fig. 12.6). A multi-sexual reproduction process (see point 3 in Fig. 12.6) exchanges those masks randomly for images from a global image pool (see point 1 in Fig. 12.6) that consists of several classes of images. Recombination strategies define which mask is exchanged by an image from which class. This reproduction is multi-sexual because more than two layers and image parents are always selected.

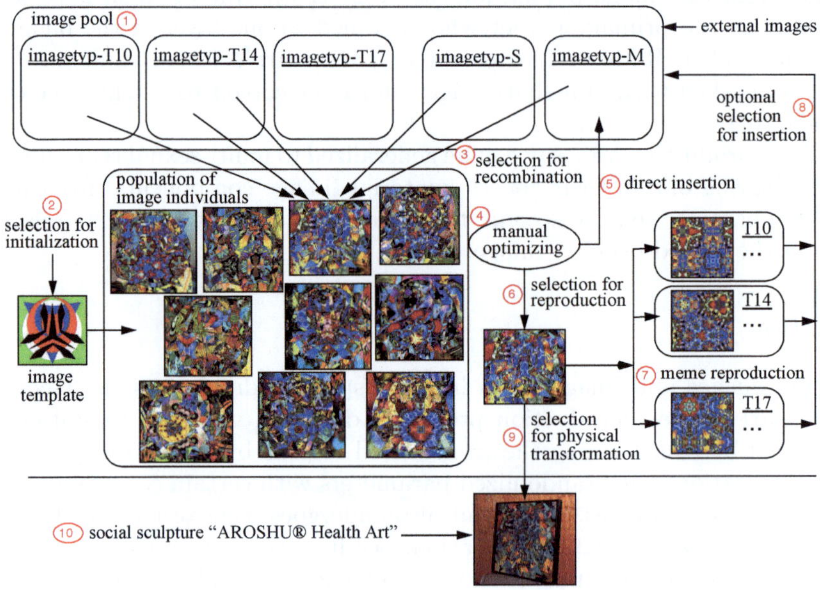

Fig. 12.6. Overview of the current evolutionary art process

After generating a population of about 100 individuals, the evaluation is done by the artist putting each image in one of three classes: "non-reproduction" class for images that do not match the aesthetic preferences and which will be deleted; "optimization" class for images that have a good overall impression but with local faults or defects which will be optimized by hand; and "direct reproduction" class for images that match the preferences. After the time-consuming manual optimization, (see point 4 in Fig. 12.6) the images from the second and third classes are directly copied into the global image pool in their own class (see point 5 in Fig. 12.6).

Additionally, they undergo a second reproduction phase where mathematical symmetry operators with random but constrained parameters are applied to them (see point 7 in Fig. 12.6). Forty to eighty meme images were generated for each symmetry operator. These images were directly inserted into the global image pool, where every symmetry operator used has its own image class. Images from the first and second reproduction processes are then available for selection in the next iteration or generation, where the same or a different image template is used.

12.3.2 Global Image Pool

A huge global image pool consisting of pixel images is provided. The images come from non-evolutionary art processes such as self-organizing painting and from previous evolutionary runs. The image pool is structured into different classes (see imagetyp-T10, T14, T17, M, and S in Fig. 12.6) depending on the origin and method of generation. Many of the image individuals from the first evolutionary art processes are included in a specific image type S, called "Spaces". These individuals are often used as background (first layer).

The idea of a predominant image or meme pool is derived from the idea of genetic load [25]: Preserved genes from the evolutionary history of a population or a species to be used now or later. These genes were originally included in the gene structure of the individuals, but in my evolutionary art process all memes were externalized in the image pool where they are used for recombination purposes. Such a predominant image pool has no close biological analogy because it represents not only all the genes of a present ecosystem, but also the whole history of such an ecosystem.

12.3.3 Initialization by Determination of an Image Template

An important building block is the use of an image template in analogy to a genome. A genome is defined by a certain number and positions of genes. A certain number of masks and their positions relative to each other exemplify the analogy in this evolutionary art process. Each mask is located on a specific layer of the image template. The masks and their composition in the template are generated by the artist and they reflect my interest in the dependencies between symmetry and symmetry breaking. In most cases, bilateral symmetry is used for the masks.

12.3.4 Recombination of Image Individuals

A population is defined by a number of image individuals. Those image individuals are generated by using a multi-sexual recombination process that randomly takes images from the image pool and exchanges the content of masks for the corresponding content of the selected images (see Fig. 12.7). This recombination process has a similarity to the multi-sexual recombination of viruses where more than two individuals recombine to build offspring. The gene pool is the set of all individuals that ever existed, which corresponds to the image pool.

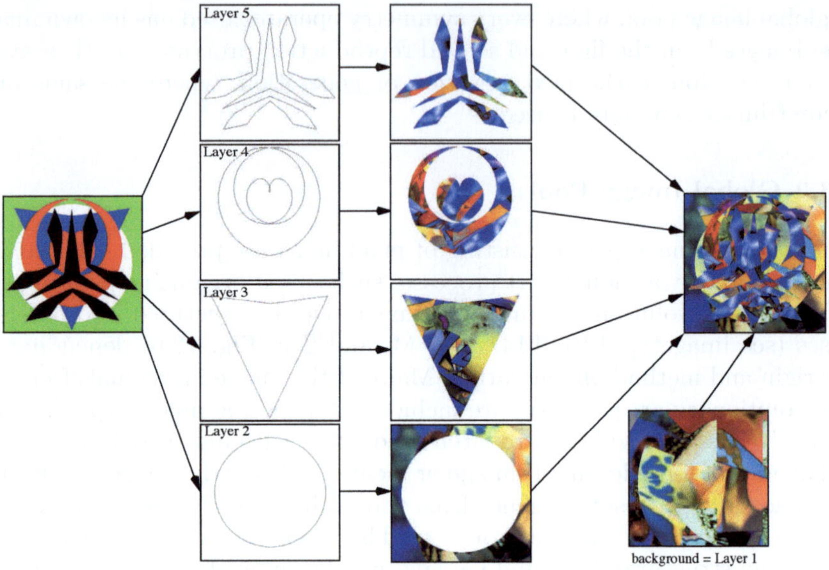

Fig. 12.7. Recombination with a template and masks

There are lots of possible recombination strategies which determine what type of image should be used for one of the masks. It is part of the artist's task to specify such strategies. An actually used recombination strategy specifies that for the background layer (layer 1) a random image is chosen from the class "Spaces from the year 2004", for layer 2 a random image is chosen from imagetyp-T14 (plane group p3m1), for layer 3 a random image is chosen from imagetyp-T14 or imagetyp-T10 (plane group p4m), for layer 4 a random image is chosen from imagetyp-T17 (plane group p6m), and for layer 5 a random image is chosen from imagetyp-M (image individuals that were directly transferred to the image pool; see point 5 in Fig. 12.6):

- layer 1: "Spaces from the year 2004"
- layer 2: image type T14
- layer 3: image type T10 or T14
- layer 4: image type T17
- layer 5: image type M.

A huge flexibility can be generated if the masks are previously transformed into paths. In this case, the images from the image pool are inserted and then undergo an RST transformation before they are transformed together with the path into a new mask or stencil.

12.3.5 Evaluation

After having generated a population of roughly 100 image individuals, the images are evaluated by the artist by putting them into one of the following classes:

- class "non-reproduction": images that do not match the aesthetic preferences, which will be deleted
- class "optimization": images that have a good overall impression but with local faults or defects; they will be optimized by hand
- class "direct reproduction": images that match the aesthetic preferences.

12.3.6 Manual Optimizing

The option of manually optimizing image individuals is specially important when paths are used, given that the probability of images with local faults can be high in this instance depending on the RST parameters. A fault mask or stencil is built when the RST-transformed image does not fully overlap its corresponding path. Image individuals with one or more of such faults are called "nonvalid". If the overall impression of such an image is good, then it is selected for the "optimization" class and the fault is reversed by hand by moving the RST-transformed image on the layer in such a way that it fully overlaps the path, followed by the merging of the image and path.

The detection of nonvalid image individuals is done manually by the artist during the evaluation; however, a script was developed which can automatically detect such individuals if a specific background color is used that is not intentionally used in any of the images. One of the drawbacks of this procedure is the production of "false positive" detections, i.e., images are marked as nonvalid because there are pixels of the specific color, though they all have valid masks. A threshold of pixels was introduced in order to minimize the false positive detections: the image is classified as nonvalid only when the number of pixels with such color is above the threshold

12.3.7 Selection for Meme Reproduction

After the optimization of image individuals, the classes "direct reproduction" and "optimization" are merged and then directly copied into the image pool in the imagetyp-M class. One of the unique features of my new evolutionary art process is that these images or a selected subset of them undergo a second stage of reproduction, the meme reproduction. In the present implementation, all images from the merged classes are selected for this second reproduction.

12.3.8 Image Meme Reproduction

This second stage of reproduction shares similarities with species that produce fruits or spores. Those fruits or spores have none or few morphological similarities with the parents but they are able to yield offspring by themselves.

Usually, parts of image individuals are selected and a whole new image can be generated from these parts using a system of simple image operations. Given that symmetry is one of my main interests, special mathematical operations (two-dimensional symmetry groups or plane groups [26]) are used to perform this task. There are 17 plane groups and four of them generate seamless images (pmm, p4m, p3m1, p6m). After experimenting in 2004 with all plane groups, three (p4m, p3m1, p6m) of the four seamless plane groups are now used in my evolutionary art process. Every symmetry group defines its own class in the global image pool. The plane group p3m1 fits my aesthetic preferences very well and it is used the most in the meme reproduction process. From every selected image individual from the first reproduction process, 80 different meme images were generated with p3m1, where p4m and p6m generate 40 each.

The generation of a meme image with p3m1 will be described next in some detail. The process begins with the selection of an image part from the source image, e.g., M04-05-08b-1-026 (rotated 90° counterclockwise) in Fig. 12.8.

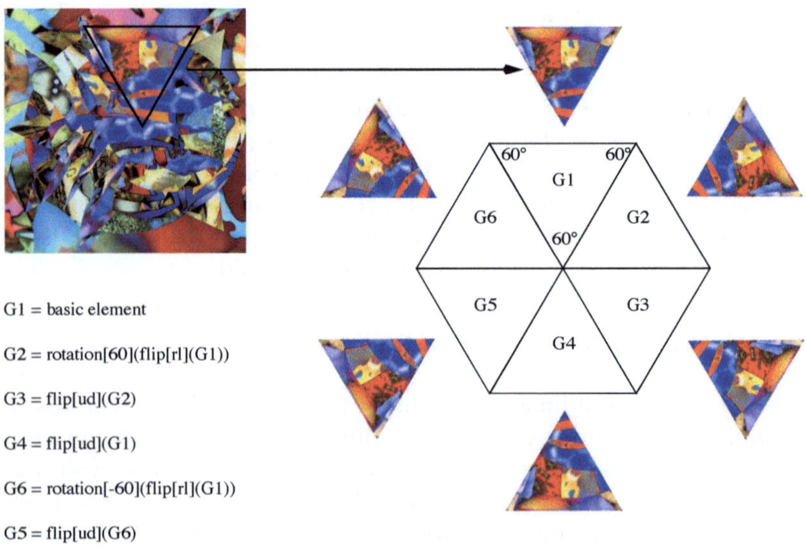

Fig. 12.8. Building blocks of a seamless plane covering with p3m1

The selection with a polygon selection operation is an equilateral triangle. Its side length is a predefined constant or a function of the side lengths of the source image (e.g., 0.8 of the infimum of the two side lengths). The position of the triangle in the image M04-05-08b-1-026 is random and different in every on of the meme reproduction processes. The selected image part serves as a basic building block, G1, that can be copied and altered with some simple geometric procedures to generate five other building blocks, G2-G6, in the following way (see Fig. 12.8):

- G2 is generated if G1 is flipped right-left and than rotated 60° clockwise (rotate[60](flip[rl](G1)))
- G3 is generated if G2 is flipped up-down (flip[ud](G2))
- G4 is generated if G1 is flipped up-down (flip[ud](G1))
- G6 is generated if G1 is flipped right-left and than rotated 60° counter-clockwise (rotate[-60](flip[rl](G1)))
- G5 is generated if G6 is flipped up-down (flip[ud](G6)).

A seamless covering of the plane is possible with those six building blocks. A meme image can be interpreted as a region of such a patterned plane and, by default, the side lengths of the meme image are the same as the side lengths of the source image (see Fig. 12.9). The resulting meme image is named according to the symmetry used to generate it (here T14 for p3m1) and is numbered, so the image in Fig. 12.9 could be copied as T14M04-05-08b-1-026-001 in the T14 class of the global image pool.

12.3.9 Optional Selection for Insertion in the Image Pool

The images generated by the meme reproduction process can be copied directly in the global image pool or can be evaluated. The direct copy option was implemented since evaluation by a human is not reasonable, due to the large amount of meme images and because of the unavailability of an aesthetic preference model that could evaluate these images with machine learning methods. This approach is also reasonable because experience has shown that meme images generated by the selected plane groups fit, in most cases, the aesthetic preferences, provided the source image was selected according to the same preferences.

12.3.10 Selection for Physical Transformation

The selection for physical transformation is not part of the evolutionary process in a strict sense, but it is part of my art process in general. Not only is the image which should be physically obtained selected here, but also are all the other aspects related to this decision: Size, materials, kind of printing, number of copies printed, etc.

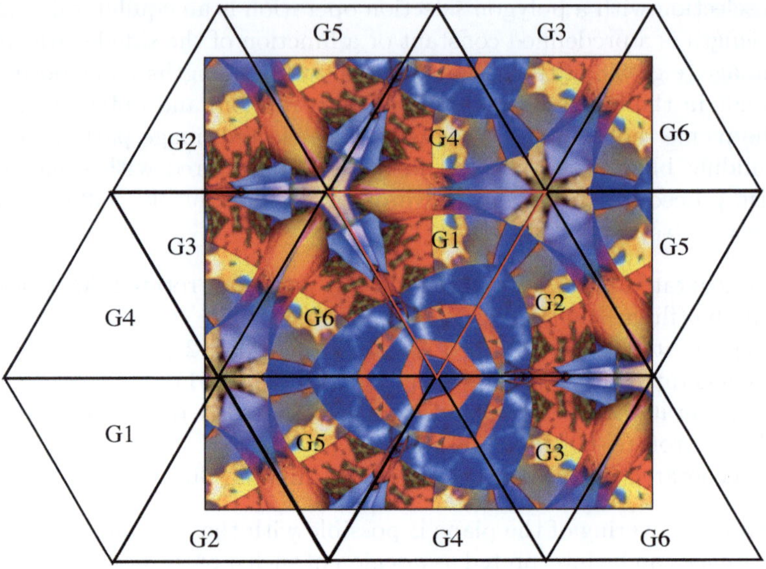

Fig. 12.9. Selection of a meme image from the seamless plane covering

12.3.11 The Social Sculpture AROSHU® Health Art

Since 2003/04 the evolutionary art process is embedded in my social sculpture "Health Art", therefore the selection for physical transformation is constrained by specific techniques and materials compatible with this ecological and health-conscious concept. First, the selected image individuals were printed with acrylic on canvas and then sealed with shellac to avoid toxic emissions from the paint. Then the canvas is integrated in the AROSHU® picture frame with the absorber material that neutralizes and/or binds a large number of gaseous air pollutants.

12.3.12 Change of Generations

In evolutionary art processes which are more closely related to the biological processes, there is a change of generation after the reproduction and selection of individuals. The selected offspring or a mixture of parents and offspring build the next generation, followed by further reproduction and selection processes. In my evolutionary art process there is no change of generation in this sense, because none of the individuals are transferred directly to the next generation. Selected individuals and the meme images are transferred instead into the global image pool. This has a biological correlation to species that produce fruits or spores, e.g., plants that live for only one year.

12.3.13 Resulting Images

Figure 12.10 shows two prototypical image individuals that were generated with this new evolutionary art process (the two image population of these examples are shown on the DVD). They include most of the factors of my current contrast aesthetics: Concrete art shapes and Informel content, biomorphic and hard-edge shapes, and shapes with global bilateral symmetry, local and global symmetries, and symmetry breaking in the content.

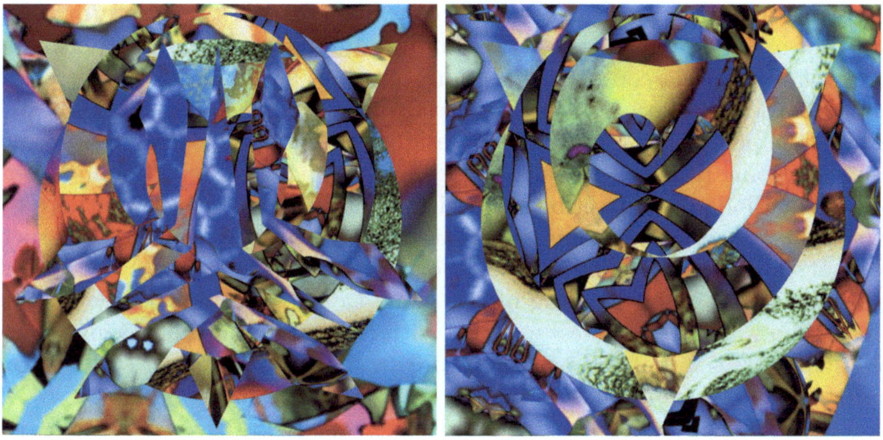

Fig. 12.10. Two examples of prototypical new image individuals: M04-05-08b-1-026 and M05-06-11-2-020

12.4 Future Plans

The continuous update of the predominant image pool with large pixel images demands much higher requirements from the underlying hardware than the use of expression-based evolutionary art methods, because the functions or programs that represent an image need much less hard disk memory. At the moment 2 TB hard disk spaces are in use; they must be upgraded at short intervals. The plans until 2010 are to use a small farm of computers and a large hard disk array to establish a balance between the recombination process of image individuals, consuming less resources, and the meme reproduction processes, consuming plenty of them.

Until then, a further development considering the used file formats has to be tackled. With the file formats used today, the image pool would grow at this point at a rate of more than 30 TB a year. The replacement of the file format used cannot be done easily, because the elements in the image pool have a specific file format which is used in the recombination operation of the image individuals. Only a reimplementation of the recombination operation would allow other file formats like JPEG 2000 (jp2, `http://www.jpeg.org/jpeg2000`). The conversion of the image pool with several hundred thousand images to jp2 is complete (September 2006) and the reimplementation of the image recombination process with ImageMagick (`http://www.imagemagick.org`) is in the process.

A further development of the evolutionary art process will focus on the image meme reproduction by reimplementing the used plane groups with ImageMagick and generalizing them. Generally speaking, methods for covering the plane or finite plane parts should be examined, where one part (or more parts) of a source image is (are) selected and a set of geometric operations are applied, such as copying, transition, rotation, and flipping. The present meme reproduction process uses seamless, periodic, and nonoverlapping covering of the plane but there is a large design space of possible nonperiodic and nonoverlapping (Penrose patterns; for tilings and patterns see [27]) and overlapping methods that might be aesthetically interesting and could perhaps be explored by genetic programming. Apart from the geometric operations such as rotation or flipping, there are topological methods that could be applied to correct overlapping covering of the plane to generate seamless coverings. There is no way for a seamless covering with regular identical pentagons (fivefold symmetry), but if the pentagons are stretched or squeezed (topological operations), then it becomes possible.

The supershape formula from Johan Gielis [22] is a generalized Superellipse Equation capable of modeling a wide range of biomorphic shapes in two or three dimensions and could be generalized to even higher dimensions. It might be worthwhile to investigate with genetic programming methods if there are generalized and derived equations with symmetries that deliver interesting biomorphic and other shapes. I have chosen for my work an a posteriori generation of shapes with bilateral symmetry, which is easily done because the specific plane group (a subpart of pmm) can be applied to all of these shapes.

A long-term goal is the introduction of aesthetic preference models. Such a machine learning model should be able to predict aesthetic judgments of a specific person (me as the artist) in a specific domain like my nonrepresentational images. This model could be used as an explicit fitness function which would constitute an important step to allow my evolutionary art processes to grow independently from me and, in the long run, to turn them from transhumanist into posthumanist art processes.

Acknowledgments

The author would like to thank Les Apps (London) for his revision of an earlier version of the text and Uwe Brahm (Saarbrücken) for his help regarding LaTeX.

References

1. Dortmund, M.O., ed. (2002). *Informel Bd.1: Der Anfang nach dem Ende.* Museum Ostwall. Dortmund
2. Dortmund, M.O., ed. (2002). *Informel Bd.2: Begegnung und Wandel.* Museum Ostwall. Dortmund
3. Dortmund, M.O., ed. (2003). *Informel Bd.3: Die Plastik – Gestus und Raum.* Museum Ostwall. Dortmund
4. Dortmund, M.O., ed. (2004). *Informel Bd.4: Material und Technik.* Museum Ostwall. Dortmund
5. Herskovic, M., ed. (2003). *American Abstract Expressionism of the 1950s – An Illustrated Survey with Artists' Statements, Artwork, and Biographies.* New York School Press. Franklin Lakes, NJ
6. Hartung, H., Krempel, U. (1981). *Hans Hartung – Malerei, Zeichnung, Photographie.* HWS Verlagsgesellschaft m.b.H. Berlin Ausstellung in der Städtischen Kunsthalle Düsseldorf und der Staatsgalerie moderner Kunst München.
7. Varnedoe, K., Karmel, P. (1998). *Jackson Pollock.* Tate Publishing. London
8. Wikipedia (2006). Selbstorganisierende Malerei. `http://de.wikipedia.org/wiki/Selbstorganisierende_Malerei`
9. Rotzler, W. (1995). *Konstruktive Konzepte. Eine Geschichte der konstruktiven Kunst vom Kubismus bis heute.* 3rd edn. ABC. Zürich
10. Thornhill, R., Gangestad, S. (1993). Human facial beauty. Averageness, symmetry and parasite resistance. *Human Nature,* **33**: 64–78
11. Braun, C., Gründl, M., Marberger, C., Scherber, C. (2001). *Beautycheck – Ursachen und Folgen von Attraktivität.* Technical report. Lehrstuhl fär Experimentelle und Angewandte Psychologie Universität Regensburg
12. Johnstone, R.A. (1994). Female preference for symmetrical males as a by-product of selection for mate recognition. *Nature,* **372**: 172–175
13. Voland, E., Grammer, K. (2003). *Evolutionary Aesthetics.* Springer. Berlin
14. Todd, S., Latham, W. (1992). *Evolutionary Art and Computers.* Academic Press. Winchester, UK
15. Ritter, H., Martinetz, T., Schulten, K. (1992). *Neural Computation and Self-Organizing Maps: An Introduction.* Addison-Wesley. Bonn
16. Kohonen, T. (1995). *Self-Organizing Maps.* Springer. Berlin 3rd edition published April 2006.
17. Bachelier, G. (1998). *Einführung in Selbstorganisierende Karten.* Tectum. Marburg
18. Rechenberg, I. (1994). *Evolutionsstrategie'94.* Frommann Holzboog. Stuttgart
19. Bachelier, G. (1998). *Einführung in Evolutionäre Algorithmen.* Tectum. Marburg
20. Bachelier, G. (1999). *Fitness-Approximationsmodelle in Evolutions-Strategien.* Tectum. Marburg
21. Gerbel, K., Weibel, P., eds. In Gerbel, K., Weibel, P., eds.: *Ars Electronica 93: Genetische Kunst – Künstliches Leben.* Linz (1993)
22. Gielis, J., ed. (2003). *Inventing the Circle – The Geometry of Nature.* Geniaal Press. Antwerpen
23. Harlan, V., Rappmann, R., Schata, P., eds. (1984). *Soziale Plastik. Materialien zu Joseph Beuys.* Achberger

24. Murken, A.H., Wiese, S.v., eds. (2006). *Heilkräfte der Kunst.* Stiftung Museum Kunst Palast Düsseldorf. Düsseldorf Ausstellung Museum Kunst Palast Düsseldorf 21.01-19.03.2006 und Museum Wiesbaden Oktober 2006 bis Februar 2007.
25. Born, J. (1978). *Evolutionsstrategien zur Numerischen Lösung von Adaptionsaufgaben.* PhD thesis. Humboldt-Universität. Berlin
26. Hahn, T., ed. (2005). *International Tables for Crystallography Volume A: Space-group symmetry.* Springer. Berlin
27. Grünbaum, B., Shephard, G.C., eds. (1986). *Tilings and Patterns.* Freeman. New York

13

Evolving Structure in Liquid Music

J. J. Ventrella

Jeffrey@Ventrella.com

Summary. A software application called "Musical Gene Pool" is described. It was designed to evolve non-linear music from an initial random soup of sounds, which play continuously. Most evolutionary music systems to date require the user to select for musical aspects in a piecemeal fashion, whereas this system is experienced as continuous music throughout the entire process, as follows: a human listener gives fitness rewards after sounds (organisms) emerge from the gene pool, take turns playing, and return back to the pool. Organisms start out unicellular (one sound), but as the listener selectively rewards random sequences deemed more musical than others, some organisms join up to form larger, multicellular organisms – which become phrases or extended musical gestures. Genetic operators of splitting, death, replication, and mutation occur in the gene pool among rewarded organisms. This results in gradual evolution of structure as the music continues to play. This emerges in response to the listener's own internal emerging musical language, based on accumulated musical memory. This structure is *liquid* – continually able to flow and rearrange to allow serendipity. While there is a limit to organism length (duration of phrases), it is proposed that the interactive scheme could be adjusted to evolve increasingly larger organisms, and hence, longer musical passages. These would essentially be mobile chunks of linear music with self-similarity in their structures – revealing the histories of their evolution.

13.1 Introduction

> Music "*...is a fluid reality. The only thing that primitive polyphony, classical counterpoint, tonal harmony, twelve-tone serial music, and electronic music have in common is the principle of giving form to noise in accordance with changing syntactic structure.*" Jaques Attali, *Noise*, p. 10.

Definitions of music that acknowledge the act of performing and listening are *phenomenological*, as contrasted with descriptions of music as "object" – as a piece of structure, possessing meaning in and of itself [1]. In this chapter, we take a phenomenological stance and elevate the role of listening. In fact, we make the act of listening *participatory* – whereby it becomes the catalyst for the generation of the music itself. Attali [2] describes music as "giving form to noise." Here is described a music generation system where form emerges from noise through interaction: the listener and an evolvable population of sounds become collaborative agents, changing over time in response to each other.

The *Musical Gene Pool* is an interactive software application which generates fluid music with no explicit beginning, middle, or end. It is seeded with a primordial soup of random sounds, and, given occasional feedback from a listener, evolves to become increasingly structured. Once the amount of structure in the gene pool has reached the highest possible level, continued listener feedback can still change the *quality* of that structure. If feedback is discontinued, the music keeps playing, maintaining the same quality.

While this experimental musical form currently requires the listener to sit at a computer and respond via mouse or keyboard clicks, the preferred usage is for the listener (or *listeners*) to be remote from the computer, possibly sitting in a comfortable chair or walking around doing some activity, with some way to provide occasional feedback using a clicker. Given sufficient population size, musical operators, and sufficient time for listening and evolving, it could produce rich and varied music — music which harnesses implicit representations of the aesthetics of the listeners who have interacted with it.

The resulting populations in the gene pool could be stored in digital files, and "run" (as in running a software simulation). These files would be extremely small compared with the size of a piece of music stored as a typical MIDI file, where the linear ordering of events maps directly to time. The advent of evolutionary music provides opportunities for non-linear forms of music storage, as proposed by Brown [3]. One can describe the Musical Gene Pool files as compressed forms of linear music: when considering the amount of repetition, theme, and variation in most music, the Musical Gene Pool stores the *seeds* of this variation in a compact form. Each time it is run, the variation unfolds, and it is never twice the same.

13.1.1 Evolutionary Music

Composers and scientists alike have taken a recent interest in evolutionary music composition. There are now conferences and publications dedicated to evolutionary music and art [4]. Burton and Vladimirova [5] provide an introduction to techniques, such as the genetic algorithm (GA) [6] and their applications to music generation. Miranda and Biles [7] provide more recent coverage of progress in evolutionary music. Some of these systems are based on the idea of an *artificial composer* – and seek to represent essential aspects of composition in some encoded form, either for automatic music generation or as a way to better understand the act of composition [8, 9]. Some systems simulate virtual ecologies in which sonic communication evolves for survival purposes and have musical value [10, 11]. Other systems acknowledge the human composer/listener as still far superior to any artificial agent. The *interactive evolution* approach uses variations on the genetic algorithm, which includes a human to provide the fitness values for a genetic algorithm. That is the approached used here.

13.1.2 Schoenberg, Cage, Reich, Eno

In advancing the art of evolutionary music, we must acknowledge the pioneers who have shaped the modern musical landscape and expanded our vocabulary of what music is or can be. Schoenberg originated dodecaphonic music: the 12-tone row and techniques for manipulating these musical seeds. While atonal music may not sink deep into the human psyche (for many people), it provides an intellectual basis for appreciation of the algorithmic nature of musical variation. John Cage opened our ears to the music of the natural world, to randomness, and to the importance of silence. Steve Reich's minimalist phase compositions place the listener in a timeless dimension where gradual change in texture becomes a primary musical perception. Brain Eno enriched contemporary pop music with technical innovations, notably tape loops generating ambient soundscapes that never repeat the same patterns. He also has helped to make popular the idea of Generative Music [12]. These composers are of course just a few of the many pioneers, but their innovations have relevance to this project.

Perhaps most important is the stance that John Cage encouraged us to take when thinking about music, as "purposeless play" – and so as with the Musical Gene Pool, the listener is encouraged to flow with the random chance that is at the bottom of the pool, and to suspend expectations and desires of how the music "should" come about. Taking this stance can have the best results, acknowledging that the listener and the gene pool are equal collaborators in the creation of the music. Using a bottom-up attitude to music generation invites serendipity, which is the creative engine of the Musical Gene Pool.

13.2 Description

The Musical Gene Pool model consists of three basic elements:

1. a population of musical organisms (the gene pool)
2. a mechanism for playing the sounds of the organisms (the *ear*)
3. listener feedback in the form of a single binary signal.

13.2.1 Organisms

The gene pool consists of hundreds of organisms. An organism is a collection of one or more cells; thus, organisms can be unicellular or multicellular. Unicellular organisms specify one sound, while multicellular organisms specify a series of sounds played over time, as in a musical phrase. Figure 13.1 illustrates a multicellular organism made of six cells, numbered 0 through 5. The lines connecting the cells represent the delays between cells as they make sounds. Notice that cell 0 in this example has a line extending to the right. This indicates the duration of a delay *before* it plays. Also notice that cell 3 has zero delay, and so it overlaps with cell 2: the two cells produce simultaneous sounds played together. Having two cells play simultaneously creates harmony. Any number of contiguous cells can have *zero* delay, to create chords.

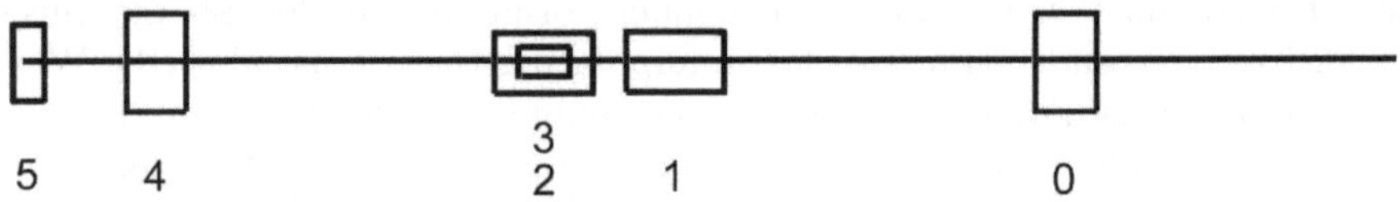

Fig. 13.1. A six-celled organism

Each cell has five attributes, the first four of which correspond to standard MIDI. These are as follows:

1. **Pitch**: the "note" of the sound. This ranges from *Pmin* to *Pmax*.
2. **Volume**: (velocity) ranges from *Vmin* to *Vmax*.
3. **Instrument**: ranges from 0 to *I*. This corresponds to the General MIDI standard mapping of instruments (such as "grand piano," "cello," etc.)
4. **Duration**: how long the sound is played. This ranges from *Dmin* to *Dmax*, in units of milliseconds. Note: this value does not apply to "one-shot" sounds, or sounds that have short sustain and decay, such as *xylophone* or *bell*.
5. **Delay**: how long the cell waits after the last cell played before it plays (indicated by the lengths of the lines in Fig. 13.1). This can be any value in the set *D* (0, 1, 2, 3, 4, 8), which is multiplied by the constant *Ds* to map it to milliseconds. *Ds* affects the tempo of the music. There are no explicit denotations of the concept of "half note," "quarter note," etc.

The exact values used in the experiment are given at the end of this section.

Random organisms are continually chosen from the population and lined up end-to-end to form a continuous stream of cells (sounds) which are played in sequence. After each organism has had its turn playing its cell's sounds, it returns back into the population. We shall now precisely define the "gene pool" as this population. It *does not* include those organisms which have left the pool and are part of the stream.

13.2.2 An Explanation by Way of the Visual Interface

The process shall be explained by way of the visual interface and the behavior of the application, which was designed to make the process intuitive. This is shown in Fig. 13.2. The gene pool is represented as the region at the bottom. A stream of organisms can be seen emerging from the pool at the bottom left, and the white arrow shows the initial direction that organisms move in after leaving the pool and taking their positions along the stream. The cells pass through the sound-playing threshold at top (the ear), and then descend back into the pool. While playing a sound, organisms move from left to right, passing through a sound-playing threshold; thus, the cells are actually heard in order from right to left. And so cell 0 (the "head cell") plays first, as indicated in Fig. 13.1.

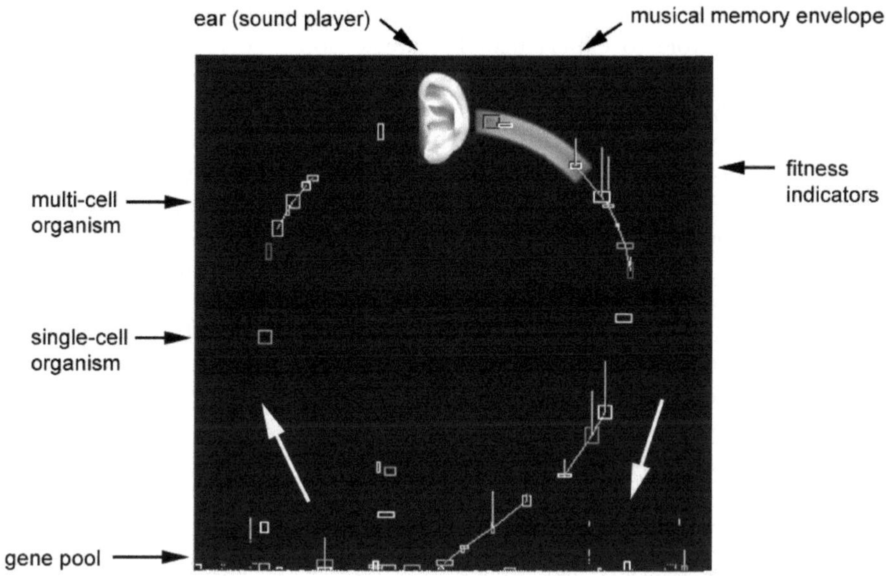

Fig. 13.2. The visual interface for the Musical Gene Pool

The stream of organisms follows a circular path which rotates clockwise at a rate of 0.0666 Hz (one rotation every 15 seconds). This rate affects the *tempo* of the music, along with the cell delay scalar Ds. Cells are visualized as rectangles. The height of the rectangle is determined by pitch, and the width is determined by duration. The color of the rectangle is specified using hue, saturation, and luminance values, as follows: hue is determined by instrument, saturation is determined by pitch, and luminance is determined by volume. This mapping, while somewhat arbitrary, does visualize all of the attributes of a cell, and ensures a substantial visual variety. This visual interface provides clarification and motivation for the listener/composer using the application. But here is an important point: the visual display is entirely unnecessary for this system to work. All that is really needed are the listener's ears and brain, and a way to provide reward. In fact, in preliminary tests with subjects, the visuals were found to be a distraction to pure musical judgment, as discussed below.

13.2.3 Listener Feedback

Many interactive evolutionary music systems developed so far use a rather piecemeal approach to evolving music: the user chooses an individual (a sound, musical fragment, etc.), listens to it, rates it, chooses another, listens, rates it, etc. – and then updates the generation to create a new population. The regimen is not unlike the standard GA, but with a human inserted into the selection stage. The Musical Gene Pool was designed to recognize that the human must be able to experience this music holistically in order to make meaningful choices. And so it provides musical continuity throughout the entire evolutionary process.

As the organisms stream through the ear, and create continuous sounds, the listener can respond to sounds recently heard by sending a binary signal (either by pressing the mouse button in the window or pressing the space-bar on the keyboard). A duration of $M = 1800$ milliseconds (just under two seconds) after a sound passes through the ear is called the "musical memory envelope," illustrated in Fig. 13.2 as the region to the right of the ear. The listener is asked to reward any sounds or sound sequences that are interesting, expressive, curious, or in any way worthy of encouragement for further experimentation. When the user issues a reward, the cells that lie in the musical memory envelope receive *fitness values*, which are visualized in Fig. 13.2 as vertical lines, or *fitness indicators*.

The envelope carries the most strength in the middle and the least strength at the beginning and end, as shown in Fig. 13.3.

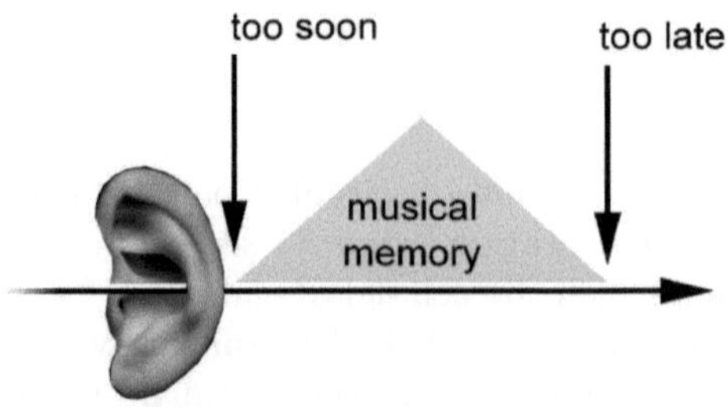

Fig. 13.3. Musical memory envelope

The strength of a cell's reward is determined by where the cell lies in the envelope. Cells that have just played and lie at the leftmost region of the envelope receive a smaller fitness value, under the assumption that they are too recent to contribute to the holistic musical experience that the listener is responding to. Cells that lie at the rightmost end of the envelope also receive a small fitness value, under the assumption that too much time has passed for this sound to have contributed to the holistic musical experience. If the sound sequences are especially desirable, and remain so for extended time, the listener can hold down on the key continuously. This is indicated by the long black rectangle in Fig. 13.4, resulting in a *plateau* of maximum fitness values. Notice the vertical lines at the bottom, which show the fitness values given to the cells (sounds) at the top.

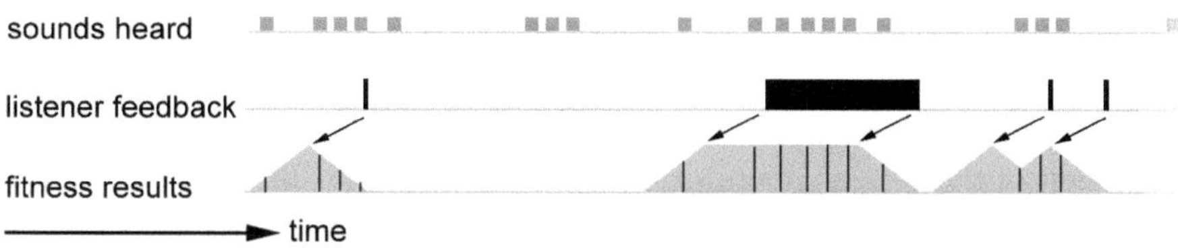

Fig. 13.4. Fitness values applied to cells

13.2.4 But Just How Long Is Musical Memory?

In reality, musical memory covers many arbitrary lengths of time, ranging from the momentary thrill of a trill to the lifelong memory of a tune. All ranges of memory contribute to one's reaction to music. Admittedly, the Musical Gene Pool only accounts for the reactions to musical experience that can occur within a few seconds. This may seem like a gross oversimplification. However, there are some subtle aspects to how listener behavior changes over time as the character of the music takes shape. As the gene pool becomes more self-similar, the listener begins to respond not just to immediate sound sequences, but also to how these sounds fit within the emerging quality of the music as a whole. The listener's internal representation of the emerging musical language becomes a factor in judgment; this is discussed in more detail later in the chapter.

The preferred duration of the musical memory envelope may vary with listeners, as well as over time while listening. Since there is no such thing as a *correct* duration, this should be made into an adjustable parameter (in a subsequent version of the software) which the listener can change at any time.

13.2.5 Genetic Operators

Besides receiving fitness values as a result of the listener-rewarding cells just heard, there is another important operation: cells automatically join up with neighboring cells occurring in the envelope (if they are not already part of a common organism). This causes all cells in the envelope to merge into the same organism. This is the *join* operator, and it is one of the genetic operators used in this system. The reason for using the join operator is that the listener has presumably responded to the ordering of these sounds, and not merely to the sounds themselves. It is meant to correspond with music experience of the sounds in combination: as a phrase, gesture, motif, or rhythmic expression. An organism can grow to up to $C = 16$ cells only, and so in the case when a join would cause an organism to become larger, the join operation is not performed.

The fitness of an organism is measured as the sum of all its cells' fitness values. After an organism with positive fitness has returned to the gene pool it has a certain number of time steps F in which it is "fertile," meaning it can either *split* or *replicate* (with chance of mutation after replication). The chance of either of these operations occurring is proportional to its fitness: the higher the fitness, the higher the chance of one of these operations occurring. An overview of the genetic operators is shown in Fig. 13.5. The *join* operation occurs outside of the gene pool and is the direct result of listener interaction. The *split* and *replicate* operations are performed while in the gene pool, and so they happen unknown to the listener. But their effects become apparent over time, after affected organisms begin emerging from the gene pool and make themselves known. These two operators are described in detail below.

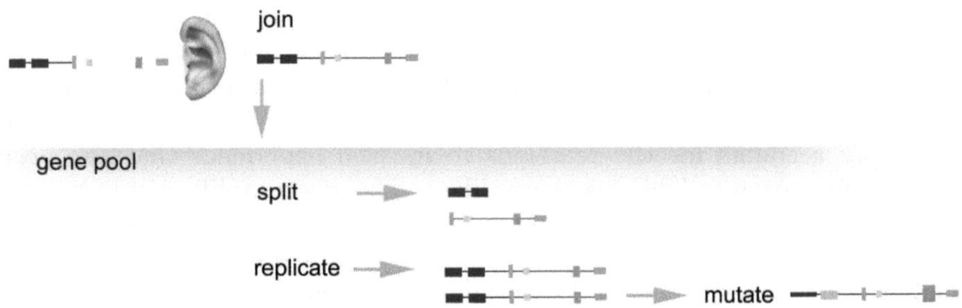

Fig. 13.5. Genetic operators

If an organism is in the gene pool, and if it has positive fitness, and if it is fertile, then there is

1. a random chance S of splitting:
   The organism is severed at some split locus cell, and becomes two organisms. The split locus is determined by randomly choosing a cell with a relatively low fitness value.
2. a random chance R of replication:
   A copy of the organism is made and added to the population.
   MUTATIONS: As soon as this organism is created, it has a random chance of any of the following mutations occurring
   Pitch shift Pm (the pitch values of all cells shift equally by a random value ranging from -12 to 12).

Instrument Homogenization *Ihm* (a cell with relatively high fitness is chosen and its instrument value is randomly copied to a percentage $H = 0.5$ of the organism's cells).

Instrument Shift *Ism* (the instrument value of all cells are shifted uniformly by a random amount in the range -5 to 5).

Octave Normalization *Om* (the average pitch value of all cells is determined. Then, any cell whose pitch has a difference with this average of more than 6 is shifted towards the average by a value of 12. This reduces large jumps in pitch, and encourages more melodic sequences).

Cell Harmonization *Hm* (a random cell is chosen and doubled. It is then given a delay of zero, and its pitch is shifted by a random amount ranging from -12 to 12).

Arpeggiate *Am* (if any cell has a delay of zero, its delay is changed to a random delay value within the set D).

Zap *Zm* (a random attribute of a random cell is changed to a random value).

Scramble *Sm* (the ordering of the cells is randomly shuffled).

Harmonize and *arpeggiate* are complimentary: harmonize tends to make organisms denser, while arpeggiate thins them out.

S and R (rates of splitting and replicating) are effectively lower, due to the nature of the algorithm. The algorithm chooses a random organism from the entire population as a candidate to apply the operator – but if that organism is not fertile, has zero fitness, or is not in the gene pool, then the operator is not applied.

Other Mutations

Towsey, et al [9] describe twenty-one "melodic features" used to manipulate melodies in a genetic algorithm-based system for automated music composition. Other evolutionary music systems employ similar melodic mutations. Currently only a handful of musical mutations are applied in the Musical Gene Pool, as described above, but others have been tried, and many more are intended to be added in subsequent versions, such as

1. *delay homogenization* (taking the delay values from some cells and copying them to other cells. This has been tried, but it is problematic as it tends to result in too many evenly-spaced delays)
2. *overlap* (taking two organisms and combining them – side-to-side, like earthworms mating – so that they overlap in time, thus creating a single, more dense organism with higher likelihood of harmonization and combined instrument sounds)
3. *stutter* (taking an arbitrary piece of an organism and generating a new organism by attaching copies of this piece end-to-end
4. *octave shift* (shifting all pitch values up or down by a value of 12)
5. *retrograde* (reversal in time, as in dodecaphony)
6. *inversion* (reversal in pitch, as in dodecaphony)

7. *retrograde plus inversion* (as in dodecaphony)
8. *pitch compression/expansion* (scaling the range of pitch values)
9. *general homogenization* (taking an arbitrary attribute, such as volume, and making all the cells' attributes take on the same value, chosen from a high-fitness cell. This has been tried, but it is problematic, as it tends to result in organisms with too much order and symmetry.)

These are just a few of the possible mutations which have been explored, or are candidates for exploration. It was found that as more mutations get added to the mix, the chance of these mutations being applied must be lowered, so as to preserve the original form and not dissolve existing structure. This is a common balancing act in many genetic-algorithm-based systems.

13.2.6 Genotype Representation

Note that the genetic operators *join* and *split* are performed at the *cell level*, meaning that a *cell* is analogous to a *gene*. And so the *genotype* of an organism would be defined as the array of cells. This is a high-level genotype representation. When a join or split occurs, it occurs between the *cells*, considered as hard units. The reason for this level of representation is to allow these genetic operators to map more easily to musical meaning. The mutations on the other hand have a more granular effect, and can change a single attribute of a cell, although here too, these mutations are still performed in recognition of the cellular organization of the genotype.

13.2.7 Extended-Time Crossover

A key ingredient in the standard genetic algorithm technique is *crossover* – the recombination of genetic material between two parent genotypes, usually to create offspring genotypes. One may ask why crossover is not used in this scheme. But in fact, an effect quite similar to crossover does occur as a result of organisms splitting and rejoining over extended time. The important difference is that this is not *sexual* reproduction in the strict sense that two parent genotypes combine genes to produce offspring genotypes. Instead, organisms reproduce *asexually* (via the replicate operator). But the fact that they can split, and rejoin with other organisms later, gives rise to the kind of experimental mixing that we normally attribute to sex. This special brand of extended-time crossover is deemed more applicable to the Musical Gene Pool, as it allows listener discretion to be a direct factor in recombination.

13.2.8 Managing Population Count

A bit of explanation concerning software implementation is in order as far as representing the population of organisms in the gene pool. An array of size P is used to store the organisms. Each organism in the array is itself represented as an array containing the values that determine its cells' attributes. Array sizes can easily be adjusted to accommodate different usage scenarios. The genetic operators of joining, replicating, and splitting affect the population array. They are not applied to any of the organisms which have left the gene pool and are part of the stream. First we explain the join operator: when organism b joins onto the end of organism a, organism a grows in length, taking copies of the cells from organism b; and then the original organism b dies. This marks the array index of organism b as *dead*, and decreases the population size by 1. Replicating and splitting, on the other hand, increase the population size by 1 each. In this case, if the population size is below the maximum P, then the first dead index in the array (resulting from a previous join operation) is chosen to store the newly created organism. If the population is already maxed out (no indices are marked dead), then a relatively low-fit organism is chosen to die, leaving room for the new organism. The relatively low-fit organism is chosen by "tournament selection" (two organisms are randomly selected, and the one with the lowest fitness is taken).

Note that even though the organisms in the population are kept in a linear, ordered array, the ordering is irrelevant to user interaction and the way the music evolves (because organisms emerge from the gene pool randomly).

At the very beginning, population size is P (the maximum size), but it quickly decreases as soon as the listener starts rewarding cells and they begin joining to form multicellular organisms. Also at first there are more of them dying than replicating or splitting. But soon after, as the gene pool starts brewing, the population size increases. In a mature gene pool it will approach and remain at or near the maximum P. Population dynamics are of course sensitive to the specific tuning of the rates of replication and splitting, in combination with the behavior of the listener, which affects the frequency of join operations.

13.2.9 Using MIDI Channels to Manage Instrumentation

The Musical Gene Pool uses the Java MIDI package. Many modern computers come with an on-board MIDI synthesizer with 16 channels. A common usage is to assign a unique instrument to each channel (or to just use the default instruments), giving a palette of 16 instruments which can play in parallel, so they can be heard overlapping in time. In order for an arbitrary number of instruments to be specified (more than 16), a technique is used in this system to approximate the effect of arbitrarily many channels. This is accomplished by cycling through the channels, incrementing a *channel count* each time a sound is played, and reassigning the instrument of that channel through a *program change event*. (Channel 10 is skipped: on many standard MIDI synthesizers, this channel is reserved for percussion sounds, where the pitch parameter is used for percussion sounds).

13.2.10 Parameters

Table 13.1 shows the complete list of all parameter values that have been chosen. These parameters were chosen to optimize the listener experience in the context of the Java applet described here. These values would be adjusted in the case of adapting this experiment to form a large, collaborative sound ecology (as described below).

Table 13.1. Parameters

Symbol	Description	Value	Units
t	Time step duration	1/30	second
P	Maximum population size	200	count
C	Max cells per organism	16	count
Ds	Delay scalar	120	milliseconds
$Dmin$	Minimum cell sound duration	10	milliseconds
$Dmax$	Maximum cell sound duration	700	milliseconds
$Pmin$	Minimum cell sound pitch	30	general MIDI
$Pmax$	Maximum cell sound pitch	90	general MIDI
$Vmin$	Minimum cell sound volume	30	general MIDI
$Vmax$	Maximum cell sound volume	127	general MIDI
I	Number of cell sound instruments	64	general MIDI
D	The set of cell delay values	0, 1, 2, 3, 4, 8	delay units
S	Split Rate	0.3	chance per time step
R	Replication Rate	0.3	chance per time step
Pm	Pitch Shift Mutation Rate	0.1	chance per time step
Ism	Instrument Shift Mutation Rate	0.05	chance per time step
Om	Octave Normalize Mutation Rate	0.2	chance per time step
Ihm	Inst. Homogenize Mutation Rate	0.5	chance per time step
Hm	Harmonize Mutation Rate	0.05	chance per time step
Am	Arpeggiate Mutation Rate	0.01	chance per time step
Zm	Zap Mutation Rate	0.05	chance per time step
Sm	Scramble Mutation Rate	0.05	chance per time step
M	Musical Memory Envelope	1800	milliseconds
H	Inst. Homogenize Percentage	0.5	chance per cell
F	Fertility Duration	500	time steps

13.3 How Musical Structure Evolves

As the term "gene pool" indicates, the organisms are free-floating: they have no predetermined positions within the population, and so they can line up in any sequence. When unicellular organisms join to form multicellular organisms they begin to form some degree of structure in terms of cell positioning, and thus in sounds occurring over time. There is an analogy to the states of matter:

a population of unicellular organisms is similar to a gas. A population with larger organisms might be seen as a liquid – having some structure, but still able to "flow" with listener response. This is illustrated in Fig. 13.6.

Fig. 13.6. Musical gas and musical liquid

13.3.1 Listening is Composing

How can composing be reduced to a simple binary act, in the form of a mouse click or keyboard strike? This may seem offensive to accomplished composers, but it is of course not meant to replace, or in any way compare to the act of composing, which requires top-down design, and involves great skill. On the contrary, this is a form of bottom-up emergence, which begins with chaos, and gradually acquires order. The nature of that order depends of course on the tastes of the listener, and relatively little skill is required (although it helps).

13.3.2 Preliminary Tests

Preliminary, informal tests were done on about six subjects, each using the Musical Gene Pool for some duration ranging from about five minutes to about 30 minutes. At the very beginning, when all organisms are unicellular, and all attributes are randomly distributed evenly over the full range, the listener is asked to simply respond to sounds and sound sequences that have some vague musical interest, so as to get things rolling. In the early stages, it has been observed that the listener will generally respond to timbre, since there are so many instrument variations, and virtually no melodic or rhythmic structure to speak of. But over time, the mutation causing instrument homogenization tends to decrease the variety of timbre, and the listener begins to respond more to instances of melodic or rhythmic structure. This is when things start to get interesting.

13.3.3 Attraction to a Tonal Center

Dodecaphonic music sought to free musical expression from the tyranny of tonality; it was one of the most significant experiments in modern music. But we have reason to believe that human ears and brains have a predisposition to melodies and harmonies which have a hierarchical structure. Theories of tonality are continually being developed, giving support to this claim [13]. The logic and hierarchy of traditional tonality is easily mapped to the overtone series, which occurs in nature [14]. The natural favoring of tonal centers is evident in the behavior of the listener of the Musical Gene Pool, based on observation. This may be enhanced since the listener is concentrating on finding musical sense, i.e., seeking order. However, there may be a purely mathematical reason for a tonal center to emerge initially; it may simply be a function of the gene pool becoming more homogeneous: a specific pitch may become more common (or perhaps more prominent based on the instrument or volume). Even without the listener gravitating towards a tonal center, this pitch may propagate in the gene pool. It is suspected that any slight increase of an arbitrary pitch will cause the listener to hear tonality (usually this pitch is heard initially as a tonic or a fifth). Once this feedback cycle begins, the tonality increases, and the listener becomes more responsive to the subtle aspects of the emerging key. Tonal center, or any musical feature for that matter, cannot be attributed only to the listener. It results from gene pool – listener feedback.

13.3.4 Attraction to Repetition

The human brain is not only good at detecting sequences of patterns, it is actually wired to do this, and on multiple layers of the neocortex [15]. And so we are sensitive to the slightest hint of repetition. If an organism has replicated and if by chance the two copies pass through the ear one right after the other, then this causes a repetition of the sound sequence over a short duration of time. Even if each organism in itself is not musically meaningful, the repetition is experienced as structure for the listener: it becomes a pattern, and this is quickly perceived. Much like the arbitrary convergence of a tonal center, some forms of musical structure may emerge simply as a result of the listener responding to repetition. Familiarity with this pattern reinforces its musical value, and it causes a feedback loop.

13.3.5 Context

An organism that has little musical meaning at one point in time for the listener may become potent at another stage based on its context. For instance, it may follow a different organism which sets the musical stage for new meaning. Also, by the time the organism comes around again, the listener may have entered into a different modality of listening, perhaps focusing on a new tonal center or a new rhythm. In either case, *context* – whether within the sequence of organisms or within the listener's mind – can change the meaning of an organism. In Darwinian terms, a change in its ecological niche may change its fitness.

13.3.6 What Kind of Music Emerges?

By now the reader may be wondering what kind of music emerges. To begin, here is what *does not* emerge: (1) specific, familiar melodies in their entirety (although snippets of familiar tunes may emerge). (2) Clearly-defined chordal structure based on traditional Western harmony (although, again, moments of chordal logic can emerge). (3) Strongly metered rhythm. What *can* emerge could be described as alternating moments of impressionistic, expressionistic, and minimalist passages, which are sometimes mediocre, and at other times quite magical. The listener can push the music towards a strongly rhythmic, staccato style, or towards a slower, softer style. Given enough effort by the listener, distinct keys can be fished out, and distinct key changes can occur as well (thanks to the pitch-shift mutation). These key changes, along with changes in instrumentation, as varying strains of organisms take their turns passing through the ear, create the *impressionistic* effect. This tends to diminish over time as the gene pool becomes more regular. A *minimalistic* effect comes about if the listener encourages a single strain of organism to populate the pool, at the expense of others. The listener can also focus on breeding a certain melodic motif, with a characteristic instrumentation and rhythm. Trying to describe the music in words cannot do it justice, and so the reader is encouraged to run the Java applet [16].

13.3.7 From Chaos to Order, Stopping at Complexity

Music offers a great illustration of complexity. Utter randomness has no informational value. The same goes for total order. For instance, a large orchestra in which every musician is rapidly blasting out random notes will result in a wash of undifferentiated cacophony – not much information content, and little musical meaning. At the opposite extreme, if all the musicians repeatedly played the same note over and over again with no variation, again there would be little information content or musical meaning. Somewhere between these extremes lies music. The bifurcation diagram [17] in Fig. 13.7 illustrates this notion.

Predictability and regularity serve as the background against which unpredictability or novelty (surprise) serves as the informational aspect of a message. The Musical Gene Pool begins at the random end of the scale. As soon as order begins to emerge (such as a replicated pattern, or the homogenization of instruments in an organism), the listener is able to begin using it as background: it takes on an environmental purpose in the musical landscape, and the surprises are read as foreground, i.e., as having musical content.

Styles in music around the world range from orderly to highly chaotic – from the simplest Gregorian chants to the free jazz of Ornette Coleman. But the Musical Gene Pool does not move in this direction. It is also the opposite of some improvisational schemes, which begin with a simple groove or motif and build increasing complexity, syncopation, and variation. Instead,

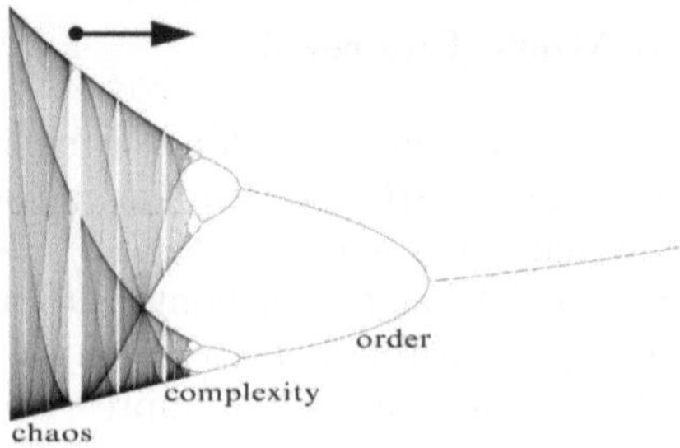

Fig. 13.7. Musical Gene Pool trajectory

the Musical Gene Pool begins with randomness, and gently introduces bits of order here and there, which the listener is invited to respond to. It is not possible to reach the exquisite mix of regularity and surprise of Beethoven, much less the degree of expressiveness. It would be cause for celebration if even brief Beethoven moments did emerge. The primary goal is emergence from total randomness to some degree of complexity, as the listener responds to pieces of emerging order. The path from chaos towards order, and stopping at complexity (and then breeding different flavors of complexity), is what the Musical Gene Pool achieves.

13.3.8 Blind Mode – the Purest Form

To use the application in the purest way, one should turn off the computer monitor, and allow only audition to determine the response, so as not to be distracted by the visuals. As an example of visual distraction, it is possible that the listener, when becoming accustomed to a family of organisms containing a large yellow square "causing" a desirable sound, will begin to respond to organisms with large yellow squares right as they pass through the ear – before even hearing them! Indeed, human vision and audition are tightly linked, especially when sound and visual stimuli occur in synchrony, creating a sense of cause and effect. And since humans are highly visual, it is possible that the active listener may become an active "watcher," without realizing it. Subjects who have tried it out have commented how very different the experience is with eyes closed.

Running this in "blind mode" would of course be less entertaining and less educational than watching flowing strings of colorful shapes meander on the screen. On the other hand, imagine yourself sitting in a comfortable chair with your eyes closed, and with a clicker in hand. You allow yourself a half hour, and all you have to do is press the clicker when you like what you hear. The chances are you will start to hear more of what you like. And perhaps you will come to like it so much that you will just drop the clicker, sit back, and enjoy.

13.4 Scaling Up

The Musical Gene Pool is considered as a first step, perhaps a prototype, for an extensive sound ecology with a large, slowly evolving population of large organisms, and a collaborative listening community. A large database of organisms could be stored on a server and made accessible online such that multiple listeners could contribute to its evolution over the span of many months. Perhaps listeners would be able to save the state of local gene pools, and then upload them to public server pools from which others could download and mix them into their own local pools.

There is an analogy to the real "musical gene pool" – the one that exists out there in the world: it is the sum total of all music throughout history, with all its variations, cultural influences, memetics, hybridizations, etc.). If the Musical Gene Pool could be made malleable and large enough, and if it could be exposed to the global Internet population, it might begin to mirror some aspects of the global musical gene pool.

This system would include the following:

Longer Organisms The maximum size of an organism is currently 16 cells, which can harness a small representation of listener aesthetics, and generate musical phrases. But ideally, the act of joining organisms should extend over larger time spans, enabling longer musical passages.

Larger Populations A population of 200 is sufficient for experimenting with a single listener, and it takes about a half hour of continuous use to reach a saturation point of musical structure. But after listening to an evolved gene pool for longer than about five minutes, the self-similarity caused by organisms and their kin replaying may be too repetitive for some ears. On the other hand, imagine a population of tens of thousands of large organisms continually evolving under the direction of many listeners. This musical ecosystem would be varied and complex indeed. This might have to be built up incrementally by adding smaller (human-sized) pre-evolved pools. A randomly seeded population which is extremely large would take prohibitively long to generate any musical satisfaction for a listener. But, a large pool which has already been seeded with organisms that were pre-evolved by many listeners would be more approachable. And it could hold immense musical variety.

More Mutations As explained above, there are many forms of musical variation that have been described in algorithmic form and used in similar evolutionary systems. Having a larger set of such mutations would expand the repertoire of possibilities for the listener and encourage more kinds of musical structure to emerge.

13.4.1 Super-organisms

Earlier we considered a population of unicellular organisms as a gas, and a population of multicellular organisms as a liquid (more structured, yet still able to flow with user interaction). Let us take this analogy to the extreme: consider what would happen if organisms were allowed to join up indefinitely, to grow in size, and to eventually freeze up into a single super-organism. What we would end up with is a single linear piece of music – a solid. This solid piece of music would no longer be interactive, but it would be an interesting artifact indeed – it would reveal the history of its own evolution in its structure, as indicated in Fig. 13.8. This organism would be made from pieces of smaller, older organisms, which themselves would be made from pieces of yet smaller, older organisms. And since there is repetition at all levels, this structure would probably exhibit a degree of fractal self-similarity.

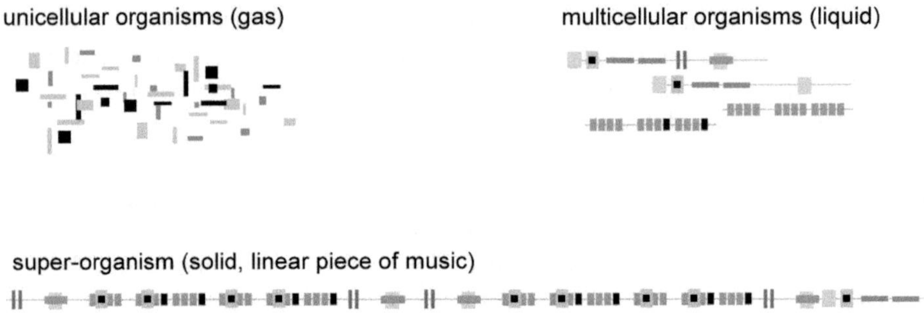

Fig. 13.8. Emergence of self-similarity in a super-organism

Does this mean that the Musical Gene Pool could evolve structure along the entire spectrum from gas to liquid to solid, resulting in one piece of linear music? Certainly not with the current interactive scheme, which is inherently liquid. The splitting operator is currently set at a constant random rate, and the maximum size of an organism is 16 cells. These two factors limit how large organisms can potentially grow. In order to grow increasingly larger organisms, there would have to be no limit to size, and the split operation would have to decrease over time as evolution progresses, until, at the very end, no organisms can split, and a single organism results, filling up the entire space of the population. But even if these changes were made, it would be difficult to evolve a super-organism due to the nature of listener feedback.

Consider a hypothetical scenario in which the listener is evolving a population of thousands of organisms: they are allowed to grow indefinitely, and the split operator has decayed to zero. Imagine that the listener has reduced the number of organisms down to only two. Now, if the goal were to end up with one super-organism, then the listener would have to wait for whatever organism that is playing to finish – for many minutes (perhaps even an hour, if the delays are long). And just when this organism leaves the ear and the other organism enters, the listener would have to issue a single reward (just in time!) in order to join them. This is not an ideal way to finish the journey.

Even though the system is not set up for this, it is hard to resist the idea of generating a super-organism with deep fractal self-similarity which stands as the evolutionary culmination of many hours of listening and rewarding. Exactly how to accomplish this is uncertain, and in fact it may be contradictory or paradoxical. If the Musical Gene Pool is inherently liquid, then once the organisms have reached a considerably large size, the idea of bottom-up emergence no longer holds, and it must give way to a form of top-down design. In this case the listener is best advised to switch to an editing interface where the remaining large organisms could be spliced together by hand.

13.5 Conclusions

The Musical Gene Pool is an experiment in blurring the distinction between listening and composing. The population of musical organisms is considered to be a collaborator in the process of emergent music. Perhaps one might argue that the Musical Gene Pool system, with its carefully tweaked operators, is more of a composer than the human participant. However, nothing could happen unless the two come together and interact. It is best to think of the human listener and the gene pool as two agents in an improvisation – a dynamic ecosystem. And while this interaction flows over time, it is intriguing to observe how musical memory accumulates in the listener's mind, and how this changes the way the listener guides the gene pool. This tool may not produce music worthy of Carnegie Hall. But it is hoped that these experiments open our ears and mind more to the psychology of listening and composing, and why it is that some sound combinations, and not others, have musical meaning.

Acknowledgements

I would like to thank Gary Walker, who taught me how to play guitar and the basics of music theory when I was ten years old, and who recently contributed ideas for this project. Also, thanks to Eddie Elliot, an artistic and technical collaborator of many years, who taught me Java, MIDI programming, and contributed ideas for this project.

References

1. Sansom, M.J. (2005). Understanding musical meaning: Interpretative phenomenological analysis and improvisation. In: *British Forum for Ethnomusicology, Annual Conference – Music and Dance Performance: Cross-Cultural Approaches, SOAS*
2. Attali, J. (1985). *Noise: The Political Economy of Music.* Vol. 16 of Theory and History of Literature. University of Minnesota Press

3. Brown, A.R. (2002). Opportunities for evolutionary music composition. In: *Australasian Computer Music Conference*, 27–34
4. Raidl, G.R., Cagnoni, S., Branke, J., Corne, D., Drechsler, R., Jin, Y., Johnson, C.G., Machado, P., Marchiori, E., Rothlauf, F., Smith, G.D., Squillero, G. (2004). *Applications Of Evolutionary Computing: EvoWorkshops 2004: EvoBIO, EvoCOMNET, EvoHOT, EvoIASP, EvoMUSART, and EvoSTOC.* Lecture Notes in Computer Science. Springer. Coimbra, Portugal
5. Burton, A.R., Vladimirova, T.R. (1999). Generation of musical sequences with genetic techniques. *Computer Music Journal*, **23**(4): 59–73
6. Goldberg, D.E. (1989). *Genetic Algorithms in Search, Optimization, and Machine Learning.* Addison-Wesley Professional
7. Miranda, E.R., Biles, J.A. (2007). *Evolutionary Computer Music.* Springer. Secaucus, NJ, USA
8. Todd, P.M., Werner, G. (1999). Frankensteinian approaches to evolutionary music composition. In Griffith, N., Todd, P.M., eds.: *Musical Networks: Parallel Distributed Perception and Performance.* MIT Press/Bradford Books. Cambridge, MA, 313–339
9. Towsey, M., Brown, A., Wright, S., Diederich, J. (2001). Towards melodic extension using genetic algorithms. *Educational Technology and Society*, **4**(2): 54–65
10. Dahlstedt, P. (2001). Living melodies: Coevolution of sonic communication. *Leonardo*, **34**(3): 243–248
11. Werner, G., Todd, P. (1997). Too many love songs: Sexual selection and the evolution of communication. In Husbands, P., Harvey, I., eds.: *Fourth European Conference on Artificial Life (ECAL97).* Cambridge, MA. MIT Press, 434–443
12. Eno, B. (1996). Generative music. Transcript of a talk. *in Motion Magazine*
13. Lerdahl, F. (2001). *Tonal Pitch Space.* Oxford University Press
14. Fink, R. (2003). *On the Origin of Music – An Integrated Overview of the Origin and Evolution of Music.* Greenwich
15. Hawkins, J., Blakeslee, S. (2004). *On Intelligence.* Times Books
16. Ventrella, J. (2006). Java applet for the musical gene pool. Online at: `http://www.ventrella.com/EvoMusic/EvoMusic.html`
17. Gleick, J. (1987). *Chaos – Making a New Science.* Penguin Books

14

A Survey of Virtual Ecosystems in Generative Electronic Art

Alan Dorin

Centre for Electronic Media Art
Faculty of Information Technology
Monash University
Clayton
Australia 3800
aland@csse.monash.edu.au
www.csse.monash.edu.au/~aland

Summary. This paper explores the application of ecosystem simulation to the production of works of generative electronic art. The aim is to demonstrate that virtual ecosystems are capable of producing outcomes that are rich, complex and interesting aesthetically. A number of artworks that employ virtual ecosystems are surveyed. The author argues that the most interesting works of generative art exhibit four basic properties: coherence and unity; multi-scaled temporal complexity; autonomous production of novelty; responsiveness to perturbation. The virtual ecosystem is assessed for its suitability as a medium for constructing generative art in light of these desirable properties. It is concluded that the ecosystem's strengths lie in its exhibition of multi-scaled complexity and its autonomous production of novelty. Whilst an artist may manipulate a simulation to retain visual and sonic coherence, the software also possesses an implicit coherence inherent in its ability to self-organize. Under some circumstances it appears that the weakness of the virtual ecosystem as an artistic medium lies in its unpredictable response to perturbation. Consequently, the paper also explores virtual ecosystems' susceptibility to external control and describes methods that have been employed to adjust the responsiveness of art works that employ them.

14.1 Introduction: Why Use Computers for Art?

It is easy for us to employ technology as its designers intended. With some effort we may even incrementally extend existing ideas. It takes considerable insight, however, to take a leap into unknown territory. In the history of art, it is exactly this approach that is documented as a string of movements towards the amorphous labyrinth that is contemporary art. It was natural for traditional artists to adopt the digital computer as a mechanical, optical and chemical mimesis for their traditional media. But simulation of this kind requires only a superficial understanding of the machine's potential. It is the purpose of this essay to explain how a deeper understanding of the computer will allow it to be used to make art that could not be made in any other way. As shall be demonstrated, the benefits of making this leap away from the mimicry of traditional artistic media to explore the unique potential of the computer are substantial. The inquiry thus begins with a question: "What is unique about computation as an artistic medium?"

The digital computer is a rapid, formal, symbol manipulation device. It is able to outperform humans in this regard by many orders of magnitude. In this capacity the machine can be considered as a sophisticated tool. However, the rate at which the symbols are manipulated by the computer is so great that the individual symbol disappears in a fluid flow of information. The human experience of this stream is akin only to that of interacting with physical, dynamical systems. Our interactions with it have the potential to be as rich and rewarding as our interactions with the physical environment. This twin view of the machine as tool and complex-adaptive system has profound implications on art.

Our interactions with computers are often at the level of the symbols the computer manipulates rather than with the machine *per se*, but experientially there need be no hard distinction between the two. Whilst some of us may enter individual symbols into a spreadsheet and read the results of calculations from its cells, in many cases the meaning of the symbols a computer manipulates is visualized or sonified, masking their "numerical-ness". The symbols' interpretation then occurs so transparently that we easily read into the machine's states traits we normally consider only in reference to the physical environment. Position, velocity, shape, colour, intensity, pitch, timbre and a host of other properties are attributed by us to the entities appearing on-screen or emanating from loudspeakers as if the computer somehow held real objects "inside" it and was offering us a window into another world. Between the extremes of a "tool" and a "window" lies a perspective that accepts the machine as a physical device and does not look *within* it for meaning, nor at its output, but *at* it as a complex adaptive system. It is this perspective that I believe has the most potential for computer-based art.

How might we program the computer so that its potential is realized? Any artist would be justified for interrupting such a train of thought (programmers like this author tend to jump in too soon). Prior to addressing this issue one ought to investigate the mode of presentation of any software that is to adopt the "complex adaptive system" mode as a means of engaging a viewer. Hence, the following subsection tackles this associated but nevertheless essential issue. The subsequent sections of the essay will address the details related to programming the computer to capitalise on its unique properties.

14.2 Presenting Visual, Generative Art

It is my belief that an audience can best experience the computer acting as a complex adaptive system when it locates the changes it witnesses as existing in the same physical space as itself. This is simple to achieve with a little thought, and bypasses the explicit interface (often employing a virtual button on a screen to be activated by a mouse-controlled cursor) between a virtual world within the computer and the world with which the observer usually interacts. With typical foresight, the theorist Jack Burnham took a similar line in his writing, anticipating a move from the symbolic realm to art works that were themselves quite literally alive. He wrote,

> "The stabilized dynamic system will become not only a symbol of life but literally life in the artist's hands and the dominant medium of further aesthetic ventures. As the Cybernetic Art of this generation grows more intelligent and sensitive, the Greek obsession with 'living' sculpture will take on an undreamed reality."
>
> *Beyond Modern Sculpture*, Burnham

The advances in AI anticipated by Burnham did not really eventuate. Neither did his vision for the obsolescence of the *objet d'art*. Nevertheless, a "Systems Aesthetic" stemming from the original ideas of Bertalanffy and closely aligned with the writings of Burnham forms the core of current Artificial Life Art and Generative Electronic Art [1]. Evolutionary Art forms a subset of these broad categories. Although all of these fields are marginal within the art world, their view of the natural world as a dynamical system remains relevant to a few artists, especially those producing technology-driven art. To some people's minds, as Burnham suggested, the works are not only symbols of life, "but literally life in the artist's hands". I will not discuss the merit of this philosophical remark here except to say that not all take it to be truthful or meaningful. Nevertheless, some Artificial Life works appear exemplary.

It would be a senseless diversion to begin the "What is *good* art?" debate here. However, the superficially argued basis upon which the following remarks are based is that the best works avoid adoption of the dominant "virtual environment" paradigm of computer games and some simulation, in favour of an examination of the potential of the computer as a dynamical system.

The medium of computation is certainly *useful* for its ability to simulate reality. This and the issues it raises are *interesting* from a philosophical standpoint. However they are less interesting from an artistic perspective. Single and multiple images have long been used to mimic and test our preconceptions about the virtual and the real. This issue has already been repeatedly examined within art. I feel that little of importance is added to the remarks already made on painting, literature and cinema by computational virtual realities.

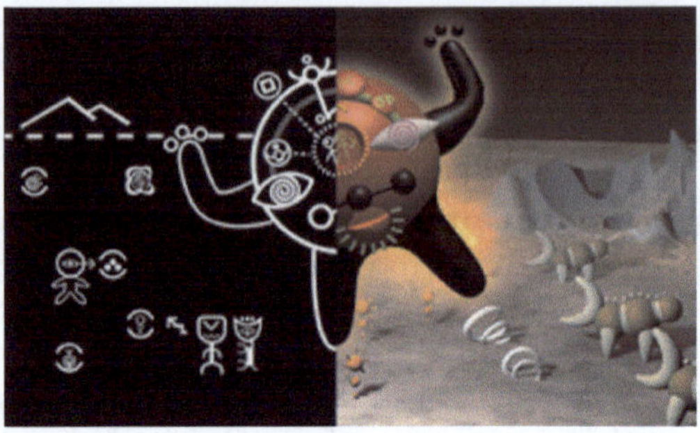

Fig. 14.1. *Iconica* (detail) interactive installation. Innocent (1999)

The modern digital computer is unique. To squander it on confronting reality in the context of art is mediocre. For instance, one popular way to utilise the computer is to simulate and visualise a three-dimensional Cartesian space. This space may contain creatures moving around a virtual world, eating one another or apparently carrying out behaviours associated with the real-world entities they simulate. Although typical of computer games such as *Spore* (Wright 2006), such worlds are also popular in interactive new-media art. The artworks *Technosphere* (Prophet and Selley 1995) and *Iconica* [2] (Fig. 14.1) are both interactive Artificial Life environments that adopt this approach. Fortunately, these two works are not *about* the virtual-real dichotomy, and each has much to recommend it. Nevertheless, I do not think that either benefits substantially from the virtual Cartesian world that it adopts.

An alternative is to avoid offering the audience an explicit VR *within* a computer and to present the machine as a physical system with its own unique properties that may have little to do with the simulation of 3D space and its contents as we know them. This offers the potential to present interpretations of our relationship with machines that I believe are truly multifaceted and unique to the medium. In this case the viewer is hidden from the symbols in the machine. The interface between the real and the virtual appears absent since the entity with which the human interacts exists in the same physical space as his body.

SAM – Sound Activated Mobile and Senster (Ihnatowicz 1968, 1970) – and more recently *Autopoieis* (Rinnaldo 2000) are works that overcome the need for humans to project themselves or their actions into a virtual space. These works are all robotic; however, the screen need not be discarded altogether. Similar experiences may be achieved using a conventional flat screen or projection onto any surface as long as the image does not give an illusion of something "in there", but a depiction of something "on there". This can be achieved by avoiding the use of the standard perspective projection. Screens may be touch or movement sensitive, or they may simply be for viewing a dynamic 2D surface. What matters is that they do not resort to virtual 3D to

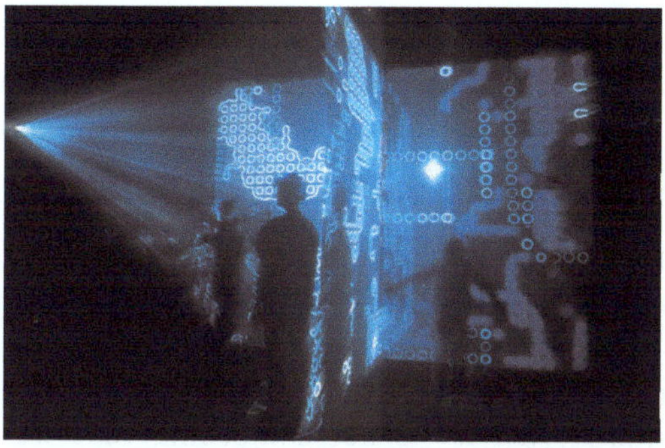

Fig. 14.2. *Eden* interactive installation. McCormack (2001)

disguise the fact that they are screens, but that they acknowledge their own limitations as surfaces and operate within these constraints.

The *Mimetic Starfish* (Brown 2000) is a work that adopts this approach by projecting the image of a starfish onto a circular tabletop for interaction with humans who place their hands on it. The positions of hands on the table are monitored by overhead video cameras and fed into the electronic system to give the illusion of the starfish's tentacles recoiling or venturing towards its human visitors. The result is quite strange but certainly engaging for many of the viewers. The starfish responds naturally to violent and gentle movements alike. As long as no contact is made directly with the projected image all seems fluid and natural. That one is playing with a ghost becomes evident when the image and human hand intersect — the tentacle is not tactile.

Screens that people can move through or around are also utilised in *Eden* [3] (Fig. 14.2) and *Remain In Light* (Haruki Nishijima 2001). Especially in Eden, the use of smoke and gauze as projection surfaces brings to the imagery a real volume through which gallery visitors can move. No longer is the visitor concerned with a computer and interpretation of its behaviour; instead he enters a space with its own logic and physical character. Here he interacts with a mysterious, misty volume of blue and purple rings and cylinders, punctuated by audible drones and trills.

The issues touched upon above are a significant part of the problem the artist faces in trying to present an innovative work of art. Without addressing these issues in some way, a work will be ill-formed. Certainly it may be successful by chance or intuition; these aspects of art making have a role to play even here. Yet in the construction of generative electronic media art such approaches are less likely to be successful than when working with more traditional media. A methodical approach will always be required to construct computational artworks. That is just the nature of the beast!

Leaving aside this issue for some time, the remaining problem the artist must face lies in manipulating the computer so that the behaviour of the image or effectors it controls is artistically relevant and interesting. Success depends on the context of the work and the aesthetic skill of the artist. Nevertheless, there are some features of the medium that will benefit any artist working with computation. These are examined in the following section.

14.3 How Can We Program the Computer to Behave as a Complex Dynamical System?

Creativity is often associated with human artistic practice; it may be one of its defining traits. Creativity is not something that we have found easy to explain from within the sciences, despite its recognised significance and despite many attempts to elucidate its virtues from the arts. When it comes to the construction of autonomous machines that exhibit such a prized human ability our engineering skills arguably fall short. The potential of the computer as a dynamical system generating patterns that we might easily associate with art may only be realised if we know how to engineer collections of instructions that allow it to exhibit creative ability. The characteristics required of it might be summarised as follows. The system must exhibit

- *Coherence and unity*
  Maintain its identity over time, despite perturbation;
- *Multi-scaled temporal complexity*
  Demonstrate complex dynamics over fine and coarse timescales;
- *Autonomous production of novelty*
  Explore large design spaces independently of human input;
- *Responsiveness to perturbation*
  Permit external events to deeply influence its behaviour.

An artist might also prefer that the system exhibit

- *Susceptibility to external control*
  Permit external (artist-laid) constraints on its behaviour.

To satisfy these requirements, it would be helpful if we could identify a model system that exhibits the characteristics we are seeking. The alternative, engineering a system from scratch, is considerably more difficult.

It appears that biology provides us with some likely candidates: cells; organisms; societies and ecological systems. Acting on the assumption that these systems operate under similar principles of continuous self-construction, the discussion that follows will focus on the ecosystem as a model for computational complex system development. We will do this only because its components (organisms) and the methods of their interaction serve as convenient examples of the relationships that might be replicated in software to allow the computer to function as a complex adaptive system useful within the context of art making.

14.3.1 The Ecosystem

The concept of the ecosystem appeared in an article by ecologist Tansley [4]. Ecosystems are groups of organisms and their abiotic environment. Inter-organism interactions take many forms, including, for instance, reproduction, communication, predation, parasitism, competition and mutualism.

Of utmost importance in determining the dynamic structure of an ecosystem are the networks by which energy and matter are transferred and transformed between organisms and their abiotic environment. Typically, energy enters an ecosystem as sunlight that is harnessed by plant photosynthesis. Plants are responsible for self-production of food. This process requires nutrients and water to be absorbed from the environment by the plants to build their physical structures. The vegetable matter that is the result of the plants' growth is consumed by herbivores that use it for metabolism to build animal matter and for locomotion. Much of the energy gained by the plants is lost in this process.

Herbivores may be consumed by carnivores. These metabolise and build their own animal matter from the bodies of the herbivores. Again, much energy is lost in the transformation. Some carnivores may be eaten by others of higher trophic level. For instance spiders may be eaten by lizards, which may be eaten by snakes, which may be eaten by birds of prey. Herbivores and carnivores alike may be consumed after their death by carnivorous (or omnivorous) scavengers. Any dead organism that is not otherwise destroyed will decay as it is consumed by bacteria and fungi. Similarly, such organisms break down the waste products of all plants and animals. These processes return the elements locked up in an organism or its waste products to the ecosystem for recycling. The energy that has been consumed along the way cannot be recovered. Much of it is dissipated as heat. For this reason, as already indicated, ecosystems require a continuous supply of energy for their maintenance.

The ecosystem is adaptive. As populations of organisms change, others in their habitat adapt also. Physical changes in the abiotic environment are coupled with changes in the population and behaviour of organisms also. As long as the energy and matter transfers within the ecosystem are maintained and balanced, the ecosystem will persist. Changes in temperature, pressure and climatic conditions impact heavily on terrestrial and aquatic ecosystems alike. The reverse is also true. That is, organisms impact heavily on their abiotic environment by moving and transforming the materials from which they are made. Foreign elements may be introduced to an ecosystem such as predators, disease or pollutants. Some abiotic components of the system may fall into short supply, for instance sunlight may be reduced by airborne particles or water may be diverted away from a habitat. As these changes occur, often as a result of events external to the ecosystem, the ecosystem is transformed, or fails drastically.

14.3.2 The Virtual Ecosystem

A *virtual ecosystem* is a software simulation of organism and environmental interactions within a real ecosystem. These have been constructed frequently within the field of Artificial Life to demonstrate biological phenomena and to offer suggestions as to how these may arise. For instance, Watson and Lovelock devised *DaisyWorld* [5] in order to demonstrate homeostasis. Virtual organisms (daisies) maintain the temperature of their model planet at a steady level.

Virtual ecosystems have also assisted us to draw more general conclusions about complex adaptive systems. *Polyworld* [6], *Tierra* [7], *Swarm* [8], *Echo* [9], *Sugarscape* [10], and *Avida* [11] all model some of the relationships between organisms listed above. In each case, the organisms are represented as either data structures for manipulation by the software or computer programs to be executed. The data structures or programs are modified by their interactions with others of their kind in a virtual environment governed by rules written by the programmer. The software therefore constrains the ecosystem's "inhabitants" within the bounds of its virtual physics and chemistry in a way analogous to that in which real organisms act in accordance with physics and chemistry. The types of interactions that may occur between a virtual ecosystem's components are explicitly determined by these constraints.

Creative and artistic applications of virtual ecosystems have also been devised. For instance, models of the morphogenesis of situated organisms, especially plants, have been based on virtual ecosystems. The technique has generated computer graphics landscapes complete with naturalistic vegetation [12]. To date, even these visually motivated simulations have largely ignored death, disease and decay. These phenomena have seldom been treated in Artificial Life or Computer Graphics, despite their obvious importance in the context of biology and virtual ecosystems alike [13].

14.3.3 The Ecosystem for Interactive Art and Play

The virtual ecosystems listed in the previous section were not implemented as dynamic artworks or games but there have in fact been several implemented for just these purposes. *Eden*, as already discussed, is an interactive artwork in which an evolving population alters the real soundscape of the exhibition as it adapts to changes in the virtual environment brought about by human movement through physical space. *Living Melodies* [14] is a sonic ecosystem in which evolutionary agents sing to one another to generate a musical composition. *Listening Sky* [15] (Fig. 14.3) and *Meniscus* (Dorin 2003) (Fig. 14.4) are two others in which agents with generative physical and aural forms roam a virtual space. Over virtual evolutionary time periods these produce offspring with characteristics inherited from their ancestors but adapted to their current situation, thereby giving rise to a visual and audible environment that changes before the human viewer. Sommerer and Mignonneau have also exhibited several virtual ecosystems as directly interactive artworks, including *A-Volve* (1993) and *Life Spacies I* and *II* (1997, 1999) (Fig. 14.5). *Nerve Garden* (Damer et al 1997) is an interactive ecosystem, this one for interaction via the WWW. Ecosystem simulations have been employed in games such as *SimLife* (Maxis 1992), *Creatures* (Creature Labs 2002), and, recently, *Spore* (Wright 2006). In short, virtual ecosystems are hardly new to those who construct computer applications as artworks and for play.

Why are virtual ecosystems helpful in the context of "creative software"? How can their utility be improved? What are the strengths and weaknesses of the existing virtual ecosystems as models for dynamic artworks? These issues are the subjects of the following section.

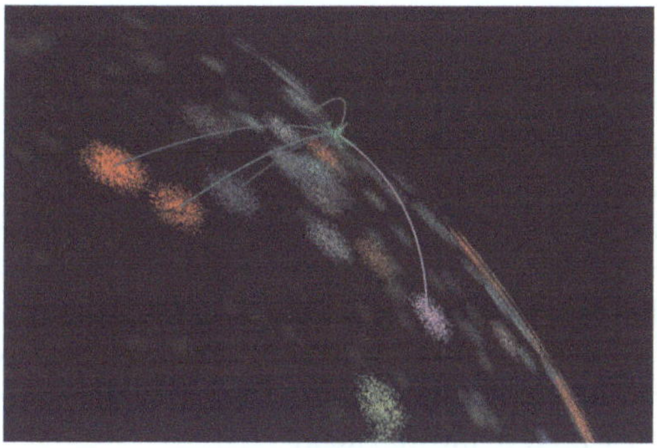

Fig. 14.3. *Listening Sky* (detail) interactive installation. Berry, Dorin, Rungsarityotin (2001)

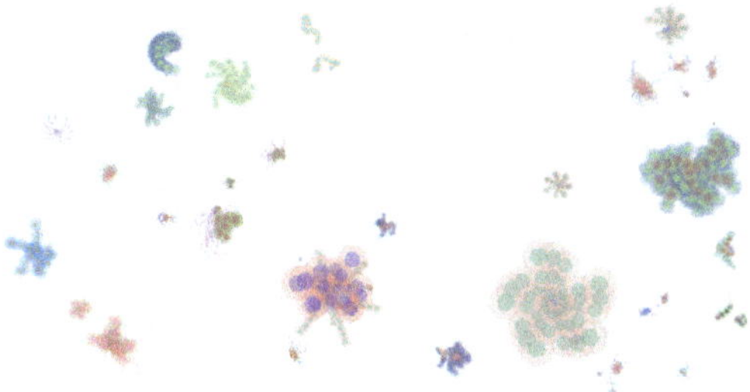

Fig. 14.4. *Meniscus* (detail) interactive installation. Dorin (2003)

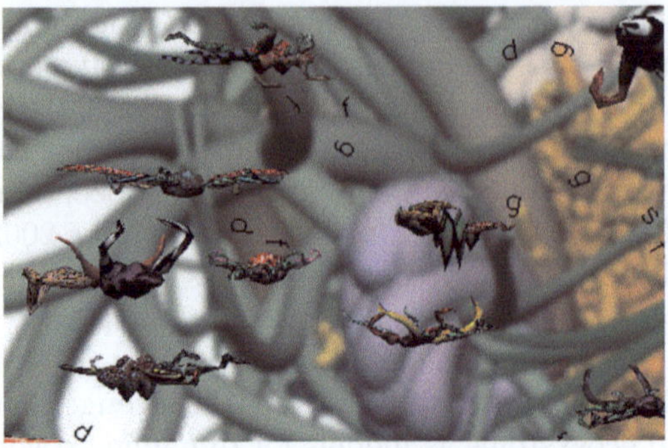

Fig. 14.5. *Life Spacies II* (detail) interactive installation. Sommerer and Mignonneau (1999)

14.3.4 Why Use Virtual Ecosystems for Making Art?

Clearly, all artists will not adopt the virtual ecosystem. The point of this section is not to convince every artist that he should utilise the technique, but to explore the potential the virtual ecosystem offers for engaging and provocative works of art.

As already indicated, it is my belief that a system for making interactive art must meet, to varying extents, a set of criteria listed above. These criteria shall now be examined individually and the virtual ecosystem assessed to gauge the degree to which it meets them.

Coherence and Unity – an Aesthetic Ideal

For an artwork to be coherent, its components must be integrated in a way that is somehow natural or fitting, so as to produce a complete artefact that is identifiable as a unit. If there is some way of viewing even a complex, composite entity that results in an observer being satisfied that the system may be treated as somehow "whole" the arrangement may be labelled *coherent*.

Given the push-me-pull-you nature of ecosystems, coherence may appear problematic. Sometimes an artist might like a work to explore a range of possibilities that may even surprise the process's designer, but which nevertheless fall within a set of predetermined constraints. Hence, in this sense a coherent ecosystem would remain true to a particular idea in its visual style, its autonomous behaviour, or perhaps its response to human interaction. With complex adaptive systems such coherence does not appear to be guaranteed; such systems are unwieldy. Sometimes they respond to perturbation smoothly, sometimes violently and unpredictably. Sometimes they disintegrate and vanish altogether. Under other circumstances their components proliferate and over-run the senses. It is really up to the artist to examine the possible outcomes on a case-by-case basis and attempt to nip problems in the bud.

For instance, mass extinctions may be handled by monitoring the population's health and artificially boosting an individual's fitness before the entire system collapses. A population that risks over-running the available resources can be capped by the timely introduction of a disease that drains the health of agents. Agent bodies that evolve to be too complex may be penalised for inefficient use of resources. All of these strategies and others have been implemented successfully in various works by the author. An abundance of other strategies is possible given a little creativity. In this sense, the maintenance of coherence is a sub-component of the requirement for artist-laid constraints that will be addressed below.

The very idea of the ecosystem as an autonomous work of art is appealing to the author from an aesthetic standpoint. The reason for this is closely tied to the implicit requirement of coherence for *any* ecosystem. The proposal therefore shifts from worrisome control issues, to the idea that an ecosystem is coherent *by definition*. As long as its pathways for energy and matter transfer and transformation are maintained, the system is a coherent biological system. If the system is perturbed too severely, it ceases to exist as a system. Within its acceptable range of perturbation the ecosystem is a fascinating, intricate conceptual network of relations between its abiotic and biotic elements. These relationships may be physical, chemical, temporal, behavioural, social, competitive or cooperative; as an artist there are countless possibilities to explore. Each possible ecosystem supports many niches to be filled and defined by components falling within the constraints imposed by the artist. Each of these elements must be uniquely adapted to mesh with all of the other components in a functional and long-lived whole, the most interesting of which are far more complex than anything that could be designed manually. If the work functions at all, it is coherent in this deep, logical sense, even if it appears to meander visually or sonically. Hence, for an artist concerned with *process* rather than superficial appearance, the ecosystem is an attractive concept to explore.

Multi-Scaled Temporal Complexity

The ecosystem is constituted of countless multi-scaled transformations of its organisms and the environments they inhabit. Changes occur in the morphology and behaviour of species over evolutionary time periods. Even if no other attributes were modelled within a software ecosystem, the potential of digital evolutionary pressure to push the system is a significant attribute of the technique.

A number of factors contribute to evolutionary pressure for change. Among these, changes driven by conditions external to the ecosystem affect its adaptive inhabitants and enforce an ongoing modification of their structures and behaviour. If organisms do not evolve to match changes in their abiotic habitat, they die out. Adaptability is required for life to continue. In addition to changes in the abiotic environment, changes of structure and behaviour amongst an organism's cohabiters demand modification over evolutionary timescales. For instance, arms races between predators and prey, competition between organisms for limited resources and cooperation between organisms to orchestrate a suitable environment also induce evolutionary change.

Recognition of the driving forces behind evolution is significant for interactive art, as these pressures must be modelled in the software ecosystem. For instance, human input may gradually alter the virtual environmental conditions of the software organisms, forcing them to adapt over evolutionary time scales. If the system must operate autonomously, a function that alters a basic property of the virtual environment over time will similarly force the agents to adapt. These strategies are adopted in Eden. Firstly, user movement around the work encourages the growth of plant-like agent food. Secondly, the amount of energy available for the growth of the food resource undergoes simulated seasonal variation. The work *Life Spacies II* [16] allows users to control the energy supply entering the virtual ecosystem by way of text messages that are decomposed into individual characters for consumption by the space's inhabitants. In each case, by forcing adaptation the software system ensures that its agents are rewarded for diverse survival strategies and that no specific strategy will suffice over long time scales.

In the work *Meniscus* the user is offered control over the water level of a simulated micro-environment. Each creature prefers a particular depth beneath the surface. If the water level is lowered beneath a creature's preferred depth, it will be "stressed" and will metabolise more rapidly than usual, possibly causing it to die prematurely. Additionally, user agitation of the water "frightens" some creatures, causing them to band together in a close-knit school. When the water settles, this may indirectly facilitate their ability to find suitable mates for reproduction. Thus, depending on the organism's individual traits, human interaction with the system drives it to change over evolutionary time periods.

The work *Diseased Squares* (Dorin 2005) (Fig. 14.6) takes a self-organized approach to driving evolutionary change that is independent of user behaviour. This work is a non-interactive ecosystem simulation for video projection in which agents are subject to infection by a co-evolving infectious disease. The disease evolves to infect agents by matching its own colour signature with one that each agent holds. The agent population evolves to counter this increased disease infectiousness by pushing its colour range away from the spectrum of disease colour signatures. The result is a continual shift in the colour signatures of diseases and agents alike.

An individual organism can be expected to undergo a number of transformations that constitute changes at a temporal scale shorter than that of the evolutionary process. Organisms are born, develop to maturity, reproduce, age, die and eventually decay. These cyclic events each involve transformation of morphology and behaviour over a period of seconds, days or years depending on the organism. To date, many of these phenomena have not been modelled within virtual ecosystems.

Fig. 14.6. *Diseased Squares* (detail) generative video installation. Dorin (2005)

Virtual birth is often instantaneous. In most systems, mating itself is an invisible process of genetic recombination and mutation that occurs outside the virtual space of the simulation. Within the *Polyworld* simulation, visible signs of mating are represented by two adjacent agents each exhibiting its desire to mate through increased blue colouration. This data is available to the agents themselves and to humans watching the simulation. There is no model of the physical transfer of genetic material in *Polyworld* or many other simulations. Usually the genotype of the evolving agents is not explicitly represented within the simulation space; it is assumed to consist of different stuff. The process of replication operates according to rules that are outside the virtual physics or chemistry that agents experience at a simulation step by a simulation step basis [17]. To some extent this varies within systems such as Ray's *Tierra* as the code that carries out replication is indeed a part of the system. The operating system that executes the code however is not accessible for alteration and remains fixed, much like the laws of chemistry remain fixed.

The absence in many simulated ecosystems of a developmental model for agent morphology is also noticeable. As a result, agents are not usually simulated with developing young in their bellies, nurturing eggs, or caring for infants. Instead, a new virtual organism miraculously appears alongside its parents, often as well equipped for survival as they are. In some cases agent controllers may develop during a lifespan. For instance, *Polyworld* organisms have neural network brains that are adjusted by experience utilising a Hebbian learning algorithm. Holland's *Echo* agents update classifier systems during their lifespan and McCormack's *Eden* agents use a similar algorithm.

In an early work by Sommerer and Mignonneau, *A-Volve* (1994), users interactively sculpt virtual creatures to be added to the ecosystem for later autonomous interaction with other agents. Creature construction utilising aesthetic evolution is another process that has been attempted in an early version of Dorin's *Meniscus*. In a later version of the work, agents lay eggs that bounce around the bottom of their watery environment in response to human movement. After sufficient bounces an egg will hatch. Eggs do not otherwise play any role in this ecosystem; for instance, scavengers cannot eat them.

In many virtual ecosystems, death results in the complete removal of an agent from the simulation. Deceased *Polyworld* agents remain in the simulation and may be consumed for energy gain by others. *Diseased Squares* agents decay over time. If they are carrying an infectious disease they may transfer it to other agents that approach during this period.

The introduction of visual or sonic developmental models into the virtual ecosystem is an obvious means of increasing the system's ability to exhibit change at the temporal scale of an agent's lifetime. There are obvious computational costs involved in implementing such a feature and to date, the only sophisticated visual developmental models of which the author is aware are those included for developing vegetation in simulated environments [12]. Various authors have modelled learning behaviour of different kinds that allow agents to change their behaviour during their lifetime.

As must now be clear, the ecosystem and its virtual counterpart may be extremely rich sources of variation over a range of timescales. It will of course fall to the individual programmer-artist to determine exactly which aspects of the system will be implemented; but there is plenty of scope for experimentation. The means through which this potential for change relates to the exploration of novelty by the system is the subject of the following section.

Autonomous Production of Novelty

Change must be associated with an exploration of interesting new ideas if the artwork is to succeed in quite the way this paper is suggesting might be desirable. A system that is capable of exploring novelty without human intervention must have a "problem space" within which humans recognise the occurrence of original and creative outcomes. The artificial ecosystem has as its implicit problem space the modes of survival of its organisms. Energy acquisition, success in locating mates and success in producing and rearing young, all drive the evolution of novel behaviours and the morphologies that facilitate them. The building blocks of real biochemistry are sufficient to construct a bewildering range of bodies and behaviours. Whilst in theory the computer is also capable of such diversity, in practice this aspect of the virtual ecosystem has proven itself to be a tough nut to crack.

To take a relevant example, there exist numerous methods for constructing procedural computer graphics models. For instance, turtle graphics, parametric modelling and particle systems are a few methods that have been employed. Within the range of possibilities for these systems, it is possible to construct an infinite variety of forms. However, to a human viewer, the vast majority of these possible forms are either not very interesting in and of themselves, or they are not significantly different from the other possible forms in the set.

For instance, it is possible to parameterise a triangle according to the lengths of its sides. Whilst even within this simple specification there are an infinite range of possible triangles, humans could not be expected to find this set uniformly interesting. Perhaps a single right-angled triangle, an isosceles triangle and an equilateral triangle would be vaguely interesting; but as for the rest of the infinite set, well, they are all "just triangles".

Unfortunately for this trivial system, it could never be expected to generate a square, let alone a fanciful kaleidoscope of thousands of intricately interwoven, multi-coloured facets. This is a large part of the problem. An ideal representation scheme in this context would be able to change the *kind* of outcome that it produces. Since in visual art it is the observer who classifies objects according to kind, the ideal system would produce different kinds of object that a human would recognise. Within these sets there should also be a range of sub-kinds that can be identified. These must be sufficiently ingenious ways of re-interpreting (for instance "triangle-ness") what we are amused or fascinated by, or at the very least interested in.

Nature's ability to generate an apparently open-ended variety of designs is truly marvellous. Shells are different *kinds* of things than leaves, which are different kinds of things than jellyfish. Certainly these objects may share characteristics, but they differ sufficiently that humans classify them as different kinds of things. Many of us have also been fascinated by the diversity within single classes of nature's constructions, even to the point of maintaining collections just of shells, rocks and butterflies, for instance. Humans are also capable of designing artefacts of a particular kind that interest other humans. Our painting collections, or even our postage stamp collections, are evidence of this. So why is the set of possible butterfly wing patterns more interesting than the set of possible triangles? How can we program the computer to generate forms as interesting as our manually designed stamps or art works?

The key is in the choice of representation scheme, the subtlety of the outcomes it is capable of generating and in the ease with which this space may be navigated from one interesting phenomenon to another whilst minimising the occurrence of uninteresting outcomes. Clearly, since evolutionary pressure is the guiding force in the process, whilst a specific representation scheme may include countless uninteresting possibilities, as long as these are unfit agents they will not proliferate in the population, often this is a desirable scenario. Unfortunately its implementation depends on the availability of at least an implicit measure of interestingness, something that has not been forthcoming. The programmer must consider also that a system can be *too* interesting, in which case it will appear noisy. A certain degree of familiarity needs to be established. Repetition is required to highlight, even to *define*, the very idea of novelty. This issue will be addressed in the following section.

There are few more general principles than those just outlined to guide the programmer in establishing a space suited for the appearance of novelty. However, a number of schemes have been developed for special purposes that may act as starting points. Dawkins' *biomorphs* [18] (Fig. 14.7) are a great

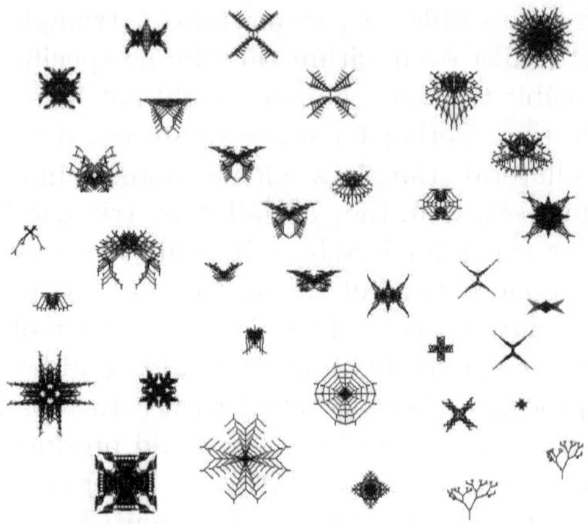

Fig. 14.7. *Biomorphs* evolved using Dawkins' *Blind Watchmaker* software

example of the complexity of models that may result from simple construction rules. A large part of their success is due to the simple forms' openness to interpretation and the significant changes in appearance that may result on any path through phenotypic space. Some suggest to us stars, others insects or trees – the human imagination is a powerful ally. In this instance, the problem space within which novelty appears is clearly defined by what appeals to the human user of the software.

The creatures of *Meniscus* share the simplicity of *biomorphs* although they are constructed specifically to mimic micro-organisms and consequently forego some of the potential Dawkins' system exhibits. *Meniscus'* agents are constructed of pairs of coloured, concentric, translucent discs, arranged along simple 2D paths. The discs are parameterised to alter their radii and the number of wiry flagella or cilia that protrude from their circumferences. In addition, the 2D paths along which they lie are parameterised so that each agent moves across the screen in a gradual sweep or a series of erratic dances. All of these characteristics are subject to artificial evolution, ensuring the work is able to explore a range of visual structures within the problem space defined by the generative system.

In contrast, the agents in sonic works such as *Eden* and *Living Melodies* gain our interest through the combination of their characteristics (musical tones or sounds) with those produced by the rest of the population. In the best of these systems the result is an orchestral population, rather than a cacophony of one-man bands. Although the agents' individual visual appearances are not interesting, and even their individual sonic behaviours are repetitive, in concert with their peers they produce a musical work or pleasing ambient texture. The work *Autumn Squares* (Dorin 2004) also takes this approach, reducing the idea to a minimal but shifting visual field. The agents are silent rectangles of different dimensions and colours that genetically drift

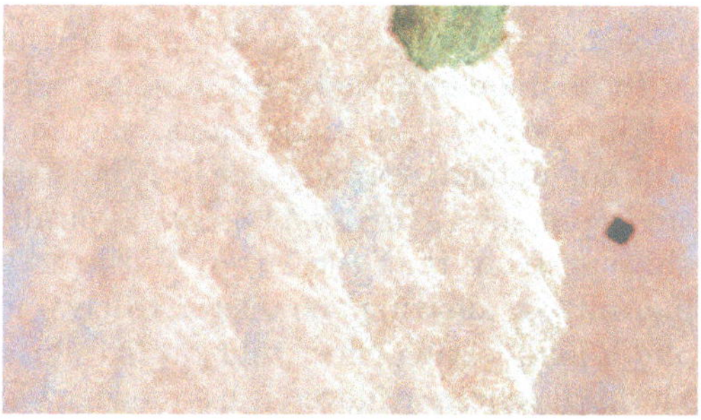

Fig. 14.8. *E-volver* (detail) generative video installation. Driessens and Vertsappen (2006)

through size and colour spaces as they glide across a dark plane. The result is a display that moves through green, red, orange, yellow and brown, forming clusters and streams, sunbursts and decaying hues. *E-volver* (Driessens and Verstappen 2006) (Fig. 14.8) takes this approach also, its agents being little more than pixel-sized specks the size of Langton's ant. Although *E-volver's* agents are invisible, each wanders across a plane reacting to the colours in its path by changing its direction and laying visible coloured paths of its own. The result of co-evolving collections of these ant-like agents is a wide range of pixel-scapes evoking satellite images of the Earth, mould growing on cheese or perhaps lichen on rocks.

More complex creatures have of course also been attempted but seldom within an independently operating virtual ecosystem. *Life Spacies* for instance constructs creatures from text entered by users. The basis for the creatures' morphology is a set of body segments built as a surface of revolution with various appendages attached. The model is capable of generating a range of visual outcomes, but perhaps it does not exhibit the diversity of Sims' aesthetically evolved creatures in *Galapagos* (1997). These two works rely on user intervention and do not autonomously generate novelty. Although neither of these systems was intended to operate in such a way, it would be interesting to discover if the genotypic space each encapsulates is sufficiently robust that it could be designed to mesh neatly within an independent virtual ecosystem.

Responsiveness to Perturbation and Susceptibility to External Control

Two desirable properties of interactive systems for art making will be addressed in this section, as they are inter-dependent. Each relates closely to the role of the human interactor. This human may be an artist constructing a work based upon the notion of an ecosystem, or a gallery visitor exploring an existing work. In either case they will have some expectations that must be met and perhaps others that an artist might prefer shattered.

As a visitor approaches an interactive new-media artwork, he expects to be able to influence the outcome of the work in some perceptible way that justifies its proffered interactivity. In some cases, the changes wrought by visitors to a work are not immediately visible. In others the visitor controls the work directly and completely. Ecosystems are typically more suited to the former end of this spectrum than the latter. With care a combination of influences may be permitted, allowing the visitor to have immediate impact on the simulation and a long-lasting effect that outlives his visit.

One way in which this has been achieved is by allowing visitors to design an agent, place it in the simulation, and watch the resulting interactions between it and the rest of the ecosystem. *A-volve* (Sommerer and Mignonneau 1993) takes this approach. The game *Spore* is similar in allowing the user to configure a creature and place it in the game world. The approach is akin to designing a character for a role-playing game. In these game-like cases however, the actions of the agent remain under the control of the designer, even if they are constrained by the traits of the agent's design. Under the ecosystem model the agent's author relinquishes control of his creation from birth.

The work *Meniscus* allows gallery visitors to alter the abiotic environment of the ecosystem by adjusting the water level of a virtual pipette. This changes the dynamic of the ecosystem in complex ways that are quite outside the understanding of the majority of gallery visitors. These deep changes also result in clear superficial visual changes in the behaviour of the agents that may be appreciated immediately.

Eden takes a similar approach by monitoring the movement of people through the exhibition space and relating this activity to the abundance of agent food in the virtual ecosystem. In this instance, the viewer is not aware of the connection between his movements and the behaviour of the ecosystem. Whilst the overall behaviour of the system is indeed influenced by human movement, this is not a transparent process and the audience is left (metaphorically) in the dark.

Some general principles of virtual ecosystem behaviour are worthy of note. Firstly, under some conditions, evidence suggests that virtual ecosystems are: (i) difficult to initiate elegantly; (ii) remarkably resilient to perturbation once running. These conclusions are based on the success of existing works that employ ad hoc initiation strategies but nevertheless continue to operate over long periods of time once running.

Boot-strapping virtual life is a difficult process to automate elegantly. The implementation of a virtual physics sufficiently complex to give rise to the emergence of replication, whilst simultaneously supporting mutation and the genotype/phenotype distinction, remains a research challenge. To bypass this requirement, Ray's *Tierra* ecosystem of replicating code fragments is initiated with a hard-coded ancestor. Pargellis' related *Amoeba* ecosystem [19] starts from a random soup of software also, but the instruction set from which its genotypes are initially thrown together is geared to make the random appearance of a replicator more likely than is the case in Tierra. Yaeger's

Polyworld has two modes of operation: one explicitly mates agents deemed successful by a hard-coded fitness function; the other allows the ecosystem to run freely. The first mode is required to boot-strap the system to the point where the free-running mode may take the reins. Without it there is little chance that agents in the initial random population will live sufficiently long to acquire energy and a mate for reproduction in order to start the evolutionary process.

Most virtual ecosystems take the easy option by building replication into the simulation as a basic primitive. That is, when two agents meet they may "decide" to mate. Replication is not a behaviour that needs to be constructed; it is an assumed characteristic of every agent. Although this allows the evolutionary process to start easily, the implementation suffers from the drawback that strategies for constructing offspring and for recombining or mutating genomes are hard-coded into the simulation by the programmer, rather than emergent from the interactions of the agents.

Hard-coding is of course a significant influence on the outcome of any ecosystem simulation, quite apart from its constraints on the possibilities for mating and reproduction. Hard-coding usually determines the range of possibilities for the evolutionary process to explore. This is quite often the most aesthetically significant aspect of any artwork that employs the technique. The constraint usually amounts to restrictions on agent morphology and the means by which agents interact with their biotic and abiotic environment through programmer-designed sensors.

The agent population may consist of coloured pixels (*E-volve*), circles (*Eden*), triangles like Reynolds' original *boids* or coloured rectangles (*Autumn Squares*). More complex collections of primitives such as groups of line segments (*biomorphs*), discs (*Meniscus*) or the virtual solids as used by Todd and Latham in *Mutator* [20] and Sims in his *Galapagos* (1997) installation are also possible. All of these choices are under the control of the programmer. It is therefore quite clear that as an artist, the virtual ecosystem is open to an enormous range of visual interpretations. Plenty of scope exists for leaving one's signature on any work that operates in this mode. In opposition to these artist-laid constraints the user's interaction through the mechanisms discussed above allow a balanced approach to constructing an artwork that is rewarding to explore, but can nevertheless express the vision of the artist who programmed it.

14.4 Conclusion

The method of presentation of an electronic media artwork and the algorithms for generating the piece are arguably the two most significant aspects of any endeavour in the computational arts. Even the strongest underlying idea will stand or fall by the artist's attention to these two aspects of art making. This essay has discussed the application of a dynamic, complex adaptive computational system based on real ecological systems to electronic art. Not every artist will wish to adopt such a methodology; however, as has been shown, the idea has merit. In particular, if an artist is seeking a generative system capable of autonomous and human-directed exploration of a constrained set of models, the virtual ecosystem is worthy of consideration. The method's main weakness lies in its unwieldiness. This is simultaneously its strength. As long as the programmer has sufficient grasp of the behaviour of his software, the system may be guided to explore spaces of interest to the artist or gallery visitor. Unpredictability then becomes a welcome ally in the construction of a work that is capable of surprising and challenging not only the viewer but even the artist who constructed it.

Regardless of the visual or sonic outcome, the underlying ecosystem-based process has about it a pleasing conceptual coherence. Such coherence is of relevance only to those whose concern is elegance at the algorithmic level. As with much generative new-media art, the elegance of the underlying process often passes over the heads of gallery visitors. Nevertheless, to an artist, such underlying unity may be desirable for its own sake.

There are many reasons to use a computer as a simple tool for making art. The issues discussed here move beyond this limited vista to follow a winding mountain path that is travelled only by computation. Our knowledge of this path, and our familiarity with the scenery through which it passes, is still in its infancy. It is my belief that the radically new understanding that computation offers is as suitable for artistic exploration as it is for scientific experimentation.

References

1. Whitelaw, M. (2004). *Metacreation: Art and Artificial Life*. The MIT Press
2. Innocent, T. (1999). The language of iconica. In Dorin, A., McCormack, J., eds.: *First Iteration, CEMA*. Melbourne
3. McCormack, J. (2001). Eden: An evolutionary sonic ecosystem. In Kelemen, J., Sosík, P., eds.: *Advances in Artificial Life, 6th European Conference*. Lecture Notes in Computer Science. Springer, 133–142
4. Tansley, A.G. (1935). The use and abuse of vegetational concepts and terms. *Ecology*, **16**(3): 284–307
5. Watson, A., Lovelock, J. (1983). Biological homeostasis of the global environment: The parable of daisyworld. *Tellus B*, **35**: 284–289
6. Yaeger, L. (1994). Computational genetics, physiology, metabolism, neural systems, learning, vision, and behavior or PolyWorld: Life in a new context. In Langton, C.G., ed.: *Proceedings of the Workshop on Artificial Life (ALIFE '92)*. Sante Fe Institute Studies in the Sciences of Complexity. Reading, MA, USA. Addison-Wesley, 263–298
7. Ray, T.S. (1992). An approach to the synthesis of life. In Langton, C.G., Tayler, C., Farmer, J.D., Rasmussen, S., eds.: *Artificial Life II*. Addison-Wesley. Reading, MA, 371–408

8. Burkhart, R., Askenazi, M., Minar, N. (2006). Swarm documentation set. `http://www.santafe.edu/projects/swarm/swarmdocs/set/set.html`
9. Holland, J.H. (1998). *Hidden Order: How Adaptation Builds Complexity (Helix Books)*. Addison Wesley Publishing Company
10. Epstein, J.M., Axtell, R.L. (1996). *Growing Artificial Societies: Social Science from the Bottom Up*. Brookings Institute
11. Adami, C., Brown, C.T. (1994). Evolutionary learning in the 2d artificial life system avida. In Brooks, R.A., Maes, P., eds.: *Artificial Life IV: Proceedings of the Fourth International Workshop on the Synthesis and Simulation of Living Systems*. Cambridge, MA, USA. MIT Press, 377–381
12. Deussen, O., Hanrahan, P., Lintermann, B., Mech, R., Pharr, M., Prusinkiewicz, P. (1998). Realistic modeling and rendering of plant ecosystems. In: *SIGGRAPH '98: Proceedings of the 25th Annual Conference on Computer Graphics and Interactive Techniques*. New York, NY, USA. ACM Press, 275–286
13. Dorin, A. (2005). A co-evolutionary epidemiological model for artificial life and death. In Capcarrère, M.S., Freitas, A.A., Bentley, P.J., Johnson, C.G., Timmis, J., eds.: *Advances in Artificial Life, 8th European Conference, ECAL*. Lecture Notes in Computer Science. Springer, 775–784
14. Dahlstedt, P. (1999). Living melodies: Coevolution of sonic communication. In Dorin, A., McCormack, J., eds.: *First Iteration, CEMA*. Melbourne, 56–66
15. Berry, R., Rungsarityotin, W., Dorin, A., Dahlstedt, P., Haw, C. (2001). Unfinished symphonies – songs of 3.5 worlds. In: *Workshop on Artificial Life Models for Musical Applications, Sixth European Conference on Artificial Life, Editoriale Bios*. Prague, Czech Republic, 51–64
16. Sommerer, C., Mignonneau, L. (1999). VERBARIUM and LIFE SPACIES: Creating a visual language by transcoding text into form on the internet. In: *VL '99: Proceedings of the IEEE Symposium on Visual Languages*. Washington, DC, USA. IEEE Computer Society, 90–95
17. Taylor, T. (2002). Creativity in evolution: individuals, interactions, and environments. In Bentley, P., Corne, D., eds.: *Creative Evolutionary Systems*. Morgan Kaufmann Publishers Inc.. San Francisco, CA, USA, 79–108
18. Dawkins, R. (1987). *The Blind Watchmaker*. W.W. Norton & Co. New York
19. Pargellis, A.N. (2000). Digital life behavior in the amoeba world. *Artif. Life*, **7**(1): 63–75
20. Todd, S., Latham, W. (1992). *Evolutionary Art and Computers*. Academic Press. San Diego

15

Complexism and the Role of Evolutionary Art

Philip Galanter

Independent Artist email@philipgalanter.com

Summary. Artists have always learned from nature. A new generation of artists is adapting the very processes of life to create exciting new works. But art is more than the creation of objects. It is also a progression of ideas with a history and a correspondence to the larger culture.

The goal of this chapter is to take a step back from the details of the technology and the consideration of specific works, and to view evolutionary art in the broader context of all art. This kind of multidisciplinary discussion requires one to be multilingual, and this chapter will use the language of scientists, humanists, artists, and philosophers. While doing so we will quickly visit complexity science, postmodernism in the arts, and the conflict between the cultures of the humanities and the sciences.

With this as a backdrop, I will introduce a new approach I call complexism. Complexism is the application of a scientific understanding of complex systems to the subject matter of the arts and humanities. We will see that the significance of evolutionary art is that it takes complexism as both its method and content. Evolutionary art is a new kind of dynamic iconography: the iconography of complexism. And complexism offers nothing less than the reconciliation of the sciences and the humanities through a higher synthesis of the modern and the postmodern.

To a certain extent this chapter participates in the modernist tradition of the art manifesto. The art manifesto is a form of speculative writing where the artist-author posits a new revolutionary creative direction for a group of artists who share a set of common interests, as well as a new worldview that offers a radical break with the past. Writers of such manifestos have included Marinetti, Kandinsky, Schwitters, Moholy-Nagy, Gropius, Breton, and others [1].

Like other manifestos, this chapter includes forward-looking assertions about work not yet started let alone completed. I have tried to identify the more speculative parts of this chapter as being part of this complexist manifesto.

15.1 Complexity Science

With the founding of the Santa Fe Institute in 1984 serving as a significant milestone, for more than 20 years scientists from diverse fields have been working together in a new way to create a new multidisciplinary understanding of systems. Under the general rubric of "complexity science" and "complexity theory" various systems, and various kinds of systems, have been studied, compared, contrasted, and mathematically and computationally modeled. An abstract understanding of systems that spans the physical, biological, and social sciences is beginning to emerge [2].

Science generally proceeds in a reductive manner, the thinking being that by breaking down complicated phenomena into their figurative (or literal) atomic parts one gains predictive and explanatory power. The problem with reductionism, however, is that it doesn't fully address the problem of putting the pieces back together again [3].

This is especially true of complex systems. When scientists speak of complex systems they don't mean systems that are complicated or perplexing in an informal way. The phrase "complex system" has been adopted as a specific technical term.

Complex systems typically have a large number of small parts or components that interact with similar nearby parts and components. These local interactions often lead to the system organizing itself without any master control or external agent being "in charge." Such systems are often referred to as being self-organizing. These self-organized systems are also dynamic systems under constant change, and, short of death or destruction, they do not settle into a final stable "equilibrium" state. To the extent these systems react to changes in their environment so as to maintain their integrity, they are known as complex adaptive systems [4].

In common language one is reminded of the saying that "the whole is greater than the sum of its parts." The weather, for example, forms coherent patterns such as thunderstorms, tornados, and hot and cold fronts, yet there is no central mechanism or control that creates such patterns. Weather patterns "emerge" all over and all at once. In the near term weather can be predicted with some accuracy, but beyond more than a few days the weather becomes quite unpredictable.

The stock market is similarly a complex system with emergent properties. Billions of shares and transactions are linked in a finite chain of cause and effect, and patterns such as booms and busts emerge from the overall system. Yet no one factor dominates or "plans" the market. Even with all of the relevant information available to the public, the stock market generates surprising and unpredictable behavior.

15.1.1 Biology and Complexity Science

For most practical purposes a falling rock can be considered as a simple physical system, and modeled with a simple formula of mass, velocity, and gravitational force. A biological system, such as a frog, is much more difficult to model and is said to be complex. In sub-geological time a rock is relatively inert and its information state is limited to position, velocity, and spin. A frog is ever changing, and an attempt to measure every body function, the tension of every muscle, the activity of every neural connection and so on would be very daunting.

As a complex system a frog can be viewed as a very large collection of more atomic units; in this case, cells. And each cell, in turn, exhibits enormous genetic complexity by creating intricate switching networks and manufacturing diverse complex proteins. Somehow these local interactions combine and create coherent macro-behaviors that are described as being emergent and adaptive, and, indeed, as being life itself.

Complex systems are typically nonlinear,[1] so in terms of control the same amount of force may yield a smaller or larger change, sometimes in ways that may seem counterintuitive. Such systems may also be chaotic, so even the tiniest difference in a system's history can result in a massive future difference [5, 6]. In a sense, as the cells go through their local interactions, the frog is an emergent phenomenon. This notion of emergence, as well as the attention paid to autocatalytic cycles and connectionist models, makes complexity a key development area in the life sciences [7].

Complexity science is an antidote to the overly reductionist tendencies of 19th century science. Areas of application in the life sciences include evolution, brain function, animal societies, metabolism, and much more. More generally complexity science impacts physics, chemistry, economics, meteorology, computer science, and more. In that complexity science seeks to abstract an understanding of systems across all of these disciplines, the study of complexity is one of integration rather than specialization [8].

Complexity science thus offers more than an incremental increase in scientific understanding. It is revolutionary in that it reverses the top-down process of reductionism, and instead offers a synthesis of bottom-up processes. In a resonant way, complexity science is revolutionary in the way it eschews specialization, and instead attempts to establish commonalities across scientific disciplines with regard to systems [8].

The question to be considered later is, if complexity science offers a revolution in the sciences, does it also offer a revolution in the broader culture?

[1] The term "nonlinear" has multiple discipline-specific meanings that can confuse an interdisciplinary discussion. In the humanities nonlinear can mean (1) disconnected, illogical, or irrational, or (2) having multiple narratives, or (3) having a viewer-driven interactive narrative, or (4) being a non-chronological presentation. In the context of complexity science, nonlinearity references (1) mathematical expressions with exponential terms (e.g., "x^n") or (2) behaviors where "the whole is greater than the sum of the parts," or (3) situations where small continuous changes result in macro-level phase changes. Examples of (3) might include solid ice melting into liquid water with a slight increase in heat, or catastrophic material failure due to a slight increase in load.

15.1.2 Quantifying Complexity

It is one thing to compare a simple system with a complex system, and quite another to compare disparate complex systems. One scientific approach is to develop a functional definition of complexity so it can be quantified, allowing the comparison of complex systems.

The observation that the state of a frog entails much more information than the state of a rock might lead one to consider information as a measurement of complexity. An earlier related attempt to better understand the quantification of information was initiated by Claude Shannon in the form of information theory [9]. For the purposes of analyzing the capacity of a given communication channel, the core idea is that the more "surprise" a given channel can exhibit the more information it contains. A corollary to this is that low information communications contain redundancies that allow compression, and high information communications with little redundancy resist compression.

Consider the following informal examples presented without mathematical rigor. A channel that simply transmits the character "a" over and over again offers no surprise, and thus no information. It can also be compressed to a few characters, by using a symbol that means "an infinite number of the following" and then the character "a." A typical English language sentence carries more information because of the variability of characters used. Such a sentence can, however, be compressed to a degree because the English language is somewhat predictable and includes some redundancy. For example, if the characters "elephan" come out of the channel, chances are good that the next character will be "t." From the point of view of information theory, a channel that offers maximal information is one that transmits perfectly random characters. Because a random signal is, by definition, entirely unpredictable, it offers no redundancy and cannot be compressed.

It's easy to see that information as measured by Shannon's information theory is not a good proxy measure for our intuitive sense of a system's complexity. The DNA that determines the metabolism, neurology and other subsystems of a frog requires structure and regularity. Making random changes to the DNA of a fertilized frog egg will certainly increase its Shannon information, but at some point it will render the egg incapable of cell division. Our intuitive sense is that a living, growing, reproducing frog egg is more complex than a dead frog egg with highly unusual DNA. Contrary to this, the Shannon measure of information would give a higher score to the "dead" randomized DNA than the more regular "living" DNA. A high Shannon measure of information does not imply a high degree of complexity.

As noted by Murray Gell-Mann [10] another approach is to consider the algorithmic complexity (AC) of a given system. Algorithmic complexity is also called the algorithmic information content (AIC), and was independently developed by Kolmogorov [11], Solomonoff [12], and Chaitin [13].

Any system that can be expressed as a deterministic algorithm can be mapped into a smallest possible program running on a general-purpose computer. (Such a computer may be considered "Turing complete" if one relaxes the formal requirement of infinite storage). In this context it is understood that by "program" we mean both the machine instructions executed and stored data processed. The algorithmic complexity of the system under consideration is simply the length of this shortest possible program without reference to the execution time.

Some systems, such as fractals, require infinite time to generate because they have infinite detail. But we don't normally think of fractals as having infinite complexity. They are simple in the sense that they exhibit self-similar structure at every scale. And, in fact, a fractal algorithm can be very compact indeed. So one might hope that AC is a good candidate for a measure of what we intuitively consider complexity. Perhaps the larger the algorithmic complexity, the more complex the system.

Unfortunately, in the case of random processes we run into the same paradox as we see in information theory. Returning to our informal example, a program to produce the character "a" over and over again can be quite short, simply a print statement within an infinite loop. The machine instructions and data to produce an English language text will be somewhat larger, but given the redundancies in the English language itself, the program can implement data compression not unlike that one would find in a ".zip" file. Nevertheless, such a program would still have a larger AC than the previous single character example. Finally, consider a program that must reproduce a string of specific random characters of equal length. The machine instructions and data would be longer still because the string would lack the redundancies of natural language, and would resist any compression scheme.

Much like the Shannon information measure, the algorithmic complexity measure is not a good proxy for our intuitive sense of complexity. A book's complexity comes from its structure and regularity as much as its diversity, and a random string of equal length is intuitively less complex. In a sense all random strings of characters are the same, and as one "randomizes" a book it becomes less complex as its intelligible coherence collapses into noise.

The Shannon information measure and algorithmic complexity both increase as a system approaches randomness. But our intuitive sense is that complexity peaks somewhere in between highly ordered highly redundant systems and highly disordered structure-less systems. In genetics and evolution, the successful complex system (species) will strike a balance between order (highly accurate DNA replication and repair) and disorder (the occasional mutation or variation through sexual crossover operations).

What is needed is something like Murray Gell-Mann's notion of "effective complexity." With effective complexity systems that are highly ordered or disordered are given a low score, indicating simplicity, and systems that are somewhere in between are given a high score, indicating complexity. Gell-Mann explains:

"A measure that corresponds much better to what is usually meant by complexity in ordinary conversation, as well as in scientific discourse, refers not to the length of the most concise description of an entity (which is roughly what AIC is), but to the length of a concise description of a set of the entity's regularities. Thus something almost entirely random, with practically no regularities, would have effective complexity near zero. So would something completely regular, such as a bit string consisting entirely of zeroes. Effective complexity can be high only in a region intermediate between total order and complete disorder." [10]

To measure effective complexity Gell-Mann proposes to split a given system into two algorithmic terms, with the first algorithm capturing structure and the second algorithm capturing random deviation. The effective complexity would then be proportional to the size of the optimally compressed program for the first algorithm that captures structure. To implement effective complexity as a practical matter Gell-Mann points out that this process is exactly what a complex adaptive system does as it learns (models) its environment. Aspects that are random, or noise, are forgotten and aspects that exhibit structure are compressed (abstracted and generalized). Structural aspects that resist compression are experienced as being complex.

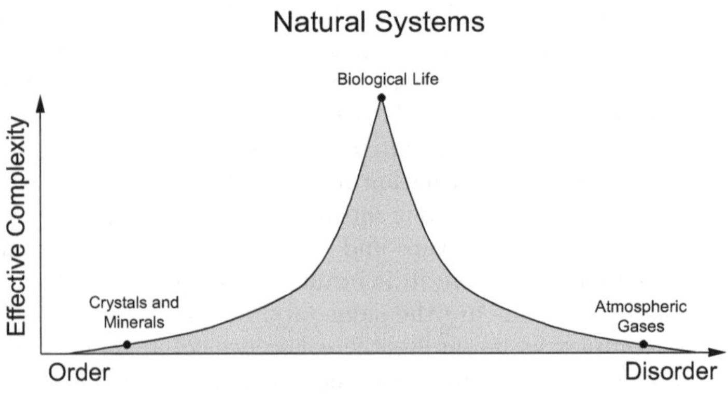

Fig. 15.1. The effective complexity of a system increases between order and disorder

As shown in Fig. 15.1. highly ordered systems from nature such as crystals, or highly disordered systems such as atmospheric gases, yield low measures of effective complexity. The robust complex adaptive systems found in nature, the living things biology takes as its subject matter, are represented at the apex of the curve. Note that the contours of the graph are meant to suggest a nonlinear increase in complexity as one progresses away from either highly ordered or highly disordered systems. Also note that the finite apex of the curve is meant to imply that the structural component of a system expressed as a program cannot be of infinite length.

The notion of effective complexity is closely related to our intuitive sense of complexity in biological systems. In the next section we will see how effective complexity also creates a context for understanding evolutionary art.

15.2 Evolutionary Art as Generative Art

The term "generative art" has gained popularity over the last decade. In an earlier paper I offered what is now perhaps the most widely quoted definition:

> "Generative art refers to any art practice where the artist uses a system, such as a set of natural language rules, a computer program, a machine, or other procedural invention, which is set into motion with some degree of autonomy contributing to or resulting in a completed work of art." [14]

The key element in generative art is the use of an external system to which the artist cedes partial or total subsequent control.

Some additional observations are worth making. First, note that the term generative art is simply a reference to how the art is made, and it makes no claims as to why the art is made this way or what its content is. Second, generative art is uncoupled from any particular technology. As will be seen in the examples that follow, generative art may or may not be "high tech."

Third, a system that moves an art practice into the realm of generative art must be well defined and self-contained enough to, in principle, operate autonomously. This doesn't, however, rule out art that is entirely handmade. This only means that control over some aspect of producing the art is handed over to an external system, and there are implicit decisions made which are not left up to the moment-to-moment intuitive choices of the artist. For example, ancient art based on tiling patterns is generative because the placements of individual tiles are not decisions made by the artisan, but rather are dictated by a manually executed symmetry-based algorithm.

Clearly evolutionary art is a type of generative art. The genetic information and competitive evolutionary process is an external system to which the artist cedes control. In some cases the artist retains tighter control by personally acting as the fitness function, and choosing in each round of breeding which individuals will reproduce, and which individuals will be removed from the gene pool. In other cases the artist will express his or her judgment as an abstraction in the form of an algorithmic fitness function, and will then allow the breeding cycle to run free. In what follows we will see that evolutionary art occupies a special position in the spectrum of generative art.

15.2.1 Generative Art in the Context of Complexity Science

Complexity science has given us a way of sorting out systems in the abstract. There are two kinds of simple systems, those that are highly ordered and those that are highly disordered. Complex systems exist in the middle ground between order and disorder.

Since generative art turns on the artist's use of a system, the insights gained from complexity science can also be used to sort out generative art.

15.2.2 Highly Ordered Generative Art

In every time and place for which we can find artifacts, we find examples of the use of symmetry in the creation of art. Reasonable people can disagree as to at what point the use of symmetry can be considered an autonomous system. But even among the most so called primitive peoples examples abound in terms of the use of geometric patterns in textiles, symmetric designs about a point, repeating border designs, and so on. Many of these are well documented by authors like Hargittai and Hargittai [15] and Stevens [16]. Additionally Washburn and Crowe have shown how specific art objects can be analyzed in terms of abstract symmetry classes, and how such classification can be a useful anthropological tool in understanding human societies [17].

The artistic use of tiling, in particular, is nothing less than the application of abstract systems to decorate specific surfaces. Leading the most notable examples in this regard are perhaps the masterworks found in the Islamic world. It is perhaps no coincidence the Islamic world also provided one of the significant cradles of mathematical innovation. It is also worth noting that the word "algorithm" has its roots in the Islamic world.

Highly ordered systems in generative art also made their appearance in innovative 20th century art. A popular contemporary tile artist, and student of the Islamic roots, was M.C. Escher. While lacking in formal mathematical training, it is clear that he had a significant understanding of the generative nature of what he called "the regular division of the plane." Without the use of computers he invented and applied what can only be called algorithms in the service of art [18].

In addition, minimal and conceptual artists such as Carl André, Mel Bochner, Donald Judd, Paul Mogenson, Robert Smithson, and Sol LeWitt used various simple highly ordered geometric, number sequence, and combinatorial systems as generative elements in their work [19, 20].

Generative art based on highly ordered systems seems ubiquitous, but can we say that generative art is as old as art? Many are familiar with the discoveries of representational cave paintings some 35,000 years old that depict animals and early man's daily life. But in 1999 and 2000 a team led by archaeologist Christopher Henshilwood of the South African Museum in Cape Town uncovered the oldest known art artifacts. Etched in hand-sized pieces of red ochre more than 70,000 years old is an unmistakable grid design made of triangular tiles that would likely be recognizable as such to Escher or generations of Islamic artists.

While the etchings, like most ancient archaeological finds, are not without controversy, many find them compelling examples of abstract geometric thinking with an artistic response. In a related article in Science anthropologist Stanley Ambrose of the University of Illinois, Urbana-Champaign says "This is clearly an intentionally incised abstract geometric design ... It is art." [21].

Two stone etchings alone cannot make the case that generative art is as old as art itself. But around the world, and throughout history, there is overwhelming evidence of artists turning to systems of iterative symmetry and geometry to generate form. Early generative art may seem unsophisticated because it is highly ordered and simple, but our complexity inspired paradigm for generative art has an important place for highly ordered simple systems.

15.2.3 Highly Disordered Generative Art

One of the earliest documented uses of randomization in the arts is a musical dice game invented by Wolfgang Amadeus Mozart. Mozart provides 176 measures of prepared music and a grid that maps the throw of a pair of dice, and a sequence number (first throw, second throw, etc.) into the numbers 1 through 176. The player creates a composition by making a sequence of random dice throws, and assembling the corresponding measures in a sequential score. Perhaps Mozart knew intuitively that purely random music isn't terribly interesting because he found a primitive way to mix order and disorder. The short pre-composed measures provide order, and the throw of the dice provide disorder [22].

Randomization in the arts came into its own primarily in the 20th century. As a young artist Ellsworth Kelly used inexpensive materials such as children's construction paper along with chance methods to create colorful collages. He was inspired to do this after observing the random patchworks that would develop in the repair of cabana tents on the French Riviera [23].

The writer William Burroughs famously used his Dada inspired "cut-up" technique to randomize creative writing. Less well known are Burroughs experiments in visual art using shotgun blasts to randomly scatter paint on, and partially destroy, plywood supports [24]. Occasionally Carl André would use a random spill technique rather than his more typical highly ordered assembly systems [19].

Perhaps the most famous advocate for the random selection of sounds in music was John Cage [25, 26]. As mentioned earlier, generative art is a long-standing art practice, but different artists may choose the same generative technique for wholly different reasons. For John Cage the motivation for randomization was a Zen inspired acceptance of all sounds as being equally worthy. For André the intent was in part to focus attention on the properties of the materials, but also to assault art-world expectations regarding composition.

It is important to remember that what generative artists have in common is how they make their work, but not why they make their work, or even why they choose to use generative systems in their art practice. The big tent of generative art contains a diversity of intent and opinion.

15.2.4 Generative Art Systems in the Context of Effective Complexity

While the term "generative art" is somewhat foreign to the art-world mainstream, both highly ordered and highly disordered generative art is bound tightly to the canon of art history. What seems lacking in the humanities is a broad understanding of systems and systems based art.

In part, it is this lack of a broad view of systems that has slowed the acceptance of complexity based generative art in the mainstream. The context can be made clear by a simple adaptation of the earlier graph. It's worth noting that some generative art systems are used to create a final static art object, and in other cases it is the actual generative system that is put on display. In any case, what are being sorted out here are the generative art systems themselves, and not necessarily the end results.

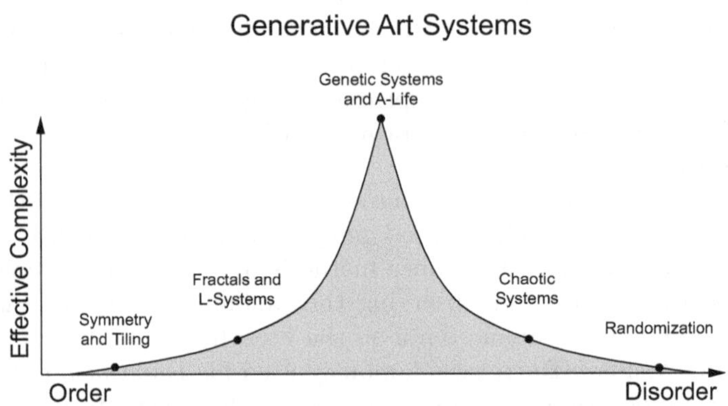

Fig. 15.2. Effective complexity used to organize various generative art systems

It has already been noted that both highly ordered generative art such as that based on symmetry and tiling, and highly disordered generative art based on randomization, are of very low complexity. Before turning to evolutionary art it is worth considering generative systems that move away from high order or disorder, but do not achieve high complexity.

Ordered systems that offer more complexity than simple applications of symmetry include fractals and Lindenmayer (or L-) systems. Fractals are mathematical objects first discovered by Benoit Mandelbrot that exhibit self-similarity at all scales. Fractals have been applied to generative art in the creation of abstract patterns as well as simulating natural objects such as clouds, riverbanks, mountains, and other landforms [27].

L-systems are grammar-based systems of axioms and production rules developed by Lindenmayer and Prusinkiewicz that can simulate the growth of branching structures in plants. L-systems have been applied to generative art in the creation of abstract patterns as well as 2D and 3D renderings of artificial trees, bushes, and flowers [28].

What fractals and L-systems have in common as systems is a structural algorithm component that is not quite as compressible as simple symmetry relationships, but is highly recursive and thus much more compressible than one might assume from the visual result.

Near the other end of the spectrum generative artists have explored chaotic feedback systems. Like all chaotic systems, those used by artists are deterministic but exhibit a nonlinear sensitivity to initial conditions. This is sometimes called "the butterfly effect" as in the hypothetical example that a butterfly in India flaps its wings and this later results in a tornado in Texas [29].

While the long-term results of a chaotic system may be so unpredictable as to seem random there is short-term predictability. The feedback mechanism is a simple structural algorithm that is highly compressible. From the point of view of effective complexity chaotic feedback systems are a bit more complex than, and not quite as disordered as, absolute randomization.

Artists who have used chaotic feedback include early video artists Steina and Woody Vasulka. The Vasulkas created dynamic systems by creating a video signal loop where the camera is pointed directly into its own display [30]. And in 1963, Hans Haacke's "Condensation Cube" (first titled "Weather Cube") displayed ever-changing patterns of evaporation and condensation the same year that Ralph Lorenz discovered chaos in weather systems [31].

15.2.5 Complex Generative Art and the Unique Position of Evolutionary Art

While systems such as the economy and the weather are indeed complex, complexity scientists frequently cite examples from life itself as being the most complex known systems, and especially the most complex adaptive systems. Evolutionary art, and other biologically inspired art, exploit models of systems that are at the apex of the effective complexity curve.

By all rights, evolutionary art should be able to transform the larger culture by offering non-specialists a new understanding of complex systems, and indeed of life itself. But while those in the arts and humanities have accepted various forms of generative art in bits and pieces, they have yet to recognize generative art as a full spectrum of complexity relationships. Without such recognition the true importance of evolutionary art is lost.

A primary observation of this manifesto is this sad fact: despite a relatively recent superficial embrace of trendy technology-based art, the arts and humanities in the 20th century have developed a growing antipathy towards science at the level of fundamental philosophy. Until the sciences and the humanities can be reconciled, it is likely that evolutionary art will be denied its crown as one of the most complex forms of generative art, and robbed of its culturally transformational power.

The following section will outline the split between the sciences and the humanities, and will offer the hope that complexity theory itself may hold the key to their reconciliation.

15.3 The Growing Rift Between Science and the Humanities

The first popular airing of the growing 20th century rift between the humanities and science is usually attributed to C.P. Snow's 1959 Rede lecture "The Two Cultures." In this lecture he captures a difference in attitude that has only become greater in the intervening years.

> "Literary intellectuals at one pole – at the other scientists, and as the most representative, the physical scientists. Between the two a gulf of mutual incomprehension – sometimes (particularly among the young) hostility and dislike, but most of all lack of understanding. They have a curious distorted image of each other. Their attitudes are so different that, even on the level of emotion, they can't find much common ground.
> ...
> The non-scientists have a rooted impression that the scientists are shallowly optimistic, unaware of man's condition. On the other hand, the scientists believe that the literary intellectuals are totally lacking in foresight, peculiarly unconcerned with their brother men, in a deep sense anti-intellectual, anxious to restrict both art and thought to the existential moment. And so on." [32]

Critics will point out that Snow's full critique is intellectually superficial and overly concerned with practical matters such as education reform and combating poverty. But if one interprets "anti-intellectual" as "anti-rational" in the above quote, at least part of Snow's critique seems to be a prescient concern about the coming conflict between philosophically rational modernism (science) and irrational post-modernism (the humanities).

Philosophically, science is rooted in the values of the Enlightenment and modernity. This includes a metaphysics of naturalism and realism, and an epistemology which trusts both experience and reason as a means to knowledge. Science is indeed a relatively optimistic enterprise in that it posits that real progress and real improvements in understanding are achievable.

As the humanities have adopted an increasingly postmodern attitude they have grown comparatively pessimistic. Veering towards a radical relativism, the postmodern humanities actively argue against progress, and against sense experience and reason as a means to knowledge. At the extreme the entire Enlightenment/scientific project is reduced to mere social construction, no better or more certain than the mythologies of other cultures now or in other times [33, 34].

15.3.1 Postmodern Antipathy Towards Science

Postmodernism, deconstruction, critical theory and the like introduce notoriously elusive, slippery, and overlapping terms and ideas. Most adherents would argue that this must be the case because each is not so much a position as an attitude and an activity; an attitude of skepticism and activity that is in the business of destabilizing apparently clear and universal propositions [35].

Where modern art aspires to progress towards the absolute, postmodern art celebrates the circulation of a plurality of ideas while denying any notion of ultimate progress towards singular totalizing views. In his foundational treatise "The Postmodern Condition" [36] Lyotard cites both political and linguistic reasons why, in his view, this must be so. In his formulation of deconstruction Derrida emphasizes this break with structuralism. He denies the notion that language corresponds to innate or specific mental representations, let alone the noumenal world. Rather, at most, language is an unfixed system of traces and differences. And, regardless of the intent of the author, texts (i.e., all media including art) always reveal multiple, possibly contradictory, meanings [37].

As part of the art manifesto aspect of this chapter I will now make a number of observations regarding postmodernism. First, it's worth noting that the effect of postmodernism on art has included a number of changes for the better. Postmodernism has offered a useful corrective to the theoretical rigidity of some modern art criticism. Postmodernism has created the basis for many new threads in art such as identity art, the leveling of high and low art, and the development of political art as activism. Most of all postmodernism has promoted racial, ethnic, and sexual diversity in art in a way that perhaps modernism should have, but seldom achieved.

But postmodern art has also introduced significant problems by keeping the world at an ironic arm's length and viewing sincerity as a naive indulgence of the past. Some find postmodern art to be overly political to the point of blind reductionism. And postmodern art at times seems to be a snake eating its own tail, as it produces increasingly insular art about art (about art,...).

Perhaps most unfortunately, art students are steeped in postmodernism without explicit exposure to its derivation and development. And, worse yet, they are not offered the philosophical alternatives. These students may take required science classes, but very few will study the philosophy of science from the point of view of Enlightenment values. And so generations of art students now take as axiomatic the conclusions of postmodern writers, most often in the form of slogans such as:

- Science is not objective discovery, it is merely social construction (after Lyotard).
- Language has no fixed meaning. There are only traces and word games (after Derrida).
- The author is dead, and any meaning is created by the reader (after Barthes).
- There is no truth, merely discourse and (political) power (after Foucault).

At this point postmodernism has become for most young artists uninspected received wisdom, and a conceptual box from which they can find little escape.

The schism between the arts and humanities reached a new high with the so-called "science wars" of the 1990s. Anxious to bolster the standing of postmodernism in the face of ongoing scientific progress, those in the humanities began to critique the scientific method as part of "science studies." Science studies both attempts to destabilize scientific knowledge, and at the same time co-opt concepts from 20th century science that could be interpreted as epistemological challenges. Targets for postmodern appropriation include Einstein's theory of relativity, quantum mechanics, the Heisenberg uncertainty principle, Gödel's theorem, and more [34].

Most of those scientists who cared to comment at all typically labeled such writing as non-science at best, and nonsense at worst [34, 38]. The debate reached fever pitch when physicist Alan Sokal's essay, published in the fashionable academic journal "Social Text," was revealed as a content-free parody of postmodern writing. It was intended to demonstrate by way of a hoax the lack of rigor in postmodern science studies [34, 39].

15.3.2 Postmodernism and Science-Inspired Art

For better or worse postmodernism, deconstruction, and critical theory are the dominant worldviews within which contemporary art theory and criticism operates. Not surprisingly most mainstream artists who approach scientific concerns do so with skepticism, irony, and political antagonism. The few artists who actively embrace scientific ideas find themselves in a sort of conceptual no-man's-land between the warring factions, and somewhat estranged from both sides.

Blais and Ippolito exhibit this alienation in their survey of some 50 technology-artists called "At the Edge of Art."[2] Coming from the subcultures of the museum and the academic art world, they express a kind of ambivalence as they praise expressive work using technology, and yet can't quite bring themselves to call it art.

[2] The author of this chapter is one of the artists profiled.

> "Far from the traditional epicenters of artistic production and distribution, creative people sitting at computer keyboards are tearing apart and rebuilding their society's vision of itself. Though they may call themselves scientists, activists, or entrepreneurs rather than poets or artists, many of these visionaries are playing the roles of Dante or Da Vinci. Unlike the Soviet artist-engineers or Happening participants of the past century, who pushed artistic practice to the edge from within the avant-garde, many of the most innovative creators of the new century hail from other disciplines." [40]

One might think that with the rise of "new media" and technology-based art artists could find shelter from postmodern skepticism. But contemporary commentary on technology-based art is firmly rooted in the postmodern critique.

One example of this is Lovejoy's "Postmodern Currents – Art and Artists in the Age of Electronic Media." This book documents the late 20th century history of media art, and is something of a standard text in art schools. Lovejoy reiterates the popular claim that somehow contemporary media technology is the physical manifestation of postmodern theory.

> "George Landow, in his Hypertext: the Convergence of Critical Theory and Technology, demonstrates that, in the computer, we have an actual, functional, convergence of technology with critical theory. The computer's very technological structure illustrates the theories of Benjamin, Foucault, and Barthes, all of whom pointed to what Barthes would name "the death of the author." The death happens immaterially and interactively via the computer's operating system." [41]

The supposed influence of critical theory on computer architecture would no doubt come as a surprise to the engineers who actually create the technology without any need to consult the guiding principles of postmodernism. And the quote is hardly an isolated idea. As the title indicates, postmodernism is the conceptual thread upon which Lovejoy strings all manner of (often unrelated) examples of technology art.

Another example is Wilson's encyclopedic survey "Information Arts – Intersections of Art, Science, and Technology." This publication includes all manner of art using digital technology, especially those which somewhat recursively address science and technology as subject matter. His embrace of postmodernism as a context for the artistic exploration of science is less committed, but he leaves no doubt about its nearly universal effect on the field, and is candid about his use of critical theory as an organizing principle for his book.

> "In recent years, critical theory has been a provocative source of thought about the interplay of art, media, science, and technology. Each of the major sections of this book presents pertinent examples

> of this analysis. However, in its rush to deconstruct scientific research and technological innovation as the manifestations of metanarratives, critical theory leaves little room for the appearance of genuine innovation or the creation of new possibilities. While it has become predominant in the arts, it is not so well accepted in the worlds of science and technology." [42]

"Not so well accepted" indeed.

The point here is not to say that Lovejoy and Wilson alone set art, and especially technology-related art, in a postmodern context. They, as careful commentators surveying technology-based art, have correctly identified postmodern ideas as dominating the field. Postmodernism continues as the currently operative paradigm in the arts, even the high-tech arts.

15.3.3 Postmodernism in Crisis

As a central part of the art manifesto aspect of this chapter I'm asserting that it is time to go beyond postmodernism. Like all waves of philosophical skepticism, postmodernism taken to its ultimate conclusion leads to an intellectual and existential dead-end. And, indeed, even in the arts and humanities there is a vague sense that postmodernism has been "played out." There are, however, few suggestions and no consensus as to what comes next. The problems, though, are glaring.

First, postmodernism is guilty of what is termed a performative contradiction. Postmodernism, as a form of skepticism, seeks to undermine all claims to knowledge by demonstrating that all propositions are merely consensual realities and word games constructed by, and relative to, a given culture. But such a claim is so epistemologically corrosive that it also undermines the ability of would-be postmodernists to make the claim in the first place. In other words, if postmodernism must allow that it too is merely a word game and a social construction without intrinsic truth-value, why should anyone take it seriously?

Second, over time it has become increasingly clear that postmodernism is, as much as anything, a specific form of politics. As philosopher Stephen Hicks points out, if postmodernism was purely an epistemological position one would expect to find postmodernists across the political spectrum from left to right. In fact, postmodernists are uniformly left wing, and for many postmodern rhetoric is first and foremost a political tool. Hicks, tracing skepticism from Rousseau to Foucault, makes a convincing case that postmodernism has become a sort of philosophical survival shelter for literate disappointed socialists. Modernism, by contrast, is politically orthogonal, and science can be embraced by both those on the left and the right [33].

Finally, postmodernism taken to its natural end, leads to a nihilism that is simply impossible to live out. It's one thing to be philosophically skeptical, but if one were to actually apply that skepticism to everyday decisions it's hard to know how one could ever leave the house. In a way related to the performative contradiction, postmodernism in practice inevitably leads to acts of philosophical bad faith and hypocrisy.

Artists who embrace Enlightenment values and science find themselves in the minority, and all too often the objects of dismissal as remnants of a long discarded modernism. This is a problem, but also an opportunity. Evolutionary artists, and other artists working with complex generative systems, are standing right where the foundation for a new bridge between the sciences and humanities must be built.

15.4 Complexism – A New Science-Friendly Paradigm for the Arts and Humanities

In this final section I would like to bring the speculative art manifesto aspect of this chapter to the fore. My proposal is that complexism is that which comes after postmodernism. Complexism is, in a sense, the projection of the world-view and attitude suggested by complexity science into the problem space of the arts and humanities. Complexism does this by providing a higher synthesis that subsumes both modern and postmodern concerns, attitudes, and activities.

15.4.1 Complexism and the Challenges of Uncertainty and Incompleteness

Complexism must provide an account that takes into consideration the changes that took place in science in the 20th century. In the move from classical to modern physics the Laplace clockwork universe was replaced with an uncertain statistical universe. No longer could one fantasize that given a full inventory of masses and velocities, one could deduce the state of the universe at any time. Quantum mechanics and Heisenberg uncertainty have forever removed that possibility. And at larger scales chaotic dynamics ensure that a deterministic universe will always, even in principle, remain unpredictable.

Complexism must also embrace the limits intrinsic to logic and mathematics as revealed by metamathematics. David Hilbert's program to deduce all mathematics using a formal grammar of provably consistent axioms was stopped dead in its tracks by Gödel's incompleteness theorem [43]. Gödel proved that in any axiomatic system there are going to be truths that cannot be proven. Resonating with independent work by Church [44], Turing demonstrated an algorithmic parallel in that there will always be programs whose end-state cannot be predicted without actually being run [45]. Chaitin extended this work to demonstrate that axiomatic systems can, in fact, contain an uncountable number of unprovable truths [46, 47].

Complexism must leapfrog the attempt by postmodern science studies to appropriate via misinterpretation these epistemologically loaded ideas. Yes, even simple physical systems are cloaked in uncertainty. And yes, there will always be mathematical truths that cannot be proven. And of course this shakes to its core the kind of early Enlightenment optimism maintained by a Laplace or a Hilbert. But none of these findings has brought science or mathematics to a halt. In fact understanding that knowledge is bracketed by uncertainty and incompleteness is in itself a major triumph of 20th century science and mathematics. And within those brackets the 20th century yielded unprecedented progress on virtually every scientific and mathematical front.

The problem is that 20th century science and mathematics have yet to be put in an appropriate cultural context. The accurate assimilation of these powerful ideas into the general culture will provide complexist artists with subject matter for many years to come.

15.4.2 Complexism and the Reconciliation of Modernism and Postmodernism

Without any specific commitment to literal Hegelian philosophy, the reconciliation of modernism and postmodernism by complexism can be best described with a thesis-antithesis-synthesis model. Remember that we are talking here about a paradigm for the arts and humanities. As such complexism is more about attitude than rigor, and more about metaphor than quantification.

Taking modernism as the thesis, and postmodernism as the antithesis, both can be described with a series of apparently irreconcilable polar opposites. For example, where modernism looks to the absolute, postmodernism emphasizes the relative, and where modernism posits progress, postmodernism denies progress. Under this scheme complexism can offer a point-by-point synthesis that in its totality suggests a new paradigm. A synthetic attempt like complexism should be expected to take many years to develop, but a first approximation is offered in Table 15.1 and in the discussion below.

Modernism	Postmodernism	Complexism
Absolute	Relative	Distributed
Progress	Circulation	Emergence & Co-evolution
Fixed	Random	Chaotic
The Author	The Text	The Generative Process
Authority	Contention	Feedback
Truth	No Truth	Incomplete truth known to be not fully knowable
Pro Formalism	Anti Formalism	Form as public process not privilege
Hierarchy	Collapse	Connectionist networks

Table 15.1. Complexism as a higher synthesis of modernism and postmodernism

Modernism, whether in the sciences or in the hands of painters such as Rothko and Pollock, reflected Enlightenment values in reaching for the absolute and the fixed. The postmodern attitude rejects the absolute, and rather posits a multivalent view of relative positions that are, ultimately, as good as random. Complexism reconciles the absolute with the relative by viewing the world as a widely interconnected distributed process. Complexism posits a systems view where processes may be neither fixed nor random, but are instead chaotic. Complexism will nurture in the broader culture a visceral appreciation of how the world can be deterministic and yet unpredictable.

Where modernism posits progress, and postmodernism rejects progress for multiple contingencies in constant circulation, complexism looks towards the emergence of co-evolved possibilities. Co-evolved entities achieve real progress in the relative context of each other, and success remains a moving target rather than a fixed end-state. In human communications the modernist ideal posited the gifted author (scientist or artist) in a demonstrable position of authority. The postmodern retort is that the reader creates the meaning of the text (experiment or artwork), and such readings should be contentious via deconstruction. In complexism the flow of information is seen to require agents acting as both authors and readers, creating a generative process based on constant mutual feedback.

Where modernism posits hierarchies, postmodernism seeks to collapse them. Complexism doesn't erase relationships, but nor does it mandate hierarchies. Complexism emphasizes connectionist models and networks, creating systems of peer agents rather than leaders and followers. Where modernism aspired to absolute truth, and postmodernism denied any possibility of truth, complexism acknowledges known limits to human knowledge, but takes seriously the incomplete and statistical scientific truths that are achievable.

15.4.3 Complexism and the Importance of Evolutionary Art

Complexism has revolutionary implications for art. For example, modern art embraced formalism, i.e., the study of significant form. Whether by representation or abstraction, formalism was celebrated as the heroic pursuit of the specially gifted artist. Postmodernism rejected formalism as a fetishistic pursuit of meaningless beauty that makes false claims to authority and privilege along the way.

Complexism rehabilitates formalism, but not as a privileged view. Complexist formalism is a public process where form is an understandable property created by underlying generative processes. Static form is no longer meaningless but rather serves as an icon for the systems from which it emerges.

It was noted earlier that some generative art uses a system "in the studio" to create an object that is displayed to an audience at a later time, while other generative art displays systems in action to an audience in real time. As useful and interesting as the former is, it is the latter that best expresses what is revolutionary about complexism. Because in its purest form generative art using complex systems is about the dynamics of complex systems.

Complexism not only rehabilitates formalism, it perhaps more importantly reintroduces the artistic notion of dynamism. As originally introduced by the Futurists, dynamism celebrated the aesthetic of the locomotive and the racecar, and called for the exploration of motion and process rather than portraying objects as being frozen in time [48].

Dynamism in complex art is the visceral appreciation of the beauty of dynamics as more fully revealed in the context of complexity. In a sense, formalism is to nouns as dynamism is to verbs. With its focus on complex generative systems, complex art encourages artists to move from art objects to art processes, i.e., from nouns to verbs.

Through the 19th century generative artists primarily used simple highly ordered systems. The 20th century saw the rise of generative art using simple highly disordered systems. In the 21st century we are starting to see an explosion of generative art using complex systems in the realm between order and disorder. Evolutionary art, at the apex of the effective complexity curve, completes the full spectrum and history of generative art.

Presented in its purest form rather than as a means to some other end, evolutionary art takes complexism as both its content and working method. Evolutionary art demonstrates the reconciliation of the sciences and humanities by providing a visceral experience of the distribution, emergence, coevolution, feedback, chaos and connectionism that are the hallmarks of the new paradigm of complexism.

Evolutionary art, especially when offered as an ongoing process rather than a static object, presents the dance of formalism and dynamism. It underscores how each arises from the other, and marks a radical shift of emphasis in art away from nouns and towards verbs.

In short, evolutionary art creates the dynamic icons by which complexism can become known and understood, and in doing so creates a new paradigmatic meeting place for the sciences and humanities.

References

1. Kolocotroni, V., Goldman, J., Taxidou, O. (1998). *Modernism: An Anthology of Sources and Documents.* Edinburgh University Press. Edinburgh
2. Waldrop, M. (1992). *Complexity: The Emerging Science at the Edge of Order and Chaos.* Simon and Schuster. New York
3. Cohen, J., Stewart, I. (1994). *The Collapse of Chaos: Discovering Simplicity in a Complex World.* Viking. New York
4. Flake, G.W. (1998). *The Computational Beauty of Nature: Computer Explorations of Fractals, Chaos, Complex Systems, and Adaptation.* MIT Press. Cambridge, MA, USA
5. Cambel, A.B. (1993). *Applied Chaos Theory: A Paradigm for Complexity.* Academic Press. Boston

6. Smith, P. (1998). *Explaining Chaos.* Cambridge University Press. New York
7. Kauffman, S.A. (1995). *At Home in the Universe: The Search for Laws of Self-Organization and Complexity.* Oxford University Press. New York
8. Bar-Yam, Y. (1997). *Dynamics of Complex Systems.* Addison-Wesley
9. Shannon, C.E. (1948). A mathematical theory of communication. *The Bell System Technical Journal,* **27**(3): 379–423
10. Gell-Mann, M. (1995). What is complexity? *Complexity,* **1**: 16–19
11. Kolmogorov, A.N. (1965). Three approaches to the quantitative definition of information. *Problems in Information Transmission,* **1**: 1–7
12. Solomonoff, R.J. (1964). A formal theory of inductive inference (part i and part ii). *Information and Control,* **7**: 1–22, 224–254
13. Chaitin, G.J. (1966). On the length of programs for computing finite binary sequences. *Journal of the ACM,* **13**(4): 547–569
14. Galanter, P. (2003). What is generative art? Complexity theory as a context for art theory. In: *International Conference on Generative Art.* Milan, Italy
15. Hargittai, I., Hargittai, M. (1994). *Symmetry: A Unifying Concept.* Shelter Publications. Bolinas, Calif. Berkeley
16. Stevens, P.S. (1981). *Handbook of Regular Patterns: An Introduction to Symmetry in Two Dimensions.* MIT Press. Cambridge, Mass.
17. Washburn, D.K., Crowe, D. (1988). *Symmetries of Culture: Theory and Practice of Plane Pattern Analysis.* University of Washington Press. Seattle
18. Escher, M.C., et al. (1982). *M. C. Escher, His Life and Complete Graphic Work.* H.N. Abrams. New York
19. Meyer, J.S. (2000). *Minimalism. Themes and Movements.* Phaidon. London
20. Alberro, A., Stimson, B. (2000). *Conceptual Art: A Critical Anthology.* MIT Press. Cambridge, Mass.
21. Balter, M. (2002). From a modern human's brow – or doodling? *Science,* **295**(5553): 247–248
22. Schwanauer, S.M., Levitt, D.A., eds. (1992). *Machine Models of Music.* MIT Press. Cambridge, MA, USA
23. Bois, Y.A., Cowart, J., Pacquement, A. (1992). *Ellsworth Kelly: The years in France, 1948–1954.* National Gallery of Art, Prestel
24. Sobieszek, R.A., Burroughs, W.S. (1996). *Ports of Entry: William S. Burroughs and the Arts.* Thames and Hudson Ltd.
25. Nyman, M. (1999). *Experimental Music: Cage and Beyond.* 2nd edn. Music in the Twentieth Century. Cambridge University Press
26. Holmes, T. (2002). *Electronic and Experimental Music: Pioneers in Technology and Composition.* 2nd edn. Routledge. New York
27. Mandelbrot, B.B. (1983). *The Fractal Geometry of Nature. Updated and augmented.* W.H. Freeman. San Francisco
28. Prusinkiewicz, P., Lindenmayer, A., Hanan, J.S., Fracchia, F.D., Fowler, D.R., de Boer, M.J.M., Mercer, L. (1991). *The Algorithmic Beauty of Plants (The virtual laboratory).* Springer
29. Casti, J.L. (1994). *Complexification: Explaining a Paradoxical World Through the Science of Surprise.* 1st edn. HarperCollins. New York
30. Steina, Vasulka, W. (2001). Instrumental video
31. Benthall, J. (1972). *Science and Technology in Art Today.* Praeger World of Art Series. Praeger. New York
32. Snow, C.P., Collini, S. (1993). *The Two Cultures.* Cambridge University Press

33. Hicks, S.R.C. (2004). *Explaining Postmodernism: Skepticism and Socialism from Rousseau to Foucault.* Scholargy Publishing, Inc.
34. Koertge, N. (2000). *A House Built on Sand: Exposing Postmodernist Myths about Science.* Oxford University Press, USA
35. Sim, S. (1999). *The Routledge Critical Dictionary of Postmodern Thought.* Routledge. New York
36. Lyotard, J.F. (1984). *The Postmodern Condition: A Report on Knowledge.* Vol. 10 of Theory and History of Literature. University of Minnesota Press
37. Caputo, J.D. (1996). *Deconstruction in a Nutshell: A Conversation with Jacques Derrida.* Perspectives in Continental Philosophy. Fordham University Press. New York
38. Sokal, A., Bricmont, J. (1999). *Fashionable Nonsense: Postmodern Intellectuals' Abuse of Science.* Picador. New York
39. Sokal, A. (2000). *The Sokal Hoax: The Sham that Shook the Academy.* University of Nebraska Press
40. Blais, J., Ippolito, J. (2006). *At the Edge of Art.* Thames and Hudson Ltd.
41. Lovejoy, M. (1996). *Postmodern Currents: Art and Artists in the Age of Electronic Media.* Prentice Hall
42. Wilson, S. (2002). *Information Arts: Intersections of Art, Science and Technology.* Leonardo Books. The MIT Press. Cambridge, Mass.
43. Gödel, K. (1934). On undecidable propositions of formal mathematical systems. In Davis, M., ed.: *The Undecidable.* Raven Press. New York, 41–71
44. Church, A. (1936). An unsolvable problem of elementary number theory. *American Journal of Mathematics*, **58**(2): 345–363
45. Turing, A.M. (1936). On computable numbers, with an application to the entscheidungsproblem. *Proceedings of the London Mathematical Society*, **2**(42): 230–265
46. Chaitin, G.J. (2006). *The Unknowable.* Discrete Mathematics and Theoretical Computer Science. Springer
47. Chaitin, G.J. (2002). *The Limits of Mathematics: A Course on Information Theory and the Limits of Formal Reasoning.* Discrete Mathematics and Theoretical Computer Science. Springer
48. Chipp, H.B., Selz, P.H., Taylor, J.C. (1968). *Theories of Modern Art; A Source Book by Artists and Critics.* Vol. 11 of California Studies in the History of Art. University of California Press. Berkeley

Part V

Future Perspectives

16

The Evolution of Artistic Filters

Craig Neufeld,[1] Brian J. Ross,[1] and William Ralph[2]

[1] Department of Computer Science, Brock University, 500 Glenridge Ave., St. Catharines, ON, Canada L2S 3A1 craig.neufeld@gmail.com, bross@brocku.ca
[2] Department of Mathematics, Brock University, 500 Glenridge Ave., St. Catharines, ON, Canada L2S 3A1 bralph@brocku.ca

Summary. Artistic image filters are evolved using genetic programming. The system uses automatic image analysis during fitness evaluation. Multi-objective optimization permits multiple feature tests to be applied independently. One unique fitness test is Ralph's bell curve model of aesthetics. This model is based on an empirical evaluation of hundreds of fine art works, in which paintings have been found to exhibit a bell curve distribution of color gradient. We found that this test is very useful for automatically evolving non-photorealistic filters that tend to produce images with painterly, balanced and harmonious characteristics. The genetic programming language uses a variety of image processing functions of varying complexity, including a higher-level paint stroke operator. The filter language is designed so that components can be combined together in complex and unexpected ways. Experiments resulted in a surprising variety of interesting "artistic filters", which tend to function more like higher-level artistic processes than low-level image filters. Furthermore, a correlation was found between an image having a good aesthetic score, and its application of the paint operator.

16.1 Introduction

This chapter presents an evolutionary art system that evolves artistic image filters. This approach differs from more conventional systems in a number of ways. Firstly, the system incorporates a novel mathematical model of aesthetics proposed by Ralph [1]. This model is based on an empirical study of fine art, in which a variety of paintings by master artists were shown to exhibit a bell-curve distribution of color gradients. By incorporating this aesthetic model in the evolutionary system, we are able to replace the human evaluation step with an automatic measurement of some aesthetic properties. This contrasts to interactive evo-art applications that rely on the artistic sensibilities of a human user to evaluate all images.

Secondly, our system is engineered to generate non-photorealistic image filters. This differs from the usual expression-based evolution of images. Image filters have several distinct artistic advantages over procedurally-generated images. Procedurally-generated images tend to be very abstract. Although this is not an inherent disadvantage, it does mean that resulting images usually lack recognizable high-level representational content, such as people, landscapes, objects, historical and social contexts, and so on. On the other hand, image filters transform an existing graphic design, painting, or photograph into something quite unique, while still inheriting the basic composition and content of the original. Therefore, a source image can be a base image which bootstraps the production of a filter that generates a new result.

The chapter is organized as follows. Section 16.2 reviews relevant background work in non-photorealistic rendering, evo-art applications, evolutionary computation, and multi-objective optimization. Section 16.3 discusses Ralph's mathematical model of aesthetics. Details of the genetic programming system, including GP language, fitness evaluation, and experimental parameters, are given in Sect. 16.4. Results are presented in Sect. 16.5. A discussion of the results is given in Sect. 16.6. Comparisons to related work are in Sect. 16.7. Concluding remarks and directions for future research are given in Sect. 16.8.

16.2 Background

Evolutionary image synthesis is well established [2, 3], and is a sub-area of the growing field of evolutionary art [4]. Historically, most evo-art is interactive, with the user taking the role of fitness evaluator [5, 6, 7, 8, 9, 10, 11]. The primary reason for supervised evolution is the significant technical obstacle in defining criteria for automatic analysis and evaluation, especially in a creative artistic context. Therefore, evo-art systems have typically required the artistic sensibilities of the user to subjectively evaluate each candidate image as generated by its evolved image expression, and assign it a score of merit. Amongst other controls, the user may manipulate a mutation rate parameter, so that the diversity of results can be accelerated or reduced as desired. This results in a genetic algorithm that takes the form of an iterative, manual tool for image exploration. Interactive evolution is less suitable for evolving preconceived styles of images, than it is as a creative tool for discovering new ones. Moreover, it can quickly exhaust the user, who must manually view and evaluate possibly thousands of images.

Automatic image evolution removes the user as an interactive fitness evaluator. The first such systems used image analysis functions evaluate rudimentary image features such as color, luminosity, and shape [12, 13, 14, 15]. These scores are then matched with those of a target image, with the intension of evolving a solution with scores as close as possible to the target. A related automated approach is in [16], which evolves procedural textures for 3D models.

Automated aesthetic image evolution has not been widely studied. However, as more research is directed towards scientific models of aesthetics (e.g., [17, 18]), their migration into evo-art application will become commonplace. Pioneering work by Baluja et al. uses an artificial neural network (ANN) as an image evaluation function within a GA [19]. Before evolution, the ANN is trained on sets of example images that have been deemed to be aesthetically appealing. Their system does generate images according to the evaluation by the ANN. It is unclear whether their ANN has learned any relevant aesthetic principles, especially given the vast quantity of training data used.

More recently, genetic programming using a fitness function encoding a model of aesthetics has been used by Machado et al. in the NEvAr system [20]. That model posits that images are aesthetically pleasing if they are both visually complex, as well as easy for the brain and visual system to perceive and interpret. Two mathematical measurements are used: (i) image complexity is measured by the JPEG compression ratio; (ii) visual self-similarity is indicated by the fractal compression ratio. Their aesthetic model was applied to the "Design Judgment Test", which is a standardized psychological test used to evaluate art appreciation [17]. Impressively, the model scored better than typical art students.

Recently, an aesthetic distance metric was proposed as a means for measuring the information proximity between candidate images and a library of images preclassified to be aesthetically pleasing [21]. Although the metric was successfully tested against user preferences during interactive image evolution, it has not been tested extensively in automatic image evolution.

16.2.1 Evolutionary Art and Image Filter Synthesis

Evolutionary computation has been used to evolve image filters. The essential difference between an image filter and a procedural image generator is that a filter transforms the source image's pixel values into new values, whereas a procedural image expression generates pixel values from scratch. Beyond this technical difference, filters and image generators are very similar, and are easily combined together.

Poli and Cagnoni use interactive GP to evolve filters that generate false color enhancements of images, which make them more suitable for visual analysis [22]. Lewis uses interactive evolution to synthesize filters to apply to video footage [23]. Genetic FX Studio [24] is an interactive system that primarily uses mutation to evolve image filters.

Machado et al. use GP to evolve image coloring filters [25]. Unlike Poli's and Cagnoni's system, they do this in an automatic environment, with the intension of creating artistically styled colorizations of grayscale images. Given the HSV channels for an image, they evolve a function that computes the hue from the brightness value. This is done by comparing computed results to desired training examples. The intension is to evolve a filter that is generalizable to other grayscale images.

Yip uses evolutionary computation to evolve image filters [26]. A genetic algorithm uses fixed-size chromosomes that translate into linear filter sequences. Yip's system performs image evaluation using a number of feature tests, which are combined into a score using user-defined weights. Automatic evaluation compares this score to that of a target image, which is taken as having desirable aesthetic qualities to be matched by the evolved filter. The goal is to find a filter sequence that results in a filtered image with similar characteristics to the target image.

16.2.2 Non-Photorealistic Rendering

Non-photorealistic rendering (NPR) is a major area of computer graphics research. The goals of NPR are less constrained than that of photorealistic rendering, since any rendering effect which is not intended to produce realism can qualify as an NPR technique. Many basic filters from computer vision and image processing can create rudimentary NPR effects [27]. More advanced techniques are interested in simulating effects as found in natural media, such as pencils, oils, and watercolors [28, 29]. NPR technology is widespread in commercial tools such as Adobe Photoshop.

Although a review of NPR technology is outside the scope of this chapter, one research paper is of note. Shiraishi and Yamaguchi present a method of automatic paint stroke rendering [30]. Given a photograph or other image, their system analyzes it in terms of color layout and image detail, and generates a rendering that appears as if it were painted with discrete brush strokes. We adopt the essential ideas from their paint stroke renderer as a primitive in our GP language.

16.2.3 Multi-Objective Optimization

A multi-objective problem is characterized by having two or more fitness criteria [31]. Multi-objective search strategies consider each feature test as an independent dimension in the search space. The common alternative is to merge scores together, usually with a weighted sum, and thereby create a single objective for the search. Weights are usually *ad hoc*, introduce bias into the search, and can be detrimental to the quality of solutions obtained for nontrivial problems.

We interpret the evaluation of images using the multi-objective approach from [14]. When filters are added to a new population, multiple feature tests will be derived for their generated images. These scores are used to determine a *Pareto ranking* of all the individuals in the population. Pareto ranks are partial orderings based on the idea of *domination*. One individual dominates another if it is at least as good in all the scores, and better in at least one. Individuals having rank 1 are undominated, and are the current best solutions in the population. Those of rank $k > 1$ are dominated by all the individuals of ranks $< k$. All the individuals in a rank are incomparable with one another.

At the end of a run, all those with rank 1 are considered as valid solutions to the problem.

After the Pareto ranks are determined, the individuals in each rank are evaluated with respect to their diversity. Filters in a rank are considered superior within that rank if they are more diverse with respect to their location in the multi-dimensional search space. Diversity scoring evaluates the proximity of each filter to its nearest neighbor in feature space. Unique filters are given better scores within the rank than those that are minor variations of each other. The desired outcome is a diverse selection of solutions.

16.3 A Mathematical Model of Aesthetics

Measurable aspects of artificial and natural phenomena often exhibit particular kinds of mathematical distributions. For example, the well known *1/f* distribution is found in diverse areas such as natural images [32] and human cognition [33]. One famous example examining 1/f noise in music is the work of Voss and Clarke [34]. They show that the differences in successive pitches in notes (pitch gradients) exhibit 1/f distributions. Furthermore, stochastically-generated music based on 1/f noise generators is more aesthetically pleasing than that generated by pure random or white noise generators.

A mathematical model characterizing aesthetic aspects of fine art has been proposed by Ralph [1]. The following gives a simplified overview of the theory. After analyzing hundreds of examples of fine art, it was found that many works consistently exhibit functions over color gradients that conform to a normal or bell curve distribution. This is seen with many artists, such has Cezanne and Seurat, who create "painterly" images.

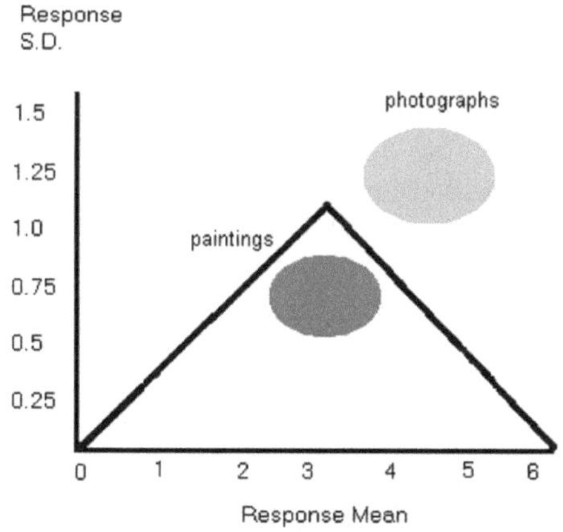

Fig. 16.1. Gradient response distributions

In Fig. 16.1, the circular area within the triangle shows the space where such paintings' gradient response measurements normally fall. This is a "sweet spot" that is a locus for the corpus of paintings studied. This normal distribution of gradient response is claimed to be difficult to realize, since it is essentially characterizing the global distribution of gradient throughout an entire image: local changes can affect the distribution found throughout the entire painting. It is hypothesized that this bell curve distribution has been an implicit aesthetic ideal of many painters throughout history. On the other hand, the visual responses of much contemporary art, photographs and graphic design work usually do not have normal distributions, and which reside outside of the triangle.

The bell curve model posits that a viewer's response to an image is largely determined by his or her psycho-neurological reaction to visual stimuli. When viewing an artwork, a viewer's visual system is stimulated by the details of the image. The bell curve model suggests that a viewer is most attracted to changes in an image, for example, the edges between different colors. The areas with constant colors are of less interest. Furthermore, larger changes are more noticeable than smaller ones. Since it is known that our nervous system tends to have a logarithmic reaction to stimuli, this model likewise treats measurements logarithmically.

The following calculations are performed on images using RGB color space. Ralph's studies, on the other hand, were performed in LAB color space. Although more precise results could be obtained if we used LAB space as well, we opted for RGB space for efficiency reasons.

The first step is to compute an image's color gradient. This is done by computing the following for each pixel (i,j) of an RGB image (ignoring the extrema row and column of the image buffer):

$$|\nabla r_{i,j}|^2 = \frac{(r_{i,j} - r_{i+1,j+1})^2 + (r_{i+1,j} - r_{i,j+1})^2}{d^2}$$

where $r_{i,j}$ is the red value at pixel (i,j). Similar computations are done for the green and blue channels. The d value is a scaling factor that is used to scale the result for images having different dimensions. We take it to be 0.1% of half the diagonal length, scaled for typical pixel densities on CRT monitors. The overall gradient or *stimulus* S is then:

$$S_{i,j} = \sqrt{|\nabla r_{i,j}|^2 + |\nabla g_{i,j}|^2 + |\nabla b_{i,j}|^2}$$

for the separate RGB channel gradients. Finally, the *response* R is computed as:

$$R_{i,j} = \log(S_{i,j}/S_0)$$

where S_0 is the threshold of detection, which is taken to be 2. If $S_{i,j} = 0$ (no change in color at a pixel), it is ignored.

Next, the distribution of the response values for an image is determined. The calculation of the distribution is based on the hypothesis that the probability that a viewer pays attention to a detail of an image is proportional to the magnitude of the stimulus that resides at that detail. Hence we use a weighted mean and standard deviation, with $R_{i,j}$ being the weight value for each response. The normal distribution of R is then estimated using a weighted normal distribution, defined by a mean (μ) and standard deviation (σ^2):

$$\mu = \frac{\sum_{i,j}(R_{i,j})^2}{\sum_{i,j} R_{i,j}} \qquad \sigma^2 = \frac{\sum_{i,j} R_{i,j}(R_{i,j}-\mu)^2}{\sum_{i,j} R_{i,j}} .$$

Once μ and σ^2 are found for an image, the actual distribution of all $R_{i,j}$ for all pixels in the image is tabulated. Using a bin width of $\sigma/100$, a histogram is calculated, where each $R_{i,j}$ updates its corresponding bin using a weight of $R_{i,j}$.

Finally, the closeness of fit between the response actual distribution and the hypothesized bell distribution is determined. This is called the *deviation from normality* or DFN. This is calculated as:

$$\text{DFN} = 1000 \sum p_i \log \left(\frac{p_i}{q_i} \right)$$

where p_i is the observed probability in the ith bin of the histogram, and q_i is the expected probability assuming a normal distribution with the computed mean and standard deviation above. When $q_i = 0$, that bin is ignored. A DFN value of 0 means that a perfect normal distribution exists, while higher DFN values indicate poorer fits to the normal distribution.

There are a number of practical advantages of the bell curve model. The DFN score is easily incorporated as a fitness score within the genetic algorithm. The bell curve model also permits a means for characterizing broad artistic styles. As discussed in [1], different styles of art are often characterized by their bell curve fit, as well as the associated mean and standard deviation of the distribution. Many paintings with good DFN's tend to have bell curves with a mean around 3.0 and a standard deviation of 0.75. Photographs have poor bell distributions, with means of around 4.2 and standard deviations of 1.2 or more. Graphic designs have even higher values. We have found that these values have some influence over general styles of images evolved by the genetic programming system. The ways in which the shape of distributions might characterize different artistic styles requires further investigation.

16.4 System and Experiment Details

Our filter evolution system is the latest variation of Gentropy, a genetic programming-based system which has been used in the past for image evolution [14, 15]. Gentropy's GP engine is the lilGP 1.1 system [35]. LilGP is written in C, and supports basic genetic programming [36].

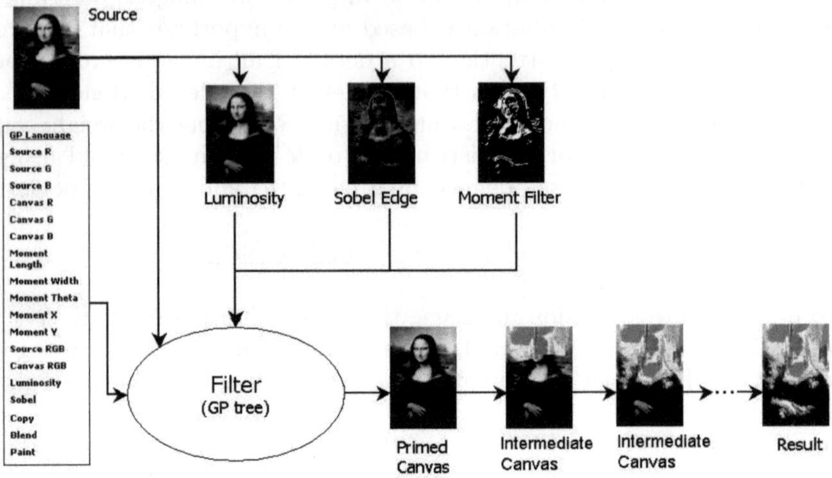

Fig. 16.2. Rendering process

Figure 16.2 shows the basic rendering scheme used by filters in the GP system. At the beginning of a run, a source image is read into the system. This is used as the training image by all candidate filters during evolution. This source image may be used as the color palette target image as well; however, another image may be used instead. The canvas is a dynamic buffer where the filter manipulates the image, and where the final filtered image will reside at the end of processing. It is initialized with the source image. Some pre-processing of the source image is also done, to create prefiltered images that will be used during rendering (see Sect. 16.4.1).

An image filter is a GP tree, which is usually a complex expression containing an assortment of language components selected from a library of functions and terminals. This expression can access both the original source image, as well as a canvas that has the intermediate output dynamically altered during processing. The filter processes the entire source image pixel-by-pixel, from top-to-bottom, and left-to-right. Before the GP tree is applied to a particular pixel location, that pixel's source RGB, moment parameters, luminosity, and Sobel filter values are made available to the corresponding terminals in the tree. The execution of a filter at a source pixel results in an RGB color generated at the root of the tree, which represents the new value of the source image pixel. This color is written to the current pixel location on the canvas. During execution, however, many functions may produce spatial changes over multiple pixels the proximity of the current pixel. For example, a single call to the paint primitive will alter a swath of pixels on the canvas. Repeated calls of the filter for multiple pixels may result in complex, iterative rendering behavior.

16.4.1 Image Preprocessing

The source image is preprocessed to create a number of filtered images. These provide some rudimentary image analyses that can be exploited by the GP filter. A luminosity filter is generated for the source image, which converts colors into grayscale intensities. It uses the conversion: $L = 0.299r + 0.587g + 0.114b$. A Sobel edge analysis is also generated [27]. The horizontal and vertical edges are computed and combined, resulting in a grayscale gradient for the edges.

The following preprocessed data are motivated by the needs of the non-photorealistic paint primitive (Sect. 16.4.2). We use the paint rendering approach described in [30], with some modifications. First, a "point image" is created from the source. These points denote the salient features of an image at which paint brush strokes might normally be placed. The points are computed by applying a threshold of 0.5 to the Sobel image, resulting in a binary image in which values equal to 1 represent points.

Next, a color difference image is computed for each non-zero point in the point image. An N-by-N area of the source image is used around each point coordinate. N is computed to be a user-specified percentage of the largest dimension of the source image. The color difference is relative color distance between the center pixel and the other pixels in the local $N \times N$ area. This results in a value between 0.0 and 1.0, where 0.0 means that the color difference is large, and higher values indicate a closer proximity of color.

Once the color difference image is generated, moment calculations are performed. These determine the length (l), width (w), angle (θ), and center coordinate offsets (Δx, Δy) of a brush stroke to be placed at that point. Should a pixel location not correspond to a computed point in the point image (i.e., the point value is 0), then these values are 0. More information about these moment calculations can be found in [30].

16.4.2 Filter Language

The GP system uses strong typing in its formulation of program expressions [37]. Strong typing requires that the computed values for all operators, and arguments for all functions, be assigned data types. The filter language uses two data types, *float* and *vector*. A float is a floating point value. A vector is a triple of floats, which is easily translated into an RGB color.

Table 16.1 lists the float operators. Operators that do not have arguments are terminals in the GP program trees. Functions have specific types for their arguments. Operators that refer to the source, canvas, or preprocessed filter data, always return values relative to the currently pixel being processed. *Ephemeral constants* are float constants that are initially created with a random number generator. However, once generated, they retain their value throughout the lifetime of their existence. *source_R* is the red channel value of the current processed pixel in the source image. The green and

Table 16.1. Selection of float operators

Name	Arg. types	Description
ephem	-	ephemeral random constants ($-1.0 \leq X \leq 1.0$)
source_R, source_G, source_B	-	source R, G, B values
canvas_R, canvas_G, canvas_B	-	canvas R, G, B values
lum	-	luminence
sobel	-	Sobel
moment_θ	-	brush stroke angle
moment_ΔX, moment_ΔY	-	X, Y offset for center of brush stroke
moment_width	-	width of brush stroke
moment_height	-	height of brush stroke
lum	v	NTSC luminance of vector
avg	f,f	average of two arguments
if	f,f,f	If $arg_1 > 0.5$, then arg_2 is evaluated, else arg_3 is evaluated

Table 16.2. RGB vector operators

Name	Arg. types	Description
ephem	-	ephemeral random vector constant ($-1 \leq R, G, B \leq 1$)
source_RGB	-	RGB vector of source pixel
canvas_RGB	-	RGB vector of canvas pixel
lum_RGB	-	NTSC luminance vector of source pixel
sobel_RGB	-	Sobel vector value at source pixel
copy	f, f	pixel at x, y displacement replaces current pixel, and its color returned as result
blend	f, f	like copy, but pixel color is averaged with current pixel
median	f	returns the median pixel value of an $N \times N$ matrix, arg is interpreted modulo 3 to determine N = 3, 5, or 7
paint	f,f,f,f,f,f	paint, color fixed
general_paint	f,f,f,f,f,f,v	paint, color computed
if	f,v,v	(see float *if*)
v_rgb	f,f,f	create a vector from three floats

blue channels are similarly defined. Likewise, *canvas_R* is the red value of the current pixel in the canvas. The *lum* and *Sobel* are the grayscale values of the luminosity map and Sobel edge filter for the source image. The *moment* $\theta, \Delta X, \Delta Y$, *width* and *height* are the moment data for the current pixel. They are normally relevant to the vector paint function, but are available to any function in the GP tree. The *if* function is a decision operator. If its first float argument value is greater than 0.5, then the second argument is evaluated, and its value is returned as a result; otherwise the third argument is evaluated and returned. Other standard math operators are used, such as $+$, $-$, \, $*$, sine, cosine, log, etc.

The vector operators are shown in Table 16.2. Ephemeral vector constants are equivalent in function to the float ephemerals. Vector versions of the source, canvas, luminosity, and Sobel values are also defined. In the case of luminosity and Sobel, the vector has three copies of the grayscale value. The copy and blend operators read a single pixel value in the proximity of the current pixel, and copy or blend it respectively with the current pixel. *median* computes a local area median value for the source pixel. The *if* operator is identical to the float version, except that vector expressions are executed and returned as results. *v_rgb* generates a vector from three float arguments.

The two remaining vector operators, *paint* and *general_paint*, are the most complex and important operators in the language. They are implementations of the paint procedure from [30]. The *paint* operator expects the following arguments:

$$paint(brush\ pattern,\ \ width,\ \ length,\ \ \theta,\ \ \Delta X,\ \ \Delta Y)$$

where *brush pattern* is a float expression that is evaluated *modulo* 5 to choose a paint brush pattern (Fig. 16.3), *width* and *height* are the width and height for the scaled brush, θ is the brush stroke orientation, and ΔX and ΔY is the offset relative to the current pixel where the center of the brush stroke should be placed. Normally, most of these values would be determined by the moment calculation described in Sect. 16.4.1. If we supplied the moment values directly to the *paint* operator as arguments, the result would be one predetermined style of paint stroke for all evolved images. A key decision, however, is to have the paint arguments take the form of evolved internal subtrees. The paint operator is supplied with whatever values are computed by these subtree expressions, as well as the current source pixel's RGB color, and paints a brush stroke accordingly. Since additional calls to the paint operator may be embedded within the argument subtree, a single call to the paint operator can involve multiple calls to itself, resulting in a complex rendering process. As will be seen, giving evolution these liberties with the arguments results in a wide diversity of rendered images.

The *general_paint* operator is identical in functionality to *paint*, except that an additional vector argument is supplied, which represents the color that the paint stroke should use. With this single enhancement, *general_paint* is afforded more flexibility in rendering than *paint*, as the latter is forced to use the source color.

16.4.3 Fitness Evaluation

After a GP filter has been applied to the source image, the rendered result is analyzed to obtain a fitness score. We use two to four separate fitness criteria in our experiments. Gentropy uses the multi-objective optimization strategy described in Sect. 16.2.3. This permits the feature tests to be considered independently, without the need for user-supplied weights.

A feature test used in all experiments is quadratic color histogram matching (CHISTQ). This permits the user to specify a desired color palette, as defined by a *color target image.* This image may or may not be the same as the source image upon which the filter is applied. The CHISTQ test is often used in image content systems such as VisualSEEk [38]. This color test converts two images into quantized color histograms, and then performs a color distance measure on the histograms. The histogram for the color target image is calculated once at the start of the run, while every filter's rendered image has a new histogram calculated for it per fitness evaluation.

The other major feature test is the bell curve aesthetic analysis, as described in Sect. 16.3. Three scores are associated with the aesthetic model – the DFN (fit to normal distribution), and the distribution's mean and standard deviation. We always attempt to minimize the DFN, and 0.0 is the lowest score possible. The mean and standard deviation are associated with the gradient distribution, and correspond to differing visual characteristics in the image. For example, a very low mean value typically means that there is little visual change in an image. Although the mean and standard deviation are computed as part of the DFN calculation, they are independent of the actual DFN score, and are taken as separate objectives in the multi-objective search space. Therefore, any combination of DFN, mean, and standard deviation can be used as feature tests.

When using a multi-objective evaluation, a subset of rank 1 solutions is given as a result. Typically, if K objective scores are used, then solutions are strong in $N < K$ scores. Sometimes, a solution can be particularly strong in one single score (e.g., color), but terrible in another score (e.g., DFN). Fortunately, the nature of multi-objective evolution is that the entire population will generally improve in all objectives, yielding results that are respectable in all measured aspects of the problem.

16.4.4 Other Experimental Parameters

Table 16.3 lists conventional GP parameters common in all experiments. Details of these parameters can be found in the literature [36]. Each experiment was run a maximum of four times with a different random number seed. Since the result of a single run is a diversity of images from the rank 1 set, not many runs are required to obtain an interesting selection of filters. Since exact solutions are virtually impossible, all runs complete to the maximum limit of 40 generations.

The remaining parameters in Table 16.3 are peculiar to Gentropy. Because image analysis with the color histogram and DFN tests is time consuming, training images are by necessity small, and the resolution given in the table is typical. The move operator moves a pixel within a Cartesian range from the currently processed pixel coordinate. We use a range of 10% of the largest

Table 16.3. Genetic programming parameters

Parameter	Value
Runs/experiment	max 4
Population size	500
Generations	40
Initialization	ramped half&half
Initial ramped tree depth	2 to 6
Max. tree nodes	200
Max. tree depth	15
Crossover rate	0.9
Mutation rate	0.1
Selection scheme	tournament (size 3)
Solutions per run	10
Gentropy parameters:	
Training image resolution	approx 230 by 150
Move operator range	10%
# paint brush textures	5
Moment: local source size	4%
Moment: color range bound	150

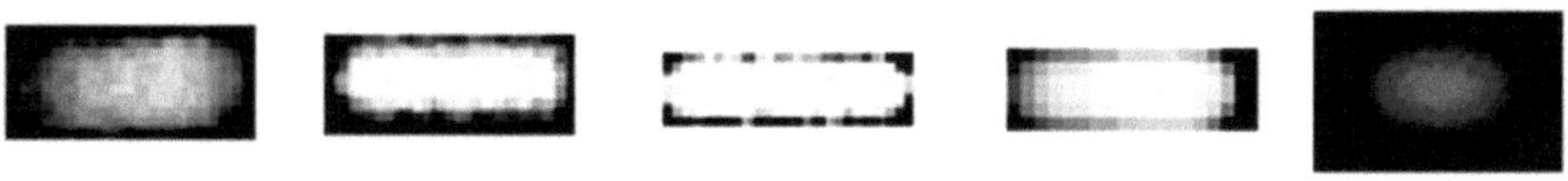

Fig. 16.3. Paint brushes

dimension of the image resolution. For the training image size in the table, this would be approximately 23 pixels. Five different grayscale paintbrush textures were used (Fig. 16.3). The moment filter's local source size is the percentage of the image's longest dimension to be used to compute the moment filter area size (see Sect. 16.4.1). This is also used as the maximum length and width of a brush stroke. The minimum dimension of a brush stroke is fixed at 2-by-2 pixel block. When generating the color difference image, the bound of similar color reflects the color distance range to consider, based on input images using 1-byte per RGB channel.

16.5 Results

This section gives example results for various experiments. To understand the nature of the aesthetic analysis, we sometimes report the DFN score and its associated mean and standard deviation scores. For efficiency reasons, the GP

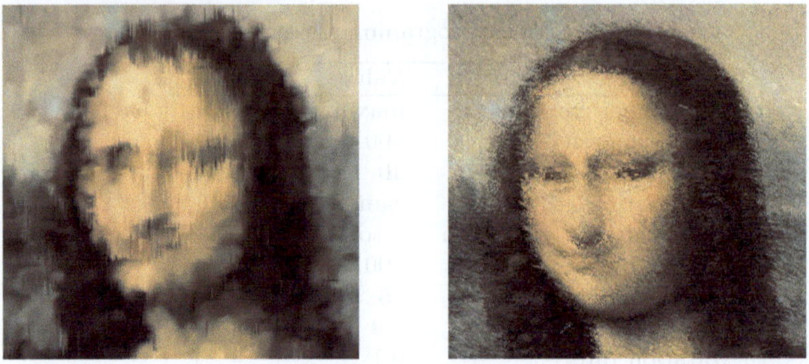

(a) DFN=4.3, MEAN=4.00, SD=1.01 (b) DFN=28.8, MEAN=4.58, SD=0.99

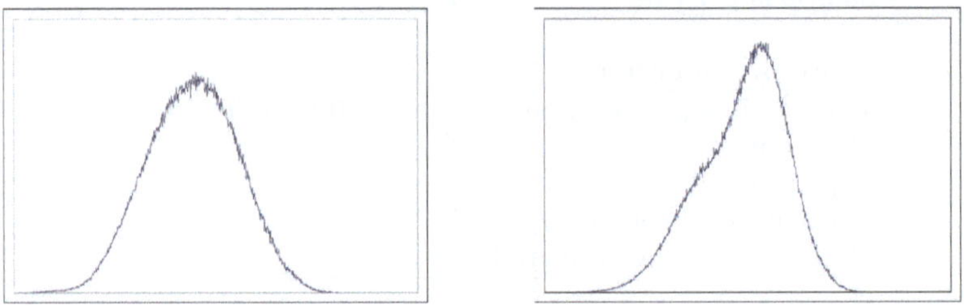

Fig. 16.4. Paint-based filters

system applies the DFN analysis to small resolution images. We display larger-resolution "test" images in this section, since they show more detail. The DFN scores are computed for the testing images using LAB color space, and after a 3×3 Gaussian blur is applied to them. The use of LAB space and Gaussian blur factor follows the scheme by Ralph [1]. Gaussian blur simulates what a viewer would see by sitting a small distance away from a monitor, rather than with their eyes against the screen. LAB space also permits comparison of our results to those studied by Ralph in Fig. 16.1.

For the examples in Fig. 16.4, we use a restricted filter language, in which the color-restricted paint operator is the only vector operator. We use the source image as the color target. The three objectives are to minimize DFN, maximize CHISTQ, and use a target mean of 3.75. These results are details from large resolution versions (1024 by 659) of smaller training images (231 by 149) used during evolution. The CHISTQ scores are in the high 0.90's, due to the color-restricted language. Filter (b) has more high frequency detail than (a), and hence has a higher DFN. The gradient response histograms for (a) and (b) are also shown. Image (a) has a more accurate bell curve than (b), corresponding to its lower DFN score.

Figure 16.5 repeats the previous experiment, but using the color target in (a), and an unrestricted language that is capable of generating new colors different from the source image. This is a challenging task for evolution, since

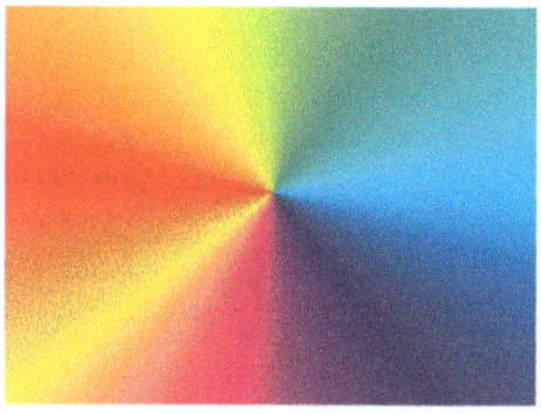

(a) Color target.

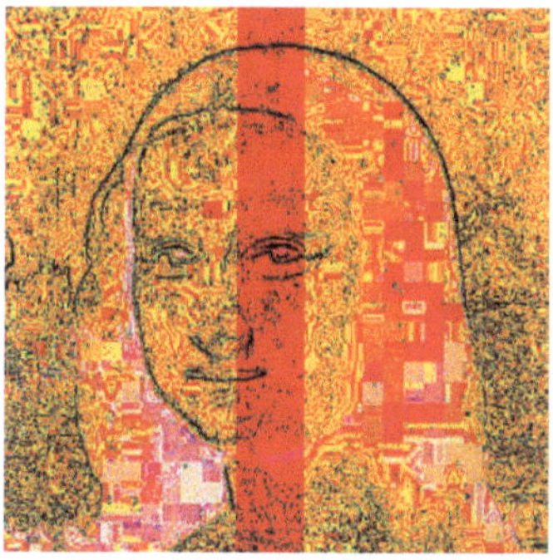

(c) DFN=119.3, CHISTQ=0.90

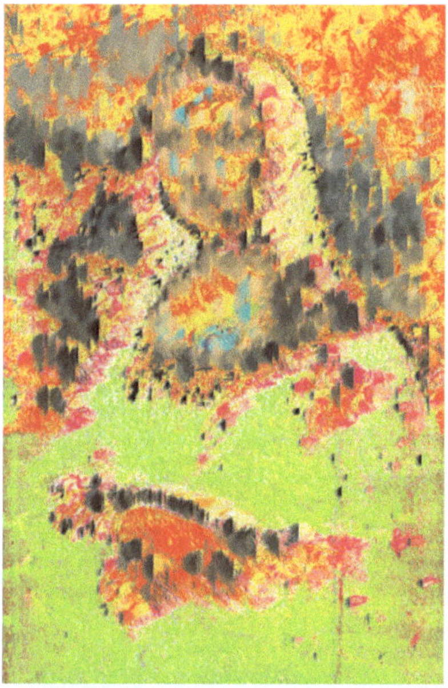

(b) DFN=77.8, CHISTQ=0.89

Fig. 16.5. Using an alternate color target

finding a good match for this rainbow color palette is detrimental to having a good DFN score, which prefers a more conservative palette with generous color gradient ranges. One interesting filter result is in (b), and its color palette is a combination of those from the source image and the color target image. An alternate solution is in (c), which found a good CHISTQ score, but by sacrificing the DFN. Such an image is typical of many results with high DFN scores. This filter did not use any paint primitive, and the result is a filter that is noisy and artificial in appearance.

Figure 16.6 shows one evolved filter applied to two different images. The target palette is in (b). The filter applied to the B&W photograph in (a) results in the colorized, painterly version in (c). This same filter is applied to the Mona Lisa in (d).

Figure 16.7 shows a variety of rendering effects possible using GP filters. They are selected from various experiments using different target and color target images, and applied to the Mona Lisa image.

Figure 16.8 shows the multi-objective performance of a single run. This experiment used four feature tests: CHISTQ, DFN, mean, and standard deviation. The DFN and CHISTQ scores are plotted for the top 10 individuals in rank 1, from generations 0, 20, and 40. The goal is to minimize DFN and maximize CHISTQ, i.e., the target marker at the bottom-right. As the run proceeds, individuals are tending to move down (lower DFN) and right

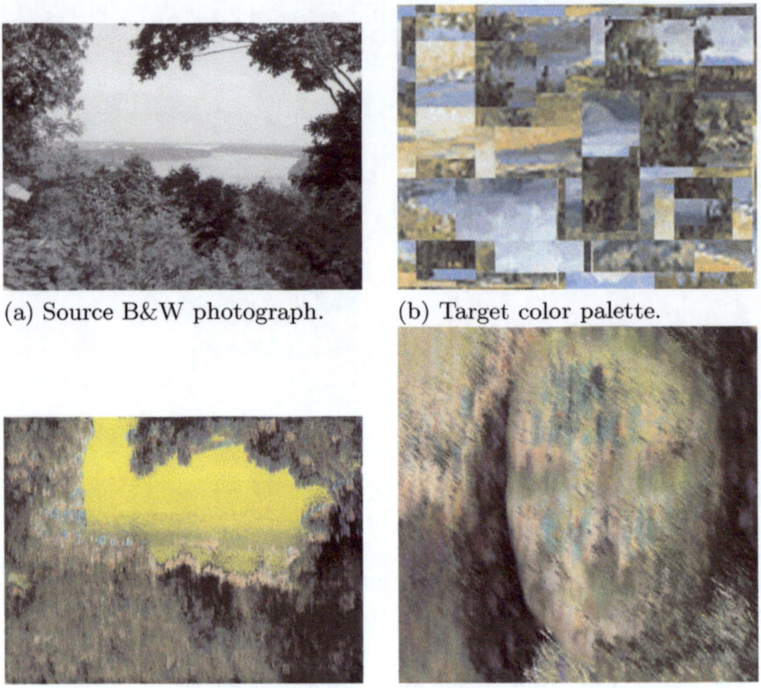

(a) Source B&W photograph. (b) Target color palette.

(c) Applied to (a). (d) Applied to Mona Lisa.

Fig. 16.6. A colorizing filter

(better color). Note that the other two unplotted tests disperse the population towards their targets scores, which detracts from satisfying the DFN and CHISTQ scores alone. For example, an individual whose color score has not improved, might have a much better mean score. The triangles at the bottom-right of the plotted group show improvements over all the generation 0 individuals.

16.6 Discussion

We do not claim that our filter evolution system guarantees the production of visually pleasing images. The results shown in Sect. 16.5 are culled from hundreds of less impressive images, to highlight exemplary results that we found interesting according to our own tastes. A great many results, including some with good scores, were not remarkable. Our feature tests are not canonical models of aesthetics, as such models do not yet exist. Rather, they are heuristic evaluations of beauty, and should not be interpreted literally. In general, lower DFNs indicate more balanced images, while higher DFNs correspond to more chaotic or boring ones. It is useful as a means to control

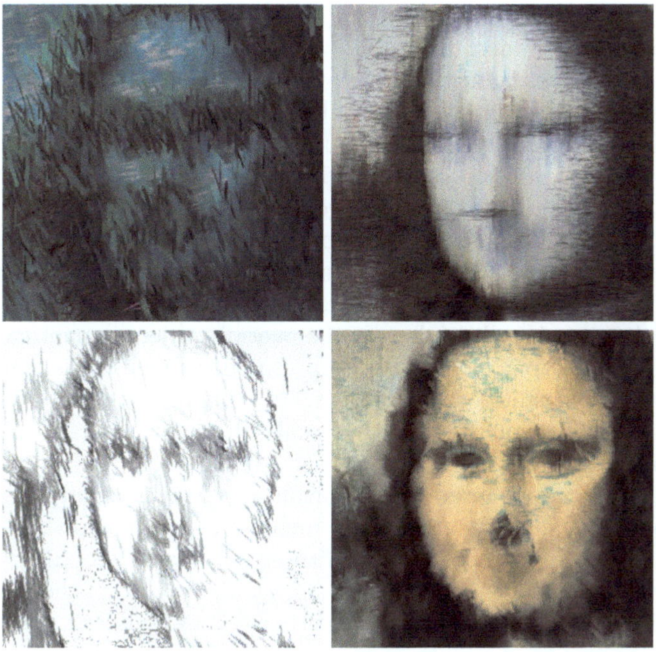

Fig. 16.7. Miscellaneous filters

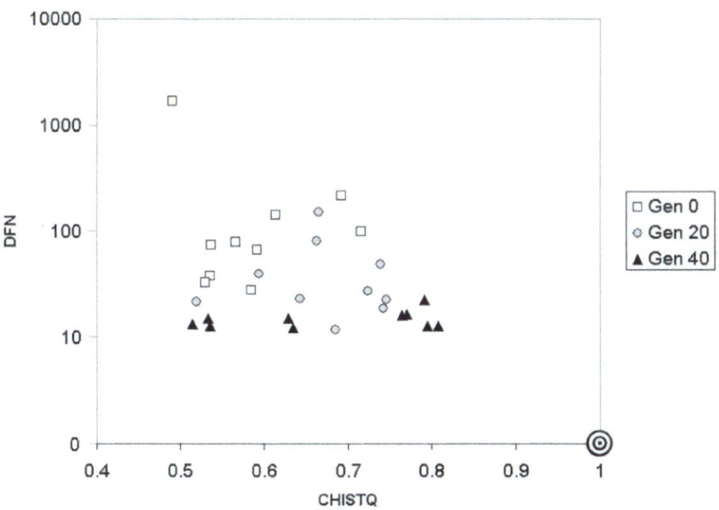

Fig. 16.8. Evolution performance for a run

the general characteristics of images, which is critical in automated synthesis, in which there is no human to watch over and guide evolution. Here, the bell gradient model plays the critical role of a "filter tamer", trying to move evolution towards areas of filter space that are *more likely* to produce balanced, harmonious, and painterly results.

Having good feature scores is an indication that an image has sound technical characteristics. For example, a good DFN score means that a level of detail exists that is similar to that found in many masterpieces. Whether such images succeed at a higher aesthetic level, however, cannot be assured. As is clear from examples in Sect. 16.5, images can be rendered in a convincing technical and painterly style, yet the overall subject matter can be alien, macabre, and horrifying. Beauty is interpretable at many levels, which are not encompassed in our suite of fitness tests.

It is worth stressing that all the results from our system are obtained entirely automatically, with no direct user influence over the direction of evolution. If the user were interactively involved, even more impressive results would be possible, since an artistically inclined person could then contribute significant aesthetic judgments to the fitness evaluation process. The current implementation does not give the user substantial control, other than setting the target images, filter language, and other GP parameters. After that, the GP system is given the freedom to search from an enormous range of filters to satisfy these criteria. Only at the end of a run, will a user determine whether the results are satisfactory. Hence, like other evo-art applications, ours uses evolution as a tool for discovery, from which many eclectic and fascinating results may arise. Ours is not a system which can be used to synthesize a filter that conforms to rigid, preconceived specifications [39].

The GP filter language is highly compositional, and permits the construction of complex image processing programs that are reactive to the visual characteristics of the source image. A larger resolution image of the source (training) image can result in a quite different rendered outcome than what occurred during training, should the large image have substantially different edge, luminosity, and color characteristics than the smaller source image. The most startling results are often obtained by applying a filter to an image different from the training image. This shows that there is a large amount of chance and discovery in our approach – qualities that have always been the strengths of evo-art applications.

16.6.1 Relationships Between the Aesthetic Model and Paint Operator

After many experiments, we suspected that there could be a correlation between the bell curve aesthetic model and the existence of paint strokes in an image: images tended to have lower DFN scores when the paint primitive was active. To help confirm this, we analyzed the source code of filters from a number of runs, to see if there is a correlation between the use of the paint

Table 16.4. Paint operator analysis

	DFN	No DFN
Average DFN:	102	232
Percent of filters with paint:	79%	53%
Avg freq of paint when used:	3.5	1.6
Avg highest depth of paint (root=1):	3.6	6.8

operator and the resulting DFN score. Two indicators that are suggestive that paint is active are the frequency of paint function calls in a program, and well as the depth of the paint calls within the GP tree. For example, a paint call residing at the root (depth = 1) is likely to be a key component in the filter.

We performed 24 runs, in which half the runs incorporated the DFN as an objective, and the other half did not. As before, the MEAN and CHISTQ were the other objectives. We analyzed the top 10 filters in each run, yielding 120 filters in total for both of the DFN and non-DFN cases.

Table 16.4 shows the result of our analysis. As expected, the runs using DFN as an objective generate solutions with lower DFNs. Nearly 80% of the solutions in these runs use a paint operator, compared to just over half of the non-DFN solutions. Filters in the DFN runs that incorporate the paint operator, use it nearly twice as frequently as the non-DFN filters. Most importantly, the DFN runs use paint much closer to the root of the tree, which suggests that it is likely instrumental in the rendering process, compared to its deeper, more covert placement in the non-DFN filters.

We speculate that the bell curve gradient distribution might be a characteristic of painting styles that exploit visible paint strokes. Many of the painting styles studied by Ralph [1], such as impressionist works, are dominated by noticeable paint strokes. We hypothesize that the visual artifact of such paint strokes is a normal distribution of the color gradient. This would help explain the correlation of paint strokes in evolved images that have active paint operators. It is also supported by the results in [40], in which procedurally generated images with low DFN's often were more painterly in appearance, even though the paint operator was not used. More research is needed.

16.7 Comparisons to Related Work

Our system is the latest incarnation of the Gentropy image evolution system [14, 15]. Related research that applies Ralph's bell curve aesthetic model to image synthesis is [40].

Yip's filter evolution system is similar in spirit and functionality to ours [26]. He also applies a suite of basic image analysis functions, and the fitness function matches these scores with the corresponding ones for a target image. All test scores are merged into a single-objective score using a weighted sum. This requires the user to define the weights, which can be complicated to do and prone to user bias. Our adoption of multi-objective Pareto ranking prevents this. His texture distribution analysis has some similarities to our bell gradient analyses. For example, both use separate mean and standard deviation scores as targets. The DFN model merges aspects of his texture and entropy analyses into a single computation. Yip's overall analysis matches distribution statistics of texture and entropy with a target image. Our use of DFN always tries to fit gradient distributions as closely as possible to a normal distribution. Yip's approach could be an interesting enhancement to ours, as we could use a source image's gradient distribution as a target for a run. Since a target image might not have a normal distribution, this would permit a variety of non-painterly images to be purposefully evolved. Yip's filters are simpler than ours, as he evolves short sequences of preset filters. This is necessitated by his use of a GA instead of GP.

Machado et al.'s color filter evolution is also comparable to our system in many ways [25]. Both systems use the GP paradigm for filter construction. They use a simpler filter language than we do, as they are only concerned with deriving spectral filters that colorize grayscale images. Our filters perform color generation, as well as spatial distortions. Their color matching test is comparable to our quadratic histogram color test.

16.8 Conclusion

This chapter is another example of using evolution for creativity exploration. Ralph's aesthetic model is a novel means of taming the characteristics of filters, and is an interesting way for establishing a preference for filters that use our paint operators. Taming the nature of filters is necessary, since automatic evolution left unchecked has the tendency to evolve wildly chaotic filters. Such results are too discordant to be visually interesting, and rarely have that inherit painterly quality found in many classical examples of fine art.

A long-term goal is to incorporate other models of aesthetics, for example, compositional balance, color selection, and (in the very long term) subject matter relevance. Because art appreciation and artistic competency rely upon the highest levels of human cognition and pattern matching, there is much research to be done in determining how human beings perceive and create art, and how these tasks might be automated on computers.

Development is progressing on a new version of Gentropy that combines automatic and supervised evolution, as well as merge filter and image generation operators. A user will be able to interactively experiment with the language, training images, fitness evaluation, and other parameters, hopefully resulting in a powerful tool for artistic creativity.

16.9 Acknowledgements

The authors thank Andrea Wiens, Han Zhu, Hai Zong, and Greg Roberts for their contributions to the development of Gentropy over the years. This research is partially funded by NSERC Operating Grant 138467-1998

References

1. Ralph, W. (2005). Painting the Bell Curve: The Occurrence of the Normal Distribution in Fine Art. *In preparation.*
2. Dorin, A. (2001). Aesthetic Fitness and Artificial Evolution for the Selection of Imagery from the Mythical Infinite Library. In: *Advances in Artificial Life – Proc. 6th European Conference on Artificial Life.* Springer
3. Whitelaw, M. (2002). Breeding Aesthetic Objects: Art and Artificial Evolution. In Bentley, P., Corne, D., eds.: *Creative Evolutionary Systems.* Morgan Kaufmann, 129–145
4. Bentley, P., Corne, D. (2002). *Creative Evolutionary Systems.* Morgan Kaufmann
5. Gatarski, R. (1999). Evolutionary Banners: An Experiment With Automated Advertising Design. In: *Proc. COTIM-99*
6. Graf, J., Banzhaf, W. (1995). Interactive Evolution of Images. In: *Proc. Intl. Conf. on Evolutionary Programming*, 53–65
7. Hemert, J., Eiben, A. (1999). Mondrian Art by Evolution. In: *Proc. Dutch/Belgian Conf. on Artificial Intelligence (BNAIC 99)*
8. Lewis, M. (2000). Aesthetic Evolutionary Design with Data Flow Networks. In: *Proc. Generative Art 2000*
9. Rooke, S. (2002). Eons of Genetically Evolved Algorithmic Images. In Bentley, P., Corne, D., eds.: *Creative Evolutionary Systems.* Morgan Kaufmann, 330–365
10. Rowbottom, A. (1999). Evolutionary Art and Form. In Bentley, P., ed.: *Evolutionary Design by Computers.* Morgan Kaufmann, 330–365
11. Sims, K. (1993). Interactive evolution of equations for procedural models. *The Visual Computer*, **9**: 466–476
12. Ashlock, D., Davidson, J. (1999). Texture Synthesis with Tandem Genetic Algorithms using Nonparametric Partially ordered Markov Models. In: *Proc. CEC*, 1157–1163
13. Ibrahim, A. (1998). *GenShade: An Evolutionary Approach to Automatic and Interactive Procedural Texture Generation.* PhD thesis. Texas A&M University
14. Ross, B., Zhu, H. (2004). Procedural Texture Evolution Using Multiobjective Optimization. *New Generation Computing*, **22**(3): 271–293
15. Wiens, A., Ross, B. (2002). Gentropy: Evolutionary 2D Texture Generation. *Computers and Graphics Journal*, **26**(1): 75–88
16. Hewgill, A., Ross, B. (2004). Procedural 3D Texture Synthesis Using Genetic Programming. *Computers and Graphics*, **28**(4): 569–584
17. Machado, P., Cardoso, A. (1998). Computing Aesthetics. In: *Proc. XIVth Brazilian Symposium on AI.* Springer, 239–249
18. Spehar, B., Clifford, C., Newell, B., Taylor, R. (2003). Universal aesthetic of fractals. *Computer and Graphics*, **27**: 813–820

19. Baluja, S., Pomerleau, D., Jochem, T. (1994). Towards Automated Artificial Evolution for Computer-generated Images. *Connection Science*, **6**(2/3): 325–354
20. Machado, P., Cardoso, A. (2002). All the Truth About NEvAr. *Applied Intelligence*, **16**(2): 101–118
21. Svangard, N., Nordin, P. (2004). Automated Aesthetic Selection of Evolutionary Art by Distance Based Classification of Genomes and Phenomes using the Universal Similarity Metric. In: *Applications of Evolutionary Computing: EvoWorkshops 2004*. Springer, 447–456 LNCS 3005.
22. Poli, R., Cagnoni, S. (1997). *Evolution of Pseudo-Colouring Algorithms for Image Enhancement with Interactive Genetic Programming.* Technical Report CSRP-97-5. School of Computer Science, University of Birmingham
23. Lewis, M. (2004). Aesthetic Video Filter Evolution in an Interactive Real-time Framework. In: *EvoWorkShops*, 409–418
24. Software, M. (2005). Geneticfx studio `http://www.mindcube.ukf.net/geneticfx/`. Last accessed May 26, 2005.
25. Machado, P., Dias, A., Duarte, N., Cardoso, A. (2002). Giving Colour to Images. In: *Proc. AISB 2002 Symposium on AI and Creativity in the Arts*
26. Yip, C. (2004). *Evolving Image Filters.* Master's thesis. Imperial College of Science, Technology, and Medicine
27. Gonzalez, R., Woods, R. (2002). *Digital Image Processing.* 2 edn. Prentice Hall
28. Gooch, B., Gooch, A. (2001). *Non-photorealistic rendering.* A.K. Peters
29. Strothotte, T., Schlechtweg, S. (2002). *Non-photorealistic computer graphics : modeling, rendering, and animation.* Morgan Kaufmann
30. Shiraishi, M., Yamaguchi, Y. (2000). An Algorithm for Automatic Painterly Rendering Based on Local Source Image Approximation. In: *Proceedings of NPAR 2000.* ACM Press, 53–58
31. Coello, C.C., Veldhuizen, D.V., Lamont, G. (2002). *Evolutionary Algorithms for Solving Multi-Objective Problems.* Kluwer
32. Tolhurst, D., Tadmor, Y., Chao, T. (1992). Amplitude spectra of natural images. *Ophthalmic & Physiological Optics*, **12**(2): 229–232
33. Pressing, J. (1999). Sources for 1/f noise effects in human cognition and performance. *Paideusis: Journal for Interdisciplinary and Cross-Cultural Studies*, **2**
34. Voss, R., Clarke, J. (1978). 1/f noise in music: Music from 1/f noise. *J. Acoustical Society of America*, **63**(1): 258–263
35. Zongker, D., Punch, B. (1995). *lil-gp 1.0 User's Manual.* Dept. of Computer Science, Michigan State University
36. Koza, J. (1992). *Genetic Programming: On the Programming of Computers by Means of Natural Selection.* MIT Press
37. Montana, D. (1995). Strongly Typed Genetic Programming. *Evolutionary Computation*, **3**(2): 199–230
38. Smith, J., Chang, S.F. (1996). Visualseek: a fully automated content-based image query system. In: *Proc. ACM-MM*, 87–98
39. Hertzmann, A., Jacobs, C., Oliver, N., Curless, B., Salesin, D. (2001). Image Analogies. In Fiume, E., ed.: *Proceedings SIGGRAPH 2001.* ACM Press, 327–340
40. Ross, B., Ralph, W., Zong, H. (2006). Evolutionary Image Synthesis Using a Model of Aesthetics. In: *Proceedings CEC-06*

17

Co-evolutionary Methods in Evolutionary Art

Gary R. Greenfield

University of Richmond, Richmond, Virginia 23173 USA ggreenfi@richmond.edu

Summary. Following the ground breaking work of Sims and Latham there was a flurry of activity in interactive artificial evolution of images. However, the move towards non-interactive evolution of images that arises by invoking fitness functions to serve in place of users in order to guide simulated evolution proceeded haltingly and unevenly. If evolutionary computational models for image evolution are indeed inspired by nature, then it is natural to consider image evolution in the broader co-evolutionary context. This chapter briefly surveys the role co-evolutionary methods have played in evolutionary computation and then examines some of the instances where it has been applied to evolutionary art. The paucity of examples leads to a discussion of the challenges faced, and the difficulties encountered, when trying to use co-evolutionary methods both in evolutionary art and artificial creativity.

17.1 Introduction

Richard Dawkins [1] is usually credited with introducing the concept of *user-guided* artificial evolution. Dawkins *Biomorphs* program was originally developed as an artificial life simulation for studying "evolvability." If fell to Karl Sims [2] to combine Dawkin's user-guided evolution concept with an imaging technique based on Koza's genetic programming [3] to create the interactive evolutionary art method known as *evolving expressions*. Sims later published several variations on this theme [4, 5]. At about the same time, user-guided evolution also found its way into an interactive evolutionary art system developed by Latham and Todd [6, 7] for generating synthetic three dimensional organic sculptures.

For Sims, an image — the *phenotype* — was generated from a LISP expression — the *genotype*. For descriptions and references concerning the many evolutionary artists who have developed their own Sims' style systems see [8, 9] as well as the survey of evolutionary art by Matthew Lewis in the first chapter of this book.

17.1.1 Non-Interactive Image Evolution

Baluja et al. [10] were the first researchers to attempt to fully automate an evolutionary art system. They designed and implemented a non-interactive system that used as a foundation a bare-bones Sims' style image generative component. First they logged images from users' interactive sessions with the Sims' style image generating component to create an image database. Images from the database were resolved to 48×48 pixels and numerically rated for their aesthetic value. Training and testing sets of images for a neural net were drawn from this database with equal representation given to low, medium, and high ranked images. After training and testing, the neural net was used to guide image evolution *without* human intervention starting from randomly generated image populations. According to the authors, the results were "somewhat disappointing" and "mixed and very difficult to quantify." They concluded it was difficult for their neural nets to learn or discern any aesthetic principles from the training sets. They also noted that their neural net's exploration of image space was "very limited and largely uninteresting" and they suggested that the greatest potential for using such automated approaches may be to prune away uninteresting images and direct the human (assistant) to more promising ones.

17.1.2 Setting the Stage

Other early attempts to non-interactively evolve artworks, most of which are also based on the Sims' image generation method [11, 12, 13], had limitations as was recognized by those authors. The primary difficulty encountered is the necessity of designing fitness functions that assign a numeric value to represent the *aesthetic* content of an image. Unless there are innate universal measures of beauty that stem directly from the mind (rather than being acquired by experience or from external sources), that apply to humans, and that one can quantify, such a static measure of aesthetic content appears to contradict our understanding of works of art. This observation sets the stage for more dynamic measures of the aesthetic value of art works. From an evolutionary art point of view it paves the way to the technique we focus upon in this chapter, co-evolution — the evolution of interacting populations.

17.2 The Origins of Co-Evolution in Evolutionary Computing

The introduction of the concept of *competitiveness* into evolutionary computation by trying to model biological principles governing predator–prey and host–parasite relationships had its antecedents in some of the earliest efforts to use simulated annealing and genetic algorithms in optimization [3]. Following claims by Ray of observing evidence of co-evolution in his ground breaking artificial life simulator *Tierra* [14], the design and implementation of a general-purpose framework for co-evolution fell to Hillis [15]. Hillis developed a clever and sophisticated co-evolutionary approach to use for studying the problem of searching for "sorting networks." Hillis' work led to the recognition and popularization of co-evolution as a mainstream tool in evolutionary computation and optimization

17.2.1 Hillis, Co-Evolution, and Sorting Networks

A sorting network is an implementation of a compare-and-swap algorithm for sorting lists $\{a_1, \ldots, a_n\}$ of fixed size n. This means that when a sorting network sorts such a list into, say, ascending order, it does so simply by specifying a sequence of ordered pairs. This is possible because a sequence of ordered pairs $(i_1, j_1), \ldots, (i_m, j_m)$ can be used to represent an m statement sequential program whose k-th statement is: `if` $a_{i_k} > a_{j_k}$ `then swap(`a_{i_k}`,`a_{j_k}`)`.

Hillis [15] developed a co-evolutionary framework for simulated evolution in an attempt to find examples of sorting networks that matched the performance of the most efficient networks that had been designed by hand to solve this sorting problem for lists of size $n = 16$. The shortest length ever achieved by hand required $m = 60$ ordered pairs. Using sorting networks for which $n = 16$ as one of his populations, Hillis' crucial observation was that a sorting network sorts all instances of the problem correctly if and only if it sorts all instances of the problem where the a_i are restricted to being either zeros or ones correctly.

The ingenuity of Hillis was four-fold. First, rather than test all 2^n zero–one instances of the problem on each candidate sorting network, Hillis maintained a small set of 20 difficult to sort test cases for each network. His co-evolving population consisted of these sets of test cases. Individual test cases were viewed as parasites attacking, or preying, upon the host sorting networks. Second, Hillis organized his sorting network population spatially by letting each network occupy a node in a two-dimensional grid. This meant that genetic diversity could be maintained through sub-populations that arose as a consequence of the local selection algorithms used to mate his sorting networks. Third, Hillis incorporated expert knowledge into his co-evolutionary system by initializing his sorting networks so that each one began with an identical list of 32 compare–swap pairs. This list of pairs duplicated the initial sorting phase that the best hand designed solutions for the $n = 16$ problem had used. Fourth, Hillis developed a sophisticated biologically inspired genotype to phenotype representation scheme. This scheme deserves further consideration due to its complexity.

Sorting Network Genotypes

Hillis constructed his sorting network genotype using 15 *pairs* of chromosomes. Each chromosome consisted of eight *codons*. Each codon was a four bit binary integer representing an index for one of the 16 elements to be sorted. Thus a genotype consisted of $2 \times 15 \times 8 \times 4 = 960$ bits. The phenotype was a list of between 60 and 120 ordered pairs to be used as compare–swap statements as explained above. By considering two codons at a time, each chromosome was parsed to furnish four ordered pairs for consideration for the sorting program. Those ordered pairs were compared with the corresponding ordered pairs from the companion chromosome. If corresponding ordered pairs were identical then only one copy became part of the sorting network otherwise both pairs became part of the network. As mentioned above, the initialization was such that the first 32 pairs from matching chromosomes were always identical. They constituted the initial sorting phase that was the expert knowledge. The genetic operators Hillis used were anti-climactic. One point crossover was implemented in such a way that a crossover point was selected for each pair of chromosomes, and point mutation was implemented in such a way that one codon per thousand was altered.

Hillis' Parasites

The parasites Hillis' used were instances of length $n = 16$ zero–one strings for the networks to sort. Each network was assigned 20 such binary strings. Since the population of networks was spatially organized, by default, these small sets of test cases were spatially organized. The "arms-race" that Hillis set in motion resulted from the fact that networks had to become better and better at sorting as the subsets of test cases were simultaneously evolving to present ever more challenging instances of the problem to sort.

The Legacy of Hillis

The title of Hillis' paper explains what his contribution to the field of evolutionary computation really meant. Hillis was not able to successfully evolve a sorting network that improved, or even matched, the lower bound of the best known network. Hillis was able to show experimentally that by using co-evolving populations of test cases he could reduce the amount of computation required to evaluate the fitness of his sorting networks while simultaneously finding shorter networks than if he simply exhaustively tested whether or not a network could sort. Therefore parasites (i.e., co-evolution) had *improved* the ability of evolutionary optimization to find shorter networks.

17.2.2 Co-Evolution and Competition

Hillis had demonstrated the advantages of co-evolution, but the effort required to implement the technique meant it was not for the faint of heart. Using an even more ambitious and elaborate genotype-to-phenotype mapping scheme, as well as a state of the art simulated physical environment, Karl Sims [16] used co-evolution in the guise of competition to evolve virtual bodies and controllers for synthetic "creatures" to showcase their behaviors when they were required to participate in contests of a simulated version of capture-the-flag. At the same time Reynold's [17] used co-evolution to evolve two populations of synthetic creatures that were paired off in pursuer–evader contests. Later Nolfi and Floreano [18] investigated a similar pursuer–evader problem occurring in a physical environment by co-evolving robots to compete in pursuer–evader contests.

Games are another natural problem domain where competition contests or suites of test cases arise. Thus we find researchers who have considered co-evolutionary approaches to evolving strategies for tic-tac-toe [19], Othello [20], Backgammon [21], and a variant of Iterated Prisoner's Dilemma [22]. Finally, in a more applications oriented vein, researchers have also considered co-evolutionary approaches to symbolic regression [23] and scheduling [24].

17.3 Artists Using Co-Evolution

With this background, we consider four "case-studies" of artists using co-evolutionary methods in evolutionary art. We restrict our attention to the visual arts. For work done in using co-evolution for music composition see [25, 26]. In this section we cover the three shorter examples. In the next section we cover the longest example.

17.3.1 Steven Rooke — Art Critics

Steven Rooke was an early adopter of Sims' image generation method using evolving expressions. The system he implemented allowed him to interactively evolve abstract images [27]. Although Rooke never published the results of his experiments, early on he attempted to non-interactively evolve images using a design that was quite different from the fitness function approaches or trained neural net approaches that had been previously tried by others. Rooke's idea was to try to co-evolve a population of art critics, which he called "image commentators," to perform the aesthetic evaluations of the images his Sims' inspired system generated.

Since Rooke always seeded his gene pools with genetically promising material,[1] he could be confident that his art critics would initially be presented with visually promising images. The job of each critic was to assign an aesthetic fitness value to every image in his image population of size 100. The training set Rooke used to obtain his initial population of critics consisted of the phenotypes of the first 20 generations of images from an evolutionary run

[1] This has been coined using the "digital amber" approach because the genetic material is extracted from archived gene banks.

that he had seeded as described above, together with *his* personal aesthetic rankings for all of the images in each of these generations.

In Rooke's experimental set-up both his images and his critics were populations of evolving expressions. Thus the same evolutionary and genetic infrastructure could be used to manage the population of images and the population of critics. Note, however, that the evolving expressions for the two populations used different sets of primitives. The critic expressions were filled, not with image processing primitives, but with location finding primitives for isolating sub-regions of the image and with statistical assessment primitives for analyzing these sub-regions. By seeding his initial image population, Rooke avoided launching co-evolution with randomly generated populations of images. Similarly, by evolving the initial random population of critics off-line until they contained at least one critic that could duplicate his fitness rankings for the first 20 generations of his training set to within an acceptable error, he avoided initially launching co-evolution with randomly generated populations of critics. To implement a co-evolutionary search for images, after each new generation of images was bred, the oldest ranked generation of images would be removed from a sliding window of 20 generations and the current generation would be added to the window using the rankings obtained by the current top-ranked critic. Thus, after 20 generations of co-evolution, the critics were in complete control. Evolution of the critics was sustained by matching their ranking ability against the fitness rankings furnished by the sliding window of 20 generations of images. Evolution of the images was sustained by the rankings of the current top-ranked critic.

Rooke let his critics guide image evolution for 300 generations. Rooke judged his art critics to have been capable of learning his aesthetics, but he abandoned this line of research because they seemed incapable of using this "knowledge" to explore new and interesting areas of image space. One plausible explanation was that Rooke's critics were being trapped in eddies of image space. Rooke, echoing the thought of Baluja et al., suggested that it might be necessary to work side by side with his critics and intervene every so often to put them back on track by reassigning *his* aesthetic fitness rankings to the images in the current sliding window, and then re-evolving the critics — an on-going human assisted co-evolution scenario.

17.3.2 Alan Dorin — Disease Models

Alan Dorin (Chap. 14) is an artist who also used a co-evolutionary model based on parasites [28, 29]. In his generative electronic art installations, parasites are modeled as virtual diseases. Dorin notes that diseases and epidemiology have played a role in literature and film in the past, and have come to prominence in contemporary art through artistic expression related to HIV/AIDS. Dorin considers the SIR epidemic model for disease which is based on the number of *susceptible*, *infected*, and *removed* members of the population and is controlled by parameters such as disease *latency* and *incubation* periods as well as, of course, the physical interactions between the members of the population.

Dorin's installations are visualizations of individuals, or *agents*, floating in a two-dimensional toroidal world. Genomes control the exploration behavior and interaction behaviors of agents. Agent survival depends heavily on age and energy level. Virtual diseases are transmitted solely through agent-agent contact. Geometry and color provide visual cues for the current status of agents as they explore, interact, and become subject to infectious diseases. In Dorin's disease population, diseases have "color signatures" plus other parameters under genotype control that affect attributes such as their latency, incubation period and *devastation*, or lethality, potential. New diseases are introduced every 100,000 update steps.

While Dorin's co-evolutionary simulation is a stand alone artificial life experimental simulation tool for studying models of the spread and elimination of diseases, it is included here because it is also an *interactive* installation art project. With further enhancement, it is expected humans will be able to affect agent behavior and will be integrated into the disease transmission process. Perhaps diseases will be spread to (virtual) agents via partial color signature matching with the clothes humans wear. This makes it a unique and forceful artistic creation.

17.3.3 Saunders and Gero — Artificial Societies

Saunders and Gero [30] use an adaptive fitness model for co-evolving Sims' style images that places it at the boundary of co-evolutionary frameworks. Their system was, in fact, designed not for its image evolution capabilities but for studying the emergence of novelty and creativity. Its goal was identifying principles behind their emergence in artificial societies. It is noteworthy for its elaborate complexity, and for its image evaluation mechanisms. It should be stressed, however, that since their system is designed to search for novelty, even though some of the images may have aesthetic content when considered from an artistic perspective, it would be unfair to judge their results solely on that basis alone.

Their evolutionary framework is agent-based. Now *each* agent has its own copy of an "off-the-shelf" Sims' style two-dimensional image generation system. For image evaluation purposes a low resolution 32×32 pixel rendering of an image obtained from one of these image generators is transformed into a black and white silhouette using an edge-detector. These silhouettes are then passed to other agent's self-organizing maps. Agent's self-organizing maps are neural networks that accept as input images presented in the 1032 bit vector silhouette format and produce as output a 6×6 array of *categories* of such transformed images. An agent's array represents its short term memory. On the basis of the comparison between the input silhouette and the category silhouettes a *novelty* value between 0 and 32 is assigned to an image. Thus an agent's evaluation of an image is a measure of "the degree to which it could not have predicted it from previous experience." This novelty value is now used as the argument for a hedonic function that determines the *level of interest* of the image.[2] The design objective is to make it possible for agents to identify similar but different artworks.

For their evolutionary framework Saunders and Gero use ten agents. If an agent has evolved an image whose level of interest exceeds a threshold then it transmits the *genotype* of that image to all of the other agents. Upon receipt agents evaluate an artwork as described above. They then have the option of immediately incorporating its genotype into their copy of the Sims' style image evolution system. The subtlety here is that an agent must evolve any genotype it receives in this manner for at least one generation before it can redistribute it as its own. The receiving agent also issues a credit to the sending agent. The ultimate goal is to place the best images in the public domain so that all agents can use this repository for evolving new, ever more creative and interesting, images using their individual copies of the Sims' style system. Thus images and agents are co-evolving. The catch is that an agent cannot place its own image in the public domain, only a recipient of that image can do so. In this sense the archives of the public domain resemble the sliding window of Rooke's image population rankings.

In [30] Saunders and Gero described experiments where agents used different hedonic functions and different thresholds for assigning creativity to their images as well as for deciding whether to place images in the public domain. Their experimental results were used to support arguments about why novelty should proceed at a measured pace and how cliques might form. From a co-evolutionary art point of view, their design is significant because of the way image fitness is both adaptive and responsive to prior events.

17.4 Gary Greenfield — Co-evolution Using Convolution Filters

Gary Greenfield was also an early adopter of the Sims' evolving expressions image generation technique. He has investigated interactive image evolution [31, 32, 33], image co-evolution [34, 9, 35], and the use of fitness functions in non-interactive image evolution [11, 36]. Here we describe in significant detail his co-evolutionary methods. For background, we first consider some evolutionary computation research of Belpaeme in digital image processing.

[2] The hedonic curves used are sums of two sigmoid functions designed in such a way that hedonic values are close to zero at the novelty extremes and peak in the novelty mid-range.

17.4.1 Background

Belpaeme [37] evolved Sims' style expressions using as primitives at the internal nodes "classical" image processing functions. His motivation was to discover new and useful digital filters.[3] His goal was to develop image classification filters for use in computer vision applications. His fitness measure was how successful a digital filter phenotype arising from an evolved expression genotype was at *distinguishing* between the images in his test set. One intriguing outcome of Belpaeme's experiment was that the expressions for the filters he evolved almost always turned out to be very small. It was as if there was somehow a hidden bias towards computational efficiency built into his fitness metric. The explanation Belpaeme offered was that chaining (i.e., iterating) classical image processing functions caused a significant loss of image information content. Thus smaller expressions had more information available to use for the classification task than larger ones. This lesson about loss of information establishes the rationale for trying to ensure that evolutionary frameworks for image analysis are kept as simple as possible.

17.4.2 Greenfield's Motivation

To spark visual interest, an image must cause our eyes to present visual anomalies to our brain. That is, a visually interesting image must be processed by our eyes in such a way that the data that is extracted and passed along to our brain has sufficient information content to allow it to be recognized as visually significant. If we think of this data extraction process as digitally filtering an image, and we assume that recognition of a processed image as visually interesting by our brain is based in part on a decision about the complexity of this processed data, then what we are assuming is that visual anomalies will be recognized by our higher level processing units, our brains, provided our digital filtering mechanisms, our eyes, can encode image complexity properly.

With this as motivation, and mindful of the "simplicity lesson" learned from Belpaeme above, Greenfield assigned elementary digital convolution filters to fixed locations of the phenotype image obtained from a genotype. He convolved small portions of the image determined by these fixed locations using the filters. Then, to determine image complexity, he compared the convolved image to the original image. He sought images for which the convolved portions of the image were significantly *different* than the original portions of the image. Since images and filters co-evolve this becomes a dynamic as opposed to a static measure of fitness.

In this context, a convolution filter is viewed as being parasitic upon an image. Its survivability is determined by how well it is able to blend in with an

[3] Since the time of the work being described in this section, evolving image processing tools such as filter banks or segmentation schemes has become standard practice.

image. This is because in order for a filter to survive, the convolved portions of the image must be nearly identical with the original portions of the image. The survivability of an image is determined by how well it is able to repel a parasite by making it visible. This is because the image complexity of the phenotype will "expose" parasites whenever the convolved portions of the image are markedly different than the original portions of the image.

An alternative way of looking at this situation arises from thinking about the way digital convolution filters work. They use the neighboring values of a given pixel to determine a new value for that pixel. Since the new value for the pixel will be compared with the original value, one might also say a filter's survivability is determined by its ability to predict pixel values, while an image's survivability is determined by how well it can foil such predictions. Further details are required to understand how and why this inspires a co-evolutionary arms race.

17.4.3 The Host Image Genotype and Phenotype

Greenfield defines an image genotype to be a symbolic expression tree E represented in postfix form. The leaf nodes are chosen from the set consisting of constants with values ranging from 0.000 to 0.999 in increments of 0.001, denoted $C0 - C999$, together with the independent variables $V0$ and $V1$. The internal nodes are chosen from sets of unary and binary primitives. A unary primitive is a function from the unit interval to itself, and a binary primitive is a function from the unit square to the unit interval. There are five unary primitives denoted $U0 - U4$ and 15 binary primitives denoted by $B0 - B14$. The arithmetic descriptions of the set of primitives may be found in [38]. Several were inspired by two-dimensional designs first proposed by Maeda [39].

Let N be the desired image resolution width and length. An $N \times N$ phenotype $h_{i,j}$ is obtained by letting $(V0, V1)$ be the point $(i/N, j/N)$ in the unit square and then, using a stack evaluation algorithm, obtaining a density value $E(V0, V1)$ in the unit interval for the pixel whose coordinates are (i, j). To visualize phenotypes as images the density values are assigned to bins which are then mapped to colors. For the purposes of co-evolution, the resolution is $N = 100$, and the color look-up table is gray scale defined by a linear ramp from black to white. This ramp is resolved into 256 equal width density bins. Figure 17.1 shows four binary primitives. Figure 17.2 shows the bottom-up image processing network that yields the phenotype from a typical genotype.

17.4.4 The Parasitic Digital Convolution Filters

Greenfield defines the genotype of a parasite to be a 3×3 matrix $(f_{i,j})$, $0 \leq i, j \leq 2$, whose integer values lie in the interval $[-P_{\max}, P_{\max}]$. The results shown here use $P_{\max} = 8$. Given a 100×100 host image with phenotypic values $h_{i,j}$ lying in the interval $[0, 1]$ extract, using as the lower left-hand corner the

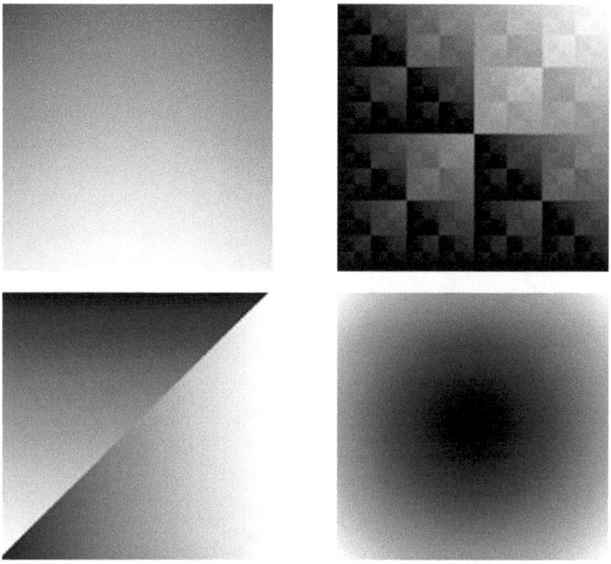

Fig. 17.1. The image phenotypes from the genotypes of four binary primitives. *Top.* The parabolic primitive `V0 V1 B13` formed using a construction for converting a continuous function defined on a closed interval (here, $F(X) = 1/2 - X^2$ on $[-1/2, 1/2]$) into a binary primitive and `V0 V1 B8`, a fractal primitive obtained by applying the bitwise and operator to corresponding digits in the arguments `V0` and `V1` after they have been expressed in binary. *Bottom.* The primitive `V0 V1 B9`, which is a pointwise version of a vector defined primitive introduced by Maeda [39] and `V0 V1 B8` whose phenotype is induced by the height function $Z = 2((X-1/2)^2+(Y-1/2)^2)$

pixel with indices determined by location (L_x, L_y), the 10×10 *patch* $p_{i,j}$ where $1 \leq i, j \leq 10$. Define the *neighborhood* of this patch to be the 12×12 region of the host image consisting of this patch surrounded by a one pixel wide border. Pass the convolution filter determined by the parasite genotype over the neighborhood to obtain the convolved patch

$$v_{i,j} = \frac{\sum_{r=0}^{2} \sum_{c=0}^{2} p_{i+(r-1),j+(c-1)} f_{i+(r-1),j+(c-1)}}{S},$$

where

$$S = 1 + |\sum_{i,j} f_{i,j}|.$$

17.4.5 The Fitness Contest

The idea is to perform pixel by pixel comparisons between pixel densities of the 10×10 patch of an image with the associated pixel densities of the 10×10

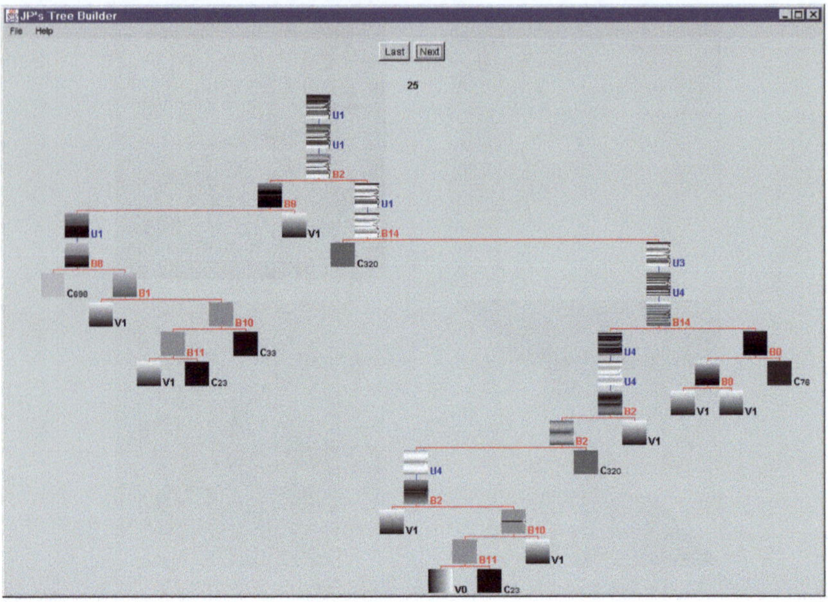

Fig. 17.2. A screen capture showing the bottom-up image processing network that yields the phenotype from the genotype in Greenfield's image generation system using the Sims' method

patch of the convolved image. The result of each pixel comparison is one or zero depending on whether the magnitude of the difference of the densities lies above or below a threshold value. More precisely, to compare a 10×10 patch $p_{i,j}$ of an image phenotype with its convolved 10×10 patch $v_{i,j}$, let

$$h = \sum_{i,j} \delta_{i,j} ,$$

where

$$\delta_{i,j} = \begin{cases} 1 \text{ if } |v_{i,j} - p_{i,j}| > \varepsilon , \\ 0 \text{ otherwise} , \end{cases}$$

and ε is the host's *exposure* threshold. The images shown here use $\varepsilon = 0.05$. Since h is integer valued with $0 \leq h \leq 100$, and the values of h are large when the two patches differ, we award h fitness points to the host image and $p = 100 - h$ fitness points to the parasite filter. If *multiple* parasites are attached to a host, each at a different location, the host's fitness is the total points awarded averaged over the number of parasites. An example of the host–parasite interaction is shown in Fig. 17.3. A visualization of the fitness calculation is shown in Fig. 17.4.

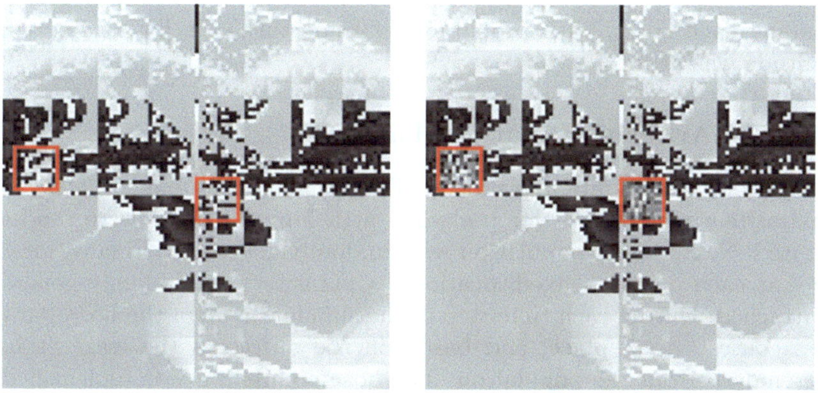

Fig. 17.3. *Left.* The phenotype of a host showing the patches where two parasites are attached. *Right.* The same host with the parasites rendered visible after convolution filtering

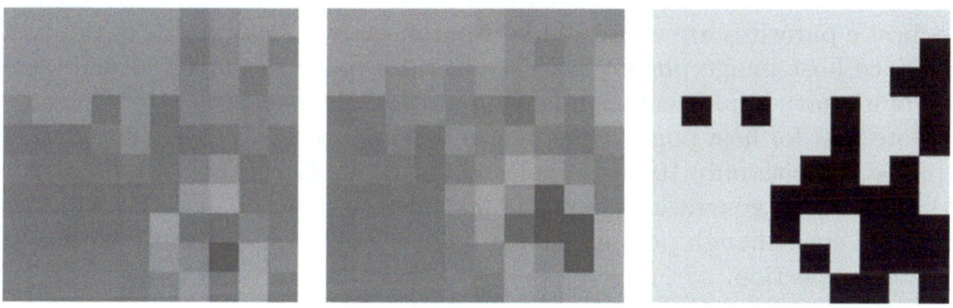

Fig. 17.4. The fitness contest calculation: The filtered patch (center) is "subtracted" from the unfiltered patch (left) — here both patches are false-colored to accentuate gradations occurring within the phenotype. After a threshold has been applied to the magnitude of the difference of the result yielding a bi-level image (right), one point is awarded to the host image for each pixel that is black and one point is awarded to the parasite filter for each pixel that is gray

17.4.6 Genetic Operators

Greenfield used standard operators from genetic programming for the host image genotypes. The recombination operator exchanged subtrees between two such genotypes, while the mutation operator examined each node stochastically to see if it should be substituted for. In keeping with spirit of digital convolution filters being viewed as primal organisms, their reproduction was accomplished by cloning parasites and then stochastically subjecting the clone to one or more transcription operators. These included, for example, exchanging two rows or columns, circularly shifting a row or a column, or exchanging two entries. All filters were passed to a point mutation operator which, upon examining each entry, with probability 0.05 perturbed it by a value whose magnitude was at most two.

17.4.7 The Artificial Evolution Simulation

Initialization was a multi-step process. First L pixel locations, or sites, – one per parasite *population* — for use when attaching parasites were randomly generated. Next, a host population was randomly generated. Finally, for each image, at each of the L fixed locations, a parasite was randomly generated and attached. During each time step of the simulation all of the host–parasite fitness contests took place, and based on the outcomes the least fit hosts were removed from the population. The host population was replenished by mating pairs of hosts. The pairs were randomly selected from the pool of survivors. For each parasite population, the least fit parasites were removed and parasite replacements were obtained by cloning and mutating as described above. Thus parasite replacement was elitist. New hosts inherited the parasites that were attached to the deceased host they replaced. Since the phenotypes of a host's parasites are expressed by filtering only a small patch of the host, and since host image phenotypes do *not* have to be displayed visually, this co-evolutionary implementation is computationally efficient.

Note that for host populations of size 30, supporting up to five populations of parasites, with only 10 hosts replaced per generation, when the simulation was run for 1000 generations, up to 10,000 hosts and 80,000 parasites would be examined even though perhaps at most ten hosts were archived (i.e., culled) for later inspection.

17.4.8 Subtleties

A potential winning strategy for a parasite is a "do nothing" strategy using the genotype

$$\begin{pmatrix} 0 & 0 & 0 \\ 0 & 1 & 0 \\ 0 & 0 & 0 \end{pmatrix}.$$

The design thwarts this by using the weighting factor of one more than the absolute value of the sum of the entries when calculating the convolution filter phenotype, and by limiting those genotype entries to a value with magnitude $P_{\max}$. The exposure threshold used to determine the fitness value can now be carefully chosen so that the parasites are at a competitive disadvantage. On the other hand the penalty is such that under certain circumstances even constant-valued image phenotypes would be deemed fit, and since this is undesirable, host populations are handicapped by placing upper and lower bounds on the size of host genomes, and by initializing host genomes in such a way that only a small percentage of constant primitives appear in the leaf nodes.

For initial random populations, fitness tends to be an all or nothing proposition. To encourage evolutionary trajectories to spiral and branch out into image space rather than go in circles, Greenfield adopted *maximin* and *minimax* tie-breaker rules. For simplicity, assume there is only one parasite population. If there is a tie in host fitness, then the winner is the host that has the larger of minimums that are taken over the set of absolute values of phenotype differences used in the fitness calculation, while if there is a tie in parasite fitness, then the winner is the parasite with the smaller of the maximums taken over this same set. The tie-breaker rule rewards partial progress towards the conflicting goals of the two populations.

Preliminary results from a partial implementation of this co-evolutionary design by Clement [40] revealed two additional flaws that should be addressed. First, a host with thin enough "banding" in the image phenotype provided too many contrasting density values for a parasite to adjust to. This was overcome by restricting the percentage of unary primitives that could appear in a host genotype thus forcing the binary primitives to shoulder more of the image survivability burden. Since the reason for using unary primitives was to promote visual *smoothing* in the phenotype, shifting the burden to binary primitives also produced better overall image contrast and fostered greater diversity within the host gene pool. Second, a host phenotype exhibiting a pattern consisting of "islands" of discontinuities is automatically very fit. These images have cloud-like structures. It was not possible to eliminate such cloud-like structures completely given the nature of the fitness contest. Indeed, "random noise" might be regarded as the limiting, stable evolutionary state reachable by a host population.

It seems ironic that even though it is simple to increase the host population size to hundreds or even thousands of individuals, there seems to be little incentive for doing so, especially in view of the difficulty of monitoring such populations. With a host population of size 30, it becomes feasible to interrupt the co-evolutionary simulation and inspect all host phenotypes, all host genotypes, and all parasite genotypes.

With the design described so far, it was quite easy for hosts to become *lethal* to parasites.[4] To strengthen parasite populations, similar to what tends to happen in nature, Greenfield made them faster evolving species than their hosts by using the method we now describe. Both host and parasite populations were too small to permit implementing the spatial mating techniques Hillis used,[5] so the following simplified model of what one might expect to occur in nature was used instead. In nature, a parasite, after initially attaching to (invading?) a host, often starts dividing and multiplying asexually until the host is teeming with parasites. These may become more and more virulent over time thanks to mutation. Since the evolved objects of interest are host images rather than parasite filters, this phenomenon was simulated by using

[4] In co-evolution the opposite problem of excessive parasite virulence is also often encountered [41].

[5] More recent research [42, 43] suggests that this feature may be the *primary* reason Hillis succeeded in improving his evolutionary computational results.

"hill-climbing." After a host was infected by a parasite, for a fixed number of intervening *parasite* generations, the parasite was cloned, mutated and evaluated but was only replaced by the mutated clone if the resulting fitness was higher. Note that the disadvantage here is that this procedure must be applied to all hosts, not just newly infected ones. But now since all hosts are being considered during each generation, the advantage is that a natural form of aging is being applied to the host population. By using a sufficient number of parasite generations, it was possible to build parasite fitness levels back up between host generations, which is remarkable considering the survivability task they face. For the images shown here parasites were bred for 20 generations between each host generation.

17.4.9 Examples of Co-evolved Images

Figure 17.5 shows two examples of the co-evolved images Greenfield's coevolutionary model provided. Figure 17.6 provides a better indication of the diversity of images that can be evolved using these techniques by offering more examples, but at a lower resolution due to space considerations.

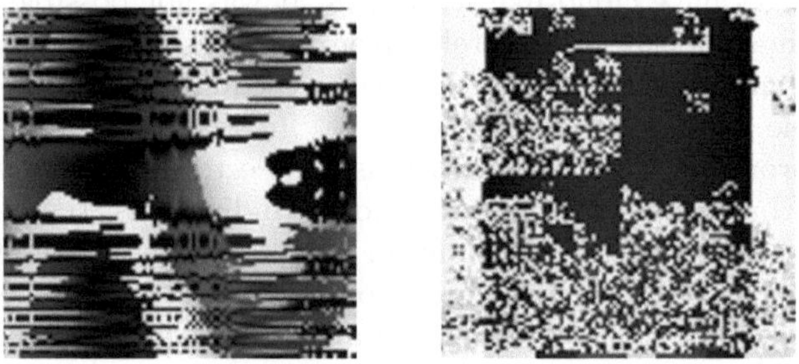

Fig. 17.5. Example co-evolved images

17.4.10 Tracing Co-evolution — Tilings

Because of the number of images considered, in order to observe the results of co-evolution, image genotypes must be culled from the host population and their phenotypes displayed. Since the results of the fitness contests can be difficult to understand and interpret it can be difficult to see how co-evolution is affecting the nature of evolved images. To consider such issues Greenfield [44] made some further modifications to his co-evolutionary framework. The principal one was dropping the elitism re-population requirement for hosts. Thus instead of retaining the most fit images (i.e., the breeding pool) after each generation, he completely replaced the host image population. This was accomplished by shrinking the image population size down from 30 to a

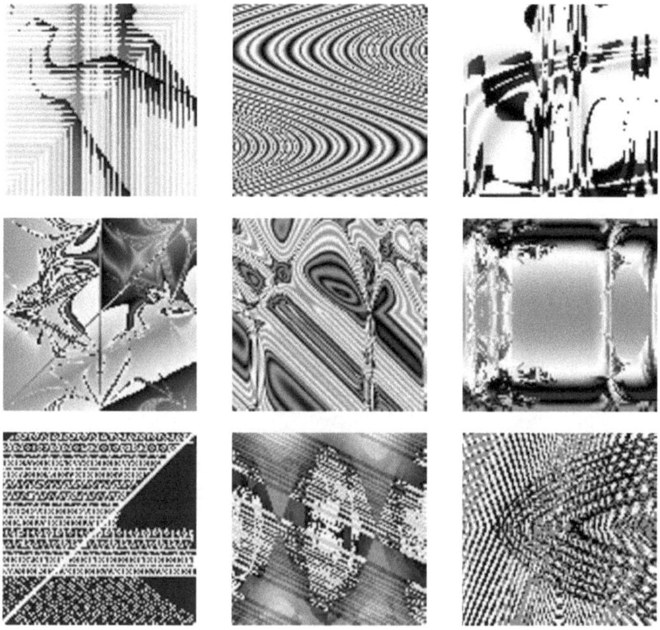

Fig. 17.6. The diversity of co-evolved imagery

breeding pool of 15 at the conclusion of each generation and then selecting and breeding, with replacement, 15 randomly selected pairs of distinct hosts drawn from that pool. Parasite population management, including intergenerational breeding to strengthen the parasites as described above, was not significantly altered. There were two parasite populations (i.e., two randomly generated fixed locations for parasites to attach to), five parasites were replaced after each host generation, and "hill-climbing" for parasites was allowed to proceed for 25 parasite generations. The number of host generations was either 500 or 1000 with the most fit host culled after every 25 (respectively 50) generations so that a 4×5 array, or "tiling", could be assembled and viewed.

Figure 17.7 shows such a tiling. Tilings were then used to identify *epochs*: intervals where the change between two successive images was significant. Once epochs were identified, the co-evolutionary simulation was re-run and the most fit images were culled every generation (respectively every other generation) during the epoch to create a 5×5 "mosaic" such as the one shown in Fig. 17.8. In this figure the epoch begins starting from the generation of the last image in the first row of Fig. 17.7. Somewhat unexpectedly, when some mosaics were viewed at full resolution they were found to be of aesthetic interest in their own right. Figure 17.9 shows such an example.

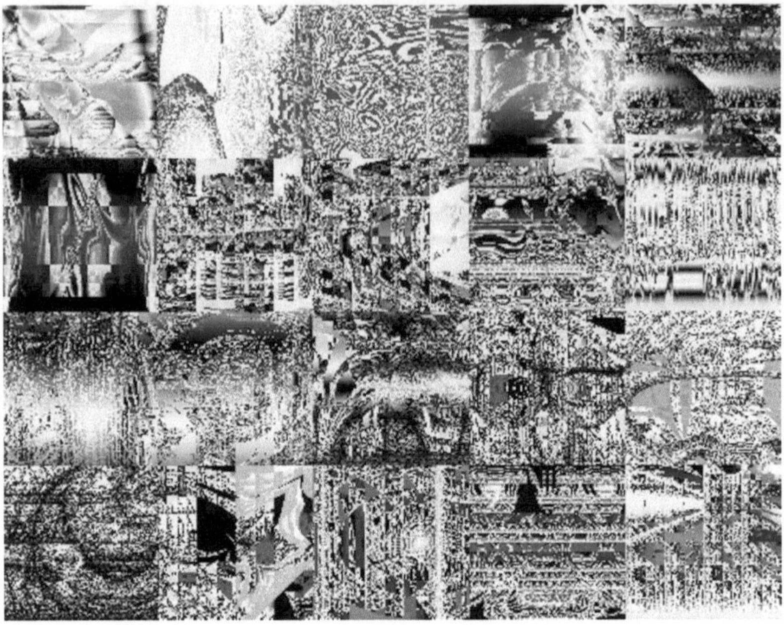

Fig. 17.7. A 4 × 5 tiling obtained by running the co-evolutionary simulation for 1000 generations and culling after every 50 generations. Chronologically, the tiling is left to right, top to bottom

17.5 The Pitfalls and Difficulties of Co-evolution

In artificial life simulations and in combinatorial optimization based on evolutionary computation, the use of co-evolution is usually justified by the desire to accelerate co-evolutionary arms races [45], to maintain population diversity [46], or both [22]. However, it has long been recognized that there are certain pitfalls and traps that must be avoided. Two critical issues Ficici and Pollack [47] identify are *evolutionary cycling* where genotypes are re-discovered over and over, and *mediocre stable states* where the co-evolving populations are constantly changing but few tangible gains are realized.

In the context of evolutionary art such issues are also of concern, but there are additional considerations. Perhaps the most important is the nature of the co-evolutionary design itself. In all of the examples we have seen: (1) it required an extraordinary effort to design a population to co-evolve in conjunction with the population of visual art works being produced by an underlying image generation system, and (2) it was difficult to find an evaluation scheme that made *artistic* sense. Much of the problem with the latter arises as a consequence of the fact that there is very little data available to suggest algorithms for evaluating aesthetic fitness. Moreover, the few algorithmic approaches that have been tried [10, 11, 12, 48] do not seem to be particularly well-suited for co-evolution. There are several interesting theories and

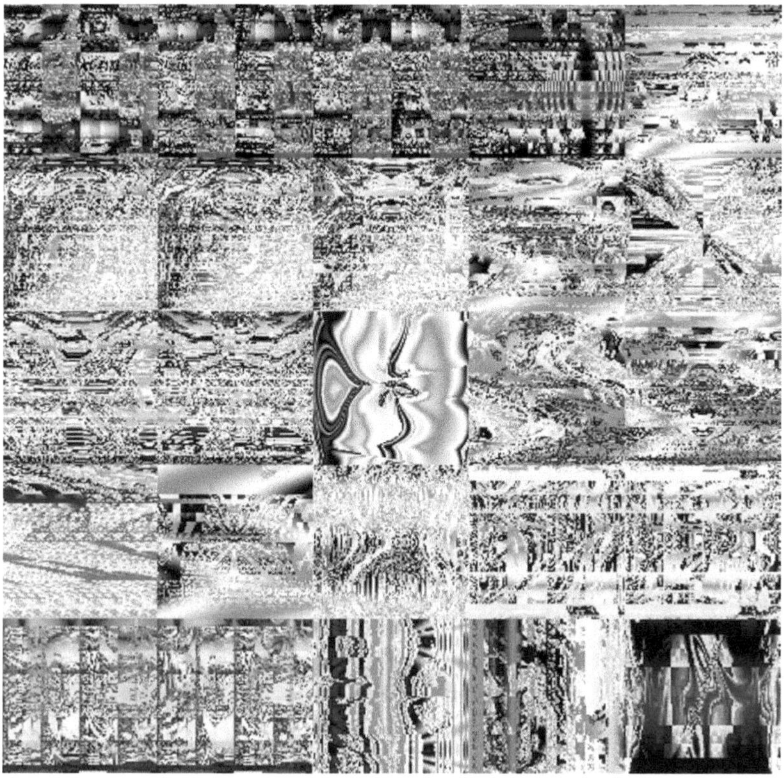

Fig. 17.8. A 5×5 mosaic induced by the tiling shown in Fig. 17.7. It was obtained by culling the most fit image from every other each generation during a fifty generation epoch commencing with generation 251 of that run. Thus the top left tile of this tiling from generation 252 is the image culled two generations after the tile appearing at the far right in the first row of Fig. 17.7, while the bottom right tile of this tiling from generation 300 coincides with the first tile in the second row of Fig. 17.7

hypotheses from psychology and cognitive science [49, 50, 51, 52] about the nature of aesthetics, but scant few clues for how to go about quantifying or assessing it. It would be desirable to have better cognitive science arguments for justifying measurements of aesthetic content.

For Greenfield, an image for which the convolved image was significantly *different* from the original furnished a dynamic measure of fitness. Fortunately, evolutionary cycling was rare, and there was evidence that evolutionary trajectories were able to escape from degenerate regions of image space following *different* evolutionary paths, hence new hosts tended to be quite different than images from earlier generations. In his co-evolutionary model, parasites chase hosts over the fitness landscape or, to put it another way, hosts ward off parasites by fleeing from them over the fitness landscape, and co-evolution causes this fitness landscape to constantly change. Such a "Red Queen Effect"

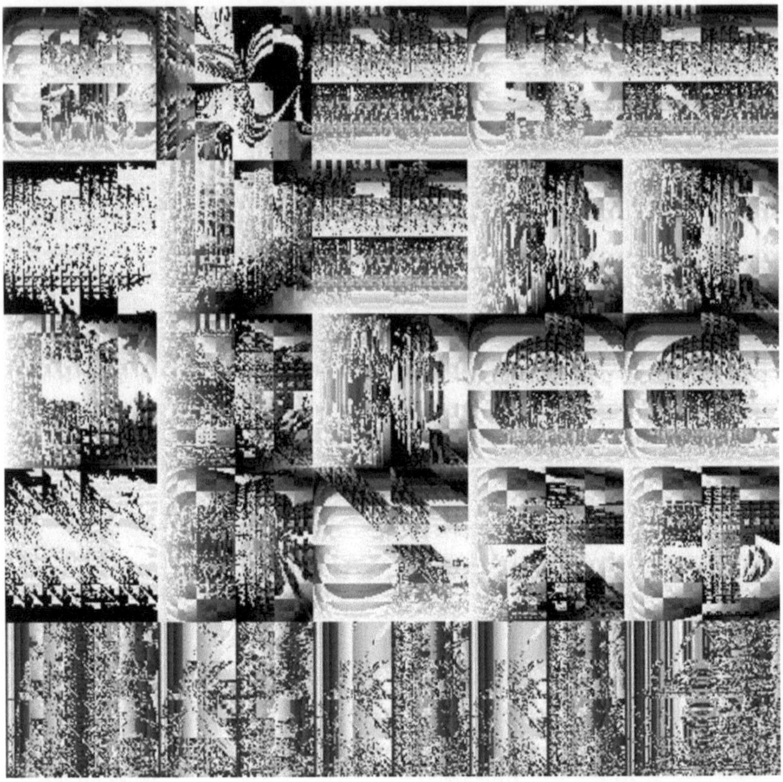

Fig. 17.9. A 5×5 mosaic made by culling the most fit image from each generation of a 50 generation epoch. Surprisingly, this mosaic exhibits some of the composition characteristics one might expect from an artist created tiling

is consistent with the results of other co-evolutionary simulations [45, 53]. However, now the problem one has to cope with is the problem of image sub-populations appearing and disappearing too quickly. As Ficici and Pollock [47] point out, most often this is caused by an imbalance between the fitness (i.e., health) of hosts and parasites. Note that this helps to explain why Greenfield found it necessary to breed his two populations at different rates.

Saunders and Gero were interested in making use of the *arms race* aspect of co-evolution as indicated by their statement that "agents influence the behavior of other agents by communicating their artworks and their evaluations of those artworks." Dorin was motivated to use co-evolution for its *diversity* features. He wanted the visual display of his interactive installation to not be too stable and boring. He observed that his "population model incorporating disease seems to maintain diversity indefinitely." There are other alternatives to consider if maintaining diversity during image evolution is the principal objective. One well-known technique is evolutionary multi-objective optimization [36]. Another approach that has not been very well studied is image "targeting" where examples are supplied by users and interacting subpopulations are dedicated to these examples [54].

Other artistic issues that would not ordinarily be considered when deciding whether or not to use a co-evolutionary framework are "color" and "style." For example, some would say the style of Greenfield's co-evolved images might fall somewhere between chaotic and noisy. This occurred even though it is well known that most Sims' style image generation systems are capable of producing a much wider range of styles. Moreover, color is extrinsic to his evolutionary model. It is a post-process and as the false-colored images co-evolved by Greenfield on the accompanying DVD show his images can look wholly different when re-colored. Therefore, if co-evolutionary methods are to become more commonplace or widespread in evolutionary art in the future, in addition to finding easier implementation pathways, better means of confronting issues such as style and color will also need to be addressed.

References

1. Dawkins, R. (1989). The evolution of evolvability. In Langton, C., ed.: *Artificial Life*. Reading, Massachusetts. Addison-Wesley, 201–220
2. Sims, K. (1991). Artificial evolution for computer graphics. *Computer Graphics*, **25**: 319–328
3. Koza, J. (1990). Evolution and co-evolution of computer programs to control independently acting agents. In Meyer, J., Wilson, S., eds.: *From Animals to Animats, Proceedings of the First International Conference on Simulation of Adaptive Behavior*. Cambridge, Massachusetts. MIT Press, 366–375
4. Sims, K. (1991). Interactive evolution of dynamical systems. In Varela, F., Bourgine, P., eds.: *Toward a Practice of Autonomous Systems: Proceedings of the First European Conference on Artificial Life*. Cambridge, Massachusetts. MIT Press, 171–178
5. Sims, K. (1993). Interactive evolution of equations for procedural models. *The Visual Computer*, **9**: 466–476
6. Todd, S., Latham, W. (1991). Artificial life or surreal art. In Varela, F., Bourgine, P., eds.: *Torward a Practice of Autonomous Systems: Proceedings of the First European Conference on Artificial Life*. Cambridge, Massachusetts. MIT Press, 504–513
7. Todd, S., Latham, W. (1992). *Evolutionary Art and Computers*. Academic Press. San Diego, California
8. Rowbottom, A. (1999). Evolutionary art and form. In Bentley, P., ed.: *Evolutionary Design by Computers*. San Francisco, California. Morgan Kaufmann, 261–277
9. Greenfield, G. (2002). On the co-evolution of evolving expressions. *International Journal of Computational Intelligence and Applications*, **2(1)**: 17–31
10. Baluja, S., Pomerleau, D., Jochem, T. (1994). Towards automated artificial evolution for computer-generated images. *Connection Science*, **6**: 325–354
11. Greenfield, G. (2002). Color dependent computational aesthetics for evolving expressions. In Sarhangi, R., ed.: *Bridges: Mathematical Connections in Art,*

Music, and Science; Conference Proceedings 2002. Winfield, Kansas. Central Plain Book Manufacturing, 9–16
12. Machado, P., Cardoso, A. (2002). All the truth about NEvAr. *Applied Intelligence*, **16(2)**: 101–119
13. Machado, P., Cardoso, A. (1998). Computing aesthetics. In Oliveira, F., ed.: *Proceedings XIV-th Brazilian Symposium on Artificial Intelligence SBIA 98.* Vol. 1515 of Lecture Notes in Artificial Intelligence. Berlin. Springer, 219–229
14. Ray, T. (1992). An approach to the synthesis of life. In Langton, C., et al., eds.: *Artificial Life II, Santa Fe Institute Studies in the Sciences of Complexity, Proceedings Volume X.* Redwood City, California. Addison-Wesley, 371–408
15. Hillis, D. (1992). Co-evolving parasites improves simulated evolution as an optimization procedure. In Langton, C., et al., eds.: *Artificial Life II, Santa Fe Institute Studies in the Sciences of Complexity, Proceedings Volume X.* Redwood City, California. Addison-Wesley, 313–324
16. Sims, K. (1994). Evolving 3d morphology and behavior by competition. In Brooks, R., Maes, P., eds.: *Artificial Life IV, Proceedings of the Fourth Interantional Workshop on the Synthesis and Simulation of Living Systems.* Cambridge, Massachusetts. MIT Press, 28–39
17. Reynolds, C. (1994). Competition, coevolution and the game of tag. In Brooks, R., Maes, P., eds.: *Artificial Life IV, Proceedings of the Fourth Interantional Workshop on the Synthesis and Simulation of Living Systems.* Cambridge, Massachusetts. MIT Press, 59–69
18. Nolfi, S., Floreano, D. (1998). Co-evolving predator and prey robots. *Artificial Life*, **4(4)**: 311–335
19. Angeline, P., Pollack, J. (1993). Competitive environments evolve better solutions to complex tasks. In Forrest, S., ed.: *Proceedings of the Fifth Interantional Conference on Genetic Algorithms.* San Mateo, California. Morgan Kaufmann, 264–270
20. Smith, R., Gray, B. (1994). Co-adaptive genetic algorithms: An example in othello strategy. In Dankel, D., ed.: *Proceedings of the 1994 Florida Artificial Intelligence Research Symposium.* Florida AI Research Society, 259–264
21. Pollack, J., Blair, A. (1998). Co-evolution in the successful learning of backgammon strategy. *Machine Learning*, **32(3)**: 225–240
22. Darwen, P., Yao, X. (2000). Does extra genetic diversity maintain escalation in a co-evolutionary arms race. *International Journal of Knowledge-Based Intelligent Engineering Systems*, **4(3)**: 191–200
23. Dolin, B., Bennett, F., Rieffel, E. (2002). Co-evolving an effective fitness sample: Experiments in symbolic regression and distributed robot control. In: *Proceedings of the 2002 ACM Symposium on Applied Computing (SAC).* Madrid, Spain. ACM Press, 553–559
24. Husbands, P., Mill, F. (1991). Simulated co-evolution as the mechanism for emergent planning and scheduling. In Belew, R., Booler, L., eds.: *Proceedings of the Fourth International Conference on Genetic Algorithms.* San Francisco, California. Morgan Kaufmann, 264–270
25. Todd, P. (2001). Simulating the evolution of musical behavior. In Wallin, N., ed.: *The Origins of Music.* MIT Press. Cambridge, Massachusetts
26. Werner, G., Todd, P. (1997). Too many love songs: Sexual selection and the evolution of communication. In Husbands, P., Harvey, I., eds.: *Fourth European Conference on Artificial Life.* Cambridge, Massachusetts. MIT Press/Bradford Books, 434–443

27. Rooke, S. (2002). Eons of genetically evolved algorithmic images. In Bentley, P., Corne, D., eds.: *Creative Evolutionary Systems.* San Francisco, California. Morgan Kaufmann, 339–365
28. Dorin, A. (2005). Artificial life, death and epidemics in evolutionary, generative, electronic art. In Rotlauf, F., et al., eds.: *Applications of Evolutionary Computing, EvoWorkshops 2005 Proceedings.* Vol. 3449 of Lecture Notes in Computer Science. Berlin. Springer, 448–457
29. Dorin, A. (2004). The virtual ecosystem as generative electronic art. In Raidl, G., et al., eds.: *Applications of Evolutionary Computing, EvoWorkshops 2004 Proceedings.* Vol. 3005 of Lecture Notes in Computer Science. Berlin. Springer, 467–476
30. Saunders, R., Gero, J. (2001). Artificial creativity: A synthetic approach to the subject of creative behavior. In Gero, J., ed.: *Proceedings of the Fifth Conference on Computational and Cognitive Models of Creative Design.* Sydney. Key Centre of Design Computing and Cognition, 113–139
31. Greenfield, G. (2000). Evolving expressions and art by choice. *Leonardo*, **33(2)**: 93–99
32. Greenfield, G. (1998). New directions for evolving expressions. In Srahangi, R., ed.: *1998 Bridges Conference Proceedings.* Arkansas City, Kansas. Gilliland Publishing, 29–36
33. Greenfield, G. (1999). On understanding the search problem for image spaces. In Sarhangi, R., ed.: *1999 Bridges Conference Proceedings.* White Plains, Maryland. Gilliland Publishing, 41–54
34. Greenfield, G. (2000). Art and artificial life — a coevolutionary approach. In Bedau, M., et al., eds.: *Artificial Live VII Conference Proceedings.* Cambridge, Massachusetts. MIT Press, 529–536
35. Greeenfield, G. (2002). Simulated aesthetics and evolving artworks: A coevolutionary approach. *Leonardo*, **35(3)**: 283–289
36. Greenfield, G. (2003). Evolving aesthetic images using multiobjective optimization. In McKay, B., et al., eds.: *Congress on Evolutionary Computation, CEC 2003.* Vol. 3. Canberra, Australia. IEEE Press, 1903–1909
37. Belpaeme, T. (1999). Evolving visual feature detectors. In Floreano, D., et al., eds.: *Advances in Artificial Life, Proceedings of the Fifth European Conference.* Vol. 1674 of Lecture Notes in Artificial Intelligence. Berlin. Springer, 266–270
38. Greenfield, G. (2000). Mathematical building blocks for evolving expressions. In Sarhangi, R., ed.: *2000 Bridges Conference Proceedings.* Winfield, Kansas. Central Plain Book Manufacturing, 61–70
39. Maeda, J. (1999). *Design by Numbers.* MIT Press. Cambridge, Massachussetts
40. Clement, D. (2000). Coevolution of evolved expressions Honor's Thesis, University of Richmond, Virginia.
41. Cartlidge, J., Bullock, S. (2004). Combating coevolutionary disengagement by reducing parasite virulence. *Evolutionary Computation*, **12(2)**: 193–222
42. Mitchell, M., Crutchfield, J., Das, R. (2006). The role of space in the success of coevolutionary learning. In Rocha, L.M., et al., eds.: *Artificial Life X: Proceedings of the Tenth Conference on the Simulation and Synthesis of Living Systems.* Cambridge, Massachusetts. MIT Press, 118–124
43. Williams, N., Mitchell, M. (2005). Investigating the success of spatial coevolutionary learning. In Beyer, H.G., et al., eds.: *Proceedings of the 2005 Genetic and Evolutionary Computation Conference, GECCO-2005.* New York, New York. ACM Press, 523–530

44. Greenfield, G. (2004). Tilings of sequences of co-evolved images. In Raidl, G., et al., eds.: *Applications of Evolutionary Computing, EvoWorkshops 2004*. Vol. 3005 of Lecture Notes in Computer Science. Berlin. Springer, 260–269
45. Cliff, D., Miller, G. (1995). Tracking the red queen: Measurements of adaptive progress in co-evolutionary simulations. In Moran, F., et al., eds.: *Advances in Artificial Life: Third European Conference on Artificial Life.* Vol. 929 of Lecture Notes in Artificial Intelligence. Granada Spain. Springer, 200–218
46. Cartlidge, J., Bullock, S. (2003). Caring versus sharing: How to maintain engagement and diversity in coevolving populations. In Banzhaf, W., et al., eds.: *Proceedings of the 7th European Conference on Artificial Life (ECAL 2003).* Vol. 2801 of Lecture Notes in Artificial Intelligence. Heidelberg. Springer, 299–308
47. Ficici, S., Pollack, J. (1998). Challenges in co-evolutionary learning; arms-race dynamics, open-endedness, and mediocre stable states. In Adami, C., et al., eds.: *Artificial Life VI.* Cambridge, Massachusetts. MIT Press, 238–247
48. Staudek, T. (2003). Computer-aided aesthetic evaluation of visual patterns. In Barrallo, J., et al., eds.: *ISAMA-BRIDGES 2003 Conference Proceedings.* Granada, Spain. University of Granada, 143–149
49. Arnheim, R. (1974). *Entropy and Art, an Essay on Order and Disorder.* University of California Press. Berkeley, California
50. Arnheim, R. (1966). *Towards a Psychology of Art, Collected Essays.* University of California Press. Berkeley, California
51. Ramachandran, V., Hirstein, W. (1999). The science of art: A neurological theory of aesthetic experience. *Journal of Consciousness Studies*, **6(1-2)**: 15–52
52. Zeki, S. (1999). *Inner Vision, an Exploration of Art and the Brain.* Oxford University Press. New York, New York
53. Paredis, J. (1997). Coevolving cellular automata: Be aware of the red queen. In Back, T., ed.: *Proceedings of the Seventh International Conference on Genetic Algorithms.* San Francisco, California. Morgan Kaufmann, 393–400
54. Wiens, A., Ross, B. (2002). Gentropy: Evolving 2D textures. *Computers and Graphics*, **26(1)**: 75–88

18

Experiments in Computational Aesthetics

An Iterative Approach to Stylistic Change in Evolutionary Art

Penousal Machado,[1] Juan Romero,[2] and Bill Manaris[3]

[1] CISUC, Department of Informatics Engineering, University of Coimbra, 3030 Coimbra, Portugal machado@dei.uc.pt
[2] Faculty of Computer Science, University of Coruña, Coruña, Spain jj@udc.es
[3] Computer Science Department, College of Charleston, Charleston, SC 29424, USA manaris@cs.cofc.edu

Summary. A novel approach to the production of evolutionary art is presented. This approach is based on the promotion of an arms race between an adaptive classifier and an evolutionary computation system. An artificial neural network is trained to discriminate among images previously created by the evolutionary engine and famous paintings. Once training is over, evolutionary computation is used to generate images that the neural network classifies as paintings. The images created throughout the evolutionary run are added to the training set and the process is repeated. This iterative process leads to the refinement of the classifier and forces the evolutionary algorithm to explore new paths. The experimental results attained across iterations are presented and analyzed. Validation tests were conducted in order to assess the changes induced by the refinement of the classifier and to identify the types of images that are difficult to classify. Taken as a whole, the experimental results show the soundness and potential of the proposed approach.

18.1 Introduction

We are interested in the development of Artificial Artists (AAs), i.e., artificial systems with artistic capabilities similar to their human counterparts. In our view, an AA should be able to perform aesthetic and/or artistic judgments – i.e., be able to assess the merits of the artworks it creates, as well as the works of other, artificial or human, artists [1] – and to adapt to the requirements of a dynamic hybrid society [2], populated by artificial and human agents. Taking this into consideration, our architecture for the development of AAs comprises two modules: a Creator and an Artificial Art Critic (AAC) [3].

Although, the results presented in this paper concern the visual domain, we are also interested in the music domain, and on the cross-transfer of concepts between both. Therefore, our approach to aesthetics in the visual domain is informed by our work in aesthetic modeling and classification in the music domain [4, 5].

We consider that the ability to learn how to perform aesthetic judgments is vital. It allows the system to be fully autonomous, and to use the works of other artists as source of inspiration [1]; also it creates some of the preconditions for stylistic change in the system's artistic performance, enabling it to explore, or set, new trends [3, 2].

The results presented in this chapter are a step in that direction. In particular, the main research goal is to develop a system that: (i) builds its own aesthetic model from a set of examples (thus allowing it to be influenced by other artists); and (ii) autonomously modifies its artistic style.

To achieve this goal, we explore an approach where the role of the creator is played by an Evolutionary Computation (EC) engine, and the role of the AAC by a classifier that uses a Feature Extractor (FE) and an Artificial Neural Network (ANN)-based Evaluator. Our proposal has two distinctive characteristics:

1. The use of an ANN to distinguish between images generated by the EC engine and a selected set of external images (e.g., famous paintings, artworks of a given style, landscape photographs, portraits, etc.).
2. The iterative execution of the following steps:
   - The EC engine tries to find images that are classified as external ones; the fitness is a function of the output of the ANN.
   - Once the EC run is over, the created images are added to the training set of the ANN as instances of internal images.
   - The ANN is trained to distinguish between the two sets.

Conceptually, this approach can be seen as a compromise between approaches with a static/global fitness function and those with dynamic/contextual fitness assignment such as co-evolutionary ones.

The external set of target images constitutes an "inspiring set", a stable attractor that is meant to ensure that the evolved imagery tends to incorporate aesthetic qualities recognized by humans. On the other hand, the systematic addition of the evolved images to the training set as "counter-examples" and the subsequent training of the ANN causes a competition between evolver and classifier, allowing us to attain a dynamic behavior. The fitness changes from iteration to iteration, hence promoting stylistic change.

The proposed approach has been tested with an external set of 3322 images of renowned painters and an internal set of EC-generated images. The employed AAC architecture [3] has been used in the music domain in author identification tasks, and in classification experiments related to aesthetic judgment [5, 6]. In the field of visual art, this architecture has been used in author identification tasks [7, 8, 9]. The employed FE incorporates ideas inspired by the use of complexity [10], fractal dimension [11, 12], and the Zipf–Mandelbrot law [13, 14, 7, 15] in both the visual and music domains.

Our experimental results show that the AACs used are able to discriminate between the two sets and to guide the EC algorithm. Conversely, in each iteration, the EC algorithm is able to find images that are classified as external. Therefore, an autonomous neuro-evolutionary framework able to perform stylistic variation is attained. In Manaris et al. [6] we explore a similar approach in the music domain.

The chapter is structured as follows: we begin with an overview of previous work on automatic fitness assignment and computational aesthetics (Sect. 18.2), and with a short overview of our previous work on fitness automation in the field of visual art (Sect. 18.2); in Sect. 18.4 we describe our approach; this is followed by a global overview of the system and an in-depth look at its main modules (Sect. 18.5); the experimental results attained in the visual domain and their analysis are presented in Sect. 18.6; next, we present the results attained in several validation tests; finally, in Sect. 18.8, we draw overall conclusions, and indicate other research directions and application areas.

We include all images generated throughout the evolutionary runs in the accompanying DVD, as well as the corresponding fitness values. Although the number of images, over 30000, is probably too large for a close inspection, browsing over them will, hopefully, allow the reader to get a better grasp of the types of imagery produced in each iteration.

18.2 State of the Art

One of the main difficulties in the application of EC to artistic tasks is the development of appropriate fitness assignment schemes.

Fitness assignment plays an important role in any EC system; artistic tasks are not an exception. Focusing on the domain of visual art, there are essentially five approaches to fitness assignment: interactive evolution – an approach that has been popularized by Karl Sims [16] (see Chap. 1 for a wider list of references); similarity based – i.e., evolving towards a specific image or images (see Chap. 1); hardwired fitness functions [17, 18, 19, 20]; machine-learning approaches [21]; and co-evolutionary approaches [12, 22] (see Chap. 17). The combination of several of the above methods has also been explored, for instance Saunders and Gero [12] use ANNs in the context of a co-evolutionary approach and Machado et al. [8, 9] combine interactive evolution with a hardwired fitness function.

Taking into account that we are interested in systems able to perform aesthetic judgments, interactive evolution and similarity-based approaches are not of particular relevance for the present chapter. The remaining approaches pose several complex problems.

Even if we consider that there is such a thing as a global aesthetic value that can be objectively measured, or that we are only interested in mimicking the aesthetic preferences of a particular user, building a hardwired function capable of assessing it is definitely a difficult task. If we take into consideration that this function will be used in conjunction with EC algorithms, which are prone by nature to explore the shortcomings of the fitness function to maximize fitness, the scenario becomes even worse.

Using a machine-learning approach can alleviate some of the burden of coding the fitness function. Nevertheless, learning to evaluate aesthetic judgments has proven to be a complex task. The work of Baluja et al. [21] is one of the few published attempts at doing so, and it is also the closest one to the approach presented in this chapter. Baluja et al. [21] use interactive evolution to build a set of evaluated images, in a later stage these images are used to train an ANN that receives as input an image and produces an evaluation. Several ANN architectures have been tested.

Although the approach is elegant, the results are far from being a success [21]. The ANN is able to train, yet it fails to generalize properly. In the best configuration found, the error in the test set is 0.2, which is only marginally superior to the results attainable by using a random function, biased to match the probabilistic distribution of the training set, to assign fitness (0.24) [21].

Independently of the fitness function being built or learned, static approaches to fitness assignment share a common problem: the EC algorithm tends to converge to a specific type of imagery that depends on the particularities of the fitness function and of the EC algorithm.

Co-evolutionary approaches overcome, to some extent, this limitation. However, it is difficult to incorporate aesthetic criteria in the evaluation scheme.[4] Even if this difficulty is overcome, ensuring that the evolved imagery relates to human aesthetics is not a trivial task. As Todd and Werner state:

> "One of the biggest problems with our coevolutionary approach is that, by removing the human influence from the critics ... the system can rapidly evolve its own unconstrained aesthetics." [23]

Taking into consideration the limited number of EC systems, in the field of visual art, where an attempt to incorporate aesthetic criteria in fitness assignment is made, it becomes relevant to consider approaches that, while not related to EC, are of pertinence to the field of computational aesthetics.

The work of Birkhoff [24] is probably the first attempt to present a formal measurement of aesthetics. Birkhoff suggests that aesthetic value results from the ratio between order and complexity, applying this principle to measure the aesthetic value of several 2D contours. The works of Moles [25], Arnheim [26, 27, 28] and Bense [29], draw upon the ideas of Birkhoff, bringing into play Shannon's [30] Information Theory. More recently, Staudek [31, 32] also presents an aesthetic theory where notions such as chaos and complexity play an important role.

Machado and Cardoso [10] use complexity estimates, based on JPEG and fractal image compression, to estimate the aesthetic value of grayscale images,

[4] A thorough description and analysis of co-evolutionary approaches in the field of visual art can be found in Chap. 17.

attaining results higher than the human average in Maitland Graves' "Design Judgment Test" [33]. This work was the basis for the automated fitness assignment scheme [17, 9] which we briefly describe in Sect. 18.3.

Svangärd and Nordin [20] also resort to complexity estimates based on compression schemes to evaluate images. Ritendra et al. [34] resort to a set of features – which includes texture, colorfulness, shape convexity and familiarity measures – and an support vector machine-based classifier to discriminate between photographs with high and low ratings, using as data source an online photo sharing Web site (Photo.net).

The concept of fractal dimension (FD) has also been considered a relevant aesthetic feature [35]. Taylor et al. [11] show the evolution of the FD of Jackson Pollock's paintings, later exploring the use of this technique to authenticate them. Finally, they study the relations between FD and aesthetics [36]. Interestingly, FD has also been used in Evolutionary Art (EA) to automate fitness assignment [37, 12].

18.3 Background Work on Automated Fitness Assignment in Visual Art

Inspired by the works of Moles [25] and Arnheim [26, 27, 28] and by studies that indicate a preference for simplified representations of the world, and a tendency to perceive it in terms of regular, symmetric and constant shapes [38, 27, 39, 40], Machado and Cardoso [10, 17, 9] have explored the following hypothesis: Aesthetic value is related to the sensorial and intellectual pleasure resulting from finding a compact percept (internal representation) of a complex visual stimulus.

This approach rewards images that are simultaneously visually complex and easy to perceive, employing estimates for the Complexity of the Percept (CP) and for the Complexity of the Visual Stimulus (CV). CP and CV are estimated through the division of the root mean square error (RMSE) by the compression ratio resulting, respectively, from the fractal (quadratic tree based) and JPEG encoding of the image.

Additionally, a temporal component is also considered [10, 17, 9]. As time passes the level of detail in the perception of the image varies. It is therefore necessary to estimate CP for different moments in time, in this case t_0 and t_1, which is attained by performing fractal image compression with increasing levels of detail. The proposed approach values images where CP is stable for different levels of detail. To capture the previously described notions the following formula was proposed [10]:

$$\text{value} = \frac{CV^a}{(CP(t_1) \times CP(t_0))^b} \times \frac{1}{\left(\frac{CP(t_1) - CP(t_0)}{CP(t_1)}\right)^c} \tag{18.1}$$

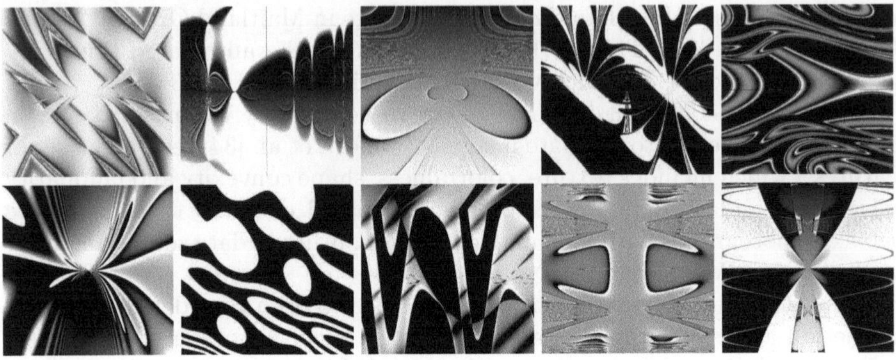

Fig. 18.1. Best individuals from 10 independent runs

where a, b and c are parameters used to adjust the importance given to each of the components. The left side of the formula rewards images that have, simultaneously, high CV and low CP estimates. The right side rewards images whose CP is stable across time. The division by $CP(t_1)$ is a normalization operation.

To apply this set of ideas in an evolutionary context, we limit the different components of the formula, as follows:

$$\text{value} = \frac{\min(\alpha, CV)^a}{\max(\beta, CP(t_1) \times CP(t_0))^b} \times \frac{1}{\max\left(\gamma, \frac{CP(t_1)-CP(t_0)}{CP(t_1)}\right)^c} \quad (18.2)$$

where α, β and γ are constants defined by the user.

Machado and Cardoso [17, 9] conducted several experiments, using the Genetic Programming (GP) engine of NEvAr[5] and (18.2) as fitness function.

The results attained with this autonomous EA system are quite surprising [17, 9]. Although the approach has several shortcomings – e.g., it only deals with grayscale images – it allows the evolution of a wide set of imagery with arguable aesthetic merit. In Fig. 18.1, we present the fittest images from several independent runs.

In a subsequent study [8, 9], a variation of this approach was used in the context of a partially interactive system. In this variation, the user was allowed to specify optimum values for CV, $CP(t_1) \times CP(t_0)$, and $(CP(t_1) - CP(t_0))/CP(t_1)$. The user was also able to intervene at any stage of the evolutionary run, supplying fitness values to the current population. The evaluations performed by the user took precedence over the ones made by the system. Using this variation it became possible to overcome some of the shortcomings of the previous approach, including the limitation to grayscale images.

[5] NEvAr stands for "Neuro Evolutionary Art". In Sect. 18.5.1 a brief overview of the system is provided.

18.4 The Approach

Succinctly, the proposed approach can be described as follows:

1. A set of *external* images is selected.
2. Using the EC system, a set of randomly generated *internal* images is created.
3. The ANN is trained to distinguish among *internal* and *external* imagery.
4. A new EC run is started. The output of the ANN is used to assign fitness. Images classified as *external* have higher fitness than those classified as *internal*.
5. The EC run stops when a termination criterion is met (e.g., a pre-established number of generations, attaining a given fitness).
6. The images generated by the EC algorithm are added to the set of *internal* images.
7. The process is repeated from step 3.

One of the key aspects of this approach is the definition of two classes of images. The first class contains *external imagery*. Images that were not created by the GP system and that are usually considered "interesting" or of "high aesthetic value". This class represents an "inspiring set". In the experiments presented in this chapter we employ a set of paintings made by famous artists. The second class contains *internal imagery*, i.e., images previously generated by the GP engine. Although part of these images may be considered interesting by some, for the purposes of the present chapter this class represents undesirable imagery – we are interested in stylistic change, therefore, in this context, images that were already created by the system are not desirable. Nevertheless, and for different purposes, the inclusion of remarkable images generated by the GP engine in the inspiring set may be appropriate.

Like Baluja et al. [21], we use ANNs to assign fitness to the evolved images. In their work, the ANN is trained to mimic the evaluations performed by users in previous interactive runs.

This poses problems, such as: (i) it is difficult to create a set of consistently evaluated images; and (ii) it is difficult to ensure that such a set is representative of the range of imagery that the system may produce. In our proposal the ANN is trained to discriminate between *internal* and *external* images. These sets can be objectively defined, which solves the first problem. Regarding the second problem, although the set of *external* images should be representative of a given type of imagery, this is arguably easier than creating a set that is representative of all the images that an EA tool can create (note that, for instance, NEvAr can, in theory, generate any image [17, 9]). Additionally, the internal set is iteratively expanded, which also contributes to overcome the second problem.

The approach of Baluja et al. [21] has another type of limitation: since the training images are generated by the GP system, even if the ANN is able to reproduce the evaluations of the user(s) (note that this was not the case

[21]), its use to assign fitness will, most likely, lead to the evolution of images that were already generated in interactive runs, or which are similar to them. Although this can be valuable, the generation of novel imagery would be far more interesting.

In our approach, the task of the evolutionary module is to evolve images that the ANN classifies as external imagery. This may be accomplished by evolving images that:

1. are similar (from the perspective of the ANN) to those belonging to the *external* set;
2. are different from the set of GP-generated images used to train the ANN (e.g., images that are entirely novel, hence dissimilar from both sets).

Once such images are found, they become part of the *internal imagery* of the system and are used to train the ANN that will be used in the next iteration, which forces the GP to explore new paths in subsequent iterations.

In the long run, there are two possible final scenarios: (i) the EC system becomes unable to find images that are classified as external; (ii) the ANN becomes unable to discriminate between internal and external imagery.

The first outcome reveals a weakness of the EC engine. This can be caused by a wide variety of factors, for instance: the set of EC parameters may be inadequate; the fitness landscape may be deceptive; etc.

In the second outcome, there are two possible sub-scenarios: (ii.a) the images created by the EC system are similar to some of the external images, which implies that the EC and the classifier are performing flawlessly; (ii.b) the images created by the EC system are stylistically different from the external imagery provided.

The second sub-scenario indicates a weakness of the classifier system. In theory, this can indicate: the existence of stylistic differences that are not captured by the set of features; that the employed ANN and training technique is not able to take full advantage of the provided features; that the settings used in the training of the ANN were not appropriate; etc.

Distinguishing between situations (ii.a) and (ii.b) may encompass some degree of subjectivity. Nevertheless, if that were the case, this difficulty alone would imply, that a considerable success was attained, i.e., an autonomous EC system capable of producing artworks that are arguably similar to those made by humans.

18.5 Description of the System

The system employed, schematically represented in Fig. 18.2, uses a GP engine to generate images and an AAC to classify them.

The GP engine, described briefly in the next section, is the same engine employed in NEvAr (a detailed description can be found in Machado and Cardoso [17, 9]). The AAC is presented in Sect. 18.5.2. The integration of both systems is discussed in Sect. 18.5.3.

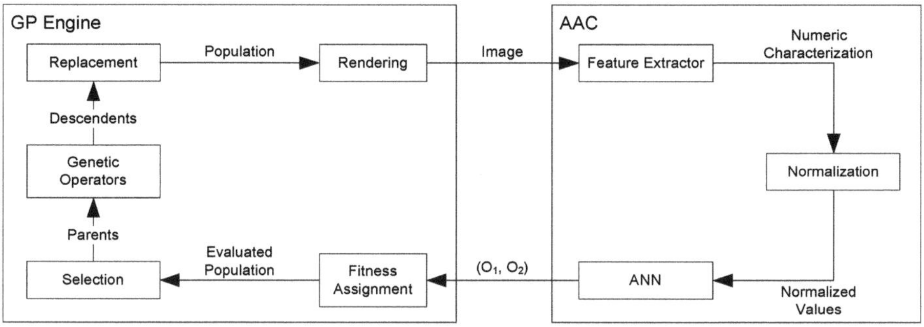

Fig. 18.2. Overview of the system

18.5.1 Genetic Programming Engine

NEvAr is an expression-based EA system (inspired by the work of Karl Sims [16]) that allows the evolution of populations of images.

NEvAr employs GP. As such, the genotypes are trees constructed from a lexicon of functions and terminals. The function set is composed mainly of simple functions such as arithmetic, trigonometric and logic operations. The terminal set is composed of two variables, x and y, and random constants. The phenotype (image) is generated by evaluating the genotype for each (x, y) pair belonging to the image. Thus, the images generated by NEvAr are graphical portrayals of mathematical expressions. As usual, the genetic operations (recombination and mutation) are performed at the genotype level. In order to produce color images, NEvAr resorts to a special kind of terminal that returns a different value depending on the color channel being processed.

The initial versions of NEvAr allowed only user-guided evolution. Later, the system was expanded by the integration of modules that allow fully or partial automation of the fitness assignment (see Sect. 18.3).

Figure 18.3 displays typical imagery produced via interactive evolution by several users.[6]

Obviously, different users may have different preferences. The tastes of a given user may also change from time to time, leading to the exploration of distinct evolutionary paths. User fatigue also tends to decrease the consistency of the evaluations. Additionally, the user may get tired of a particular type of imagery; therefore, novelty may become more important to the user than the aesthetic qualities of the image.

Although user-guided evolution is characterized by subjectivity, by inconsistency, and by the search for novelty, the interaction between system and user typically results in a type of image, an identifiable *signature* (in the sense defined by Cope [41]). This signature depends on the particularities of NEvAr

[6] Further samples can be found on NEvAr's Web site: `http://eden.dei.uc.pt/~machado/NEvAr/index.html`.

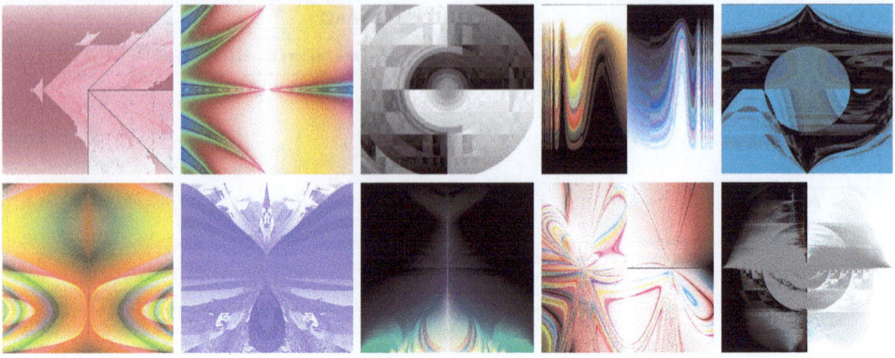

Fig. 18.3. Examples of images generated with NEvAr by different users

(primitives, genetic operators, genotype–phenotype mapping, etc.) and on the evaluations performed by the user that directly affect the fitness landscape. Nevertheless, in theory, any image can be generated [17, 9] and, therefore, stylistic change is possible.

18.5.2 Artificial Art Critic

Our AAC architecture [3] has been used in the field of visual art for author identification tasks [7, 8, 9]. In the musical domain it was tested in experiments on author identification, and in pleasantness and popularity prediction [5, 6].

It is composed of two modules, an FE and an Evaluator. The FE makes an analysis of the image, measuring several characteristics that are thought to be aesthetically relevant. Based on the collected measurements, the evaluator, implemented by means of an ANN, performs the classification task.

The current version of the feature extractor includes two types of complexity estimates based on JPEG and fractal compression. As in previous work, (Sect. 18.3) the ratio between the RMSE and the compression rate is used to estimate complexity. The fractal and JPEG estimates are calculated at three levels of detail, which is accomplished by establishing different upper bounds for the error per pixel.

The image is split into its Hue, Saturation and Value channels. For each channel the FE calculates the above-mentioned features. Inspired by previous results attained with similar metrics in music classification [4], the FE also comprises Zipf-based metrics. Namely, the rank-frequency (Zipf [42]) distribution (slope and linear correlation, R2, of the trendline) of the Hue, Saturation and Value.

Additionally, for each channel, the FE also determines:

1. The average value of each channel;[7]

[7] Since the Hue channel is circular, we compute its average angle.

2. The standard deviation of the value (STD).

For the Value channel, the FE also estimates the FD of the image, edges, and horizontal and vertical edges. Each of these measurements results in two values, the FD and the linear correlation with the FD.

The FD is measured using an approach similar to the one employed by Taylor et al. [11]: the image is converted to black and white and the FD estimated using the box-counting technique. To calculate the FD of the edges, a Sobel filter is employed to detect them (see e.g., [43]) and the FD of the resulting image is calculated.

In Table 18.1 we present the different groups of features and the components of the image to which they are applied.

Table 18.1. Characteristics considered by the FE and components of the image to which they are applied

Feature	Image	Hue	Saturation	Value
JPEG complexity	X	X	X	X
Fractal complexity		X	X	X
Average and STD		X	X	X
Zipf distribution and corresponding R2		X	X	X
FD and corresponding R2				X

To determine the variation of the considered characteristics, we partition the image into five regions of the same size – the four quadrants, and an overlapping central rectangle – and compute the previously described measurements for each partition. This process yields a total of 246 measurements.

This FE is an improvement over the one used in previous experiments that did not include an evolutionary component [7, 8, 9]. Taking into account the results attained in those tasks, we decided to use a similar one to discriminate between internal and external imagery. The main difference between the FE used in previous experiments and the current one is the measurement of the FD of several characteristics of the image.

The evaluator is composed of a feed-forward ANN with one hidden layer. We resorted to Stuttgart Neural Network Simulator (SNNS) [44] for training purposes. Standard backpropagation was employed. The values resulting from the feature extractor are normalized between 1 and −1. We adopt an architecture similar to the one used in author identification experiments. We use ANNs with one input unit per feature, 12 units in the hidden layer and 2 units in the output layer (one for each category).

18.5.3 Integration of the AAC and GP Engine

The fitness of the images is determined by the output of the AAC and requires five steps: (i) rendering the image; (ii) extracting the features; (iii) normalizing the feature values and feeding them to the ANN; (iv) determining the ANN output; (v) calculating the fitness value.

In essence, the ANN is trained to perform a binary classification task. This creates a problem: a fitness landscape composed exclusively by values close to zero or close to one will definitely cause problems for the GP system. In other words, a binary classification is not adequate to guide evolution, intermediate values are necessary.

To overcome this difficulty, while training the ANN, we allow differences between desired and obtained output values. If the difference is below the maximum tolerated error threshold, then it is propagated back as being zero (i.e., non-existent). In the experiments presented in the following sections the maximum tolerated error is set to 0.3. This allows us to get outputs that are not in the limits of the $[0, 1]$ interval, creating a smoother fitness landscape.

We use ANNs with two output neurons. The activation value of the first neuron, O_1, determines the degree of belonging to the class of selected external images. The activation of the second output neuron, O_2, determines the degree of belonging to the class of internal images.

Considering this architecture – and a maximum tolerated error of 0.3 – it is possible to devise fitness functions to evolve images that:

1. are classified as belonging to one category and not to the other (one neuron with an activation value above 0.7 and the other with an activation below 0.3);
2. are simultaneously classified as belonging to both categories (both neurons with an activation above 0.7);
3. are not classified as belonging to any of the categories (both neurons with an activation below 0.3);
4. the ANN is unable to classify with certainty (both neurons with an activation value in the $[0.3, 0.7]$ interval).

We are interested in evolving images that are classified as belonging to the set of paintings considered, $O_1 \geq 0.7$, and as not belonging to the set of NEvAr images, $O_2 \leq 0.3$. A suitable fitness function for this goal is as follows:[8]

$$\text{fitness} = \left[\frac{1 + (O_1 - O_2)}{2}\right]^2 \times 10. \tag{18.3}$$

Accordingly, an image that results in an ANN output of $(0.3, 0.7)$, thus being marginally considered as a NEvAr image, has a fitness of 0.9. Conversely, an image that is in the threshold of being classified as a *painting*, i.e., that results in an ANN output of $(0.7, 0.3)$, has a fitness of 4.9. In other words, a fitness value in the $[0, 0.9[$ interval corresponds to images that are classified as NEvAr's; in the $[0.9, 4.9]$ interval to images that the ANN is unable to classify; and in the $]4.9, 10]$ interval to images classified as paintings by the ANN.

[8] The multiplication by 10 is a scaling operation performed to allow an easier integration with the user interface.

18.6 Experimental Results

In this section we present some of the experimental results attained with our approach.

As previously stated, one of the key issues of our approach is the iterative methodology used, i.e., once an evolutionary run ends, the images generated by NEvAr are added to the set of internal images and the ANN is retrained.

For the purpose of the current paper, we are mainly interested in analyzing the differences, in terms of produced imagery, that occur from iteration to iteration, which implies presenting the images obtained in each of them. This necessity, coupled with space constraints, makes it infeasible to present results from several independent experiments. Therefore, we focus on a single experiment, paying particular attention to the first and last iterations.

18.6.1 Experimental Setup

The settings of the GP engine are presented in Table 18.2. The settings are similar to those used by default when NEvAr is run in interactive mode [17, 9]. The images are rendered in full color, at a resolution of 128×128 pixels. External images of higher dimension are resized to 128×128 for feature extraction.

To calculate the complexity estimates used in the FE, the images are compressed at three different levels of detail by setting the maximum error per pixel to 8, 14 and 20. These values were determined empirically in previous tests.

One of the sub-goals of our experiments is the assessment of the relevance of some aspects of the FE, namely the relevance of the features concerning color information and the importance of the features gathered from the partitions of the images.

Table 18.2. Parameters of the GP engine. See Machado and Cardoso [17, 9] for a detailed description

Parameter	Setting
Population size	50
Number of generations	50
Crossover probability	0.8 (per individual)
Mutation probability	0.05 (per node)
Mutation operators	sub-tree swap, sub-tree replacement, node insertion, node deletion, node mutation
Initialization method	ramped half-and-half
Initial maximum depth	5
Mutation max tree depth	3
Function set	$+, -, \times$, /, min, max, abs, neg, warp, sign, sqrt, pow, mdist, sin, cos, if
Terminal set	X, Y, scalar and vector random constants

To serve this goal, we employ different combinations of features, which result in ANNs with different input layers. The first group of ANNs includes features pertaining to the three color channels of the image. The second group of ANNs uses features related to the Saturation and Value channel. The information contained in the Hue channel is only relevant when the saturation and value are taken into consideration. In addition, Hue is circular by nature, which creates difficulties in the measurement of several features. For these reasons, the information extracted from the Hue channel is likely to be less reliable. The third group only considers the Value channel, thus analyzing the grayscale version of the image.

We gather the same set of features for the entire image and for its partitions, which results in some degree of redundancy. It is, therefore, important to assess the relevance of the information gathered from the partitions. To do so, we further divide the three groups above into ANNs which use features relative to the partitions and those which do not.

Overall, we employ six ANN architectures. The particularities of each are summarized in Table 18.3. In Table 18.4, we present other relevant parameters relative to the ANNs.

For each considered architecture we perform 30 independent repetitions of the training stage, in order to get statistically significant results. For each of these repetitions we randomly create training, test and validation sets with, respectively, 70%, 10%, and 20% of the patterns. The same randomly created sets are used for the different architectures. The training of the ANNs is halted when one of the following criteria are met: 1000 training cycles, or an RMSE in both the training and test sets lower than 0.005. These parameters were empirically established in previous experiments.

Table 18.3. Features considered in each ANN

Artificial Neural Network	1	2	3	4	5	6
Color channels	3	3	2	2	1	1
Partitions	yes	no	yes	no	yes	no
Number of features	246	41	186	31	108	18

The number of internal images increases from iteration to iteration, while the number of external images remains constant. This creates a disproportion between the two classes, which could jeopardize training. To avoid this problem we use a one-to-one class distribution scheme [44]. During training, the ANN is exposed to the same number of patterns from each class, by including repetitions of patterns from the class of lower cardinality in the training set (this does not affect the test or validation sets).

We also wish to detect at what stage the different ANNs become unable to fully distinguish between the two classes. For this purpose we carry out an additional test in which all the patterns are included in the training set. In

Table 18.4. Parameters relative to the ANNs and their training

Parameter	Setting
Number of architectures	6
Activation function	logistic
Output function	identity
Initialization of weights	random, $[-0.1, 0.1]$ interval
Learning function	backpropagation
Learning rate	0.3
Momentum	0
Update function	topological order
Maximum n. of training cycles	1000
RMSE limit (train and test sets)	0.005
Shuffle weights	yes
Class distribution (training set)	one-to-one

this case, the ANN training is halted after 5000 training cycles or when an RMSE of zero is reached. From here on we will call this specific test "*Entire Corpus*".

The generation of the 2500 images of each iteration takes, approximately, 4.5 hours. The creation and rendering of one population takes an average of 15 seconds, 0.3 seconds per image. Feature extraction is a time-consuming process, taking, on average, 6 seconds per image. The ANN training is even more time-consuming, depending on the number of patterns, the 30 training runs for a single architecture can take up to 12 hours. All time estimates where performed using a Pentium Mobile at 1.8 GHz.

Initial Sets

The initial sets of external and internal images play an important role in the performance of our system. We use an external set containing 3322 paintings of the following artists: Cézanne, de Chirico, Dalí, Gaugin, Kandinsky, Klee, Klimt, Matisse, Miró, Modigliani, Monet, Picasso, Renoir, van Gogh. The images where gathered from different online sources. The rationale was to collect a wide and varied set of artworks.

The set of internal images is created using NEvAr to generate 7 initial random populations of size 500. In order to obtain a more representative set of internal images, these generations were created using different upper bounds for the tree depths. Additionally, in order to avoid a bias towards simplicity in the internal set of images, a primitive that generates random noise in two of the populations (2 and 7) is used.

Although the images were created randomly, some of the phenotypes may appear more than once. The same can happen throughout iterations.

We performed tests in which these repetitions were removed, arriving to the conclusion that it was not advantageous to do so. Considering our goals, images that occur frequently in one iteration should be avoided at all costs in subsequent ones. Having repeated instances of "popular" images ensures that these have more influence on the training of the ANN than others. Therefore, classification errors are unlikely to happen in images that become popular, avoiding a future convergence of the EC to these images.

The existence of repetitions implies a partial overlap between the training, test and validation sets. Consequently, there is a bias in the ANN results. To overcome it, we performed a set of independent validation experiments, presented in Sect. 18.7.

In what concerns the external set, repetitions were avoided. Nevertheless, it is relatively common for an artist to paint several versions of the same motif. In these cases, and in order to avoid the subjectivity of deciding what was sufficiently different, we decided to include the different variations.

18.6.2 First Iteration

In this section we present the experimental results attained in the first iteration. An in-depth analysis of the results concerning the training of the ANN and of the relative importance of the different groups of features, of this and further iterations, will be published in the future.

In Table 18.5 we provide an overview of the results attained in training, for the different ANN architectures, presenting the average number of training cycles, the average RMSE and its STD for the training, test and validation sets. The results are calculated from the 30 independent training repetitions made for each of the 6 architectures.

Table 18.5. Overview of the ANNs' training results in iteration 1

			Training		Test		Validation	
Network	Features	Cycles	avg	std	avg	std	avg	std
1	246	733.3	.0001	.0001	.0065	.0027	.0069	.0017
2	41	863.3	.0010	.0016	.0079	.0037	.0086	.0025
3	186	940.0	.0001	.0007	.0108	.0035	.0102	.0022
4	31	926.6	.0021	.0011	.0088	.0043	.0098	.0025
5	108	1000.0	.0005	.0005	.0212	.0060	.0232	.0041
6	18	1000.0	.0125	.0028	.0214	.0057	.0225	.0049
Average		910.5	.0027	.0011	.0128	.0043	.0135	.0029

We are also interested in the number of images that are incorrectly identified. In Table 18.6 we provide an overview of these results considering a "winner-takes-all" strategy, i.e., the output neuron with the highest activation value determines the category in which the corresponding image is classified. We present the average number of misclassified images and its STD for the test, training and validation sets. The last two columns of the Table concern

Table 18.6. Average number of misclassified patters in iteration 1. The training, test and validation set have, respectively, 4775, 682 and 1364 patterns

	Training			Test			Validation			Entire Corpus	
Network	avg	std	%	avg	std	%	avg	std	%	Ext.	Int.
1	.1	.2	.001	2.9	1.9	.430	6.5	2.4	.475	-	-
2	1.9	3.6	.040	3.7	2.2	.545	8.7	2.9	.635	-	-
3	.4	1.9	.008	6.2	2.5	.911	11.3	2.9	.828	-	-
4	2.6	2.6	.054	3.9	2.7	.574	9.2	3.6	.672	-	-
5	1.0	1.5	.020	10.2	3.4	1.491	22.6	4.5	1.660	-	-
6	36.1	7.0	.756	10.8	3.4	1.581	21.9	5.0	1.604	6	5
Average	7.0	2.8	.147	6.3	2.7	.922	13.4	3.6	.976	1.00	.83

the *Entire Corpus* test. They depict the number of external images classified as internal (Ext.) and the number of internal images classified as external (Int.).

A brief perusal of Tables 18.5 and 18.6 shows that most of the ANNs successfully discriminate between internal and external images. The average RMSE in test and validation is lower than 0.0232 for all ANNs. Additionally, the average percentage of correctly classified images always exceeds 98.43%.

There are no statistically significant differences between the RMSEs attained in the test and validation sets,[9] which tends to indicate that the ANNs are generalizing properly.

The comparison between the RMSEs attained by the ANNs that use information gathered from the three color channels and those that only use information from the Saturation and Value reveals statistically significant differences for test, train and validation sets. Comparing the ANNs that resort to the Saturation and Value channels with those that only use Value also shows statistically significant differences for the three sets.

The analysis of the results of the ANNs that use features gathered from the images' partitions (ANNs 1, 3 and 5) with those that do not points out the following: although significant differences exist when we consider the RMSEs achieved in training, there are not statistically significant differences in the results attained in the test and validation sets. This indicates that, in the considered experimental conditions, the information gathered from the images' partitions is not relevant for generalization purposes.

To confirm the experimental results described above, we performed several control experiments. In these tests we randomly assigned a category to all the patterns used in the different sets. The experimental results indicate misclassification percentages of, roughly, 50% for the test and validation sets, regardless of the architecture, thus confirming that the previously described results do not arise from some implicit bias in the methodology.

[9] The statistical significance of these results, and subsequent ones, was determined through the Wilcoxon–Mann–Whitney test. Confidence level of 0.99.

Considering the above experimental findings – which suggest that the information associated with the different color channels is relevant for generalization purposes, while the information gathered from the images' partitions is not – we chose the second architecture to guide the evolutionary algorithm. This architecture employs a relatively low number of features (41), which was also relevant for our choice. To assign fitness, we select the ANN with the lowest average RMSE across training, test and validation, among the 30 trained ANNs corresponding to the second architecture.

Analysis of the EC Results

Figure 18.4 depicts the best individual of each population and the corresponding fitness values. In order to provide a better overview of the full range of imagery produced in the run we selected some examples, which are presented in Fig. 18.5. These images have a fitness higher than 4.9, which means that the ANN is classifying them as external (see Sect. 18.5.2).

The comparison between the images produced and the ones from the internal set reveals that, while the images of the internal set tend to have very low or very high complexity, the fittest images found during the run tend to have intermediate levels of complexity.

This result was expected. Randomly generated images of small depth tend to be simple. That is why we used a noise generation primitive in two of the seven random populations of the initial internal set. However, the inclusion of the noise primitive resulted frequently in mostly random images, which by definition have high complexity. Since images of intermediate complexity are frequent in the external set and rare in the internal one, it is only natural that the ANN has chosen this path to discriminate between both.

The EC algorithm found images that the ANN classifies as external without difficulties. From the fourth population onwards the fitness of the best individual is above 4.9, from the tenth population onwards the best individual has a fitness above 9.

18.6.3 Intermediate Iterations

Once an iteration is over, the 2500 images produced by the GP engine are added to the internal set and the ANNs retrained. As previously stated, we use a class distribution of one-to-one. The number of external images does not grow, but the set of internal images keeps expanding. Therefore, in each training cycle the ANNs are only exposed once to each internal pattern; the number of times they are exposed to each external pattern steadily increases from iteration to iteration.

To ensure that the initial conditions are the same for all iterations, we use a fixed random seed. Therefore, the initial population, albeit randomly generated, is the same for all iterations. This ensures that the variations in

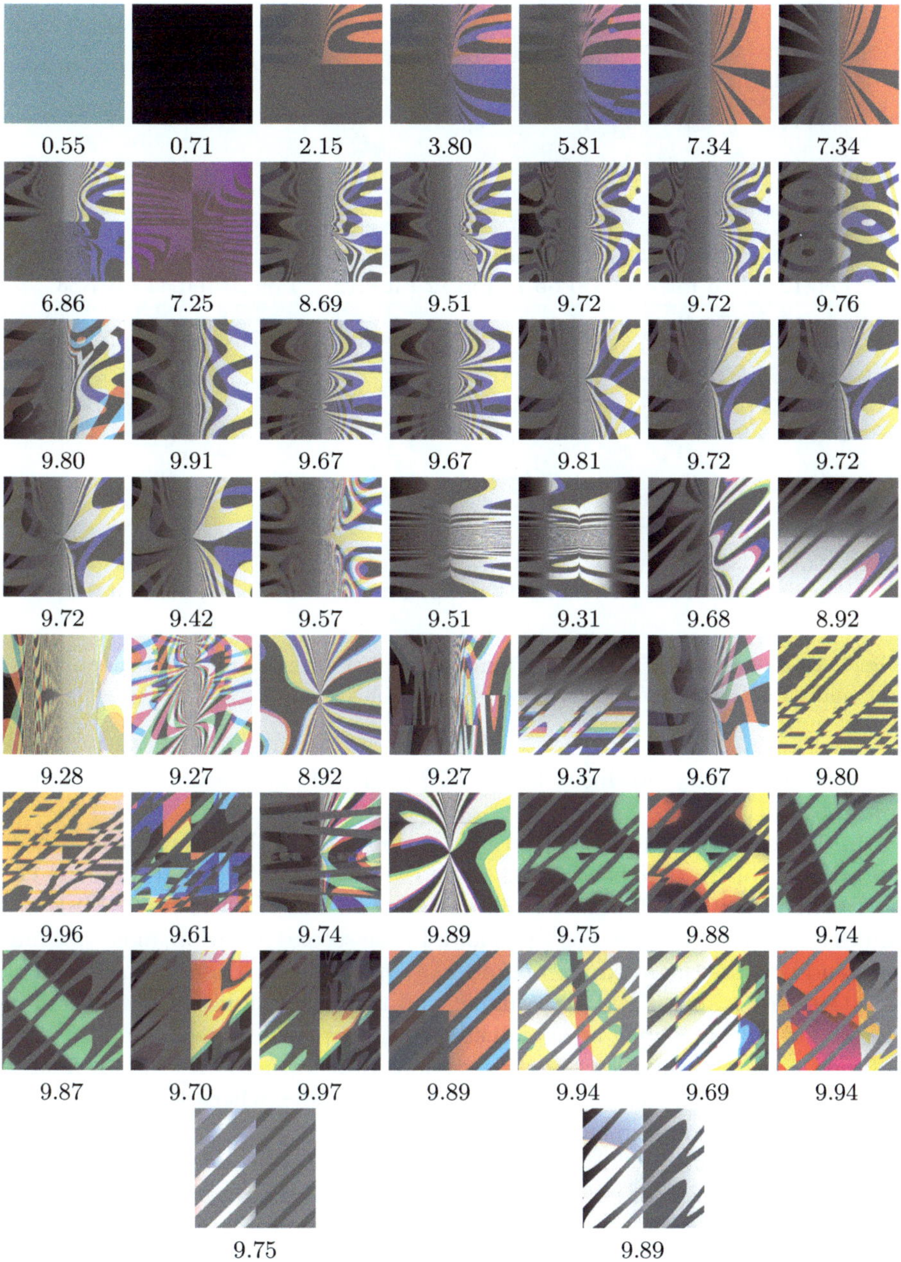

Fig. 18.4. Fittest individual from each population of the first iteration. The image in the upper-left corner corresponds to population 0; remaining images in standard reading order. The numbers indicate the fitness values

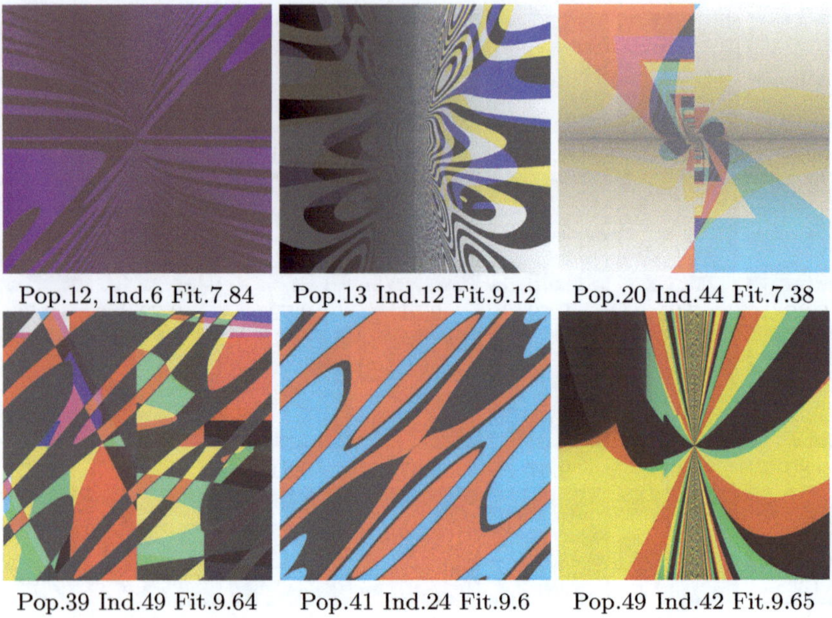

Fig. 18.5. Selected images from the first iteration (Pop=population, Ind=individual, Fit=fitness attributed by the ANN)

the type of imagery produced by the GP engine do not result from different initial conditions.

In Tables 18.7 and 18.8 we provide a synthesis of the results attained in the training of the ANNs with the second architecture for iterations 1 to 12.

In the first iteration, most training runs end because the test RMSE becomes lower than the specified threshold. In the second iteration, most training runs end because the maximum number of cycles is met. Therefore, in the first iteration, the training RMSE is higher and test and validation lower than in the second one. This may be explained by a higher correlation among the test, training and validation sets in the first iteration – where all internal images are randomly generated – than in the second one – where the internal set contains 3500 random images and 2500 evolved ones.

The increase of test and validation RMSE in the second iteration is temporary. The addition of new images resulting from evolutionary runs leads to better generalization since the set becomes more representative.

As can be observed, from the third iteration onwards the RMSE and the percentage of misclassified images remain relatively stable for the training, test and validation sets. The main exception to this trend is the sudden, and statistically significant, increase in the training RMSE and the misclassification percentage from iteration 11 to 12. Due to this difference in performance,

Table 18.7. Overview of the training results in iterations 1 to 12 of the ANNs with the second architecture

		Training		Test		Validation	
Iteration	Cycles	avg	std	avg	std	avg	std
1	863.3	.0010	.0016	.0079	.0037	.0086	.0025
2	953.3	.0003	.0009	.0113	.0039	.0111	.0024
3	913.3	.0003	.0007	.0082	.0025	.0082	.0018
4	943.3	.0003	.0009	.0090	.0028	.0095	.0020
5	823.3	.0005	.0009	.0074	.0029	.0083	.0021
6	920.0	.0003	.0006	.0081	.0024	.0079	.0018
7	930.0	.0005	.0005	.0088	.0027	.0085	.0022
8	886.7	.0004	.0005	.0079	.0026	.0079	.0014
9	880.0	.0007	.0008	.0076	.0024	.0077	.0017
10	940.0	.0006	.0009	.0083	.0025	.0084	.0011
11	893.3	.0008	.0006	.0079	.0026	.0079	.0019
12	916.7	.0016	.0017	.0085	.0026	.0085	.0025

Table 18.8. Average number and percentage of misclassified patterns attained by the ANNs with the second architecture in iterations 1 to 12. The column "Patterns" shows the total number of patterns in each iteration

		Training			Test			Validation			Entire Corpus	
Iteration	Patterns	avg	std	%	avg	std	%	avg	std	%	Ext.	Int.
1	6822	1.9	3.6	.040	3.7	2.2	.545	8.7	2.9	.635	-	-
2	9322	.9	3.4	.013	7.4	2.8	.798	14.2	4.2	.759	-	-
3	11822	.9	2.4	.011	6.5	2.7	.552	13.3	3.8	.564	-	-
4	14322	.8	2.8	.008	8.9	3.4	.624	19.0	4.6	.665	-	-
5	16822	2.1	4.3	.018	8.8	4.0	.524	19.7	4.8	.586	-	-
6	19322	.8	1.4	.006	11.1	3.7	.572	20.9	5.5	.542	-	1
7	21822	2.5	3.6	.017	12.8	4.5	.586	25.6	6.5	.586	-	1
8	24322	1.6	3.0	.009	13.2	4.5	.545	26.9	4.8	.552	-	-
9	26822	2.6	4.2	.014	14.4	5.1	.537	27.4	6.3	.511	-	1
10	29322	4.2	5.8	.021	16.8	5.4	.574	34.5	5.3	.589	-	3
11	31822	5.7	4.3	.026	17.1	6.2	.537	35.5	9.9	.557	-	1
12	34322	16.6	25.1	.069	19.8	5.7	.578	39.6	11.8	.577	-	6

we decided to stop our iterative approach in order to perform a more detailed analysis.

In the next section we present the results attained by the EC algorithm in iterations 2 to 11. The ANNs of iteration 12 are analyzed in Sect. 18.6.4.

Analysis of the EC Results

In Fig. 18.6 we present the fittest individual from populations 0, 10, 20, 30, 40 and 50, for iterations 2 to 10. In Fig. 18.7 we present selected examples from these iterations.

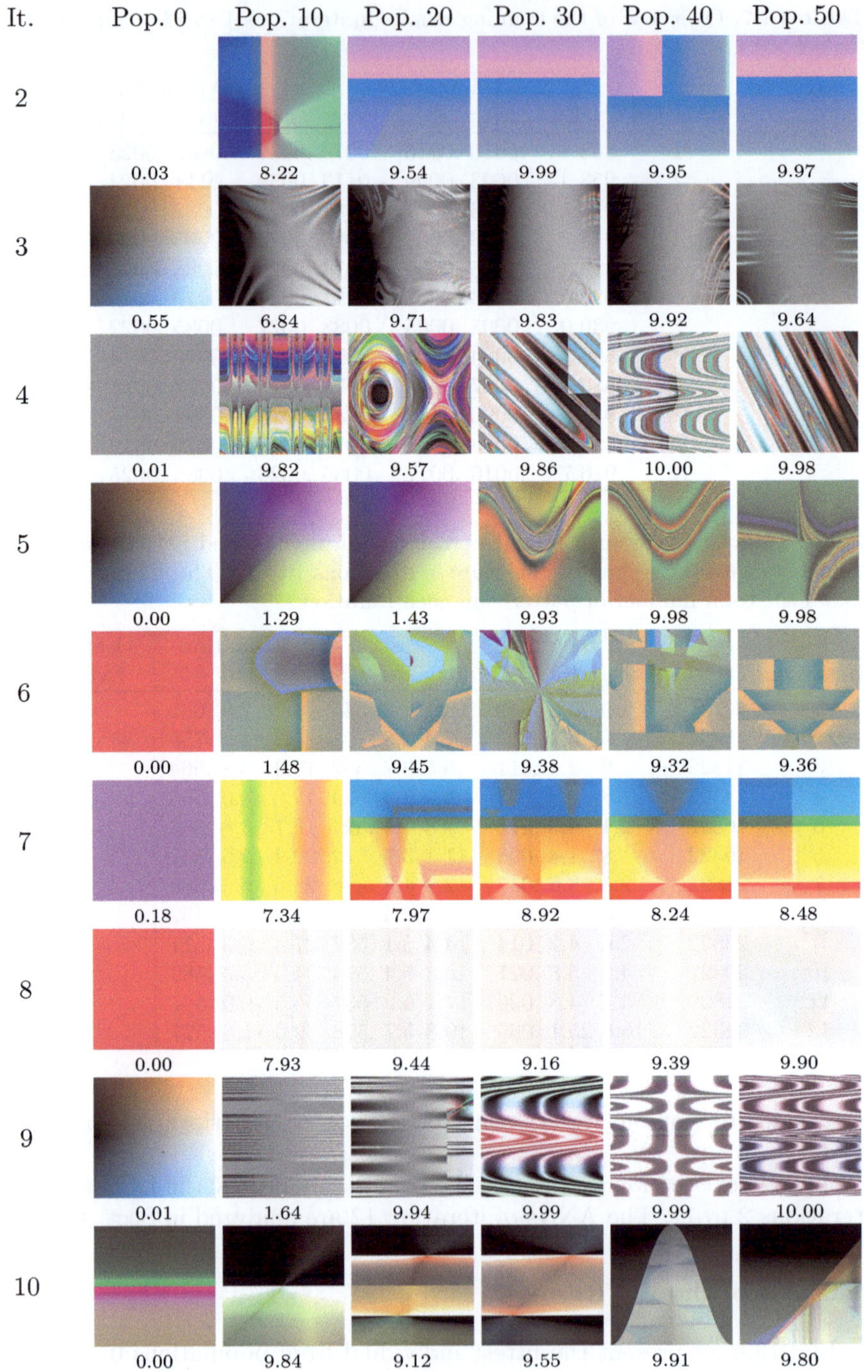

Fig. 18.6. Fittest images from populations 0, 10, 20, 30, 40, 50 of Iterations 2–10

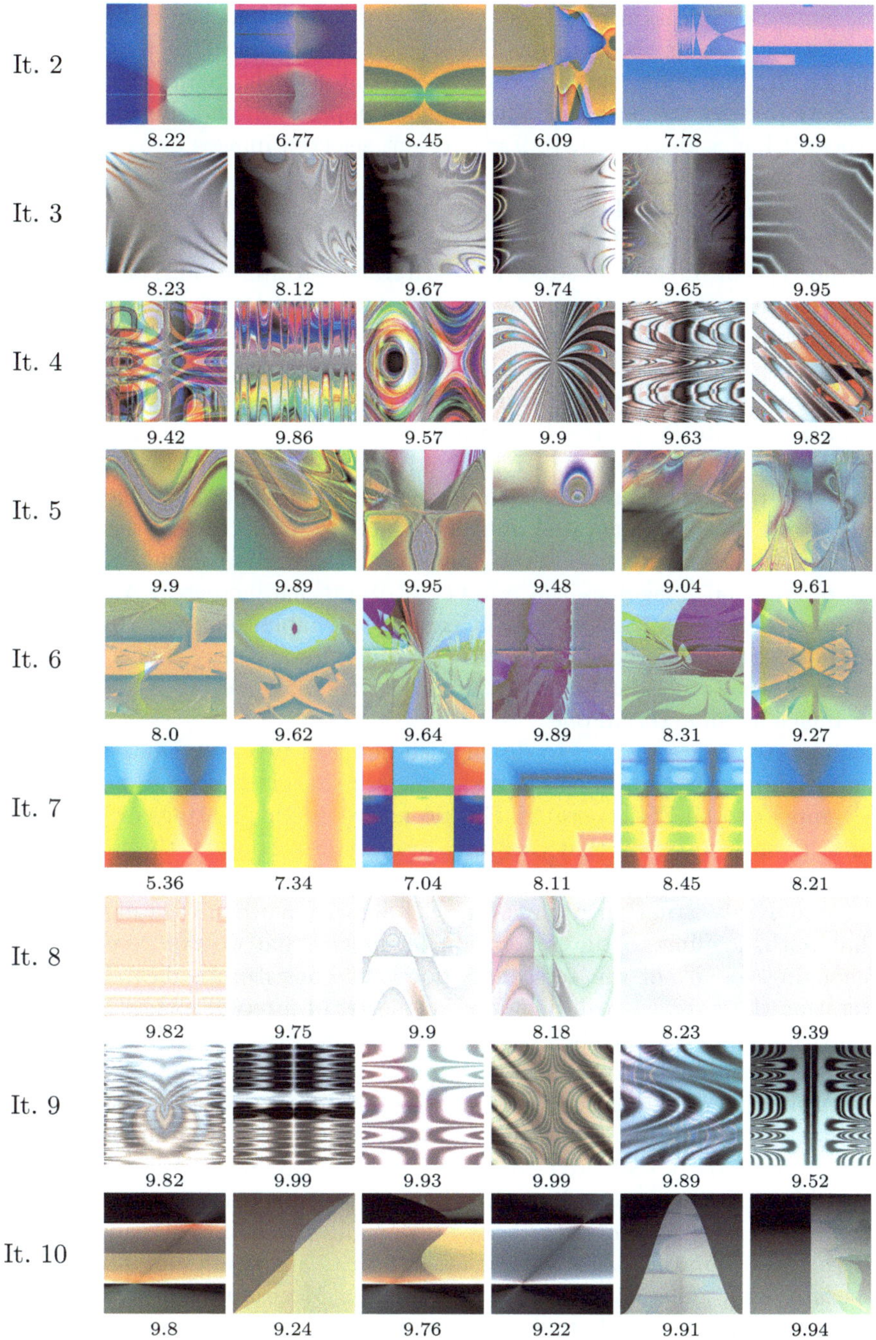

Fig. 18.7. Selected images from Iterations 2 to 10

Since the addition of the images of iteration 11 to the internal set led to the increase of the training RMSE and misclassification percentages on the twelfth iteration, this iteration is presented with greater detail. In Fig. 18.8 we present the best individual of each population and the corresponding fitness value, while in Fig. 18.9 we present selected images from the eleventh iteration.

By nature, the analysis of visual results entails some degree of subjectivity. We believe, however, that it is safe to say that there are significant differences in the type of imagery produced from iteration to iteration. For instance, in the eleventh iteration the EC algorithm converged to a style, characterized by the use of specific hues and by the low saturation values, that diverges from those explored in previous iterations. Considering that one of our main goals was to attain stylistic variation in an autonomous EC framework, the unlikeness of iterations is a key result.

We are not however, just interested in change. The inclusion of a fixed aesthetic reference frame is also a key aspect of our approach. It is therefore important that the generated imagery relates to human aesthetics.

One would expect to observe imagery that gets increasingly closer to the set of external images as the number of iterations increases. Although this may be the case in the long run, it is not reasonable to expect this approach to the aesthetic reference to be steady. To understand why this is the case, it is important to ponder about the reasons that may lead an ANN to classify an image as an external one.

The ANNs are trained to distinguish between two sets. However, conceptually, three sets can be considered, images that: (i) appear to be paintings; (ii) appear to be EC-generated; (iii) do not resemble paintings or EC created ones. Even if an ANN that can fully discriminate between the first two sets exists, occasionally this ANN will classify images of the third set as paintings.

When this situation occurs, the EC algorithm will, most likely, explore that path, leading to the generation of images that do not resemble those belonging to any of the sets. This does not constitute a flaw, in the next iteration these images will be added to the set of internal images and the EC algorithm will no longer be able to explore that path. It does mean, however, that the "approach" to the aesthetic reference frame is not steady.

A simplified example may help in the clarification of the previous statements. Let us consider that only two features exist (x, y), and that external images are closely scattered around the point $(4, 3)$ while the considered internal images are scattered around $(6, 4)$. A possible classifier for this system is: $x \leq 5.5 \rightarrow \textit{external}$, $x > 5.5 \rightarrow \textit{internal}$. Using this classifier can lead to the evolution of images with $x \cong 4$, the EC algorithm can also overcompensate, e.g., generating images with $x \cong 1$. More importantly, y is a free variable, anything can happen in that dimension, e.g., an image with $(0, 10)$ would be classified as external. As such, considering a Euclidian space, the generated images are not necessarily closer to the set of external images than those belonging to the internal set.

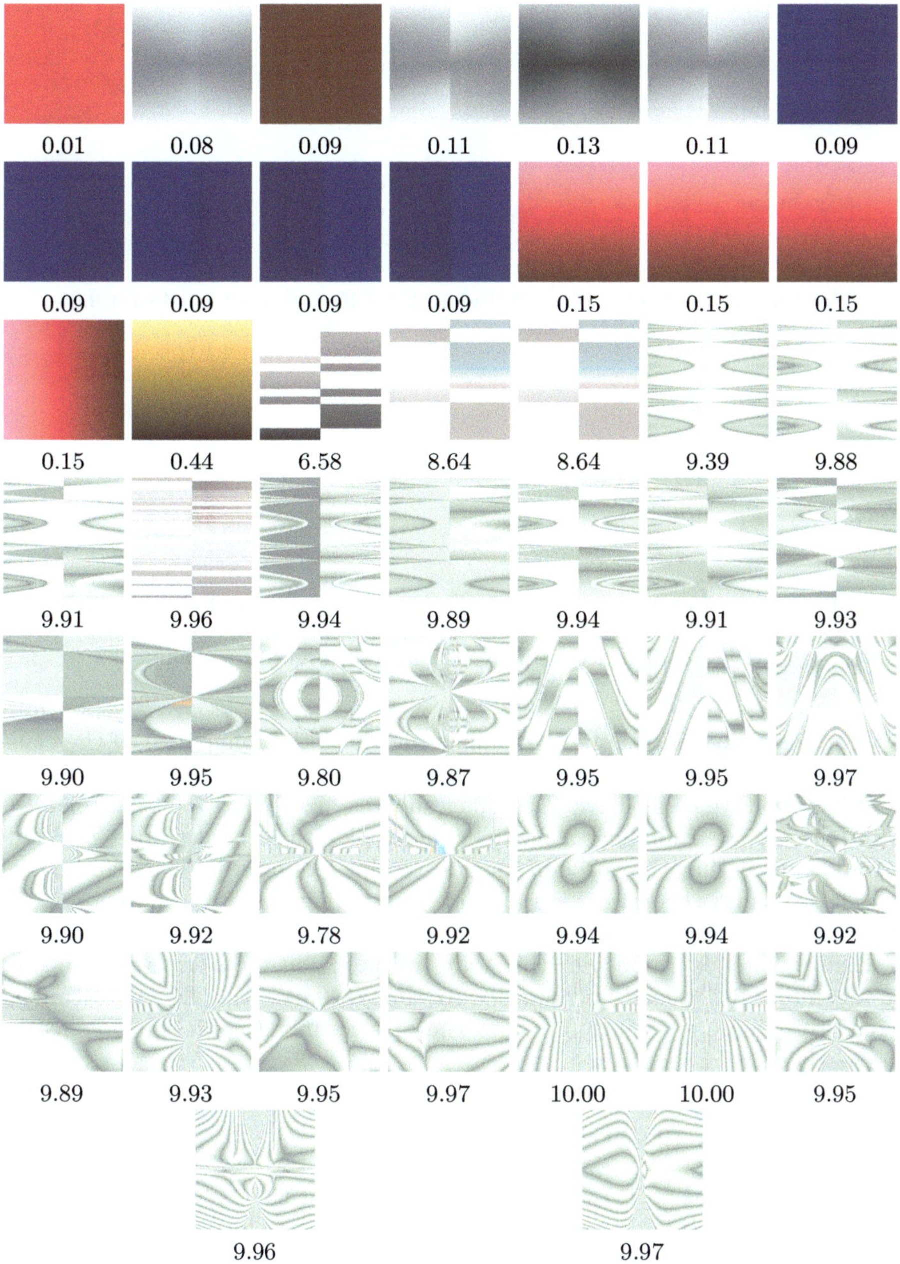

Fig. 18.8. Fittest individual from each population of the eleventh iteration

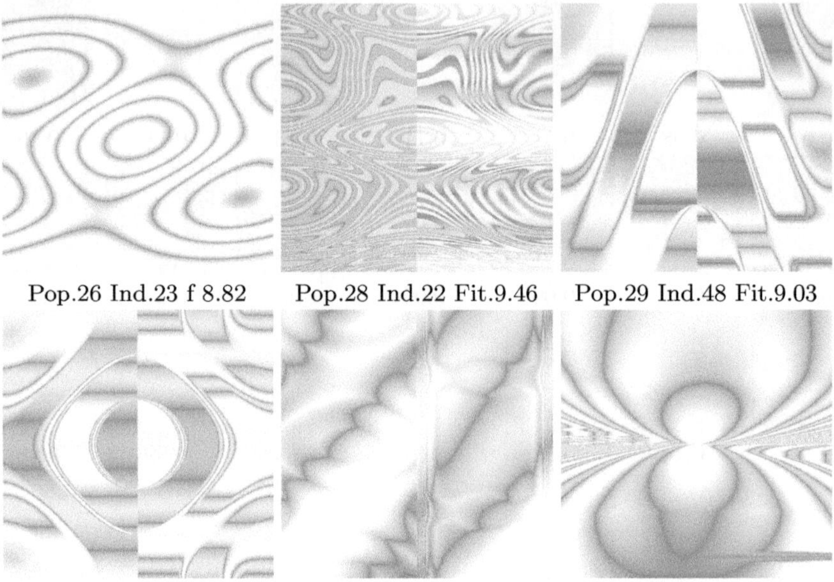

Pop.26 Ind.23 f 8.82 | Pop.28 Ind.22 Fit.9.46 | Pop.29 Ind.48 Fit.9.03

Pop.30 Ind.25 f 9.8 | Pop.37 Ind.35 Fit.9.47 | Pop.40 Ind.31 Fit.9.89

Fig. 18.9. Selected images from the eleventh iteration

The successive addition of new images leads to the refinement of the classifier. For instance, assuming that images with $x \cong 1$ were generated, in the next iteration we could have a classifier such as "$2.5 \leq x \leq 5.5 \rightarrow external$". Alternatively, we could have a classifier that took into account feature y. What is important is that the space of images classified as internal is expanding.

Thus, from a theoretical standpoint – assuming that the EC engine and the AAC are adequate and always able to cope – the combination of a fixed aesthetic reference frame with the ANN training, and the iterative expansion of the internal set leads necessarily to change (since the EC algorithm is forced to explore new paths) and to the erratic, but certain convergence to the aesthetic reference frame.

18.6.4 Iteration 12 – Training Stage

In Tables 18.9 and 18.10 we provide a synthesis of the experimental results attained in the training stage of iteration 12 for the 6 architectures considered.

The results presented in these tables show that most ANNs were able to achieve high discrimination rates across training, test and validation sets. All ANN architectures attain average classification percentages higher than 97.62 in training, test and validation.

The comparison of the training results attained in the first and twelfth iteration is interesting. There are statistically significant differences in training

Table 18.9. Overview of the ANNs' training results in iteration 12. The entries in bold indicate statistically significant differences between the results attained in this iteration and the corresponding ones of the first iteration

			Training		Test		Validation	
Network	Features	Cycles	avg	std	avg	std	avg	std
1	246	580.0	.0001	.0001	**.0052**	.0017	**.0058**	.0015
2	41	916.7	**.0016**	.0017	.0085	.0026	.0085	.0025
3	186	866.7	0	.0001	**.0071**	.0018	**.0077**	.0020
4	31	1000.0	**.0035**	.0014	**.0117**	.0028	**.0107**	.0022
5	108	1000.0	.0008	.0010	.0222	.0038	.0224	.0048
6	18	1000.0	**.0268**	.0027	**.0330**	.0083	**.0332**	.0071
Average		893.9	.0055	.0011	.0146	.0035	.0147	.0033

Table 18.10. Average number and percentage of misclassified patterns in twelfth iteration. The training, test and validation set have, respectively, 24025, 3432 and 6864 patterns

	Training			Test			Validation			Entire Corpus	
Network	avg	std	%	avg	std	%	avg	std	%	Ext.	Int.
1	0	0	0	12.9	5.2	.376	28.4	7.9	.414	-	-
2	16.6	25.1	.069	19.8	5.7	.578	39.6	11.8	.577	-	6
3	.08	.43	.000	17.1	4.2	.499	36.2	9.4	.528	-	-
4	44.2	23.7	.184	28.7	7.2	.836	50.8	11.0	.740	2	55
5	9.8	11.2	.041	51.0	9.1	1.485	101.3	21.9	1.476	-	8
6	416.5	56.0	1.734	81.3	21.2	2.370	163.3	37.9	2.380	23	461
Average	81.2	19.4	.338	35.1	8.7	1.024	70.0	16.7	1.019	4.17	88.33

RMSE for all architectures (2, 4, and 6) that do not use information gathered from the images' partitions. Taking into consideration that the ANNs used to guide evolution have the second architecture, these results reveal that the GP engine is able to find images which are found difficult to classify by the ANN guiding evolution. The fourth and sixth architectures use a subset of the features used in the second, which explains the decrease of performance observed.

For the architectures using partition information architectures, the differences in training RMSE are not significant. Most features considered in these architectures are not present in the second one. As such, there was not a specific evolutionary pressure on these features, and consequently their performance in training was relatively unaffected.

The increase of cardinality of the training sets allowed the ANNs with the first and third architectures (the ones that have a higher number of features) to achieve better generalization. For the ANNs with the second architecture, in spite of the increased difficulty in training, the performance in the test and the validation sets is similar to that attained in the first iteration. The same does not apply to the ANNs with the fourth and sixth architecture, whose performance is significantly worse than that attained in the first iteration. The performance of the ANNs with the fifth architecture appears to be unaffected. This is probably due to the low degree of overlap between the features considered in this architecture and in the second.

Nevertheless, it is important to remember that the ANNs of the first and twelfth iterations are not being tested on the same sets. The ANNs of the first iteration would attain poor results if tested on the validation sets of the twelfth.

18.7 Independent Validation Experiments

The existence of repeated patterns induces a bias in the experimental results presented in the previous section. Therefore, we conducted a series of control experiments in order to understand better the changes induced by the iterative refinement of the internal set of images. We are mainly interested in comparing the performances of the ANNs used to guide the evolution in iteration 1 and 11.

To achieve this goal we employ three sets of images. The first comprises 2000 images, made by artists that were not on the training set, from a collection of painting masterpieces [45]. The second consists of images retrieved with Google image search using the keyword "painting", containing the first 947 hits that do indeed correspond to paintings. In the context of an "Artificial Art" event, several students used NEvAr in interactive mode to evolve a large number of images, submitting their favorite ones to the online gallery associated with the event.[10] The third set comprises the 278 images submitted (a sample of these set can be found in Fig. 18.3).

In Table 18.11 we provide a synthesis of the results attained in these experiments, presenting the percentage of images classified as external, following a winner-takes-all strategy, attained by the ANNs used in the first and eleventh iteration.

These results suggest that the fixed aesthetic reference frame provided by the external set is achieving its task, allowing both ANNs to discriminate between images that may be classified as paintings and images that were created with NEvAr.

Table 18.11. Percentage of images classified as external by the ANNs used to guide evolution in iterations 1 and 11, and difference among them

Set	Iteration 1	Iteration 11	Difference
Painting masterpieces	99.68%	96.88%	−2.80%
Images retrieved with Google	96.41%	90.92%	−5.49%
User-guided evolution	17.99%	10.07%	−7.91%

[10] `http://sion.tic.udc.es/jornadas/`

When these results are compared with those attained in the validation sets of iterations 1 and 11, where these ANNs correctly classify roughly 99.5% of the images, a difference in performance can be observed. Several factors may contribute to it:

1. The sets used in the interactions have artworks by the same painters and images from the same evolutionary runs. Therefore, the correlation between the training and validation sets of each iteration is stronger than the correlation between the training set and the images used in these experiments.
2. The images of the external set used to train the ANNs are artworks of renowned artists. The images retrieved from Google originate from a wide variety of sources (e.g., amateur works, child art, etc.), which also explains why the results attained with these images are worse than those attained with the collection of masterpieces.
3. The images resulting from interactive evolution are those selected by the users, i.e., images that were considered remarkable by them. As such, the percentage of atypical images in this set is likely to be higher than the percentage of atypical images in the entire evolutionary run.

Comparing the results of the ANN of the first iteration with those of the eleventh reveals a decrease of the percentage of the images classified as external (2.80% and 5.49%, respectively). On the other hand, the increase in performance in the set resulting from user-guided evolution is 7.91%, a value that surpasses the differences observed in the other sets.

When combined, these results indicate that the ANN from iteration 11 is able to refine its capacity to recognize internal imagery without seriously hindering its performance in a set of external images that was not used in training, i.e., the ANN appears to be able to keep the provided aesthetic reference frame and to generalize properly, which confirms the experimental findings of the previous sections.

18.7.1 Borderline Images

We are also interested in determining which images are the most difficult to classify. To achieve this goal we conducted two different experiments. In both cases, the training set is composed of 100% of the images of the external set, of the initial random internal set, and of the images generated in generations 1 to 11 (inclusive).

In the first test, we do not employ a class distribution. Due to the different cardinalities of the sets, the ANN is exposed to, approximately, 10 internal images for each external one. In the second test we employed a class distribution of 10 to 1, which means that the ANN is exposed to, roughly, 100 external images for each internal image. The rationale is the following: in the first test the ANN is exposed to more internal images, as such it will tend to misclassify external ones. Conversely, in the second test, the ANN will tend to misclassify internal images.

We employed the second architecture. The parameters used in training are similar to those used in the "Entire Corpus" tests, the exception being the use of a lower learning rate (0.1) and a higher number of training cycles (10000). In this case, for each experiment, 30 repetitions were performed.

In the first experiment, on average, 2.60 internal images were classified as external, and 4.56 external images were classified as internal. In the second experiment, an average of 2.93 internal images are misclassified, while no external images are misclassified.

The external images that are misclassified most frequently are: Salvador Dalí, "Fried Egg on the Plate Without the Plate" (1932), "Battle in the Clouds" (1979); Pablo Picasso, "Paul as a Pierrot" (1925); Amedeo Modigliani "Nude — Anna Akhmatova" (1911) and "Stone Head" (1910); Henri Matisse, "La Musique" (1910).[11]

These results were, to some extent, unexpected. One could assume that the ANN would tend to misclassify external images that resemble those created by the EC algorithm. Instead, the misclassification errors occur in images that are atypical in the scope of the considered external set.

Dalí's artwork, "Fried Egg on the Plate Without the Plate" and Picasso's "Paul as a Pierrot" are, in the employed version, images of little detail and texture. "Battle in the Clouds" is a stereoscopic work, which is odd in the present context. The artwork "Nude — Anna Akhmatova", by Modigliani is a pencil on paper drawing, while "Stone Head" is a sculpture. Both stand out for obvious reasons in a set composed mainly of paintings. Matisse's work "La Musique" can also be considered atypical in regard to the remaining images that compose the set. In addition, the image was saved at a low resolution, which may cause perturbations of the features values.

The internal images that are misclassified most frequently are presented in Fig. 18.10. Although one can argue that some of these images are more similar to paintings than the images typically created with NEvAr, the comparison between these images and those generated throughout the runs shows that they are, above all, uncommon.

It is interesting to notice that three of these images were previously selected to illustrate the types of imagery produced during the iterative runs (see Figs. 18.5 and 18.7). By browsing the book's DVD the reader can verify that these images stand out from the images of their iteration, capturing the attention of the viewer, which alone grants them more chances of being selected.

Overall, the results presented in this section confirm that the ANNs are able to generalize properly and to identify correctly images that are stylistically consistent with the set of internal or external images.

[11] For copyright reasons we are unable to reproduce these images, nevertheless the interested reader will easily find them on the Web.

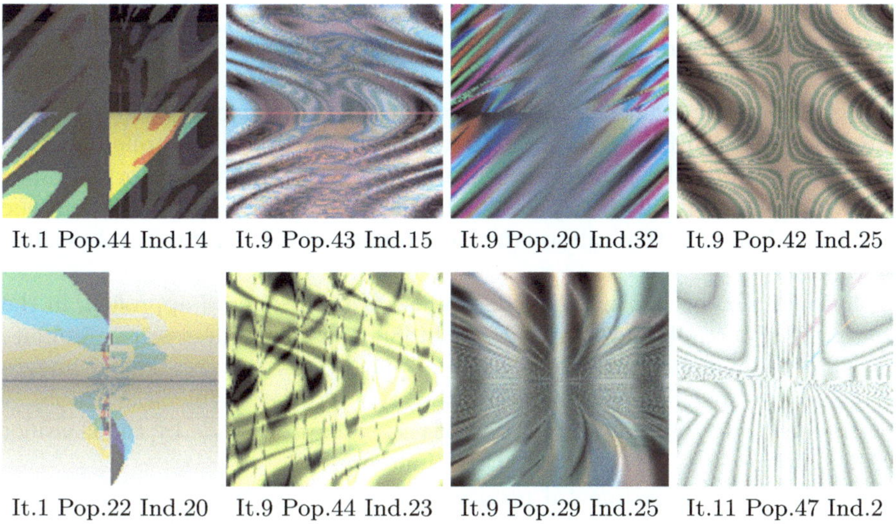

Fig. 18.10. Internal images that are most frequently misclassified

18.8 Conclusions

We have presented a novel approach that relies on the competition between a classifier and an EC algorithm to promote the iterative refinement of the classifier and to change the fitness landscape of the EC.

The use of a training set that contains human-made artworks and evolutionary ones is one of the key ingredients of our approach. The inclusion of a static aesthetical reference frame composed of human-made artworks provides a stable attractor across evolutionary runs, fostering the production of imagery that relates to human aesthetics. The systematic addition of evolutionary artworks to the training set fosters the refinement of the classifier, promoting stylistic change from one evolutionary run to the other.

The experimental results attained point towards the following results: stylistic change was achieved; the classifiers are able to discriminate between internal and external imagery, attaining success rates above 97.5% in the validation sets; the iterative refinement of the training set, by the addition of the images created by the EC system, gave rise to more discerning classifiers.

The experimental results attained in the independent validation tests confirm these findings, showing the following: the classifiers are able to classify properly images, human-made or artificial, that are not related to the employed training sets, attaining success rates above 89%; that the classifiers can also be used to identify images that stand out from the remaining images of the set.

Although the approach was primarily designed for stylistic change, it can be used for different goals. One of the most obvious applications is its use to identify shortcomings of classifier systems (e.g., face recognition ones), through the evolution of patterns that are misclassified.

It can also be used to evolve images that match the aesthetic preferences of a given user or set of users. This goal might be attained by replacing the external set of artworks by a set of artworks that match these preferences. In the present paper, the search was oriented to images outside the normal range of NEvAr, which is inherently a difficult task. Using the same approach, one could search images that, although characteristic of NEvAr, are highly valued by the user(s).

It could also be worth exploring the use of the proposed approach, in the context of a partially automated EA tool [8], to assign fitness or to eliminate undesirable imagery. Another possible application is the creation of images that mimic a specific style, including the style of other artificial art tools. A further possibility is the combination of the evaluation made by the classifier with those made by hand-coded fitness functions.

Although the experimental results attained so far are promising, there is still room for improvement. The feature extractor is probably the module that will undergo more changes in the near future.

As previously mentioned, the FE used has limitations in the handling of color information, in particular Hue. The transition to a perceptually uniform color space may mitigate this problem. Following the same set of ideas explored in our research in the musical domain [5, 6], the inclusion of metrics specifically designed to characterize relevant aspects of the images' coloring, such as color consonance or color neighborhood, may also play an important role. The inclusion of features that deal with aspects such as the distribution of the points of interest, texture and contour analysis, can also be a significant improvement.

Due to the considerable computational effort associated with feature extraction and image rendering, we were forced to use a working resolution of 128×128, which may be too small to allow a good characterization of the images, in particular of the external ones, and the evolution of more refined artworks.

Exploring different ways to map the output of the classifier to fitness values may also prove relevant. In particular, since the analysis of the connection weights of the different ANNs suggests that different strategies are being employed to classify images, using a set of ANNs to guide evolution, instead of using just one, may contribute to a smoother fitness landscape. The replacement of the ANN by an evolutionary classifier is also an interesting possibility.

Although our system has now, in some sense, the ability to "see", it lacks the ability to wander. More precisely, the external images are supplied by us. It would be both interesting and conceptually relevant to let our system navigate through the Internet, collect images, build its own aesthetic references, etc. Alternatively, connecting the system to a camera or TV in order to retrieve images from the "real world" is also an intriguing possibility.

Acknowledgements

The authors would like to acknowledge Santiago Gonzalez for the integration of the AAC and NEvAr, and for his help on the collection of data and on the setting of the experimental environment. Antonio Seoane provided the scripts used in the analysis of the experimental results. Patrick Roos wrote the code upon which the calculation of the FD is based. Jorge Tavares revised the original version of this paper and provided insightful comments, suggestions and ideas. Alejandro Pazos, Amílcar Cardoso, Antonino Santos, Dwight Krehbiel, Dallas Vaughn, Luca Pellicoro and Marisa Santos made relevant contributions to previous projects upon which the presented work is based, and to related ones. This work was partially supported by research project XUGA-PGIDIT04TIC105012PR.

References

1. Machado, P., Cardoso, A. (1997). Model proposal for a constructed artist. In Callaos, N., Khoong, C., Cohen, E., eds.: *First World Multiconference on Systemics, Cybernetics and Informatics, SCI97/ISAS97*. Caracas, Venezuela, 521–528
2. Romero, J. (2002). *Metodología Evolutiva para la Construcción de Modelos Cognitivos Complejos. Exploración de la Creatividad Artificial en Composición Musical.* PhD thesis. University of Corunha. Corunha, Spain (in Spanish)
3. Romero, J., Machado, P., Santos, A., Cardoso, A. (2003). On the development of critics in evolutionary computation artists. In Günther, R., et al., eds.: *Applications of Evolutionary Computing, EvoWorkshops 2003: EvoBIO, EvoCOMNET, EvoHOT, EvoIASP, EvoMUSART, EvoSTOC*. Vol. 2611 of LNCS. Essex, UK. Springer
4. Manaris, B., Purewal, T., McCormick, C. (2002). Progress towards recognizing and classifying beautiful music with computers — MIDI-encoded music and the Zipf–Mandelbrot law. In: *Proceedings of the IEEE SoutheastCon*. Columbia, SC
5. Manaris, B., Romero, J., Machado, P., Krehbiel, D., Hirzel, T., Pharr, W., Davis, R. (2005). Zipf's law, music classification and aesthetics. *Computer Music Journal*, **29**(1): 55–69
6. Manaris, B., Roos, P., Machado, P., Krehbiel, D., Pellicoro, L., Romero, J. (2007). A corpus-based hybrid approach to music analysis and composition. In: *Proceedings of the 22nd Conference on Artificial Intelligence (AAAI 07)*. Vancouver, BC
7. Machado, P., Romero, J., Santos, A., Cardoso, A., Manaris, B. (2004). Adaptive critics for evolutionary artists. In Günther, R., et al., eds.: *Applications of Evolutionary Computing, EvoWorkshops 2004: EvoBIO, EvoCOMNET, EvoHOT, EvoIASP, EvoMUSART, EvoSTOC*. Vol. 3005 of LNCS. Coimbra, Portugal. Springer, 435–444
8. Machado, P., Romero, J., Cardoso, A., Santos, A. (2005). Partially interactive evolutionary artists. *New Generation Computing – Special Issue on Interactive Evolutionary Computation*, **23**(42): 143–155

9. Machado, P. (2007). *Inteligência Artificial e Arte.* PhD thesis. University of Coimbra. Coimbra, Portugal (in Portuguese)
10. Machado, P., Cardoso, A. (1998). Computing aesthetics. In Oliveira, F., ed.: *Proceedings of the XIVth Brazilian Symposium on Artificial Intelligence: Advances in Artificial Intelligence.* Vol. 1515 of LNCS. Porto Alegre, Brazil. Springer, 219–229
11. Taylor, R.P., Micolich, A.P., Jonas, D. (1999). Fractal analysis of Pollock's drip paintings. *Nature*, **399**: 422
12. Saunders, R. (2001). *Curious Design Agents and Artificial Creativity — A Synthetic Approach to the Study of Creative Behaviour.* PhD thesis. University of Sydney, Department of Architectural and Design Science Faculty of Architecture. Sydney, Australia
13. Manaris, B.Z., Vaughan, D., Wagner, C., Romero, J., Davis, R.B. (2003). Evolutionary music and the Zipf–Mandelbrot law: Developing fitness functions for pleasant music. In Günther, R., et al., eds.: *Applications of Evolutionary Computing, EvoWorkshop 2003: EvoBIO, EvoCOP, EvoIASP, EvoMUSART, EvoROB, and EvoSTIM.* Vol. 2611 of LNCS. Springer, 522–534
14. Machado, P., Romero, J., Manaris, B., Santos, A., Cardoso, A. (2003). Power to the critics — A framework for the development of artificial art critics. In: *IJCAI 2003 Workshop on Creative Systems.* Acapulco, Mexico
15. Manaris, B., Machado, P., McCauley, C., Romero, J., Krehbiel, D. (2005). Developing fitness functions for pleasant music: Zipf's law and interactive evolution systems. In Rothlauf, F., et al., eds.: *Applications of Evolutionary Computing, EvoWorkshops 2005: EvoBIO, EvoCOMNET, EvoHOT, EvoIASP, EvoMUSART, EvoSTOC.* Vol. 3449 of LNCS. Lausanne, Switzerland. Springer, 498–507
16. Sims, K. (1991). Artificial evolution for computer graphics. *ACM Computer Graphics*, **25**: 319–328
17. Machado, P., Cardoso, A. (2002). All the truth about NEvAr. *Applied Intelligence, Special Issue on Creative Systems*, **16**(2): 101–119
18. Greenfield, G. (2002). Color dependent computational aesthetics for evolving expressions. In Sarhangi, R., ed.: *Bridges: Mathematical Connections in Art, Music, and Science; Conference Proceedings 2002.* Winfield, Kansas. Central Plains Book Manufacturing, 9–16
19. Greenfield, G. (2003). Evolving aesthetic images using multiobjective optimization. In McKay, B., et al., eds.: *Congress on Evolutionary Computation, CEC 2003.* Vol. 3. Canberra, Australia. IEEE Press, 1903–1909
20. Svangård, N., Nordin, P. (2004). Automated aesthetic selection of evolutionary art by distance based classification of genomes and phenomes using the universal similarity metric. In Günther, R., et al., eds.: *Applications of Evolutionary Computing, EvoWorkshops 2004: EvoBIO, EvoCOMNET, EvoHOT, EvoIASP, EvoMUSART, EvoSTOC.* Vol. 3005 of LNCS. Coimbra, Portugal. Springer, 445–454
21. Baluja, S., Pomerlau, D., Todd, J. (1994). Towards automated artificial evolution for computer-generated images. *Connection Science*, **6**(2): 325–354
22. Greenfield, G.R. (2002). On the co-evolution of evolving expressions. *International Journal of Computational Intelligence and Applications*, **2**(1): 17–31
23. Todd, P.M., Werner, G.M. (1999). Frankensteinian approaches to evolutionary music composition. In Griffith, N., Todd, P.M., eds.: *Musical Networks: Parallel Distributed Perception and Performance.* MIT Press, 313–340

24. Birkhoff, G. (1933). *Aesthetic Measure*. Harvard University Press
25. Moles, A. (1958). *Théorie de L'Information et Perception Esthétique*. Denoel
26. Arnheim, R. (1956). *Art and Visual Perception, a Psychology of the Creative Eye*. Faber and Faber. London
27. Arnheim, R. (1966). *Towards a Psychology of Art/Entropy and Art — An Essay on Disorder and Order*. The Regents of the University of California
28. Arnheim, R. (1969). *Visual Thinking*. University of California Press. Berkeley, CA
29. Bense, M. (1965). *Aesthetica. Einführung in die neue Aesthetik*. Agis (reprinted by Baden-Baden, 1982)
30. Shannon, C.E. (1951). Prediction and entropy of printed english. *Bell System Technical Journal*, (30): 50–64
31. Staudek, T. (2002). *Exact Aesthetics. Object and Scene to Message*. PhD thesis. Faculty of Informatics, Masaryk University of Brno
32. Staudek, T., Linkov, V. (2004). Personality characteristics and aesthetic preference for chaotic curves. *Journal of Mathematics and Design*, **4**(1): 297–304
33. Graves, M. (1948). *Design Judgement Test*. The Psychological Corporation. New York
34. Datta, R., Joshi, D., Li, J., Wang, J.Z. (2006). Studying aesthetics in photographic images using a computational approach. In: *Computer Vision – ECCV 2006, 9th European Conference on Computer Vision, Part III*. LNCS. Graz, Austria. Springer, 288–301
35. Aks, D., Sprott, J.C. (1996). Quantifying aesthetic preference for chaotic patterns. *Empirical Studies of the Arts*, **14**: 1–16
36. Spehar, B., Clifford, C.W.G., Newell, N., Taylor, R.P. (2003). Universal aesthetic of fractals. *Computers and Graphics*, **27**(5): 813–820
37. Wannarumon, S., Bohez, E.L.J. (2006). A new aesthetic evolutionary approach for jewelry design. *Computer-Aided Design & Applications*, **3**(1-4): 385–394
38. Wertheimer, M. (1939). Laws of organization in perceptual forms. In Ellis, W.D., ed.: *A Source Book of Gestalt Psychology*. Harcourt Brace. New York, 71–88
39. Tyler, C.W., ed. (2002). *Human Symmetry Perception and Its Computational Analysis*. Lawrence Erlbaum Associates
40. Field, D.J., Hayes, A., Hess, R.F. (2000). The roles of polarity and symmetry in the perceptual grouping of contour fragments. *Spatial Vision*, **13**(1): 51–66
41. Cope, D. (1992). On the algorithmic representation of musical style. In Laske, O., ed.: *Understanding Music with AI: Perspectives on Music Cognition*. MIT Press. Cambridge, Massachusetts, 354–363
42. Zipf, G.K. (1949). *Human Behaviour and the Principle of Least Effort: An Introduction to Human Ecology*. Addison-Wesley
43. Kittler, J. (1983). On the accuracy of the Sobel edge detector. *Image Vision Computing*, **1**(1): 37–42
44. Zell, A., Mamier, G., Vogt, M., Mache, N., Hübner, R., Döring, S., Herrmann, K.U., Soyez, T., Schmalzl, M., Sommer, T., et al. (2003). *SNNS: Stuttgart Neural Network Simulator User Manual, Version 4.2*. Technical Report 3/92. University of Stuttgart. Stuttgart
45. Directmedia (2002). 10000 Meisterwerke der Malerei — von der Antike bis zum Beginn der Moderne. DVD-ROM

19

Facing the Future: Evolutionary Possibilities for Human-Machine Creativity

Jon McCormack

Centre for Electronic Media Art
Monash University
Clayton 3800
Victoria, Australia
jonmc@csse.monash.edu.au
www.csse.monash.edu.au/~jonmc

Summary. This chapter examines the possibilities and challenges that lie ahead for evolutionary music and art. Evolutionary computing methods have enabled new modes of creative expression in the art made by humans. One day, it may be possible for computers to make art autonomously. The idea of machines making art leads to the question: what do we mean by 'making art' and how do we recognise and acknowledge artistic creativity in general? Two broad categories of human-machine creativity are defined: firstly, machines that make art like, and for, humans; and secondly, machines that make 'art' that is recognised as creative and novel by other machines or agents. Both these categories are examined from an evolutionary computing perspective. Finding 'good' art involves searching a phase-space of possibilities beyond astronomical proportions, which makes evolutionary algorithms potentially suitable candidates. However, the problem of developing artistically creative programs is not simply a search problem. The multiple roles of interaction, environment, physics and physicality are examined in the context of generating aesthetic output. A number of 'open problems' are proposed as grand challenges of investigation for evolutionary music and art. For each problem, the impetus and background are discussed. The paper also looks at theoretical issues that might limit prospects for art made by machines, in particular the role of embodiment, physicality and morphological computation in agent-based and evolutionary models. Finally, the paper looks at artistic challenges for evolutionary music and art systems.

> In the last analysis all intelligibility and all intelligent behaviour must hark back to our sense of what we are, which is, necessarily, on pain of regress, something we can never explicitly know.
>
> — Dreyfus and Dreyfus [1]

19.1 Introduction

The idea of using Evolutionary Computing (EC) techniques to make art, or aid our understanding of creativity, is a relatively new one. The majority of research in what is termed Evolutionary Music and Art (EMA) has been carried out over the last fifteen years.[1] In this fifteen-year time frame many talented EMA researchers and artists have inspired us with their achievements and stimulated us to imagine new possibilities for art and creativity. The most successful role of EMA research to date has been to assist the artist or designer in exploring spaces of intricate combinatorial complexity. This research has led to new forms of computer-generated aesthetics. The role of the creator has shifted from the direct creation of artefacts to the design of processes that create artefacts: an approach dubbed 'metacreation' by theorist Mitchell Whitelaw [2].

While the last fifteen years have seen many successes, it is interesting to speculate on future directions for the field. Thus, the aim of this chapter is to look forward to the next 15 years of research and beyond. It is not inconceivable that in 15 years time we may have machines that can autonomously create what is widely considered to be original art.[2] These machines may develop their own lines of creative enquiry, producing results that are not derivative of some existing human style or genre, but exhibit a high degree of independent artistic creativity. In addition to making new art, these systems may help us understand more about human creativity and novelty in general. This is a goal in the tradition of classical artificial intelligence, which sought to better understand human cognition by building machines that exhibited 'intelligent' behaviour. Autonomous art-making systems, if they ever exist, will bring into question the primacy of human creativity, the concept of authorship, and the role of creativity in human (and machine) culture.

Such ideas might make for interesting speculation. However, what I believe is a more likely (and ultimately a more creatively rewarding) scenario is one of *human-computer synergistics*, where the machine enables modes of creative thought and activity currently unattainable. The machine does not do this alone — the human will remain a vital part of the creative process.

Regardless of whether you subscribe to the 'machine as independent creative intelligence' or 'machine as a synergetic partner to the human artist'

---

[1] I am aware of evolutionary and cybernetic art experiments that significantly predate this current period; however, I will leave a thorough 'pre-historical' analysis for another paper.

[2] If we consider Harold Cohen's *Aaron* as such a system, that time arrived many years ago [3]; however, the art produced by Aaron is highly constrained in terms of the aesthetic variety it can attain independently of the rules programmed into it. While what Aaron produces might be considered art (as are many of the works produced by computational processes), few would consider Aaron itself an artist. Indeed, Cohen explicitly states, 'I have never, in fact, claimed that AARON is a creative program' [4].

scenario, this chapter will focus on challenges I believe will be important to address in order to advance the field (and perhaps determine which scenario is more appropriate). To this end, I will propose a series of 'grand challenges' in EMA for the next fifteen years.[3] I believe meeting these challenges will be necessary if we are to successfully approach either of these speculative futures. These grand challenges, or 'open problems', are certainly not the only ones faced by researchers and are not claimed to be definitive or exclusive to EMA. Indeed, researchers in neighbouring fields such as artificial life and evolutionary computing face similar challenges, and it is likely that research from many other disciplines will help to inform EMA research over the coming decades.

It is the goal of this chapter to catalyse our thinking about EMA, to 'ignite the fire' as W. B. Yeats proposed as the role of the educator. But, in addition to igniting the fire, I will also attempt to 'fill the pail' by offering some possible ways in which we can address the challenges that I am proposing.

19.2 The First Problem: Defining Creativity and Art

Open Problem 1 *To devise more formalised and objective definitions of 'art', 'artistic creativity' and 'novelty'. To understand the processes behind these terms in greater detail than exists today, from a perspective suited to developing computational models that simulate creative behaviour. The definitions should be broad enough to cover a variety of artistic practices and acts, but with sufficient detail to make them practically useful in advancing EMA research.*

The premise in creating and researching EMA is that problems involving art making and artistic creativity are *non-trivial*. But what exactly do we mean by terms such as 'art making' and 'creativity'? What separates art from non-art? What is art? This seemingly simple question finds a multitude of answers.

'The arts' form an essential part of human society and culture. Even in times when our survival may be threatened (such as war), we turn to art for solace, understanding, and a sense of community. Governments, groups and individuals invest considerable resources in the arts. We build expensive, iconic buildings in which to exhibit and perform our art. We go to great lengths to preserve and share art with other members of our community, even the art of other communities and cultures. Our school education programs feature training and appreciation of music, performance, visual art and sculpture. Many people devote much of their lives to learning a musical instrument or mastering painting. The ability to skilfully play an instrument, or to create a visceral and emotive painting, for example, is much sought after and respected in society. In day-to-day life, we seem to have little difficulty in deciding what is 'creative', what is 'art' and what is not. However, this judgement is neither

[3] Parts of this chapter are based on material originally published in [5].

universal nor binary — we all have opinions not only on what art is, but also on the quality of the artworks themselves, reflecting our culture, personal 'taste' and social sophistication. However, when we seek a more formal, quantitative and objective definition, things get, well... complicated.

19.2.1 Art and Novelty

The first problem is that 'art' (a relatively new word, historically speaking) actually encompasses a diverse variety of human activity. It includes painting, drawing, photography, installation, conceptual art, performing art, music, literature, poetry, cinema and architecture. Some of these kinds of art have been around for much of human history, others enabled more recently through technology. Some, such as architecture, serve purposes in addition to just being art. In Western culture, we also draw a distinction between so-called 'high art' and 'low art', with high art given greater cachet by some.

Forming a unifying definition of such a broad range of activities is difficult, despite each being readily accepted as art. Even if we restrict our definition to one particular form of art, the problem doesn't get much easier. This is because, in contemporary Western society at least, almost *anything* can be classified as art, including: a can of human excrement; an empty space; a room with just a light switching on and off; four minutes and 33 seconds of silence.[4] These are all descriptions of highly reputable works of modern and contemporary art. To further highlight this definitional quagmire: a number of extremely valuable 'readymade' works of art are typically mistaken for everyday objects of little aesthetic or financial value when considered out of context: Andy Warhol's *Brillo Boxes* and Marcel Duchamp's *Fountain* being historically important examples. Any definition of art that exclusively considers the output (the art object or act) will be incomplete. It is necessary to consider *context* and *process* as well. While necessary however, these features are not sufficient for an all-encompassing definition. Views of what is and is not art vary across cultures, time and even individuals within the same culture and time. It is a subjective, moving classification; influenced by experience, fashion, personal taste and culture. A detailed analysis of the causal networks that inform these features currently remains an intractable problem. In summary, a formal, universal definition of art appears impossible.

As we shall see, an important property of art is that it involves *novelty*, so it isn't surprising that a static classification of art is limiting. Since artists are continually developing new art, and this art is often *novel relative to what has come before*, the boundary of art constantly shifts into new areas. In addition, since the sources of this novelty include a combination of physical artefacts, human culture, and subjective experience, expecting a formalised understanding for all the possibilities of this phase-space will be challenging.

[4] The works are, respectively, Piero Manzoni: *Artist's Shit*; Yves Klein: *The Void*; Martin Creed: *Work No. 227: The lights going on and off*; John Cage: *4' 33"* (three movements).

The problem of the 'all-inclusive' approach to a definition of art is twofold. Firstly, the approach is 'top-down', trying to devise a description based on subjective classification of existing exemplars. Secondly, this classification is formed principally through the writing and research of art theorists, art critics, art gallery curators and artists. An analysis of the literature from these groups reveals much contradiction and a focus on the subjective view of the individual critic or theorist [6].[5]

What might be more fruitful, and certainly more appealing to EMA research, is a 'bottom-up' analysis, with a focus on cause rather than effect. To this end, we should seek our understanding of art from the perspectives of human ethology and evolutionary theory. Creative practices and rituals such as body decoration, story telling, music making, and so on, are communal: assisting in social cohesion. The ethnologist and cultural anthropologist Ellen Dissanayake suggests that the practice of 'making special' distinguishes things from the everyday to build social groupings and teach the value of mutual achievement [7, 8]. Individual skills at creative practices may serve as indicators for potential mates [9].

19.2.2 Artistic Creativity

Equally as vexed is the issue of creativity. In broad terms creativity involves the generation of something *novel* and *appropriate* [10]. In the context of art, however, defining what is 'appropriate' requires expert knowledge of what constitutes art. As we have seen, this is problematic. Humans naturally seek novelty in their environment, being drawn to particular spatio-temporal patterns that provide 'stimulus novelty' [11]. In many cases of art making, these novel spatio-temporal patterns appear to arise from new combinations of existing atomic elements. For example: a musical score is a combination of notes; a building is a combination of bricks; poetry is a combination of words; a digital image is a combination of pixels. The precise arrangement of these atomic elements in space and time being of crucial importance. Yet when considering *how* these patterns come about, creative goals are not normally considered in terms of the combinatorial arrangement of primitives. Composers don't normally *think* about how to arrange from a set of individual notes into a composition; visual artists don't normally conceptualise image making in terms of how to arrange a set of pixels.

The idea of combinatorial arrangement of primitive or atomic elements is important for many EMA systems, and a natural approach in purely *structural* terms. However, recent theories of human cognition do not view creativity in terms of a combinatorial approach. Terry Dartnall calls the belief that 'creativity is the creative combination or recombination of previously existing elements' *combinationism* [12, p. 14]. This understanding is based on the

[5] Many critics and theorists make the implicit assumption that their own conscious experience of an artwork is identical to all of those who experience the work.

intuition that *nothing can come from nothing*; hence we require a 'combination or recombination of what we already had'. That is, one cannot create something new from nothing. However, creativity is not combinationism in Dartnall's view. Rather, it begins with knowledge, skill and abilities, and it is from these faculties that creativity *emerges*. The challenge is to account for how these cognitive properties give rise to creative output, an issue to be further examined in Sect. 19.7.

If a non-combinational model of creativity is correct, it may account for why combinatorial EMA systems do not exhibit the novelty of human creativity. Further, if there is something non-computational in this explanation, computers, as we currently define them, could never be considered autonomous creative agents in the way humans are.

19.3 Classification of EMA Research

Research in EMA has covered a variety of problems in aesthetics, creativity, communication and design. Broadly speaking, much of the research and results to date have been exploratory rather than theory driven. Some common methodologies include:

- use technique X from complexity research to make images or music, where X might be cellular automata, self-organised critical systems, swarm models or generative grammars, for example;
- use aesthetic selection to evolve X, where X is image, 3D form or music, for example;
- devise a suitable fitness function to automate the evolution of X, where X is image, form or music.

Certainly there have been many successes using these strategies. However, even in this glib set of scenarios there is a sense that these strategies are a combination of ideas from other disciplines applied to the context of art-making. The role of the following sections is to ask what else might be possible and to encourage a stronger theoretical basis for EMA. Before we look at these other possibilities, it is important to define some broad categories of EMA research, which will assist in structuring the analysis to follow.

19.3.1 Categories of EMA Research

Researchers in EMA may come from a mathematical or computing background or from a visual art, sound art, or music composition background, or may possess skills across several disciplines. What I feel is important to distinguish however is not the researcher's primary discipline, but rather the *goals* of the research itself. These goals I divide into two broad categories:

i) EMA systems whose intent is to generate art that is appreciated by a human audience. Their success will be normally evaluated on the quality of their artistic output or understanding. These I call 'art-making/understanding' systems as their primary consideration is to make art or help us understand human art;
ii) Research that explores the concept of artistic creativity in general. These systems attempt to evolve artistic behaviour under a more general definition. As such, the 'art' produced may not be recognised or considered art by a human audience. These I call 'artificial creative' systems.

The first category is where the majority of current systems lie. The desire to make art for *people* to experience will normally motivate those who design such systems. Their goal will be to create a system that produces an output we *recognise and evaluate* as visual art, music, performance, architecture, poetry, etc. As with conventional art, the output may be highly individual and distinctive in style, specific to a particular researcher, artist, or computational system. These systems are typically highly specialised with much domain-specific knowledge and personal meta-heuristics involved (the 'no free lunch' theorem at work again [13]). Other research — still in this first 'art making/understanding' category — may look at aesthetic problems in a more general sense or attempt to produce a broader range of aesthetic output, not just one particular individual's 'style'. Whatever the result, the general premise is that the research is oriented around what humans would ascribe aesthetic properties to, irrespective of the intended research question.

The second category is more problematic, and potentially more challenging than the first. Here, artistic creativity is considered in an open context, appreciated by entities other than people as 'aesthetic'. We can understand aesthetic behaviour in a sense that is not exclusive to humans. Bowerbirds, for example, create elaborate decorative constructs around their nests that serve no direct survival advantage, but rather act as displays to attract mates. EMA research in this second category attempts to look at creativity in a culture- and species-independent way.

Artificial life (AL) proposed to look at life and living systems more broadly, beyond 'life-as-we-know-it', investigating instantiation in non-biological media, such as computation [14]. Similarly, 'artificial creative' systems examine artistic creativity in non-biological systems, typically computational, agent-based systems. This agenda might even include the possibility of discovering new forms of art ('art-as-it-could-be'). That is, artistic products or systems created and analysed by synthetic autonomous agents. While this may seem an appealing goal, it is highly likely that it will suffer from the same epistemic problems that artificial life went through [15, 16]: for example, how could we recognise creative behaviour in artificial systems if it were significantly different from our own experience of what creative behaviour is? Nonetheless, even if a theory of artistic creativity in general might be unachievable, it is likely that such research could provide new insights into behaviours we currently observe in humans and other animals. These 'artificial creative' systems are examined in more detail in Sect. 19.12.

Having defined these two categories, let us now focus on the first; that is, we wish to use evolutionary methods to create and understand art appreciated by humans. Before tackling this class of art making/understanding, let us get a feel for the scale of the problem we are up against. The following sections will focus on visual art images as examples; however, the reader should find that the arguments apply to almost any other (digitally representable) media, including music.

19.4 Everyimage

People understand the expression 'finding a needle in a haystack' as indicating that a problem is very difficult because it involves searching through a lot of things (probably too many) to find what one is after. Evolutionary music and art might be described this way — as researchers, we're trying to find the aesthetically satisfying needle from the data haystack of computation and algorithm. As we shall see, this is an understatement. So let us begin with a simple thought experiment. How difficult it is to find the good art using computational representations and processes? How hard is it to find the *Mona Lisa*[6] from the set of all possible images?

We will restrict our art to be two-dimensional, pixel-based images (the standard way images are stored on a computer). Initially this seems like a relatively simple subset of what might constitute art. However, the following argument can be adapted to any form of digitally representable media, irrespective of type or resolution (including non-visual representations, such as music).

The discrete, pixel-based image is curiously deceptive in terms of its complexity. A modest 500 $\times$ 400 pixel image, for example, contains only 200,000 pixels and is easily stored and manipulated on any modern computer. How-

[6] Readers might be perplexed with my continual use of the *Mona Lisa* as an exemplar artwork in this chapter. I am not suggesting researchers try to evolve an image that is literally the *Mona Lisa*. I use the *Mona Lisa* for a variety of reasons, including a kind of postmodern irony. In the canons of Western Art, this image is broadly recognised as an exemplary example of fine art. It has been around for long enough to be reasonably sure it is not the product of a fad or distortion of what constitutes art, albeit in a classical, Western sense. It is widely known and instantly recognised as an archetypal art image (which has lead to its appropriation and manipulation by other artists). What is even more well known than the image itself, is that it is a 'great' work of art, so its social cachet as art is even greater than its artistic value as a painting.

ever, the space of possible images that can be represented within those 200,000 pixels is, as we shall see, *Vast.*[7]

Imagine if we were to iterate through every possible 500×400 pixel image, starting with all bits of each pixel set to 0 (the 'all black' image), changing bits one by one, until all bits for each pixel are 1 (the 'all white' image). In between the all 0s image and the all 1s image, would be a (partially) fascinating journey, because if we were able to do this, along the way we'd see every image that has ever been, or ever will be taken by anyone, anywhere! Every great (and not so great) work of visual art is in there, past, present and future, as are images of political assassinations, nude celebrities (even ones that have never posed nude), serial killers, animals, plants, landscapes, buildings, every possible angle and perspective of our planet at every possible scale and all the other planets, stars, galaxies in the universe, both real and imaginary. Pictures of next week's winning lottery ticket, and of you holding that winning ticket.

There are pictures of people you've never met or seen before (even in pictures, although there are many pictures of you with them, even looking at pictures of you looking at them). There are pictures of you and me together with our arms around each other like we've been best friends for years (even if we've never met), and pictures of you as a child sitting on my knee while I read what looks like a copy of this book to you.

Pictures of you at every moment of your life from conception to your death. It's not just you: there are pictures of every person who has ever existed at every stage of his or her life, from atomic close-ups to long shots. There are even some group portraits of all your ancestors (although admittedly at 500×400 pixels it is hard to make out a lot of detail). Then there are pictures of people that have never existed, along with pictures of people in situations that have not happened to them in reality. Then, there are all of these images (and many more) with every Photoshop filter ever invented (even the expensive third-party ones and even ones that haven't been invented yet), applied in every possible combination! And that's just a tiny fraction. *Every possible image.* Here is the image version of Borges' *Library of Babel.*[8]

Within this library of all possible images, along with all these interesting images, are many more that are not so interesting. So along with the *Mona Lisa*, for example, are all the *Mona Lisa* copies with just one pixel different (there are 3.35×10^{12}, or *three trillion*, of these). Then there are the ones with just two pixels different, and so on. In some versions, only parts of the image can be recognised as the *Mona Lisa.* Many others are just abstract patterns or shapes; some just look like noise or random bits of colour. Clearly, for each image that we know to be 'interesting' there are a lot of others that

---

[7] I adopt Daniel Dennett's notation of capitalising the V to signify the sublime scale of the word used in this context; parts of this section draw their inspiration from a similar discussion on genotype–phenotype space in [17, Chap. 5].

[8] The story of an imaginary library containing all possible 410-page books [18].

are almost as interesting, and as we get more and more distant from the interesting ones there soon comes a point where they are clearly not as good, eventually bearing little or no resemblance to the initial, interesting image.

Nonetheless, being able to generate every possible image sounds like a good idea, one that we could make a lot of money from (imagine selling all those nude celebrity images to tabloid newspapers without having to actually go out and take them!). However, before you rush off to start writing the program to iterate through this set, it is important to understand how big the number of all possible 200,000 pixel images is. Even though each image is relatively small, with millions of them easily stored on a modern hard disk, the number, or *phase-space* of all possible images is very big. At 24 bits per pixel (the standard for colour images) its about 9.5×10^{1444943}. How long would it take to iterate completely through this phase-space? Lets be optimistic and imagine that every particle in the universe[9] is a supercomputer and can compute one billion images per second (we'll conveniently ignore the problem of how we'd actually look at them). Each particle[10] has been computing images since the universe began. How many images have been computed in total, i.e., how far have we progressed from the all black starting image through all possible 500×400 pixel images since the universe began? Fifty percent? Ten percent? One percent? The answer is approximately 2×10^{-105}%. Yes, 105 0s to the right of the decimal place; in practical terms, basically none! Here we see the Vastness of combinatorial explosion, which occurs in all sorts of problems, not just images. It seems our financial security from tabloid photo sales has been put on hold.

What if we were to simplify the problem? Reduce the resolution (even low-resolution images of nude celebrities might fetch a good price). Reduce the bit depth — black-and-white might be good enough. Would that make it possible to iterate through in a practical time? Unless you're willing to accept very tiny bitmap images, the answer is, unfortunately, no. If you were prepared to spend your entire working life looking at images at a rate of one per second, you should just be able to look at all possible 5×5 pixel binary images. Before you attempt this, here's what the *Mona Lisa* looks like as a 5×5 pixel bitmap (magnified ten times):

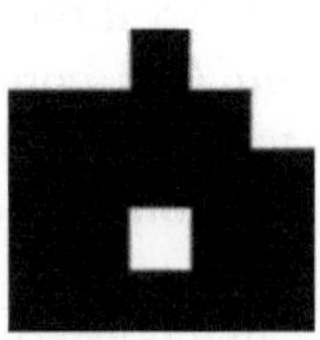

[9] For the purposes of this exercise, we assume there are 10^{80} particles in the universe — a reasonable approximation based on current estimates.

[10] I assume the number of particles in the universe is fixed over the lifetime of the universe; forgive me, this is only a thought experiment after all.

Pity the more ambitious fools who went one pixel higher in each dimension — they'd have only seen less than 1% of their set of possible 6×6 pixel binary images by the time they die.

It really is impossible to comprehend the size of this space of all possible images, even in relative terms, despite it being a finite set. Astronomical proportions, such as the size or age of the universe, don't come anywhere near to the measure of how big this space is. It is beyond the sublime, yet a computer can generate any image from this set, so each image has the possibility of actually existing.

It is also interesting to observe that we could combine still images from the *everyimage* set in certain sequences to generate movies. So from the set of all possible 500×400 pixel images we could generate the set of all possible 500×400 pixel movies of some length. Since we have potentially every possible image, we also have every possible movie (including all the 'directors cuts', even if they were never made!). The catch is that to make a sequence we may need to duplicate some of the images (i.e., some of the frames might be the same).

This idea of duplication means that we could also build a 500×400 pixel image by tiling four 250×200 pixel 'quarter' images together. If our 250×200 pixel image set contains all possible images, this would include all the possible 'quarter' images from the set of possible 500×400 pixel images, the only condition being that in certain cases we will have to repeat some of the 250×200 images. For example, the 'all-black' 500×400 pixel image can be made by repeating the 250×200 pixel 'all-black' image four times. Why stop here? The set of all possible 125×100 pixel images could form the set of all 500×400 pixel images by using 16 of them at a time. If we follow this to its full regress, we end up with just two single-bit images: one containing a 0 and the other a 1. This is the binary universal image. It is capable of representing all possible images, and is easily searchable iteratively. The problem is that all possible images at this resolution collapse to either all black or all white, highlighting an important issue that will recur throughout this chapter, that of information and physicality. We need a certain amount of information (pixel resolution in this case) before we can physically start to recognise and distinguish images in some meaningful way. The resolution and recognition is dependent on the physicality of viewing — something that has evolved under constraints of efficiency, utility and fidelity [19]. Tiling or combining these 1-bit images together gives us all possible images at any resolution and bit depth; however, the difficulty is in knowing *which* bit to put *where*.

I hope I have now convinced you (if you actually needed any convincing) that the size of the search space for these types of problems is impractical for any kind of exhaustive search. The chances of randomly flipping bits with the hope of coming up with the *Mona Lisa* or even a nude celebrity are unimaginably *Small*. This is one reason why more sophisticated search methods, such as evolutionary computing methods, might be useful. But before we tackle that issue, there is one more important question to ask: Of the set of all possible images, what fraction would actually be 'interesting' images? That is, ones that we might actually want to spend some time looking at. Would this fraction be greater than or less than the fraction of 'junk' images (ones that we're not interested in looking at)?

Of course, interest is such an arbitrary thing at the micro level. I might be more interested in looking at pictures of my family rather than of a family I don't know. A medieval historian might be more interested in medieval castle pictures than modern architecture; a medical researcher might have a fancy for tumour images. However, these micro variations in interest don't matter statistically in the macro landscape of images humans create and have interest in. Additionally, what is interesting varies over time: you might find the first few fractal images you see interesting, but after seeing many fractal images your interest may wane — this behaviour characterised by the *Wundt curve* [20].

While it is difficult to pin down the exact number, it is clear that the fraction of interesting images from the *everyimage* set is extremely Small. If you need proof, try randomly generating 500 × 400 pixel images for a few hours and see how many interesting ones you find.

The problem of 'the possible and the actual' is well known in biology.[11] There are a large number of images that are actually interesting, but this set, even if a little fuzzy around the edges, is only a tiny fraction of all possible images. That's why random bits don't in general produce interesting images and why our brains are such good classifiers. The question is, can we automate the classification of images that are actually interesting from all possible images?

19.5 Inference, Clustering and Synthesis Models

A common method of tackling this problem would be to use some form of statistical, neural or other machine learning model. Let us imagine an idealised version of this system — a *supermodel* in the terminology of Allison [21]. The model analyses a large quantity of high-quality art images. A series of learned parameters are estimated from the model (see Fig. 19.1). These may suggest clusters around genres, artists, visual styles and so on. Hence we have been able to form some multi-dimensional classification of artistic images. This model would be very useful, because it could tell us what was good art and what was rubbish. More practically, it may be able to resolve disputes over authenticity, being able to determine if a newly discovered painting was the work of a great master or merely a clever fake.

Given an appropriate parameterised model, our attention could next be turned to the synthesis of high quality art images. In theory, it should be

[11] Many different DNA sequences are *logically* possible, fewer *physically* possible; a significantly smaller number still actually exist in biology.

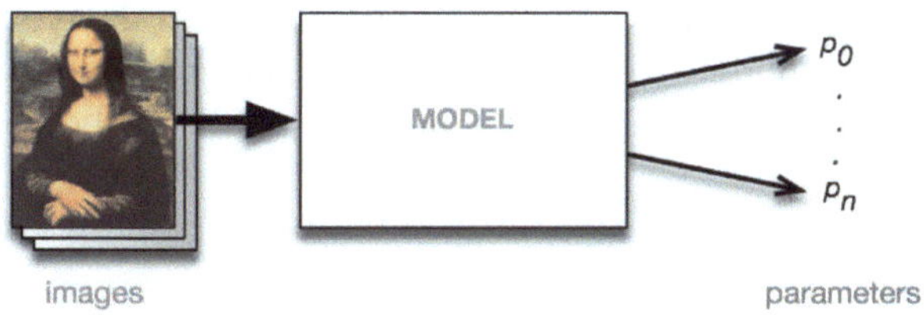

Fig. 19.1. A idealised clustering/classification system. Images are input into the model, resulting in a series of learned parameters $p_0 \dots p_n$

possible with the appropriate parameter settings to synthesise images using this model. That is, we now have a 'black box' that when primed with the appropriate parameter settings could give us the *Mona Lisa* (Fig. 19.2). Further manipulation of the parameters might even give us new images, reminiscent of a particular artist or style, but with no exact correspondence to any of the input images. That is, by exploring the parameter space around or near particular clusters we might find new possibilities, perhaps some that may be recognised as significant works of visual art.

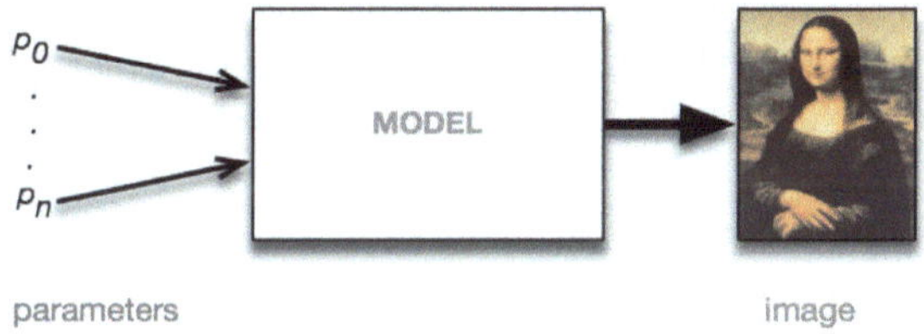

Fig. 19.2. A 'black box' synthesis model

The parameters (shown as $p_0, \dots, p_n$ in the figure) are, of course, crucial. The most naïve model would have as many parameters as there are bits that make up all the pixels. This naïve model is capable of generating any image, but as we saw in Sect. 19.4, its parameter space is intractable. Models with fewer parameters may be more tractable, but not necessarily capable of generating all the interesting images (e.g., the extreme case where a single parameter produces just the *Mona Lisa*). An ideal synthesis model will have few parameters and only produce 'interesting' images as output, i.e., we want to maximise the ratio

$$Q = \frac{\text{\%of all interesting images output}}{\text{size of parameter phase-space}} \tag{19.1}$$

Q being a kind of 'quality factor' of the model. The problem with many existing systems is either

i) the gamut of 'interesting' images the model can produce is limited, usually due to the model being too simplistic (not capable of representing a sufficient number of interesting images — the 'only the *Mona Lisa* model');
ii) the size of the parameter space is too big to find the interesting images (the 'naïve model');

The majority of systems will lie somewhere between these two extremes.

19.5.1 Evolutionary Search Models

The synthesis model of Fig. 19.2 encapsulates the model that is used in many EMA systems to generate music or visual images. In this scenario, the artist or programmer designs some form of parameterised system. The choice of parameters represents the *genotype* of the system. The system generates output, typically in the form of sound or image (the *phenotype*). Normally the number of parameters is very large, making an incremental or ordered search of the entire parameter space impractical; hence the use of better search methods such as genetic algorithms or aesthetic selection. The problem is one of 'search for interesting phenotype'. This approach is shown in Fig. 19.3. That is, we have some parameterised model that we wish to explore in order to find the most aesthetically interesting images within the parameter landscape. The problem in many cases is that the value of Q is too low; that is, there are too many parameters or not enough interesting images.

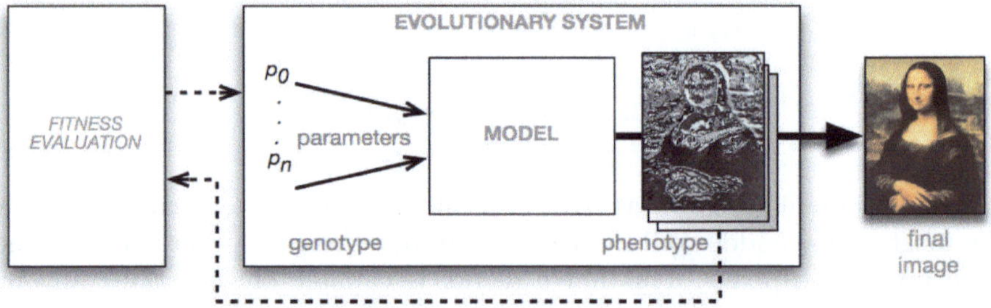

Fig. 19.3. An evolutionary synthesis model with explicit use of fitness evaluation

In this case, our model is slightly less 'black box' than before, because it shows explicitly that fitness evaluation is taking place. In the case of interactive aesthetic selection, a person will perform this evaluation. For example, in the well-known interactive evolution system of Karl Sims [22], his model used Lisp expressions, the parameters being a set of functions and constants arranged in a parse tree, with fitness evaluation being performed by the user. Other systems have attempted to remove or diminish (or assist, depending on your perspective) the user's role in fitness evaluation (see [23] for a survey). This means providing an evaluation of fitness based on some machine-representable algorithm.

For evolutionary aesthetic search there are two primary considerations:

i) the evaluation of the fitness of phenotypes produced by the system;
ii) the design of the generative system that creates the phenotypes and its parameterisation.

For the model outlined in Fig. 19.3, I believe this is a natural division of the overall problem of using evolutionary systems to 'make art'. However, for reasons I will outline in Sect. 19.8, I think there are better models than this one. Nonetheless, this is a popular and well-explored method [23] and is worthy of examination. We have already seen that for consideration (ii) we seek a high Q value; but what kinds of models will give a high Q value? This will be examined in Sect. 19.7, with consideration (i) explored in the next section.

19.6 Aesthetic Fitness Evaluation

The first consideration is the evaluation of phenotype fitness. As previously discussed, there are two basic approaches:

i) Have a human perform the fitness evaluation, normally by selecting one or more of the most aesthetically interesting phenotypes from a small population at each generation;
ii) Use some form of automated (i.e., machine representable) fitness measure.

Some systems may use a combination of these, but in the majority they remain distinct approaches to fitness evaluation. I will now examine each in detail.

19.6.1 Interactive Aesthetic Fitness Evaluation

Interactive aesthetic selection[12] presents the possibility of searching for beautiful or interesting phenotypes in any parameterised system through human evaluation of fitness. In practical terms however, aesthetic selection can only perform a limited search within a certain class of phenotypes, not necessarily all possible phenotypes that can be generated by any non-trivial system.[13] This is particularly the case when the genotype or phenotype space-time complexity is very high, as with expression trees. The methodology itself tells us

[12] Also known as *interactive selection*, *aesthetic evolution* or *interactive evolution*.
[13] By non-trivial system I am speaking of any parameterised system where the genotype and phenotype spaces cannot be explored practically by iterative or other simple search methods.

little about artistic creativity in general, and does not really offer *the* most beautiful or interesting images from any non-trivial system.

Interactive aesthetic selection has a number of problems:[14]

1.) People can only perform meaningful subjective comparisons on a small number of phenotypes (typically < 16).
2.) Human fitness evaluation is slow (compared to a machine), forming a bottleneck in the evolutionary process.
3.) Small population size and evaluation bottleneck (1 and 2 above), combined with mutation and single-parent generational selection, do not effectively balance the search between exploration and exploitation; this is one of the genetic algorithm's principal strengths as a search method [25, p. 29]. Adding crossover operators along with adapting mutation and crossover probabilities may reduce this imbalance, as would fitness ranking,[15] since the search is biased towards exploitation.[16]
4.) Genotype–phenotype mappings are often not uniform (i.e., a minor change in genotype may produce a radical change in phenotype).
5.) The size and complexity of genotypes in any real-time system is limited. It is difficult to distinguish between a genotype that uses a lot of resources to do nothing (such as a recursive null op) and one that uses a lot of resources to do something interesting (analogous to the halting problem).

These limitations are indicative of why interactive selection can't find the Lisp expression that generates the *Mona Lisa*. The human doing the selecting is limiting the effectiveness of the GA as a search technique. Moreover, representation and resources limit the generation scheme, its mapping and its complexity.

Such difficulties have led researchers to try to devise schemes that remove some or all of these limitations while still providing the ability to find interesting phenotypes within the parameterised system's gamut of possibilities. One approach has been to change the interface and selection relationship between user(s) and phenotype [26] rather than removing human subjectivity from the process completely. While successful for the situation in which it was devised, this method is not generally applicable to all interactive selection problems.

Genotype–phenotype mapping has also been researched. One interesting approach has been to evolve genotypes that represent some computational process, which is itself generative. That is, the genotype specifies the process

[14] For other opinions about difficulties with interactive selection see [24] and [2].

[15] This is problematic because fine-grain aesthetic ranking is difficult for most people, particularly when the fitness distribution is small.

[16] The author has observed that a common approach when using interactive selection is for the user to select the parent from the first or second generation as the formative archetype for successive generations, e.g., 'that phenotype looks like a tree, so I'll select it and try and evolve a tree' — the exploration side of the GA has been diminished from this point onwards. Hence the search is highly sensitive to initial selections.

of construction and then the construction process builds the phenotype. As the construction process itself is evolvable rather than fixed, more complex outcomes are possible [27].

To address the problems of subjective fitness evaluation by humans, the main alternative is to try to formalize the fitness function, so a machine rather than a human can perform it.

19.6.2 Formalised Aesthetic Fitness Evaluation

Open Problem 2 *To devise formalised fitness functions that are capable of measuring human aesthetic properties of phenotypes. These functions must be machine representable and practically computable.*

Many of the difficulties outlined in the previous section could be minimised or eliminated if we were able to devise a machine-representable fitness function for aesthetics. However, to date no general formal function has been found for 'interesting' or 'beautiful', for example.

As a subject of study, aesthetics has long been considered by a number of disciplines, predominantly art theory and philosophy. More recently, science has embarked on a number of studies of aesthetics and the creative processes used to facilitate and judge aesthetics. Let us now look at some basic aesthetic measures from a variety of disciplines.

There have been some noble attempts to *measure* aesthetic properties; however, given the difficulty of defining art in terms of objects alone (as discussed in Sect. 19.2), it is not surprising that many consider the proposition of measuring aesthetics conceptually flawed. The mathematician G. D. Birkhoff famously proposed an 'aesthetic measure', $M = O/C$, where O is aesthetic order and C is complexity [28]. Birkhoff defined ways of measuring order and complexity for several different categories of art, including two-dimensional polygons and vases, paintings by the great masters, architecture and even poetry. Clearly, the formula favours order (a square having a higher M value than an octagon, for example). Birkhoff's measure failed to capture aesthetic qualities with any generality, being described more as a measure of 'orderliness', and his decision to focus on this property as an aesthetic one in itself is problematic [29] (i.e., it imposes an assumed aesthetic judgement *a priori*).

Much has been made of many so-called 'harmonious proportions' observed both in nature and art. A continuing theme in art, architecture and design is the use of special proportions, such as the golden ratio (≈ 1.618) as a basis for structural beauty in the designed form. This particular ratio has been documented in the architecture of Stonehenge (twelfth to sixteenth centuries, B.C.), in the ancient Greek architecture of the fifth century, B.C., through the Renaissance and to the present day. Studies by Fechner in the late nineteenth century, and later by Lalo in 1908, claimed that the majority of people surveyed have a natural preference for rectangles proportioned to the golden ratio [30, pp. 6–7].

The golden ratio is also found in a variety of natural objects, including the spiral phyllotaxis observed in flower heads and pinecones, the spiral growth of seashells and the body proportions of animals (as studied by D'Arcy Thompson, for example, [31]). The fact that the ratio occurs naturally supposedly provides evidence of its 'universal' aesthetic value.[17]

A detailed study of proportional harmonies in nature, art and architecture was undertaken by the architect György Doczi, who showed special harmonic relationships in natural and artificial structures, with particular emphasis on the golden ratio [34]. Doczi also showed how musical systems exhibit similar harmonic relationships, thus establishing an aesthetic connection between natural form and musical scales. He proposed a new term *dinergy*, because while many terms 'refer to aspects of the pattern-forming process of the union of opposites... none expresses its generative power'. Doczi's key emphasis was that in nature harmonies are dynamic generative processes that result from the union of opposites, this union forming harmonious proportions.

In another classic study, Robert Bringhurst describes how harmonic relations from music and nature serve as a basis for page layout and typographic structure on the printed page [35]. Such relationships date back to medieval times and the earliest days of book design.

Despite many studies emphasising these special ratios and harmonic proportions, we need to be careful about the significance of projecting such ratios as art universals, or even as important properties of what constitutes artistic intent. A special issue of the journal *Empirical Studies of the Arts* in 1997 found little convincing evidence for the golden ratio as an art universal, highlighting methodological flaws and cultural bias in previously positive studies [36]. Martin Kemp suggests that attempts to ascribe divine proportions as key compositional features of Renaissance art is nonsense: 'there is no evidence that Renaissance and Baroque artists used such surface geometry in constructing their paintings' and 'there is quite a fashion for drawing fat lines on thin reproductions of Renaissance paintings' [37]. This issue is further analysed in the recent book by Edward Tufte, who examines a number of attempts to map geometric structures to various canons of visual art, finding many of them lacking in coherence (in some cases, opposing mappings may work equally well with the same artwork or the mapping breaks down in three-dimensions — the original space of the sculptural works examined). Tufte concludes that 'there must be an explanatory tightness of the mapping in relation to the image' and that mappings should be 'specific, coherent, credible and testable' [38].

While artists have used such proportions deliberately, in a number of cases this may have been prompted by the publication of books with exaggerated claims about the significance of such ratios, particularly those that have appeared throughout the twentieth century and are widely used as textbooks in art and design schools.

[17] It turns out that the ratio appears in natural shapes due to optimality in self-organizing packing structures [32, 33].

In addition to harmonious structure and special ratios, the art canon is rich with compositional rules and structures that form a standard component of classical training in visual art. Some of these rules include

- The *rule of thirds* in figure/ground or land/sky relationships: division of the frame into thirds is a simple harmonic compositional device.
- *Compositional optical balance*, where the position and area of key figures within the image form a balanced visual counterpoint. That is, the image is structured so that one can see optical balance between the colour, area and location of the figures in the scene and the aspect ratio of the image itself. A classic example is Gainsborough's *Mr. and Mrs. Andrews* (1750), where the landowner, his seated wife and the large tree at the extreme left of the image form a counterpoint to a distant group of trees on the right.
- *Axis and focal point*, where strong visual elements (such as lines or edges) in the image draw the eye to the important or central features, providing a pathway that leads the eye 'into' the picture.
- *Entrance and exit*, where compositional structure provides a path for the eye to follow: a point of entry, a path around and a point of exit. With poor entrance and exit, the eye is confused, constantly moving more or less randomly over the image as the viewer tries to read its visual composition. Good entrance and exit allows the eye to follow a natural pathway around all the elements of the image, without getting lost.
- *Light and shade*: using contrast as a compositional device can be a powerful aesthetic device. The eye is more sensitive to the coherence of brightness in an image than colour purity or saturation (which is why, for example, a photographic negative is difficult to read).

19.6.3 Other Science Studies of Art

A large number of scientific studies of art and aesthetics have been undertaken. Here I will briefly mention just a few.

Frequency distributions, such as Zipf's Law, have been used as the basis of aesthetic measures [39]. Factors such as the fractal dimension of the image have also been considered, most famously seen in the paintings of Jackson Pollock [40].

Evolutionary psychologist Nicholas Humphrey sees a formal similarity in that way humans are drawn to beauty and a hungry dog is drawn to saccharine — there is an innate desire to find beauty in certain constructs of 'likeness tempered with difference' (note the relation to Birkhoff's measure), 'thematic variation' and 'the metaphor of rhyme' [11]. Aesthetic preference results from a biological predisposition in humans and animals to seek useful classification of structures in the world around them. Beautiful structures facilitate classification since they provide evidence of possible taxonomies that are useful for our survival and easy to understand.

A study by Ramachandran and Hirstein proposed 'a theory of artistic experience and the neural mechanisms that mediate it' in the *Journal of Consciousness Studies* [41]. Their experiments suggest that visual art provides super-stimuli that excite certain regions in the brain more strongly than natural stimuli, and that artists consciously or unconsciously develop rules or principles to 'titillate these visual areas of the brain'. Like the evolutionary psychologists, Ramachandran and Hirstein seek to find universals that define aesthetic response in humans. Their thesis is in part based around the *peak-shift principle* from animal learning. Artworks are in some sense caricatures of prototypes, with the exaggeration or difference from the prototype resulting in a form with relevant features that are more prominent than in the prototype form itself.

In a more recent book, Ramachandran proposed 'ten laws of art which cut across cultural boundaries'. These include peak shifting, grouping, contrast, isolation, perceptual problem solving, symmetry, abhorrence of coincidence or generic viewpoints, repetition, rhythm, orderliness, balance and metaphor [42]. A number of these properties have also been identified in other studies.

Some of the rules discussed here may be better suited to figurative or to abstract imagery. Particular genres of art or 'paradigm shifts' in Kuhnian terminology deliberately exploit, ignore or selectively break rules. In terms of using them for aesthetic fitness measures it is not simply a matter of selecting weights for a set of rules and observing the results, as there appear to be higher-level relationships that affect the use of each rule.

When using rule-based measures such as symmetry, contrast, grouping, balance, etc., it is easy to devise programs that will generate images that satisfy all these criteria without the need to search using evolutionary methods. That is, there are too many images that easily satisfy such simple criteria; hence the use of evolution via such weighted fitness functions alone may be of limited benefit.

19.6.4 Problems with Aesthetic Measure

Many of the features listed in the previous sections have formed, or may form, the basis of machine representable aesthetic fitness functions. Certainly, they are useful starting points in developing aesthetic measures. The difficulty is that it is easy to generate images that satisfy many of these compositional rules or harmonious proportions; yet the images themselves either

- seem to lack a 'certain something' that would convince the majority of people that they are art; or
- are limited by the representational scheme used to create the pictures, so reasonably 'aesthetic' images may be evolved; but they are all of a certain style; that is, they are not capable of fully exploiting the novelty that might fit the given measures.

Why is this the case? By definition, aesthetic measures will focus on the *measurable features* of aesthetic objects. These are commonly geometric properties, dimension, proportion, fixed feature categories, organizational structure, etc., such as those discussed in the previous sections. The basis for using any such feature or property is that it can be objectively and directly measured from the artwork. However, there are many things considered important to aesthetic theory that cannot be measured directly. These features or properties are generally *interpreted* rather than measured, often in a context-sensitive way.

Even something as simple as colour perception is context sensitive, the human perception of colour changing according to the composition of neighbouring colours. In short, many artworks are successful because they are conceptualised through the *perceptual* properties of sound or image. Since machines don't share the perceptual consciousness of humans, the best we can attain is to try to establish formalised rules based on phenomenological experience and empirical experiment. This assumes phenomenological experience is more or less similar amongst humans.

The issue of interpretation extends to the semantics of an artwork. For example, Sect. 19.6.2 looked at the use of harmonious proportions (such as the golden ratio) in nature, art and music as a commonly observed measurable property of aesthetic objects. While these measures are interesting and revealing properties of many different types of structures, they say nothing about the *semantics* of the structure itself. What matters is not only that ancient Greek temples exhibit similar geometric golden ratios, but also the context of their form in relation to Greek and human culture, the meaning and significance to the observer and the perceptual physicality (the interpreted physical relation between observer and observed). It seems that such easily measurable general properties are used at the expense of details that are difficult to measure. Scientific theories deliberately choose levels of abstraction applicable for physical laws to be 'universal'. This has been a reasonably successful strategy for the physical universe. For aesthetic laws, however, it appears that general abstractions or simplistic physical measures may not be sufficient. Moreover, as was discussed in Sect. 19.2, the idea of combining or recombining basic primitives is contrary to some cognitive theories of creativity.

This raises another problem in current thinking about aesthetic measure: that the phenotype can be evolved and measured in isolation from its environment. I will return to this issue in Sect. 19.8, when we consider more closely the situated embeddedness of human art making and its structural and semantic coupling with the environment.

19.7 Parameterised Systems in Music and Art

The first of our primary considerations at the end of Sect. 19.5.1 was in finding algorithms that measure aesthetic fitness. This is really what we wanted from the system shown in Fig. 19.1: a model capable of clustering aesthetically pleasing images, thus enabling us to determine the aesthetic quality of an image, at least in relation to the learnt dataset. In terms of the overall model, Fig. 19.3 is superfluous because it is really encapsulated by Fig. 19.2 (the parameters are the parameters of the evolutionary algorithm). The second consideration, then, is what is inside the 'black box': what should our model be?

The previously mentioned system of Karl Sims generated images using Lisp expressions evolved by aesthetic selection [22]. In essence these expressions were a combination of basic arithmetic operations and standard mathematical functions such as trigonometric and fractal functions. Even with a limited number of such expressions, the gamut of possible images is extremely large. However, it turns out that typically all of the images produced by such a system are of a certain 'class' — that is, they all look like images made using mathematical expressions. While, for example, a Lisp expression for generating the *Mona Lisa* certainly exists,[18] no such expression has been found by aesthetic selection.

Steven Rooke extended the aesthetic selection system of Karl Sims [43]. He did not change the basic methodology (evolving images created from expressions by aesthetic selection); rather, he added a range of additional functions to further increase the gamut of *easily searchable* possibilities. That is, complexity (cf. sophistication, 'interestingness') was built into the base primitive rather than being evolved by aesthetic selection (in essence trying to increase his model's Q value from (19.1)). Certainly, Rooke's images looked different and more complex than those of Sims, but they were still of a certain class (images made using an expanded set of mathematical functions), exhibiting the underlying traits of the predominantly fractal functions that defined them.

Indeed, in all uses of aesthetic selection the results produced are 'of a certain class'; that is, they exhibit strong traits of the underlying formalised system that created them (the parameterised system). A natural, but unsuccessful strategy has been to increase the scope and complexity of primitives in the parameterised system, making it easier to find more complex possibilities in the phenotype with a low-complexity genotype. Systems of more than trivial complexity cannot be exhaustively searched. Genotype structures such as trees present a difficulty for aesthetic selection because of competing constraints between tree size and node function complexity. Increasing node function complexity gives more complex images with a smaller tree size. On the other hand, the variety of images that can be produced increases with tree depth: bigger trees will always offer more possibilities than complex function nodes. Evolving deep trees from scratch using aesthetic selection is extremely tedious. Even using automated fitness functions, the exponential increase in

[18] In fact, many Lisp expressions for generating the *Mona Lisa* exist, but what we would like is the smallest expression possible. Hence, the problem is related to information compression.

complexity as tree depth increases means that the total search space soon becomes intractable, even for genetic algorithms.

In all systems, the design of the parameterised system is limited by the creativity of the artist or programmer, in that she must use her creativity to come up with representations and parameterisations she thinks will lead to interesting results within the constraints imposed by the implementation and method. The search process has shifted up a level (from parameters to mechanisms), but it is still a search problem that needs to be undertaken by humans: it cannot (yet) be formalised, and hence, automated.

What is needed then is a system capable of introducing novelty *within itself.* The physical entities of the earth are capable of such a task, in that they are able to create an emergent physical replication system. This is achieved from the bottom up, in a non-teleological process of self-assembly and self-organization. It is possible because atoms, molecules, genes, cells and organisms are all physical entities and part of the same system. This issue will be examined more closely in Sect. 19.8.

Open Problem 3 *To devise a system where the genotype, the phenotype and the mechanism that produces phenotype from genotype are capable of automated and robust modification, selection and, hence, evolution.*

19.8 Embedded, Embodied and Structurally Coupled

The idea of measuring aesthetics in isolation, and even the use of classification techniques as a methodology for successfully and fully understanding artistic creativity, is, I believe, an incomplete one. Certainly these studies tell us many useful things, and when used in an evolutionary sense they have been, and surely will be, capable of many interesting and worthwhile discoveries about art and creativity. However, what is also useful is what these methods *do not* tell us.

To understand this, let us take a step back and consider how an image such as the *Mona Lisa* comes about. Painting is a physical activity involving feedback connections between hand, brush, canvas and eye. A painting emerges as a result of physical interaction with, and perception of, the painting itself as it is being created. That is, even if the artist has representations or ideas of what she will paint (a plan), the process of painting involves interaction, evaluation and perception during the process of creating the image. This process, at some point, comes to an end and the painting is 'finished'. Determining when the image is complete is a possible outcome of the interaction involved in creating the image (other environmental and resource factors may also come into play).

The embodied painter, paint, canvas, brushes, etc. are all *embedded* in a physical environment. These elements are *structurally coupled.* Moreover, there are many causal chains that contribute to even the simplest act of marking a canvas. These chains extend widely into the environment, encompassing the societal and environmental. Physicality imposes many constraints (limiting what is physically possible from what is logically possible), the structural coupling and causal chains further limiting what is actually possible from what is physically possible. From the Vast set of all possible images, our physicality, chemistry, biology and sociology all act as constraints on the images we create from that set. We have also previously considered that creating an artwork involves the phenomenology of sensation.

Considering agents as embodied, embedded and structurally coupled is counter to the standard 'mainstream' Cartesian approach to cognitive science [44]. It involves deeper consideration beyond the simple fact that creative intelligence requires a body. *Morphological computation* suggests that forms of intelligence are embodied in the functional morphology of the system itself [45].

We can apply these ideas to the way we conceptualise EMA systems. In Fig. 19.4a we see the standard interactive evolution model. Here the genotype and phenotype are conceptually distinct entities (conceptual entities map neatly to algorithms and data structures). This conceptual distinction corresponds to consideration of the genotype and phenotype as having de-coupled ontologies — each exists in a separate conceptual space linked by a one-way information flow. Selection is performed by the user (or automated by a fitness function) which is again conceptually distinct from the phenotype and genotype.

Figure 19.4b shows the addition of an environment in which the phenotype may be embedded. Importantly, the genotype is still disconnected from this space. A system comprised of a simulated physical environment with evolving creatures operating under Newtonian physics (e.g., [46, 47]) is a popular example. While the environment and physical simulation affects the phenotype, the genotype remains conceptually and ontologically distinct, and hence is unaffected by the physical simulation. In pragmatic terms, the data structures representing the genome do not move with the phenotype or undergo any kind of physical simulation — they exist in some kind of ethereal 'other space' that is linked to the physical simulation via one-way information flows.

Figure 19.4c is a further 'enhancement' of this paradigm, where selection is no longer determined by a conceptually distinct fitness evaluation. Here, the environment itself is an implicit fitness evaluator with phenotype survival linked to efficiency or resource discovery and utilisation. A common example of this style of conceptualisation is the 'ecosystem' model [48] where entities exist in a simulated ecosystem with a well-defined conservation of energy.

The final model in Fig. 19.4d is what I believe to be the most important model for future creative evolutionary systems. In this model, the genotype, the phenotype and the mechanism that produces phenotype from genotype are all conceptually embedded and structurally coupled to the environment (Open Problem 3). The production of phenotype from genotype is not considered in terms of unidirectional information flows; rather, it mirrors a morphological model of natural development. Selection is implicit and operates as a result of the particular environmental and physical model.

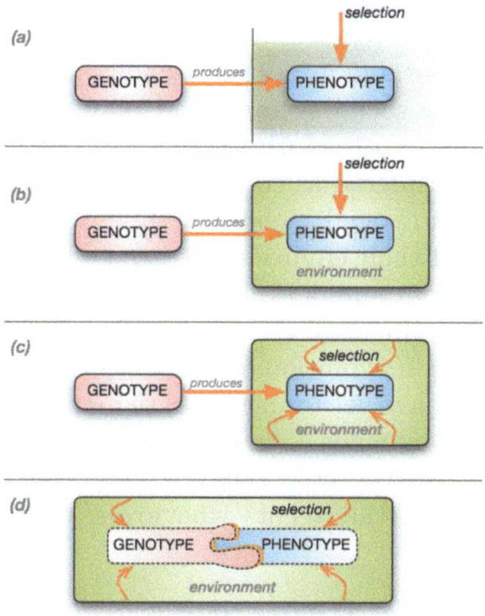

Fig. 19.4. Different conceptual approaches to evolutionary systems

In the context of EMA, such a system will not be limited by a fixed genotype representation, as is the case with current systems. That is, we aim to devise a system that does not solely produce images of mathematical functions or biomorphs or any particular class of phenotype, due to a fixed parameterised representation. Rather, the genotype, its interpretation mechanism and the phenotype exist conceptually as part of a singular system capable of automated modification. Any such system must be *robust* in the sense that it is tolerant of modification without complete breakdown or failure. A similar challenge has been posed in artificial life research for the evolution of novel behaviours [49].

It might be argued that the phenotypes produced by DNA are 'of a certain class' (i.e., biological organisms); however, DNA is able to build organisms, which in the appropriate environment are capable of open-ended creative behaviour. These systems exploit dynamical hierarchies to achieve their complexity. To date, no computerised system has robustly demonstrated such behaviour.

19.9 The Role of Environment

Different forms of creative behaviour are practiced across all human cultures, but art making is ubiquitously a social activity, heavily influenced by culture and environment [50]. Modes of artistic practice favoured in one culture may be close to unrecognisable in another. Fads, fashion and style also play important roles in human social systems and play a role in determining the acceptability and popularity of creative acts.

Organisms can be considered as complex systems that adapt to their ecological, environmental and social niches. In this way, creative systems could be considered 'mirrors' of their environment; so if we build a better and more complex environment in our simulation, we should expect the creative agents that populate that environment to reflect this complexity and detail. Despite an abundance of research in evolutionary biology, social sciences and psychology, most EMA systems have yet to incorporate many of these environmental, cultural and mimetic phenomena into their world view. The design of environments from which creative behaviour is expected to emerge is at least as important as the design of the agents who are expected to evolve this behaviour.

Open Problem 4 *To define creative universes that can be implemented in computer simulation. These universes may be highly pragmatic and individual, and even simplistic.*[19]

19.10 Is EMA Really Art?

In answer to the question 'what is art?' physicist and philosopher Abraham A. Moles somewhat jokingly said that anything exhibited in art galleries is art [52]. That is, art is what people (usually experts) currently deem appropriate to be exhibited in a place publicly recognised for exhibition and appreciation of 'art'. While there have been many exhibitions of computer-generated and evolutionary art, these categorisations focus on technological fascination, as opposed purely to artistic sentiment or merit.

Some common criticisms of EMA from the art world to date is that

- it is creatively and aesthetically naïve, crude or primitive;
- it is unaware of the visual or acoustic research undertaken and documented by arts practitioners and theorists, particularly over the last 150 years;
- it is too dependent on the technological world-view and the limitations it brings to conceptualising creative works;
- it is technologically fetishistic;

[19] Conway's *Game of Life* is a good example of a simple universe with complex emergent behaviour in a non-creative context [51]; but the test of a good universe here is that it is capable of emergent, individually creative behaviour.

- it lacks the human subtlety or sensitivity of conventional artworks;
- those who create it have a narrow, Western classical or modernist understanding of art.

These are important criticisms to address. But they should not become constraints, for as we have already seen, the opinion of what art is is often contradictory in the art world.

If EMA art is to mature, it needs to become recognised as art for what it is, in addition to how it was made.

Open Problem 5 *To create EMA devices and systems that produce art recognised by humans for its artistic contribution (as opposed to any purely technical fetish or fascination).*

One could consider this a new version of the *Turing test*, where artistic outcomes of EMA systems might be compared alongside those of humans. If the 'art world' cannot tell the difference, or at least considers both worthy of the title 'art', then the test has been passed.

This test still allows EMA to have its own new aesthetic qualities or be part of a wider 'movement' in machine-based or generative art. As previously stated, Western art is characterised by continuing change and innovation, with movements and styles fluctuating in acceptance and popularity. However, human systems of art theory and appreciation do consider these factors (along with many others) in deciding what is art — so if EMA seeks acceptance by the art world, these systems should be able to accommodate it.

Research into EMA should include developing systems and devices capable of being recognised by the art community as successful art-generating devices, irrespective of the technical methodology used to create them. This leads to an important component of the solution to this open problem: how to make good instruments.

19.11 The Extended Interface

Let us consider the class of evolutionary systems designed specifically for use as art-making machines. Humans have been able to devise numerous musically or visually creative physical devices. When a competent musician interacts with a cello or piano for example, it becomes clear that the instrument acts as a physical cognitive extension of the performer. In a cybernetic sense, musician and instrument are one, with brain, body and instrument intimately linked as a performance system. Similarly, a seemingly simple tool such as the pencil is capable of a vast array of artistic possibility when placed in the right hands. These creative systems exploit the brain's plasticity in incorporating physical tools and cultural practices as cognitive extensions. This idea is based on theories of 'extended mind', rooted in Cybernetics research and championed today by researchers such as Andy Clark and Mike Wheeler [53, 44].

If we compare artistic tools such as pencils and pianos to most creative computer software, we typically find the software lacking. Mimicry (such as painting software) is common, and while such systems do offer greater convenience and flexibility over their physical counterparts, they lack a true sense of immediacy, physical tactility and environmental interaction.

We might consider the way most people interact with (and author) software as *physically passive* in the sense that it is predominantly a conceptual exercise, like writing. In essence computers are symbol manipulators, so programming languages require the programmer to conceptualise in terms of symbols and the processes that act on them. Take a look at someone hunched over a keyboard, mouse and computer screen: his physical movement and interaction is highly constrained — little taps on the keyboard and jittery mouse movements — the interface tools mere intermediary inconveniences between expressive intent and result. This mode of interaction gives little to physical expression.

This is not a request for 'usability' or the incorporation of Human-Computer Interaction (HCI) principles into software design. It is one for conceptualising software as a *performance instrument* — one that is, in the words of Golan Levin, 'instantly knowable, and indefinitely masterable' [54]. Anyone can pick up a pencil and begin using it; however, it may take years of training and practice to master and achieve creative results of significance. One should hope for similar possibilities in the next generation of evolutionary digital tools.

As with a physical instrument, software places constraints on the scope of the interactions and possibilities it permits. However, the possibilities offered within the constraints define the creative potential of that tool. It is therefore imperative to consider the constraints carefully when designing creative tools. As software has few obvious physical constraints, one needs to conceptualise differently, working within and through the constraints to achieve the best outcomes.

Where do evolutionary systems fit into this proposal? One argument is that many generative computational systems potentially offer highly unique and novel phase-spaces, capitalising on the emergent properties these systems typically display. However, the difficulty is in locating these novel phase-spaces and exploring them intuitively: moving the system from one state to another in ways that are creatively rewarding (composition) and surprising (improvisation). To do this effectively, one must feel an intimacy with the system (possibly gained over years of exploration and practice) that allows one to instinctively anticipate how to 'play' the system in order to get the best results [55]. Equally as important is the mapping of algorithmic phase-space to visual and/or sonic output. A common methodology has been to consider process and output as conceptually distinct phenomena; an alternative is to unify process, its control and its output when conceptualising such systems. This will lead to a tighter conceptual coupling between aesthetics and process.

Open Problem 6 *To devise unique kinds of evolutionary 'software instruments' that offer the possibility of deep creative engagement and enable the creative exploration of generative computational phase-spaces.*

Evolutionary and adaptive systems will assist in the exploration and search of these phase-spaces, guiding without dictating, being plastic (in the way that the brain is plastic), leading human and machine to a synergistic embrace of new possibilities. In these modes of engagement with machines, we may really see some astonishing results, opening possibilities beyond those offered by current physical instruments. The challenge is to make a 'software instrument' that equals or exceeds traditional instruments in terms of creative possibility. We will know we have succeeded when these tools are used by many, mastered by few; subject to study in art and music schools; and embraced by cultural institutions as significant new art forms. It would be easy to argue that this is already the case for some computer tools; however, a closer analysis shows it is really only part of the broader automation of society and culture that the computer has enabled over the last fifty years. Yes, artists and designers now work with computers, but in most cases this has been with software that mimics traditional tools (pencils, cameras, piano keyboards), rather than offering media and results unique to computation.

19.12 Artificial Creative Systems

I now turn to the creative activity of artificial systems. As discussed earlier (Sect. 19.3.1), this differs fundamentally from those systems designed to produce art that is recognised and appreciated by humans. Artificial creativity extends Langton's idea of artificial life being 'life-as-it-could-be' [14]. Evolutionary artificial agent simulations are a popular tool for artificial life research [56]. Recently, some researchers have begun to look at creative behaviour in artificial systems.

We have already discussed issues of artistic creativity in Sect. 19.2. In developing computational models of creativity, Partridge and Rowe require that creativity involves production of something novel and appropriate [57]. In addition, novelty may exist relative to the individual (Boden's *P-creativity*), and for society or the whole of human culture (*H-creativity* in Boden's terminology) [58]. In the case of agent simulation this is relative to an individual or population. For their computational model of creativity, Partridge and Rowe see novelty involving the creation of new representations through emergent memory. Such a facility enables a recognition of novelty in terms of past events.

Rob Saunders evolved artificial agents capable of 'creative' behaviour using a co-evolutionary strategy of curious agents and critics [59]. Agents responded in terms of a psychological theory of interest to novel behaviour.

Most systems involved in the generation of novelty do so by appropriate recombination of basic primitives. This is a 'combinatory' emergence of complex wholes constructed from combinations of irreducible primitives. It is 'one-way' in the sense that once the primitives and their combinatory rules are specified, the resultant combinations have no effect on the primitives themselves: there is no feedback from the macro-states to the micro-states. The set of primitives and their functions are fixed; hence the set of possible outcomes is determined exclusively by the combination of these base primitives. In any computer simulation this set of possible outcomes will be a fixed, finite set, although as we have seen, it may be beyond astronomical proportions in size.

In the case of *creative emergence*, fundamentally new primitives enter the system [60]. Clearly, this distinction relates to Open Problem 3, where we want the emergence of new primitives in our system, not just the combination of a fixed set. Therefore, the main question is, can new primitives arise in a computational simulation, and if so, how?

By necessity, primitives in a computer program must be symbolic. While it is easy to dynamically add new symbols, automating the production of new interpretations of these symbols is difficult in any non-trivial sense. In fact, in any modern programming language it is impossible, because symbols must ultimately be interpreted in a semantic context, determined by the programmer/observer, not the program. There are two related issues at play here:

i) How to conceptualise and then abstract a creative process in a way suited to computer simulation;
ii) The difference between a computational simulation and a physical instantiation.

In general, our conceptualisation process involves some form of *observation frame* and sets of *state spaces*. By necessity, all non-trivial models will involve abstraction (hence simplification and reduction) and recontextualisation, normally by analogy. In any physical instantiation we automatically get physics (and chemistry, biology, etc.) thrown in 'for free'. In fact, we cannot avoid it. Computational simulation is a physical process, but in terms of the *interpretation* of the simulation (the instantiation of the model), any physics (and chemistry, biology, etc.) must become an explicit part of the model, i.e., they do not come 'for free'. We might hope that if the simulation is sophisticated enough at one level (e.g., physics), other levels (e.g., chemistry, biology) will emerge in the simulation without the need to explicitly include them in our model. Organisms are physical entities, down to the atomic level and beyond. Complete simulation at this level is currently practically impossible. Hence the search for appropriate models and abstractions suitable for practical simulation is crucial. Moreover, there are arguments from philosophy regarding the ontology of emergent levels [61], so any one-way, bottom-up simulation, no matter how complete or low-level, may not capture the essential properties of higher levels. A debate continues about the significance of emergence and the limitations of computer simulation in realising emergent processes [62].

As an example of the process of abstraction and recontextualisation, we could abstract the process of drawing using a robot 'turtle' that can move and draw with a pen [63], and then recontextualise the concept of 'creative behaviour' by trying to get the robot to create new and appropriate drawings through interaction with its environment. Creating novel drawings is easy (random movement would provide this). The more difficult problem is in finding what is appropriate in terms of them being labelled creative? Creative novelty must be defined *relative to what has come before*. Each random drawing may be new, but relative to each other, they are not new (in statistical terms). As a first step, we would like to get out of the system non-trivial behaviours that we did not explicitly put into the system. It has been suggested that this involves the concept of agency in some minimal form [64]. More research is needed on how we can define creative behaviour in artificial systems, perhaps even some formal (measurable) properties, so we can quantify what is currently determined largely by observation and opinion.

Open Problem 7 *To create artificial ecosystems where agents create and recognise their own creativity. The goal of this open problem is to help understand creativity and emergence, to investigate the possibilities of 'art-as-it-could-be'.*

To date, computational creativity has largely relied on psychological theories of creativity. As neuroscience advances our understanding of creative behaviour, and we explore simulated creativity in artificial life models, new and better theories can be developed. The challenge for researchers in EMA is to convincingly demonstrate the autonomous emergence of agents capable of generating and recognizing novelty in their interactions. By necessity, this will involve an understanding of creativity beyond that which currently exists.

19.13 Art Theories of Evolutionary Music and Art

Finally, any research involving music or art must be mindful of theories related to such practices from the disciplines themselves. Even studying these theories from an anthropological perspective is likely to shed light on the nature of creativity and aesthetics. Human culture and art is constantly changing and evolving — practices accepted today as art may not have received such acceptance in the past. Evolutionary and generative art is no exception. If this art is to progress, there must be critical theories to place the field in context and to understand it and its practitioners in the broader art world.

Open Problem 8 *To develop art theories of evolutionary and generative art.*

It is important to distinguish between *art theory* and *art criticism*. Art criticism is based on how to evaluate art within some critical framework. Art theory is not like scientific theory in that its use for prediction or general explanation is minimal. There do not seem to be any laws of art that will predict artists' behaviour, or that explain the 'evolution' of art history by detailing what 'succeeds' in making a work beautiful or significant. For the products of EMA to be accepted as art, there must be some artistic theory associated with them. Some developments have begun in this area [2].

19.14 Conclusions

This chapter has covered a wide range of issues regarding problems and challenges for EMA. As stated in the introduction, many of these issues are the opinion of the author and are intended to stimulate debate rather than be definitive statements on the research agenda for EMA. No doubt, others will find different issues for investigation. My bias has been towards creating systems that work in synergetic tandem with the human artist, rather than autonomous mimics of human creativity. If there is one thing to be acknowledged, it is that there are still many fascinating and deep issues in EMA, ripe for further investigation. Along with developments in evolutionary computing, artificial life and cognitive science, EMA inspires a greater appreciation of human creativity, novelty, and emergence. Most importantly, EMA has the potential to expand our concept of what it means to 'make art'. If, over the next fifteen years, we can meet the challenges touched upon in this chapter, EMA research will certainly have made significant, invaluable contributions to both sides of the art and science divide.

Acknowledgements

I would like to thank the editors for their advice and feedback on earlier versions of this manuscript. I am also indebted to the following people for valuable discussions: Lloyd Allison, Peter Bentley, Jon Bird, Tim Blackwell, Paul Brown, Alan Dorin, Alice Eldridge, Mark d'Inverno, Janis Jefferies, Gordon Monro, Jane Prophet and William Latham. Parts of this manuscript were completed while I was a visiting researcher at Goldsmiths College, University of London. I would like to thank Prof. Mark d'Inverno for hosting my visit.

References

1. Dreyfus, H.L., Dreyfus, S.E., Athanasiou, T. (1986). *Mind Over Machine: The Power of Human Intuition and Expertise in the Era of the Computer.* Free Press. New York
2. Whitelaw, M. (2004). *Metacreation: Art and Artificial Life.* MIT Press. Cambridge, Mass.
3. Cohen, H. (1995). The further exploits of Aaron, painter. *Stanford Humanities Review*, **4**: 141–158
4. Cohen, H. (1999). Colouring without seeing: A problem in machine creativity

5. McCormack, J. (2005). Open problems in evolutionary music and art. In Rothlauf, F., Branke, J., Cagnoni, S., Corne, D.W., Drechsler, R., Jin, Y., Machado, P., Marchiori, E., Romero, J., Smith, G.D., Squillero, G., eds.: *Applications of Evolutionary Computing, EvoWorkshops 2005: EvoBIO, EvoCOMNET, EvoHOT, EvoIASP, EvoMUSART, and EvoSTOC.* Vol. 3449 of Lecture Notes in Computer Science. Lausanne, Switzerland. Springer, 428–436
6. Carey, J. (2005). *What Good are the Arts?* Faber and Faber Limited. London
7. Dissanayake, E. (1988). *What is Art For?* University of Washington Press. Seattle
8. Dissanayake, E. (1995). *Homo Aestheticus: Where Art Comes From and Why.* University of Washington Press. Seattle
9. Miller, G.F. (2000). *The Mating Mind: How Sexual Choice Shaped the Evolution of Human Nature.* William Heinemann. London
10. Partridge, D., Rowe, J. (2002). Creativity: A computational modeling approach. In Dartnall, T., ed.: *Creativity, Cognition, and Knowledge: An Interaction.* Praeger, 211–238
11. Humphrey, N.K. (1973). The illusion of beauty. *Perception*, **2**: 429–439
12. Dartnall, T., ed. (2002). *Creativity, Cognition, and Knowledge: An Interaction.* Praeger. Westport, Connecticut
13. Wolpert, D.H., Macready, W.G. (1997). No free lunch theorems for search. *IEEE Transactions on Evolutionary Computation*, **1**(1): 67–82
14. Langton, C.G. (1989). Artificial life. In Langton, C.G., ed.: *Artificial Life.* Vol. 6 of SFI Studies in the Sciences of Complexity. Addison-Wesley, 1–47
15. Pattee, H.H. (1988). Simulations, realizations, and theories of life. In Langton, C.G., ed.: *Artificial Life.* Vol. VI. Addison-Wesley, 63–77
16. Bonabeau, E.W., Theraulaz, G. (1994). Why do we need artificial life? *Artificial Life*, **1**: 303–325
17. Dennett, D.C. (1995). *Darwin's Dangerous Idea: Evolution and the Meanings of Life.* Simon & Schuster. New York
18. Borges, J.L. (1970). The library of babel. In Yates, D.A., Irby, J.E., eds.: *Labyrinths.* Penguin Books. Harmondsworth
19. Dennett, D.C. (1991). Real patterns. *Journal of Philosophy*, **88**: 27–51
20. Berlyne, D.E. (1971). *Aesthetics and Psychobiology.* Appleton-Century-Crofts. New York, N.Y.
21. Allison, L. (2002). *Model Classes.* Technical Report 2002/125. School of Computer Science and Software Engineering, Monash University. Clayton, Victoria, Australia
22. Sims, K. (1991). Artificial evolution for computer graphics. *Computer Graphics*, **25**(4): 319–328
23. Takagi, H. (2001). Interactive evolutionary computation: Fusion of the capabilities of ec optimization and human evaluation. *Proceedings of the IEEE*, **89**: 1275–1296
24. Dorin, A. (2001). Aesthetic fitness and artificial evolution for the selection of imagery from the mythical infinite library. In Kelemen, J., Sosík, P., eds.: *Advances in Artificial Life.* Vol. 2159 of LNAI. Prague. Springer, 659–668
25. Eiben, A.E., Smith, J.E. (2003). *Introduction to Evolutionary Computing.* Natural Computing Series. Springer
26. McCormack, J. (2002). Evolving for the audience. *International Journal of Design Computing*, **4** Available on-line: `http://www.arch.usyd.edu.au/kcdc/journal/vol4/index.html`.

27. Kitano, H. (1990). Designing neural networks using genetic algorithms with graph generation system. *Complex Systems*, **4**: 461–476
28. Birkhoff, G.D. (1933). *Aesthetic Measure.* Harvard University Press. Cambridge, MA
29. Scha, R., Bod, R. (1993). Computational aesthetics. *Informatie en Informatiebeleid*, **11**: 54–63
30. Elam, K. (2001). *Geometry of Design: Studies in Proportion and Composition.* Number 107 in Design briefs. Princeton Architectural Press. New York, N.Y.
31. Thompson, D.W. (1942). *On Growth and Form.* 2nd edn. Cambridge University Press. Cambridge
32. Douady, S., Couder, Y. (1992). Phyllotaxis as a physical self-organized growth process. *Phys. Rev. Lett.*, **68**: 2098–2101
33. Douady, S., Couder, Y. (1996). Phyllotaxis as a dynamical self organizing process (part i, ii, iii). *Journal of Theoretical Biology*, **139**: 178–312
34. Doczi, G. (1981). *The Power of Limits: Proportional Harmonies in Nature, Art and Architecture.* Shambhala (Distributed by Routledge & Kegan Paul). London
35. Bringhurst, R. (1992). *The Elements of Typographic Style.* Second edition edn. Hartley & Marks. Vancouver, BC
36. Holger, H. (1997). Why a special issue on the golden section hypothesis?: An introduction. *Empirical Studies of the Arts*, **15**
37. Kemp, M. (2004). Divine proportion and the holy grail. *Nature*, **428**: 370
38. Tufte, E.R. (2006). *Beautiful Evidence.* Graphics Press LLC. Cheshire, Connecticut
39. Manaris, B., Machado, P., McCauley, C., Romero, J., Krehbiel, D. (2005). Developing fitness functions for pleasant music: Zipf's law and interactive evolution systems. In Rothlauf, F., Branke, J., Cagnoni, S., Corne, D.W., Drechsler, R., Jin, Y., Machado, P., Marchiori, E., Romero, J., Smith, G.D., Squillero, G., eds.: *Applications of Evolutionary Computing, EvoWorkshops 2005: EvoBIO, EvoCOMNET, EvoHOT, EvoIASP, EvoMUSART, and EvoSTOC.* Vol. 3449 of Lecture Notes in Computer Science. Lausanne, Switzerland. Springer, 489–507
40. Taylor, R.P., Micolich, A.P., Jonas, D. (1999). Fractal analysis of Pollock's drip paintings. *Nature*, **399**: 422
41. Ramachandran, V.S., Hirstein, W. (1999). The science of art: A neurological theory of aesthetic experience. *Journal of Consciousness Studies*, **6**: 15–51
42. Ramachandran, V.S. (2003). *The Emerging Mind.* Reith lectures. BBC in association with Profile Books. London
43. Rooke, S. (2002). Eons of genetically evolved algorithmic images. In Bentley, P.J., Corne, D.W., eds.: *Creative Evolutionary Systems.* Academic Press. London, 339–365
44. Wheeler, M. (2005). *Reconstructing the Cognitive World: The Next Step.* MIT Press. Cambridge, Mass.
45. Pfeifer, R., Bongard, J. (2006). *How the Body Shapes the Way We Think: A New View of Intelligence.* MIT Press. Cambridge, MA
46. Hornby, G.S., Pollack, J.B. (2001). Evolving l-systems to generate virtual creatures. *Computers & Graphics*, **26**: 1041–1048
47. Sims, K. (1994). Evolving virtual creatures. In: *Computer Graphics.* ACM SIGGRAPH, 15–22
48. Dorin, A. (2007). A survey of virtual ecosystems in generative electronic art. In Romero, J., Machado, P., eds.: *The Art of Artificial Evolution.* Springer

49. Taylor, T. (2002). Creativity in evolution: Individuals, interactions, and environments. In Bentley, P.J., Corne, D.W., eds.: *Creative Evolutionary Systems.* Academic Press. London, 79–108
50. Brown, D.E. (1991). *Human Universals.* McGraw-Hill. New York
51. Berlekamp, E.R., Conway, J.H., Guy, R.K. (1982). *Winning Ways for your Mathematical Plays.* Vol. 2. Academic Press. New York
52. Nake, F. (1994). How far away are we from the first masterpiece of computer art? In Brunnstein, K., Raubold, E., eds.: *IFIP 13th World Congress 94.* Vol. 2. Elsevier Science, B.V.. North-Holland, 406–413
53. Clark, A. (2003). *Natural-Born cyborgs: Minds, Technologies, and the Future of Human Intelligence.* Oxford University Press. New York
54. Levin, G. (2000). *Painterly Interfaces for Audiovisual Performance.* Master of science thesis in media arts and sciences. MIT. Boston
55. Eldridge, A.C. (2005). Cyborg dancing: Generative systems for man-machine musical improvisation. In Innocent, T., ed.: *Proceedings of Third Iteration.* CEMA. Melbourne, 129–141
56. Packard, N.H. (1988). Intrinsic adaption in a simple model for evolution. In Langton, C.G., ed.: *Artificial Life.* Los Alamos, NM. Addison-Wesley, 141–155
57. Partridge, D., Rowe, J. (1994). *Computers and Creativity.* Intellect. Oxford, England
58. Boden, M.A. (1994). What is creativity? In Boden, M.A., ed.: *Dimensions of Creativity.* MIT Press. Cambridge, MA, 75–117
59. Saunders, R., Gero, J.S. (2001). Artificial creativity: A synthetic approach to the study of creative behaviour. In Gero, J.S., ed.: *Proceedings of the Fifth Conference on Computational and Cognitive Models of Creative Design.* Sydney. Key Centre of Design Computing and Cognition, 113–139
60. Bird, J. (2004). Containing Reality: Epistemological Issues in Generative Art and Science. In: *Impossible Nature: The Art of Jon McCormack.* Australian Centre for the Moving Image, 40–53
61. Emmeche, C., Køppe, S., Stjernfelt, F. (1997). Explaining emergence: Towards an ontology of levels. *Journal for General Philosophy of Science*, **28**: 83–119
62. Bedau, M.A., McCaskill, J.S., Packard, N.H., Rasmussen, S., Adami, C., Green, D., Ikegami, T., Kaneko, K., Ray, T.S. (2000). Open problems in artificial life. *Artificial Life*, **6**: 363–376
63. Abelson, H., DiSessa, A.A. (1982). *Turtle Geometry: The Computer as a Medium for Exploring Mathematics.* The MIT Press series in artificial intelligence. MIT Press. Cambridge, Mass.
64. Bird, J., Stokes, D. (2006). Evolving minimally creative robots. In Colton, S., Pease, A., eds.: *Proceedings of The Third Joint Workshop on Computational Creativity (ECAI 06)*, 1–5

Index

Natural Computing Series

H.-P. Schwefel, I. Wegener, K. Weinert (Eds.): **Advances in Computational Intelligence. Theory and Practice.** VIII, 325 pages. 2003

A. Ghosh, S. Tsutsui (Eds.): **Advances in Evolutionary Computing. Theory and Applications.** XVI, 1006 pages. 2003

L.F. Landweber, E. Winfree (Eds.): **Evolution as Computation.** DIMACS Workshop, Princeton, January 1999. XV, 332 pages. 2002

M. Hirvensalo: **Quantum Computing.** 2nd ed., XI, 214 pages. 2004 (first edition published in the series)

A.E. Eiben, J.E. Smith: **Introduction to Evolutionary Computing.** XV, 299 pages. 2003

A. Ehrenfeucht, T. Harju, I. Petre, D.M. Prescott, G. Rozenberg: **Computation in Living Cells. Gene Assembly in Ciliates.** XIV, 202 pages. 2004

L. Sekanina: **Evolvable Components. From Theory to Hardware Implementations.** XVI, 194 pages. 2004

G. Ciobanu, G. Rozenberg (Eds.): **Modelling in Molecular Biology.** X, 310 pages. 2004

R.W. Morrison: **Designing Evolutionary Algorithms for Dynamic Environments.** XII, 148 pages, 78 figs. 2004

R. Paton†, H. Bolouri, M. Holcombe, J.H. Parish, R. Tateson (Eds.): **Computation in Cells and Tissues. Perspectives and Tools of Thought.** XIV, 358 pages, 134 figs. 2004

M. Amos: **Theoretical and Experimental DNA Computation.** XIV, 170 pages, 78 figs. 2005

M. Tomassini: **Spatially Structured Evolutionary Algorithms.** XIV, 192 pages, 91 figs., 21 tables. 2005

G. Ciobanu, G. Păun, M.J. Pérez-Jiménez (Eds.): **Applications of Membrane Computing.** X, 441 pages, 99 figs., 24 tables. 2006

K.V. Price, R.M. Storn, J.A. Lampinen: **Differential Evolution.** XX, 538 pages, 292 figs., 48 tables and CD-ROM. 2006

J. Chen, N. Jonoska, G. Rozenberg: **Nanotechnology: Science and Computation.** XII, 385 pages, 126 figs., 10 tables. 2006

A. Brabazon, M. O'Neill: **Biologically Inspired Algorithms for Financial Modelling.** XVI, 275 pages, 92 figs., 39 tables. 2006

T. Bartz-Beielstein: **Experimental Research in Evolutionary Computation.** XIV, 214 pages, 66 figs., 36 tables. 2006

S. Bandyopadhyay, S.K. Pal: **Classification and Learning Using Genetic Algorithms**. XVI, 314 pages, 87 figs., 43 tables. 2007

H.-J. Böckenhauer, D. Bongartz: **Algorithmic Aspects of Bioinformatics.** X, 396 pages, 118 figs., 9 tables. 2007

P. Siarry, Z. Michalewicz (Eds.): **Advances in Metaheuristics for Hard Optimization.** Approx. 496 pages, 66 figs., 83 tables. 2008

J. Knowles, D. Corne, K. Deb (Eds.): **Multiobjective Problem Solving from Nature. From Concepts to Applications**. XVI, 410 pages, 178 figs., 53 tables. 2008

J. Romero, P. Machado (Eds.): **The Art of Artificial Evolution. A Handbook on Evolutionary Art and Music.** XVIII, 460 pages, 169 figs., 30 tables and DVD-ROM. 2008

MIX
Papier aus verantwortungsvollen Quellen
Paper from responsible sources
FSC® C105338

If you have any concerns about our products,
you can contact us on
ProductSafety@springernature.com

In case Publisher is established outside the EU,
the EU authorized representative is:
Springer Nature Customer Service Center GmbH
Europaplatz 3, 69115 Heidelberg, Germany

Printed by Libri Plureos GmbH
in Hamburg, Germany